T0210859

Communications in Computer and Information Science 1034

Commenced Publication in 2007
Founding and Former Series Editors:
Phoebe Chen, Alfredo Cuzzocrea, Xiaoyong Du, Orhun Kara, Ting Liu,
Krishna M. Sivalingam, Dominik Ślęzak, Takashi Washio, and Xiaokang Yang

Editorial Board Members

More information about this series at http://www.springer.com/series/7899

Constantine Stephanidis (Ed.)

HCI International 2019 - Posters

21st International Conference, HCII 2019
Orlando, FL, USA, July 26–31, 2019
Proceedings, Part III

 Springer

Editor
Constantine Stephanidis
University of Crete
and Foundation for Research
and Technology – Hellas (FORTH)
Heraklion, Crete, Greece

ISSN 1865-0929 ISSN 1865-0937 (electronic)
Communications in Computer and Information Science
ISBN 978-3-030-23524-6 ISBN 978-3-030-23525-3 (eBook)
https://doi.org/10.1007/978-3-030-23525-3

This Springer imprint is published by the registered company Springer Nature Switzerland AG
The registered company address is: Gewerbestrasse 11, 6330 Cham, Switzerland

Foreword

The 21st International Conference on Human-Computer Interaction, HCI International 2019, was held in Orlando, FL, USA, during July 26–31, 2019. The event incorporated the 18 thematic areas and affiliated conferences listed on the following page.

A total of 5,029 individuals from academia, research institutes, industry, and governmental agencies from 73 countries submitted contributions, and 1,274 papers and 209 posters were included in the pre-conference proceedings. These contributions address the latest research and development efforts and highlight the human aspects of design and use of computing systems. The contributions thoroughly cover the entire field of human-computer interaction, addressing major advances in knowledge and effective use of computers in a variety of application areas. The volumes constituting the full set of the pre-conference proceedings are listed in the following pages.

This year the HCI International (HCII) conference introduced the new option of "late-breaking work." This applies both for papers and posters and the corresponding volume(s) of the proceedings will be published just after the conference. Full papers will be included in the *HCII 2019 Late-Breaking Work Papers Proceedings* volume of the proceedings to be published in the Springer LNCS series, while poster extended abstracts will be included as short papers in the HCII 2019 *Late-Breaking Work Poster Extended Abstracts* volume to be published in the Springer CCIS series.

I would like to thank the program board chairs and the members of the program boards of all thematic areas and affiliated conferences for their contribution to the highest scientific quality and the overall success of the HCI International 2019 conference.

This conference would not have been possible without the continuous and unwavering support and advice of the founder, Conference General Chair Emeritus and Conference Scientific Advisor Prof. Gavriel Salvendy. For his outstanding efforts, I would like to express my appreciation to the communications chair and editor of *HCI International News,* Dr. Abbas Moallem.

July 2019   Constantine Stephanidis

HCI International 2019 Thematic Areas and Affiliated Conferences

Thematic areas:

- HCI 2019: Human-Computer Interaction
- HIMI 2019: Human Interface and the Management of Information

Affiliated conferences:

- EPCE 2019: 16th International Conference on Engineering Psychology and Cognitive Ergonomics
- UAHCI 2019: 13th International Conference on Universal Access in Human-Computer Interaction
- VAMR 2019: 11th International Conference on Virtual, Augmented and Mixed Reality
- CCD 2019: 11th International Conference on Cross-Cultural Design
- SCSM 2019: 11th International Conference on Social Computing and Social Media
- AC 2019: 13th International Conference on Augmented Cognition
- DHM 2019: 10th International Conference on Digital Human Modeling and Applications in Health, Safety, Ergonomics and Risk Management
- DUXU 2019: 8th International Conference on Design, User Experience, and Usability
- DAPI 2019: 7th International Conference on Distributed, Ambient and Pervasive Interactions
- HCIBGO 2019: 6th International Conference on HCI in Business, Government and Organizations
- LCT 2019: 6th International Conference on Learning and Collaboration Technologies
- ITAP 2019: 5th International Conference on Human Aspects of IT for the Aged Population
- HCI-CPT 2019: First International Conference on HCI for Cybersecurity, Privacy and Trust
- HCI-Games 2019: First International Conference on HCI in Games
- MobiTAS 2019: First International Conference on HCI in Mobility, Transport, and Automotive Systems
- AIS 2019: First International Conference on Adaptive Instructional Systems

Pre-conference Proceedings Volumes Full List

34. CCIS 1033, HCI International 2019 - Posters (Part II), edited by Constantine Stephanidis
35. CCIS 1034, HCI International 2019 - Posters (Part III), edited by Constantine Stephanidis

http://2019.hci.international/proceedings

HCI International 2019 (HCII 2019)

The full list with the Program Board Chairs and the members of the Program Boards of all thematic areas and affiliated conferences is available online at:

http://www.hci.international/board-members-2019.php

HCI International 2020

The 22nd International Conference on Human-Computer Interaction, HCI International 2020, will be held jointly with the affiliated conferences in Copenhagen, Denmark, at the Bella Center Copenhagen, July 19–24, 2020. It will cover a broad spectrum of themes related to HCI, including theoretical issues, methods, tools, processes, and case studies in HCI design, as well as novel interaction techniques, interfaces, and applications. The proceedings will be published by Springer. More information will be available on the conference website: http://2020.hci.international/.

General Chair
Prof. Constantine Stephanidis
University of Crete and ICS-FORTH
Heraklion, Crete, Greece
E-mail: general_chair@hcii2020.org

http://2020.hci.international/

Contents – Part III

Learning Technologies

HCI in Transport and Autonomous Driving

New Trends in Social Media

NET-EXPO: A Gephi Plugin Towards Social Network Analysis of Network Exposure for Unipartite and Bipartite Graphs

Muhammad "Tuan" Amith, Kayo Fujimoto, and Cui Tao[⊠]

University of Texas Health Science Center at Houston, Houston, TX 77030, USA
cui.tao@uth.tmc.edu

Abstract. Social network analysis (SNA) concerns itself in studying network structures in relation to individuals' behavior. Individuals may be influenced by their network members in their behavior, and thus past researchers have developed computational methods that allow us to measure the extent to which individuals are exposed to members with certain behavior within one's social network, and that be correlated with their own behavior. Some of these methods include *network exposure model*, *affiliation exposure model*, and *decomposed network exposure models*. We developed a Gephi plugin that computes and visualizes these various kinds of network exposure models called NET-EXPO. We experimented with NET-EXPO on some social network datasets to demonstrate its pragmatic use in social network research. This plugin has the potential to equip researchers with a tool to compute network exposures in a user friendly way and simplify the process to compute and visualize the network data.

Keywords: Social network analysis · Network exposure model · Affiliation exposure model · Visualization · Gephi · Human computer interaction · Software · Network science · Public health

1 Introduction

An old adage, *"[w]hen the character of a [wo]man is not clear to you, look at [their] friends"*, assumes that each individual is reflected by their interactions by another human being. Within the field of social network analysis (SNA), graph-based networks that represent relational structures can provide comprehension into their relations to individual-level behaviors/attributes. A graph is a mathematical model connecting nodes to elucidate a network structure. While representing individual people as nodes (or actors) within a graph and the connection between nodes as relationships (or ties), these graphs can provide methods to garner insight into the social network composed of a population of interest.

© Springer Nature Switzerland AG 2019
C. Stephanidis (Ed.): HCII 2019, CCIS 1034, pp. 3–12, 2019.
https://doi.org/10.1007/978-3-030-23525-3_1

SNA is "set of techniques used to understand these relationships and how they affect behavior" [1]. By representing these social structures as networks, researchers can apply various mathematical and graph-based methods to quantify structural characteristics and their relation to behavioral attributes of a population. Network methods such as computing centrality measures [2,3] or complex methods such as community detection [4] can reveal behavioral information in a social network. As a graph structure, we can potentially visualize the network to further assess and communicate important findings to a wider audience.

We introduce a software add-on that we developed for a popular open source visualization software called Gephi [5]. We will also summarize the network exposure models that the software add-on is based on.

1.1 Network Exposure Model

The *network exposure model* aims to assess a degree to which an individual is exposed to his or her network members with certain attributes or behaviors [6–9]. It has been grounded in the diffusion of innovation theory [10], and modeling network influence by constructing the weight matrix W_{ij} were discussed [11]. Network Exposure (E_i) is defined in the equation below (Eq. 1).

$$E_i = \frac{\sum_j W_{ij}\, y_j}{\sum_j W_{ij}}, for\ i, j = 1, \ldots, N, i \neq j \tag{1}$$

From Eq. 1, a network influence is represented by relationships from individuals i (ego) to j (alter) in the form of a weight matrix W_{ij} (with i indexing row and j indexing column) that is matrix multiplied by $y_j (i \neq j)$ that represent each network member j's value in his or her behavioral variable (either coded as 0 or 1), and divided by row sum of $\sum_j W_{ij}$, to normalize the resulting exposure value. Here, E_i represents the resulting vector of network exposure, yielding the proportion of a connecting network members with certain behavior or attribute y_j.

1.2 Affiliation Exposure Model

Affiliation exposure, developed by our co-author (KF) and colleagues [12,13], have been employed in various social network analysis research [12–16]. *Affiliation exposure model* extends the *network exposure model* by replacing a weight matrix W_{ij} with a one-mode actor-by-actor co-affiliation matrix C_{ij}. The co-affiliation matrix is a result of a projection of (or conversion from) a two-mode affiliation matrix A_{ij} where actor i index row and event j index column. Mathematically, this projected co-affiliation matrix C_{ij}, is computed by the matrix multiplication of a bipartite graph as a matrix A_{ij}, by its transposed form A'_{ij}, i.e., $C_{ij} = (A_{ij} \cdot A'_{ij})$. The off-diagonal entries of the resulting co-affiliation matrix, representing the number of common events each pair of actors jointly affiliated. C_{ij} (where $i \neq j$) is used to compute affiliation exposure (See Eq. 2). Values in the on-diagonal entries represent the number of total event each actor affiliated, that will not be used in affiliation exposure computation, but used as a control variable in regression analysis [12].

$$F_i = \frac{\sum\limits_j C_{ij}\, y_j}{\sum\limits_j C_{ij}}, for\ i,j = 1, \ldots, N, i \neq j \qquad (2)$$

Analogous to *network exposure model*, the resulting vector F_i measures the percentages of events in which actors co-affiliates with actors of a specific behavioral attribute y_j.

1.3 Decomposed Network Exposure Model

Decomposed network exposure model is another network exposure derivative developed by our co-author (KF) and colleagues that allows us to incorporate multiple network influences, by including two network weight matrices of the same population that can be decomposed into overlapped versus non-overlapped network influence [17,18]. We will focus on *decomposed network exposure* for using two one-mode networks as an example, but future implementation for NET-EXPO will support combinations of one one-mode network and one two-mode network [18] and two two-mode networks [17].

$$D_{i,overlap} = \frac{\sum\limits_j \{sgn(X_{ij})\, W_{ij}\}\, y_j}{\sum\limits_j \{sgn(X_{ij})\, W_{ij}\}}\ for\ i,j = 1, \ldots, N,\ i \neq j \qquad (3)$$

$$D_{i,non-overlap} = \frac{\sum\limits_j \{[1 - sgn(X_{ij})]\, W_{ij}\}\, y_j}{\sum\limits_j \{[1 - sgn(X_{ij})]\, W_{ij}\}}\ for\ i,j = 1, \ldots, N,\ i \neq j \qquad (4)$$

Equations 3 and 4 defines the *decomposed network exposure model* for two one-mode networks, X_{ij} and W_{ij}. The model involves generating a matrix from a weight matrix (X_{ij}) and converting the elements into binarized elements $sgn(X_{ij})$, and also generating the inverse form of $1 - sgn(X_{ij})$, i.e., switching 0 to 1, and 1 to 0. To derive an overlapped decomposed exposure component to a certain behavior $(D_{i,overlap})$, we preform element-wise multiplication between the binary matrix $sgn(X_{ij})$ and another weight matrix W_{ij}, and then compute the standard procedure for network exposure (matrix multiply the resulting dot-multiplied matrix by the behavior vector y_j), that will yield overlapped network exposure component between two networks. To derive non-overlapped decomposed exposure component to a certain behavior, we subtracted the binarized elements $sgn(X_{ij})$, from a square matrix with all off-diagonal elements 1, and everything else being identical to the computation of Eq. 3.

1.4   Research Objectives

Using the aforementioned models discussed, we intend to harness Gephi, a network visualization tool, to display and compute the various network exposure measures. Through the visualization of these measures, network researchers can potentially analyze and have an insight to better understand various network influences of individuals or events/places on specific individual nodes in a network.

Currently, the Gephi plugin repository do not offer any support for the discussed network exposure models of various forms. To accomplish our objective, we developed a software add-on for Gephi that computes the models and allows the users to exploit the Gephi's visualization tools to display the models. We will demonstrate and discuss NET-EXPO's functionality using published datasets from well-known studies to reveal various network influences through the visualizations.

2   Material and Method

2.1   NET-EXPO

NET-EXPO was developed using the Gephi plugin API and leveraged a Java matrix library, EJML (Efficient Java Matrix Library)[1]. We implemented the computations for these models and integrated it within the Gephi framework. We also implemented some basic user interface features for the user to instruct Gephi on how to process the data. This included three basic configuration panels (See Fig. 1) for the three exposure models where each tab is reserved for each model computation.

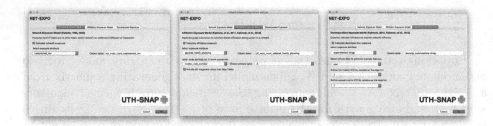

Fig. 1. NET-EXPO's configuration panel for *network exposure*, *affiliation exposure*, and *decomposed network exposure models*

---

[1] http://ejml.org.

2.2 Sample Network Datasets

We utilized three network datasets from previous research to demonstrate the visualization potential of the plugin. One dataset originated from research studying online network data of sex escorts and their customers from a Brazilian forum [19]. The other dataset came from Rogers and Kincaid [20] that involved the adoption of family planning methods in South Korean villages. The third dataset came from Teenage Friends and Lifestyle Study and focused on a friendship network of teenagers and their behavioral attributes [21–24]. For convenience, we used an excerpt of their network of 50 school girls[2].

3 Results and Discussion

The plugin was tested on Gephi v0.9.2 on an Apple Mac Pro® machine (8-core 2.4 GHz Intel processor, 64 GB RAM, and AMD Radeon™HD 7950 3 GB video card). We optimized the memory allocation for Gephi (up to 4 GB) to accommodate large network graphs.

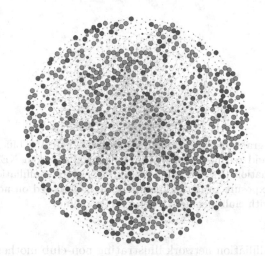

Fig. 2. Unidirected graph of network exposure visualized through NET-EXPO. The size of the node indicates network exposure to unprotected sexual activity. Green nodes represent the sex workers and the pink nodes represent the sex clients. (Color figure online)

Figure 2 represents a one-node network of both escorts and clients, with ties representing a sexual partnership (W_{ij}). The behavioral attribute y_j was the unprotected sexual activity, which we defined as having either anal or oral sex without a condom (1 for unprotected sex and 0 for protected sexual contact).

---

[2] https://www.stats.ox.ac.uk/~snijders/siena/s50_data.htm.

The network displays a visualized graph through NET-EXPO that represents a unidirected sexual network between escorts/sex workers (green nodes) and their clients (pink nodes), with the node size representing the degree to which individuals are exposed to risk of disease infection through unprotected sex activity. This network visualization shows the amount of exposure to partners that engaged in unprotected sex. The size of the nodes indicates the exposure value (i.e. the larger the value, the larger the node size). Also the dataset for this network spanned 6 years and amounted to a large network size that stalled the performance. We relegated to using a subset (first two years of data collected) for demonstration purposes.

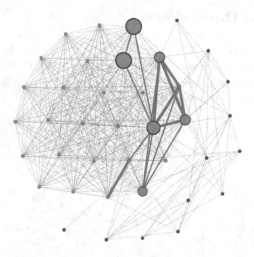

Fig. 3. Unidirected graph of Korean village mothers where the blue nodes represent non-club members and red nodes represent club members from NET-EXPO. Green lines are the co-affiliation ties and gray lines are the non-co-affiliation ties. The size of nodes indicates exposure to family planning methods based on non-club members shared interaction with club members. (Color figure online)

Figure 3 is an affiliation network illustrating non-club mothers (blue nodes), who share an interaction with members of a "Mother's Club" (red nodes). The village network shown in Fig. 3 is the converted co-affiliation matrix (C_{ij}) projected from a two mode network (A_{ij}) of non-club mothers i (first mode) and encounter with club mothers j (second mode). The y_j vector was the adoption of family planning methods of the non-club mothers (1 for adopting and 0 for not adopting). The size of the nodes indicate the magnitude of the affiliation exposure. NET-EXPO also facilitates the creation of new links (co-affiliation) based off the projected matrix with values assigned to each of them (off-diagonal values). This particular network employs line thickness to denote the strength of the co-affiliation (green lines in Fig. 3).

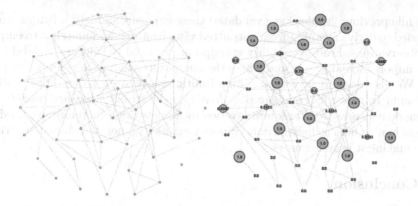

Fig. 4. Two network exposure visualizations of teenage drug use resulting from *decomposed network exposure model* computation from NET-EXPO.

Figure 4 presents two visualizations for *decomposed network exposure model*. The one-mode friendship network of the first year (X_{ij}) and the one-mode friendship network of second year (W_{ij}) were overlapped. The behavior attribute vector y_j is binary value indicating whether the individual ever experimented with drugs (1 for yes or 0 for no). The left network of the figure $(D_{i,overlap})$ shows the measure of exposure to drug use with a friendship network of two years. The right side network $(D_{i,non-overlap})$ of the figure reveals the measure of exposure to drug use where the friendship network was not over the span of two years. The gray nodes represent teen girls who experimented with drugs, and the light orange nodes are teen girls who never experimented with drugs. The left network did not yield any exposure value, but the right network revealed exposure to experimental drug use. Again, the size of the nodes indicate the exposure strength with the values as labels assigned to each node.

With NET-EXPO, users can harness the Gephi platform to measure and visualize *network exposure*, *affiliation exposure*, and *decomposed network exposure*. With minimum effort, network researchers could extrapolate exposure data and their visualizations using a graphical interface provided through the Gephi platform. We showed NET-EXPO's functionality using open network datasets - sex escort network (*network exposure*), family planning network from a Korean villages (*affiliation exposure*), and a friendship network of teens (*decomposed network exposure*).

While previous studies have validated these exposure models, a future study is needed to derive meaning from outputted visualizations and match it to empirical observations. From a usability standpoint, we need to address scalability if users import large datasets and where the computations may take longer to process. We also need to investigate some limitations relating to workflow within the Gephi framework. For example, *decomposed network exposure models* for two-mode networks would require two two-mode networks, therefore, we need to address how to best utilize the data import formats to generate complex matrices while making it easy for users.

4   Conclusion

In this paper, we introduce a Gephi plugin called NET-EXPO that visualizes networks to help understand influences and the impact of affiliations among the nodes that represent individuals. netdiffuseR, a CRAN package for the R statistical environment, implements algorithms to compute network diffusion statistics including network exposure models, and other network diffusion statistics [25]. Our co-author (KF) published a STATA script module called AFFILIATION-EXPOSURE for *affiliation exposure model* [26]. In comparison with AFFILIATIONEXPOSURE, NET-EXPO aims to offer an extended network exposure model computations with the ease of click and point. As a Gephi plugin, it can leverage the WYSIWYG[3] approach to visualize and manage network data. This makes NET-EXPO an ideal tool for non-technical users to be introduced to network exposure models and reach a large audience base who use Gephi. With NET-EXPO, we demonstrated the use of this plugin using three network datasets to manifest visualizations for *network exposure model, affiliation exposure model*, and *decomposed network exposure model*. The plugin is available on Github[4] for open source under the Apache License 2.0. In the future, we plan on addressing scalability for large networks, testing usability with novice users, and furthering the utility of visualizing network exposure models. NET-EXPO will be extended to include a wider array of network exposure models and computation of longitudinal network exposure models [27].

Acknowledgments. This research was supported by the UTHealth Innovation for Cancer Prevention Research Training Program (Cancer Prevention and Research Institute of Texas grant # RP160015), the National Library of Medicine of the National Institutes of Health under Award Number R01LM011829, and the National Institute on Alcohol Abuse and Alcoholism (1K99AA019699), and the National Institute of Mental Health of the National Institutes of Health under Award Numbers R01MH100021.

References

1. Valente, T.W.: Social Networks and Health: Models, Methods, and Applications. Oxford University Press, New York (2010)

---

[3] *What you see is what you get.*
[4] https://github.com/UTH-Tuan/NET-EXPO.

2. Freeman, L.C.: Centrality in social networks conceptual clarification. Social Netw. **1**(3), 215–239 (1978)
3. Newman, M.E.: The mathematics of networks. New Palgrave Encycl. Econ. **2**(2008), 1–12 (2008)
4. Blondel, V.D., Guillaume, J.L., Lambiotte, R., Lefebvre, E.: Fast unfolding of communities in large networks. J. Stat. Mech.: Theory Exp. **2008**(10), P10008 (2008)
5. Bastian, M., Heymann, S., Jacomy, M., et al.: Gephi: an open source software for exploring and manipulating networks. Icwsm **8**(2009), 361–362 (2009)
6. Marsden, P.V., Friedkin, N.E.: Network studies of social influence. Sociol. Methods Res. **22**(1), 127–151 (1993)
7. Burt, R.S.: Social contagion and innovation: cohesion versus structural equivalence. Am. J. Sociol. **92**(6), 1287–1335 (1987)
8. Valente, T.W.: Network models of the diffusion of innovations. Comput. Math. Organ. Theory **2**(2), 163–164 (1996)
9. Valente, T.W.: Network models and methods for studying the diffusion of innovations. Models Methods Soc. Netw. Anal. **28**, 98 (2005)
10. Rogers, E.M.: Diffusion of Innovations. Simon and Schuster, New York (2010)
11. Leenders, R.T.A.: Modeling social influence through network autocorrelation: constructing the weight matrix. Soc. Netw. **24**(1), 21–47 (2002)
12. Fujimoto, K., Chou, C.P., Valente, T.W.: The network autocorrelation model using two-mode data: affiliation exposure and potential bias in the autocorrelation parameter. Soc. Netw. **33**(3), 231–243 (2011)
13. Fujimoto, K., Unger, J.B., Valente, T.W.: A network method of measuring affiliation-based peer influence: assessing the influences of teammates' smoking on adolescent smoking. Child Dev. **83**(2), 442–451 (2012)
14. Papachristos, A.V., Wildeman, C., Roberto, E.: Tragic, but not random: the social contagion of nonfatal gunshot injuries. Soc. Sci. Med. **125**, 139–150 (2015)
15. Wipfli, H.L., Fujimoto, K., Valente, T.W.: Global tobacco control diffusion: the case of the framework convention on tobacco control. Am. J. Public Health **100**(7), 1260–1266 (2010)
16. Myneni, S., Fujimoto, K., Cobb, N., Cohen, T.: Content-driven analysis of an online community for smoking cessation: integration of qualitative techniques, automated text analysis, and affiliation networks. Am. J. Public Health **105**(6), 1206–1212 (2015)
17. Fujimoto, K., Wang, P., Valente, T.W.: The decomposed affiliation exposure model: a network approach to segregating peer influences from crowds and organized sports. Netw. Sci. **1**(2), 154–169 (2013)
18. Fujimoto, K., Valente, T.W.: Alcohol peer influence of participating in organized school activities: a network approach. Health Psychol. **32**(10), 1084 (2013)
19. Rocha, L.E.C., Liljeros, F., Holme, P.: Information dynamics shape the sexual networks of Internet-mediated prostitution. Proc. Natl. Acad. Sci. U.S.A. **107**(13), 5706–5711 (2010)
20. Rogers, E.M., Kincaid, D.L.: Communication networks: toward a new paradigm for research (1981)
21. West, P., Sweeting, H.: Background, rationale and design of the west of scotland 11 to 16 study. MRC Medical Sociology Unit Working Paper, no. 52 (1996)
22. Michell, L., Amos, A.: Girls, pecking order and smoking. Soc. Sci. Med. **44**(12), 1861–1869 (1997)
23. Michell, M.P.L.: Smoke rings: social network analysis of friendship groups, smoking and drug-taking. Drugs: Educ. Prevent. Policy **7**(1), 21–37 (2000)

24. Pearson, M., West, P.: Drifting smoke rings. Connections **25**(2), 59–76 (2003)
25. Yon, G.V., et al.: netdiffuser: Network analysis for diffusion of innovations (2016)
26. Fujimoto, K.: AFFILIATIONEXPOSURE: stata module to compute an affiliation exposure model using two-mode actor(row)-by-event(column) network data. Statistical Software Components, Boston College Department of Economics, June 2011
27. Valente, T.W., Dyal, S.R., Chu, K.H., Wipfli, H., Fujimoto, K.: Diffusion of innovations theory applied to global tobacco control treaty ratification. Soc. Sci. Med. **145**, 89–97 (2015)

Investigating the Determinants of Users' Willingness to Pay for Answers on Q&A Platforms

Jia Gu[✉] and Lili Liu

College of Economics and Management,
Nanjing University of Aeronautics and Astronautics, Nanjing, China
{gujia,llili85}@nuaa.edu.cn

Abstract. Charging for answers on Q&A platforms is gaining popularity in Mainland China. For the purpose of making profit, understanding the determinants of users' willingness to pay for answers is crucial for Q&A platforms, yet remains unclear. To narrow the research gap, this study develops an extended UTAUT framework, which integrates trust and long tail effect. In particular, the impacts of seven antecedents are empirically investigated, including performance expectancy, effort expectancy, social influence, facilitating conditions, trust towards answer providers, trust towards the Q&A platform, and long tail effect. Data was collected from 123 Chinese Q&A platform users (all of them have paid for answers) and analyzed with SPSS 22.0. Findings indicate that users' willingness to pay is positively influenced by performance expectancy, facilitating conditions, trust towards the Q&A platform, and long tail effect. The potential theoretical and practical contributions are discussed.

Keywords: Q&A platforms ·
Unified Theory of Acceptance and Use of Technology (UTAUT) · Trust ·
Long tail effect · Willingness to pay

1 Introduction

Charging for answers on Q&A platforms is gaining popularity in Mainland China. The traditional Q&A platforms in mainland China (e.g., Baidu Knows, Sougou Ask, and Sina Love Question) are organized under free mode, where answers are free and accessible to any user, and the majority of revenue comes from advertisements. However, as the volume of content increases, the quality of answers in Q&A platforms are diluted [2], which requires questioners to spend more time and effort on filtering appropriate answers [8]. When the user's initial enthusiasm fade away, providing monetary incentives is an effective method to encourage users answering questions on Q&A platforms [24]. In recent years, Q&A platforms have been undergoing a tremendous transformation from providing free answers to charging for answers. Q&A platforms charging for answers have completed the screening of users to a certain extent because users willing to pay tend to have higher loyalty [13]. Questioners can enjoy better knowledge services, while respondents have the opportunity to become popular when they successfully realize their cognitive surplus [25]. For example, by paying to answer providers in Zhihu live and

C. Stephanidis (Ed.): HCII 2019, CCIS 1034, pp. 13–20, 2019.
https://doi.org/10.1007/978-3-030-23525-3_2

Fenda, questioners are able to enjoy timely and high-quality knowledge. The charging mode is also beneficial for answer providers (e.g., getting monetary rewards and social reputation for providing answers) [9, 22] and Q&A platforms (e.g., sharing the payment from questioners, motivating users to provide answers, maintaining the sustainability of the platform) in different ways.

As a relatively new phenomena, little is known about the key factors that affecting user's purchase behavior on Q&A platforms. Drawing on the Unified Theory of Acceptance and Use of Technology (UTAUT) [19], this study investigates how performance expectancy, effort expectancy, social influence, and facilitating conditions influence users' willingness to pay for answers on Q&A Platforms. Following prior studies, trust [4, 6] and long tail effect [18] are added as additional antecedents of willingness to pay, in order to generate fruitful findings with an extended UTAUT model. We seek to shed light on future studies on online paid knowledge. The results of this paper not only can contribute to future literature on online paid knowledge, but also can provide insights for Q&A platforms to better serve users, to motivate more users becoming knowledge providers, to increase the business income of Q&A platforms thus help the platform retain.

2 Theoretical Background

The Unified Theory of Acceptance and Use of Technology (UTAUT) model integrates various theories and research into a unified theoretical model to explain the adoption of technology, which has been widely accepted [23]. Four independent variables have been identified in the original UTAUT model, including performance expectancy (*the degree to which an individual believes that using the system will be helpful in job performance, and users seem to be more motivated to use and accept new technology if they perceive that this technology is useful*), effort expectancy (*the ease of using a system*), social influence (*the degree to which an individual perceives that important others believe he/she should use a new system*), and facilitating conditions (*organizational and technical support needed to use a new system*) [19].

There are many attempts that integrate additional variables to the UTAUT model [4, 6, 18]. For instance, trust has been proved as a key factor that affects users' willingness to pay [23], which has been studied in various papers. A lack of trust may discourage online consumers from participating in e-commerce [3], and online trust is positively related to the customer online purchase intention [5]. Therefore, we integrate trust with UTAUT model in this paper. In addition, long tail effect is considered as a prominent strength of e-commerce. It has been discussed by researchers as a specific characteristic of online shopping, and proved to be an important factor influencing consumers' willingness to pay [18]. Hence, long tail effect is added as an additional antecedent of willingness to pay in this study.

3   Research Model and Hypotheses

The research model is graphically represented in Fig. 1. In the following section, hypotheses are discussed in more details.

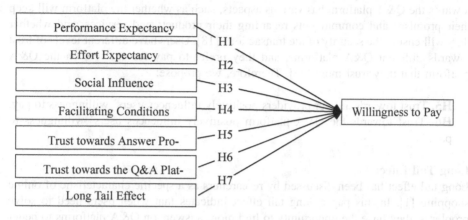

Fig. 1. Research model

UTAUT Hypotheses

In this study, willingness to pay is described as the possibility that a user pays for answers on Q&A platforms [7], which can be used as an important indicator to predict consumer behavior [16]. Users' problems will get solved by referring to other people's experience and professional answers on Q&A platforms, which help them achieve personal development [25]. In addition, by paying for answers online, users can get satisfactory answers faster, which improves their work efficiency. Operating the Q&A platform and paying for answers on the platform is not difficult. If users find the payment system easy to operate, they are more willing to pay on the Q&A platform. Moreover, when deciding whether pay for answers or not, people are always influenced by previous users' behavior. If individuals perceive stronger support from their significant others (their friends and relatives), they are more willing to pay on Q&A platforms. Finally, facilitating conditions such as smart phones, Internet, required knowledge and online customer support will also affect users' willingness to pay [18]. Therefore, we hypothesize:

H1. Performance expectancy positively influences users' willingness to pay.
H2. Effort expectancy positively influences users' willingness to pay.
H3. Social influence positively influences users' willingness to pay.
H4. Facilitating conditions positively influences users' willingness to pay.

Trust Towards Answer Providers and Trust Towards the Q&A Platform

Trust refers to the degree to which a user considers an e-business solution as credible, or a user's likelihood of believing others [12], which has been proved as a key factor that affects users' willingness to pay [21]. In this study, trust consists of two sub-dimensional constructs: trust towards answer providers and trust towards the Q&A platform. On one hand, based on the questioners' own preference and needs, they may develop higher level of trust towards a specific respondent, and pay for the answers provided by this respondent rather than alternatives [25]. On the other hand, trust towards the Q&A platform has various aspects, such as whether the platform will keep their promises and commitments regarding their products and services, and whether they will ensure the security of the transactions [18]. Users have different levels of trust towards different Q&A platforms, and they prefer to pay for answers on the Q&A platform that they trust more [25]. Therefore, we propose:

H5. Trust towards answer providers positively influences users' willingness to pay.
H6. Trust towards the Q&A platform positively influences users' willingness to pay.

Long Tail Effect
Long tail effect has been discussed by researchers as a specific characteristic of online shopping [1]. In this paper, long tail effect indicates that when users need to solve problems, they have the opportunity to find more answers on Q&A platforms to better meet their needs than offline. There are more answer providers on online Q&A platforms than offline, and users can select reliable people (based on their own perception) to answer their questions. It is suggested that long tail effect is positively associated with consumers' purchase behavior [18]. Therefore, we hypothesize:

H7. Long tail effect positively influences users' willingness to pay.

4 Research Methodology

4.1 Measurements

A questionnaire was designed to collect data. All the measurement items were first compiled in English, and then translated into Chinese. Two bilingual researchers translated the questionnaire back and forth for three times, during this process inconsistent translations were corrected. All of the items were adapted from prior studies, in order to ensure the content validity. Measurement items for performance expectancy, effort expectancy, social influence, and facilitating conditions were adapted from Venkatesh et al. [20]. The scales for trust towards answer providers, trust towards the Q&A platform, and long tail effect were modified from Singh et al. [18], while the items for willingness to pay were adapted from Pavlou et al. [16]. In this paper, the wording of the measurement statements was modified to better adapt to Q&A platforms. The questionnaire was designed based on a 7-point Likert scale that ranged from 1 (Strongly Disagree) to 7 (Strongly Agree) [14].

4.2 Data Collection

This survey was distributed by the Questionnaire Star Platform. People who had paid for answers on Q&A platforms were selected as respondents. Eventually, we received 123 valid samples. As a general rule, the minimum sample size should be at least five times as many observations as the number of variables to be analyzed [10]. Therefore, our sample size of 123 is sufficient.

Respondents' demographic information was summarized in Table 1. In conclusion, 56.1% of the respondents were female while 43.9% of them were male. More than 40% of the respondents were between 26 and 35 years old. 79.7% of the samples had Bachelor's degree. 32.5% of the samples' monthly income was between 5000 and 10000 yuan. In general, most of our respondents were young and middle-aged women with good educational background and upper middle income. Furthermore, 69.1% respondents preferred to use Zhihu live compared with other Q&A platforms, mainly because the platform was easy to operate, question would be answered very fast, and the answers were of high quality. Majority of the respondents (81.3%) paid for knowledge and skill-related answers.

Table 1. Respondent demographics.

Item	Category	Frequency	Percentage (%)
Gender	Male	54	43.9
	Female	69	56.1
Age	Under 18	6	4.88
	18–25	37	30.08
	26–35	59	47.97
	36–45	19	15.45
	46 and above	2	1.63
Education	High school and below	21	17.07
	Bachelor's degree	98	79.67
	Master's degree and above	4	3.25
Monthly income	Below 1500 yuan	16	13.01
	1500–3000 yuan	20	16.26
	3001–5000 yuan	34	27.64
	5001–10000 yuan	40	32.52
	Above 10000 yuan	13	10.57
Most frequently used paid Q&A platform	Fenda	7	5.69
	Zhihu live	85	69.11
	Value	9	7.32
	Sina Weibo Q&A	20	16.26
	Others (CSDN)	2	1.63
Type of paid content	Knowledge and skills	100	81.3
	Life experience	17	13.82
	Entertainment	6	4.88

4.3 Data Analyses and Results

Data was analyzed using SPSS 22.0. Reliability and validity of all constructs were examined. Reliability reflected the consistency of the measurements [10], which was assessed by Cronbach's alpha. The threshold value used to evaluate Cronbach's alpha was 0.60 [15]. In this paper, Cronbach's alpha for all constructs were greater than 0.6, indicating good reliability. Besides, factor analysis was conducted to examine validity. The KMO value was 0.918, greater than 0.6, implying that the data was valid [11]. The explanatory rate of cumulative variance after rotation was 69.143% (greater than 50%), signifying that information can be extracted effectively [10].

   Since multiple scale questions were used to test each construct, we calculated the average value of each items associated with a particular construct to generate new variables for SPSS analysis, including willingness to pay, performance expectancy, effort expectancy, social influence, facilitating conditions, trust towards answer providers, trust towards the Q&A platform, and long tail effect. First, we used correlation analysis to examine the correlation between willingness to pay and the other variables (Pearson correlation coefficient was checked). The correlation values between willingness to pay and seven antecedents exceeded 0.5 at a significant level of $p < 0.01$, indicating that there were significant positive correlations between them and we could conduct regression analysis [17]. Results of the regression analysis were shown in Fig. 2, in which performance expectancy ($\beta = 0.21$, $p < 0.05$), facilitating conditions ($\beta = 0.29$, $p < 0.001$), trust towards the Q&A platform ($\beta = 0.24$, $p < 0.05$), and long tail effect ($\beta = 0.23$, $p < 0.01$) were positively associated with willingness to pay, which accounted for 66.7% variance of it. However, effort expectancy, social influence, and trust towards answer providers had no significant impact on willingness to pay. Hence, H1, H4, H6, and H7 were supported, while H2, H3, and H6 were not supported.

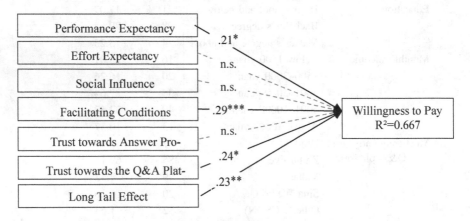

Fig. 2. Structural model

5   Contribution

The main purpose of this study was to examine the determinants of users' willingness to pay for answers on Q&A platforms. Findings confirmed that performance expectancy, facilitating conditions, trust towards the Q&A platform, and long tail effect were positively related to willingness to pay. However, notably, effort expectancy, social influence, and trust towards answer providers had no significant effect on willingness to pay. Effort expectancy reflects the ease of using the platform to pay for answers. Though the Q&A platforms and payment systems are easy to operate, users have to make additional effort (e.g., go through the payment process) to access the answers, which is more complex compared with obtaining free answers. Besides, users might make the purchase decision by themselves, rather than considering the suggestions from others, which could be a possible explanation on the insignificant relationship between social influence and willingness to pay. While using the Q&A platforms, users care more about the answers rather than answer providers, thus we failed to find a significant relationship between trust towards answers providers and willingness to pay. Moreover, it is difficult to find useful and real information about an answer provider on Q&A platforms.

This empirical study in one of the first that integrates trust (including trust towards answer providers and trust towards the Q&A platform) and long tail effect with UTAUT model to investigate users' willingness to pay for answers on Q&A platforms, thus makes contribution to the online paid knowledge literature. Practically, findings of this study provide helpful insights for managers of Q&A platforms. First, 81.3% of our respondents have paid for knowledge and skill-related answers. The Q&A platforms could recommend knowledge or skill-related Q&A collections to the questioners, most likely they will pay for the collections. Second, improve customer service quality to ensure that users' questions can be solved fast and efficiently. Third, Q&A platforms not only should strictly examine the qualification and professional competence of answer providers, but also need to ensure the security of the payment system. Finally yet importantly, Q&A platforms should adopt incentive mechanism to motivate more people becoming knowledge providers, in order to provide users with a broader selection of answers.

Acknowledgement. This study was supported by the Fundamental Research Funds for the Central Universities: No. NR2018002 awarded to second author and the Creative Studio of Electronic Commerce in Nanjing University of Aeronautics and Astronautics.

References

1. Brynjolfsson, E., Hu, Y., Simester, D.: Goodbye pareto principle, hello long tail: the effect of search costs on the concentration of product sales. Manage. Sci. **57**(8), 1373–1386 (2011)
2. Cathy: Zhihu.Com, bridging the gap of growing knowledge sharing demand in china. In: Harvard Business School Digital Initiative (2017)
3. Chen, Y.-H., Barnes, S.: Initial trust and online buyer behaviour. Industrial Manag. Data Syst. **107**(1), 21–36 (2007)

4. Cheng, D., Liu, G., Qian, C., Song, Y.F.: Customer acceptance of internet banking: integrating trust and quality with UTAUT model. In: IEEE International Conference on Service Operations and Logistics. IEEE (2008)
5. Ling, K.C., Chai, L.T., Piew, T.H.: The effects of shopping orientations, online trust and prior online purchase experience toward customers' online purchase intention. Int. Bus. Res. **3**(3), 63–76 (2010)
6. Codyallen, E., Kishore, R.: An extension of the UTAUT model with e-quality, trust, and satisfaction constructs. In: ACM SIGMIS CPR Conference on Computer Personnel Research: Forty Four Years of Computer Personnel Research: Achievements. ACM (2006)
7. Dodds, W.B., Monroe, K.B., Grewal, D.: Effects of price, brand, and store information on buyers. J. Mark. Res. **28**(3), 307–319 (1991)
8. Feng, E.: Chinese tech apps trade knowledge for cash. Financial Times (2017)
9. Guo, S., Guo, X., Fang, Y., Vogel, D.: How doctors gain social and economic returns in online health-care communities: a professional capital perspective. J. Manag. Inform. Syst. **34**(2), 487–519 (2017)
10. Hair, J.F., Black, W.C., Babin, B.J., Anderson, R.E.: Multivariate Data Analysis, 7th edn. Pearson, London (2009)
11. Kaiser, H.F.: A second generation little jiffy. Psychometrika **35**(4), 401–415 (1970)
12. Keat, T.K., Mohan, A.: Integration of TAM based electronic commerce models for trust. J. Am. Acad. Bus. **5**(1/2), 404–411 (2004)
13. Keith, M., Santanam, R., Sinha, R.: Switching costs, satisfaction, loyalty and willingness to pay for office productivity software. In: Proceedings of 43rd Hawaii International Conference on System Sciences (HICSS). IEEE Computer Society (2010)
14. Likert, R.: A technique for the measurement of attitudes. J. Arch. Psychol. **22**(140), 1–55 (1932)
15. MacCallum, R.C., Roznowski, M., Corinne, M.M., Reith, J.V.: Alternative strategies for cross-validation of covariance structure models. Multivar. Behav. Res. **29**(1), 1–32 (1994)
16. Pavlou, P.A., Fygenson, M.: Understanding and predicting electronic commerce adoption: an extension of the theory of planned behavior. MIS Q. **30**(1), 115 (2006)
17. Pearson, K.: Notes on the history of correlation. Bimetrika **13**(1), 25–45 (1920)
18. Singh, M., Matsui, Y.: How long tail and trust affect online shopping behavior: an extension to UTAUT2 Framework. Pac. Asia J. Assoc. Inform. Syst. **9**(4), 1–24 (2017)
19. Venkatesh, V., Morris, M.G., Davis, G.B., Davis, F.D.: User acceptance of information technology: toward a unified view. MIS Q. **27**, 425–478 (2003)
20. Venkatesh, V., Thong, J.Y., Xu, X.: Consumer acceptance and use of information technology: extending the unified theory of acceptance and use of technology. MIS Q. **36**(1), 157–178 (2012)
21. Wang, W.-T., Wang, Y.-S., Liu, E.-R.: The stickiness intention of group-buying websites: the integration of the commitment–trust theory and e-commerce success model. Inform. Manag. **53**(5), 625–642 (2016)
22. Wasko, M.L., Faraj, S.: Why should i share? Examining social capital and knowledge contribution in electronic networks of practice. MIS Q. **29**(1), 35–57 (2005)
23. Zhou, T., Lu, Y., Wang, B.: Integrating TTF and UTAUT to explain mobile banking user adoption. Comput. Hum. Behav. **26**(4), 760–767 (2010)
24. 蒋楠, & 王鹏程: 社会化问答服务中用户需求与信息内容的相关性评价研究——以"百度知道"为例. 信息资源管理学报(3), 35–45 (2012)
25. 赵宇翔, 刘周颖, & 宋士杰. :新一代知识问答平台中提问者付费意愿的影响因素探究. 数据分析与知识发现, **2**(8), 16–30 (2018)

Internet Use and Happiness: An Updated Review of Literature

Richard H. Hall$^{(\boxtimes)}$

Missouri University of Science and Technology, Rolla, MO, USA
rhall@mst.edu

Abstract. The purpose of this research is to review the literation on the relationship between internet use and happiness, updating a previous review [1], and
building upon a series of longitudinal studies following this initial review [2–4].
Reasons for studying happiness, and happiness definitions and measurement are
discussed. This is followed by a discussion of early research which found a
negative relationship between internet use and happiness, followed by studies
indicating a more positive relationship, supporting a "stimulation hypothesis"
that poses that the internet can act to facilitate face-to-face interactions. More
recent research has focused on social networking. With some important exceptions, these most recent studies continue to find that internet use is positively
related to happiness, while identifying a number of important mediating and
moderating variables, such as experience with the internet and social networking;
wealth; health; number of "friends"; the nature of interactions; extroversion, and
the ways in which users represent themselves online.

Keywords: Internet · Happiness

1 Why Study Happiness and the Internet?

Following the dawn of the new millennium, research on happiness increased dramatically, largely spurred on by the fact that people increasingly rate happiness as a major
life goal. For example, recent surveys have indicated that the strong majority of people
across many countries rate happiness as more important than income [5]. Lyubomirsky
[6] sums this research up, "…in almost every culture examined by researchers, people
rank the pursuit of happiness as one of their most cherished goals in life" (p. 239).

In addition, there is a large body of evidence that suggests situational factors, in
particular wealth, play a surprisingly small role in determining happiness. Some suggest that this may be the result of society moving into a post-materialistic phase, where
basic needs have been largely met for many in industrialized countries, so pursuit of
self-fulfillment becomes more important [5].

Finally, there are number of studies that indicate that happy people, in general, have
a positive effect on society. For example, there is evidence that happier people are more
successful and socially engaged [6]. Happy people are healthier, as well. For example,
in a synthetic analysis of 30 studies, Veenhoven [7] found that the effect of happiness is
comparable to the effect of not-smoking on longevity in healthy populations.

© Springer Nature Switzerland AG 2019
C. Stephanidis (Ed.): HCII 2019, CCIS 1034, pp. 21–27, 2019.
https://doi.org/10.1007/978-3-030-23525-3_3

affective expression). Time spent on the Internet was negatively related to both happiness measures; information gathering was positively related to Flourishing scores; and affective expression was unrelated to happiness.

Internet Use and Happiness: A Longitudinal Analysis [3]. This was an extension of the 2016 study (above), which explored the relationship between happiness and Internet use. The Internet Use Scale (IUS), developed in the previous study, was administered to college students along with the Flourishing Scale and the Satisfaction with Life Scale; and three new open-ended questions. I compared changes in the relationship between these measures, and their mean values, across the two samples, and carried out qualitative analyses of the open-ended questions. Results indicated that those who reported spending less time on the internet, less time expressing emotions, and more time checking facts, scored higher on measures of happiness. Further, participants found negative affective expression on the Internet particularly aversive. Finally, those with lower happiness scores were more likely to report playing on-line games; and those with higher happiness scores were more likely to identify Internet disinformation as aversive.

Internet Use and Happiness: A Replication and Extension [4]. This study was an extension of the two previous studies, which explored the relationship between happiness and Internet use. The Internet Use Scale (IUS) was administered to college students along with the Flourishing Scale and the Satisfaction with Life Scale. I compared changes in the relationship between these measures, and their mean values, across the three samples; assessed the relationship between use factors and happiness over-all, combining data from all samples; and evaluated the relationship between individual usage scale items and happiness. Results indicated that those who reported spending less time on the Internet, and less time expressing negative emotions scored higher on measures of happiness. There was also some indication that those who spend time checking facts on the Internet are happier, but the effect was not as strong nor consistent.

4.2   Highlights of Recent Research

- In a survey of more than 800 Dutch Adolescents, Valkenburg and colleagues [17], assessed students experience with a social networking site, by questioning participants regarding the number of reactions to their on-line profiles, the tone of the interactions, the number of real-life friendships established through the site, self-esteem, and wellbeing. They found that the number of interactions and the tone (more positive than negative) significantly predicted wellbeing; while the time spent on the site, and the real-life relationships established, did not.
- Kim and Lee [18] surveyed Facebook users. They assessed number of Facebook friends, and perceived social support from Facebook. Survey items were also included to determining the way in which users represented themselves (positively versus honestly). They found that number of Facebook friends, perceived social support from Facebook, and positive self-representation predicted happiness. They also found an interaction between self-representation and social support in

predicting happiness. That is, honest self-representation predicted happiness, so long as the user perceived strong social support from Facebook.

- In a comprehensive study which included a survey, as well as a daily diary of social network use, Oh and colleagues [19] examined the relationship between a number of social networking use variables with life satisfaction. They found that the degree of positive affect users felt while using social network sites (SNS) predicted life satisfaction, and the number of Facebook friends indirectly predicted life satisfaction, as mediated by positive affect.

- Penard and colleagues [20] utilized a part of the European Value Survey for a large population in Luxenburg to assess the relationship among a number of internet use variables, socioeconomic (SES) variables, and happiness. Controlling for a number of SES variables, the researchers found that those who reported not-using the internet in the past three months reported less happiness. This relationship remained significant, but was greatly reduced when controlling for income and health satisfaction, indicating that the relationship was strongest for those who scored low on income and health satisfaction. They also found the relationship was strongest for those who were younger.

- In another recent study [21] students were asked to carry out a task with the option of checking social media sites (multi-tasking) while completing the task. They also included a survey, which measured happiness, "technostress" and logged the amount of time students spent on the distraction task (visiting social media sites). They found that the amount of time spent on the social media sites predicted technostress scores, and both technostress and time on social media were negatively and significantly related to happiness.

- Lissitsa and colleagues [22] carried out a large-scale longitudinal exploration utilizing an annual government survey in Israel. They found that internet use was positively related to life satisfaction, controlling for a number of SES variables. The relationship was particularly strong for those with health problems and with lower incomes. They also found the strength of the relationship decreased over time from 2003–2012.

- In a study carried out in Finland [23], a large number of Facebook users were surveyed and their number of friends was recorded from their Facebook sites. Although well-being and number of Facebook friends was significantly correlated, the relationship was not significantly related when controlling for extroversion, indicating those with more friends tend to be more extroverted and extroverts scored higher on measures of life satisfaction.

- In a recent large-scale survey carried out in the Netherlands, social network use was not significantly related to happiness, and the relationship was even negative, when users were particularly unsatisfied with their social contacts [24].

- Finally, a recent review of this literature, indicates that factors that impact the internet/happiness relationship can be conceived of as four factors/channels: Effect on time usage, availability of new activities, access to new sources of information, and enhanced communication [25].

References

1. Hall, R.H., Banaszek, A.: The internet, happiness, and social interaction: a review of literature. In: Nah, F.F.-H. (ed.) HCIB 2014. LNCS, vol. 8527, pp. 166–174. Springer, Cham (2014). https://doi.org/10.1007/978-3-319-07293-7_16
2. Hall, R.H.: Internet use and happiness. In: Nah, F.F.-H., Tan, C.-H. (eds.) HCIBGO 2016. LNCS, vol. 9751, pp. 37–45. Springer, Cham (2016). https://doi.org/10.1007/978-3-319-39396-4_4
3. Hall, R.H.: Internet use and happiness: a longitudinal analysis. In: Nah, F.F.-H., Tan, C.-H. (eds.) HCIBGO 2017. LNCS, vol. 10294, pp. 213–222. Springer, Cham (2017). https://doi.org/10.1007/978-3-319-58484-3_17
4. Hall, R.H.: Internet use and happiness: a replication and extension. In: Nah, F.F.-H., Xiao, B.S. (eds.) HCIBGO 2018. LNCS, vol. 10923, pp. 465–474. Springer, Cham (2018). https://doi.org/10.1007/978-3-319-91716-0_37
5. Diener, E., et al.: New measures of well-being. In: Diener, E. (ed.) Assessing well Being, vol. 39, pp. 247–266. Springer, Dordrecht (2009). https://doi.org/10.1007/978-90-481-2354-4_12
6. Lyubomirsky, S., King, L., Diener, E.: The benifits of frequent positive affect: does happiness lead to success. Psychol. Bull. 6, 803–855 (2005). https://doi.org/10.1037/0033-2909.131.6.803
7. Veenhoven, R.J.: Healthy happiness: effects of happiness on physical health and the consequences for preventive health care. J. Happiness Stud. 9, 449–469 (2008). https://doi.org/10.1007/s10902-006-9042-1
8. Diener, E.: Subjective well-being: the science of happiness and a proposal for a national index. Am. Psychol. 55, 34–43 (2000). https://doi.org/10.1037/0003-066X.55.1.34
9. Myers, D.G.: The funds, friends, and faith of happy people. Am. Psychol. 55, 56–67 (2000). https://doi.org/10.1037/0003-066X.55.1.56
10. Freedman, J.: Happy People: What Happiness Is, Who Has It, and Why?. Harcourt Brace Jovanovich, New York (1978)
11. Magnus, K, Diener, E.: A longitudinal analysis of personality, life events, and subjective well-being. Paper Presented at the 63rd Annual Meeting of the Midwestern Psychological Association, Chicago, IL (1991)
12. Lyubomirsky, S., Ross, L.: Hedonic consequences of social comparison: a contrast of happy and unhappy people. J. Pers. Soc. Psychol. 73, 1141–1157 (1997). https://doi.org/10.1037/0022-3514.73.6.1141
13. Kraut, R., Patterson, M., Lundmark, V., Kiesler, S., Mukopadhyay, T., Scherlis, W.: Internet paradox: a social technology that reduces social involvement and psychological well-being? Am. Psychol. 53, 1017–1031 (1998). https://doi.org/10.1037/0003-066x.53.9.1017
14. Cummings, J., Butler, B., Kraut, R.: The quality of online social relationships. Commun. ACM 45, 103–108 (2002). https://doi.org/10.1145/514236.514242
15. Kraut, R., Kiesler, S., Boneva, B., Cummings, J., Helgeson, V.: Internet paradox revisited. J. Soc. Issues 58, 49–74 (2002). https://doi.org/10.1111/1540-4560.00248
16. Valkenburg, P.M., Peter, J.: Online communication and adolescent well-being: testing the stimulation versus the displacement hypothesis. J. Comput.-Mediat. Commun. 12, 1169–1182 (2007). https://doi.org/10.1111/j.1083-6101.2007.00368.x
17. Valkenburg, P.M., Peter, J., Schouten, A.P.: Friend networking sites and their relationship to adolecscents' well-being and social self-esteem. CyberPsychol. Behav. 9, 584–590 (2006). https://doi.org/10.1089/cpb.2006.9.584

18. Kim, J., Lee, J.R.: The Facebook paths to happiness: effects of the number of Facebook friends and self-presentation on subjective well-being. CyberPsychol. Behav. Soc. Netw. **6**, 359–364 (2011). https://doi.org/10.1089/cyber.2010.0374
19. Oh, J.H., Ozkaya, E., LaRose, R.: How does online social networking enhance life satisfaction? The relationships among online supportive interaction, affect, perceived social support, sense of community, and life satisfaction. Comput. Hum. Behav. **30**, 69–78 (2014). https://doi.org/10.1016/j.chb.2013.07.053
20. Penard, T., Poussing, N., Suire, R.: Does the internet make people happier? J. Socio-Econ. **46**, 105–116 (2013). https://doi.org/10.1016/j.socec.2013.08.004
21. Brooks, S.: Does personal social media usage affect efficiency and well-being? Comput. Hum. Behav. **46**, 26–37 (2015). https://doi.org/10.1016/j.chb.2014.12.053
22. Lissitsa, S., Chachasvili-Bolotin, S.: Life satisfaction in the internet age – changes in the past decade. Comput. Hum. Behav. **54**, 107–206 (2016). https://doi.org/10.1016/j.chb.2015.08.001
23. Lonnqvist, J., Deters, F.G.: Facebook friends, subjective well-being, social support, and personality. Comput. Hum. Behav. **55**, 113–120 (2016). https://doi.org/10.1016/j.chb.2015.09.002
24. Arampatzi, E., Burger, M.J., Novik, N.: Social network sites, individual social capital and happiness. J. Happiness Stud. **19**, 99–122 (2018). https://doi.org/10.1007/s10902-016-9808-z
25. Castellacci, F., Tveito, V.: Internet use and well-being: a survey and a theoretical framework. Res. Policy **47**, 308–325 (2018). https://doi.org/10.1016/j.respol.2017.11.007

HCI Design Principles and Visual Analytics for Media Analytics Platform

Ajaz Hussain[1]([✉]), Sara Diamond[1], Steve Szigeti[2],
Marcus A. Gordon[1], Feng Yuan[1], Melissa Diep[1], and Lan-Xi Dong[1]

[1] Visual Analytics Lab, OCAD University,
100 McCaul St, Toronto, ON M5T 1W1, Canada
{ahussain, sdiamond}@ocadu.ca
[2] University of Toronto, 3359 Mississauga Road,
Mississauga, ON L5L 1C6, Canada
steve.szigeti@utoronto.ca

Abstract. Media industries and advertisers are increasingly turning to big data analytics to better understand audience media consumption patterns, as evidenced by Canada's *Globe and Mail*'s applications *Sophi* and *TasteGraph* [1, 2]. Data analytics and interface design provide complementary perspectives for large datasets. HCI design principles have been applied to Business Intelligence (BI) platforms, including techniques which filter and summarize large data sets, and are equally relevant to media informatics platforms for advertisers, buyers, sellers, and planners [1, 7–9]. This analysis becomes more challenging when managing highly scalable and multi-dimensional audience survey data [3–6]. According to Dewdney and Ride visualization tools are essential for effective decision making in the communications industry as these ease cognitive load and decision-making [15]. Kirk proves that a visualization system becomes a successful tool when it builds on the user's extant domain knowledge, providing enhanced insights [13]. The research aims to leverage visualization design principles as defined by Tulp and Meirelles [6, 7] and in order to improve the UI/UX and visual analytic capabilities of a leading media analytics platform providing planners, advertisers, and media buyers with an interface to better understand their audience. We have analyzed and assessed the different application report parameters that explore television and radio survey datasets from a leading analytics firm. We propose design prototypes which are comprised of enhanced symbolic icons [9] through badges and glyphs, consistent colours [10], and layouts which maintain a visual hierarchy and filtration techniques [10, 11, 14] in order to minimize information clutter and cognitive overload. We propose a variety of interface designs that address user needs using HCI, heuristic design principles and novel visualization techniques [6, 7, 12, 15]. Next steps include validating our design prototypes through rigorous user testing and building high fidelity prototypes.

Keywords: HCI design principles · Visual analytics · Big data analytics · Media analytics platform · User experience and engagement

© Springer Nature Switzerland AG 2019
C. Stephanidis (Ed.): HCII 2019, CCIS 1034, pp. 28–35, 2019.
https://doi.org/10.1007/978-3-030-23525-3_4

1 Introduction

In an effort to better understand audience media consumption patterns, content producers, distributors and advertisers increasingly look to the collection and analysis of large data sets. This challenge has been addressed through various means, such as the *Globe and Mail*'s development and implementation of applications such as *Sophi* and *TasteGraph* [1, 2]. This Canadian national newspaper, a producer and distributor of content, employs *Sophi* to provide editors with visualizations of readers' engagement with articles, and *TasteGraph* which provides a means to group and correlate readers' interests in order address the needs of advertisers. These software platforms are key tools, necessary for analyzing large data sets and providing business intelligence. Sun et al. define Business Intelligence (BI) as, "the process of collecting, organizing and analyzing data to discover, visualize and display patterns, knowledge, and intelligence as well as other information within the data" [22]. Analysis becomes more challenging when managing highly scalable and multi-dimensional audience survey data [3–6]. Human Computer Interaction (HCI) design principles have been applied to BI platforms, including techniques which filter and summarize large data sets, and are equally relevant to media informatics platforms for advertisers, buyers, sellers, and planners [1, 7–9]. According to Dewdney and Ride, human culture has become increasingly reliant upon the visual dimension of human sense perception in communication, hence visualization tools are essential for effective decision making as these both ease cognitive load and support decision making [15].

The research described in this paper aims to leverage HCI design principles and effective data visualization techniques in order to improve the user interface and experience (UI/UX) in addition to the visual analytic capabilities of a media analytics platform (acronym MAP). MAP (i) provides planners, advertisers, and media buyers with a web-based interface with which to analyze their audience and (ii) aggregates audience (television and radio) behavioral data gathered from scalable, heterogeneous, multi-dimensional survey data.

In the growing field of media analytics, platforms need to provide instantaneous feedback, tracking and summary measures to effectively serve a range of users [1]. Our preliminary observations and analysis of MAP saw value in revising an interface in order to improve interaction. We have not yet undertaken user testing of our designs, and draw these conclusions from product comparisons and visualization best practices.

2 Literature Review

In this section, we discuss heuristic design principles, data visualization techniques, business and marketing insights.

2.1 Heuristic Design Approach and User-Friendly Interfaces

Jakob Nielsen describes ten usability heuristics: visibility of system status; a match between the system and the real world; user control and freedom to navigate; consistency and standards; error prevention; support to recover from errors; recognition rather than personal recall; flexibility to serve different levels of users; aesthetic and minimalist design; excellent help and documentation [8]. A heuristic approach to visualization involves an evaluation of these principles at every level of the design process as Zuk et al. suggest [16]. McCarthy argues that designers of a media analytics and marketing platform, like any other application, must use iterative prototyping to improve the product in response user testing, rather than trying to adapt users to the product [17]. Cairo shows that when designers create visualization elements, they are successful when they first determine the tasks that users must perform, then apply a diverse range of visual analytical techniques, and finally iteratively test and improve prototype designs [9]. It is not enough to present data in a general format, the information needs to be presented in a way that allows the users to absorb, process and extract further insights in ways that are relevant to their domain knowledge [19]. Yau explains that graphics are meant to be more than visually attractive; they need to be understandable and functional to users to gain insights [24]. Keim et al., like Nielson in an earlier era, emphasize the need for analysts to understand the sources of their decisions, making data and information processing transparent [8, 23].

2.2 Data Visualization and Analytics Techniques

Data visualization transforms complex datasets into meaningful insights allowing the user to identify patterns, trends and dataset composition, including interrogating the quality of the data. We consider five salient visual elements and groupings in our observations of the MAP interface. These represent areas of improvement that address heuristics, provide data visualization in context, respect the knowledge of the user, while enhancing user comprehension, efficiency, accuracy and support strategic thinking:

- *Badges & Glyphs* – Gray et al. propose various strategies that summarize the key aspects of an interface in order to help analysts summarize a context [10]. Depending on user interaction, for each parameter the size, color and opacity changes to illustrate the icon that is being selected [2].
- *Headline Figures* – While not strictly a visualization technique, headline figures provide "a powerful comparative message assume that viewers understand the range of good/bad for that metric" [10].
- *Charts & Graphs* – As Munzer and Meirelles [7, 14] indicate, providing variations in graph types will allow the user to gather further insight into the data displayed and will improve visual perception and pattern recognition according to Kirk [13]. In the proposed design prototypes, we provide a variety of charts and graphs creating alternate views of the same data.
- *Parameter Filtering* – Andrienko et al. support filtering techniques that eliminate clutter and occlusions, allowing the user to reduce clusters and to focus on relevant datasets on the dashboard [12]. They emphasize the use of filters to differentiate aspects of a data set [12]. Customize the interface will lead to an enhanced level of recognition and understanding.

2.3   Highly Dimensional Data Analysis Through Visual Insights

Ware shows that details on the screen become less prominent when there is a high contrast level between colours [11], an approach we adopted in our prototypes. In addition, we made use of interactive visualization in order to provide a direct summary of the user's analytical inquires. Edge et al. create visualizations allowing the user to navigate between data acquisition, processing, analysis and reveal the AI algorithms that process the data, using a visualization dashboard [3]. Text and visual information should present complementary perspectives in summarizing the datasets of the report. These tools should work together to enhance the data insight. Presenting a diverse range of communication techniques can help analysists absorb information rapidly and allow businesses to make timely decisions, as Lavalle et al. note [18].

Meirelles offers a three-stage model of perception that occurs when users gather insights from highly dimensional data that are effectively organized through data visualization [7]. In the first stage the user engages in rapid parallel processing to, "extract basic features", followed by, "slow serial processing stage to extract patterns and similar structures". Finally, in the third stage they obtain goal-oriented information that is displayed in a few succinct visuals that can be held, "in working visual memory" of the user [7]. The spacing, positioning and order of survey data into visual information can present users with a variety of insights with the data [21]. The users of MAP require accurate comprehension of television and radio datasets that are presented in tables and report summaries in a form that relates to their culture of use and tasks. It is important to present the information as a story and focus on the results and datasets that relate to the users' analysis needs [9]. As Kirk notes, when interpreting highly scalable survey data results, the interface should contain clear labels and provide context to each visualization to amplify recognition [13] and it should avoid redundant icons and features that take away the user from the important information as Munzer proves [14].

3   Methodology and Proposed Design Prototypes

In this section, we discuss the proposed interface designs that make use of heuristics and various visualization techniques with the intention of enhancing cognitive efficiency and insights [7]. MAP is comprised of two modules containing a variety of visual interfaces, (i) an interface for parametric selection to create a report, and (ii) the report itself.

3.1   Observation and Analysis of Input Interface

The interface for generating reports employs multiple rows and columns which allow users to select and compare different program and stations according to various variables (such as trends, rating, audience reach, and population by minute).

Figure 1 provides a side-by-side comparison of the existing input interface (on the left) with our proposed design prototype (on the right). The annotations ❶, ❷, ❸, and ❹ correspond to the discussion below.

Fig. 1. Input interface of *Creating New Program List Report*

1. *Data Range*: **Users must choose a date range to undertake their analysis.** The predefined and custom date range options are currently not in the same format, with predefined dates presented as a pull-down list and the custom date selection using a calendar visualization. We propose a calendar visualization for both options to maintain consistency (see Neilson's heuristics and Andrienko et al.'s visualization methods [8, 12]). For additional interface consistency, the "Add" button should always be included in both the predetermined and custom option.

2. *Audience*: **Users need to compare different demographic categories' consumption of media content on different stations.** In the existing interface, there is no indication of the searchable demographic categories. Our prototype follows Nielsen's recommendations and maintains a consistent and standardized style [8].

3. *Program Filter*: **In order to understand and compare audience numbers for specific programs, the user must choose the number of airings of a program.** In the existing interface, there's a field to select the minimum number of airings for the programs by manually inputting a number or using arrows to increase or decrease the number of minimum airings. Our research proposes the simplified approach by showing distinct group-based air range values, like 1–3, 4–6, 5+, to establish a scalable view for the user as suggested by Gray et al. [10].

4. *Dayparts*: Users chose segments of the day, understood as "dayparts" to consider stations, programs and audience demographics in relation to time periods. Using Ware's guidelines, we propose that visualizations be constructed using common scales [11]. This strategy improves the display of the predetermined dates and custom dates section, where the visual representations differ. The predetermined pull-down list of dates should be accompanied by a symbol to help the user visualize the date ranges as Cairo et al. suggest [9]. A visual relationship can be created using iconic representation of real-world objects like a clock design that accompanies the calendar visualization to help the user recognize the action needed.

3.2 Observation and Analysis of Output Interface

A key purpose of the report is the identification of programs which situate the target audience in relation to the viewing rates. When multiple audiences are selected for the report, the target audience groups are compared to the overall viewership of each program. Figure 2 presents the side-by-side comparison of existing generated output report interface (on-the-left) with proposed design prototype (on-the-right). We discuss salient design gaps annotated as ❶, ❷, and ❸, with proposed solutions (see below).

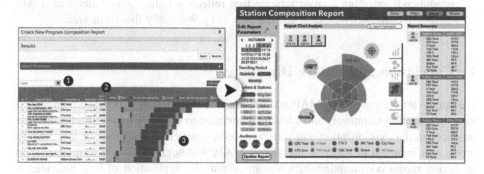

Fig. 2. Output interface of *Station Composition Report*

Of significance is our change of visualization strategies. We propose replacing a tree map strategy with a sunburst chart, "with layers to show relative contributions to the whole [10].

1. *Chart Mode*: It allows users to either view the full report summary table or hide the composition bar graph to view the data behind the graph visualization; they cannot be viewed simultaneously. In addition, when exporting the report only the raw data will be transferred to a spreadsheet (not the visualization). In the proposed design, we provide the ability to visualize and interpret the resulted report by variety of visual analytics, as suggested by Gray et al. [10] and LaValle et al. [18] that there needs to be a variety of visual charts and graphs in report summaries. Users need the ability to easily process the information and not rely on the numbers and tables alone for analysis. For instance, Fig. 2 represents a *Station Composition Report* allowing the user to identify the radio stations that reflect the target audience in relation to overall listenership. We used headline figures, as suggested by Andrienko [12] and Meirelles [7] to represent variables such as listener's age-groups and radio stations. In addition, the meaningful key insights from data are extracted and displayed in a summary table grouped by age, and stations. Users can select different charts and graphs based on their context and preferences.

2. *Selection Highlighting*: The "100% Mode" button changes the graph from single viewership rates to the highest composition levels for the selected target audience, but in the current design it is not clear as only the graph changes. Each audience category can be selected to make the composition bar graph reflect the particular audience compared to the program/station name, yet it is not clear which target is being shown. To improve the level of information processing, we instead display the visualizations along common scales [9].

3. *Colour Scheme*: The composition bar graph generates random colours, with the exception of the light blue colour that is reserved for the first target audience. Gray et al. suggests varying the opacity of categories in order to clearly indicate the choices [20]. We apply this technique to audience selection in the table. Ware recommends selecting a color scheme that reflects a light colour palette as it will enhance the distinctiveness of the datasets [11]. We apply this technique.

4   Conclusion and Future Directions

We conducted an analysis of MAP and highlighted areas which benefit from enhanced data visualization techniques and additional attention to HCI heuristics. Employing best practices in data visualization and interface design, we created a series of low fidelity prototypes intended to improve the use of MAP. Although MAP is a tool specific to analyzing media consumption data, we argue that the application of best practices is essential to all business analytics tools. We must strive to ensure that tools for data analysis, regardless of domain, be accessible, navigable, and intuitive. Having created low fidelity prototypes based on existing literature, our research will now progress to the validation stage and conduct user testing to evaluate the prototypes. Through this process we intend to iterate our designs with the intention of building high fidelity prototypes which will lead to further evaluation and refinement.

References

1. Peter, J., Szigeti, S., Jofre, A., Edall, G., Diamond, S.: The Sophi HUD: a novel visual analytics tool for news media. OCAD University Open Research Repository (2017)
2. Karawash, A., et al.: TasteGraph: a visual analytics tool for profiling media audiences' tastes. In: Proceedings of the IEEEVis, InfoVis, Berlin (2018)
3. Edge, D., Larson, J., White, C.: Bringing AI to BI: enabling visual analytics of unstructured data in a modern business intelligence platform. In: Extended Abstracts of the 2018 CHI Conference on Human Factors in Computing Systems, p. CS02. ACM, April 2018
4. Delen, D., Moscato, G., Toma, I.L.: The impact of real-time business intelligence and advanced analytics on the behaviour of business decision makers. In: 2018 International Conference on Information Management and Processing (ICIMP), pp. 49–53. IEEE, January 2018
5. Marjanovic, O., Dinter, B., Ariyachandra, T.R.: Introduction to the minitrack on organizational issues of business intelligence, business analytics and big data (2018)
6. Tulp, J.W.: Designing for small and large datasets. In: Bihanic, D. (ed.) New Challenges for Data Design, pp. 377–390. Springer, London (2015). https://doi.org/10.1007/978-1-4471-6596-5_20
7. Meirelles, I.: Hierarchical structures: trees. In: Design for Information: An Introduction to the Histories, Theories, and Best Practices Behind Effective Information Visualizations, pp. 5–15. Rockport publishers (2013)
8. Nielsen, J.: 10 usability heuristics for user interface design. Nielsen Norman Group **1**(1) (1995). https://www.nngroup.com/articles/ten-usability-heuristics/

9. Cairo, A.: The Truthful Art: Data, Charts, and Maps for Communication. New Riders, San Francisco (2016)
10. Gray, C.C., Teahan, W.J., Perkins, D.: Understanding out analytics: a visualization survey. J. Learn. Anal. School Comput. Sci. (2017). https://research.shadowraider.com/jspui/handle/1471/19
11. Ware, C.: Color. In: Information visualization: perception for design, pp. 95–138. Morgan Kaufmann (2013)
12. Andrienko, G., Andrienko, N., Bak, P., Keim, D., Wrobel, S.: Visual analytics infrastructure. In: Andrienko, G., Andrienko, N., Bak, P., Keim, D., Wrobel, S. (eds.) Visual Analytics of Movement, pp. 103–129. Springer, Heidelberg (2013). https://doi.org/10.1007/978-3-642-37583-5_4
13. Kirk, A.: The context of visualization. In: Data Visualization: A Successful Design Process. Packt Publishing Ltd. (2012)
14. Munzer, T.: What's vis, and why do it? In: Visualization Analysis and Design, pp. 1–18. AK Peters/CRC Press (2014)
15. Dewdney, A., Ride, P.: Digital media as a subject. In: Curran, J. (ed.) The Digital Media Handbook, pp. 18–28 (2014). Chap. 2
16. Zuk, T., Schlesier, L., Neumann, P., Hancock, M. S., Carpendale, S.: Heuristics for information visualization evaluation. In: Proceedings of the 2006 AVI Workshop on Beyond Time and Errors: Novel Evaluation Methods for Information Visualization, pp. 1–6. ACM, May 2006
17. McCarthy, J., Wright, P.: Technology as Experience. MIT Press, Cambridge (2007)
18. LaValle, S., Lesser, E., Shockley, R., Hopkins, M.S., Kruschwitz, N.: Big data, analytics and the path from insights to value. MIT Sloan manage. Rev. **52**(2), 21 (2011)
19. Garrett, J.J.: Elements of User Experience: User-Centered Design for the Web and Beyond. Pearson Education, London (2010)
20. Gray, J., Chambers, L., Bounegru, L.: The Data Journalism Handbook: How Journalists Can Use Data to Improve the News. O'Reilly Media, Inc., Newton (2012)
21. Tourangeau, R., Couper, M.P., Conrad, F.: Spacing, position, and order: interpretive heuristics for visual features of survey questions. Public Opin. Quart. **68**(3), 368–393 (2004)
22. Sun, Z., Sun, L., Strang, K.: Big data analytics services for enhancing business intelligence. J. Comput. Inform. Syst. **58**(2), 162–169 (2018)
23. Keim, D., Kohlhammer, J., Ellis, G., Mansmann, F.: Mastering the information age solving problems with visual analytics (2010). http://www.vismaster.eu/wp-content/uploads/2010/11/title-page-to-chapter-1.pdf
24. Yau, N.: Choosing tools to visualize data. In: Visualize This: The FlowingData Guide to Design, Visualization, and Statistics, pp. 53–89 (2015)

Beautifying Profile Pictures in Online Dating: Dissolving the Ideal-Reality Gap

Takuya Iwamoto[1,2,3](✉) and Kazutaka Kurihara[2,3]

[1] Cyberagent, Inc., Abema Towers 40-1 Udagawacho,
Shibuya-ku, Tokyo 153-0042, Japan
iwamoto_takuya_xa@cyberagent.co.jp
[2] Japan Adcanced Institute of Science and Technology,
1-1 Asahidai, Nomi, Ishikawa 923-1292, Japan
[3] Tsuda University, 2-1-1 Tsuda-Cho, Kodaira-shi, Tokyo 187-8577, Japan

Abstract. With the drastic expansion of the online dating service market, attractive profile pictures are vital in the competitive world of dating. To attract others using these pictures, photo editors are helpful. However, enhanced profile pictures produce an ideal-reality gap. The more a profile picture is beautified, the wider is the gap between the image and the actual person, which can cause discomfort when two users meet in person. A solution to the gap problem is the gradually reversing the beautified image to the non-edited image over time, which was supported by our first experiment which tested if subjects could notice the gradual changes in given profile pictures over certain time. Additionally, we conducted an experiment, where one group saw gradual changes of a beautified image while another just saw the beautified image, and finally, the subjects' minds to meet the model on the image was compared. This paper discusses both the experiments.

Keywords: Online dating · Love · Profile picture

1 Introduction

Since the release of Windows 95 and match.com, an international online dating service, the internet has become a major way to find potential matches. A survey conducted by Stanford University in 2010 reported that about 20% of heterosexual couples met online, which is ranked third following meeting through friends and in bars/restaurants [1]. From the same survey, approximately 70% of same-sex couples meet online, and this method of meeting has been ranked the first.

Bigger the dating service market becomes, more the competition to obtain attractive matches become keen. One possible approach to attract other users among online dating services is editing profile pictures.

Every online connection begins with a person's profile. Making a profile attractive is indispensable to receiving messages from target users. Aside from the usual self-introduction, a profile picture is important for attracting dating candidates. A research study of various dating services found that the attractiveness of a profile picture is positively related to the profile owner's popularity and the number of messages received

© Springer Nature Switzerland AG 2019
C. Stephanidis (Ed.): HCII 2019, CCIS 1034, pp. 36–41, 2019.
https://doi.org/10.1007/978-3-030-23525-3_5

[2]. An easy way for users to make their profiles more appealing is to use a photo editing app. Due to the user-friendly interfaces and functions of photo editors, users can easily enhance their profiles. Photo editors have become especially popular among women, and there is some merit to that since these enhancements do appear to motivate target users to contact them. However, the key problem is that enhanced profiles are estranged from a person's actual appearance, which can create problems when people meet in real life. For example, a person may feel depressed because of the gap between another person's real appearance and decorated profile photo.

Our first study showed that human beings are not good at noticing subtle changes over time. Such a phenomenon is called "changing blindness" in which humans lack the ability to detect visual changes [3]. Taking this changing blindness into account, our team proposed a plan to mitigate any discomfort when two users meet in person by gradually changing the beautified images back into the original images through frequent communication. This paper provides the results of the first experiment that tested if subjects could identify the gradual changes in given profile images as well as an explanation of an extended experiment.

2 Pilot Study

The word "beautifying" means that user makes their photos look more beautiful. The extent of beautification can be expressed as the difference between images before and after beautification. To examine the perceptual ability of human beings to gradual changes in images, we conducted an experiment where the subjects were shown beautified images that gradually shifted to the original images over time.

Preparation of Beautified Image
To prepare pairs of pre- and post-enhanced images, three women (A, B, and C) were instructed to take photos of themselves and to beautify their images by editing them.

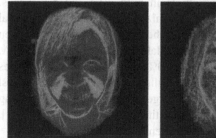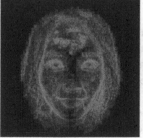

A)Age in the 30s: takes selfies rarely   B) Age in the 30s: takes selfies rarely   C)Age in the 20s;takes selfies frequently

Fig. 1. Color mapping of edits made to three participants' pictures (Color figure online)

The difference in each pair of images is visualized in Fig. 1. A pixel is colored one of the three colors: black, red, or yellow. A black pixel shows no change in the before and after images. A red pixel represents a slight change, while a yellow pixel symbolizes a large change. Each woman has a unique approach to beautify their images or has a different combination of the parts of their faces that they especially change. In the case of female A, her forehead was shrunk and her nasolabial fold or laugh lines were blurred. For the female B, her eyes were enlarged, the contour of her face was slimmed, and her forehead was randomly blurred. Finally, the female C made her eyes bigger while reducing the width of her nose [4].

There were mainly seven heavily edited areas in the participants' faces, which were represented as seven yellow sections in their faces in Fig. 1. Test subjects were shown the women's images over eight days, beginning with the beautified image which gradually reverted to the original image by the eighth day. Throughout the experiment, the seven parts were used as reference to see if the test subjects could figure out which part of the women's faces were changed.

2.1 Procedure

Ten subjects, five females and five males, participated in the experiment. The subjects watched 30 and 5 s videos for each prepared image three times (i.e., they watched 6 different videos three times and so they watched 18 videos in total). In the videos, the beautified image gradually dissolved or reverted to the original, non-edited images over a five or thirty second period. The subjects were informed in advance that the images of the women would undergo change but were not told what was altered. For each video, subjects were asked to identify the parts of the face that was changed and they had three chances to explain the query.

2.2 Result

Table 1 shows a summary of the subjects' performance in identifying changes in photo images A, B, and C during their viewing of the 5 s and 30 s videos. A score of each cell in the table indicates the number of subjects who could recognize the difference in a specified area of face after a certain number of tries. For example, for eyes in C, no subjects could identify the changes despite six trials in both 30 s and 5 s videos. Further, in the case of image A, 40% of subjects recognized the change in nasolabial fold but no one could not identify the changes in the forehead. In theory, there were ten subjects who could identify the changes in both the nasolabial fold and forehead for A, so there were 20 potential identifications. The value of 20% under the block A indicates that four out of 20 possible identifications were fulfilled. Theoretically, each test subject can notice 7 different changes. Taking the average of the numbers of noticing changes in heavily edited areas for each subject, the resulting score was 1.2 out of 7 [1]. There is no subject who could notice more than two identifications [1].

2.3 Discussion

From the results above, the average score of identifying changes in heavily edited areas was 1.2. Additionally, gender differences did not affect the identification score for changes in the face. Averages of the identification scores calculated after being grouped by gender did not differ at all [1]. Therefore, in the first experiment, we concluded that

Table 1.

	Nasolabial fold	Forehead	Eyes	Forehead	Outline	Eyes	Nose
30s	A		B			C	
1st try	1	0	0	0	0	0	0
2nd try	2	0	0	0	1	0	0
3rd try	1	0	1	2	0	0	0
	40.0%	0.0%	10.0%	20.0%	10.0%	0.0%	0.0%
	20.0%		13.3%			0%	
5s	A		B			C	
1st try	0	0	0	0	0	0	1
2nd try	0	0	0	0	1	0	0
3rd try	1	0	0	0	0	0	1
	10.0%	0.0%	0.0%	0.0%	10.0%	0.0%	20.0%
	5.0%		3.3%			10%	

the modifications of beautified images into non-edited images tended to be unnoticed as long as the speed of changes was gradual [1].

3 Extended Experiment

Second experiment lasting 10 days was conducted involving 22 male test subjects between 18 and 28 years old. The subjects were divided into two groups: the controlled group were shown the same beautified image for 10 days straight; the experimental group were shown the beautified image on the first day; thereafter, they saw progressively unedited images until day 8. Figure 2 lists what the group B saw in chronological order. Further, subjects in group B were shown the non-edited picture once a day for the last 3 days of the experiment. Finally, on the last day of the experiment, both groups were shown the non-edited profile picture and asked to rate on a 7-point Likert.

Fig. 2. Gradual changes of the fully beautified image (left) into the non-edited image (right) over eight days

Result of Group B scale their interesting in meeting the model on the photo. We hypothesized that less group A would agree to meet the model as compared to group B because group A were just shown the beautified image continuously for 10 days while group B was gradually introduced to the non-beautified image. Besides, because only group B was shown gradual changes of the images through the period, we asked them if they had recognized the subtle changes in the images.

3.1 Result

The result of the additional question for group B was that 2 out of 12 subjects in group B answered positively. The results of the extended experiment on groups A and B are shown in Fig. 3. The outcome was completely opposite to the hypothesis. Statistically, the result shows that group A scored an average of 5.2 (with 7 representing a strong desire to meet the model and 1 representing no desire at all), and group B scored 3.2. The t-test's result had a p-value of 0.009, representing a significant value. We intend to conduct extensive experiments to further investigate the reasons for this unexpected result.

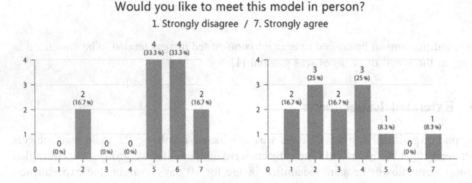

Would you like to meet this model in person?
1. Strongly disagree / 7. Strongly agree

Fig. 3. Result of the question for group A and B

4 Conclusion

We proposed a plan to mitigate the discomfort caused by the difference between a beautified profile picture and the real-life appearance of the person when two users of online dating services meet in person. A possible solution is slowly reversing the beautified image to the original image through frequent communication. As part of a preliminary study, this paper provides the results of an experiment that tested whether the test subjects can perceive the differences in profile pictures when shown gradual changes from edited to non-edited photos. The subjects watched 30 and 5 s videos of the gradual shifts for 10 subjects and then were asked to identify the differences. The outcome was that one test subject could only identify 1.2 out of 7 heavily edited areas on an average. In real-time online dating, it is common for users to communicate online for a long time before meeting in person. Since the users will see profile pictures over a much longer period than the experimental conditions set up by us, it is expected that a gradual swap from the beautified to non-edited photo will go nearly undetected. After the initial study, we conducted a 10-day experiment that tested whether the subjects would want to meet someone in an image that has gone through a gradual change to the non-edited profile picture, rather than an abrupt change in the images shown. Surprisingly, the result was opposite to our hypothesis. The group that was abruptly shown a non-beautified picture responded more positively to meeting the model than the group that was subtly introduced to the non-edited photo. In the future, we would like to conduct further experiments that delve into why the result mentioned above turned out to be so. More importantly, we plan to prepare a communication tool that resembles a chatroom in a dating service, and we will study the effect of the gradual changes from the beautified photos to natural photos on real-life first impressions. Finally, by introducing the reversing method in real services, we would like to reduce the discomfort caused by the ideal-reality gap between beautified and real images when two users meet in real life.

References

1. Rosenfeld, M.J., Thomas, R.J.: Searching for a mate the rise of the internet as a social intermediary. Am. Sociol. Rev. **77**(4), 523–547 (2012)
2. Rudder, C.: Dataclysm: Love, Sex, Race, and Identity-What Our Online Lives Tell Us about Our Offline Selves. Broadway Books, New York City (2015)
3. Simons, D.J.: Current approaches to change blindness. Vis. Cogn. **7**(1–3), 1–5 (2000)
4. Iwamoto, T., Kurihara, K., Esora, M., Nishimoto, K.: Towards soft landing in an online dating service: bridging the ideal–real gap. In: Proceedings of the 8th Augmented Human International Conference (AH 2017), p. 37 (2017)

Emotion Recognition in Social Media: A Case Study About Tax Frauds

Stefanie Niklander(⊠)

Universidad Autónoma de Chile, Av. Pedro de Valdivia 425, Santiago, Chile
stefanie.niklander@uautonoma.cl

Abstract. Analyzing and understanding the relation of emotions and human computing interaction has become a necessity today. Indeed, sentiment analysis tools have gained special attention during the last years in order to facilitate and support the understanding and study of human affections. In this paper, we analyze an important Chilean tax fraud case by combining sentiment analysis and critical discourse analysis. We take as a case study, the tweets of the year 2018 that contain the #SQM hashtag. This case involves tax fraud and violations of political campaign laws. People from different political parties created fake invoices, which are then paid by SQM to be illegally used onto political parties violating campaign finance laws. Interesting results are obtained where we identify which topics and persons have a negative or positive connotation in the readers.

Keywords: Sentimental analysis · Critical discourse analysis · Opinion mining · Social media

1 Introduction

Analyzing and understanding the relation of emotions and human computing interaction has become a necessity today. Indeed, sentiment analysis tools have gained special attention during the last years in order to facilitate and support the understanding and study of human affections [1]. Despite the great advances in the interpretation of emotions, the existence of ironies and sarcasms in speeches make the automatic analysis a hard task. Identifying these two rhetorical figures is very difficult, so it is necessary to explore other research techniques to have a complete analysis. Emotions are present in every text produced by people, but they become even more present when the issues are controversial.

In this paper, we will analyze an important Chilean tax fraud case by combining sentiment analysis and critical discourse analysis. Critical discourse analysis (CDA) is a type of discourse analytical research that primarily studies the way social power abuse, dominance, and inequality are enacted, reproduced and resisted by text and talk in the social and political context. Critical discourse take explicit position and thus want to understand, expose social inequality. CDA aims ultimately to make a change of the existing social reality in which discourse is related in particular ways to other social elements such as power relations, ideologies, economic and political strategies and policies [2].

C. Stephanidis (Ed.): HCII 2019, CCIS 1034, pp. 42–44, 2019.
https://doi.org/10.1007/978-3-030-23525-3_6

We take as a case study, the tweets of the year 2018 that contain the #SQM hashtag. This case involves tax fraud and violations of political campaign laws. People from different political parties created fake invoices, which SQM then paid. Owners of those fake invoices then transferred those funds onto political parties violating campaign finance laws. SQM (Sociedad Química y Minera de Chile) is a Chilean chemical company and a supplier of plant nutrients, lithium and industrial chemicals. The company was under investigation for the aforementioned concern. Interesting results are obtained where we identify which topics and persons have a negative, positive or neutral connotation related to this case. This paper is organized as follows: Sect. 2 presents the problem, results and discussion. Conclusions and some lines of future directions are given at the end.

2 Discussion and Results

Within social networks and various websites, million users express their opinion daily. Many of the opinions in these media remain anonymous. Knowing what each person and with which sense wrote them might help for business or marketing as well as in political issues. The evaluation is done on two stages, in the first one the data is analyzed via SentiStrength [3], which performs automatic sentimental analysis on texts, while in the second one, discourse analysis is employed. By using sentiment analysis we can recognize whether or not a text is positive, negative or neutral and with CDA we can infer the point of view of tweets towards a particular target.

When we apply emotional computing (via SentiStregth) to the SQM tweets we can observe that people comment are very critical with the hashtag 2018, since 52.5% of the comments were rated as negative. However, 44.5% of them were positive and 3% neutral. Notwithstanding the foregoing, we were able to verify that there are errors in the data just delivered, in the sense that the tool could not recognize the ironies present in the tweets. 9.5% of the tweets posted as positive contained ironies in their content (Table 1).

Table 1. Polarity statistics in SQM tweets

Positive	44,50%
Negative	52,50%
Neutral	3%

When analyzing the #SQM hashtag through the Critical discourse analysis (CDA), we would see the discontent of the Chilean population against the SQM case. This discontent is due to the fact that none of those accused of committing fraud obtained judicial penalties. The tweets complain about the existing impunity in this case and claim for a justice that applies penalties to all equally. In addition, there is a constant call for no more corruption in Chile. The above is manifested through the constant use of the #nomáscorrupción (#nomorecorruption) hashtag in their tweets.

It is striking that no differences are made by political sectors. It is said that everyone is corrupt, regardless of his or her political party. This causes indignation and loss of confidence in politicians in general. This is aggravated when the response of the institutions, as is the case studied, acts with a lack of transparency, without telling the truth or giving explanations that are not very credible.

Finally, most of people who comment with the #SQM asks that the national resources must be returned to all Chileans. They ask that the company be nationalized and stop being a group of Chilean businessmen.

3   Conclusions

In this paper we study the combination of sentimental analysis and CDA, with the purpose of enriching the analysis and obtaining more reliable data. We observed that the population has acquired a great amount of information on the network and is also a recipient and transmitter of opinions. Citizens can answer political power and demand from politicians a degree of transparency superior to that of the past. To continue observing these phenomena we consider it is necessary to enlarge the corpus for enriching the research and for obtaining definitive results.

References

1. Fairclough, N.: El análisis crítico del discurso como método para la investigación en Ciencias Sociales. In: Wodak, R., Meyer, M. (eds.) Métodos de análisis crítico del discurso, pp. 179–203. Gedisa, Barcelona (2003)
2. Buimer, H.P., Bittner, M., Kostelijk, T., van der Geest, T.M., van Wezel, R.J.A., Zhao, Y.: Enhancing emotion recognition in VIPs with haptic Feedback. In: Stephanidis, C. (ed.) HCI 2016. CCIS, vol. 618, pp. 157–163. Springer, Cham (2016). https://doi.org/10.1007/978-3-319-40542-1_25
3. Thelwall, M., Buckley, K., Paltoglou, G., Cai, D., Kappas, A.: Sentiment strength detection in short informal texts. J. Am. Soc. Inf. Sci. Technol. **61**, 2544–2558 (2010)

Investigating the Usage Patterns and the Implications of Young Adults' Social Media Usage in South Africa

Shanay Paideya[1]([✉]), Adheesh Budree[1], and Shivani Arora[2]

[1] University of Cape Town, Cape Town 7700, South Africa
shanaypaideya@gmail.com, adheesh.budree@uct.ac.za
[2] Delhi University, Delhi, India
dr.shivani.research@gmail.com

Abstract. Social media has rapidly grown and become a prominent and integral part of our daily lives. Social media usage has various effects on users. The purpose of this research is to provide an insight on the current social media usage patterns of young adults in South Africa and to explore the implications of social media usage on social interactions. A survey was conducted and the data gathered from 103 participants was analysed. The usage pattern analysis found that most users are followers rather than posters. The following factors were found through exploratory factor analysis: social media dependency, social interaction impact and false self-comparison/impress. It was found that social media usage affects face-to-face conversations and therefore affects the quality of relationships. It was also found that these factors are linked to social norms.

Keywords: Social media · Implications · Usage patterns · Young adults

1 Introduction

Internet access in developing countries is rapidly increasing which has helped bridge the "digital divide", giving people a platform to express their views and giving them a sense of self-empowerment [1]. It has created a vast amount of opportunities for users, due to its extensive capabilities such as providing educational and development opportunities, as well as given rise to the use of social media [1].

South Africa, a developing country, has a population of approximately 57.2 million people [3]. Approximately half of the South African population is present online, there is an estimated 21 million internet users in South Africa [4]. Facebook is ranked the most used social media platform with 2.2 billion users worldwide [5]. It is also the most used platform in South Africa with 16 million active users [6].

Social media has influenced the way people interact and socialize impacting their daily lives [2]. It does not require any prior training/skills to be used and is easily accessible giving it a wide user base [9]. There are various reasons and influencing factors that make people utilize social media and some are common while others vary depending on different factors [7]. Personal influencing usage factors can include personality or human satisfying needs [8]. There are also external influencing factors

© Springer Nature Switzerland AG 2019
C. Stephanidis (Ed.): HCII 2019, CCIS 1034, pp. 45–57, 2019.
https://doi.org/10.1007/978-3-030-23525-3_7

such as the intention of use, capabilities of the social media site or the ease of use of the site. Different users may be influenced by different factors in different contexts and environments, therefore influencing their usage patterns [9]. The use of social media has various implications on its users [10].

1.1 Classification of Social Media

There are various types of social media platforms that have a combination of functionalities that allow users to interact in different ways [9]. Various social media platforms, such as Facebook, Twitter, WhatsApp, LinkedIn, YouTube and Instagram help facilitate user actions [11]. These platforms are classified by a type depending on the content generated and the way in which users engage on the platform, since new platforms are constantly evolving and new ones being created, the following model can be used to classify social media platforms based on users' presence/media richness and self-presentation/self-disclosure [2] (Fig. 1).

		Social presence/ Media richness		
		Low	Medium	High
Self-presentation/ Self-disclosure	High	Blogs	Social networking sites (e.g., Facebook)	Virtual social worlds (e.g., Second Life)
	Low	Collaborative projects (e.g., Wikipedia)	Content communities (e.g., YouTube)	Virtual game worlds (e.g., World of Warcraft)

Fig. 1. Classification of social media by self-presentation/self-disclosure and social presence/media richness [2]

1.2 Classification of Social Media Users

Social media users can be classified as posters or followers on social media. Posters are defined as users that post a lot of content and are often seen as influencers. Followers generally don't post content as often but generally appreciate the content posted by "posters" [8]. The following reasons presented in [8] were proposed to explain why users engage in social media and the behaviour they portray on social media, based on the type of user they are and what they use social media for [12]. The 4 main reasons identified were relationship, self-media, creative outlet and collaboration, and the two types of users are posters and followers.

	Relationship	Self-media	Creative outlet	Collaboration
Poster	Self-presentation, Develop relationship	Have an impact, Promote one's self	Hobby sharing, Showcase of creativity	Help others establish reputation/fame
Follower	Develop relationship	Fans of celebrities, Update news and information	Aesthetic content, Entertainment	Learn new things, Find answers/help

Fig. 2. Reasons users engage on social media based on the type of user [12]

1.3   Factors that Influence Social Media Usage

Social media can be used for various activities such as communication, socializing, creating online communities, content creation and sharing, collaboration, marketing for businesses and various other activities [1] therefore serving as a platform for users to express themselves [13]. Various influencing factors and users' individual differences that impact the use of social media, can be factors such as age, gender, personality traits [7], level of computer literacy, trust of the site, ease of use and social influences [12]. Various influencing factors will be discussed below.

Personality. Personality traits influence Facebook usage habits [7]. The Five-factor model, which has been used in multiple studies [12], is based on the theory that an individual's personality can be analysed by determining how they rank in 5 bipolar factors: extraversion, agreeableness, openness to new experiences, conscientiousness and neuroticism. Several of the Big 5 factors have been found to be associated with the way individuals interact with each other and maintain social relationships [7]. A study was conducted in Australia, by [7] applying the personality model to Facebook and found that some of these factors are associated with certain Facebook usage patterns [14]. The study aimed to identify the personality characteristics associated with being a Facebook user or non-user and to determine whether these characteristics are related to the user's usage patterns. The results showed Facebook users are more likely to be narcissistic and extraverted but tend to have stronger feelings of family loneliness. They have higher levels of narcissism, leadership and exhibitionism than non-users. It was also found that non-users of the site are more likely to be conscientious, shy and socially lonely. Overall, it was found that personality characteristics are associated with differential preferences for particular types of Facebook features.

Human Satisfaction Needs.   A large and significant part of social media is the "social" factor and understanding how this shapes social media [11]. Social norms and basic human needs have remained the same over many years [15]. Human behavior is

Autonomy	Feeling like you are the cause of your own actions rather than feeling that external forces or pressures are the cause of your actions.
Competence	Feeling that you are very capable and effective in your actions rather than feeling incompetent or ineffective.
Relatedness	Feeling that you have regular intimate contact with people who care about you rather than feeling lonely and uncared for.
Physical thriving	Feeling that your body is healthy and well taken care of rather than feeling out of shape or unhealthy.
Security	Feeling safe and in control of your life rather than feeling uncertain and threatened by your circumstances.
Self-esteem	Feeling that you are a worthy person who is as good as anyone else rather than feeling like a "loser."
Self-actualization	Feeling that you are developing your best potential and making life meaningful rather than feeling you are stagnant and that life does not have much meaning.
Pleasure-stimulation	Feeling that you get plenty of enjoyment and pleasure rather than feeling bored and under-stimulated by life.
Money-luxury	Feeling that you have plenty of money to buy most of what you want rather than feeling like a poor person who has no nice possessions.
Popularity-influence	Feeling that you are liked, respected, and have influence over others rather than feeling like a person whose advice or options nobody is interested in.

Fig. 3.   The basic needs for human satisfaction [16]

governed by the satisfaction of these needs [16]. The way in which these needs are satisfied has changed over the years, social media becoming one of the channels for this [8]. There exists 10 candidate needs that are satisfying to human nature and are ranked as follows 8:

"To derive a set of candidate needs for the study, we drew from a variety of psychological theories. As a foundation we used Deci and Ryan's self-determination theory of motivation (1985, in press), which specifies that people want to feel effective in their activities (competence), to feel that their activities are self-chosen and self-endorsed (autonomy), and to feel a sense of closeness with some others (relatedness)" [16]. The identified needs that are satisfying to human nature can be categorized by the reason of social media use and the type of user [7], which can be seen in the table below (Fig. 4).

	Relationship	Self-media	Creative outlet	Collaboration
Poster	Relatedness, Self-esteem	Popularity-influence, Money-luxury	Self-actualization, Competence	Competence, Self-actualization
Follower	Relatedness	Self-esteem, Relatedness	Pleasure-stimulation	Autonomy

Fig. 4. Table combining the type of user and human satisfaction needs [8]

Uses and Gratifications of Using Facebook. The use and gratification theory explains that the psychological and social needs motivate users to utilize different social media platforms based on the functionalities available to the user [17]. "The basic premise of uses and gratifications theory is that individuals will seek out media among competitors that fulfills their needs and leads to ultimate gratifications" [18]. Combining the work of [18] and [17], the following are the factors derived as the top 10 uses and gratification themes: social interaction, information seeking, pass time, relaxation, entertainment, expression of opinions, communicatory utility, convenience utility, information sharing, surveillance/knowledge about others.

1.4 Social Norms

Social interactions are governed by social norms which have existed for many years, they are a set of unwritten rules that govern social interactions and behaviour which are considered acceptable by society [15]. These norms originate from individual attitudes and behaviour to create group norms which are accepted by a group consensus and on the other hand these norms influence an individuals' attitude and decisions consequently shaping, constraining and redirecting behaviour. There are also various influencing factors on social norms, such as societal approval and establishing status. Social norms also vary depending on the group that establishes the norm and the environment of the individual [19]. These norms are shared amongst groups that usually share common values. A norm may not be inherently good or valuable but it gets passed along depending on the values accepted by people. Social norms can help shape the desire to act effectively, build and maintain relationships with others and maintain self-image [15]. There are two types of social norms: injunctive and descriptive norms. Injunctive norms are perceived moral rules of a group, they are what is accepted and seen as appropriate behaviour. Descriptive norms, also known as typical behaviour, are the norms that are actually followed, and help reflect the kind of behaviour that is prevalent in a given setting [20].

It is human nature to want to fit in and be accepted by society. Humans are motivated to behave in ways that are effective in achieving their goals and this behavior is influenced by the environment in which they exist [15]. When people conform to norms, this results in positive external benefits such as inclusion and approval from the group they conform to and establishing a high or acceptable status within this group [20]. People are social beings [11], they aim to build and maintain relationships with those around them by following the norms of the group of people they wish to be a part of. To be a part of this group and accepted, they also need to maintain self-image. These social constructs and interactions have existed for many years and continue to exist in the world today [11]. These existing concepts have been integrated with social media as it has become a new environment for socialization [8]. Measuring norms can be done in two ways by observing the behaviour over time or individuals can be asked to report on their behaviour, by answering specific questions provided [21].

2 Research Design

The purposes for using an inductive approach are to (a) condense raw data into a brief, summary format; (b) establish clear links between the evaluation or research objectives and the summary findings derived from the raw data; and (c) develop a framework of the underlying structure of experiences or processes that are evident in the raw data [22]. The study aimed to explore the influence of social media on social interactions. A quantitative strategy was best suited for this study as it aimed to quantify data and generalise results from a sample of the population of South Africa.

The target population for this study is South African social media users, aged 18–25. This group was chosen as it has the largest active social media user group [13] and are more technologically aware [13], therefore they will be more comfortable and able to participate in an online questionnaire. The South African population is 57.2 million, with approximately 21 million internet users. There are an estimated 16 million Facebook users and about 3 million users aged between 18–25 years [6]. Facebook is the most used social media platform so Facebook users were chosen as the target population because the number of general social media users was difficult to obtain. For the purposes of this study with a population size of 3 million users, a 95% confidence level and 5% margin of error, a good representation will be 385–400 respondents. There were only 117 respondents to the questionnaire, therefore analysis had to be conducted on this set of data as it was the best representation obtained.

Online Questionnaires were used as it was assumed that respondents have internet access since they are social media users, making it convenient for them to respond to the survey. Online questionnaires can be freely distributed, making it easier to obtain a large sample and makes the storing of the recorded data centralized and consistent [25]. Online questionnaires ensured confidentiality allowing for respondents to feel comfortable to provide honest and open feedback [24]. Google forms was the medium used to collect data for this study.

Participation in the study was voluntary and users were guaranteed anonymity. Participants were informed about the background of the study and its purpose in the cover letter of the questionnaire. Participants were required to give consent before proceeding to participation in the study.

2.1 Research Questions and Objectives

The main goal of this study is to investigate the implications of social media use on the social interactions of young adults in South Africa. This will be achieved by:

- investigating user's social media usage patterns
- analysing the implications social media has on users' social interactions

These goals will be achieved by addressing the following questions:

The main research question is:

What is the impact of social media on social interactions of Facebook in South Africa, on users aged 18–25?

Research sub-questions:

- What is the Facebook usage pattern of young adults (18–25 year olds) in South Africa?
  To answer this question the following questions need to be answered:
  - How much time do users spend daily, using social media?
  - What activities do users engage in on social media and which is the most frequent activity engaged in?
- What implications does the use of social media use have on social interactions?
  - Do people ignore their work/daily activities because of social media usage?
  - Do people pay more attention to their phones during a conversation?
  - How do other people's online presence influence users?

2.2 Hypotheses

The following hypotheses were developed to answer the research sub-questions posed and formulated based on the literature that has been researched.

Hypotheses for the usage pattern:

H1: Social media users use social media every day and spend approximately 4 h a day using social media.
H2: Users spend more time scrolling through content posted by others, than updating their statuses and posting pictures.
Hypotheses for the implications of the use social media:

H3: People prioritize their work/daily activities over social media usage.
H4: People are easily distracted by checking their phones during a conversation.
H5: Other people's online behaviour affects users' self-esteem and self-presentation.

3   Research Analysis and Findings

The demographic information gathered for this study was the age and gender of the participants. Statistical analysis was carried for the first half of the analysis to gain an insight on the usage patterns of social media users in South Africa. Exploratory factor analysis was carried out for the second part of the analysis to assist with gaining an insight on the implications of social media usage.

Demographic Information. The age and gender of the participants was recorded to ensure participants were in the correct age category and to ensure a diverse group of individuals. The research yielded 117 respondents but 12% (n = 14) of responses had to be disregarded as these respondents were in the wrong age category, therefore only 103 responses were used for this study. Out of the 103 responses, there were 39.81% (n = 41) male respondents, 58.25% (n = 60) female and 1.94% (n = 2) chose not to specify.

Statistical Analysis. Statistical analysis helps identify patterns and trends in data that has been collected [25], therefore it was used for the first part of the analysis as the first aim of this study was to look at the usage patterns of social media users.

How Often Users Glance at Their Phone. Users were asked to choose a time interval that most appropriately described how frequent they glanced at their mobile phones to check for notifications. Approximately 33.98% (n = 35) of respondents reported that they glance at their phones every 10–20 min, approximately 27.18% (n = 28) reported they glance within 5-10 min and 18.45% (n = 19) respondents every 20–30 min. Therefore majority of users, 79.61% (n = 82), glance at their phones at least every 30 min. 2.91% (n = 3) of respondents admitted to looking at their phone every minute, 13.59% (n = 14) of respondents every hour and the 3.88% (n = 4) that specified how often they glance at their phones, stated they would at more than an hourly rate.

Rank Activities Engaged in on Mobile Phones. Users were asked to rank the activities they engage in on their mobile phones, the 6 activities that were presented in the survey were: social networking, music/videos, email, news applications, online shopping and online gaming. Respondents were required to rank these activities on a scale of 1–6 where 1 represented most frequent and 6 represented the least frequent.

The results indicate the most frequently engaged-in activity on mobile devices is social networking, followed by listening to music/watching videos, then email, news applications, online shopping and lastly online games.

Likeliness to Use Social Media on a Typical Day. Users were asked to indicate their likeliness of social media usage on a typical day, using a scale of 1–5 ranging from 1 - very likely to 5 - very unlikely. The results showed that majority 65.05% (n = 67) of respondents reported that they are very likely to use social media on a typical day. 8.74% (n = 9) were likely, 5.83% (n = 6) neutral, 6.8% (n = 7) unlikely and 13.59% (n = 14) very/highly unlikely.

Amount of Time Spent Using Social Media. Since the study intends to gain insight on the usage patterns of social media users, respondents were asked to indicate the amount of time they spend using social media, it can be seen that 91.26% (n = 94) of users spend 1–6 h utilizing social media. Only 2.91% (n = 3) spend less than 1 h and 6.80% (n = 6) spend more than 6 h using social media on a typical day.

A better insight on what activities users engage in on social media can be gauged from the following 2 questions that were asked.

Amount of Time Posting Content. First users were asked how many hours they spend posting content and only 2.92% (n = 3) respondents said they spend more than 2 h posting content on social media, where 0.97% (n = 1) spent 2–4 h, 0.97% (n = 1) spent 4–6 h and 0.97% (n = 1) spends more than 6 h. 97.01% (n = 100) respondents reported that they spend 0–2 h posting content on social media.

Activities Engaged in While Using Social Media. Users were then asked to rank the activities they engage in from most frequently to least frequently. The results show that the activity that is engaged in most frequently is scrolling through content, followed by posting pictures which is closely followed by the updating of statuses.

3.1 Exploratory Factor Analysis

Since an exploratory approach was used, exploratory factor analysis was carried out to analyse the data. EFA is a complex multivariate statistical approach involving many linear and sequential steps, which is used to uncover the underlying structure of a relatively large set of variables and identify the relationships between measured variables [26]. The survey presented a set of 24 statements, also referred to as items, based on the literature and required the respondents to declare how suitable each statement applied to them on a scale of 1–5, this is how these variables were measured. Therefore the exploratory factor analysis method was best suited for this study. IBM SPSS Statistics, an analysis software program was used to perform this part of the analysis and extract the factors. The guidelines and steps proposed by [25] was used for the factor analysis.

First a correlation matrix was created to show the relationship between the items that were presented to the respondents. The variables with high inter-correlations could be measuring an underlying variable, called a factor [25]. Each item is compared with every other item and gets a value between −1 and 1, the higher the value, the stronger the relationship is between the items and the lower the value, the weaker the relationship is between the items. Bruin [25] recommends inspecting the correlation matrix (often termed Factorability of R) for correlation coefficients over 0.30. The factor loadings can be categorised using another rule of thumb as ±0.30 = minimal, ±0.40 = important, and ±.50 = practically significant. It is also recommended that the ratio of the data sample and variables be a 1:5, 1:10 or 1:20 [26]. The ratio for this study was 1:4.29.

Before extracting factors, several tests need to be conducted to ensure the data can be accurately analysed and to assess the suitability of the data for factor analysis [26]. The Kaiser-Meyer-Olkin (KMO) test is used to measure the adequacy of the sample. The first test that was conducted was the KMO test which is recommended when the variable ratio is less than 1:5. The KMO index ranges from 0 to 1, with a value greater than 0.5 which is considered to be suitable for factor analysis. The second test conducted was the Bartlett's Test of Sphericity which should be significant ($p < .05$) for factor analysis to be suitable [25]. The table below shows the KMO of Sampling Adequecy and Bartlett's Test of sphericity produced by IBM SPSS (Fig. 5).

KMO and Bartlett's Test		
Kaiser-Meyer-Olkin Measure of Sampling Adequacy.		0.716
Bartlett's Test of Sphericity	Approx. Chi-Square	896.236
	df	276
	Sig.	0.000

Fig. 5. Results of KMO and Bartlett test

The results indicate that the KMO is >0.5 and the Bartlett's Test of Sphericity significance is <0.05, therefore the data collected was suitable for factor analysis.

Once the data was deemed suitable for factor analysis, the factor extraction process followed. Multiple extraction techniques and rules exist, and it is suggested that multiple approaches should be used for factor extraction [24]. The approaches used in this study are: the Scree test, Kaiser's criteria (Eigenvalue > 1) and the cumulative percent of variance extracted.

The cumulative Percentage of variance and Eigenvalue > 1 rule varies across disciplines of research as no fixed threshold exists, some researchers believe factors should be stopped when at least 95% of the variance is explained and some have as low as 50–60% [26]. The results of this study show a cumulative percentage of variance 24.29% and a total of 8 factors have an eigenvalue > 1, which was taken from the Total variance table.

The Scree test approach plots the eigenvalues with the components and helps the researcher determine how many factors will be extracted. A Scree plot was produced, giving affirmation that 8 factors would be extracted.

A component matrix was then created, showing the relationship between the factors and the individual components.

The next step was to create a rotation matrix, this helps determine which items relate to which factor, items may relate to more than one factor but will relate more to one of the factors. Orthogonal rotation was used for this analysis.

The final step of this process is to check the reliability of these factors by using Cronbach's alpha. The Cronbach's alpha is a measure of internal consistency, how closely related the items in a factor are. This involves calculating the Cronbach's alpha of each factor that has been extracted, if the value is greater than 0.7, the factor is reliable, if not the factor should be removed. After calculating the Cronbach's alpha for each factor and it could be seen that there are only 3 credible factors.

List of the Items Categorized by Factors
Factor 1: Social media dependency

- I spend more time on social media than I think I should.
- I ignore my work because of social media usage.
- My family tells me that I spend too much time on my phone.
- I keep my phone out and present during any conversation.
- I can't imagine my life without using social media.

Social media dependency is when users are reliant on the use of social media and prioritize social media above priorities or obligations.

Factor 2: Social interaction impact

- I feel disrespected when my friends phub. (Phubbing – using a phone during a conversation and ignoring the person talking to me)
- I feel unheard when my friends phub.
- I feel disconnected when my family/friends glance at their phones during a conversation
- I feel my friends phub all the time.

This factor looks at the impact of others actions on the individual, focusing on in-person/physical interactions.

Factor 3: False self-compare/impress

- I wish my life was as 'exciting' as my friends'.
- I want the world to know I have a great life.
- I 'like' a post to please the 'friend' who posted it.
- Too many pictures posted by someone irritates me.
- I admire my friends' pictures posted online.

The false self-compare/impress factor categorizes the items that drive the person's behaviour where they may present a false persona to impress others or compare to others.

4   Data Results

The results showed that people glance at their phones at least every half an hour. They are also highly likely to use social media on a daily basis. 91.26% (n = 94) of respondents claimed to spend 1–6 h using social media daily but the results also showed that users spend only 0–2 h of posting content, therefore supporting H1. When asked to rank the activities they carry out the most when using social media, it was found that scrolling through content was ranked as the highest, these results support H2. These participants can be classified as followers based on [8]'s definition.

When presented with various activities to engage in on mobile devices, social media was ranked as the most frequent activity. The use of social media satisfies all basic human needs and gratifications as identified by [16] and [18]. The other activities can only satisfy some of the basic needs and therefore social media is shown to take preference above other activities. The watching of videos and listening to music ranked second as this satisfies the entertainment or pleasure stimulation need. The use of email gives the gratification of social interaction as it is used for communication purposes. The use of news applications ranked fourth which satisfies the need to seek out information. Online shopping was ranked fifth and (satisfies) the money-luxury need, and lastly, online gaming also satisfies the pleasure stimulation need. The ranking of these activities show which human satisfaction needs are valued more above others.

The exploratory factor analysis, produced the following factors: social media dependency, social interaction impact and false self-compare/impress. The first research sub-question based on the implications of social media use, questions whether people prioritize social media or other obligations and the hypothesis stated that people stick to their obligations but the results do not support H3 as it is the highest contributing factor meaning that people do prioritize social media over their obligations. This ties in with the first factor, social media dependency. The second factor that was extracted is the social interaction impact, this factor supports H4 which ties in with the study conducted by [23] and also claimed that this is influencing the quality of relationships as there is a shift from deep meaningful conversations to shallow short conversations due to the presence of a distraction. Factor 3 is about the false presentation of an individual on social media due to the fact that they want to be impressionable on social media, therefore H5 is also supported and this is influencing users' online behaviour.

These 3 factors can be linked to the 3 main social norms that were discussed where factor 1 links to the norm, act effectively, factor 2 relates to building and maintaining relationships and factor 3 is related to self-image. The usage patterns showed an excessive amount of social media usage and these users being classified as followers due to their online behaviour of predominantly scrolling content compared to posting content, therefore high social media usage has an impact on a user by making them dependable on social media, influencing their in-person social interactions and impacting their online self-presentation.

5 Conclusion

Prior research has extensively studied the reasons behind why people use social media. These include the personality, human satisfaction needs, gratifications, the technology acceptance model and a few others. Social media is growing rapidly and does have an impact on its users. An online survey was conducted and the data of 103 respondents were analysed. This study focused on participants aged 18–25 who were South African, social media users.

The first aim of this study was to investigate the usage patterns of social media users, by doing so this gave an insight to the amount of time people spend using social media and what activities they engage in while using social media. Statistical analysis was carried out to gain insight on the data gathered for this part of the study, which showed users spend a lot of time using social media but most of this time spent scrolling through content rather than posting content.

The second aim of this study was to determine the impact social media has on its users. Through an online questionnaire, data was gathered and analysed using

IBM SPSS. The results showed that the use of social media does have an impact on its users. The factors that were identified were social media dependency, the impact on social interactions and the impact on self-compare/impress, which can be linked to the 3 social norms which are to act effectively, build and maintain relationships and maintaining a self-image. All hypotheses besides H3 were supported by the results of the study and therefore answered all proposed research questions.

References

1. Ali, A.H.: The power of social media in developing nations: new tools for closing the global digital divide and beyond. Harv. Hum. Rights J. **24**, 185–219 (2011)
2. Haenlein, M., Kaplan, A.M.: Users of the world, unite! The challenges and opportunities of social media. Bus. Horiz. **53**, 59–68 (2010)
3. Worldometers: Worldometers: Population. http://www.worldometers.info/world-population/south-africa-population/. Accessed 19 Mar 2018
4. Shapshak, T.: Forbes. Retrieved from Tech: South Africa has 21 million internet users, mostly on mobile, 19 July 2017. https://www.forbes.com/sites/tobyshapshak/2017/07/19/south-africa-has-21m-internet-users-mostly-on-mobile/#60a093521b2d. Accessed 29 Dec 2018
5. Statista: Number of monthly active Facebook users worldwide as of 4th quarter 2017 (in millions). Retrieved from Internet: Social Media & User-Generated Content. https://www.statista.com/statistics/264810/number-of-monthly-active-facebook-users-worldwide/. Accessed 22 Nov 2018
6. Business Tech: How many people use Facebook, Twitter and Instagram in South Africa. Retrieved from Business Tech, 18 September 2017. https://businesstech.co.za/news/internet/199318/how-many-people-use-facebook-twitter-and-instagram-in-south-africa/. Accessed 29 Dec 2018
7. Ryan, T., Xenos, S.: Who uses Facebook? An investigation into the relationship between the Big Five, shyness, narcissism, loneliness, and Facebook usage. Comput. Hum. Behav. **27**(5), 1658–1664 (2011)
8. Zhu, Y.-Q., Chen, H.-G.: Social media and human need satisfaction: implication for social media marketing. Bus. Horiz. **58**(3), 335–345 (2015)
9. Ainin, S., Jaafar, N.I., Tajudeen, F.P.: Understanding the impact of social media usage among organizations. Infom. Manag. **55**, 30–321 (2018)
10. Dennis, J., Michikyan, M., Subrahmanyam, K.: Can you guess who I am? Real, ideal, and false self-presentation on Facebook among emerging adultd. Emerg. Adulthood **3**(1), 55–64 (2015)
11. Fuchs, C.: Social Media: A Critical Introduction. SAGE Publications Ltd., London (2017)
12. McElroy, J., Moore, K.: The influence of personality on Facebook usage, wall postings, and regrets. Comput. Hum. Behav. **28**(1), 267–274 (2012)
13. Fuchs, C.: Internet and Society: Social Theory in the Information Age. Routledge, New York (2008)
14. Azucar, D., Marengo, D., Settani, M.: Predicting the Big 5 personality traits from digital footprints on social media: a meta-analysis. Pers. Individ. Differ. **124**, 150–159 (2018)
15. Cialdini, R.B., Trost, M.R.: Social influence: social norms, conformity and compliance. Social influence: Social norms, conformity, and compliance. In: Gilbert, D., Fiske, S., Lindzy, G. (eds.) The Handbook of Social Psychology, vol. 2, McGraw-Hill, Boston (1999)
16. Elliot, A.J., Kasser, T., Kim, Y., Sheldon, K.M.: What is satisfying about satisfying events? Testing 10 candidate psychological needs. J. Pers. Soc. Psychol. **80**(2), 325–339 (2001)

17. Lee, C.S., Ma, L.: News sharing in social media: the effect of gratification and prior experience. Comput. Hum. Behav. **28**, 331–339 (2012)
18. Whiting, A., Williams, D.: Why people use social media: a uses and gratifications approach. Qual. Mark. Res. **16**, 362–369 (2013)
19. Denny, E., Mackie, G., Moneti, F., Shakya, H.: What are social norms? How are they measured? UNICEF, San Diego (2015)
20. Bukowski, M.W., Laursen, B., Rubin, K.H.: Handbook of Peer Interactions, Relationships and Groups. The Guilford Press, New York (2018)
21. Jackson, J.: A conceptual and measurement model for norms and roles. Pac. Sociol. Rev. **9**, 35–48 (1966)
22. Thomas, D.R.: A general inductive approach for analyzing qualitative evaluation data. Am. J. Eval. **27**(2), 57–75 (2006)
23. Cheng, L., Genevie, J., Misra, S., Yuan, M.: The iPhone effet: the quality of in-person social interactions in the presence of mobile devices. Environ. Behav. **48**(2), 275–298 (2016)
24. Evans, J.R., Mathur, A.: The value of online surveys. Internet Res. **15**, 195–219 (2015)
25. Bruin, J.: Newtest: command to compute new test. UCLA: Statistical Consulting Group (2006). https://stats.idre.ucla.edu/stata/ado/analysis/. Accessed 29 Dec 2018
26. Brown, T., Onsman, A., Williams, B.: Exploratory factor analysis: a five-step guide for novices. Aust. J. Paramed. **8**(3), 1–13 (2012)

HCI in Business

Human Computer Interaction with Multivariate Sentiment Distributions of Stocks Intraday

Lamarcus Coleman[1,2]([⊠]) and Mariofanna Milanova[1]

[1] Department of Computer Science, University of Arkansas at Little Rock,
Little Rock, AR 72204, USA
{lrcoleman1, mgmilanova}@ualr.edu
[2] Gradient Laboratories Inc., Little Rock, AR 72204, USA

Abstract. In this work we show that the sentiment of the broader stock market, namely the S&P 500, is related to the activity of individual stocks intraday. We introduce a concept we term as embedded context which is an approach to improving unigram language models for restricted use cases. We use a Gaussian Mixture Model to create different sentiment regimes (i.e. distributions) of the broader market over our training period and perform an analysis of the return and volatility characteristics of each stock per each regime. We create an intraday momentum trading strategy using a moving average and Relative Strength Index (RSI) over our testing period with no consideration to our prior sentiment regime analysis which serves as our baseline model. We then create an updated version of our intraday trading strategy which considers the sentiment regime of the broader market. Our results show an improvement in each stock's intraday strategy performance as a result of considering the broader market's sentiment regime.

Keywords: Sentiment analysis · Gaussian Mixture Model · Stock market prediction

1 Introduction

Prior works have shown that there exists some relationship between the public's mood and movement within the stock market. We pose a key question, "Why is there a relationship between the mood of the public and movement in stock prices?" We believe that this relationship is indicative of traders, or market participants, and not the general public.

Though prior works have collected substantial data on general Twitter users and did not specify whether or not those users were actual market participants, our thought experiment suggests this is not necessary to build a model capable of associating sentiment to changes in asset prices. Consistent with our reasoning, we suggest that for the purpose of stock price prediction using the sentiment of the market, only the mood of traders, or actual market participants is needed to engender a predictive system.

We have also found that while much work has been conducted relative to the sentiment of the assets and its effect on price changes, to the best of our knowledge, no

© Springer Nature Switzerland AG 2019
C. Stephanidis (Ed.): HCII 2019, CCIS 1034, pp. 61–66, 2019.
https://doi.org/10.1007/978-3-030-23525-3_8

prior work has studied whether or not the sentiment of the broader market can be used to predict changes in the prices of individual stocks on neither a daily or intraday basis. In lieu of this, we form our first research question for testing. Can it be concluded that there exists a relationship between the sentiment of the broader market and that of individual stocks using only information from likely market participants?

We introduce a novel idea we term embedded context. The premise of this idea is that the key fallacy of a simple unigram model can be circumvented by increasing the specificity of the model. Within a standard unigram model, the tokens can take on different connotations dependent upon prior and subsequent words. Our idea of embedded context suggests that the specification of model creation to a specific use case could limit these possible contexts and thus embed a discrete meaning of each word into a unigram model. Relative to this work, we achieve this by (1) only searching for tweets from likely market participants and (2) creating a custom vocabulary specific to market participants and the interpretation of their sentiment. Thus forming our second research question, "Can embedded context be used to circumvent the issue of context in unigram models for restricted use cases?"

2   Literature Review

Bollen et al. [1] posed the question "Is the public mood correlated over even predictive of economic indicators?" This work surveyed whether or not collective mood states from Twitter were correlated with the Dow Jones over time. Bollen [1] used Granger Causality Analysis to determine the correlation between past Dow values and prior mood states to daily closing Dow prices. A Self Organizing Fuzzy Neural Network was used for prediction of market prices to capture the non-linear relationship.

Nisar and Yeung [7] studied the relationship between political sentiment and movements in the FTSE 100 on a daily basis. They too derived sentiment using data from Twitter.

Kordonis et al. [4], basing their work on the prior work of Pak and Paroubek (2016), studied the effectiveness of Naïve Bayes Bernouli Classification and SVMs for sentiment analysis. They conducted a correlation analysis between tweets and market movement and used this correlation for the forecasting of stock prices.

Mittal and Goel [6] found tools such as Opinion Finder and SentiWordnet, which has been used in other studies, infeasible and thus developed their own sentiment analysis system. They too used a Self-Organizing Fuzzy Neural Network for daily Dow price prediction. A trading strategy was constructed based on the prediction of the model.

Patel et al. [8] used a variety of Neural Network models on different sectors of the Bombay Stock Exchange. They learned that the prediction of prices is better framed as a classification task.

Jermann [3] studied the influence of executive tweets on market movement. Analysis was conducted on word and sentence level features. A Naïve Bayes bag of words model served as the baseline and a Neural Network was used for comparison. The work illustrated a high degree of specificity in tweet collection by focusing only on tweets from individuals that contained the name of their company within the description of their profile.

Davda and Mittal [2] used NLP to create a trading strategy around news headlines. They used Yahoo Finance as a source for news and scraped price data from Google Finance. Lee et al. [5] studied the significance of text analysis for stock price prediction. While other researchers focused on breaking news events disseminated via Twitter and other sources, Lee et al. focused on news events reported in companies' 8-K filings, or the required filing for significant events within a company.

Si et al. [9] designed a Semantic Stock Network (SSN). This network constituted of nodes (i.e. stocks) and which were connected by edges of which constituted the co-occurrence of nodes mentioned frequently within tweets. They used a labeled topic model to model the tweets and network structure at each node.

Trastour et al. [10] used Latent Dirichlet Allocation to extract topics from news articles. The inputs to their model were daily and monthly proportions of articles per each topic. They used these inputs to predict the daily and monthly crude oil prices.

3   Methodology

We began by collecting daily price data for the SPY ETF, our four stocks, Adobe (ADBE), AT&T (T), General Electric (GE), and Wells Fargo (WFC) over the period of January 1, 2018 to June 1, 2018. We also collected intraday data on the five minute timeframe for each of our four stocks.

After splitting our data into training and testing sets, we created a list of every trading day in the 2018 calendar year and used the Twitter Standard API to retrieve tweets for the SPY, using the $SPY symbol, for each day in our training period.

A market regime consists of a distinct period or subset of activity within a larger interval of market activity. We chose a Gaussian Mixture Model to model this phenomenon. A Gaussian Mixture Model, depicted by the equation below, is a model used to capture the effects of multimodal distributions. In short, as the equation depicts, the GMM is a collection or linear combination of multiple distributions.

$$P(x) = \pi\_(1)\ N(\mu\_1, \sigma\_1) + \pi\_(2)\ N(\mu\_2, \sigma\_2) + \pi\_(k)\ N(\mu\_k, \sigma\_k)$$

- P(x) - probability x stock return came from specific regime/distribution
- π - weight of N_k distribution
- μ_k - mean of k distribution
- σ_k - covariance matrix of k distribution

This model allowed us to capture the effects of market returns being generated by different regimes or distributions.

We created our regimes over our training period by (1) preprocessing and scoring our SPY Tweets by building a custom vocabulary, (2) computing the mean and variance of the SPY, and (3) passing each of these into our GMM. The use of the custom vocabulary was a means to distinguish market participants and is illustrative of what we term embedded context, or the use of unigrams within discrete contexts.

Once our regimes were created, we computed the mean return and variance for each of our stocks over our training period and group these per the regime of the broader market. The Fig. 1 below is an example of this analysis.

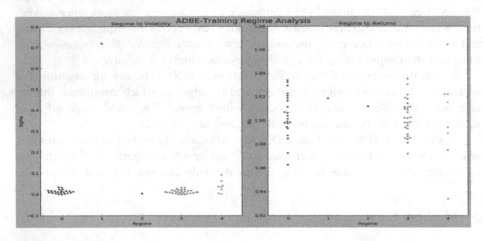

Fig. 1. Regime analysis; Displays the volatility (left) and Returns (right) of each sample drawn from its respective distribution (i.e. regime) for Adobe (ADBE) stock

We also surveyed whether or not there existed some correlation between our stocks and regimes. We normalized our stock returns and regimes to perform this study but found no significant correlation. Below is a correlation matrix from this analysis (Fig. 2).

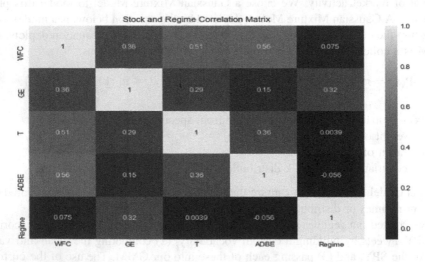

Fig. 2. Displays a correlation matrix for each stock and the regimes.

To test our hypotheses, we first developed an intraday momentum trading strategy over our testing period which did not consider our market regime analysis. This served as our baseline model. Next, we developed a market regime version of our intraday trading strategy of which considers the market's sentiment regime. Our results are displayed below (Figs. 3 and 4).

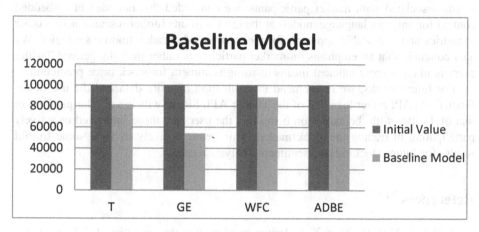

Fig. 3. Baseline model

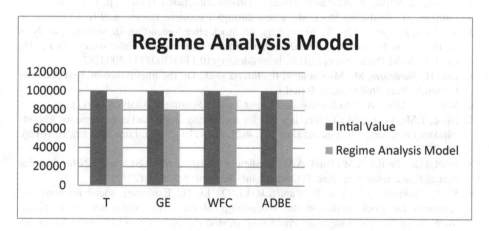

Fig. 4. Regime analysis model

We found that the regime analysis model improved the performance of the intraday strategy across all stocks. ADBE's performance improved by 12%, GE by 47%, WFC by 7%, and T improved by 12%.

4   Conclusion

Based on the findings of our experiment, we conclude that a relationship exists between the sentiment regime of the broader market and individual stocks intraday. Given that our sentiment regimes were created using tweets specific to (1) the broader market via the $SPY Twitter query, (2) and used of a custom vocabulary of positive and negatives words associated with market participants, we concluded that our idea of embedded context for unigram language models at the least warrants further research across other industries and is a viable approach for the creation of intraday trading strategies. We also conclude that an emphasis on market participants rather than the general Twitter users is likely a more efficient means of using sentiment for stock price prediction.

For future works, we recommend the collection of more data and the use of the StockTwits API rather than that of the Twitter API. StockTwits is a similar platform to that of Twitter with the exception being that the users are those interested or actively participating in trading the stock market. This venue is likely to yield some fruitful results for future stock market sentiment analysis research.

References

1. Bollen, J., Mao, H., Zeng, X.-J.: Twitter mood predicts the stock market. J. Comput. Sci. **2**(1), 1–8 (2011). https://doi.org/10.1016/j.jocs.2010.12.007
2. Davda, A., Mittal, P.: NLP and Sentiment Driven Automated Trading, p. 41 (2008)
3. Jermann, M.: Predicting Stock Movement through Executive Tweets, p. 9 (n.d.)
4. Kordonis, J., Symeonidis, S., Arampatzis, A.: Stock price forecasting via sentiment analysis on Twitter. In: Proceedings of the 20th Pan-Hellenic Conference on Informatics - PCI 2016, pp. 1–6. ACM Press, Patras (2016). https://doi.org/10.1145/3003733.3003787
5. Lee, H., Surdeanu, M., MacCartney, B., Jurafsky, D.: On the Importance of Text Analysis for Stock Price Prediction, p. 6 (n.d.)
6. Mittal, A., Goel, A.: Stock Prediction Using Twitter Sentiment Analysis (2011)
7. Nisar, T.M., Yeung, M.: Twitter as a tool for forecasting stock market movements: a short-window event study. J. Financ. Data Sci. **4**(2), 101–119 (2018). https://doi.org/10.1016/j.jfds.2017.11.002
8. Patel, H.R., Parikh, S.M., Patel, A.M.: Prediction model based on NLP and NN for financial data outcome revelation. Res. J. Comput. Inf. Technol. Sci. **5**, 5 (2017)
9. Si, J., Mukherjee, A., Liu, B., Pan, S.J., Li, Q., Li, H.: Exploiting social relations and sentiment for stock prediction. In: Proceedings of the 2014 Conference on Empirical Methods in Natural Language Processing (EMNLP), pp. 1139–1145. Association for Computational Linguistics, Doha (2014). https://doi.org/10.3115/v1/D14-1120
10. Trastour, S., Genin, M., Morlot, A.: Prediction of the crude oil price thanks to natural language processing applied to newspapers, p. 5 (n.d.)

Research on Design Service Mode of Industrial Transformation and Upgrading Driven by Design—Setting China's Yangtze River Delta Region as an Example

Wei Ding, Defang Chen, Yan Wang$^{(\boxtimes)}$, Junnan Ye, and Dadi An

East China University of Science and Technology,
130 Meilong Road, Xuhui District, Shanghai, China
dw.6789@163.com, 2351962834@qq.com, 54756432@qq.com,
2723241@qq.com, 61915633@qq.com

Abstract. Under the background of economic globalization, knowledge economy and service economy play increasingly important roles in the process of social development. China is the most representative developing country in the world where traditional manufacturing enterprises are transforming from OEM and ODM to OBM and OSM. It will have more chances in China to drive the transformation and upgrading of various industries and help more regions achieve the goal of overall upgrading and balanced development through by design.

This paper will explore and study the mode of design driving industries transformation and upgrading from the perspective of service economy. Firstly, this study summarizes and analyzes the relevant modes of design driving industries transformation and upgrading at home and abroad through literature retrieval, market research and analysis. Based on above description and discussion, the industrial design service mode which is suitable for the transformation and upgrading of the Yangtze River Delta industry is been put forward. Secondly, the mode includes four domains: government, industry, university and research institute. Different transformation tasks of the four domains and the logical relationship of the interactions between the four domains are brought forward, which will produce effective ways and means to help the traditional manufacturing enterprises achieve the goal of transformation and upgrading driven by design. Finally, the advanced enterprise of the Yangtze River Delta of China-SAIC Group is taken as an example to verify the scientificity and operability of the mode.

In conclusion, effective mode reference and method of application are been provided for traditional manufacturing enterprises to realize industrial transformation and upgrading through innovative design.

Keywords: Industrial transformation and upgrading · Design service mode · China's Yangtze river delta region

C. Stephanidis (Ed.): HCII 2019, CCIS 1034, pp. 67–74, 2019.
https://doi.org/10.1007/978-3-030-23525-3_9

1   Theoretical Research on Design-Driven Industrial Transformation and Upgrading at Domestic and Abroad

1.1   Overview of Theoretical Research at Domestic and Abroad

Verganti [1] first proposed the concept of design-driven innovation, which is together with the two innovation-driven forms of technology promotion and market pull proposed by Dosi [2]. Design-driven innovation has become the three driving factors of enterprise innovation. Chinese scholar Hongbo Lai pointed out that among the three innovation drivers, most of the traditional manufacturing enterprises in China now use market-driven innovation strategy mode and technology-driven innovation strategy mode, while the design-driven innovation strategy mode is few to be used. A large part of China's local manufacturing industries is in a state of low homogenization of products and a low-level development of low-end price wars.

As for how to drive industrial transformation and upgrading through design, Allen [3] et al. believe that product design and process reengineering can reduce the manufacturing time and cost of enterprises. Case studies by Battistella et al. show that design-driven innovation not only changes products but also promotes business model innovation [4]. Chinese scholar Xuan Huang et al. believe that the development status of China's manufacturing industry determines that many industries are more suitable to use the form of industrial design innovative products, which has the advantages of low research and development cost, high productization efficiency, short commercialization cycle and stronger timeliness [5]. Hongbo Lai et al. found that product design can affect customers' product perception and brand perception through empirical research [6]. At the same time, Hongbo Lai believes that design is of great significance for manufacturing enterprises to enhance independent innovation ability, improve products and brands' added value, transform and upgrade [7].

Thus, through design process, China's manufacturing enterprises could drive the market innovation in a short time under the premise of low cost, low risk. Finally the industry will be transformed from a vicious competition of low-end prices to a benign competition of high-end products.

1.2   Overview of Theoretical Research at Domestic and Abroad

According to the summary in the above chart, at present, the research on design-driven industrial transformation and upgrading mainly focuses on product design, marketing, science and technology, but rarely involves the perspective of "government-industry-colleges-research institutions" (Table 1).

Table 1. The mode of design-driven industrial transformation and upgrading is summarized in 11 references.

11 references explore the mode of design-driven industrial transformation and upgrading										
Literatures / Perspective	1	2	3	4	5	6	7	8	9	10	11
Culture					√						
Resources		√				√	√				
Products' design	√	√	√	√		√	√	√			√
Government										√	√
Colleges										√	
Enterprises		√						√		√	
Research institutes											
Marketing	√	√	√	√	√	√	√	√	√		
Service design								√	√		
Sci-tech	√	√	√	√	√					√	√
Management			√				√				√

2 Background of Manufacturing Industry in Yangtze River Delta Region

2.1 Regional Advantages in the Transformation and Upgrading of the Manufacturing Industry in the Yangtze River Delta Region

The Yangtze river delta is a region with rapid economic development, high degree of resource accumulation and relatively perfect urban governance in China. At the same time, the region has also actively issued design support policies, built a creative exchange platform, and carried out design-related activities, which was making the Yangtze river delta a national leader in design applications.

2.2 Problems and Deficiencies in the Manufacturing Industry in the Yangtze River Delta

The manufacturing industries in the Yangtze river delta have already started to use the application of design, but there are still many problems and deficiencies. The specific problems are as following:

The Limitation of the Design Thinking. The ideological understanding of design is limited in two aspects: the first is that manufacturing enterprises are still not fully aware of the importance of design for transformation and upgrading; the another one is excessive use of design, resulting in a lot of unnecessary waste.

The Cultivation of Design Talents Urgently Needs to be Improved. The quality of design talents is still at a low level, and there is still much room for improvement in the influence and innovation exploration ability of designers.

The Industrial Standards of Design Application Need to be Improved. At present, the industrial standards, laws and regulations of the design industry in the Yangtze river delta region are still not perfect and lack of macro-control mechanism. The industrial standards, market and government regulation are important and necessary.

The Cooperation Mode of Design Is not Deep and Sound Enough. The mode of " industry-colleges-research institutions" cooperation in the Yangtze river delta region is very common, but the form of cooperation is relatively simple, at the same time, the effect of cooperation is not deep enough. There is no systematic and scientific mode of cooperation, either.

3 Construction of Industrial Design Service Organizational Structure Mode of "Design-Driven Industrial Transformation and Upgrading" in the Yangtze River Delta Region

3.1 Theoretical Basis

According to the theory of gradient process, the quality of industrial structure is the main factor to measure the level of economic development in all regions, especially the development stage of the leading industry sector in the industrial life cycle [8].

From the perspective of Marxist theory of social development, the contradiction between the economic foundation and the superstructure are both the fundamental driving force for social development. If we want to realize all-around industrial transformation and upgrading, system reform is the fundamental power to promote all the transformation.

3.2   The Content of Industrial Design Service Mode of "Design-Driven Industrial Transformation and Upgrading"

In the whole model, government, industry, colleges and scientific research institutions perform their respective functions but synergistically integrate with each other. The Chinese government is not only the main body of its own political reform, but also the main body of other transformations. The goal of school transformation is to cultivate new talents needed by the time and to solve the current situation of mismatch between talents and the market. The purpose of research institution transformation is to apply targeted research results to the government, industry and schools. The purpose of industrial transformation is to enhance the value of the industry itself and create higher and longer term earnings, which is also the ultimate goal of other transformations. Design plays a central role in the whole transformation system and applies the transformation in various fields to the industry through the practice of design, so as to verify the role of other transformations and drive the industrial transformation.

The Role of Government in the Process of Industrial Transformation and Upgrading. In the process of system rationalization, the government should guide the formation of professional ethics of the design industry with the macroscopic guiding role of the government and system constraints. At the same time, the government should establish a design incentive mechanism to further stimulate the vitality of "design center" and promote the construction of creative ecological cycle system as well. The crucial point of the government's macro-control is to optimize the regional spatial structure, establish a regional design center integrating design resources, design talents, design exhibition and other design elements, and then spread the design power to other regions regularly. The government should also adjust the industrial distribution actively, measures to local conditions, balance the industrial proportion in the region, give full play to the cultural advantages of different enterprises and avoid serious industrial isomorphism.

The Role of Manufacturing Industries in the Process of Industrial Transformation and Upgrading. In the production process, the manufacturing enterprises should improve the proportion of product design and bring more quality sense of enjoyment to users in some small details. By means of industrial design, the level and added value of small commodities can be improved to solve the problems of insufficient creativity and low added value, so as to promote the transformation and upgrading of small commodity industries. The combination of creative innovation and traditional manufacturing industries brought by the design brings personalized experience to users, making the product become the carrier of cultural communication and spiritual communication (Fig. 1).

The Role of Schools in the Process of Industrial Transformation and Upgrading. Under the background of government policies and in combination with the development trend of the moment time, the design major of the university will conduct in-depth research on the development path of the manufacturing industry, and establish a set of design theory system from ideas to marketing, including the training of professional knowledge of design and the overall view of manufacturing, as well as the trend grasp

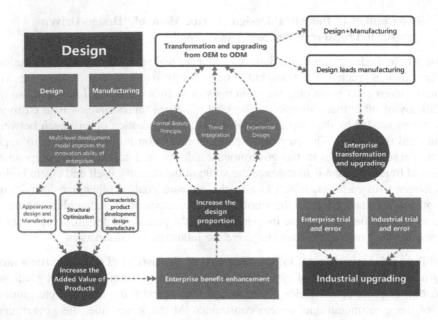

Fig. 1. Design promotion mechanism for the transformation and upgrading of manufacturing-oriented industries

and innovation training. Colleges should also build the creative talent training mechanism of high compatibility with the moment time, high plasticity, being opening and scientific, expressed in theoretical research, design, design of risk assessment, marketing, and other dimensions design of the corresponding training plan; at the same time establish deep cross cooperation with the enterprise from point to surface, making the enterprise get of university research results; and then bring students market experience and highly professional knowledge theory system; finally, the establishment of big data information center can not only train students to grasp the development of The Times, but also use scientific data to help enterprises to invest in the design of the lowest risk.

The Role of Scientific Research Institutions in the Process of Industrial Transformation and Upgrading. The industrial design and research institutions should constantly release characteristic design results based on local advantageous industries. They also need to carry design ideas into the production process to enhance the design capacity of the manufacturing industry, and provide support services for the transformation of design results for micro and small enterprises with a large number and a wide range, so as to improve their growth environment. The intellectual property protection platform should be established to protect the legitimate rights and interests of the enterprise to which the design belongs to ensure the normal operation of creative capital. Research institutions should build intellectual property display and trading platforms to better connect industrial needs and creative resources, and help enterprises realize the transformation from manufacturing-driven to innovation-driven (Fig. 2).

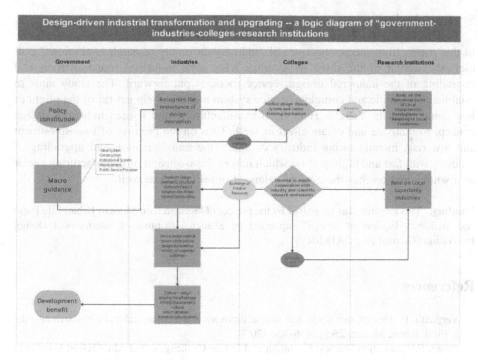

Fig. 2. Design promotion mechanism for the transformation and upgrading of manufacturing-oriented industries

4 Construction of Industrial Design Service Organizational Structure Mode of "Design-Driven Industrial Transformation and Upgrading" in the Yangtze River Delta Region

Shanghai automotive group co., ltd. is the largest listed automobile company in China's A-share market. SAIC's synergistic integration of industrial system advantage is one of its core competitiveness. Under the background of national design policy, SAIC covers the national well-known colleges and universities with "industry-university-research institutions" cooperation, and the design competition for college students combined multiple design ideas from colleges and universities, which improved innovation ability. SAIC are paying much more attention to the status of industrial design in the industry and continuously introducing the design of the leading trend of industry to lead to drive the whole auto industry innovation. Due to its core innovation competitiveness, SAIC has outstanding innovation ability in many fields of the automobile industry, and its business scale and service capability are in a leading position in the domestic industry.

5   Conclusion

In this paper, from the perspectives of "industry-university-research institutions" politics, the design of the drive in Yangtze river delta industrial transformation and upgrading of the industrial design service mode is put forward. The study aims to establish a scientific and complete service system model to help get rid of the plight of low competition in Yangtze river delta manufacturing, and it uses industrial design concept to innovate and create effect as well. Thus on the premise of low investment and low risk, manufacturing industry complete the transformation and upgrading of industry with fast and high quality, which makes the ascension of manufacturing sector as a whole, and reaches the goal of balanced development as well.

Funding. This research was supported by the project of "Research on Modern Urban Life Form and Intelligent Equipment Design" supported by Shanghai Institute of International Design Innovation (Granted No. DA18304).

References

1. Vergantir, F.: Design, meanings, and radical innovation: a meta model and a research agenda. J. Prod. Innov. Manag. **25**(5), 436–456 (2008)
2. Dosig, F.: Innovation Studies: Evolution and Future Challenges, 2nd edn. Oxford University Press, London (2013)
3. Allen, R.S.F.: Porter's generic strategies: an exploratory study of their use in Japan. J. Bus. Strat. **24**(1), 69–89 (2007)
4. Battistellacbiottog, F., Detoniaf, S.: From design driven innovation to meaning strategy. Manag. Decis. **25**(5), 436–456 (2008)
5. Xuan, H.: Exploration of industrial design mode to assist enterprise transformation. In: Design Drives Business Innovation: 2013 Collected papers of Tsinghua International Design Management Conference (Chinese portion), Department of Industrial Design, School of Fine Arts, Tsinghua University, June 2013
6. Hongbo Lai, F.: Empirical study on the impact of design-driven product innovation on customer perception and purchase intention. Res. Dev. Manag. **28**(04), 22–30 (2016)
7. Hongbo Lai, F.: Design driven innovation system construction and industrial transformation and upgrading mechanism research. Sci. Technol. Prog. Countermeasures **34**(23), 71–76 (2017)
8. Qi, B.: Study on the strategy of economic modernization in the Yangtze river delta. East China Normal University (2012)

Lexicon-Based Sentiment Analysis of Online Customer Ratings as a Quinary Classification Problem

Claudia Hösel[(✉)], Christian Roschke, Rico Thomanek, and Marc Ritter

University of Applied Sciences Mittweida, 09648 Mittweida, Germany
hoesel@hs-mittweida.de

Abstract. Online customer reviews are not only an important decision-making tool for customers, they are also used by e-commerce providers as a source of information to analyze customer satisfaction. In order to reduce the complexity of evaluation comments, written reviews are additionally represented by evaluation stars in many evaluation systems. Numerous studies address the sentiment recognition of written reviews and view polarity recognition as a binary or ternary problem. This study presents the first results of a holistic approach, which takes up the combination of customer reviews with evaluation points realized in platform-dependent evaluation systems. Sentiment analysis is regarded as a quinary classification problem. In this study, 5,000 customer evaluations are analyzed with lexicon-based sentiment analysis at document level with the target to predict the evaluation points based on the determined polarity. For sentiment analysis the data mining tool RapidMiner is used and the categorization of the sentiment polarity is realized by using different NLP techniques in combination with the sentiment dictionary SentiWordNet. The supervised learning algorithms k-Nearest Neighbor, Naïve Bayes and Random Forest are used for classification and their classification quality is compared. Random Forest achieves the most accurate results in conjunction with NLP techniques, while the other two classifiers provide worse results. The results suggest that a stronger scaling of polarity requires a stronger differentiation between classes and thus a more intensive lexical preprocessing.

Keywords: Natural language processing · Sentiment analysis · Classification · Supervised learning methods

1 Introduction

In business-to-consumer e-commerce, customer evaluations represent an important source of information – both for customers and for e-commerce providers. At the customer level, the social proof of customer evaluations is an important decision-making aid for purchasing decisions [1]. Around two thirds of online shoppers read customer reviews before buying products in online shops [2]. For

© Springer Nature Switzerland AG 2019
C. Stephanidis (Ed.): HCII 2019, CCIS 1034, pp. 75–80, 2019.
https://doi.org/10.1007/978-3-030-23525-3_10

e-commerce providers, customer reviews are an important component in the sale of products and services, as they allow conclusions to be drawn about customer satisfaction, among other things. E-commerce providers such as *Amazon.com, Inc.* [3], therefore operate – mostly platform-dependent – rating systems in order to extract moods and emotions from the reviews. An intellectual extraction of this information is hardly possible, especially for large e-commerce providers, due to the large number of reviews. Consequently, an automated evaluation is required, which is realized by means of opinion mining. Opinion mining, a field of text mining, deals with the automated extraction and evaluation of opinions from texts and uses various techniques for sentiment recognition [4]. One opinion mining technique is the sentiment analysis. Sentiment analysis uses various natural language processing (NLP) methods, such as tokenization or stemming, to analyze the sentiment of a text or the emotional attitude to an object contained in the text [5]. A fundamental problem of sentiment analysis is the categorization of sentiment polarity. Natural-language texts can contain valence shifts – for example through negation or intensification – which are usually easily understood by humans, but not by computational systems [6]. Recent research attempts to address this problem through lexicon-based preprocessing, mostly using existing sentiment dictionaries.

Prakoso et al. 2018 explicitly investigate in their study the effects of lexicon-based preprocessing on the accuracy of sentiment classification when using supervised machine learning algorithms and note that sentiment analysis with lexicon-based preprocessing achieves higher accuracy in all classification models [7]. Existing approaches from the domain of lexicon-based sentiment analysis, such as Alkalbani et al. 2017 [8], Fang and Zahn 2015 [9], Lin et al. 2018 [10], regard sentiment recognition as a binary or ternary classification problem. However, a stronger scaling of the polarity seems to make sense especially for the sentiment recognition of customer ratings, since existing – especially platform-dependent – rating systems mostly combine metrics such as written review and integer rating system. Research approaches that scale the polarity more strongly usually refer to selected social media channels and can only be transferred to other fields of application to a limited extent due to their specific functionalities. El Alaoui et al. 2018 present a lexicon-based approach for the sentiment analysis of tweets, which distinguishes seven polarity classes and uses the specific functionalities of the microblogging service, such as re-tweets or likes, in addition to a sentiment lexicon, when determining polarity [11].

Based on this approach, the question arises to what extent the specific functionalities of evaluation platforms can be used for the sentiment determination of customer evaluations. The first step is to determine to what extent the points or stars awarded by customers via rating systems reflect the opinions expressed in the written evaluations. The present study takes up this problem and presents a first state of work. Starting from the assumption that platform-dependent rating systems from e-commerce providers combine rating comments with a five-level star-scaled rating system, sentiment recognition is regarded as a quinary classification problem.

2   Methods

This study uses a data set from "Kaggle" [12] with around 400,000 customer ratings of unlocked mobile phones. Each of these devices was reviewed on *Amazon.com, Inc.* [3] and also rated by customers there. The data set is adjusted for unneeded attributes as well as missing values and balanced with regard to the attribute "Rating". This attribute is based on an integer star-scaled system where the highest rating can be five stars and the lowest rating one star. After cleansing and normalizing the data set, each rating level is represented by the same amount of elements. For resource-related reasons, 1,000 elements are used per rating level; the data set used in this study therefore contains 5,000 elements.

The methodology applied is divided into four process steps. As shown in Fig. 1, various NLP techniques are used during data preprocessing to clean up the text, structure it and convert it into a machine-readable form. The tokens of the document are then used to generate a vector that represents the document numerically and thus makes it usable for mathematical operations. The weighting of the terms is done by the combined method "Term Frequency – Inverted Document Frequency" (TF-IDF). This method takes into account the frequency distribution of terms in the corpus and weights terms on the basis of frequency and differentiations [13]. In the next step, the features extracted from the texts are used to predict the sentiment. For classification the machine supervised models k-Nearest Neighbor (k-NN), Naïve Bayes and Random Forest will be implemented, evaluated by a tenfold leave-one-out cross validation and the quality of classification will be compared between the models.

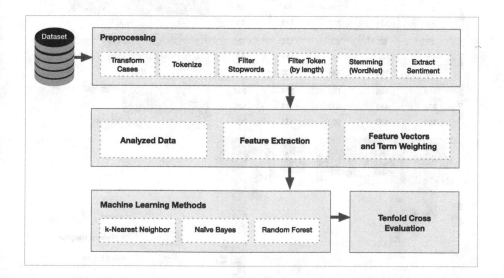

Fig. 1. Flow of process methods

The entire process was realized with the data mining tool RapidMiner 9.1 [14]. For polarity detection, the extension SentiWordNet 3.0 [15] is implemented in RapidMiner. SentiWordNet is a open source lexical resource developed for opinion mining applications [16]. The mood-bearing expressions in the text are identified and coded in relational scale.

3   Results and Discussion

In this study, a sentiment analysis with lexicon-based preprocessing of online customer ratings is carried out with the aim of predicting the integer star-scaled ratings provided by the customers based on the written reviews. For the quinary classification problem the classifiers k-Nearest Neighbor, Naïve Bayes and Random Forest are used and their accuracy is compared. Figure 2 shows the results of the classifiers.

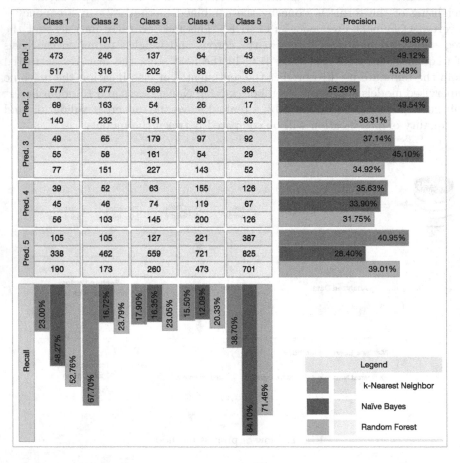

Fig. 2. Results of the classifiers k-Nearest Neighbor, Naïve Bayes and Random Forest

The classifier *k-Nearest Neighbor* classifies customer ratings by sentiment with an accuracy of 32.56%. The highest precision of 49.89% is achieved by k-NN in class 1, but the probability that a customer rating actually belonging to class 1 will be recognized and correctly classified is only 23.00%. The lowest precision of 25.29% is achieved in class 2. However, the corresponding recall value shows that a customer rating belonging to this class is recognized and correctly classified by k-NN with a probability of 67.70%.

Naïve Bayes achieves an accuracy of 35.49% on the quinary classification problem. The highest precision with 49.54% is achieved by the classifier in class 2. Nevertheless, the probability that a customer rating actually belonging to class 2 is recognized and correctly classified is only 16.72%. The lowest precision with 28.40% is class 5. However, the corresponding recall value of 84.10% shows that a customer rating belonging to this class is highly likely to be recognized and correctly classified.

The *Random Forest* classifier achieves a total accuracy of 38.27%. The highest precision of 43.48% is achieved in class 1. In addition, a customer rating belonging to this class is recognized with a probability of 52.76% and classified correctly. The lowest precision of 31.75% is achieved by the classifier in class 4. The associated recall value of 20.33% shows that a customer rating belonging to this class is recognized and correctly classified with a relatively low probability.

The low precision and recall values achieved by the classifications indicate that the individual classes could not be clearly distinguished from each other. The reason for this could be the small amount of training data used. Due to technical limitations, the data set was limited to 5,000 elements. Each class contained 1,000 elements and thus a relatively small number for training. In addition, the lexicon-based preprocessing was carried out with a cross-domain sentiment dictionary, which could have led to the fact that the sentiment of domain-dependent terms was not correctly recorded and classified.

4   Conclusion

The aim of this study was to make initial statements on the extent to which the points or stars awarded by customers via rating systems reflect the opinions expressed in the written reviews. The sentiment recognition of online customer ratings was considered a quinary classification problem. In order to gain initial insights, a lexicon-based sentiment analysis was combined with the machine learning algorithms k-Nearest Neighbor, Naïve Bayes and Random Forest. The results of the classifiers were evaluated with tenfold cross-validation and then compared. Random Forest achieved the highest accuracy with 38.27%, followed by Naïve Bayes with 35.49%. Although k-Nearest Neighbor delivered the lowest overall accuracy of 32.56%, it achieved the best predictive accuracy in three out of five classes. Naïve Bayes achieved the highest accuracy in two out of five classes. Due to the limitations described in the previous chapter, the focus of the continuation of this study will be on the delimitation of the individual classes. A first step could be to adapt the sentiment dictionary to the specific domain. The sentiment of words or subsets can vary depending on the context. Words that are positive in one domain (e.g. the horror movie was scary) may be negative in another domain. The use of a domain-specific dictionary therefore seems to be useful for the differentiation of the individual classes. In the present study, a sentiment analysis was carried out at document level. In future research, opinion mining techniques will also be applied at sentence and aspect level in order to obtain more precise results.

References

1. Plottek, K., Herold, C.: Micro moments als entscheidender moment im rahmen einer zunehmend fragmentierteren customer journey. In: Rusnjak, A., Schallmo, D.R.A. (eds.) Customer Experience im Zeitalter des Kunden, pp. 143–176. Springer, Wiesbaden (2018). https://doi.org/10.1007/978-3-658-18961-7_5
2. Bitkom: Shopping digital – Wie die Digitalisierung den Handel tiefgreifend verändert. Technical report (2017). https://www.bitkom.org/sites/default/files/file/import/171124-Studienbericht-Handel-Web.pdf
3. Amazon. https://www.amazon.com
4. Scholz, T.: Opinion mining für verschiedene Webinhalte. In: Scherfer, K., Volpers, H. (eds.) Methoden der Webwissenschaft, pp. 63–81. Schriftenreihe Webwissenschaft, Lit, Berlin (2013)
5. Medhat, W., Hassan, A., Korashy, H.: Sentiment analysis algorithms and applications: a survey. Ain Shams Eng. J. 5(4), 1093–1113 (2014)
6. Ziegler, C.N.: Automated capture of strategic knowledge on the web, p. 160. Albert-Ludwigs-Universität Freiburg i. Br., Freiburg i. Br. (2010). http://www2.informatik.uni-freiburg.de/~cziegler/papers/Habil-Thesis.pdf
7. Aryo Prakoso, A., Winantesa Yananta, B., Fitra Setyawan, A., Muljono: A lexicon-based sentiment analysis for Amazon web review. In: 2018 International Seminar on Application for Technology of Information and Communication, pp. 503–508. IEEE (2018)
8. Alkalbani, A.M., Gadhvi, L., Patel, B., Hussain, F.K., Ghamry, A.M., Hussain, O.K.: Analysing cloud services reviews using opining mining. In: IEEE 31st International Conference on Advanced Information Networking and Applications (AINA), pp. 1124–1129. IEEE (2017)
9. Fang, X., Zhan, J.: Sentiment analysis using product review data. J. Big Data 2(1), 1–14 (2015)
10. Lin, B., Zampetti, F., Bavota, G., Di Penta, M., Lanza, M., Oliveto, R.: Sentiment analysis for software engineering: how far can we go? In: The 40th International Conference, pp. 94–104. ACM Press (2018)
11. El Alaoui, I., Gahi, Y., Messoussi, R., Chaabi, Y., Todoskoff, A., Kobi, A.: A novel adaptable approach for sentiment analysis on big social data. J. Big Data 5(1), 1–18 (2018)
12. Kaggle. https://t1p.de/rk88
13. Baeza-Yates, R., Ribeiro-Neto, B.: Modern Information Retrieval, pp. 29–30. Addison Wesley (1999)
14. Rapidminer. https://rapidminer.com
15. SentiWordNet. http://sentiwordnet.isti.cnr.it/
16. Pang, B., Lee, L.: Briefly noted. Comput. Linguist. 35(2), 311–312 (2009)

Exploration of Virtual Reality-Based Online Shopping Platform

Yu-Chun Huang[1]([⊠]), Shan-Ya Hu[1,2], Ssu-Ting Wang[1,2],
and Scottie Chih-Chieh Huang[2]

[1] Tatung University, 40 Section 3 Zhongshan North Road, Taipei, Taiwan
ych@gm.ttu.edu.tw
[2] National Tsing Hua University, 101 Section 2 Kuang-Fu Road,
Hsinchu, Taiwan

Abstract. The first online shopping transformed traditional shopping experience with the development of computer and network in 1984. In traditional shopping, people are able to physically interact with the products by multitude of senses: sight, hearing, taste, smell, and touch before making a purchase. In contrast, online shopping is totally different: people are restricted by the size of 2D screen and can only use the "browser to search keywords" or the "classification" to find the products of interest. Both shopping behaviors have their advantages to satisfy human beings. Therefore, the challenge of this research lies in how to create a more natural online shopping platform by incorporating online shopping and physical shopping? This research aims to use Virtual Reality (VR) device as an alternative bridge to break the boundaries between physical and virtual shopping stores. Our long term project is to create a *"VR online shopping platform system"*. While this research focuses on the preliminary stage to explore the simulation of VR online shopping platform, the future study will implement the system and apply it to Amazon and evaluate the possibility and feasibility.

Keywords: Online shopping · Virtual Reality

1 Introduction

Computer and internet have changed our spatial experience, and created a new space—"virtual space" (Liu 2001). To understand how human beings in the digital age experience new virtual space, researchers compare the experience between physical space and virtual world (Mitchell 1996; Liu 2001; Huang 2002). Virtual space is defined as imagination of artificial world and could serve as an alternative way to represent drawings, graphics, perspectives or nowadays animation, movie and online media (Huang 2002).

Meanwhile, the technology of Virtual Reality (VR) was invented to improve realistic experience in virtual space (Sutherland 1968) and has been widely discussed and used since 1990 (Mazuryk and Gervautz 1996). There are three main elements in VR: immersion, interaction and imagination (Burdea and Coiffet 1994). To make the VR experience approaching reality, "3D computer simulation acoustic scenes" has become an important component of VR environment (Vorländer 2007). In combination

© Springer Nature Switzerland AG 2019
C. Stephanidis (Ed.): HCII 2019, CCIS 1034, pp. 81–88, 2019.
https://doi.org/10.1007/978-3-030-23525-3_11

with internet, a social network-based VR platform—Second Life (SL)—was created (Dawood et al. 2009) and used to enhance the 2D art experience in physical museums (Huang and Han 2014).

In late 20th century, Cyberspace rapidly became an alternative 'place' where daily human activities (such as economic, cultural, educational, and online-shopping) take place (Kalay 2006). The first online shopping system—"TV shopping" was created by Aldrich in 1979. Jane Snowball became the first TV shopping user to successfully make a purchase from TESCO website at home in 1984 (Kasana and Chaudhary 2014). In 1995, eBay and Amazon created the earliest and widely used online shopping platform (Kimberly 2007). By 2000, online shopping has been pervasive into our everyday lives. Most researchers focused on the issue of online shopping behaviors (Jarvenpaa and Todd 1997; Suelin 2010), shopping preferences (Wu 2003; Overby and Lee 2006) and shopping privacy (Hoffman et al. 1999; Miyazaki and Fernandez 2001). However, there is little emphasis on the differences in shopping environment between physical and virtual space through the perspective of "architecture space".

2   Problem and Objective

Since 1980, with the advent of personal computer (PC), and the development of Internet, the first "online shopping" was made possible. In 1984, the first online shopping behavior—TV shopping behavior started to challenge the traditional shopping. In traditional shopping, people are able to directly interact with the products through multitude of senses: sight (ophthalmoception), hearing (audioception), taste (gustaoception), smell (olfacoception or olfacception), and touch (tactioception) before making decisions (see Fig. 1).

On the contrary, online shopping is different: customers are restricted to the size of 2D screen and use the "browser to search keywords" or use the "classification" to find the products of interest. The number of items shown on the screen could be limited to approximately five products per page (see Fig. 1). However, users are able to quickly navigate among different shopping stores (e.g. drugstore, supermarket, shopping mall…etc.). Moreover, through internet, users could easily browse the items/stores across the world, which is not achievable in the physical world.

However, there are many limitations in current online shopping—the shopping experience, shopping environment, interface, or even the screen size are totally different from the physical shopping stores. The challenge of this research lies in the creation and simulation of online shopping from physical shopping experience. How can we create a more intuitive natural online shopping platform by incorporating the physical experiences into the virtual space?

VR has recently become a popular and inexpensive device and could be widely incorporated into multiple fields, including entertainment, health and architecture of our daily lives. Coates (1992) defined VR as an electronic simulation of environments experienced via head mounted eye goggles to enable users to interact in realistic 3D situations. This could be used as an alternative bridge to blend the boundaries between physical and online shopping stores. Our project is to create a "*VR online shopping platform system*". Here, we present the preliminary stage: explore the possibility of VR

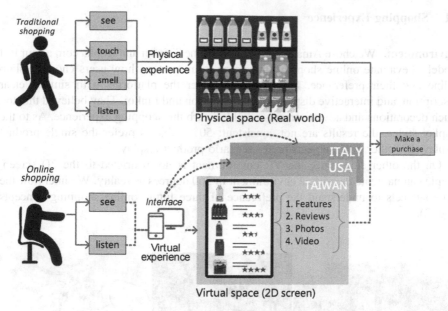

Fig. 1. Comparison between traditional shopping and online shopping

online shopping platform. The objective of this research is to create a "scenario of VR online shopping platform" according to the experience of online shopping, physical shopping and playing PS4 VR games.

3 Methodology and Steps

The project of "*VR online shopping platform*" has two stages: "the exploration of VR online shopping" and "VR online shopping platform". Since this is an ongoing project, the research we only discuss the first stage—"the exploration of VR online shopping". There are two steps for the methodology:

Step 1. Discussion of Shopping Experience and VR Manipulation.
In order to understand the advantages of online shopping, we designed a sequence of experiments to discuss the user's shopping experience. The experiments include: questionnaire, observation and interview.

Step 2. Scenario of VR Online Shopping
We created a scenario to demonstrate the concept based on the results of Step 1.

4 Discussion of Shopping Experience and VR Manipulation

Our experiments recruit ten people, between age of 20–40, with over one year of online shopping experience, as our subjects. The experiments included "questionnaire", "observation" and "interview".

4.1 Shopping Experience

Environment. We chose Amazon, Pinkoi, PChome Taiwan and Books.com as our test model to evaluate online shopping interfaces to understand how users chose to shop online and their preference. Most subjects prefer the platforms with simple, clear description, and interactive display, such as Amazon and Pinkoi. They believed that too much decorations and advertisements would disturb the shopping experience. As to the display styles, the results are not consistent: 50% subjects prefer the single product display, the other 50% subjects prefer scenario product display.

On the other side, since the VR environment is not restricted to the 2D screen, people can navigate the virtual environment in 360 degrees as reality. We interview the same subjects to understand the preference of three future online shopping concepts (Fig. 2).

Fig. 2. Concept of VR environment

90% of the subjects prefer the miniature scene as the future online shopping environment. The best thing is that users can quickly take a glance of the whole category in one shot because of the enhancement of the viewport. Also, the users are able to navigate between different stores around the world.

Shopping Process. As in the traditional shopping space, users need to follow the paths and the category signs to find the products. There is usually one kind of categories to display products in one day. Nerveless, same as online shopping, the users are able to quickly switch the filter to find the products by "key words", "multiple categories", "price" or "review". Regarding the filter priority, we found users set "price" most frequently, and followed by "brand" and "review". Every user agreed that the filter option augmented the efficiency of online shopping.

Final Decision, Assistant and Shopping with Friends. It was not possible to physically test the products, thus, most users relied on the "review of the products" (especially the numbers of stars), "comparison of products" and "online-assistant" to make the final decision before purchasing. As to the shopping assistant, the users would like to shop alone but only when they needed. For the shopping list, most users do not prefer to share the shopping list to the public, but they were happy to shop with specific friends or family. Nevertheless, some subjects prefer shopping with friends or family but some are not.

4.2   VR Manipulation

To explore the possibility of VR manipulation, we study the most immersive game—"*Batman: Arkham VR*" through PS4 VR device. We chose ten subjects (same as previous experiments) to navigate the VR world. By wearing the VR headset, every user is able to completely immersive into the virtual world. The users are able to interact with the 360-degree display scene around themselves based on the system—"6DoF (six degrees of freedom)" which plots your head in terms of your X, Y and Z axis to measure head movements forward and backwards, side to side. In the VR game "*Batman: Arkham VR*", the users can naturally and smoothly make the actual poses interacting with the virtual environment as well as in reality: such as "hold and drag a box", "hold and flip the postcard" and "pick up/drop off and push" or "see and turn the head" (see Table 1.).

Table 1. Controller in VR world

Action	Description	Controller	Demonstration
Hold + and drag	The user pressed the button and drag the mortuary cabinet.		
Hold + flip	The user pressed the button and pick up a postcard and flip to the back.		
Hold + throw out	The user pressed the button and throw out the darts.		
Release + touch/push	The user touched the vial from the table		
See + turn head	The user is turning head to browse the environment around him in virtual world.		

5   Scenario of VR Online Shopping

5.1   Features of VR Online Shopping Platform

Based on the result of our study, the "VR online shopping platform" includes the following features:

1. Environment: Since most users preferred simple interface without frame or decorations, we built the glass-like display as the interface in 3D environment. Also, we started with a miniature viewport to make the users easily filter the stores, features, prices around the world.
2. Interaction: In virtual reality, users could naturally use hands grab a product and simply rotate the product smoothly in order to see the detail of the products.
3. Shopping assistant: We use the voice control avatar to be the shopping assistant (like Siri on iPhone). The assistant will be available whenever requested.
4. Social network: The system is connected to social network and the users can send the requests to other individuals to shop together.

5.2   Scenario Demonstration

We built a scenario to demonstrate the possibility of VR online shopping platform based on the features included above. The scenario demonstration is as below:

Emily wanted to buy a pair of headphones, so she wore the VR headset and hold two controllers to get into the VR online shopping. First, she started at the home spot with multiple shopping ports (by category). She turned left her head and call "Amy" to wake up the assistant and commended by saying "find headphones" (Fig. 3A). The environment switched to the headphone show room. Emily started to go shopping in the 360-degree display scene. She used her hand to grab a highly-rated headphone—'Urbanear' (Fig. 3B), the related floating descriptions were displayed and attached to the product (Fig. 3C). Since she was still undecided and wanted to review all other high-rated headphones, she pressed the four-stars icon to pull out all four-stars headphone (Fig. 3D). Finally, she decided her favorite headphone and she easily put it into the shopping cart. Emily would like to shop around the clothes, so she swiped out to go back to home spot (Fig. 3E). She selected the brand—'Uniqlo' (see Fig. 3F), the environment changed to the Uniqlo store. Then she wiped left to browse the clothes. Suddenly a banner showed up—"her best friend Yumi requested to join her shopping" (Fig. 3G). Emily responded "yes" to accept the request (Fig. 3H). Finally, Emily was shopping together with Yumi (Fig. 3I).

Fig. 3. Scenario demonstration

6 Concluding Remark

Through the scenario, we expect the users to smoothly, conveniently and appropriately shop at the VR, and even better than physical experience. Simulating a realistic shopping mall that people might get used to could be easier. Our research incorporates virtual reality and challenge to provide a more natural and intuitive shopping place for human by creating a VR online shopping platform. VR world is not limited by the restrictions in the real world, such as the gravity, size and style. Our research is still an undergoing project with multiple ideas yet to be tested in a real VR online shopping system. Our future study will apply the system to Amazon and evaluate the possibility and feasibility.

References

Burdea, G., Coiffet, P.: Virtual Reality Technology. Wiley, New York (1994)

Coates, G.: Program from Invisible Site—a virtual sho, a multimedia performance work presented by George Coates Performance Works, San Francisco, CA (1992)

Dawood, N., Benghi, C., Lorenzen, T., Pencreach, Y.: Integration of urban development and 5D planning. In: Proceedings of the 9th International Conference on Construction Applications of Virtual Reality, Sydney, Australia, pp. 217–228 (2009)

Fitzpatrick, G.: Evolving HCI from Where to Where? OZCHI 2005, Canberra, Australia, 23–25 November 2005

Huang, C.P.: A Body-surrounding study in physical, virtual and mental space, Doctoral dissertation (2002)

Huang, Y.-C., Han, S.R.: An immersive virtual reality museum via second life. In: Stephanidis, C. (ed.) HCI 2014. CCIS, vol. 434, pp. 579–584. Springer, Cham (2014). https://doi.org/10.1007/978-3-319-07857-1_102

Hoffman, D.L., Novak, T.P., Peralta, M.: Building consumer trust online. Commun. ACM 42(4), 80–85 (1999)

Jarvenpaa, S.L., Todd, P.A.: Consumer reactions to electronic shopping on the world wide web. Int. J. Electron. Commer. 1(2), 59–88 (1997)

Kalay, Y.E.: The impact of information technology on design methods, products and practices. Des. Stud. 27(3), 357–380 (2006)

Kasana, M.J., Chaudhary, M.N.: A comparative study of eBay and Amazon in online shopping. Int. Res. J. Commer. Arts Sci. 5(2), 263–275 (2014)

Kimberly, P.: News & World Report (2007)

Liu, Y.-T.: Spatial representation of design thinking in virtual space. In: Gero, J.S., Tversky, B. (eds.) Visual and Spatial Reasoning in Design II, Key Centre of Design Computing and Cognition, University of Sydney, Australia, pp. 25–40 (2001)

Mazuryk, T., Gervautz, M.: Virtual reality-history, applications, technology and future (1996)

Mitchell, W.J.: City of Bits: Space, Place, and the Infobahn. The MIT Press (1996)

Miyazaki, A.D., Fernandez, A.: Consumer perceptions of privacy and security risks for online shopping. J. Consum. Aff. 35(1), 27–44 (2001)

Myers, B.A.: A brief history of human computer interaction technology. ACM Interact. 5(2), 44–54 (1998)

Overby, J.W., Lee, E.J.: The effects of utilitarian and hedonic online shopping value on consumer preference and intentions. J. Bus. Res. 59(10–11), 1160–1166 (2006)

Suelin, C.: Understanding consumer purchase behavior in the Japanese personal grooming sector. J. Yaşar University 5(17), 2910–2921 (2010)

Sutherland, I.E.: A head-mounted three dimensional display. In: Proceedings of the Fall Joint Computer Conference, Part I, 9–11 December 1968, pp. 757–764 (1968)

Weiser, M., Brown, J.S.: The Coming Age of Calm Technology (1996). http://www.ubiq.com/hypertext/weiser/acmfuture2endnote.htm

Wu, S.I.: The relationship between consumer characteristics and attitude toward online shopping. Market. Intell. Plann. 21(1), 37–44 (2003)

Vorländer, M.: Auralization: Fundamentals of Acoustics, Modelling, Simulation, Algorithms and Acoustic Virtual Reality. Springer Science & Business Media, Heidelberg (2007). https://doi.org/10.1007/978-3-540-48830-9

Smart Omni-Channel Consumer Engagement in Malls

George Margetis[1]([✉]) [iD], Stavroula Ntoa[1],
and Constantine Stephanidis[1,2]

[1] Foundation for Research and Technology – Hellas (FORTH),
Institute of Computer Science (ICS), Heraklion, Crete 70013, Greece
{gmarget, stant, cs}@ics.forth.gr
[2] Department of Computer Science, University of Crete, Heraklion, Greece

Abstract. Retail stores and in particular malls are going through a recession period, resulting among others from the change in customers' shopping habits and the shift towards e-commerce. Proposed strategies to alleviate this situation require manifold solutions, especially for malls, as they constitute ecosystems featuring both commercial and social activities. This paper proposes a model following an omni-channel consumer engagement approach, and blending at the same time the physical and digital shopping experience through an extended reality technology framework. The main benefits of the proposed approach are that it can be easily deployed in existing malls, as well as that it combines benefits from both physical and virtual shopping, being flexible to serve in the best possible way the evolving needs of customers. In this respect, malls of the near future can become appealing again to a wide consumer base and regain their lost allure.

Keywords: Smart malls · Consumer engagement · Augmented reality · Virtual reality · Omni-channel

1 Introduction

In the last few decades, the advent of new digital capabilities that have been interweaved in our everyday life has changed people's lifestyle in the retail domain. Furthermore, much of our time has been given over to busier lives, urging people towards the use of online services for purchasing goods, rather than visiting physical stores or malls. It has become common sense that malls "were built for patterns of social interaction that increasingly don't exist"[1], while analysts estimate that by 2022 one out of every four malls in the U.S. could be out of business, as a consequence of the changing purchasing trends. The malls of the future must be transformed into consumer engagement spaces, designed to meet the needs of new generations of shoppers[2]. A counter measure for avoiding this ominous future of the bricks-and-mortar malls is

---

[1] http://time.com/4865957/death-and-life-shopping-mall/.

[2] https://www.atkearney.com/retail/article?/a/the-future-of-shopping-centers-article.

© Springer Nature Switzerland AG 2019
C. Stephanidis (Ed.): HCII 2019, CCIS 1034, pp. 89–96, 2019.
https://doi.org/10.1007/978-3-030-23525-3_12

retailers and mall owners to listen to new generations' trends and behaviours and adapt their retail strategies towards new paradigm shifts, where technology would play a prevalent role.

Over the last few years, retailers in most countries have already adopted their selling strategies in order to enable consumers to research, compare, purchase, and return products across multiple channels, a move that is extremely challenging from the companies' perspective[3]. Such an effort demands coordination and integration across the entire retail ecosystem orchestrated as a unified omni-channel process, in which malls can constitute a fundamental part, regaining their popularity. To that end, there is a need for the integration of digital technologies to transform activities, processes, actors, and goods from analogue to digital with the aim to facilitate new forms of value creation [1]. This digitalization cannot occur in isolation, so physical assets will continue to play a key role by means of omni-channel logic [2]. Furthermore, although omni-channel retailing has some features that are related to e-commerce, it provides an unprecedented opportunity to understand not just customer transactions but also customer interactions such as visits to the store, likes on Facebook, searches on websites, and check-ins at nearby establishments [3]. Hence, companies can nowadays harness their customers' big data analytics and conclude to personalized selling experiences for their products, according to each individual customer.

This paper reports an ongoing work regarding the set-up of a new kind of smart omni-channel consumer engagement space, which can be easily deployed on existing malls and provide personalized retailing experiences through an extended reality technology framework. The purpose of the discussed work is to develop an onmnichannel purchasing chain for the customers, commencing the purchase process by recommending new products that fit to the customers according to their consuming profiles, involving a diversity of communication channels and facilitating them to examine and try them, while looking for other related products.

2   The Role of Smart Malls in Omni-Channel Retailing

Indisputably, the role of malls should be reconsidered today, acquiring a new orientation to support omni-channel retailing. In this respect, it is important to consider how customer experiences are shaped, what the assets of traditional stores are when compared to online stores, as well as what the requirements that need to be fulfilled are to adopt an omni-channel approach.

The determinants of customer experience have been reported to include the social environment, the service interface, the retail atmosphere, the assortment, the price, and promotions (including loyalty programs) [4]. Malls, by design, mainly rely on the social determinant to achieve highly satisfactory customer experiences. For example, customers often visit a mall with friends or family members. This establishes a social shopping experience that can affect a customer's own experience, as well as that of fellow customers. On the other hand, in a physical store one customer demanding

---

[3] https://www.strategyand.pwc.com/media/file/The-2017-Global-Omnichannel-Retail-Index.pdf.

attention from the sales person can take away from the experience of another customer also needing help. To that end, the proposed approach suggests that customer experiences can be fostered by new forms of malls that harness high-end technology in combination with the physical space, in a way that customers' physical presence is seamlessly merged with digital interaction.

Another important asset of bricks-and-mortar stores versus e-commerce is that customers can see, feel, touch and try the product, as well as experience the shop atmosphere (e.g. the space layout, the music, the decoration). Harnessing technology, such as interactive screens, augmented reality, and "magic mirrors," as well as technologies for stores' employees (e.g. tablets), gives an opportunity to use the store as a place to provide a personal experience that will attract customers, regardless of the channel used [5].

The omni-channel approach introduces four key differences in channel organization [6]: first, it involves more channels; second, it implies a broader perspective as it includes not only channels but also customer touch points; third, it induces the disappearance of borders between channels; and most importantly, fourth, customer brand experience – the focal differentiator of omni-channel retailing – is highly specific. In this respect, a smart mall can smoothly blend in this fusion of multi-channelled retailing, providing 'click and collect' solutions, where a customer orders a product online or via other channels and collects it in-store. Such an approach reduces e-fulfilment costs since the customers do the 'hard work' by collecting the product themselves and removes the need for delivery couriers [7]. This, Cross-Channel Integration (CCI), which includes showrooming as part of the retail chain, can also drive customers' reactions to retailers' strategy, toward reducing retailer uncertainty in providing attractive offers, conserving time and effort [7].

Taking into account the potential role of smart malls in the retailing of the future, a smart omni-channel consumer engagement system is reported, aiming to tackle the challenges that have emerged through the new forms of retailing and customers purchasing behaviours. The conceptual approach of the proposed system has its foundations on a CCI approach through which customers: (i) are being recommended with new products that fit their preferences; (ii) are able to browse through a wide collection of products and make their selections using a diversity of channels; (iii) go to the mall where they can try the selected products (physically and virtually) and eventually buy them along with other products that can be bought onsite or ordered; and (iv) engage in social activities in the physical or virtual world.

3 Smart Omni-Channel Mall Overview

The proposed smart omni-channel approach is discussed through a scenario, developing in five episodes. Each scenario-episode presents different features of the proposed system, which integrates omni-channel shopping and fuses physical-world with virtual-world shopping to create an integrated customer experience.

Episode 1: Unpacking [Home]. Alicia has bought *OmniSh*, the omni-channel smart shopping kit, which supports her shopping activities through various shopping channels. *OmniSh* comes with a variety of accessories according to the customer's preferences, such as Kinect, AR glasses, VR headset, or none of the above. Alicia bought the plain just-software version. She downloads the software and easily installs it on her Xbox console and smartphone. Within a few minutes she is ready to enjoy her shopping through *OmniSh*. First, standing in front of her Kinect, she initiates a full-body scan, so that the system makes the appropriate measurements and creates her profile featuring a virtual avatar. The next step is to set her preferences. Alicia allows the system to monitor her buying preferences as performed through *OmniSh*, in order to receive personalized suggestions and potentially interesting offers.

Episode 2: Couch Shopping [Home]. Alicia is currently watching her favourite TV series when she receives a notification on her phone informing her that, according to a promotion activity called "Late Night", retail items are offered at half-price. She selects to view the items on offer. *OmniSh* suggests that a specific blouse, which is available on her size, can be combined with a pair of trousers she already owns. The price is tempting, so Alicia decides to try the item on. She stands up, while her avatar is presented on the TV screen wearing the blouse. Alicia turns around, thinks about it for a while, and decides to order the blouse. She is not absolutely certain about how the blouse will look on her, so she decides to pick up the order from the mall, where she can actually try it on.

Episode 3: I Want That Advertisement Look [On the Go]. Alicia is waiting for the train, part of her daily commuting routine. While waiting, she notices on the board across an advertisement for a nice pair of shoes. Using the *OmniSh* on her smartphone she takes a photo and adds it to her wish list. As the train arrives she does not have enough time to look further, so she decides to do that later.

Episode 4: Competition for an Employee's Attention and How to Avoid It [Mall]. Alicia goes to the mall, to pick up her order. She enters the mall, which is *OmniSh* compatible. The application offers directions toward the store where she can try and eventually purchase the blouse she has ordered. While heading to the store, she receives an alert, that a pair of shoes similar to that in her wish list is available in a nearby store. She decides to visit this nearby store first and try the shoes on. Unfortunately, there are too many customers in the shop and the employee, who initially brought the shoes she asked for, is now busy. Alicia would like to ask if there are any other colours available for that particular pair of shoes. Instead, she deploys the *OmniSh* application and through its AR feature, she explores the additional shoes colours and checks how they would look on her. She also finds extra information and tips. Eventually, she orders them through the application and continues her shopping. She indicates that she will come back later to purchase them, when the store will be less crowded. A notification will be sent to her as soon as her order is ready, indicating the estimated waiting time.

Episode 5: Mirror, Mirror on the Wall [Mall]. Eventually she reaches the store, where her blouse is, and enters the dressing room to try it on. The dressing room features a mirror, which is technologically enhanced, and allows her to browse through other items of the store or in other *OmniSh* compatible stores, and virtually try them on. The mirror suggests other items that could be combined with her blouse. Alicia virtually tries on a nice skirt, however she is quite uncertain about it. She wishes she had been accompanied by her friend Samantha. Fortunately, the mirror features a telepresence functionality, which can bring her friend with her virtually in the fitting room. Alicia calls Samantha, who gladly joins through her VR headset. The two friends discuss for a while and Alicia decides that she will not buy the skirt.

Samantha feels totally immersed in the store atmosphere even hearing the same music that plays through the store loudspeakers. She looks around for a while and finds a nice pair of earrings that she would like to buy. Instantly, she changes the look of her avatar to her favourite dress that she plans to match with the earrings. Alicia encourages Samantha to buy them, and suggests to pick them up along with the blouse that she will buy. Samantha purchases the items and a while later Alicia picks up both orders.

4 The Smart Omni-Channel Customer Engagement System

The envisaged smart omni-channel customer engagement system aims to provide a cross-channel approach, enabling customers to complete product selection and purchase anywhere (their home, on the go and at the mall). Furthermore, the process of finding out and buying a product is complemented with additional customer needs, such as socializing, resulting in an elevated customer experience. The design of the system is based on four fundamental steps that should be accomplished for any customer, independently of their location and the technical means used: (i) recommend products to the customer, (ii) enable the customer to browse through a variety of products and categories, (iii) make it feasible for the customer to try products (either physically or virtually when possible), and (iv) give alternatives to order and buy products.

Figure 1 depicts the conceptual model of the smart omni-channel consumer engagement system, aiming to address the aforementioned requirements. It comprises the necessary *intelligence* for assisting customers during their exploration for new products, as well as multi-modal and alternative mechanisms which facilitate customers in trying the selected products, combining them with other relevant or suggested items, and eventually purchasing them. These mechanisms are mainly based on Augmented Reality, Virtual Reality and Mixed Reality approaches, which are collectively referred to as X-Reality (Extended Reality) or XR applications [8].

The system keeps customers' preferences and purchasing behaviours in the **user model** component of the architecture, which is being continuously updated with users' choices, browsing patterns and purchases. Additionally, this component keeps the body metrics of the customer that are needed for virtually applying apparel and accessories via the X-Reality fitting room. The user model is used by the **recommendation engine** component, which encompasses the necessary intelligence of the system in order to bring in to the customers' view products that are potentially interesting for them. Furthermore, the recommendation engine is able to suggest alternatives and combinations of products that fit to the current customers' selections.

The AR e-shop component makes the e-commerce functionalities of the system available in a diversity of devices (e.g. mobile, desktop PCs, tablets); it also features AR characteristics, which can prove very helpful for customers' assistance wherever

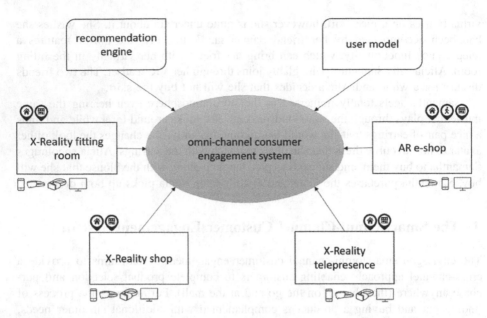

Fig. 1. Smart omni-channel customer engagement system conceptual architecture

they are located. Specifically, through this component customers can be notified for new products that meet their interests (through the recommendation engine), browse for products, select some, order and purchase them. Additionally, the AR functionality of the component can prove to be very helpful, when customers want to have more information regarding a physical product that lies in front of them (in a store of the mall). For example, if customers are looking at a pair of shoes, they can use their mobile phone to scan it and see its availability in the store, save it for later so that they order it online, or watch through their mobile screen how it would look in other colours or combined with outfits already owned by the customers, by displaying their *hologram* wearing the shoes and outfits (based on their body metrics that the system has already stored).

The X-Reality components of the system aim at providing advanced customer experiences over a cross-channel multimodal manner. Specifically, the **X-Reality virtual shop** can be accessible by the customers, via a diversity of devices including VR headsets, AR glasses, or TV screens that can be located either at the customers' homes or at the mall. Users can virtually navigate in a 3D virtual store space and browse a diversity of products and categories that have been personalized according to the pertinent user model, and eventually select and order products. In case of apparel and accessories, customers are able to virtually try them on through the **X-Reality fitting room**, over a concept very similar to [9]. Moreover, this component is able to render the customer wearing virtual apparel and accessories in combination with the physical ones that the customer wears when using the system. To this end, the system is able not only to recommend products that match with the ones that the customer is trying on, but also to display how this combination will look like on the customer per se. The **X-Reality telepresence** can cast any person in distance in the X-Reality virtual shop, providing a realistic social experience to the customer by virtually bringing them in contact with friends of family members, in order to discuss their product choice and help them to select what to purchase.

5 Conclusions and Future Work

Motivated by shifts in current lifestyle and shopping behaviour, as well as by the resulting adverse effects on retailing and malls in particular, this paper has presented an approach for enhanced consumer engagement. The proposed model adopts the omni-channel approach and advocates the integration of physical with virtual shopping facilities towards facilitating and elevating the shopping experience. As a result, benefits stemming from shopping in physical retail stores are retained. Such benefits include the physical interaction with products, experiencing the store atmosphere interacting with employees, as well as socialization with family and friends. At the same time, the blended physical-virtual approach adopted ensures that customers can bypass inconveniences that often occur when shopping in physical stores, such as long queues or lack of a specific product. Finally, the virtual shopping features facilitate among others shopping anytime and from anywhere, personalized suggestions and promotion activities, as well as social activity through friends' telepresence. The main benefit of the proposed approach is the breadth of shopping options (physical and virtual) that can be interchanged or combined to better suit each customer's needs.

The work described in this paper is still ongoing and the proposed model is currently under development. Future steps include its small- and full-scale deployment in actual malls, with the aim to iteratively evaluate and improve the model and the services provided.

References

1. Hagberg, J., Sundstrom, M., Egels-Zandén, N.: The digitalization of retailing: an exploratory framework. Int. J. Retail Distrib. Manag. **44**(7), 694–712 (2016)
2. Frishammar, J., Cenamor, J., Cavalli-Björkman, H., Hernell, E., Carlsson, J.: Digital strategies for two-sided markets: a case study of shopping malls. Decis. Support Syst. **108**, 34–44 (2018)
3. Brynjolfsson, E., Hu, Y.J., Rahman, M.S.: Competing in the Age of Omnichannel Retailing. MIT, Cambridge (2013)
4. Verhoef, P.C., Lemon, K.N., Parasuraman, A., Roggeveen, A., Tsiros, M., Schlesinger, L.A.: Customer experience creation: determinants, dynamics and management strategies. J. Retail. **85**(1), 31–41 (2009)
5. Piotrowicz, W., Cuthbertson, R.: Introduction to the special issue information technology in retail: Toward omnichannel retailing. Int. J. Electron. Commer. **18**(4), 5–16 (2014)
6. Verhoef, P.C., Kannan, P.K., Inman, J.J.: From multi-channel retailing to Omni-channel retailing: introduction to the special issue on multi-channel retailing. J. Retail. **91**(2), 174–181 (2015)

7. Zhang, J., Farris, P.W., Irvin, J.W., Kushwaha, T., Steenburgh, T.J., Weitz, B.A.: Crafting integrated multichannel retailing strategies. J. Interact. Market. **24**(2), 168–180 (2010)
8. Li, Y., Liu, H., Lim, E.T., Goh, J.M., Yang, F., Lee, M.K.: Customer's reaction to cross-channel integration in omnichannel retailing: the mediating roles of retailer uncertainty, identity attractiveness, and switching costs. Decis. Support Syst. **109**, 50–60 (2018)
9. Birliraki, C., Margetis, G., Patsiouras, N., Drossis, G., Stephanidis, C.: Enhancing the customers' experience using an augmented reality mirror. In: Stephanidis, C. (ed.) HCI 2016. CCIS, vol. 618, pp. 479–484. Springer, Cham (2016). https://doi.org/10.1007/978-3-319-40542-1_77

TradeMarker - Artificial Intelligence Based Trademarks Similarity Search Engine

Idan Mosseri[1,2], Matan Rusanovsky[1,3], and Gal Oren[1,2(✉)]

[1] Department of Computer Science,
Ben-Gurion University of the Negev, P.O.B. 653, Be'er Sheva, Israel
{idanmos,matanru,orenw}@post.bgu.ac.il
[2] Department of Physics, Nuclear Research Center-Negev,
P.O.B. 9001, Be'er-Sheva, Israel
[3] Israel Atomic Energy Commission, P.O.B. 7061, Tel Aviv, Israel

Abstract. A trademark is a mark used by a company or a private human for the purpose of marking products or services that they manufacture or trade in. A restriction on the use of the trademark is necessary to enable sellers and manufacturers to build a reputation for themselves, to differentiate themselves from their competitors and thereby promote their businesses. In addition, the restriction also serves consumers and prevents their misuse by a name similar to another product. This restriction is done through the formal examination and approval of the trademarks. This process entails trademark examination against other approved trademarks which is currently a long manual process performed by experienced examiners. Current state-of-the-art trademark similarity search systems attempt to provide a single metric to quantify trademark similarities to a given mark [6–11]. In this work we introduce a new way to carry out this process, by simultaneously conducting several independent searches on different similarity aspects - *Automated content similarity*, *Image/pixel similarity*, *Text similarity*, and *Manual content similarity*. This separation enables us to benefit from the advantages of each aspect, as opposed to combining them into one similarity aspect and diminishing the significance of each one of them.

Keywords: Artificial intelligence · Computer vision · Deep learning · Trademark · Image search

1 Introduction

The main function of patent offices is to provide legal protection of industrial intellectual properties through the registration of patents, designs and trade-

This work was supported by Google, Israel Ministry of Justice, National Digital Israel Initiative and the Lynn and William Frankel Center for Computer Science. Patent Pending, "Similarity Search Engine for a Digital Visual Object", IL/18-ORP/38222, Request No. 262220.

© Springer Nature Switzerland AG 2019
C. Stephanidis (Ed.): HCII 2019, CCIS 1034, pp. 97–105, 2019.
https://doi.org/10.1007/978-3-030-23525-3_13

marks [1]. Granting a right to intellectual properties depends on the examination of the specific application. An examination is essential to ensure the exclusivity for said property [2].

The current examination process [3] is done manually and slowly, using human trademark examiners - who are required to conduct a massive search in a large unordered database, while deciding whether there is any similarity between the trademark submitted via application and the already approved marks [4]. Automation of the examination process using Artificial Intelligence with the supervision of trademark examiners can provide a solution for the above problem with greater ease and higher accuracy.

For example, VisionAPI [5] is a computer vision tool based on powerful machine learning models, that enables users to understand the content of an image by features extraction. VisionAPI also makes it possible to detect popular product logos within an image through the *logo detection* feature. However, we claim that VisionAPI's logo detection feature can not be used solely for the trademark examination process, since it is able to detect only popular logos from a closed set of images that is under the supervision of Google (and not under some state's patent office control). In addition, as we show in Fig. 1, VisionAPI manages to not only quickly be mistaken by a small attribute change (color change, for example), but also to point similarity to only a small set of logos (even one only), such that many other possible similar logos do not appear in the result list.

(a) Extremely well-known similar trademarks

(b) Stadt Brühl logo, extremely similar to Beats logo, incorrectly classified (c) Stadt Brühl logo, after a color change, incorrectly classified

Fig. 1. VisionAPI's performance on extremely similar logos.

Another platform that provides image similarity search is LIRE [6–8], but it does not involve learning, thus we find it less suitable for finding similar abstract (deep) features, and therefore is less capable of finding visual and structural similarities in images.

Showkatramani et al. [9] utilized the usage of Convolutional Neural Networks (CNN) for the extraction of features that then were used by a variant of a nearest neighbor algorithm for finding trademarks with similar features. Another example is *TrademarkVision, trademark.vision1, trademark.vision2* which is a deep learning-based reverse visual search platform that identifies similar trademarks to a mark. However, despite the fact that the usage of deep-learning enables the detection of abstract features, the fact that the above systems are not based upon different similarity aspects or/and averages those aspects into a single list causes information loss - as will be explained next.

Although it seems that all the above systems provide a good solution for the *image similarity* problem, the formal definition of *trademark similarity* is far more complex [12] - trademarks are considered to be similar if they are *deceptively similar*. Thus, one can conclude that there may be several different metrics that the human eye uses to quantify similarities between trademarks - the main ones are the following: Visual similarity - *do the two trademarks look visually similar?*, Semantic/Content similarity - *do the two trademarks contain the same semantic content?* or Text similarity - *do the two trademarks contain similar text?*.

An improvement to the automatic examination process might be to examine the trademarks ordered by a range of similarity aspects. We use this separation in this work in order to focus on the best results from each category/aspect rather than searching through an unorderly mixture of them. We do so as we concluded that it is not feasible to average the different similarity aspects without losing information, as each of those represent a different domain of similarity, thus averaging all of the results will yield in a loss of accuracy and similarity precision. Since accuracy is the top restriction, we found the separate lists to be the optimal solution to the *trademark similarity* problem, even though there might be a bit faster ones.

2 Similarity Aspects

TradeMarker is an Artificial Intelligence based Trademarks Similarity Search Engine, that allows conducting simultaneously several independent search queries, each query examining a different similarity aspect. We next describe the work-flow of the system, as well as the different similarity aspects used by TradeMarker: Automated content similarity, Image/pixel similarity, Text similarity, and Manual content similarity.

2.1 Work-Flow

The system works in the following manner: After inserting the desired trademark image, the system performs said search queries and displays four independent output windows, corresponding to the four aspects mentioned above. In each of these windows, the most similar trademarks are presented in the order of their similarity to the input trademark. The work-flow of the system is presented in Fig. 2. As can be seen, Human-Computer Interaction is necessary in order to determine which of the trademarks are similar to the given mark, based on the ordered lists. However, this manual similarity check is minimized due to the ordered fashion in which the output is displayed.

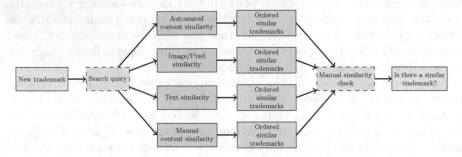

Fig. 2. The search engine performs four different search queries corresponding to the four similarity aspects of the system.

2.2 Automated Content Similarity

Similarly to the work presented by Showkatramani et al. [9] and TrademarkVision [10, 11], the first similarity aspect, automated content similarity, uses machine learning models (e.g., such as Googles VisionAPI technology which helps derive insight from images using Google's pre-trained models), in order to extract features from images, and then find images with similar features. Automated content similarity may work as follows. First, extracting image attributes and their content as tags from a received image that represents a trademark, combined with the already approved trademarks from the database. Then, comparing the tags of the received trademark with the ones of the already approved trademarks, and finally displaying them ordered by similarity score. This similarity aspect is intended to find similar objects between the images, thus finding *semantic* similarities between the trademarks. Figure 3 presents an example of tag extraction that was made by Google VisionAPI.

2.3 Image/Pixel Similarity

The second aspect, image/pixel similarity, uses the platform provided by Clarifai's technology [13, 14], in order to find visual similarities between images. It uses Computer Vision and Deep Learning techniques to display trademarks ordered by visual similarity to the input mark, based on pre-trained machine learning models. This similarity aspect is responsible for catching visual and structural similarities of the images.

(a) Input logo   (b) Logo's labels   (c) Logo's web   (d) Logo's logos

Fig. 3. An example of tag extraction made by Google VisionAPI.

2.4 Text Similarity

The third aspect, text similarity, orders approved trademarks by the similarity of the text they may contain to the text in the new trademark being examined. To quantify such text similarity, algorithms such as Dice's Coefficient, Levenshtein distance, Jaccard Similarity or Cosine Similarity can be used [15]. For example, the Dice's Coefficient algorithm returns a fraction between "0" and "1", which indicates the degree of similarity between the two strings (e.g., a first string refer to text that may appear in the examined trademark and the second string refers to the text that appear in each relevant approved trademark). Wherein "0" indicates completely different strings, "1" indicates identical strings. The comparison is case-insensitive. Naturally, this similarity aspect is in charge of finding textual similarities between trademarks.

2.5 Manual Content Similarity

The fourth aspect, manual content similarity, is the same as the existing examination trademark method. Namely, it allows a user (e.g., a trademark examiner) to manually classify the trademark with the desired tags from the Vienna Classification system [3], and then to go through all other trademarks that had already been approved and classified with the same tags. This method only reduces the amount of trademarks to examine, rather than the previous methods that present the trademarks in an ordered fashion. Thus, allowing the examiner to focus only on the most similar trademarks, and then to decide whether there is an already approved trademark that is similar to the input trademark.

3 Test Case

In Fig. 4 we present the performance of TradeMarker on Starbucks logo. The output of the tool is divided to the different similarity aspects. In this test case we present only the *first* 24 results, exactly as shown in the tool's four different windows. More results can be presented in the order of similarity by user's demand. In addition, we note that one can combine the output of Manual content similarity with the output of any other aspect by displaying the trademarks from that aspect with the same manual content that was given. Thus having the output trademarks with the given manual content, ordered by visual/text and (automate) content similarities.

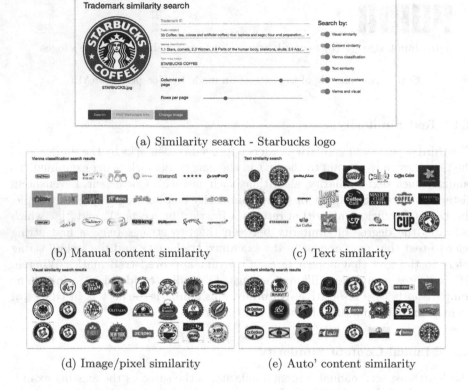

(a) Similarity search - Starbucks logo

(b) Manual content similarity   (c) Text similarity

(d) Image/pixel similarity   (e) Auto' content similarity

Fig. 4. TradeMarker's performance on Starbucks logo.

4   Evaluation

The Israeli Patent Office evaluated the performance of TradeMarker, and the results are shown in Fig. 5.

The test performed in the following manner. The examiners provided hundreds of pairs - test trademark and a counterpart similar trademark that is expected to show up after querying TradeMarker with the test trademark. We then decided on a threshold in which the expected counterpart trademark of a successful test trademark may reside. This is important, since if the expected trademark appears, but as the last result - it is practically impractical, as going through all trademarks to find similarities is not feasible in large databases, and specifically in the Israeli trademarks database, where there are more than 130 thousand registered trademarks.

We therefore found that going through 200 trademarks manually is reasonably representative but yet not too large amount of trademarks to examine.

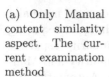

(a) Only Manual content similarity aspect. The current examination method

(b) Only Auto' content similarity aspect

(c) Only Image/pixel similarity aspect

(d) TradeMarker, using all four similarity aspects in overlap

Fig. 5. The results of the search engines on the tests that were performed by the Israeli Patent Office. True is when a similar trademark has displayed in the first 200 results, given some trademark.

We note that without TradeMarker (only Manual content similarity), just 30% of the pairs were found to be successful, or in other words, in only 30% of the test trademarks the expected counterpart trademark was found in the first 200 similar trademarks. However, using TradeMarker we managed to elevate the success rate to more than 70%. We stress that not only that TradeMarker performed better than the current examination process in the tests by a factor of 2.5, it also was able to find similarities that the old system could not even detect. We estimate that in 10% of the searches the manual tagging is losing the ability to describe all the image features, as the Vienna Classification is bounded in about 150 categories.

5   Architecture

TradeMarker was built using the M.E.A.N stack architecture. Using Angular 6 for the front-end development, NodeJS and ExpressJS to build the back-end server and MongoDB as the database. As said previously, TradeMarker uses services provided by Calrifai and Googles Vision API for catching structural (visual) and semantic (content) similarity. These interfaces and the communication

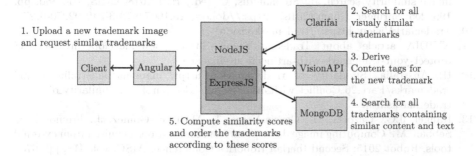

Fig. 6. The architecture of TradeMarker.

between the front and back-end of the system are done using a restful API. The architecture is summarized in Fig. 6.

6 Conclusion

Currently, trademarks examination is a long process that requires manually examining lots of unordered trademarks and the usage of techniques requiring experienced examiners. In this work we introduced several similarity aspects - Automated content similarity, Image/pixel similarity, Text similarity and Manual content similarity - on which we conduct search queries on. Automated and manual content similarities are responsible for catching semantic similarities, while image/pixel similarity is responsible for structural similarities, in contrast to text similarity that seeks for textual similarities and has no correlation to visual similarities. This separation made it possible to fully utilize the advantages of each aspect, as opposed to search through an unorderly mixture; just through one or an average of them, and thus suffer from a reduction in the significance of similarity between trademarks according to different aspects.

References

1. Israeli Trademarks Department, Departments/Trademarks. http://www.justice. gov.il/En/Units/ILPO
2. Trade Marks Ordinance 5732–1972, s. 8; 11(9); 11(13); 11(14)
3. Vienna Classification. http://www.wipo.int/classifications/vienna/en
4. ILPO Annual Report 2016, p. 50 [in Hebrew]
5. Google VisionAPI. https://cloud.google.com/vision
6. Lux, M., Chatzichristofis, S.A.: LIRE: Lucene image retrieval: an extensible Java CBIR library. In: Proceedings of the 16th ACM International Conference on Multimedia. ACM (2008)
7. Lux, M.: Content based image retrieval with LIRe. In: Proceedings of the 19th ACM International Conference on Multimedia. ACM (2011)
8. Lux, M.: LIRE: open source image retrieval in Java. In: Proceedings of the 21st ACM International Conference on Multimedia. ACM (2013)
9. Showkatramani, G., Nareddi, S., Doninger, C., Gabel, G., Krishna, A.: Trademark image similarity search. In: Stephanidis, C. (ed.) HCI 2018. CCIS, vol. 850, pp. 199–205. Springer, Cham (2018). https://doi.org/10.1007/978-3-319-92270-6_27
10. TrademarkVision. https://trademark.vision
11. NVIDIA article about TrademarkVision. https://news.developer.nvidia.com/ protect-your-trademark-with-artificial-intelligence
12. IP Australia, Similarity of trade marks. http://manuals.ipaustralia.gov.au/ trademarks/Part_26_Conflict_with_other_Signs_-_Section_44/5._Similarity_of_ trade_marks.htm
13. Rangel, J.C., Cazorla, M., García-Varea, I., Martínez-Gómez, J., Fromont, É., Sebban, M.: Computing image descriptors from annotations acquired from external tools. Robot 2015: Second Iberian Robotics Conference. AISC, vol. 418, pp. 673–683. Springer, Cham (2016). https://doi.org/10.1007/978-3-319-27149-1_52

14. Zeiler, M.D., Fergus, R.: Visualizing and understanding convolutional networks. In: Fleet, D., Pajdla, T., Schiele, B., Tuytelaars, T. (eds.) ECCV 2014. LNCS, vol. 8689, pp. 818–833. Springer, Cham (2014). https://doi.org/10.1007/978-3-319-10590-1_53
15. Gomaa, W.H., Fahmy, A.A.: A survey of text similarity approaches. Int. J. Comput. Appl. **68**(13), 13–18 (2013)

Analysis of the Relation Between Price Range, Location and Reputation in Japanese Hotels

Kohei Otake[1(✉)] and Tomofumi Uetake[2]

[1] School of Information and Telecommunication Engineering,
Tokai University, Tokyo, Japan
otake@tsc.u-tokai.ac.jp
[2] School of Business Administration, Senshu University,
Tokyo, Kanagawa, Japan
uetake@isc.senshu-u.ac.jp

Abstract. Recently, in response to the spread of the CGM, reputation such as numerical online rating and textual online review has begun to exert a big influence on hotel conversion rate and room rate. Therefore, hotel manager must consider not only factors such as the facilities, brand, competitors, and sales channels but also its reputation when formulating hotel's sales strategy. However, it is not clear how reputation affects hotel management practices in Japanese hotels. In this research, we analyzed the relation between price range, location, and reputation to clarify the impact on reputation. We collected the hotel information from "Travelko", the typical Japanese travel comparison site. Additionally, we use statistical data on tourism resources possessed by each prefecture for analysis. First, we tried to categorize prefectures using statistical data. Moreover, we conducted the multiple regression analysis to clarify the impact on the reputation for the four clusters. Based on our analysis, we clarified the relation between price range, location and reputation in Japanese hotels.

Keywords: Hotel management · Reputation · Multi-dimensional scaling · Multiple regression analysis

1 Introduction

Recently, hotel management has become more complex in response to changes in the external environment shown below [1].

- Growth of OTAs (Online Travel Agents)
- Growth of LCC (Low Cost Carrier)
- Changes in sales methods of flight tickets
- Changes in the traveler's consciousness

Moreover, in response to the spread of the CGM (Consumer Generated Media), reputation (e.g. word of mouth) such as numerical online rating and textual online review has begun to exert a big influence on hotel conversion rate and room rate [2, 3]. Therefore, hotel manager must consider not only factors such as the facilities, brand,

C. Stephanidis (Ed.): HCII 2019, CCIS 1034, pp. 106–114, 2019.
https://doi.org/10.1007/978-3-030-23525-3_14

competitors, and sales channels but also its reputation when formulating hotel's sales strategy.

However, at the present time, it is not clear how reputation affects hotel management practices in Japanese hotels (Fig. 1). In this research, we analyzed the relation between price range, location and reputation to clarify the effects of reputation.

Fig. 1. Factors to formulate hotel's sales strategy

2 Datasets

In this study, we analyze Japanese hotels using the following data.

- Hotel data extracted from "Travelko"
  "Travelko", the typical Japanese travel comparison sites, collects information from over 700 travel booking sites, and hotel information is also abundantly listed [4]. We collected the hotel information (name, location, price range, number of rooms and reputation (numerical online rating)). The acquired data is the data at August 2017. Consequently, we collected about 20,000 Japanese hotel information.
- Statistical data on tourist spots and number of visitors
  As information on tourist spots and the number of visitors, we used open data published by the Ministry of Land, Infrastructure, Transport and Tourism [5]. Statistical data includes the total number of tourist spots, the number of tourist spots for each type of tourist spot, the number of visitors for each type of tourist spot, and the situation at the time of travel. These pieces of information are organized by prefectures in Japan. In this study, we used data from July-September (2014), which is generally the high season of travel.

3 Analysis of the Relation Between Price Range, Location and Reputation

We analyze in the following procedure.

1. Basic aggregation of datasets
2. Classification of prefecture using statistical data
3. Analysis of the relationship between the price range, the number of hotel rooms and the reputation value for each classified cluster

3.1   Basic Aggregation of Datasets

First, we perform basic aggregation and grasp data outline about hotel data and statistical data on tourist spots and number of visitors. Table 1 shows the details of the hotel data. In this study, we targeted 15,938 hotels except hotels with no reviews. Figure 2 shows the distribution of price range.

Table 1. Details of the hotel data extracted from "Travelko"

Type of information	Outline of information
Price range	Standard rate per adult price range (9 levels)
Hotel location	Address, Zip code
Reputation value	Average of 5 ratings for a hotel (This value is comprehensively evaluated based on the ratings of multiple evaluation sites)

As shown in Fig. 2, the largest price range is 5,000 to 8,000 yen, which accounts for 34% of the total. Focus on the reputation value (average), the lowest value was 2.4 and the highest value was 5. Moreover, the hotel which has a value of less than 3 was about 2% of the whole.

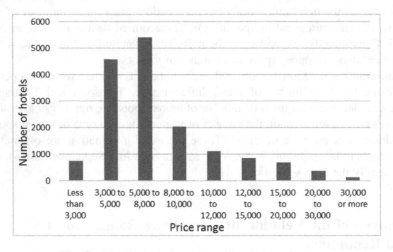

Fig. 2. Distribution of number of hotels by price range

Next, we show an overview of statistical data on tourist spots, the number of visitors and, travel situation. Japan is generally divided into 47 prefectures. In this study, we used data on 43 prefectures excluding 4 prefectures (Osaka, Fukui, Nagasaki, Okinawa) that were not included in the data report. Table 2 shows the details of the statistical data.

Table 2. Details of the statistical data for each prefecture

Type of Information	Outline of information
Tourist spots	Total number of tourist spots
	Number of tourist spots in each of six genres (Nature, History and Culture, Hot spring and Health, Sports and Recreation, Urban Tourism, Other spots.)
	Number of festivals and events
Number of visitors	Total number of visitors
	Total number of visitors per six genres
	Total number of visitors to festivals and events
Travel situation	Average number of travel companions
	Average number of visits per person
	Average expenditure per person (yen)
	Average number of visited prefectures per person

The characteristics of each prefecture are shown in Fig. 3. The left side of Fig. 3 shows the total number of tourist spots, and right side shows the total number of visitors.

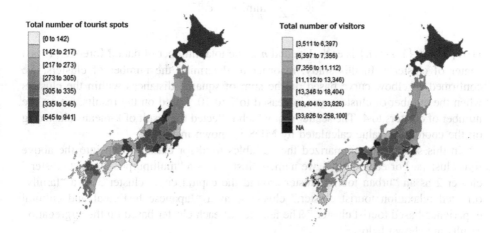

Total number of tourist spots
- [0 to 142)
- [142 to 217)
- [217 to 273)
- [273 to 305)
- [305 to 335)
- [335 to 545)
- [545 to 941]

Total number of visitors
- [3,511 to 6,397)
- [6,397 to 7,356)
- [7,356 to 11,112)
- [11,112 to 13,346)
- [13,346 to 18,404)
- [18,404 to 33,826)
- [33,826 to 258,100]
- NA

Fig. 3. The total number of tourist spots by prefecture (Left Side), and the total number of visitors by prefecture (Right Side)

It can be said that the total number of tourist spots and the total number of visitors are positively correlated (Pearson's correlation coefficient: 0.70). However, some prefectures (e.g. Fukuoka and Kyoto) have many visitors per tourist spot, and some prefectures (Niigata, Okayama) have a small number of visitors per tourist spot.

3.2   Classification of Prefecture Using Statistical Data on Tourist Spots, Number of Visitors and, Travel Situation

In this section, we try to categorize prefectures using statistical data on tourist sites and the number of visitors, because it is possible to carry out a comprehensive analysis by collectively for each prefecture with similar tourist resources and travel conditions.

First, we perform MDS (multi-dimensional scaling) [6], using the statistical data on the tourist spots, the number of visiting, and travel situation shown in Table 2. MDS is a method that performs dimensional reduction and arranging relationships between variables in a two-dimensional or three-dimensional space. Based on the distance or similarity, similar variables are placed nearby, and others are placed far away. It is possible to consider the structure of data. In this study, we calculate two-dimensional coordinate values by MDS using a total of 20 variables: information on tourist spots (8 variables), information on the number of visitors (8 variables), and information on travel situations (4 variables). Here, we used standardized Euclidean distance as the distance between variables.

Next, we perform the k-means clustering [7] to classify prefectures using the coordinate values calculated by MDS. k-means method is a kind of non-hierarchical clustering, which is one of the most famous techniques. This method divides data X into arbitrary k clusters by finding the cluster center that minimizes the evaluation function ϕ in Eq. (1).

$$\phi = \sum_{x_j \in X} \min_{i \in k} \left\| x_j - c_i \right\|^2 \tag{1}$$

Here, $x_j, j \in \{1, \cdots, n\}$ is each data and n is the total number of data. Moreover, c_i is a center of cluster i. In this study, in order to determine the number of clusters, we confirmed an elbow curve based on the sum of squared distances within the clusters when the number of clusters was increased to 2 to 10. Based on the results, we set the number of clusters to 4. The scatter plot which reflected the result of k-means clustering on the coordinate value calculated by MDS is shown in Fig. 4.

In this study, we summarized the variables used for classification into the above four clusters. For each cluster, we named cluster 1 as a "multipurpose tourist cluster," cluster 2 as an "urban tourist cluster around the capital city," cluster 3 as a "family-oriented relaxation tourist cluster," cluster 4 as a "Japanese historical and cultural experience-based tourist cluster." The features of each cluster based on the aggregation results are shown below.

1. **Multipurpose Tourist Cluster**
   There is no big feature about tourist base even if it sees relatively. The number of tourist spots is below average against 4 clusters. The number of visitors is relatively high for "Sports and Recreation" and "other spots."
2. **Urban Tourist Cluster Around the Capital City**
   This cluster contains prefectures with many tourist spots. It specializes in tourist spots of "History and Culture" and "Sports and Recreation." Moreover, many events and festivals are held in this cluster. The number of visitors is more than

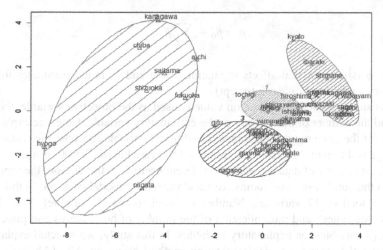

Fig. 4. Scatter plot of clustering results using prefecture coordinate values

twice as many as other clusters. In particular, the number of visitors for "Sports and Recreation" and "Urban Tourism" are overwhelming compared to other clusters. Characteristically, the average expenditure per person is overwhelmingly lower than in other clusters. Additionally, this cluster includes prefectures located around the capital, such as Tokyo and Osaka.

3. **Family-Oriented Relaxation Tourist Cluster**
   This cluster has the largest number of "Hot Spring and Health" tourist spots compared to other clusters. Focusing on the number of visitors, in addition to "Hot Spring and Health" with many tourist spots, there are also many visitors to "Nature." As for travel situations, the average number of companions is the largest. In addition, the average expenditure per person is about 2,000 yen higher than other clusters.

4. **Japanese Historical and Cultural Experience-Based Tourist Cluster**
   This cluster has a relatively large number of "History and Culture" tourist spots within this cluster. Although the number of tourist spots in "History and Culture" is small compared to other clusters, the visitor is the second largest. The number of festivals and events is the smallest.

3.3 Analysis of the Relationship Between the Price, the Number of Hotel Rooms and the Reputation Value for Each Cluster

In this section, we analyze the relationship between the price range, the number of hotel rooms, and the reputation value for the four clusters in Sect. 3.2. Specifically, we conduct the multiple regression analysis to clarify the impact on the reputation for the four (Eq. (2)).

$$y = \beta_0 + \sum_{i=1}^{n} \beta_i x_i \qquad (2)$$

Here, x_i is a factor that affects reputation value and β_i is the parameter for each explanatory variable (β_0 is an intercept).

In this study, we set the reputation value is used as the objective variable, the price range, and the number of hotel rooms as the explanatory variable. Here, the explanatory variables for the price range are expressed as dummy variables because the width of the price range is different. Moreover, we removed the variable of "30000 or more," which was the least number of data records, as a reference variable. In addition, the reputation value and the number of hotel rooms are standardized for model creation. In this study, we used a total of 17 variables, Number of hotel rooms (1 variable), Price Range dummy (8 variables), and multiplication of the number of hotel rooms and price range variables (8 variables) as explanatory variables. In this study, we selected explanatory variables by the stepwise variable selection method based on AIC (Akaike's Information Criterion).

We show the results of the models created for each cluster. Table 3 shows the values of the partial regression coefficients in the model for each cluster. Here, we show explanatory variables significant (based on a p-value < 0.05) among the explanatory variables selected by four models. The coefficient of determination for each model was around 0.20.

Table 3. The value of the partial regression coefficient in a multiple regression model about four clusters

Explanatory variables	Cluster 1	Cluster 2	Cluster 3	Cluster 4
Intercept	1.065	1.020	0.832	0.802
Number of Hotel Rooms (NR)	0.059	−0.119	−0.242	−0.018
Less than 3,000 (P1)	−1.844	−1.937	−1.648	−1.585
3,000 to 5,000 (P2)	−1.576	−1.540	−1.414	−1.280
5,000 to 8,000 (P3)	−1.063	−1.030	−0.924	−0.814
8,000 to 10,000 (P4)	−0.807	−0.759	−0.596	−0.393
10,000 to 12,000 (P5)	−0.751	−0.635	−0.503	−0.343
12,000 to 15,000 (P6)	−0.591	−0.402	−0.409	−0.271
15,000 to 20,000 (P7)	–	−0.230	−0.163	–
NR * P1	–	0.311	0.274	0.248
NR * P2	–	0.172	0.261	0.123
NR * P3	−0.162	0.125	–	–
NR * P4	−0.311	–	–	–
NR * P5	−0.313	–	–	–
NR * P6	−0.330	–	–	–

From the value of the partial regression coefficient shown in Table 3, we consider the effect of the reputation for each cluster. The overall trend is that the price range and the evaluation of the word are linear. On the other hand, focusing on the number of hotel rooms, the value of the partial regression coefficient is positive for "Multipurpose Tourist Cluster" and the others are negative. In other words, "Multipurpose Tourist Cluster" large-scale hotels tend to be highly evaluated and, in another cluster, small-scale hotels tend to be highly evaluated. Focusing on the interaction variables of "Multipurpose Tourist Cluster", when the price range is high, and the number of rooms is large the evaluation drops. From the above, consumer tends to favor large-scale, low prices hotel in "Multipurpose Tourist Cluster" compared to other clusters.

Focusing on the price range, "Urban Tourist Cluster around the Capital City" and "Family-Oriented Relaxation Tourist Cluster" are particularly appreciated for hotels in the high price range (P6 and P7). Especially in "Family-Oriented Relaxation Tourist Cluster", the partial regression coefficient of the number of hotel rooms is strongly negative. "Family-Oriented Relaxation Tourist Cluster" has the largest number of "Hot Spring and Health" tourist spots compared to other clusters. It can be inferred that high-class Japanese inn that families can stay calmly are supported. From the above, consumer tends to favor small-scale, high prices hotels in "Family-Oriented Relaxation Tourist Cluster" compared to other clusters. The same tendency can be said for "Urban Tourist Cluster around the Capital City," but since there are many prefectures located around the capital, it is inferred that luxury city hotels are supported.

Focusing on "Japanese Historical and Cultural Experience-Based Tourist Cluster," middle price range (P4 and P5) has a high partial regression coefficient evaluated compared to other clusters. The partial regression coefficient of the number of hotel rooms is almost 0, the tendency is close to "Multipurpose Tourist Cluster." However, "Japanese Historical and Cultural Experience-Based Tourist Cluster," a large number of tourists to "History and Culture" tourist spot. It can be inferred that the hotel in the middle price range received high evaluation when it was evaluated from the viewpoint of convenience to the tourist spot rather than the grade of the hotel.

4 Conclusion

In this paper, we focused on the typical Japanese travel comparison sites "Travelko" and analyzed the relation between price range, location, and reputation to clarify the impact on reputation. Based on our analysis, we clarified following points.

- There is a positive correlation between price range and reputation (numerical online rating).
- The above correlation differs in intensity depending on regions and tourism resources.
- Ratings for the same price range also differ depending on the genre of the tourist spot in the vicinity.

References

1. Uetake, T., Sasaki, I., Aoki, A.: Impact of reputation on revenue management at Hotels. In: 3rd International Tourism and Hospitality Management Conference (ITHMC), International Tourism and Hospitality Management Conference (2017). https://www.ithmc.com/sites/default/files/ithmc_2017_abstract_book_v2.pdf
2. Edwin, T.N., Dipendra, S.: Towards a model of electronic word-of-mouth and its impact on the hotel industry. Int. J. Hospitality Tourism Adm. 17(4), 472–489 (2016)
3. Wang, M., Liu, Q., Robert, C., Shi, W.: How word of mouth moderates room price and hotel stars for online hotel booking, an empirical investigation with expedia data. J. Electron. Commer. Res. 16(1), 72–80 (2015)
4. Travelko. https://www.tour.ne.jp/. Accessed 27 Mar 2019
5. Statistical data on tourist spots and number of visitors. http://www.mlit.go.jp/kankocho/siryou/toukei/irikomi.html. Accessed 27 Mar 2019
6. Kruskal, J.B.: Multidimensional scaling by optimizing goodness of fit to a nonmetric hypothesis. Psychometrika 29(1), 1–27 (1964)
7. MacQueen, J.: Some methods for classification and analysis of multivariate observations. In: Proceedings of the Fifth Berkeley Symposium on Mathematical Statistics and Probability, vol. 1, pp. 281–297 (1967)

Adopting an Omnichannel Approach to Improve User Experience in Online Enrolment at an E-learning University

Pablo Rebaque-Rivas[✉] and Eva Gil-Rodríguez

Technology Department, Universitat Oberta de Catalunya,
Parc Mediterrani de la Tecnologia (edifici B3), Av. Carl Friedrich Gauss,
508860 Castelldefels, Spain
{prebaque, egilrod}@uoc.edu

Abstract. In this research article, we present the initial results of our case study on improving user experience (UX) in a fully online enrolment process at an e-learning university, the Universitat Oberta de Catalunya (UOC). Our main conclusion is that an omnichannel approach is necessary for improving prospective students' UX. To obtain our results, we made use of three different data sources, which allowed us to map a current and future customer journey. These sources were: (1) quantitative data on the main stages in the process at which prospective students drop out; (2) field diaries compiled by prospective students over the course of the enrolment process and a co-creation workshop with the same prospective students; and (3) the UOC's perspective, gathered from workshops and interviews with University staff responsible for the enrolment process. Comparing the current journey with the ideal journey, we will demonstrate that significant improvements can be made to prospective students' UX in online enrolment via an omnichannel approach. We discovered a need for improved channel coordination (e.g. information transfer between channels), greater availability and a wider range of channels (inbound and outbound, telephone vs. chatbot), personalization and adaptation of channel content according to the stage prospective students have reached in the process, and the ability to choose the channel that best meets their needs (chatbot for commonly asked questions vs. real people for more complex or specific queries). In view of our results, we would especially highlight technological and organizational changes as the next steps to take.

Keywords: Costumer journey · Omnichanel user experience ·
Online enrolment process · Online university

1 Introduction

In this article we present a case study of the Universitat Oberta de Catalunya (UOC), in which we show the preliminary results on improving the omnichannel [1] user experience among prospective students during the enrolment process.

The UOC is an e-learning university and the vast majority of its processes and activities, including the enrolment process, take place via its information systems.

© Springer Nature Switzerland AG 2019
C. Stephanidis (Ed.): HCII 2019, CCIS 1034, pp. 115–122, 2019.
https://doi.org/10.1007/978-3-030-23525-3_15

The University offers official bachelor's and master's degree programmes accredited by the Spanish Ministry of Education, as well as UOC-certified courses in the form of postgraduate, master's degree and specialization programmes. Based in Barcelona but with a presence throughout Spain and internationally, the University currently has 47,195 students and the number of enrolments has risen by 7.9% in the last year.

Despite this increase, various information and data sources reveal that the enrolment process is over-complicated and not always successful for users, with around 50% of users dropping out at certain stages of the process.

This led us to analyse the customer journey during the enrolment process, from the moment prospective students discover the UOC and seek information on the courses and programmes on offer to the moment they successfully enrol. By doing so, we were able to identify the primary pain points along the customer journey. We collected quantitative data on the process, and on the perspective of applicants with respect to the enrolment process, as well as that of the different UOC departments taking part in that process. In this article, we will focus on the data collected in relation to management, articulation and coordination of the channels encountered by applicants during the enrolment process and how these impact on prospective students' user experience.

We will go on to present the state of the art of the subject of this article, followed by an explanation of the methodology and key results related to the omnichannel approach. Finally, we will highlight the key conclusions, implications for the current journey, and future lines of action.

2 State of the Art

In recent years, omnichannel has superseded the multichannel approach, offering the consumer a more consistent and seamless shopping or service experience [1].

Omnichannel aims to deliver a seamless customer experience, regardless of the channel [2]. Customers expect a consistent, uniform, integrated service experience, irrespective of the channel they use. They want to move seamlessly between channels according to their preferences, their present situation, the time of day or the type of product [2].

This omnichannel perspective has been employed extensively to improve the customer experience in the retail industry [1, 3, 4], with examples also found in the health centre sector [5].

One way to encourage an omnichannel approach is by mapping a customer journey [6]. This concept has been giving many definitions, all of which tend to emphasize one particular element [6], but the customer journey is essentially a tool that determines the stages and experiences a customer goes through during the service or shopping process. Omnichannel has been widely used to understand and improve services and processes and, essentially, to provide the customer with the best customer service experience [6–8]. By mapping the customer journey, it is possible to identify the channels available to users, how users make use of these, and the difficulties encountered along the way. As a result, there are two key factors in a good omnichannel experience: (1) reducing the risk of losing the customer during the customer journey by providing a unified and integrated customer service experience; and (2) encouraging the customer to continue on their journey with the company by providing seamless and intuitive cross-channel transitions at each touchpoint to match customer preferences, needs and behaviour [9].

The majority of articles found in the literature on the higher education enrolment process concentrate on identifying the factors and motivations that lead prospective students to choose one university as opposed to another. Generally speaking, these are quantitative studies and studies based on literature review, with the focus on physical universities [10–15]. Other studies attempt to analyse which types of marketing strategies or activities are most effective in recruiting new students [16, 17]. Finally, a couple of articles analyse how to improve the usability of web-based enrolment systems, that is, the interfaces that allow users to search, select and register for study programmes [18, 19].

Nevertheless, we found no articles which were based on an end-to-end analysis of the process of enrolment at an online university, nor which used a customer journey map to improve this process and examine the impact of the effective deployment and coordination of the channels involved.

3 Methodology

We used three sources of information to map the customer journey: quantitative data on the enrolment process, the perspective of prospective students attempting to enrol and the perspective of the UOC itself.

We collected quantitative data on the primary crash locations to be able to determine the crash hot spots in the enrolment process. We also took into consideration a satisfaction survey conducted annually among persons who have demonstrated an interest in studying at the UOC (that is, who have completed an online application for information via the UOC website). The purpose of the survey is to determine why these persons failed to complete the enrolment process.

A field diary method [20] and a co-creation workshop were used with prospective students to determine their experience in the actual process of approach, first contact, information and enrolment at the UOC, as well as to appreciate the process from their point of view.

We contacted persons who had applied for information via the UOC application form, given that these were prospective applicants for enrolment on one of the study programmes offered by the UOC, and invited them to describe their experience during the enrolment process using a field diary. Specifically, we asked them to relate the stages they went through in order to enrol at the UOC and indicate how they found the experience. This enabled us to obtain some 4,000 units of experience. Only 61 of the initial 112 users completed the study. Of those who completed the study, 30 went on to successfully enrol and 31 did not.

A co-creation workshop was held with the eleven Barcelona residents who successfully enrolled. The purpose of the workshop was twofold: (1) to further investigate the key points of the enrolment process, and (2) to map the ideal enrolment process.

Finally, nine interviews and two workshops were conducted with the different department heads involved in the enrolment process on behalf of the UOC (marketing, promotion, support line, tutors and in-person and electronic services) in order to determine how the current enrolment process is perceived from an operational and organizational point of view and to identify key problems.

4 Results

The different methods employed enabled us to map a customer journey of the enrolment process, determining which channels are involved and how they are involved, as well as identifying a number of pain points. These pain points refer to different areas including process agility, usability and design of certain interfaces, quality of content, platform errors, and the need for new functionalities and tools that would streamline and facilitate the process for both prospective students and the University's internal management. As we have stated above, in this article we will concentrate on the pain points which are related to the articulation, coordination and management of the channels identified in the enrolment process, and which to some degree impair prospective students' UX.

4.1 Current Journey

A key outcome was to be able to define the journey of the person taking part in the enrolment process, from the moment they discover the UOC to completion of the process. The key milestones along the journey will be defined in this section, and the key pain points in Sect. 4.2 below.

1. Discovery stage: prospective students discover the UOC through adverts in the media or on social media, web searches, word of mouth, etc.
2. Information stage: prospective students seek information on the study portfolio offered by the UOC, its educational model, prices, enrolment method, etc. They can opt to apply for information from the UOC website, which will alert the call centre to telephone the prospective student to provide further information and promote the University. They can also visit one of the UOC's physical centres[1].
3. Admission stage: prospective students apply for admission to the University using an online form. This also allows them to access the University's Virtual Campus for prospective students and enrol from there. The platform is a smaller version of the Virtual Campus available during the academic year, intended to publicize the virtual learning environment and steer prospective students in the direction of enrolment.
4. Enrolment stage: prospective students enrol from the Virtual Campus platform and pay for the enrolment using an online payment form. They have the option to contact a tutor via an online tutoring classroom, forums and email. This service is intended to provide academic guidance, including advice on choice of subjects, enrolment suggestions, etc. Having enrolled, students must present the relevant admissions documents.
5. Start of the semester: students can now access the full version of the Virtual Campus and the virtual classrooms.

---

[1] The UOC centres are service and promotional hubs; most are located in the Cataluña region.

Prospective students can complete any of the above milestones by telephoning or appearing in person at one of the University's centres. During the admission and enrolment stages, these centres function as alternatives when users comes up against problems or difficulties. A support service is also available to resolve queries and difficulties; the entry window to the service is an online form, and subsequent communications are made by email.

4.2   Pain Points Related to Omnichannel

We will now address the principal problems encountered on the customer journey, with respect to the use and management of the channels available during the enrolment process.

- Users receive communications from up to eight different emitters via different channels (web interface, outgoing telephone, tutoring forums, email, UOC centres, etc.), but the emitters are not fully coordinated in the execution of these communications.
- A standard enrolment process can involve as many as thirty communications including telephone conversations, sms, messages in tutoring forums and emails on different subjects including: (1) support service responses; (2) feedback from actions such as a request for information, an admissions application, or enrolment acceptance; (3) welcome messages; (4) tutor communications; (5) conversations with a tutor; (6) promotional emails (offers, etc.); (7) reminders of procedural requirements (presentation of documentation, payments due, etc.); and (8) academic and informative bulletins about the UOC.
- Content is offered via different channels and (1) is presented differently depending on the channel, creating inconsistency; (2) is sometimes provided at an inappropriate time (information users do not yet need is sometimes provided ahead of time, or necessary information is not provided); (3) is not usually personalized; and (4) rarely informs users of the next steps to follow to proceed with their enrolment process.
- Lack of definition of channels: the functions of some channels (tutor, UOC centre, support service for the resolution of queries) are not clearly defined and can overlap, leading to prospective students using them indiscriminately.
- Difficulties in contacting the UOC during the information and admission stages. Users are not adequately informed of how to make contact, nor is this made easy, and so users make use of channels unprepared for the demand. The online admissions form, for example, does not advise prospective students how to contact the UOC.
- Knowledge of a particular prospective student is not shared among the different departments – support line operators and tutors, for example – and so applicants are obliged to repeat information they have already supplied to the UOC.
- Users experience a number of stoppages during the enrolment process. These are often related to the system's slow provision of responses or solutions to users' situations, problems or queries. This is especially serious at moments of high demand or urgency, such as during the final few days of the enrolment period.

5 Conclusions

The current enrolment process used by the UOC is over-complicated, involving a number of different stages, and applicants are required to interact with different channels in order to successfully enrol at the University. Some channels can be avoided – it is possible to enrol without contacting the support line or the tutors, for example. However, when users do make contact via the different channels, frictions arise which affect applicants' UX.

Our view is that the different findings place the focus on the following four interrelated improvement factors.

1. **The need for improved channel coordination**, since the problem is often not so much the channel itself. Going beyond specifying and adapting what is communicated and at what stage of the journey, a coordinated and collaborative union of the different channels is needed. Communication with applicants may be constant, but it fails to be effective because of this lack of coordination with respect to frequency and type of content across the different channels. The lack of coordination also throws another problem into relief, and that is that no information transfer takes place between the different areas that deal with applicants.
2. **Greater availability and a wider range of channels (inbound and outbound, telephone vs. chatbot).** These findings show that the availability of channels during the enrolment process tends to be more unidirectional (from the UOC to applicants) than bidirectional, because of either the lack of a channel or the difficulty in finding one. This frequently causes applicants to utilize an inappropriate channel. One short-term solution could be to make UOC contact details more visible on the different web spaces that make up the milestones along the user journey. In the middle term, a chatbot could be made available to allow prospective students to make more immediate contact with the UOC. In the long term, we envisage the chatbot being the sole window to tutoring and support services.
3. **Personalization and adaptation of channel content according to the stage the prospective student has reached in the process.** If the enrolment process were a conversation between applicants and the UOC, it would be a difficult conversation because of the number of messages received by users and the lack of time-appropriate content emitted by the UOC. This "conversation" could be facilitated and streamlined by rationalizing and personalizing the content, and making it stage appropriate. To do so, once again there is a clear need for coordination between channels, which would allow the information offered to users to be released in a progressive and coordinated manner.
4. **User ability to choose the channel that best meets their needs: chatbot for commonly asked questions vs. real people for more complex or specific queries.** The enrolment process is complex, especially in relation to the specific individual characteristics of each applicant (admissions documents, grants, validations, etc.). Related to point 2 above, a chatbot could resolve straightforward or common queries. When queries become more complicated, the chatbot could refer users to a human figure, via chat or telephone.

While these solutions could make inroads toward an improvement in the omnichannel user experience and impact positively on enrolment rates, implementation is complicated. Basically, because these conclusions reveal a need for more coordination and collaboration between the departments involved, in such a way that partial objectives do not hinder the overall objective of achieving users' successful enrolment. This organizational transformation would have an impact on a number of levels, from clear governance and communication from senior management to a shared roadmap and new performance dashboards, backed by new incentive structures to facilitate cooperation, and a leader of a cross-unit team responsible for the customer journey and implementation of the various improvement initiatives [21].

References

1. Lazaris, C., Vrechopoulos, A.: From multichannel to "omnichannel" retailing: review of the literature and calls for research. In: 2nd International Conference on Contemporary Marketing Issues (ICCMI), Athens (2014)
2. Piotrowicz, W., Cuthbertson, R.: Introduction to the special issue information technology in retail: toward omnichannel retailing. Int. J. Electron. Commer. **18**(4), 5–16 (2014)
3. Verhoef, P.C., Kannan, P.K., Inman, J.J.: From multi-channel retailing to omni-channel retailing. Introduction to the special issue on multi-channel retailing. J. Retail. **91**(2), 174–181 (2015)
4. Brynjolfsson, E., Hu, Y.J., Rahman, M.S.: Competing in the age of omnichannel retailing. MIT Sloan Manag. Rev. **54**(4), 23–29 (2013)
5. Kronqvist, J., Leinonen, T.: Redefining touchpoints: an integrated approach for implementing omnichannel service concepts. In: Pfannstiel, M.A., Rasche, C. (eds.) Service Design and Service Thinking in Healthcare and Hospital Management, pp. 279–288. Springer, Cham (2019). https://doi.org/10.1007/978-3-030-00749-2_16
6. Følstad, A., Kvale, K.: Customer journeys: a systematic literature review. J. Serv. Theor. Pract. **28**(2), 196–227 (2018)
7. Moon, H., Han, S.H., Chun, J., Hong, S.W.: A design process for a customer journey map: a case study on mobile services. Hum. Factors Ergon. Manuf. Serv. Ind. **26**(4), 501–514 (2016)
8. Bernard, G., Andritsos, P.: A process mining based model for customer journey mapping. In: Proceedings of the Forum and Doctoral Consortium Papers Presented at the 29th International Conference on Advanced Information Systems Engineering (CAiSE 2017) (2017)
9. Peltola, S., Vainio, H., Nieminen, M.: Key factors in developing omnichannel customer experience with finnish retailers. In: Nah, F.F.-H., Tan, C.-H. (eds.) HCIB 2015. LNCS, vol. 9191, pp. 335–346. Springer, Cham (2015). https://doi.org/10.1007/978-3-319-20895-4_31
10. Dao, M.T.N., Thorpe, A.: What factors influence Vietnamese students' choice of university? Int. J. Educ. Manag. **29**(5), 666–681 (2015)
11. Obermeit, K.: Students' choice of universities in Germany: structure, factors and information sources used. J. Mark. High. Educ. **22**(2), 206–230 (2012)
12. Simões, C., Soares, A.M.: Applying to higher education: information sources and choice factors. Stud. High. Educ. **35**(4), 371–389 (2010)

13. Kanonire, T.: How students choose university: personal and institutional factors. In: Downing, K., Ganotice Jr., F.A. (eds.) World University Rankings and the Future of Higher Education, pp. 252–265. IGI Global, Hershey (2016)
14. Walsh, S., Cullinan, J.: Factors influencing higher education institution choice. In: Cullinan, J., Flannery, D. (eds.) Economic Insights on Higher Education Policy in Ireland. Palgrave Macmillan, Cham (2017)
15. Giacomo, C., Martina, G., Mariella, P.: Factors and information sources influencing students' consumer behaviour: a case study at an Italian public university. Int. J. Manag. Educ. **12**, 351 (2018)
16. Kucharski, M., Szopa, R., Halemba, P.: Marketing determinants of the choice of field of studies. Mark. Sci. Res. Organ. **25**(3), 41–57 (2017)
17. De Sabanto, A.L.R., Forcada, J., Zorrilla, P.: The marketing orientation as a university management philosophy: a framework to guide its application. Cuadernos de Gestión (2017)
18. Tchouakeu, L.-M.N., Hills, M.K., Jarrahi, M.H., Du, H.: On-line course registration systems usability: a case study of the e-Lion course registration system at the Pennsylvania State University. Int. J. Inf. Syst. Soc. Change **3**(4), 38–52 (2012)
19. Estevez, R., Rankin, S., Silva, R.: A model for web-based course registration systems. Int. J. Web Inf. Syst. **10**(1), 51–64 (2014)
20. Bolger, N., Davis, A., Rafaeli, E.: Diary methods: Capturing life as it is lived. Annu. Rev. Psychol. **54**, 579–616 (2003)
21. Bianchi, R., Cermak, M., Dusek, O.: More than Digital Plus Traditional: A Truly Omnichannel Customer Experience. McKinsey Insights (2016)

An Approach to Conversational Recommendation of Restaurants

Nicola Sardella, Claudio Biancalana, Alessandro Micarelli,
and Giuseppe Sansonetti$^{(\boxtimes)}$

Department of Engineering, Roma Tre University, Via della Vasca Navale 79,
00146 Rome, Italy
{ailab,gsansone}@dia.uniroma3.it

Abstract. In this paper, we propose an approach based on the integration of a chatbot module, a location-based service, and a recommendation algorithm. This approach has been deployed for restaurant recommendation, tested on a sample of 50 real users, and compared with some state-of-the-art algorithms. The preliminary experimental results showed the benefits of the proposed approach in terms of performance. An ANOVA test enabled us to verify the statistical significance of the obtained findings.

Keywords: Conversational recommender systems ·
Location-based services · Cold-start

1   Introduction and Background

In the common vision of future smart city, the user will be able to communicate directly with the available services [10,11]. As a result, there will be more and more conversational recommender systems (CRSs), namely, systems capable of inferring the user's preferences though dialogues in natural language. In this paper, we propose a system based on the integration of three different technologies: *(i)* a chatbot system, that is, an online human-machine dialogue system based on natural language [5,22]; *(ii)* a location-based service (LBS), that is, a system that exploits the user's current location to provide her with an added value [4,28]; *(iii)* a recommender system (RS), that is, a system able to provide personalized suggestions related to items (i.e., products or services) of possible interest to the target user [26,30]. The research question behind this study was to verify whether a system that contains the three above technologies is able to get better results in terms of performance compared to traditional RSs. To answer this research question, a chatbot for restaurant recommendations has been designed and implemented, which takes into accounts some features of the user's current context [2], including her location.

Despite the likely spread of CRSs in the future, the conversational recommendation is an emerging field with few contributions in the research literature. Among the most authoritative works there is the one proposed by

© Springer Nature Switzerland AG 2019
C. Stephanidis (Ed.): HCII 2019, CCIS 1034, pp. 123–130, 2019.
https://doi.org/10.1007/978-3-030-23525-3_16

Christakopoulou *et al.* [8], in which a CRS is proposed, whose theoretical foundation relies on probabilistic matrix factorization models [16,27]. In [20] the authors describe a CRS based on an end-to-end deep learning architecture, while the CRS proposed in [24] leverages PageRank with Priors for generating the recommendations and an explanation mechanism able to justify the proposed suggestions.

2   The Proposed Approach

From a technological point of view, the developed application consists of two subsystems (see Fig. 1). On the one hand, we can find a chatbot system, consisting of a proxy in charge of filtering the user's messages. Those messages can be managed directly from the DialogFlow[1] service used to identify entities and intent of the bot, and to connect a WebHook to the system for the proper management of the answers. Messages can also be sent to a service that uses the Telegram APIs[2] in order to process messages that cannot be processed by DialogFlow and to customize the user interface through the use of buttons and an inline keyboard. On the other hand, we can find a web application designed to monitor data and information obtained during the user-chatbot transactions, and to manage the experimentation phase. Those two subsystems share the same non-relational database (i.e., MongoDB[3]), which contains the user's data, the transactions occurred with the chatbot, and the restaurant information extracted

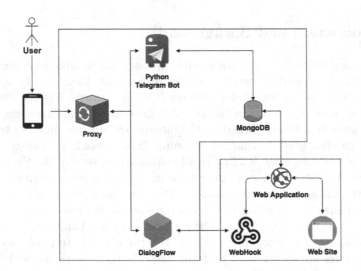

Fig. 1. The overall system architecture consisting of two subsytems.

---

[1] https://dialogflow.com/.
[2] https://core.telegram.org/.
[3] https://www.mongodb.com/.

through the Facebook Graph APIs[4]. The chatbot involves two fundamental operations: the request of recommendation and the extraction of user's feedbacks. A classic user-based nearest-neighbor collaborative filtering approach has been used to implement the recommendation algorithm. This algorithm provides two phases of recommendation. The first phase analyzes the user's demographic data with the aim of extracting 50 similar users from a dataset obtained through an online survey that allowed us to ask each user for her demographic information and preferences in terms of kinds of cuisine. This survey was realized also to mitigate the *cold-start problem* (e.g., see [26]) that is commonly associated with pure collaborative RSs when new users and/or new items are involved. The similarity is calculated using the *Pearson's correlation coefficient*, which can be calculated using the formula described as follows:

$$sim(a,b) = \frac{\sum_{d \in D}(v_{a,d} - \bar{v}_a)(v_{b,d} - \bar{v}_b)}{\sqrt{\sum_{d \in D}(v_{a,d} - \bar{v}_a)^2}\sqrt{\sum_{d \in D}(v_{b,d} - \bar{v}_b)^2}}$$

where

- a and b are users;
- D is the set of demographic information;
- $v_{a,d}$ is the value (converted to numeric form) of the demographic information d of the user a;
- $\bar{v}_a$ is the average value of the demographic information for the user a.

After the similarity calculation among users, the system returns a list of 50 users more similar to the active one and the relative types of cuisine preferred by everyone. During the second phase, the above list is reranked. The order of this list depends again on the value of Pearson's correlation coefficient, this time computed by analyzing the types of cuisine preferred by the user and the tags of the restaurant descriptions, as follows:

$$sim(a,b) = \frac{\sum_{t \in T}(r_{a,t} - \bar{r}_a)(r_{b,t} - \bar{r}_b)}{\sqrt{\sum_{t \in T}(r_{a,t} - \bar{r}_a)^2}\sqrt{\sum_{t \in T}(r_{b,t} - \bar{r}_b)^2}}$$

where

- a and b are users;
- T is the set of information regarding types of cuisine and tags;
- $r_{a,t}$ is the normalized rating of the type of cuisine or tag t of the user a;
- $\bar{r}_a$ is the average value of the standardized rating of the cooking types and tags, for the user a.

From this list ranked according to the similarity between users, the types of cuisine to be recommended are extracted. Thereafter, the system works as follows. The chatbot module recognizes the intent of recommendation by analyzing words contained in the message, such as "I'm hungry" or "Suggest me a restaurant".

---

[4] https://developers.facebook.com/docs/graph-api.

Once the intent is recognized, five recommended types of cuisine are suggested to the user. Based on the current time, the system determines whether the user is going to the restaurant for lunch or dinner. Then, based on the position automatically extracted from the LBS, the system proposes to the active user a set of restaurants in the surroundings. The system shows the user such restaurants ranked according to the recommended types of cuisine. The user can scroll through the results and view the attached pictures and, when satisfied, she can select her favorite restaurant. The feedback is generated through a pushed, scheduled service, which requires that the user expresses an opinion by means of a message in natural language and according to a five-point Likert scale. This rating is, then, combined with the results of the sentiment analysis performed on the reviews in natural language, in order to evaluate the overall feedback, which can be positive, neutral, or negative [12,14]. The obtained results will influence the future recommendations to that specific user.

3   Experimental Evaluation

In order to evaluate our system, we performed several experimental tests, in which 50 volunteer participants were interviewed. For the sake of brevity, we report only a part of it. Specifically, our RS (denoted as **Pearson** in Fig. 2) was compared with three other algorithms:

CosSim: a variant of the algorithm implemented in our chatbot, which exploits the *cosine similarity* instead of the Pearson's correlation coefficient to calculate the similarity between users;

Distance: a RS based only on the distance between the restaurant and the user's current position;

Rating: a RS based only on the reviews of the restaurant extracted from its Facebook page.

The experimental results show the perceived accuracy of each tested algorithm, in terms of *Precision, Recall,* and *F-measure* (see Fig. 2). It can be noted that most users much preferred the types of cuisine recommended by our system (both Person and CosSim versions) compared to those recommended by the others two RSs (Distance and Rating). Finally, a statistical significance test was performed on the achieved data. Specifically, we carried out the *ANalysis Of VAriance (ANOVA)* test to determine if the differences in the experimental results were relevant or due purely to chance (i.e., *null hypothesis*). For each of the four algorithms we evaluated first the number of recorded ratings, then the average of the F-measure. This data allowed us to calculate the intergroup sum of squares and the intragroup sum of squares. It was, therefore, possible determine the value of the F_{test} variable, considering two degrees of freedom equal to 3 and 156, respectively. This value was 24.89. It was, then, compared with the values of a random variable F_{crit} of Snedecor obtained by considering the same degrees of freedom. The critical value is the number that the F variable must overcome to reject the null hypothesis. In our case, F_{crit} is equal to 2.66.

Being $F_{test} \gg F_{crit}$, it was therefore possible to reject the null hypothesis and definitively claim that the algorithm implemented in the chatbot was the most efficient one.

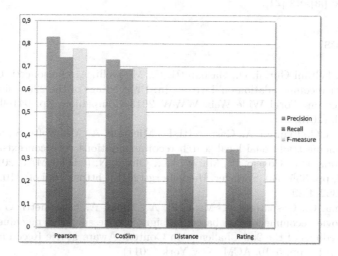

Fig. 2. Results of a comparative analysis between our approach (Pearson) and three other recommender systems.

4 Conclusions

In this paper, we have described a chatbot able to recommend restaurants to the target user, based on some contextual elements, including her current location. A WebHook has been implemented in order to manage the dialogue with the chatbot. Furthermore, we have implemented one algorithm for recommendation and one algorithm for evaluating user's feedbacks by exploiting the sentiment analysis of the reviews expressed in natural language. An online survey allowed us to collect an initial dataset, thus alleviating the cold-start problem as well. The experimental tests, which involved a sample of 50 real users, enabled us to conclude that our approach is able to obtain better results than other three approaches, in terms of Precision, Recall, and F-measure. Such findings were verified for statistical significance by performing the ANOVA test, which enabled us to reject the null hypothesis that foresees the absence of differences between the four algorithms.

Our research work has just begun, so there are many possible developments that we plan to achieve in the near future. First of all, we would like to enrich the profile of the target user with further information related, for instance, to her affective state [6,25], as well as to the real nature [13,15] and temporal dynamics [1,29] of her attitudes. Moreover, we would like to enhance the extraction of her real interests by analyzing her activity on the Web [19] and on social media [9], as well as equipping the system with an image recognition module [23] that can help in acquiring her preferences. Finally, we could integrate the chatbot services in recommender systems of itineraries among points of interest including restaurants [17,18], and in RSs of different items, such as news [7], movies [3], and scientific papers [21].

References

1. Arru, G., Feltoni Gurini, D., Gasparetti, F., Micarelli, A., Sansonetti, G.: Signal-based user recommendation on Twitter. In: Proceedings of the 22nd International Conference on World Wide Web, WWW 2013 Companion, pp. 941–944. ACM, New York (2013)
2. Biancalana, C., Flamini, A., Gasparetti, F., Micarelli, A., Millevolte, S., Sansonetti, G.: Enhancing traditional local search recommendations with context-awareness. In: Konstan, J.A., Conejo, R., Marzo, J.L., Oliver, N. (eds.) UMAP 2011. LNCS, vol. 6787, pp. 335–340. Springer, Heidelberg (2011). https://doi.org/10.1007/978-3-642-22362-4_29
3. Biancalana, C., Gasparetti, F., Micarelli, A., Miola, A., Sansonetti, G.: Context-aware movie recommendation based on signal processing and machine learning. In: Proceedings of the 2nd Challenge on Context-Aware Movie Recommendation, CAMRa 2011, pp. 5–10. ACM, New York (2011)
4. Biancalana, C., Gasparetti, F., Micarelli, A., Sansonetti, G.: An approach to social recommendation for context-aware mobile services. ACM Trans. Intell. Syst. Technol. 4(1), 10:1–10:31 (2013)
5. Biancalana, C., Gasparetti, F., Micarelli, A., Sansonetti, G.: Social semantic query expansion. ACM Trans. Intell. Syst. Technol. 4(4), 60:1–60:43 (2013)
6. Bologna, C., De Rosa, A.C., De Vivo, A., Gaeta, M., Sansonetti, G., Viserta, V.: Personality-based recommendation in E-commerce. In: CEUR Workshop Proceedings, vol. 997. CEUR-WS.org, Aachen (2013)
7. Caldarelli, S., Feltoni Gurini, D., Micarelli, A., Sansonetti, G.: A signal-based approach to news recommendation. In: CEUR Workshop Proceedings, vol. 1618. CEUR-WS.org, Aachen (2016)
8. Christakopoulou, K., Radlinski, F., Hofmann, K.: Towards conversational recommender systems. In: Proceedings of the 22nd ACM SIGKDD, KDD 2016, pp. 815–824. ACM, New York (2016)
9. D'Agostino, D., Gasparetti, F., Micarelli, A., Sansonetti, G.: A social context-aware recommender of itineraries between relevant points of interest. In: Stephanidis, C. (ed.) HCI 2016. CCIS, vol. 618, pp. 354–359. Springer, Cham (2016). https://doi.org/10.1007/978-3-319-40542-1_58
10. D'Aniello, G., Gaeta, A., Gaeta, M., Loia, V., Reformat, M.Z.: Collective awareness in smart city with fuzzy cognitive maps and fuzzy sets. In: IEEE International Conference on Fuzzy Systems (FUZZ-IEEE), pp. 1554–1561, July 2016
11. D'Aniello, G., Gaeta, M., Reformat, M.Z.: Collective perception in smart tourism destinations with rough sets. In: 3rd IEEE International Conference on Cybernetics (CYBCONF), pp. 1–6, June 2017
12. Feltoni Gurini, D., Gasparetti, F., Micarelli, A., Sansonetti, G.: A sentiment-based approach to Twitter user recommendation. In: CEUR Workshop Proceedings, vol. 1066. CEUR-WS.org, Aachen (2013)

13. Gurini, D.F., Gasparetti, F., Micarelli, A., Sansonetti, G.: iSCUR: interest and sentiment-based community detection for user recommendation on Twitter. In: Dimitrova, V., Kuflik, T., Chin, D., Ricci, F., Dolog, P., Houben, G.-J. (eds.) UMAP 2014. LNCS, vol. 8538, pp. 314–319. Springer, Cham (2014). https://doi.org/10.1007/978-3-319-08786-3_27
14. Feltoni Gurini, D., Gasparetti, F., Micarelli, A., Sansonetti, G.: Analysis of sentiment communities in online networks. In: CEUR Workshop Proceedings, vol. 1421, pp. 17–20 (2015)
15. Feltoni Gurini, D., Gasparetti, F., Micarelli, A., Sansonetti, G.: Enhancing social recommendation with sentiment communities. In: Wang, J., et al. (eds.) WISE 2015. LNCS, vol. 9419, pp. 308–315. Springer, Cham (2015). https://doi.org/10.1007/978-3-319-26187-4_28
16. Feltoni Gurini, D., Gasparetti, F., Micarelli, A., Sansonetti, G.: Temporal people-to-people recommendation on social networks with sentiment-based matrix factorization. Future Gener. Comput. Syst. **78**, 430–439 (2018)
17. Fogli, A., Micarelli, A., Sansonetti, G.: Enhancing itinerary recommendation with linked open data. In: Stephanidis, C. (ed.) HCI 2018. CCIS, vol. 850, pp. 32–39. Springer, Cham (2018). https://doi.org/10.1007/978-3-319-92270-6_5
18. Fogli, A., Sansonetti, G.: Exploiting semantics for context-aware itinerary recommendation. Pers. Ubiquit. Comput. (2019)
19. Gasparetti, F., Micarelli, A., Sansonetti, G.: Exploiting web browsing activities for user needs identification. In: International Conference on Computational Science and Computational Intelligence, vol. 2, pp. 86–89, March 2014
20. Greco, C., Suglia, A., Basile, P., Semeraro, G.: Converse-Et-Impera: exploiting deep learning and hierarchical reinforcement learning for conversational recommender systems. In: Esposito, F., Basili, R., Ferilli, S., Lisi, F. (eds.) AI*IA 2017. LNCS, vol. 10640, pp. 372–386. Springer, Cham (2017). https://doi.org/10.1007/978-3-319-70169-1_28
21. Hassan, H.A.M., Sansonetti, G., Gasparetti, F., Micarelli, A.: Semantic-based tag recommendation in scientific bookmarking systems. In: Proceedings of the 12th ACM Conference on Recommender Systems, RecSys 2018, pp. 465–469. ACM, New York (2018)
22. Kucherbaev, P., Psyllidis, A., Bozzon, A.: Chatbots as conversational recommender systems in urban contexts. In: Proceedings of the International Workshop on Workshop on Recommender Systems for Citizens, CitRec 2017, pp. 6:1–6:2. ACM, New York (2017)
23. Micarelli, A., Neri, A., Sansonetti, G.: A case-based approach to image recognition. In: Blanzieri, E., Portinale, L. (eds.) EWCBR 2000. LNCS, vol. 1898, pp. 443–454. Springer, Heidelberg (2000). https://doi.org/10.1007/3-540-44527-7_38
24. Narducci, F., de Gemmis, M., Lops, P., Semeraro, G.: Recommender systems in the internet of talking things (IoTT). In: Proceedings of the Poster Track of the 11th ACM Conference on Recommender Systems (RecSys 2017), Como, 28 August 2017
25. Onori, M., Micarelli, A., Sansonetti, G.: A comparative analysis of personality-based music recommender systems. In: CEUR Workshop Proceedings, vol. 1680, pp. 55–59. CEUR-WS.org, Aachen (2016)
26. Ricci, F., Rokach, L., Shapira, B.: Recommender Systems Handbook, 2nd edn. Springer, New York (2015). https://doi.org/10.1007/978-0-387-85820-3
27. Salakhutdinov, R., Mnih, A.: Probabilistic matrix factorization. In: Proceedings of the 20th International Conference on Neural Information Processing Systems, NIPS 2007, pp. 1257–1264. Curran Associates Inc., USA (2007)

28. Sansonetti, G.: Point of interest recommendation based on social and linked open data. Pers. Ubiquit. Comput. (in press)
29. Sansonetti, G., Feltoni Gurini, D., Gasparetti, F., Micarelli, A.: Dynamic social recommendation. In: Proceedings of the 2017 IEEE/ACM International Conference on Advances in Social Networks Analysis and Mining, ASONAM 2017, pp. 943–947. ACM, New York (2017)
30. Sansonetti, G., Gasparetti, F., Micarelli, A., Cena, F., Gena, C.: Enhancing cultural recommendations through social and linked open data. User Model. User-Adap. Inter. **29**, 121 (2019)

Differences in Customers' Interactions with Expert/Novice Salesclerks in a Bespoke Tailoring Situation: A Case Study on the Utterances of Salesclerks

Masashi Sugimoto[(✉)] , Yoichi Yamazaki, Fang Zhang, Saki Miyai, Kodai Obata, Michiya Yamamoto , and Noriko Nagata

Kwansei Gakuin University, 2-1, Gakuen, Sanda, Hyogo 6691337, Japan
sugimoto.masashi@kwansei.ac.jp

Abstract. When we make decisions, we do not always decide by ourselves, but sometimes rely on recommendation systems. Previous recommendation systems focused on the accuracy of the recommendation. More recently, human-centered recommendation systems have garnered attention. The human-centered recommendation is especially important in a context wherein mass customization lets users personalize what they buy. However, how people tackle a vast amount of decision-making in the context of personalization has not yet been revealed. In this research, we focused on bespoke tailoring, which relies on salesclerks to help customers acquire what they want. We investigated the ways that customers interact with human recommenders (salesclerks). The results showed that expert salesclerks limited the number of options which customers have at a time, and that they reassured the customers about the suitability of their choices after they made their decisions. These results indicate that qualified recommenders in bespoke tailoring help customers by avoiding choice overload and evoking the customers' positive emotions. These findings are especially helpful for a recommendation system in a situation in which personalization can lead to the realization of customer needs and wants.

Keywords: Recommendation system · Feeling and image · Bespoke design

1 Introduction

Sometimes we make decisions by ourselves, and other times, we accept advice from others about what to do. Such advisors include both humans (professional salesclerks, experts in their fields, and friends) and nonhumans (recommender systems on the computer). With the help of these advisors, we can make better choices, even in a field, where lack sufficient knowledge or experience.

This kind of advice is becoming more and more important in the industry 4.0 society, where mass customization furnishes us with various choices. In such a society, we are exposed to a multitude of options and must repeatedly make decisions. Individuals in demanding decision-making situations can be supported by technical assistance [1], one feature of industry 4.0. This technical assistance is expected to

© Springer Nature Switzerland AG 2019
C. Stephanidis (Ed.): HCII 2019, CCIS 1034, pp. 131–137, 2019.
https://doi.org/10.1007/978-3-030-23525-3_17

facilitate decision-making and lead users to better outcomes, via the interaction between humans and computers.

In decision-making activities, such as shopping, people evaluate a given item, not only in terms of its functional properties, but based on the kind of feeling and image (*kansei* in Japanese) the item evokes it [2]. The importance of *kansei* factors is heightened in an industry 4.0 society, thanks to mass customization, which enables people to select what they want through multiple stages of decision making. Although *kansei* is an important factor in human decision making, no computer-based recommender systems that consider *kansei* factors have yet been implemented. To realize one's *kansei*, it is essential to consider various options and modes of personalization.

Therefore, this study focuses on actual recommendation scenes between humans and investigates their mode of realizing the products' personalization. In particular, we pay attention to the recommenders' respective levels of ability. The results of this study demonstrate the optimum method of generating a computer system that recommends choices, from a *kansei* viewpoint. To grasp the whole scene's characteristics, we used a case study approach.

2 Related Works

2.1 Recommender Systems

Recommender systems are an example of computerized decision-making support. Recommender systems are "software tools and techniques providing suggestions for items to be of use to a user" [3]. It selects an appropriate choice among various items and decreases the user's cost of choosing.

Many studies have focused on recommender systems. Although the best recommender systems naturally provide accurate recommendations, some studies have indicated that even an accurate recommendation is not sufficient [4]. Other studies indicate the importance of human factors in rendering the recommendation: one study attaches importance to user centric directions [5]; another values a deeper understanding of users' information-seeking tasks [6]; and still another emphasizes the importance of the coverage and serendipity of recommender system output [4]. They have emphasized factors related to the human factors, and this suggests the importance of considering recommender systems from the human perspective.

Recommendations are not always provided by computers. Recommendations from humans, such as salesclerks, experts in the field, or doctors are very typical. Human recommendations decrease decision maker's cost of choosing, in much the same way that recommendation systems do.

One area in which human recommendations function usefully is bespoke design, especially bespoke tailoring. In bespoke tailoring, unlike ready-to-wear, garments are designed through the interaction between the customers and salesclerks. Thanks to that, not only can customers acquire garments in their exact size, but their every preference can also be reflected in the garment. This feature of bespoke tailoring compels customers to make a lot of choices as they buy their garment. Considering this feature, bespoke tailoring can be defined as a communication-based and decision-making process that operates as well as the computer-based recommendation systems described above.

2.2   Consumer Decision Making

Decision making is a psychological process of choosing one option from two or more alternatives. In most decision making, it is not possible to examine all possible alternatives (maximization) because cognitive resources are limited. Instead, most decision makers stop searching when they arrive at the choice that satisfies them (satisfaction) [7]. Another perspective divides the decision-making process into multiple stages (multistage decision strategy) [8]. In the multiple decision strategies, the first step involves reducing the number of the alternatives by a non-compensatory strategy, to minimize the cognitive cost. This allows for a more fine-grained analysis of the relevant information.

Psychology and economics research has investigated consumer decision making, from among the decision-making processes. Consumer decision making is affected by various factors, which include not only the function of the products, but also more affective factors, such as emotion [9] and brand similarity [10]. The effect of these affective factors was not investigated in the context of recommendation systems.

3   Customers' Interactions with Expert/Novice Salesclerks in a Bespoke Tailoring Situation

3.1   Method

Participants. Three male salesclerks and 4 male customers participated in the survey. They were recruited at a sales fair of a suit manufacture company. One salesclerk was an expert, with over 10 years of experience in bespoke tailoring. The other two were novices, who had been engaged in bespoke tailoring for fewer than five years.

Procedure. In the survey, a customer ordered a bespoke tailored suit while consulting with a salesclerk (Fig. 1). First, the customer selected the suit materials and then determined the design of the details of the suit (overall figure, number of front buttons, cloth backing, etc.) After that, the customers were measured by the salesclerk. The whole bespoke tailoring process took approximately 30 to 60 min. All aspects of customer-salesclerk interactions, including their utterances, were recorded.

3.2   Results

Object Phase of Analysis. As described in the procedure, bespoke tailoring can be divided into three phrases: suit material selection, detail design, and measurement. We focused on the suit material selection process, wherein customers face a vast number of choices.

Fig. 1. An example of actual bespoke tailoring. A salesclerk and a customer (or customers) design the suit through interaction.

Interactions with Expert Salesclerks

Case #1. (salesclerk A) The customer is a 34-year-old male.

At the beginning of the bespoke tailoring process, salesclerk A asked some questions to get a grasp of the customer's desires. He asked the customer very concrete questions, such as when he would be wearing the suit (at the office), and which color he preferred (gray, close to black). After that, salesclerk A selected some suit materials that met the customer's specifications. After the customer selected the suit material, salesclerk A provided verbal support for the decision ("I like it, I think this is good").

Case #2. (salesclerk A) The customer in is a 67-year-old male.

As in case #1, salesclerk A first determined the customer's desires through conversation. Before selecting a suit material, the customer explained his needs and wants (comfortable design, as he needed to wear a waist corset, a bright navy suit material that he had never had, and formal design) in response to the salesclerk's questions. After the customer selected the suit material, salesclerk A provided verbal support for the decision ("It's fine because the suit is double-breasted").

Interaction with Novice Salesclerks

Case #3. (salesclerk B) The customer in is a 48-year-old male.

As in the case of the expert salesclerk, salesclerk B grasped the customer's wants at the beginning of the bespoke tailoring interaction, but to a more limited extent (navy close to black). In the process of suit material selection, salesclerk B leaves all choice to the customer, failing to limit the number of alternatives. During suit material selection, the customer, and not salesclerk B, took the initiative in making the selection and salesclerk B responded to the customer's choice afterwards. Rather, salesclerk B encouraged the customer to keep comparing materials repeatedly. After the customer had made a decision regarding suit material, salesclerk C demonstrated no clear support for the selection, simply saying, "I see."

Case #4. (salesclerk C) The customer in is a 19-year-old male.

As in the other cases, salesclerk C inquired about the customer's wants (darker color and plaid), but in an abstract way ("What kind of suit materials do you like?"). During suit material selection, salesclerk C indulged in long (over 30 s) periods of silence 14 times, during which the customer continued searching for the right suit material with his family members. Like salesclerk B, salesclerk C offered no clear support for customer's selected suit material, and just said, "You like this? O.K."

4 Conclusion

4.1 Summary of the Results

There were clear differences between the customer interactions with expert salesclerks and novice salesclerks. The expert salesclerk limited the number of the choices of suit materials faced by customers. In addition, he justified the customer's decision by voicing his approval of the customer's choice he made it. By contrast, the novice salesclerks let the customers confront a vast number of choices. They also failed to validate the customer's choice.

Limiting the number of choices is a good way of decreasing the choice overload. Previous research shows that too many options causes choice overload and decreases the selector's satisfaction with the option that he ultimately selects [11]. This overload has also been studied in the context of knowledge communication between experts and decision makers (information overload) [12]. At the sales fair, more than 100 suit materials were available in the suit material selection. In addition, customers must select the various components of the suit: the number of buttons; the color of the cloth backing; the shape of the lapel and the vent; and so forth. Although these various options represent a heavy cognitive cost to customers, the expert salesclerk managed weight of the load by presenting only some of the available options to the customer. This is exactly the process upon which multistage decision strategy [8] is premised. The salesclerk first helps the customers limit their number of options and then moves onto detailed processing.

It is possible for choice justification to yield a positive effect for customers. Buying behavior is not a task that can be calculated by an algorithm that guides customers to reach the "best" outcome, but by a heuristic, with which they can arrive at a "sufficiently good" outcome. These characteristics of buying behavior make it difficult for customers to reassure themselves of the viability of what they have bought. This difficulty is more pervasive in the current society, where customers are able to choose whichever options they desire, thereby satisfying their feelings and image of what they prefer [2]. Thanks to the reassurance provided by the expert, it was possible to evoke customers' positive emotions, which are known to facilitate a purchase [9].

The characteristics of the experienced salesclerk, relative to those of the novice salesclerks, are analogous to the human information processing in decision making (Fig. 1). This analogy is possible, rendering the recommendation of the expert salesclerk more useful, reliable, and agreeable, and perhaps the one element needed to make computer-based recommendation systems a success (Table 1).

Table 1. The characteristics of the human decision-making process and recommendation of expert/novice salesclerk

Types of processing or recommendation system	Initial decision-making	After decision-making
Human decision making in purchase	Reducing information-processing and making more fine-grained analysis [8]	Seek information supporting choices in the item they purchased [13]
Expert salesclerk	Limiting the number of choices that customers have at one time	Choice justification
Novice salesclerk	Exposing customers to vast information	No support

4.2   The Novelty of the Present Research

In the previous research on recommendation systems, the accuracy of the recommendation has been attracting attention. However, in industry 4.0 society, wherein customers can purchase commodities that have been tailored to their preferences, customers must make a lot of choices, even when they can rely on recommendation systems. In this research, we revealed how the expert salesclerk reduces the costumer's cognitive cost and avoids choice overload. This mode of interaction can be applied to the design of computer-based recommendation systems.

4.3   Future Directions

In future research, we must address two problems: quantitative analysis and the need for an investigation of factors related to the customers.

In quantitative research, factors such as the rate of purchase and levels of customers' satisfaction should be explored. Implementing these analyses will facilitate more detailed and objective discussions.

The present analysis focused solely on the recommenders' side and investigated the interaction in terms of the experience of purchasing from salesclerks. Previous research has indicated that, in addition to the quality of the products, the character of the customer affects customer decision making [14] and domain-specific emotion there [15]. Introducing factors related to the customers would allow for a more revealing account of the interactions between them and salesclerks.

Considering these factors will be a help to realize a better recommender system in industry 4.0.

Acknowledgements. This research was supported by JST COI Program, "Center of Kansei-oriented Digital Fabrication".

References

1. Hermann, M., Pentek, T., Otto, B.: Design principles for Industrie 4.0 scenarios. In: 49th Hawaii International Conference on System Sciences (HICSS), Koloa, pp. 3928–3937. IEEE Computer Society (2016)
2. Nagamachi, M.: Kansei engineering as a powerful consumer-oriented technology for product development. Appl. Ergon. **33**(3), 289–294 (2002)
3. Ricci, F., Rokach, L., Shapira, B.: Recommender Systems Handbook. Springer, Heidelberg (2010). https://doi.org/10.1007/978-0-387-85820-3
4. Ge, M., Delgado-Battenfeld, C., Jannach, D.: Beyond accuracy: evaluating recommender systems by coverage and serendipity. In: Proceedings of the Fourth ACM Conference on Recommender Systems, pp. 257–260. ACM, Barcelona (2010)
5. McNee, S.M., Riedl, J., Konstan, J.A.: Being accurate is not enough: how accuracy metrics have hurt recommender systems. In: CHI 2006 Extended Abstracts on Human Factors in Computing Systems, Montreal, pp. 1097–1101. ACM (2006)
6. McNee, S.M., Riedl, J., Konstan, J.A.: Making recommendations better: an analytic model for human-recommender interaction. In: CHI 2006 Extended Abstracts on Human Factors in Computing Systems, Montreal, pp. 1103–1108. ACM (2006),
7. Simon, H.A.: Administrative Behavior: A Study of Decision-Making Processes in Administrative Organisations. The Macmillan Company, New York (1948)
8. Takemura, K.: Protocol analysis of multistage decision strategies. Percept. Mot. Skills **77**(2), 459–469 (1993)
9. Sherman, E., Mathur, A., Smith, R.B.: Store environment and consumer purchase behavior: mediating role of consumer emotions. Psychol. Mark. **14**(4), 361–378 (1997)
10. Grewal, R., Cline, T.W., Davies, A.: Early-entrant advantage, word-of-mouth communication, brand similarity, and the consumer decision-making process. J. Consum. Psychol. **13**(3), 187–197 (2001)
11. Iyengar, S.S., Lepper, M.R.: When choice is demotivating: can one desire too much of a good thing? J. Pers. Soc. Psychol. **79**(6), 995–1006 (2000)
12. Eppler, M.J.: Knowledge communication problems between experts and decision makers: an overview and classification. Electron. J. Knowl. Manag. **5**(3), 291–300 (2007)
13. Ehrlich, D., Guttman, I., Schönbach, P., Mills, J.: Postdecision exposure to relevant information. J. Abnorm. Soc. Psychol. **54**(1), 98–102 (1957)
14. Obata, K., Sugimoto, M., Nagata, N.: Optimization of motorcycle riders categorization based on emotion using decision tree analysis. In: Proceedings of the 11th IEEE Pacific Visualization Symposium (PacificVis 2018), Kobe, p. 136. IEEE (2018)
15. Sugimoto, M., Yamamoto, M., Nagata, N.: The emotions evoked during individual voluntary manufacture: their characteristics and the timing of their evocation. Trans. Hum. Interface Soc. **21**(1), 85–96 (2019). In Japanese with English abstract

Empirical Research on New Retail Servicescape Based on Experience Perspective

Ruiguang Tan[1](✉) and Jiayi Liu[2]

[1] School of Art Design and Media,
East China University of Science and Technology, M. BOX 286 No. 130,
Meilong Road, Xuhui District, Shanghai 200237, China
1981995@qq.com
[2] College of Fashion and Design, Donghua University,
No. 1882, West Yanan Road, Shanghai 200051, China
elynliu@foxmail.com

Abstract. Verify the impact of each dimension of the new retail servicescape on customer experience, and then propose the optimization strategy of the new retail. Firstly, the existing research results of business servicescapes are extracted. Secondly, the characteristics of new retail servicescapes are integrated. Then, based on physical variables, perceptional variables and social variables, data are obtained through questionnaire survey. The three dimensions all have different degrees of influence on the new retail servicescape, among which physical variables are the most important, followed by perceptional variables and social variables. Based on the research results, it is found that the application of new technology has changed those elements of the servicescape such as the layout, the combination of different business etc. The expansion of virtual servicescapes also changes the role of physical servicescapes in the retail ecology, making the physical retail servicescape more inclined to serve the daily life of the community. In addition to being a fast logistics stronghold, the physical servicescape is also a place to enrich user experience and enhance user stickiness.

Keywords: Servicescape · New retail · Dimension · Customer experience

1 Introduction

In the field of commercial services, the factors affecting user experience are mainly divided into commodity, environment and services. At present, the focus of user research has turned from commodity to servicescape integrated environment, service and other contents. All kinds of servicescapes design based on these three elements become more and more common, such as shopping center, theme hotel, theme park, theme exhibition hall, bookstore, even library, hospital and so on. As a service institution, the social utility of new retail is also affected by the corresponding servicescape. Based on the relevant research of servicescapes and the particularity of new retail, this paper takes commercial supermarkets as example to study the influence of various factors in the new retail servicescape on users, so as to provide enlightenment for subsequent research and management practice.

C. Stephanidis (Ed.): HCII 2019, CCIS 1034, pp. 138–145, 2019.
https://doi.org/10.1007/978-3-030-23525-3_18

2 Relevant Literature Review

2.1 Servicescape

Bitner [1] used "servicescape" to refer to various carefully designed and controlled environment elements such as the external environment and internal environment of the service place (including layout and design, logo and decoration, material, color, graphics, temperature, smell, music, etc.). Baker et al. (1994) incorporated interpersonal and social cues into the scope of servicescape. Tombs and McColl-kenedy (2003 and 2004) proposed the social-servicescape model, and they incorporated the customer's emotional response and cognition into the scope of servicescape. Rosenbaum et al. (2005) incorporated "social symbolic elements" (such as symbols and items that can stimulate customers' sense of belonging and identity) that could convey specific social meanings into the scope of servicescape. Rosenbaum (2009) incorporated the attention restoration theory to reveal the important role of natural elements in servicescape in the field of public health, and incorporated natural elements into the category of servicescapes. Harris et al. (2010) proposed that network servicescape was all environperceptional factors in network service delivery, including interface aesthetics, functional layout, financial security and other dimensions. In this paper, in order to correspond to the traditional physical servicescape, the network servicescape is called "virtual servicescape".

2.2 "New retail" Servicescape

At present, there are few studies on "new retail servicescape", and the existing studies mainly focus on "the influence of new retail model on servicescapes" and "the influence of new retail model on user experience and user behavior". Compared with the traditional retail model, the main feature of "new retail" is omni-channel selling based on Internet technology through the integration of online, offline and logistics to develop potential flow, making the production, circulation and service process more efficient. Yan [2] believes that "new retail" enterprises focus on the transformation and upgrading of online and offline, in-store and out-of-store, services and channels, which makes the online integrative intelligent network and the offline precise experience can achieve bidirectional integration. At the same time, as online shopping has greatly met the customers' demands of expanding commodity categories and decreasing time costs, offline shopping is mainly used to meet other different demands, such as differentiation of categories, entertainment, culture, new experience, social activity, self-esteem, etc. Chang et al. [3] believe that new retail is no longer just an exchange channel, but more "entertainment" and "social". All of these require enterprises to better understand consumers and provide them with "better experience". The concept of retail industry has changed from "price retail" to "experiential retail".

2.3 Servicescape Dimension

The division of servicescape dimensions can be seen in the study of M.J. Bitner at the earliest. She divides various elements into three dimensions, namely atmosphere, layout, signs and decorations. Baker et al. [4] proposed that people and social factors should also be paid attention to, and they divided research dimensions into three aspects, namely ambient cues, design cues and social cues. Rosenbaum and Massiah (2011) further expanded the servicescape model on the basis of Bitner (1992) and proposed four main dimensions of servicescape: physical dimension, social dimension, socially-symbolic dimension and natural dimension [5]. In the era of mobile Internet and Internet of everything, the role of physical servicescape in the retail has changed a lot. In the past, the dimensionality division of servicescapes focused on visible factors, but in the era when the technical force reconstructs the business, more and more invisible and hidden factors are influencing the user experience. In the variable design of this paper, the dimensions designed by Rosenbaum and others were deleted or modified, and the "socially-symbolic dimension" was integrated into the "perceptional dimension". As shown in Table 1.

Table 1. Dimensions and subitems of servicescape

Dimensions	Subitems	
	Symbol	Name
Physical variables (P)	Ph1	Spatial accessibility
	Ph2	Spatial arrangement
	Ph3	Sufficient lightning
	Ph4	Leisure facilities
	Ph5	Self-service facilities
	Ph6	Recreation facilities
	Ph8	Information facilities
	Ph9	Intelligent cashier
	Ph10	Diversity of commercial activities
	Ph11	Online shopping
Perceptional variables (M)	Pe1	Outdoor environment
	Pe2	Interior environment
	Pe3	User interface design
	Pe4	Lightning atmosphere
	Pe5	Decorations
	Pe6	Clothes of service staff
	Pe7	Cleanliness level
	Pe8	Smell
	Pe9	Noise
	Pe10	Music
	Pe11	Temperature
Social variables (S)	S1	Manner of service staff
	S2	Share and comments of other customers
	S3	Cultural communication and exchange
	S4	Timeliness of getting help from service staff
	S5	Social density

3 Empirical Research

3.1 Overall Design

This research mainly uses the questionnaire survey method, puts forward various factors affecting the new retail service through the generalization and summarization of the research results related to the servicescape combined with the new retail, and analyzes the importance degree of various segmentation variables in the new retail servicescape factors from the perspective of perception. In the process of questionnaire setting, Likert scale was used to measure the importance degree of customers' perception. 5 indicates that feelings are very important, 1 indicates that feelings are completely worthless, and the perception importance degree of each level decreases step by step. In order to ensure the diversity and dispersion of samples, this research takes the new retail users in Shanghai area as samples. The similar characteristics of these new retail stores are (1) technology-driven efficiency improvement (2) online-offline integrated selling (3) service-oriented selling and format integration. The questionnaire was conducted in November 2018. Main user sample groups were distributed in two supermarkets, Fresh Hema and Yong Hui Super Species. Each store issued 120 copies of the questionnaire, a total of 480 copies. 476 questionnaires were collected through random distribution and on-site recycling in the above supermarkets, and 75 invalid questionnaires were removed. The total number of valid questionnaires was 401 (the actual effective rate was 84.2%).

3.2 Questionnaire Analysis

Reliability Analysis: In order to ensure the reliability of the questionnaire, Cronbach (α coefficient) was used to test the reliability of the questionnaire when analyzing the result, and SPSS was used for analysis. The result showed that the α coefficient of whole questionnaire was 0.875, higher than 0.7, indicating that the questionnaire design was reasonable and effective. The results of questionnaire reliability analysis are shown in Table 2.

Table 2. Reliability analysis

Dimension	Sub-item	α coefficient
Physical variables	11	0.787
Perception variables	11	0.743
Social variables	5	0.756
All sub-items	27	0.852

Mean Value and Standard Deviation Analysis: In general, the mean value can be used to simply judge the user's attention to a certain sub-item. Users' recognition of the influence of the corresponding sub-item on the service effect in the new retail servicescape can be shown in this questionnaire. Usually, a high mean value reflects the users' high degree of recognition in the influence of the corresponding item, while a low mean value reflects the users' low degree of recognition in the influence of the corresponding item. The analysis results (see Table 3) show that the mean value of most sub-items in the questionnaire is above 3, which proves that users recognize the influence of most sub-items in the effect of new retail services, and the standard deviation of all sub-items is close to 1, indicating that users' opinions are relatively unified, so the survey results can reflect the actual cognition of users.

Table 3. Mean value and Standard deviation analysis

Dimension	Symbol	Section	Mean value	Standard deviation
Physical variables	Ph1	1–5	3.654	0.827
	Ph 2	1–5	2.810	0.847
	Ph 3	1–5	3.612	0.893
	Ph 4	1–5	3.845	0.857
	Ph 5	1–5	3.756	0.801
	Ph 6	1–5	3.012	1.082
	Ph 8	1–5	3.403	0.823
	Ph 9	1–5	3.412	1.032
	Ph 10	1–5	3.503	0.823
	Ph 11	1–5	3.024	1.016
Perception variables	Pe1	1–5	3.695	1.031
	Pe 2	1–5	3.812	0.893
	Pe 3	1–5	3.723	0.803
	Pe 4	1–5	3.374	0.912
	Pe 5	1–5	3.086	1.052
	Pe 6	1–5	3.552	0.824
	Pe 7	1–5	3.921	0.836
	Pe 8	1–5	3.665	0.801
	Pe 9	1–5	2.858	0.814
	Pe 10	1–5	2.775	0.945
	Pe 11	1–5	3.124	0.816
Social variables	S1	1–5	3.910	0.883
	S2	1–5	2.572	0.912
	S3	1–5	3.786	1.052
	S4	1–5	3.903	0.803
	S5	1–5	3.625	0.912

Validity Test: The validity test can analyze the overall structure of the questionnaire, so as to know whether the questionnaire can truly measure the corresponding results. In general, the KMO appropriate test value test value of SPSS can be used as the main measurement index. Through analysis, the KMO value of this questionnaire is 0.815, indicating that the questionnaire has good validity, and the $KMO > 0.7$, which is suitable for factor analysis. In addition, Bartlett's Test of Sphericity should be used before factor analysis to verify the feasibility of factor analysis of the questionnaire. According to the requirement of factor analysis, the sample size is 5 times of the number of sub-items (27), the minimum sample size of this survey is 135, the effective sample size is 401. The sample size conform to the requirements of the factor analysis. In addition, the chi-square significance probability is less than 1%, indicating that there is a strong correlation between the data, which is suitable for factor analysis. The specific results are shown in Table 4:

Table 4. New retail store servicescape KMO value and Bartlett's Test

Sampling enough KMO measure		0.815
Bartlett's Test of Sphericity	Approximate chi-square	9645.426
	df	386
	Sig.	0.000

In factor analysis, the cumulative variance contribution rate is 62.814% after separating out the common factors with the first 5 characteristic roots larger than 1. At the same time, the results of rotating component matrix obtained by the method of Varimax also confirmed that the Physical variables, perceptional variables and Social variables divided by the questionnaire were reasonable.

4   Results Analysis and Countermeasures

New retail is a change in the retail ecology. It provides users with better quality experience through more efficient restructuring of product service, procurement, inventory, distribution, market, user relationships, partner network, organizational structure and other aspects. In terms of servicescapes that are closely related to users, it involves physical servicescapes and virtual servicescapes, and new retail is a service that integrates both. To some extent, the positioning of physical servicescapes in the whole new retail ecology is different from that of traditional retail. The big data of virtual servicescapes has an impact on the selection and placement of offline products, while physical servicescapes focus more on experience – namely behaviors that require people's participation, such as social contact, catering, entertainment and learning.

4.1   The Influence of Physical Variables on the Effect of New Retail Services

Physical variable is the core of the new retail reform. When researching the two new retail supermarkets, users have high recognition for leisure facilities, self-service facilities, intelligent cashier, and diversified business forms, which have big differences with the traditional commercial supermarket. Leisure facilities, self-service facilities and diversified business forms increase the attraction to users and meanwhile improve the time of users staying in the supermarket, while smart cashier deepens users' participation in the retail process, improves the speed and saves time. Users' attitudes towards amusement facilities and online shopping (including fast logistics distribution) are differentiated, which is largely related to the composition of users. Parents with children and their elders prefer amusement facilities, while young people are more used to online shopping. There is a certain relationship between intelligent cashier and the diversity of business forms. If users can use their mobile phones to scan the QR code and pay at any time in the supermarket or even pay without feeling, they can enjoy the products immediately, which will greatly improve their freedom of action. Computer vision and machine learning techniques are used to create stores where users can pick up whatever they want and go. The integration of online and offline shopping enables people to experience products on the spot without the constraint of carrying products.

It is found in the survey that users hope to increase the cultural functions of such places and improve the quality of life experience, so that such servicescapes can become places to kill time outside the family rather than just to buy things, and their simple purchase behavior can be realized through online servicescapes. It's suggested that On the one hand, stores can provide cultural support through the diversity of the commercial forms, such as exhibition specially for the life scene: put cooking culture books and form a complete set of equipment in the food area, or put some culture related books and collocation of tea sets, wine glass, etc. in the beverage area. At Coop, a Milan supermarket of the future, each food has its own story. Supermarkets have installed screens above their shelves that will display detailed information about food as the user touches an item, or even as his or her hand gets closer and closer. On the other hand, more macro themes can be considered to plan the servicescapes, such as integrating the concepts of life culture museum and cooking museum into the design of commercial places, so as to add cultural atmosphere to the servicescape and make the commercial space become a place with strong stickiness.

4.2   The Influence of Perceptional Variables on the Effect of New Retail Services

The perceptional variable mainly examines the perceptual experience of servicescapes to users, who have high recognition for environperceptional art design and user interface design. Environperceptional art, user interface, products and services constitute a community of quality. In fact, people's perception of environperceptional art design implies space art, commodity display, lighting atmosphere and other elements. It seems that the new retail servicescape is functionally different from the traditional retail, but in fact, people's feelings in the space are influenced by technology imperceptibly. For example, the intelligent cashier system saves the space of a large row of cashier desk, people can move in and out of space more easily; the products pushed according to the network big data are more refined, making the shelves in the new retail commercial supermarket more humanized and the space more intimate. These Spaces are more suitable for staying and living with other business forms such as catering and entertainment, rather than just buying commodities.

According to the results of perceptional variables, users have higher requirements on the environperceptional art design, user interface design and environperceptional cleanliness of business servicescapes. The quality of the servicescapes can be improved by means of setting the theme of environperceptional art, creating lighting with set atmosphere, matching decorations and clothing of service personnel according to the theme of art, so as to awake the sense of identity and pleasure of users, expand the scope of the servicescape involved by users, extend the staying time of users, increase the consumption quantity and other commercial purposes. Emotional design requires that the physical objects of the servicescape produce "meaning", not just objects. However, the visual objects that can point to the meaning are often those cultural symbols that are well known to people. Therefore, the emotional design of the servicescape aiming at the theme will enhance the affinity and attraction of the site.

4.3   The Influence of Social Variables on the Effect of New Retail Services

Social variables are one of the important variables in the study of servicescapes. In many servicescapes, social variables can have a direct impact on the service effect. Social variables are reflected in both offline and online servicescapes. Results show that service personnel friendliness is a very important impact factor, which is consistent with everyday cognitive. At the same time, the timeliness of getting help from service personnel in the servicescape, cultural communication and exchange, and social density are also important factors. Among them, cultural communication and exchange refers to the cultural communication and exchange activities related to the content of the servicescape held in the site, such as the knowledge lecture, propaganda and exchange combined with certain products or lifestyles. Such activities can increase the cultural attraction of the servicescapes.

Commercial space needs to create a socialized servicescape and use social factors to improve users' experience. Main methods come from creating social scene and inspiring users to carry out cultural exchanges. This involves the spatial layout, network social scene, interactive facilities, cultural event design and other aspects of the servicescape. Social scenes and cultural exchanges are conducive to users participation and stimulate network communication.

References

1. Bitner, M.J.: Servicescapes: the impact of physical surroundings on customers and employees. J. Mark. **56**, 57–71 (1992)
2. Yan, X.: Logical Implications and Development Trends of "New Retail", Social Science Front (2018)
3. Chang, M., Su, J.: What is the "New" in New Retail? People's Forum (2018)
4. Baker, S.M., Holland, J., Kaufman-Scarborough, C.: How consumers with disabilities perceive "welcome" in retail servicescapes: a critical incident study. J. Serv. Mark. **21**(3), 160–173 (2007)
5. Rosenbaum, M.S., Massiah, C.: An expanded servicecape perspective. J. Serv. Manag. **22**(4), 471–490 (2011)

A Comparative Study of Servicescape in the Mobile Internet Era – Taking Carrefour and Hema Fresh Store as Examples

Ruiguang Tan[1($\boxtimes$)] and Jiayi Liu[2]

[1] School of Art Design and Media,
East China University of Science and Technology, M. BOX 286, No. 130,
Meilong Road, Xuhui District, Shanghai 200237, China
1981995@qq.com
[2] College of Fashion and Design, Donghua University,
No. 1882, West Yanan Road, Shanghai 200051, China
elynliu@foxmail.com

Abstract. The servicescape strategy in the mobile Internet environment has created new opportunities for enterprise operation. Through comparative studies of two enterprises—Carrefour and Hema Fresh Store, the paper explored the impacts of scene technologies and servicescape construction to customer experience under the mobile internet environment. The study is developed through the aspects of servicescape dimension, customer sensory perception and behavior intention. The results showed that the connotation of physical dimension, perceptional dimension, social dimension of servicescape have been extended under the applied of context technologies. With the help more sensory perceptions of customers, and then impact customers' psychological and behavioral intentions, thus enable enterprises to achieve better market performance.

Keywords: Mobile Internet environment · Context technology · Servicescape · Sensory perception · Customer experience

1 Introduction

Profound changes have taken place in social life forms and business operation modes with the rapid development of mobile Internet and intelligent terminal technologies. Service scenarization have become the source of differential competitive advantages of enterprises. The connotation of the servicescape is expanded under the mobile Internet environment. User-centered servicescape can be constructed with cloud computing, big data and other technologies, which can change users' thinking mode and behavior habits. This paper starts with the definition of the servicescape concept, then analyzes the evolution of the connotation of the servicescape in the mobile Internet environment and the customers experience to the servicescape. On this basis, the specific strategies of servicescape are suggested for enterprises to enhance customer experience.

C. Stephanidis (Ed.): HCII 2019, CCIS 1034, pp. 146–152, 2019.
https://doi.org/10.1007/978-3-030-23525-3_19

2 Literature Survey

2.1 Servicescape Concepts and Dimension

Bitner initially defined the servicescape as the physical and social environment of the service venue [1]. With the development of the Internet, the concept of servicescape is extended to the network, and the servicescape is divided into "physical servicescape" and "virtual servicescape". In the era of mobile Internet, the integration of "physical servicescape" and "virtual servicescape" is realized, promoting the innovation of servicescape. Technologies such as mobile devices, social media, big data, sensors and positioning systems are applied to servicescape, enabling consumers to experience unprecedented personalized and intelligent services.

Rosenbaum and Massiah proposed four main dimensions of servicescape, namely physical dimension, social dimension, socially-symbolic dimension and natural dimension [2]. The physical dimension refers to the visual and measurable elements of sensory stimuli; the social dimension refers to the influence of service personnel, customers and their emotions in the servicescape; the socially-symbolic dimension refers to the signs, symbols and handicrafts that have special symbolic meaning for some groups in the servicescape; natural dimension reveals the natural stimulation factors in servicescape that can help customers to restore health and relieve fatigue.

2.2 The Impact of Servicescape on the User Experience

Hooper found that servicescapes had an impact on users' perception of service quality and behavioral intention [3]. Existing research on user experience focuses on how to use consumers' five senses to empower products and brands, including smell, music, design, taste and material, etc., which can enhance consumers' comprehensive ability to identify and experience different corporate characteristics and servicescapes. Scholars have studied the influence of such factors as the space design, background music, lighting, smell and product texture on user experience, and it is found that servicescape elements will significantly affect users' sensory experience and consumption decision-making behavior.

Based on the above literature review, the dimensions of servicescape in the mobile Internet environment and its influence on user experience can provide inspiration for enterprises to apply servicescape strategy, and the "user experience theory" can also provide clues to explain users' sensory perception patterns. However, what changes have taken place in the dimensional connotation of servicescapes in the mobile Internet environment? How does the customer experience change in the face of servicescape information from online and offline channels? Do technological elements such as social media, location-based systems and mobile devices help enhance the user experience? There is lack of empirical evidence to support and theoretical explanation.

3 Analytical Framework

3.1 Theoretical Framework

According to the literature analysis, it can be found that servicescapes in the mobile Internet environment need to consider the supporting factors, servicescapes dimensions and the content of user experience. Based on the clues of users' perception to analyze the servicescape construction, more accurate explanation of users' experience in the mobile Internet environment can be made. With the emergence of cross-boundary connectivity in a variety of industry servicescapes, it is necessary to re-establish the model to analyze users' experience and behavioral tendency in this context. This paper, based on literature research, early focus interviews and case studies, and on the "stimulus-organism – response" paradigm (S-O-R), proposes improvements to Rosenbaum and Massiah's (2011) servicescape model and Krishna's (2012) sensory marketing theory [4].

3.2 Research Propositions

In the mobile Internet environment, with the help of mobile devices, social media, big data, sensors and positioning system technologies, the boundaries of servicescapes have been greatly expanded, and the integration of virtual servicescapes and physical servicescapes has taken place. The positioning of servicescapes has changed in the entire business ecosystem. Traditional theories believe that user experience mainly comes from the feelings, emotions and cognition triggered by the information stimulation of the servicescape, and these information channels include vision, hearing, smell, taste and touch. But the reality is that the user experience is much broader. How to expand the connotation of servicescape dimension by scene technologies? How have scene technologies changed the user experience? This paper explores the above questions through a comparative study of two cases. Selected cases include Fresh Hema and Carrefour. One is a commercial supermarket developed by Internet enterprises focusing on the development of virtual servicescapes, and the other is a traditional commercial supermarket that introduces virtual servicescape to improve operation.

4 Case Comparative Study

4.1 Selection and the Basis of Research Method

This paper focuses on the changes of servicescape under the current mobile Internet environment, and it needs to explain and summarize the servicescape construction mode and its effect on user experience. Compared with the experimental method that requires direct and accurate control of the event process, this paper considers that the user's experience of the servicescape, whether virtual or physical, is a relatively complex process that takes place in the context of real life and is difficult to control the relevant factors. Therefore, this paper adopts the case study method. Compared with single-case study design, multi-case study takes up more research resources and time, but the conclusion derived from multiple cases is often considered more convincing, so the whole study is often considered to be more able to withstand scrutiny. Therefore, this paper hopes to verify the basic logic of the analysis framework through multiple case studies, and summarize the basic rules of how servicescapes trigger user experience and response.

4.2   Case Selection and Background Research

In order to select the appropriate cases for study, consider the following criteria: First, the case enterprise uses new technologies to deepen servicescape construction, including virtual servicescape and physical servicescape; Second, the case enterprise material can be collected in the published materials; Third, the servicescape of the case enterprise is familiar to most consumers, which facilitates the description of their sensory perception; Fourth, there are some common points between different cases in terms of products, service categories and consumer demands. Finally, two cases were selected, namely Fresh Hema and Carrefour. Fresh Hema is a new data and technology driven retail platform owned by Alibaba group. Carrefour, a pioneer of hypermarkets and the largest retailer in Europe, has been using technology to improve its service in recent years.

Case data collection methods in this paper include: (1) data analysis of relevant case database literature; (2) open and structured in-depth interviews; (3) direct observation and participatory observation. The in-depth interview subjects are 158 interviewees who are familiar with the case study and have consumption experience, aged between 18 and 65, among which 44% are male and 56% are female. Undergraduates and postgraduates account for 22%, educators and researchers for 8%, white-collar workers for 28% and people in other fields for 42%. Direct observation and participatory observation were carried out in Carrefour and Fresh Hema in Shanghai to investigate their servicescapes and the application of new technology. This paper adopts the qualitative research to archive and sort out all kinds of data collected, including documents, pictures, interview records, video and photos, etc. The data are encoded according to the cases and data types, so as to facilitate the subsequent case data analysis.

5   Analysis and Discussion

5.1   The Expansion of Servicescape Dimensions Connotation

Through case comparison, it is found that the introduction of new technologies expands the connotation of servicescape dimension. Traditional servicescape dimensions are generally divided into physical dimension, social dimension, social-symbolic dimension and natural dimension. "Sales of physical goods" is the entire content of traditional retail. However, in the new retail, a large number of life-related services, experiences, scenarios, emotions, culture, health and other non-physical contents may be sold. Therefore, this paper proposes to modify the dimension of servicescape, divide it based on the user experience, and merge the two dimensions of "social-symbolic" and "natural" into "perceptional dimension". In this way, the "physical dimension" refers to the physical and functional aspects of the servicescape, which includes internal and external environmental functional design, functional layout, business format combination, lighting, cleanliness, technology, environmental facilities, equipment and other elements; "perceptional dimension" is the part of servicescape that plays a role in user perception, including "environmental style", "social symbol", "spatial atmosphere", "sense of belonging", "aesthetics" and other elements; "Social dimension" refers to the part of the servicescape where users interact with others.

Physical Dimension of the Servicescape

In the mobile Internet environment, many traditional fields are integrated with emerging information communication technologies, making users can freely switch and connect between online platforms and offline environments, and the information flow further across the boundaries of time and space. New technology helps consumers comprehensively improve their functional experience in servicescapes, such as electronic price tag, blockchain product traceability, cashless self-service payment, mini program code scanning payment, mini program online shopping, rapid logistics, etc. The change of payment method also changes the functions in the servicescapes accordingly. In the traditional supermarket, people have to queue to pay at the cashier desk before using the goods outside. But now, in the supermarket, people can buy the goods by scanning QR code with their mobile phone, so that they can immediately enjoy it. The fresh ingredients they bought can be processed in the supermarket and then eat. The functional layout of the servicescapes has changed a lot. The combination of various business forms has become very free. The supermarket is not only a place to sell commodities, but also a place for gathering, eating, working and cultural exchange. The free switching and fusion of virtual servicescape and physical servicescape bring users great freedom and self-realization. Users can experience and purchase goods in the physical servicescape, and place orders in the virtual servicescape, and set the delivery time and place, so as to save more time for experiential activities. The servicescape of Fresh Hema is the direct motivation for consumers to purchase, which promotes the application of its application program. Carrefour also began to seek changes in the servicescape revolution, and cooperated with Tencent to introduce new technologies and change the user experience.

Perceptional Dimension of the Servicescape

The perceptional dimension of servicescape contains the aesthetic quality, social symbol, somatosensory, emotion and other elements, which is the dimension to investigate the user's perceptual experience in the servicescape. The application of technologies directly changes the function of the servicescape and indirectly brings about the change of users' perceptual experience, such as high-tech aesthetics, leisure atmosphere, social atmosphere, fashion atmosphere in servicescape, and fluent and quick shopping process, etc. Due to the use of new technologies, great changes have taken place in the pattern of the supermarket, especially there is no cashier desk in the entrance. The supermarket has become a kind of free life space, users do not have to queue to pay, which saves a lot of energy and time, and they can sit down to have a drink, chat with friends, or enjoy food. The high-tech and exquisite environment design attracts more young users, who have higher requirements for quality but are not sensitive to price. They like to share novel experiences on social media, which promotes the spread of the brand. Therefore, the design of the servicescape will try to meet people's desire to share, to create an artistic consumption environment and socialized life scene. Fresh Hema appears very different with the traditional supermarket from the beginning. It has become a place of fashion life, a kind of urban living room. Carrefour still looks like a traditional supermarket. But in 2018, Carrefour also began to seek for change, it proposed to take the new direction of retail, reduce the size of the supermarket, increase the proportion of experience, and expand the cyber marketing channels.

Social Dimension of the Servicescape
The social dimension of the servicescape includes the staff and services, cultural exchanges and other elements related to human behaviors that the servicescape provides to users. In the physical servicescape of Fresh Hema, social activities often include cultural promotion, diet culture activities, cooking skill classes and competitions. The community life in the virtual servicescape includes the food experience sharing written and released by users, and the notices of offline activities. Users can attract thumb up users and comments by publishing food experience in the online community. The more likes and comments they attract, the more they can participate in other online and offline activities of Fresh Hema, thus driving more users to join in. The social dimension of Carrefour's servicescape is simply reflected in the service personnel without relevant cultural support and offline activities. Its virtual servicescape is also a simple sales platform without users' social functions.

5.2 User Experience of Servicescapes

The introduction of scene technology has changed two aspects of user experience.

First, convenience, such as the change of payment method, which reduces the queuing process. The integration of online, offline market and logistics gives users great freedom. For example, in Fresh Hema, users can experience goods in the store, place an order through the application program, and specify the delivery time and place. Then they can have a cup of coffee, chat and eat in the store. The goods ordered will be transported to the distribution center by the picker through the suspension chain distribution system, and then sent to the designated place by the deliveryman. The Internet technology is used to track users' footprints, analyze their preferences, and push personalized products and services to users with big data, which improves users' consumption efficiency.

Second, the innovative format combination experience. As the virtual servicescapes expands, the physical servicescapes have to redefine its capabilities in the value chain. Virtual servicescapes mainly provides pure shopping function. In addition to shopping, physical servicescapes are more like a "user experience center", a forward position of brand experience and promotion. Therefore, it is a general trend to make physical servicescapes more refine, social, entertainment and experimental. Physical servicescapes innovation can update user experience, stimulate user to share, spread brand experience, expand user flow, and enhance user stickiness. Therefore, in addition to the application of new technologies, there will be more and more innovative combinations of different commercial activities, and the boundaries of user experience will continue to expand. Through the study of the above two cases, it is found that the physical servicescape of Fresh Hema is better connected with users. Carrefour has also started to set up a combination with local technology enterprises to expand the virtual scene, reconstruct the physical servicescape, reduce the size of the supermarket, improve the business activities combination experience, and enhance the stickiness of users.

References

1. Bitner, M.J.: Servicescapes: the impact of physical surroundings on customers and employees. J. Mark. **56**(2), 57–71 (1992)
2. Rosenbaum, M.S., Massiah, C.: An expanded servicescape perspective. J. Serv. Manag. **22**(4), 471–490 (2011)
3. Hooper, D., Coughlan, J., Mullen, M.R.: The servicescape as an antecedent to service quality and behavioral intentions. J. Serv. Mark. **27**(4), 271–280 (2013)
4. Krishna, A.: An integrative review of sensory marketing: engaging the senses to affect perception, judgment and behavior. J. Consum. Psychol. **22**(3), 332–351 (2012)

An Experiment of the Impacts of Workplace Configuration on Virtual Team Creativity

Xinlin Yao[1], Xixi Li[2(✉)], and Cheng Zhang[3]

[1] Nanjing University of Science and Technology, Nanjing, China
[2] Tsinghua University, Beijing, China
ciciattsinghua@gmail.com
[3] Fudan University, Shanghai, China

Abstract. Enabled by advances in information and communication technologies, virtual team has been serving as an effective form to unite knowledge workers beyond various physical and social constraints for more than one decade. Nevertheless, some organizations recently started to question the effectiveness of virtual team. Scholars also argued that virtual team members remain embedded in their situated surroundings and configuration of virtual team members situating in different workplaces would be even more complicated. This study intends to solve this emerging puzzle that is not yet considered in prior work. We draw on literatures of physical workplaces and virtual team creativity and propose a research model to investigate the influence of workplace configuration on virtual team creativity and the influential mechanism of interaction balance among virtual team members. A laboratory experiment is designed to test the proposed research model and hypotheses. We discuss the potential theoretical contributions and practical implications in the end.

Keywords: Workplace configuration · Virtual team · Team creativity · Team ambidexterity · Team interaction

1 Introduction

Virtual team (or geographically distributed team) has become a common practice in modern organizations to reduce travel costs and leverage talents globally [1]. Enabled by the proliferation of information and communication technologies (ICTs), virtual team members could communicate and coordinate on team-based tasks even separated geographically, temporally, and organizationally [2, 3]. In other words, virtual team serves as an effective collaboration form leveraging knowledge workers beyond various physical and social constraints; ICTs seems make physical workplaces irrelevant to team member interaction as well as performance in the virtual team context [4]. Empowered by the ubiquitous computing infrastructures, virtual team members can communication and collaborate almost anytime and anywhere (e.g., home, café, airports, etc.) [5–7]. Up to 70% of the workforce globally are now working from home at least one day a week [8].

Nevertheless, some organizations started to question the utilitarian benefits of virtual team. For instance, Yahoo stopped the work-from-home policy in 2013 [9] and

© Springer Nature Switzerland AG 2019
C. Stephanidis (Ed.): HCII 2019, CCIS 1034, pp. 153–160, 2019.
https://doi.org/10.1007/978-3-030-23525-3_20

IBM called thousands of employees back to offices to work "shoulder to shoulder" in 2017 [10]. Scholars argued that virtual team members remain embedded in situated surroundings when communicating with distant members through ICTs, and the situated physical workplaces possibly influence their participation in and contribution to virtual teams [11–13]. Furthermore, individual members of virtual teams could possibly situate in different types of workplaces (e.g., office, home, hotel lobby) at the same time. Thus, we expect there exists a configurational effect of virtual team members' workplace composition on virtual team performance, which is yet to call for attention from information systems (IS) scholars [14].

Toward this end, we are particularly interested in the influence of workplace configuration on virtual team creativity and the influential mechanism of interaction balance among virtual team members. We design a laboratory experiment to test the proposed research model and two hypotheses.

2   Theoretical Background

2.1   Effects of Physical Workplaces

Physical workplaces – arrangements of material objects and stimuli in the places where employees engage in daily job performance – can have tremendous employees' attitudes, behaviors, and interaction with others [15]. The degree of physical enclosure is one of fundamental characteristics of workplaces and helps classify two main categories of workplaces, i.e., private and public workplaces [15, 16].

Literature from environmental psychology suggests that private and public workplaces differentially influence the situated employees' communication behaviors and task performance. For instance, in private workplaces, employees usually experience privacy protection, and thus demonstrate cognitive concentration and better task performance [17–19]. Meanwhile, private workplaces create difficulties in communication among employees, thereby hindering collaboration effectiveness [18]. On the contrary, public workplaces facilitate communication and co-operation among colleagues because of removed physical barriers and improved transparency [16]. Open square-like workplaces especially provide visibility to each other and encourage interaction, which contributes to employee creativity in task performance [20]. However, employees also perceive crowdedness and noise in the public workplaces, which could be possibly harmful to employees' cognitive concentration and perceived privacy and endangers their work performance [21].

Following the lines of argument, we expect that virtual team members are also subject to the influences in their situated physical workplaces. Particularly, we are to investigate the influence together with the influential mechanisms of workspace configuration on virtual team creativity.

2.2   Team Creativity and Ambidexterity

Team creativity refers to generation of innovative and useful ideas by a group of individuals who work interdependently [22]. As virtual team becomes a common practice in organization management, virtual team creativity also attracts much research attention, though still at an early stage of theory development [1]. Prior studies investigated virtual team creativity in terms of idea generation [23] and obtained mixed findings when examining various physical factors that influenced virtual team creativity, e.g., technology use, team members' knowledge diversity and geographic dispersion [24, 25]. Therefore, some other scholars approached the phenomenon of interest from social and cognitive processes that take place in the virtual team context [26].

Our study follows the social and cognitive perspective on virtual team creativity and conceives interaction among virtual team members as a process, which involves various activities that might occur repeatedly and/or flexibly to realize specific needs or goals of teams [26]. Furthermore, such interactive activities within teams are often characterized by achieving contradictory needs or goals, such as exploration and exploitation, differentiation and integration, divergence and convergence; team creativity is resulted from tensions, paradoxes, or dilemmas [27]. The concept of ambidexterity from organizational learning literature has been extended to explain team creativity to understand teams' ability to manage and meet conflicting demands in processes towards creativity [27, 28]. At the team level, ambidexterity could be achieved through composing team members with various skills and cognitive styles to meet conflicting needs during the collaboration processes [27]. For instance, scholars have found that the most innovative teams included creative members, conformists, and members who were highly attentive to details [29].

Taken together, we understand the virtual team creativity from a process perspective and expect that a virtual team with higher level of ambidexterity would be more likely achieve success in team creativity.

3 Research Model and Hypotheses

3.1 Effects of Workplace Configuration on Virtual Team Creativity

According to previous studies, we expect that members of virtual team would be influenced by their situated physical workplaces. Specifically, the private workplace would increase virtual team member's level of concentration to the ongoing task but might hinder communications with the distant partners [18, 19]. On the other hand, the public workplace would facilitate the divergent thinking and interpersonal communications [16, 20].

Furthermore, based on the theory of ambidexterity in team creativity [27], we expect the virtual team ambidexterity could be achieved through composing members with different cognitive styles and communication behaviors due to being situated in different types of workplaces. Therefore, we expect that a virtual team with members in both the private and public workplace would be more likely to success in team creativity comparing with virtual teams whose members are in same type of workplaces. We hypothesize this as follows (see Fig. 1):

Hypothesis 1 (H1): Configuration of private and public workplace will influence virtual team creativity, showing that virtual teams with members situate in both the

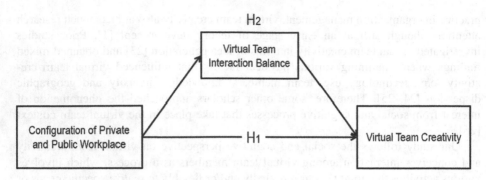

Fig. 1. Research model

private and public workplaces will achieve a higher level of creativity than the teams with members all in private (or public) workplaces.

3.2   The Mediating Role of Virtual Team Interaction

From a process perspective, team creativity is an inherently social cognitive process at the team level including various activities for achieving different even conflicting demands [27]. In the context of virtual teams, the interaction among team members are mainly or fully mediated through ICTs. Thus, we expect interactions among virtual team members will mediate the effects of workplace configuration on virtual team creativity. Based on the theory of ambidexterity in team creativity [27], we expect that the virtual team ambidexterity would be embedded in the balance of virtual team interactions, such as the balance of divergence and convergence. Taken together, we hypothesize this as:

Hypothesis 2 (H2): The balance in virtual team interaction will mediate the influence workplace configuration on virtual team creativity, showing that virtual teams with members in both private and public workplaces will have a higher level of interaction balance, and consequently contributes to virtual team creativity.

4   Research Design

4.1   Workplace and Configuration

As mentioned earlier, our study focuses on the differences between private and the public workplaces, which reflects the fundamental characteristic of the level of physical enclosure in physical environment [15, 16]. Therefore, we plan to consider the private study room and the hotel lobby as representatives for private and public workplaces, respectively.

We design three configuration modes of workplaces. Configuration Mode 1 refers to the configuration model where all virtual team members locate in public workplaces separately; in Configuration Mode 2, two team members work in public workplaces and two others in private workplaces; in Configuration Mode 3, all team members with in their own private workplaces. As such, we are able to examine the effects of configuration of private and public workplace on virtual team creativity.

4.2 Experimental Task

To measure the creativity of virtual team and reflect key features in the practical virtual team context, we will employ the digital problem-solving tasks as the experimental task. The experimental tasks will be redesigned from a computer game named "Contraption Maker" that enables multiple players collaboratively solve a given puzzle, which has been widely used in studying team collaboration and computer-mediated communication [30].

During the experiment, four team members will share the screen of the task in real time, which helps to monitor other members' attentions and moves. Team members also share the team-level goal of assembling a machine collaboratively to reach the goal that is marked with a flag. To reach the goal, they could move and connect the machine parts to trigger sequential events in the game.

To evaluate the creativity of each virtual team, we encourage team members produce as many as possible unique solutions within the time limit. The number of unique solutions of the experimental task is used to measure the level of virtual team creativity. However, only successful unique solutions will be counted for each team.

4.3 Experimental Procedure

We proposed and presented the experimental procedure in Fig. 2. Participants will be recruited from a major public university in China. In the preparation stage, participants will form four-person team once they arrived. Following an ice-breaking team building, participants will be asked for launching a chat group in WeChat for communicating during the experiment. Then, they will be orally introduced on procedures and requirements according to the printed experiment script. In the end of preparation, the whole team will be randomly assigned to one of the three configuration modes and each member will be randomly assigned to one workplace as well.

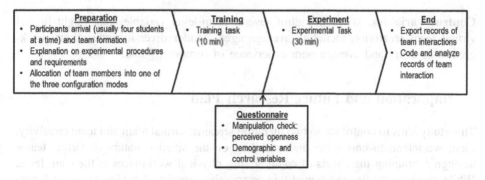

Fig. 2. Proposed experimental procedure

Participants will experience a training task in 10 min before entering the experimental task for getting familiar with the game environment, followed a questionnaire on manipulation check and control variables. The experimental task has 30 min. All interactions during the experimental task will be recorded and exported for coding and analyzing after the experiment. Each participant will receive a 40 RMB (about 6 USD) gift card of a local grocery store as reward.

4.4   Measures

Manipulation Check. We will use one item as the manipulation check to evaluate participants' perception of the situated workplace: "How do you think about the degree of openness of your situated workplace? [1 Very Private—7 Very Public]".

Virtual Team Creativity. Virtual team creativity will be measured with the number of unique successful solutions of the experimental task of each team.

Coding Scheme for Team Interactions. We will employ the scheme in [31] as the initial coding scheme for virtual team interactions in the experimental task, which concerned both divergence and convergence (see Table 1). The final scheme will be revised and established based on the real records. The balance in team interactions will be measure with the commonly used Blau's index [32].

Table 1. Initial coding scheme for team interactions

Category	Description	Example
Divergence	Task Instruction or task request	"Choose the part then move it."
	Information discovery statement	"I have a new idea."
Convergence	Acknowledgements	"Got it."
	Corrections or clarifications	"The ball should be put on the top."
	Confirmations of activity	"OK, I'm done with this."
	Task questions	"Which one should I use?"

Control Variables. We will control several team-level variables that might impact virtual team creativity, including average ages, gender diversity, educational background diversity and average prior experience of computer game.

5   Implication and Future Research Plan

This study aims to contribute to two literature streams: virtual team and team creativity. First, we intend to enrich the understanding on the situated nature of virtual teams through examining the effects of configurating physical workplaces at the team level. While previous studies mentioned this perspective, empirical evidences are still nascent. Second, we intend to contribute to the knowledge on virtual team ambidexterity through configuring different types of workplaces in the virtual team context and investigating features of virtual team interactions. We expect our results will provide valuable implications for managers effectively allocate resources in situating individual team members to different workplaces when composing and motivating virtual teams.

Our future research will investigate the dynamisms embedded in virtual team interactions and reveal the underlying mechanisms transmitting the influences of workplace configuration on team creativity. The experiment we proposed here will be further improved and conducted for data collection.

References

1. Gilson, L.L., Maynard, M.T., Jones Young, N.C., Vartiainen, M., Hakonen, M.: Virtual teams research: 10 years, 10 themes, and 10 opportunities. J. Manag. **41**(5), 1313–1337 (2015)
2. O'Leary, M.B., Cummings, J.N.: The spatial, temporal, and configurational characteristics of geographic dispersion in teams. MIS Q. **31**, 433–452 (2007)
3. Dubé, L., Robey, D.: Surviving the paradoxes of virtual teamwork. Inf. Syst. J. **19**(1), 3–30 (2009)
4. Giddens, A.: NowHere: Space, Time, and Modernity. University of California Press, Berkeley (1994)
5. Felstead, A., Jewson, N., Walters, S.: The shifting locations of work: new statistical evidence on the spaces and places of employment. Work Employ Soc. **19**(2), 415–431 (2005)
6. Hislop, D., Axtell, C.: Mobile phones during work and non-work time: a case study of mobile, non-managerial workers. Inf. Organ. **21**(1), 41–56 (2011)
7. Jarrahi, M.H., Nelson, S.B., Thomson, L.: Personal artifact ecologies in the context of mobile knowledge workers. Comput. Hum. Behav. **75**, 469–483 (2017)
8. Browne, R.: 70% of people globally work remotely at least once a week, study says, CNBC, 30 May 2018. https://www.cnbc.com/2018/05/30/70-percent-of-people-globally-work-remotely-at-least-once-a-week-iwg-study.html. Accessed 02 Mar 2019
9. Tkaczyk, C.: Marissa Mayer breaks her silence on Yahoo's telecommuting policy, Fortune, 19 April 2013. http://fortune.com/2013/04/19/marissa-mayer-breaks-her-silence-on-yahoostelecommuting-policy/. Accessed 02 Mar 2019
10. Kessler, S.: IBM, remote-work pioneer, is calling thousands of employees back to the office, Quartz, 21 March 2017. https://qz.com/924167/ibm-remote-work-pioneer-is-calling-thousands-ofemployees-back-to-the-office/. Accessed 02 Mar 2019
11. Cramton, C.D., Hinds, P.J.: Subgroup dynamics in internationally distributed teams: Ethnocentrism or cross-national learning? Res. Organ. Behav. **26**, 231–263 (2004)
12. Rennecker, J.A.: The situated nature of virtual teamwork: understanding the constitutive role of place in the enactment of virtual work configuration. Syst. Organ. **2**(3), 115–139 (2002). Sprouts: Working Papers on Information Environments
13. Sarker, S., Sahay, S.: Implications of space and time for distributed work: an interpretive study of US–Norwegian systems development teams. Eur. J. Inf. Syst. **13**(1), 3–20 (2004)
14. Yao, X., Li, X., Zhang, C., Ling, H.: Fueling virtual teams with creativity through composition of private and public workspaces. In: 38th International Conference on Information Systems, Seoul (2017)
15. Elsbach, K.D., Pratt, M.G.: 4 the physical environment in organizations. Acad. Manag. Ann. **1**(1), 181–224 (2007)
16. De Been, I., Beijer, M.: The influence of office type on satisfaction and perceived productivity support. J. Facil. Manag. **12**(2), 142–157 (2014)

17. Brennan, A., Chugh, J.S., Kline, T.: Traditional versus open office design: a longitudinal field study. Environ. Behav. **34**(3), 279–299 (2002)
18. Heerwagen, J.H., Kampschroer, K., Powell, K.M., Loftness, V.: Collaborative knowledge work environments. Build. Res. Inf. **32**(6), 510–528 (2004)
19. Bloom, N., Liang, J., Roberts, J., Ying, Z.J.: Does working from home work? Evidence from a Chinese experiment. Q. J. Econ. **130**(1), 165–218 (2014)
20. McCoy, J.M., Evans, G.W.: The potential role of the physical environment in fostering creativity. Creativity Res. J. **14**(3–4), 409–426 (2002)
21. May, D.R., Oldham, G.R., Rathert, C.: Employee affective and behavioral reactions to the spatial density of physical work environments. Hum. Resour. Manag. **44**(1), 21–33 (2005)
22. Shalley, C.E., Gilson, L.L., Blum, T.C.: Matching creativity requirements and the work environment: effects on satisfaction and intentions to leave. Acad. Manag. J. **43**(2), 215–223 (2000)
23. Alnuaimi, O.A., Robert, L.P., Maruping, L.M.: Team size, dispersion, and social loafing in technology-supported teams: a perspective on the theory of moral disengagement. J. Manag. Inf. Syst. **27**(1), 203–230 (2010)
24. Gibson, C.B., Gibbs, J.L.: Unpacking the concept of virtuality: the effects of geographic dispersion, electronic dependence, dynamic structure, and national diversity on team innovation. Adm. Sci. Q. **51**(3), 451–495 (2006)
25. Tzabbar, D., Vestal, A.: Bridging the social chasm in geographically distributed R&D teams: the moderating effects of relational strength and status asymmetry on the novelty of team innovation. Organ. Sci. **26**(3), 811–829 (2015)
26. Perry-Smith, J.E., Mannucci, P.V.: From creativity to innovation: the social network drivers of the four phases of the idea journey. Acad. Manag. Rev. **42**(1), 53–79 (2017)
27. Bledow, R., Frese, M., Anderson, N., Erez, M., Farr, J.: A dialectic perspective on innovation: conflicting demands, multiple pathways, and ambidexterity. Ind. Organ. Psychol. **2**(3), 305–337 (2009)
28. Gupta, A.K., Smith, K.G., Shalley, C.E.: The interplay between exploration and exploitation. Acad. Manag. J. **49**(4), 693–706 (2006)
29. Miron-Spector, E., Erez, M., Naveh, E.: Team composition and innovation: the importance of conformists and attentive-to-detail members. Acad. Manag. J. **54**(4), 740–760 (2011)
30. Katz, A., Te'eni, D.: The contingent impact of contextualization on computer-mediated collaboration. Organ. Sci. **18**(2), 261–279 (2007)
31. Espinosa, J.A., Nan, N., Carmel, E.: Temporal distance, communication patterns, and task performance in teams. J. Manag. Inf. Syst. **32**(1), 151–191 (2015)
32. Blau, P.M.: Inequality and Heterogeneity: A Primitive Theory of Social Structure. Free Press, New York (1977)

Study on the Effect of App Reverse Cycle Propagation Under Multi-screen Propagation

Yuhui Zhang, Zhengqing Jiang$^{(\boxtimes)}$, and Rongrong Fu

East China University of Science and Technology, Shanghai, China
y51180012@mail.ecust.edu.cn,
jiangzhengqing@ecust.edu.cn, muxin789@126.com

Abstract. According to the definition of thermodynamics, the transfer of heat source from a cryogenic body to a high-temperature body is called reverse circulation phenomenon. In the field of communication, App, as a representative of the flourishing new media, carries out advertising communication through the declining traditional media represented by TV media, which is also seen as a "reverse cycle" of communication phenomenon. In the era of multi-screen communication, the audience's attention is distracted, and the effect of App's advertising communication through TV media needs to be evaluated. Based on the situation of multi-screen communication and taking Chinese variety shows as an example, this paper explores the factors affecting the propagation effect of App's "reverse cycle". The corrcoef function in MATLAB is used to test the reliability and validity of variables, and then the hypothesis is verified by structural equation model. Finally, the key indicators affecting the communication effect are obtained.

Keywords: Multi-screen communication · APP · Reverse cycle ·
TV communication

1 Introduction

In thermodynamics, the phenomenon of reverse circulation of heat source from low temperature object to high temperature object is also reflected in the field of propagation. We regard the traditional media represented by TV as the low temperature object in the process of communication, and the new media platform represented by APP as the high temperature object in the process of communication.

With the development of mobile Internet, the new media platform represented by App has gradually become the main force of advertising communication with its strong communication situation. At the same time, the App market is fiercely competitive, the cost of online promotion is increasing, and the development of a certain level of App requires new channels of communication to gain more users and traffic. Therefore, Internet companies will turn their attention to the stable TV media to increase the App. The exposure. Therefore, we regard the advertisement of the new media representing "high temperature objects" to the TV media representing "low temperature objects" as a kind of "reverse cycle" phenomenon of communication.

C. Stephanidis (Ed.): HCII 2019, CCIS 1034, pp. 161–168, 2019.
https://doi.org/10.1007/978-3-030-23525-3_21

In the era of multi-screen communication, audiences can learn more about TV program information and participate in interaction through various media, such as mobile phones and computers. They also miss out on advertising information because of other media. Therefore, the effect of App's advertising through TV programs is worth exploring. This paper mainly makes the following contributions: 1. Investigate the audience's information on the spread of App on TV media. 2. Select the influencing factors of the effect of App on TV media, and finally establish the impact indicators that affect the effectiveness of App in TV media.

2   Preparation of Your Paper

"Reverse circulation" is a concept in thermodynamics. Thermal cycles are usually divided into forward and reverse cycles according to the direction and effect of the cycles. Unlike the positive cycle of transforming heat energy into mechanical energy, which enables the outside world to get work, the reverse cycle refers to the cycle of heat from low-temperature heat source to high-temperature heat source [1].

The research of "multi-screen communication" originated from the "three networks convergence" in 2013, that is, the telecommunication network, radio and television network and the Internet through technological transformation to achieve resource sharing and mutual compatibility, and gradually integrated into a unified information and communication network. Jay and David Heltz mentioned that the way we watch TV has changed dramatically over the past decade. People check their e-mails, discuss the latest events from reality shows on social media, browse the Web and find actors they know on TV. Interaction designs that fail to take this into account may distract viewers from TV programs and reduce their memory of what they see [2]. In the environment of multi-screen communication, the changes of media relations and user identity have played a profound role in the communication effect. The evaluation of the communication effect is no longer a unilateral evaluation of TV ratings, but also a multi-faceted consideration from the psychological dimension of the network platform and users.

On the research of advertising communication effect, Guo Qingguang mentioned the influence of opinion leaders on communication effect in his Communication Course: opinion leaders, as the relay and filter link of media information and influence, have an important impact on mass communication [3]. In his book Media and Society - A Critical Perspective, Graham Burton of Britain puts forward that the debate on the relationship between advertising and media mainly focuses on the television media. He believes that because the Internet can better target individual audiences, the cost of online advertising is actually more expensive than television advertising [4].

3   The Influencing Factors Framework of App's "Reverse Cycle" Communication Effect

The framework consists of three parts: extracting the factors affecting the communication effect of App in TV media, establishing the factors evaluating the communication effect of App in TV media, and establishing the framework of "reverse circulation" communication effect of App.

Extraction of Factors Affecting the Effect of App's Communication in TV Media
The author divides the influencing factors into four dimensions: communication platform, communication brand, communication mode and communication audience.

- **Communication Platform: The nature of communication platform.** The audience regard their favorite media platform as a trustworthy brand, and the communication platform itself assumes the role of a trust endorsement of program advertising implantation brand.

- **Communication brand: Product category**, product category may affect the advertising communication effect, and has a high degree of correlation with the audience's acceptance. **Earlier evaluation of products by audiences.** Some scholars believe that the audience's memories and perceptions of unfamiliar products or brands will increase significantly after watching advertisements; more scholars believe that familiar brands will lead to higher recall rate, more positive advertising attitude and stronger willingness to buy.

- **Communication Mode: The saliency of brand information.** There are many definitions of advertising saliency. This paper uses Gupta's definition. Saliency is the size of brand information appearing in movies or games, the central degree appearing in the screen, the duration, etc. [5]. Generally speaking, the more prominent the advertising information is, the better its dissemination effect will be; however, over-prominent placement will reduce the audience's evaluation of the brand or product. **Consistency between Brand Information and Program Content.** The result of Homer's research shows that the significant implanted brand may make consumers disgust and discomfort because of its obvious implantation intention, rigid form and disturbance of the plot, and then lead to consumers' negative attitudes [6]. **Star effect.** Star effect has a strengthening effect on the dissemination of advertising information in TV programs, especially when stars and endorsement brands show high-frequency interactive behavior. **Implantation mode.** Double coding theory holds that information is input into human brain through both language and visual channels at the same time, and memory is relatively easy; App can get better transmission effect through the dual implantation of sound and vision in the program. **Targeting information.** In the face of the serious distraction of the audience's attention from multiple screens, the advertising information must be designed with pertinence in order to attract the audience's attention.

- **Communicate audience: Demographic characteristics.** The degree of input of the audience, advertising psychology believes that the audience will play a significant role in the collection of information and the ability to process information in a strong investment state, which will have a direct impact on the effectiveness of advertising and the purchase behavior of the audience. **Consumer innovation.** A large number of studies confirm that consumer innovation has a significant impact on advertising effectiveness, and consumer innovation plays an active role in advertising cognition and behavior.

Establish Factors That Assess the Effectiveness of App in TV Media

- Ad impression: The first impression of the audience on the ad largely determines the degree of love for the app, which in turn generates the impulse to buy.
- Brand Emotion: The audience's affection for the app affects whether the audience believes that the app is consistent with its own positioning, thus affecting consumer behavior.
- App download rate and retention rate: The download amount of the app after the program is broadcasted directly reflects the effect of the advertisement.

Establish an App "Reverse Loop" Propagation Effect Framework
As shown in Fig. 1, according to the 11 hypothetical indicators of influencing factors and three indicators of evaluating communication effect, the author establishes the framework of App's "reverse circulation" communication effect from the four dimensions of media, brand, mode and audience.

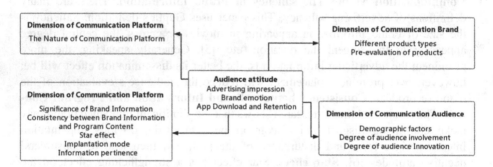

Fig. 1. The influencing factors of App's "Reverse Cycle" communication effect (Source: LNCS 5412, p. 323)

4   Empirical Analysis on the Influencing Factors of App's "Reverse Cycle" Communication Effect

This paper takes Fast Hand App and Pingduo App as examples to empirically analyze the influencing factors of App's communication effect in TV media. The author conducted a questionnaire survey on the effect of fast-hand App's dissemination in the program and a questionnaire survey on Pindo App's dissemination in the program of "Running Bar" and the audience of "Extreme Challenge" respectively. 200 valid questionnaires were collected, and the data processing results were as follows:

4.1   Reliability and Validity Analysis of Sample Data

A. Reliability Analysis
Using matlab to make regression line analysis, the specific treatment methods (taking the nature of the communication platform as an example): the grade is 1–7, then the contribution of the score from 1–7 to the problem is –0.99, –0.66, –0.33, 0.33, 0.66 and

0.99, respectively. For the nature of the communication platform, the number of -0.99 is 2, -0.66 is 0, -0.33 is 5, 0 is 44, 0.33 is 51, 0.66 is 35, 0.99 is 63. Using corrcoef function in matlab, the code is as follows:

$$X = [-0.99, -0.66, 0.33, 0, 0.33, 0.66, 0.99];$$
$$Y = [0.0116, 0, 0.0232, 0.2209, 0.2558, 0.1744, 0.3139];$$
$$Z = \text{corrcoef}(X, Y);$$
$$\text{Cout} \ll Z;$$

If $Z = 0.5748$ is found, then the probability that this problem will be recognized in the population is 0.5748. Similarly, several other influencing factors can be dealt with.

For the data processing of advertising communication effect, all scores are positively correlated, and the impact index of advertising impression is significantly higher than other problems (Data results are shown in Table 1).

Table 1. The influencing index of the factors of app communication effectiveness.

Influence factor	Index
Advertising impression	0.529
Brand emotion	0.4573
App download and retention	0.3425

B. Validity Analysis
By analyzing the validity of the questionnaire to determine whether the questionnaire is an effective questionnaire. The data obtained after the KMO and Bartlett test on the questionnaire are shown in Table 2.

Table 2. Sample data KMO and Barlett test results

Kaiser-Meyer-Olkin measure of sampling sufficiency		0.876
Barlett sphericity test	Estimated Chi-square distribution	10892.78
	df	987
	Sig.	0.03

It can be seen that the value of KMO is $0.876 > 0.700$; the value of Barlett's spherical test is $sig = 0.03 < 0.05$, which shows that there is a good correlation between variables, so the data can be used for factor analysis.

4.2   Factor Analysis Affecting the Effect of App in TV Programs

In the question setting of the questionnaire, questions 1 to 5 are descriptive statistics, questions 6 to 19 are independent variable factors, and questions 20 to 26 are dependent variable factors.

A. Independent Factor Analysis

When the eigenvalue of the independent variable is greater than one, the independent variable can be selected as the primary independent variable. The following Table 3 is the initial eigenvalues and accumulations of the individual independent variable factors after the spss analysis, and the extracted square sums are accumulated.

Table 3. Independent variable extraction square sum

Question number	Total	Percentage of variance	Percentage of accumulation
question 11	9.5655	8.038	8.038
question 12	20.7892	17.47	25.508
question 15	14.9641	12.575	38.083
question 17	22.1548	18.617	56.7

It can be seen from the processed data that the problem XI, the question 12, the question fifteen, and the question 17 are the highest among all the questions, so these questions can be taken as the main independent variables.

B. Dependent Variable Factor Analysis

In the experiment, the factors that are the dependent variables are: Question 20, Question 21, Question 23, Question 24, Question 25, and Question 26. The corresponding variables are: I can recall the main content of the Quick App. The advertisement of the Quick App in the program makes me use the impulse. I am very impressed with the slogan of the Quick App. I think the Quick Hand is an app that records life and expresses itself. After watching the advertisement, I will download the Quick App, and after the program is broadcast, I use/keep the Quick App for more than a week, and after the program is broadcast, I use/reserve the Quick App for more than one month. The data processing method is the same as above.

Table 4. Dependent variable extraction square sum

Question number	Total	Percentage of variance	Percentage of accumulation
question 23	1.0897	2.362	2.362
question 24	4.0754	8.834	11.196
question 25	11.7318	25.429	36.625
question 26	29.2379	63.375	100

It can be seen from the Table 4 that the variances generated by Question 23 to Question 26 are large, so they can be classified into two categories for processing:

- Stimulating people's desire to download immediately after watching the show, but not actually downloading to bring economic effects;
- People will actually download and use the app after watching the show, which will bring real economic effects (flow contribution).

4.3 Structural Equation Analysis Affecting the Effect of App in TV Programs

In order to better determine whether the variable will have a causal relationship, we use the structural equation model for confirmatory factor analysis. We use the SEM model for processing (Table 5).

Table 5. Initial model fitting indicator table

Index	Chi-square	Df	Chi-square/df	CFI	NFI	IFI	TLI	RMSEA
Model fit criteria	1827.7	223	$5.082 \approx 5$	$0.9023 > 0.9$	$0.876 > 0.8$	$0.815 > 0.8$	$0.819 > 0.8$	$0.0716 < 0.08$

Further analysis of the SEM model to find the standardized path coefficients under the influence of various factors, as shown in the following Table 6:

Table 6. Standardized path coefficients of SEM model fast hand APP

question number	ensemble	effect model	specific impact description	non standardized path coefficient	standardized path coefficient
question 12	online influence		online influence on download impulse	0.082	0.082
question 15			offline influence on download impulse	-0.0021	-0.0021
question 11	offline influence		online influence on download	0.00721	0.00721
question 17			offline influence on download	0.231	0.231
question 19					

In the same way, the data processing of the factors affecting the effect of the iPad on the TV media is as follows (Table 7):

Table 7. Standardized path coefficients of SEM model fight more APP

question number	ensemble	effect model	specific impact description	non standardized path coefficient	standardized path coefficient
question 10	online influence		online influence on download impulse	0.083	0.083
question 12			offline influence on download impulse	0.0032	0.0032
question 13					
question 15					
question 11	offline influence		online influence on download	0.00998	0.00998
question 17			offline influence on download	0.927	0.927
question 19					

Since the value of the normalized path coefficient is greater than 0.08, a significant correlation will be exhibited. From the above two tables, the impact of the two online aspects of question 12 (significant degree of brand information) and question 15 (adjustment of advertisement and program) will stimulate the audience's desire to download. In addition, the indicator star effect It has a certain effect on the audience's desire to download a lot of apps; the impact of the three lines of question 11 (product type), question 17 (audience evaluation of products beforehand), and question 19 (consumer innovation). The actual download behavior of the audience has an impact.

5   Conclusion

In this work, we studied the issue of App's advertising on TV media in the context of multi-screen communication. With the advent of the multi-screen era, the form and communication pattern of the media have undergone major and profound changes. By screening and extracting the influencing factors of communication effects, this paper finally establishes the key indicators that affect the effect of App "reverse cycle". The study believes that after viewing the advertisements in the variety shows, the audience has a great effect on the instant download impulse of the App and the download amount in a short period of time, which provides acceptable results for evaluating the effect of the App on the TV media. As people gradually become accustomed to accepting information dissemination in a multi-screen situation, it is necessary to establish an evaluation system for the effect of App on TV media, which provides a reference for decision makers to make more effective information dissemination decisions.

Acknowledgments. We wish to thank all test participants for taking part in our research. This research was supported by The State Administration of Press, Publication, Radio, Film and Television, Publishing and Development (East China Normal University) Key Laboratory Open Project Fund Project (ECNUP-KF201806), Shanghai Science Education Development Foundation Funded Project (2201802), Shanghai Design IV Summit Open Fund Funded project (DA18302).

References

1. Shen, W.: Identification of Common Molecular Subsequences. Higher Education Press, Beijing (1983)
2. Vanattenhoven, J., Geerts, D.: Multimed. Tools Appl. **76**, 5661 (2017). https://doi.org/10.1007/s11042-016-3646-1
3. Guo, Q.: Communication Course, pp. 189–190. Renmin University Press, Beijing (1999)
4. Burton, G.: Media and Society: A Critical Perspective. Tsinghua University Press, Beijing (2007)
5. Zhou, N., Wang, D.: Can significant embedded advertising bring better brand attitudes: a study on the significant impact mechanism of embedded advertising. Nankai Bus. Rev. **17**(02), 142–152 (2014)
6. Liu, D.: The Impact of Brand-Content Fitness on Brand Cognition and Attitudes in Embedded Advertising, Master, Hunan University (2013)

Learning Technologies

Guidelines on Context Integration: Developing Technological Solutions Communication for Education Professionals

Janaina C. Abib[✉], Ednilson G. Rossi[✉], and Rafael S. Pena[✉]

Federal Institute of São Paulo, Araraquara, São Paulo, Brazil
{janaina, ednilsonrossi}@ifsp.edu.br,
rafamaic1337@gmail.com

Abstract. This article presents a project that arose from the need to design applications with natural interactions for professionals in the field of education, who have long working days and who mix personal and social activities together with professional activities. The project is based on the Design Process Model for Health Applications: Integrating Contexts and Adding Abilities (ICAH, in Portuguese), developed to guide and support the work of application developers for health professionals who care for patients in need of long-term care [1–3]. Its objective is to validate the guidelines of integration of contexts proposed in the ICAH Model applied to education professionals. To fulfill the proposed objective, the ICAH Model was used for the definition and collection of requirements for an application of communication and dissemination of information in the educational environment. The application was developed from research and observations of professionals who worked in a professional education institution during the year 2018. The application provides the disclosure of information related to extracurricular events and activities and official communications that are part of the Institution. The observations and feedbacks collected by the application gave us indications that the application was effectively adopted by education professionals. The content of the information that had favorable feedback was, in its majority, information that added extracurricular contents and social events of the Institution, evidencing the mix of contexts in the educational environment.

1 Introduction

1.1 Contextualization

The current situation reflects that the work environment of education professionals, as well as all those professionals who deal with constant and long-term care, is conducive to the construction of a new identity and reference for these professionals, who incorporate their personal and social activities to professional activities and build cooperative relationships with their peers beyond the professional environment. To incorporate technological resources that are naturally inserted in the workflow of these professionals, without being obstacles in their routines, but that support them in the performance of their tasks, a model of design process and a set of guidelines has been developed, supporting the development of systems and applications for these professionals. The ICAH Design Process Model was developed during the works [1–5] and was used as a reference in this project.

The development of this project arose from the need to design applications with natural interactions for professionals in the field of education who have long working days and who mix personal and social activities with professional activities. The natural interactions, in this project, are defined as the way in which the user exchanges information with applications and technological resources in an instinctive and transparent way, without worrying about the peculiarities of the application or manipulated technological resource [2, 4].

What is intended is that the development of these applications allows a result that integrates the different contexts in which these professionals are: professional, personal and social, considering their abilities through the experience of using technological resources and the exchange of experiences among them. Knowing the complexity that is expected to be found in a person and their actions in the real environment, the existing typical design models and approaches that are based on the standard user idea (or medium), such as those discussed in [6, 7, 12], aren't specifically indicated for the understanding of human interaction, although they serve the purpose of generating and setting conventions – it's always necessary to refine, search or create new models and approaches [8]. In addition, the use of personal technological resources, such as mobile devices, in the professional environment allows the experience of using these resources to be used to stimulate the abilities of the professional and promote personal, social and professional integration in the work environment, incorporating the concepts of Bring Your Own Device (BYOD) defined and presented in [10, 11, 13] and Bring Your Own Application (BYOA), defined and presented in [9] to that project.

To fulfill the proposed objectives, the ICAH Model was used for the definition and development of an application of communication and dissemination of information in the educational environment. The application was developed from research and observations of professionals who acted in a professional education institution, during the year 2018. The application provides the disclosure of information related to events, extracurricular activities and official communications that are part of the Institution. The information is disseminated by education professionals, through displays installed in areas of coexistence of the Institution, as well as a totem that was strategically positioned so that officials and students can comment on the importance and usefulness of the information disclosed. The opinions collected served as feedback for professionals to analyze the importance and necessity of the information available on the displays and could refine the type of information disclosed.

The observations made, information data and feedbacks collected by the application gave us indications that the application was effectively adopted by education professionals. The content of the information that received favorable feedback was, in its majority, information that added extracurricular contents and social events of the Institution, evidencing the mix of contexts in the educational environment. The suggestions collected with education professionals showed us that in order to improve and expand the application's functionalities, such as future work, it's interesting to promote access to the application also by mobile devices.

1.2 Objective

The objective of this project is to validate a set of guidelines applied to ICAH that guides and supports the work of application developers with natural interaction for professionals in the field of education.

It's believed that applying these guidelines during the process of developing applications for the education professional will support the lifestyle of this professional in the constant and long-term care of students, facilitating the management and integration of professional, social and personal contexts for that professional. As the focus of this research is on the process of designing applications with natural interaction, both interaction designers and developers (designers and systems analysts) benefit from the validation of guidelines for the integration of contexts, so they're treated in this job, as designers or application developers.

The specific objectives are:

- Understand how education professionals use their own technological resources for professional activities;
- Know the abilities of education professionals in the use of technological resources;
- Understand how is the dynamics of communication and information exchange between a group of education professionals;
- Apply the ICAH design process model in the creation of evolutionary prototypes for education professionals, following the guidelines of integration of contexts that guide the application of the model;
- Evaluate, with a case study, the use of evolutionary prototypes by education professionals.

2 Development

This project was developed in two steps: the lifting of the requirements, according to ICAH Model and the elaboration, execution and analysis of the results of the Case Study, which included the development of the application.

2.1 First Step - Requirements Survey

Based on the understanding of the ICAH Model and the guidelines proposed in the model, the requirements for the development of a prototype to aid the communication and dissemination of information in a teaching institution were raised.

The guidelines proposed in the model are divided into two domains: the context integration domain and the skill addition domain. The two areas present common objectives to facilitate the appropriation of the artifact to be developed: to the extent that the integration of contexts occurs, users become aware of the use of technologies and applications in different contexts, in addition to the effective adoption of these technologies and applications; and the extension of the use of these technologies and applications favors the exchange of experiences and expands the abilities of the users involved in the design process. In this project the guidelines of the Domain of Context

Integration were used, which emphasize the actions to be executed during the design process, actions that guide the designers on what aspects, related to the different contexts of the user, should be considered. The actions taken in this project are described below.

(A1) Make clear the purpose of the design process. Before initiating the first session of the interaction design process, a conversation with the user group was promoted to explain what and how the design process and its activities would be carried out.

(A2) Promote a quick socialization before the design sessions (ice breaking). The design sessions began with a socialization activity and each participant was encouraged to present what they expected to happen at the end of the session.

(A3) Identify what electronic communication services are used. Technological resources were identified that were used for communications at work and outside of work, as well as the types of messages, annotations, information and reminders that users share with each other.

(A4) Promote short intervals during the design sessions. The small intervals were made during almost all the design sessions and the developers took advantage of these moments to observe the behavior of the users and how the interaction was between them.

(A5) Promote design for appropriation. It was important the active participation of the users, which allowed to elaborate a flexible and easy to use design, favoring the appropriation of technological resources.

(A6) Observe and promote the integration between users, in the professional context and outside of it.

(A7) Identify the lead user. The education professionals who directed the validations during the development of the solution were identified and encouraged the use of the innovations adopted.

The presented guidelines monitor the clearer development model activities and facilitate the work of developers and designers during the application development process.

2.2   Case Study

During the studies of the ICAH Model and the collection of requirements - based on the model, we found the need to develop a system for the dissemination of information and news in a public way on the campus of Araraquara, the Municipal Chamber of São Paulo, Brazil.

This observation guided the development of the COMMUNIQUE-SE system, a responsive WEB system. The system, as well as its characteristics and form of use, is presented below.

COMUNIQUE-SE System

The system developed aims to manage and organize information transmitted to the community of the Institution in its public displays. Today, the Institution has two displays for the dissemination of information and news and the content disclosed is not managed or controlled in an automated way. In addition, the system has a feedback functionality: for some selected information and news, community members can leave their opinion about the disclosure, choosing if what is being disclosed is useful or not.

To access the system and make available an information or news, the user, who in that first moment is the director of the institution, needs to make the access validation, through previously registered login and password.

After logging in, the list of registered releases is displayed and can be managed. In a menu you can access all the features of the system. On this system screen, in addition to the list of registered announcements, it's also possible to view, edit or delete a specific communication, with text and image (Fig. 1). It's interesting to note that the announcements are presented on the display screen of the displays during the period in which they're valid - with dates of initial and final display.

Fig. 1. Communication inclusion

In the presentation of the statement, the information or the news is shown and, if it's a communication of feedback, a range of evaluation on the usefulness of the information or the news (Fig. 2).

Fig. 2. Communication and evaluation range

When the statement presents the range of feedback, the members of the community of the Institution can register their opinion and for each opinion, the images of the evaluation range are filled, showing the number of opinions received, in terms of percentage. The collection of opinions is done on a totem with monitor and keyboard for the election (Fig. 3).

Fig. 3. Opinion collection totem

The GALLERY functionality allows to insert a set of images to appear in the displays in the form of an image carousel when there is no active communication, that is, when no information or news is in the viewing period, so the selected images are displayed in the galleries. You can create several image galleries and select which ones will be active and ready to be displayed. You can also remove and change a gallery at any time.

3 Discussion and Conclusion

As a final result for this research project, context integration guidelines were validated for the development of applications aimed at education professionals and application developers can use these guidelines as support during the development of applications, facilitating the definition and creation of applications. The validation occurred with the use of the guidelines for the definition and development of the interaction design used in the case study. And the identification of the problems and needs of the users interviewed and participants of the activities proposed in the ICAS Model gave indications of the needs to be addressed in the system developed.

The results obtained, according to the specific objectives were:

– Understanding how education professionals use their own technological resources for professional activities and their abilities in the use of technological resources was achieved through interviews, observations and questionnaires with these professionals. In addition, we analyzed how communication happens between education professionals, between professionals and students and with the management, in general.

- Application of the ICAS Model during all the work, in the surveys and interviews, with observation techniques and following the guidelines defined in the model. Thus, it was also possible to define and understand the needs and problems that these professionals reported.
- Validation of the model, as education professionals approved the iterative and evolutionary prototypes that were developed.
- Preparation of a case study, providing the creation of the COMMUNIQUE-SE system, which may be adopted by the educational institution to disseminate information and news. Also, as the COMUNIQUE-SE system has a feedback functionality, it will allow to analyze and evaluate the usefulness of the information and news disclosed.

Thus, as this project had the development of a system for education professionals, the system can be widely used by the institution's staff to disseminate news and information and obtain a feedback related to the news and information disclosed.

References

1. Abib, J.C.: Integração de Contextos e habilidades Pessoais, Sociais e Profissionais no Desenvolvimento de Soluções Tecnológicas para o Profissional da Saúde, 184 p. Tese (Doutorado) – Universidade Federal de São Carlos, 19 October 2016. (in Portuguese)
2. Abib, J., Anacleto, J.: Guidelines to integrate professional, personal and social context in interaction design process: studies in healthcare environment. In: Kurosu, M. (ed.) HCI 2015. LNCS, vol. 9169, pp. 119–131. Springer, Cham (2015). https://doi.org/10.1007/978-3-319-20901-2_11
3. Abib, J.C., Anacleto, J.C.: Integrating contexts in healthcare: guidelines to help the designers at design process. In: 30th ACM/SIGAPP Symposium on Applied Computing (SAC 2015), pp. 182–184, Salamanca (2015)
4. Abib, J.C., Anacleto, J.C.: Interaction design process for healthcare professionals: formalizing user's contexts observations. In: XIV Simpósio Brasileiro sobre Fatores Humanos em Sistemas Computacionais (2015)
5. Abib, J.C., Anacleto, J.C.: Modeling a design process to natural user interface and not ICT users. In: The 18th ACM Conference on CSCW: WORKSHOP Doing CSCW Research in Latin America: Differences, Opportunities, Challenges, and Lessons Learned (2015)
6. Anacleto, J.C., Fels, S.: Lessons from ICT design of a healthcare worker-centered system for a chronic mental care hospital. In: Proceedings of the ACM Conference on Human Factors in Computing Systems (CHI 2014), Canada (2014)
7. Anacleto, J., Fels, S.: Adoption and appropriation: a design process from HCI research at a brazilian neurological hospital. In: Kotzé, P., Marsden, G., Lindgaard, G., Wesson, J., Winckler, M. (eds.) INTERACT 2013. LNCS, vol. 8118, pp. 356–363. Springer, Heidelberg (2013). https://doi.org/10.1007/978-3-642-40480-1_22
8. Barbosa, S.D.J., Silva, B.S.: Interação Humano-Computador. Rio de Janeiro, Elsevier, série Editora Campus – SBC Sociedade Brasileira de Computação, p. 384 (2010). (In Portuguese)
9. Chase, J., Niyato, D., Chaisiri, S.: Bring-your-own-application (BYOA): optimal stochastic application migration in mobile cloud computing. In: IEEE Global Communications Conference (GLOBECOM), pp. 1–6 (2015)

10. Earley, S., Harmon, R., Lee, M.R., Mithas, S.: From BYOD to BYOA, phishing, and botnets. IT Prof. **16**(5), 16–18 (2014)
11. French, A.M., Guo, C., Shim, J.P.: Current status, issues, and future of bring your own device (BYOD). Commun. Assoc. Inf. Syst. **35**, 191–197 (2014)
12. Hix, D., Hartson, H.R.: Developing User Interfaces: Ensuring Usability through Product and Process, p. 416. Wiley, New York (1993)
13. Lee, Jr., J.R., Crossler, R.E.: Implications of monitoring mechanisms on bring your own device (BYOD) adoption. In: Proceedings of the 34th International Conference on Information Systems (2013)

Labenah: An Arabic Block-Based Interactive Programming Environment for Children. The Journey of Learning and Playing

Bushra Alkadhi(✉), Sarah Alsaif, Alhanouf Alangri, Fatima Alkallas, Hatoun Aljadou, and Noura Altamimi

Department of Software Engineering, College of Computer and Information Sciences, King Saud University, Riyadh, Saudi Arabia
balkadhi@ksu.edu.sa

Abstract. From the phone alarm that wakes us up to the social media applications that keep us connected to people around the world, technology became an integral part of our daily life. Recently, communities have realized that coding is an essential skill that everybody should acquire regardless of their age and specialty. Investing in young generations has a profound effect on building communities and their digital capabilities. Coding gives children huge competitive advantages that improve logical thinking, problem solving and encourage creativity. Given the lack of high quality educational programming resources for children especially in Arabic, this could be a challenging process.

Labenah is an Arabic edutainment application that provides children with an interactive environment to learn coding principles. It adopts block-programming where visual blocks are built together to control objects and create scenarios. Among all other existing applications, Labenah considers gamification and other important concepts that motivate children to practice important skills through an enjoyable journey between learning and playing. Children can create their own media-rich projects and undertake multi-level challenges to practice important programming concepts. Attracting such a young age requires extensive validation and user involvement; therefore the team adopted User-Centered Design (UCD) development model where potential users and stakeholders are actively engaged during each phase of the development. We discuss the participatory design approach that we followed while developing Labenah and how it affected the outcomes. Children, parents, and teachers were involved through semi-structured interview and observation sessions and surveys. Design considerations to be taken into account while designing for children are also discussed.

Keywords: Block-programming · Children · Edutainment · User-centered design

1 Introduction

For a long time, programming was limited to certain groups of people in technical fields but nowadays, programming became an essential skill that everybody should learn and acquire regardless of their age. Living in a fast pace world where technology

© Springer Nature Switzerland AG 2019
C. Stephanidis (Ed.): HCII 2019, CCIS 1034, pp. 179–187, 2019.
https://doi.org/10.1007/978-3-030-23525-3_23

is taking the lead, individuals will be more involved in creating these technologies in different levels. However, research studies have shown that the effect of learning how to program goes beyond that in making individuals better thinkers and communicators [1]. It improves logical thinking, critical thinking, and problem solving, [2, 3].

Many researchers have agreed that learning how to code in a young age is especially important to the child's development process and therefore, integrating programming throughout all educational levels since early ages is valuable and fruitful. It boosts the child's creativity as it allows him/her to think differently and outside the box [4]. Coding may also involve working within a team in a collaborative environment, which will create a positive impact on the child's communication skills and work ethics. According to Wesley (2006), "Students who participate in collaborative learning and educational activities outside the classroom and who interact more with faculty members get better grades, are more satisfied with their education, and are more likely to remain in college" [5]. Additionally, a study on a primary school in UK has concluded that communication skills and self-confidence were notably enhanced by the process of planning, designing, creating, and fixing of computer applications [6].

As mentioned earlier, programming used to be considered as a separate job by itself and for a long time, it was limited to technology specialists and a small group of people. As a result, not enough effort was dedicated to simplify programming. Instead, learning that skill was a purely technical process that requires a strong background in math and logic besides the ability to understand the symbolic structure of the program. Based on that, we came up with Labenah which is an Arabic block-based interactive programming environment for children to help them learn and practice basic programming concepts through a journey of learning and playing.

This paper discusses Labenah application and the adopted participatory design approach that we followed. It is organized as follows: the first section discusses block programming and some of the previous work while the second section describes an exploratory design approach that has been adopted while developing the application and the evaluation process.

2 Related Work

2.1 Block Programming

As learning technologies and online platforms evolved, programming material became accessible to wider range of people and more non-tech individuals got engaged in programming activities. However, taking into consideration the importance of learning programming from a young age, text-based programming might not be the perfect start for young children. Just like math and science, children need first to know and exercise the main concepts behind programming before knowing how exactly the commands should be written in a symbolic way [7]. Therefore and with the rapid rise and increasing interest in teaching and learning programming in an early age, researchers and decision makers have been studying the most effective ways to understand programming and how it is learned especially for children. What is the proper age to start learning how to program, what cognitive skills are essential to perceive such concepts, and what outcomes are we expecting from this learning journey. Answering these questions was critical to achieve the best outcomes.

Block-based programming has been recognized as a simple interactive way to introduce coding and as a stepping-stone to traditional text-based programming. It was first introduced in Scratch application by MIT's Lifelong Kindergarten lab [4]. Children can create a program by building visual blocks together in a logical way connecting different objects and programming components such as actions, events, and operators.

Block-based programming environment enhance learnability for novices as it simplifies the problem of dealing with difficult vocabularies and reduce the high cognitive load involved in coding. Research has shown that learning programming using blocks has a notable effect on perceiving the traditional textual language later on. A study on 10th grade students learning C# and Java languages has concluded "those who had taken a Scratch course in 9th grade learned more quickly, understood loops better, and were more engaged and confident than their peers who had not" [8].

2.2 Existing Applications

Although a couple of programming applications around the world have been adopting block-based programming for children (see Fig. 1), there is a lack of such applications that support Arabic language specifically for non-English speaking kids. Arab children will have to spend a tremendous amount of time on learning and mastering English in order to set up and learn coding. Additionally, besides the design and usability issues found in some of these applications, most of them mainly focus on the educational aspect without considering the entertainment and gamification factor in the process not mentioning the required lab settings and equipment that are expensive to build or rent.

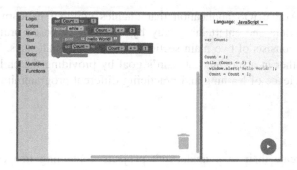

Fig. 1. Block programming sample by blocky [9].

2.3 Learning Through Playing

The inspirational quote of the great scientist Benjamin Franklin: "Tell me and I forget. Teach me and I remember. Involve me and I learn." emphasizes the importance of involvement and practical application in the learning process. Teaching children applied important concepts like programming is challenging especially with the traditional way of teaching and the complicated written codes. Not to mention the lack of high quality Arabic applications in this area designed for children. They will not be able to conceive such concepts without simplifying them and adding an entertainment factor.

Playing can help children learn and grow through imagination and sense of adventure. Because it is enjoyable, children may become very absorbed in what they are creating and learning. It promotes essential skills such as problem solving, self-expressing, teamwork, and sharing [10].

Gamefication

In today's digital generation, gamification has become an effective way to boost motivation and engagement by encouraging different behaviors [11]. Gamification is the utilization of game elements and game thinking in non-game situations [12].

Generally, players get quickly engaged in the game they play. Reaching this level of engagement is one of the main challenging goals in education and other child development activities, in fact motivating learners to ponder and keep them engaged throughout the learning process is not simple. Therefore, gamification concepts have been highly adopted in education and other systems to achieve their goals [12].

There are a few fundamental game elements that are used in successful application of gamification in education which are categorized into self-elements and social-elements. Self-elements could be points, levels, or achievement badges. These elements get users to focus on competing their knowledge and recognizing self-achievement. Social-elements focus on interactive competition such as leaderboards that motivate the user and share the his/her progress and achievements [11].

3   Overview of Labenah

Labenah is an Arabic iOS application that enables children to learn programming concepts in a simple and entertaining way by using block-based programming language. Labenah consists of two main sections: stories and challenges. These sections complete each other in achieving Labenah's goal by providing the child with a comprehensive experience of learning and practicing different programming concepts and skills.

3.1   Stories

Children can create their own media-rich projects containing images, sounds and animation as stories or games to communicate ideas and creativity. They can drag and drop different objects and choose templates that are previously designed and ready to use (see Fig. 2). These objects can be controlled through a set of blocks where each one represents a command such as arrow (right, left, up, down), if-else, and loops.

Fig. 2. Creating a story in Labenah

3.2 Challenges

Because children love adventures, Labenah provides them with multi-level challenges and problems that test different programming concepts. The child undertakes several levels of directed challenges where he/she is asked to solve some parts of the riddle using block programming (see Fig. 3). This will help him/her to develop strong problem solving and critical thinking skills and to practice what he/she has learnt. We also believe that gamification and competition are strong factors in the learning process, accordingly the child can compete and compare results with his/her friends in a stimulating and entertaining competitive environment (see Fig. 4).

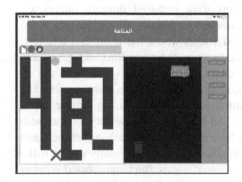

Fig. 3. The maze challenge.

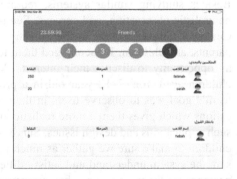

Fig. 4. Creating a group competition.

4 Participatory Design Approach

Following an appropriate software methodology is a critical requirement for success. It ensures that the software system meets requirements and quality goals in addition to controlling development cost and time [13]. Labenah mainly targets children. Attracting such a young age requires extensive validation and user involvement. Therefore, the team adopted the User-Centered Design (UCD) development model where potential users were actively involved during each phase of the project development.

The standard that has been followed is the ISO 13407: Human-centered design process which "provides guidance on achieving quality in use by incorporating user-centered design activities throughout the life cycle of interactive computer-based systems" [14] (Fig. 5).

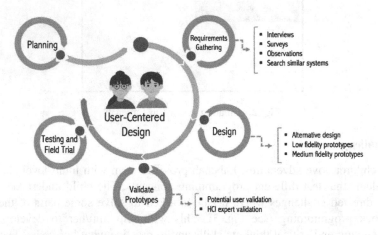

Fig. 5. UCD cycle for Labenah application

4.1 Requirements Gathering and Evaluation

Besides studying similar systems, requirements were gathered through interviews, naturalistic observation, and surveys. Semi-structured interviews took place at Riyadh Center of Gifted Students in the ministry of education where the team met teachers, parents, and children. It encouraged them to freely share their opinions and gave them an opportunity to discuss their interests. Moreover, observations were conducted on children aged from 7–12 year old in a programming course in the same center. The team's goal was to observe users in their natural behavior while using similar applications which gives them a more realistic view and feedback on how they interact with such applications and design issues. Surveys where also distributed among teachers and children to make sure we gather as much information as possible. Finally and to make sure the system understand and satisfy different users' needs, the team created number personas for the system users that encapsulate their characteristics, needs and behavior.

Several key requirements for the application were derived based on that:

- Should support Arabic language as there is a huge lack of such programming applications in the Arab world.
- Needs to be implemented on a device that is reachable for children such as iPad.
- Should be easy to use.
- Enables children to customize the objects they use.
- Includes more gamification as children need to be motivated enough to spend more time on the application.

- Encourages communication and collaboration through sharing stories and competition with peers.
- Supports different levels of programming concepts and challenges to reach wider audience and to help the child to progress.

4.2   Design Process

After examining existing applications and getting some useful input from stakeholders including teachers, parents, and children, we moved into our ideation phase where we analyzed the requirements furthermore to come up with a proper design of the system.

Since the team is adopting the UCD development methodology and to ensure the usability of the designed user interface especially for children, the team started by designing and discussing two different low fidelity prototypes in a brainstorming session. Low fidelity prototype is a sketch of the detailed functionalities of the system. It focuses on translating the design ideas into tangible artifacts rather than the visual appearance of the system. These designs were translated later on to two medium fidelity prototypes which is a high interactive prototype focuses on the design aspect of the system where the appearance is very close to the final product. It is usually designed when there is a need to test the design with real users.

These medium fidelity prototypes were evaluated in a validation session by 10 children and an HCI expert for design recommendation. Children were selected based on age, gender, and programming experience. The validation intends to determine the extent to which an interface facilitates a child's ability to complete routine tasks. Children were asked to complete the primary tasks using both medium fidelity prototypes and captured their navigational choices, task completion rates, average time per task, questions and feedback. The sessions were recorded and analyzed to identify potential areas for improvement in Labenah.

After analyzing the session and based on the recorded data, the first prototype had better results compared to the second prototype. Children found it easier to use and more interactive. More importantly, most of the children found Labenah very exciting especially the challenges ideas (Figs. 6 and 7).

Fig. 6. Labenah homepage (First prototype)   **Fig. 7.** Labenah homepage (Second prototype)

5 Conclusion

Labenah application will pave the way and open new horizons for more programming activities. It could be used at home or classrooms especially that communities nowadays are moving towards involving programming as a main course in elementary school.

More valuation sessions will be carried out with children, parents, and teachers to evaluate and test Labenah. Future work would involve enhancements on the design and features that Labenah supports. The team will always be looking to keep it interactive and usable to achieve the goal of making programming easy and accessible to all community groups especially children.

Acknowledgement. We would like to thank Riyadh Center for Talented Students in the Ministry of Education for the opportunity to join one of their courses to observe and interview children, teachers and parents. We are also really thankful to all the individuals and organizations who helped us to reach this aim.

References

1. Fessakis, G., Gouli, E., Mavroudi, E.: Problem solving by 5–6 years old kindergarten children in a computer programming environment: a case study. Comput. Educ. **63**, 87–97 (2013). https://doi.org/10.1016/j.compedu.2012.11.016
2. Proulx, V.: Computer science in elementary and secondary schools. In: Informatics and changes. Presented at Learning open Conference on Informatics and Changes in Learning, pp. 95–101, Austria (1993)
3. Futschek, G.: Algorithmic thinking: the key for understanding computer science. In: Mittermeir, R.T. (ed.) ISSEP 2006. LNCS, vol. 4226, pp. 159–168. Springer, Heidelberg (2006). https://doi.org/10.1007/11915355_15
4. Maloney, J., Peppler, K., Kafai, Y., Resnick, M., Rusk, N.: Programming by choice: urban youth learning programming with scratch. In: Proceedings of the 39th SIGCSE Technical Symposium on Computer Science Education, pp. 367–371 (2008). https://doi.org/10.1145/1352135.1352260
5. Burke, A.: Group work: how to use groups effectively. J. Effective Teach. **11**(2), 87–95 (2011). https://uncw.edu/jet/articles/Vol11_2/Burke.pdf. Accessed 12 Oct 2018
6. Clements, D., Gullo, D.: Effects of computer programming on young children's cognition. J. Educ. Psychol. **76**(6), 1051–1058 (1984). https://doi.org/10.1037/0022-0663.76.6.1051
7. Weintrop, D., Wilensky, U.: To block or not to block, that is the question: students' perceptions of blocks-based programming. In: Proceedings of the 14th International Conference on Interaction Design and Children, pp. 199–202 (2015). https://doi.org/10.1145/2189835.2189849
8. Bau, D., Gray, J., Kelleher, C., Sheldon, J., Turbak, F.: Learnable Programming: Blocks and Beyond (2017). https://doi.org/10.1145/3015455
9. Blockly, A.: JavaScript library for building visual programming editors. Start building your Blockly app. Google For Education. https://developers.google.com/blockly/. Accessed 14 Nov 2018
10. Zosh, J., et al.: Learning through play: a review of the evidence (2017). https://doi.org/10.13140/rg.2.2.16823.01447

11. Huang, W., Soman D.: A Practitioner's Guide to Gamification of Education. University of Toronto, pp. 5–13 (2013)
12. Boer, P.: Introduction to Gamification. Charles Darwin University, pp. 4–13 (2013)
13. Georgiev, V., Stefanova, K.: Software development methodologies for reducing project risks. Econ. Altern **2**, 104–113 (2014)
14. Bevan, N.: UsabilityNet: Methods: ISO 13407. Usabilitynet.org (2006). http://www.usabilitynet.org/tools/13407stds.htm. Accessed 26 Oct 2018

Creating a Community of Scholars: Outcomes and Interventions of a Four-Year Community College STEM Scholarship Program

James Braman[1(✉)], Barbara Yancy[1], and Sylvia Sorkin[2]

[1] School of Technology, Art and Design, Computer Science/Information Technology, Community College of Baltimore County, 7201 Rossville Boulevard, Rosedale, MD 21237, USA
{jbraman,byancy}@ccbcmd.edu
[2] School of Mathematics and Science, Mathematics, Community College of Baltimore County, 7201 Rossville Boulevard, Rosedale, MD 21237, USA
ssorkin@ccbcmd.edu

Abstract. This project describes degree and other outcomes after four years of a specific S-STEM scholarship program at the Community College of Baltimore County (CCBC), located in Maryland USA [1]. This scholarship program was aimed at increasing degree attainment at the community college level in Science, Technology, Engineering, and Mathematics (STEM) related fields. From Fall 2014 through Spring 2018, 101 fulltime CCBC students majoring in specific STEM fields received S-STEM scholarships for one or more semesters through NSF funding. This paper highlights previous research [1] and presents demographics of the CCBC awardees, including transfer and graduation rates. In addition, emphasis will be placed on community building and interaction, student interventions and results of spatial visualization skills testing (PSVT:R) and practice. As all students remained in the program due to its successful implementation, student success strategies will be discussed.

Keywords: Scholarships · STEM · Faculty mentoring · Transfer · Spatial skills

1 Introduction

Following our previous research [1] this paper highlights main components of an S-STEM scholarship program at the Community College of Baltimore County (CCBC). CCBC is a public two-year college with three main campuses and three extension centers. The Fall 2015 combined credit enrollment at CCBC was 22,179 students of which 29% were full-time students. Thirty-nine percent (39%) of the credit students were African American, and 60% of credit students were female. In FY 2016, CCBC awarded 2,194 associate degrees. From Fall 2014 through Spring 2018, 101 full-time CCBC students (34 female and 67 male) majoring in specific STEM fields were awarded renewable Math and Computer Inspired Scholars (MCIS) semester scholarships through NSF funding [1]. Awardees retained their scholarships for one or more semesters with the average length of 2.6 semesters. Eligible major programs for

C. Stephanidis (Ed.): HCII 2019, CCIS 1034, pp. 188–192, 2019.
https://doi.org/10.1007/978-3-030-23525-3_24

MCIS included the following transfer and career programs: Computer Science, Engineering, Mathematics, Physics, Information Systems Security, Engineering Technology, Information Technology, and Network Technology. Over half of the 101 awardees were majoring in Engineering and Computer Science. Thirty-four percent of awardees were female. These awardees have been highly successful in graduating with associate degrees or transferring to 4-year institutions.

The distribution of all credit students at CCBC in Fall 2014 by racial/ethnic group as self-described at course registration was as follows: White 45%, Black 39%, Asian 7%, Hispanic/Latino 5%, and Other/Unknown 4% [2]. In Fall 2015, CCBC had 42.3% Pell enrollment compared to 34.8% Pell enrollment at all Maryland community colleges. Minority groups that have been under-represented in STEM fields nationally are represented among the 101 MCIS awardees from Fall 2014 through Spring 2018 in proportions close to their population percentage at CCBC. In particular, 38% of the 101 awardees self-identified as White, 37% as Black, 20% as Asian, 5% as Multiple Races, and 1% as Hawaiian/Pacific Islander. Among all these, 5% were Hispanic/Latino. A total of 259 (81F/178 M) semester scholarship awards were made over four years, for the $540,000 of scholarship funds. The average semester award was $2,124, but each semester the individual awards were fixed percentages of each awardee's remaining unmet financial need after other awards and subsidized loans were taken into consideration, therefore, award amounts ranged from $80 to $5140 per semester.

2 Intervention Highlights

To increase student success and to foster a community of support, several activities were implemented as part of the scholarship. These activities included aspects of faculty-based mentoring, spatial visualization training, student involvement in leadership and volunteering roles. These interventions contributed to increased retention and completion with a specific focus on minority students and females. During the four-year grant period, there were no MCIS dropouts from the program. In addition to the major themes described below, several one-day workshops focusing on STEM programs, including guest speakers, optional internships for awardees, CCBC Technology presentation, Engineering and Mathematics Pathway workshops on resume writing, monthly mentoring of all awardees by STEM faculty, and monthly luncheon workshops were included as interventions.

2.1 Faculty Mentoring

Awardees were paired with a faculty mentor from their academic discipline and were required to meet periodically during the semester. These meetings aimed at improving student/faculty interaction and to provide a sense of support. Meetings often involved discussions of courses, preparing for future internships and employment, and other discipline-specific topics. To keep track of these meetings, mentoring agreements were used to document what actions the student needed to take before the next meeting and what was discussed. These meetings also served as advising meetings where students could discuss difficulties during the semester, course plans, and other items that the mentor could help address. Students were typically paired with the same faculty member across multiple semesters if possible.

2.2 Spatial Skills Training

Research suggests that spatial visualization abilities are essential for success in STEM fields such as in engineering, chemistry, computing, and mathematics [3–5]. As a unique component of the program MCIS scholarship students were required to participate in completing the Purdue Spatial Visualization Test: Visualization of Rotations (PSVT:R) each semester. Students took the timed 20-minute test in order to assess their spatial ability. Students that scored less than 70% on the test were asked to participate in weekly to bi-weekly workshops to practice their visualization skills. Workshops consisted of practice sessions of visualization skills and examining 3D shape rotations. At the end of the semester, students took the PSVT:R again. Scholarship criteria was not based on spatial skills scores. Workshops evolved to an online format as CCBC was one of the community college partners to the Spatial Skills Instruction Impacts Technology Students (SKITTS) project an online version of the test and workshops was used [4], and [6]. The online version of the course included video lectures, video examples, PowerPoint notes, practice and additional sketching exercises that were assigned based on the Spatial Course Learning Resources [3].

Forty-seven of the students scored at or above the 70% threshold yielding a 46.5% pass rate on the first attempt. Fifty-four students were strongly encouraged to participate in the spatial skills workshops. After completing the workshops, there was an average positive change of 16 points, for students retaking the PSVT:R. The average of the highest scores obtained from all students was 67.6%. From this group, the average highest score for females was 62.3% and 70.3% for males. Examining all post PSVT:R scores, 63 students or 62.4%, reached or exceeded the 70% threshold. These workshop series also provide a sense of community between other students and faculty.

2.3 Leadership and Volunteer Service

An additional component of the MCIS scholarship program was encouraging students to participate in the service and volunteer opportunities. The service component of the program allows the opportunity to gain valuable leadership skills, become more involved on campus, build resumes, and expand their network. As an example, The Student Ambassador Program is a leadership opportunity for MCIS scholars who are dedicated to serving and representing the college. In this role, students would assist in campus tours, serve as representatives and perform duties at various CCBC campus and community events. Some Computer Science/Information Technology, Information Systems Security, and Network Technology students volunteered by working in the student Homework Lab. Students are required to assist in the lab for a few hours each week assisting other students, answering questions, monitoring equipment and more. Several awardees volunteered as tutors for self-paced developmental mathematics classes.

3 Transfer Four-Year Institutions

The MCIS scholarship program encouraged awardees to continue their STEM studies at four-year institutions. There are numerous local universities in the area as well as connections to many other institutions. CCBC hosts numerous college fairs throughout the year to assist students in selecting transfer schools. MCIS students had additional presentations on transfer options and tips at several events. To assist awardees to complete bachelor's degrees in these fields, the MCIS project proposal stated that 20% of scholarship funds would "follow" awardees who had transferred. MCIS scholarship funding was awarded to former awardees who had earned an associate's degree, or at least 45 credits, in an MCIS-eligible program at CCBC before transferring to a four-year institution. In addition, students kept their STEM faculty mentor while transitioning to the four-year college. Those that transferred to a four-year institution from CCBC with an associate's degree, or at least 45 credits in an eligible STEM program, were given the option of retaining their MCIS scholarship for up to an additional 2 semesters. This enabled students to reach greater success in a STEM field by drawing attention to the possibility of transfer to a four-year school.

Due to the large number of MCIS awardees who transferred, in some semesters the percent of available funding allocated for transfer awards was as high as 32%. However, due to the higher costs of attendance at a four-year institution (compared to attendance at CCBC), the percentage of their unmet financial need that was awarded to transfer awardees was never as high as the percentage for awardees still at CCBC. Of the 259 (81F/178 M) semester scholarship awards that were made over four years, 85 (24F/61 M) were transfer awards made to former CCBC MCIS awardees who had transferred to a four-year institution to pursue a bachelor's degree.

4 Conclusions and Future Work

Sixty-four percent of the 101 total MCIS awardees transferred to a 4-year institution, and an additional 19% have earned an associate degree but did not transfer to a 4-year institution. 64% of the 101 MCIS awardees have earned associate degrees, and 19% have earned bachelor's degrees (as of July 2018) and 69% have earned at least one of these degrees. Considering all 101 awardees to date from Fall 2014 through Spring 2018, as of July 2018, a total of 64 (21F/43 M) awardees (63%) have transferred to 4-year colleges/universities. Overall, 62% (21/34) of the female awardees and 64% (43/67) of the male awardees have transferred. Considering all 101 MCIS awardees, at the end of Year Four, 44% of female awardees were in either COSC or ENGR major programs, and 63% of male awardees were in those two programs.

Bachelor's degrees have been earned by 19 awardees to date, including 21%of female awardees and 18% of male awardees. Additionally, another 43 (14F/30 M) MCIS awardees were enrolled at transfer institutions in 2018. For the 19 MCIS awardees who have earned bachelor's degrees, the elapsed time from initial CCBC entry to bachelor's degree attainment has ranged from 44 months to 119 months, with a median time of 60 months (5.0 years), and an average time of 65 months (5.4 years). These times are expected to increase as additional MCIS awardees earn bachelor's degrees. Research by Shapiro et al. suggests that bachelor's degree earners with no associate's degree, but with prior enrollment in 2-year institutions, the average time elapsed to bachelor's degree was 6.0 years [7].

Implementation of this project has yielded significant insights into interventions that were beneficial to student success, community building, degree attainment, and transfer. Although this program has been concluded, the benefits to the students and faculty have been significant. Lessons learned from these interventions can be used in other campus programs to benefit students as they are applied to other initiatives on campus. We continue to make revisions and further analyze data and track success rates of the program.

Acknowledgment. This material is based upon work supported in part by the National Science Foundation under award DUE-1356436. Opinions expressed are those of the authors and do not necessarily reflect the views of the NSF.

References

1. Sorkin, S., Braman, J., Yancy, B.: Interim awardee outcomes after four years of a STEM scholarship program. Inf. Syst. Educ. J. **17**(1), 49–63 (2019). http://isedj.org/2019-17/, ISSN: 1545-679X
2. MHEC Maryland Higher Education Commission.: Trends in enrollment by race and gender: Maryland Higher Education Institutions (2007–2016) (2017). http://mhec.maryland.gov/publications/Documents/Research/AnnualReports/2016EnrollRaceandGender.pdf
3. Sorby, S.: Educational research in developing 3-D spatial skills for engineering students. Int. J. Sci. Educ. **31**(3), 459–480 (2009)
4. Metz, S., Jarosewich, T., Sorby, S.A.: Adapting tested spatial skills curriculum to on-Line format for community college instruction: A critical link to retain technology students (SKIITS) (2016). https://www.asee.org/public/conferences/78/papers/18066/download
5. Gagnier, K., Fisher, K.: Spatial thinking: A missing building block in STEM education (2016). http://edpolicy.education.jhu.edu/wpcontent/uploads/2016/07/Spatialthinkingmast headFINAL.pdf
6. Sorby, S.A., Metz, S., Jarosewich, T.: Online spatial skills instruction for community college students in technical education. In: 71st Midyear Meeting Proceedings of ASEE Engineering Design Graphics Division (2016). https://sites.asee.org/edgd/wp-content/uploads/sites/22/2017/12/Part12-Sorby-Metz-Jarosewich.pdf
7. Shapiro, D., Dundar, A., Wakhungu, P.K., Yuan, X., Nathan, A., Hwang, Y.: Time to degree: A national view of the time enrolled and elapsed for associate and bachelor's degree earners (Signature Report No. 11). National Student Clearinghouse Research Center, Herndon, VA (2016). https://nscresearchcenter.org/signaturereport11/

Facilitating Deep Learning Through Vertical Integration Between Data Visualization Courses Within an Undergraduate Data Visualization Curriculum

Vetria L. Byrd$^{(\boxtimes)}$ (iD)

Purdue University, West Lafayette, IN 47907, USA
vbyrd@purdue.edu

Abstract. There is significant research underway on pedagogical approaches to data visualization that include teaching data visualization in various classroom settings, short-form data visualization instruction, the use of active learning, and the use of design patters for teaching and learning for data visualization. Most data visualization courses are taught independent of a major which might explain the lack of research in the area of vertical integration of visualization courses. This paper shares a method for facilitating deep learning through vertical integration between data visualization courses within an undergraduate data visualization curriculum. The data visualization process, concepts and techniques are introduced in a gateway course during students' second year of study. Students enrolled in the gateway course for the data visualization major collaborate with other data visualization majors taking a senior level course on a visualization challenge with real-world application. The collaboration facilitates deep learning through vertical integration between the two classes. Students from both classes form a team to compete in a data visualization challenge as part of an annual technology conference in Indianapolis, Indiana. Participation in the team is voluntary. Students who compete in the visualization challenge work with faculty mentors from both classes and practice near-peer mentoring. This paper will provide insight into how the curricular constructs of the data visualization process and deep learning combine to facilitate vertical integration between data visualization courses.

Keywords: Data visualization · Deep learning · Vertical integration · Education

1 Introduction

The ability to transform data into insight is a necessary 21st century skill. The abundance of data drives the need for knowledgeable individuals with experience transforming complex data into valuable insight. To be competitive in the data driven workforce, students must be introduced to the process of visualizing data early and often. Armed with this process knowledge, students must be able to apply concepts and

C. Stephanidis (Ed.): HCII 2019, CCIS 1034, pp. 193–201, 2019.
https://doi.org/10.1007/978-3-030-23525-3_25

techniques learned in class to real-world situations, work effectively in a collaborative environment, and apply their knowledge of data visualization in an integrative way.

The Computer Graphics Technology Department at Purdue University, addresses this issue by offering an undergraduate major in Data Visualization [1–3]. The vertical integration of upper and lower level courses within the major facilitates opportunities for students at various levels in the program to work together, and learn from each other in a team based, collaborative environment.

There is research underway on pedagogical approaches to data visualization that include teaching data visualization in various classroom settings [4–6], short-form data visualization instruction [7], the use of active learning [8], and the use of design patterns for data visualization teaching and learning [9]. These approaches are implemented and introduced in existing courses, untethered to a major, which might explain the lack of targeted research in the area of vertical integration of visualization courses. This paper will provide insights on the curricular constructs and parallels with the data visualization process and deep learning [10] that combine to facilitate vertical integration between data visualization courses.

1.1 Data Visualization Process

The process of visualizing data is known to be messy, iterative, and complex [11]. A description of the teaching approach by which data visualization is taught at the undergraduate level at Purdue has been detailed in other manuscripts [2, 3] and summarized here. The data visualization process [12] sometimes referred to as the visualization pipeline [13] is a multi-stage process of creating visual representations of data [13]. We adopt the visualization process presented by Fry [12] for introducing data visualization to undergraduates. Fry's method consists of seven stages that include: getting data, breaking the data into its component parts, removing all but the data of interest, exploring the data for patterns, creating visual representations of the data, improve some part or component of the visualization and lastly, adding functionality to enable the viewer to engage with the data. Each stage plays an important role in data visualization and builds on the intricate relationships that exist among and between the stages in the process. Understanding this process is crucial to creating visualizations that provide meaningful insight.

1.2 Vertical Integration

The concept of vertical integration can mean many things [14]. Vertical integration strategies have been applied in engineering [15], health care [16], agriculture [17], media [18], business [19] and supply chain processes [15]. For example, in manufacturing, vertical integration describes consolidating agencies involved in different stages of product development [20]. In the educational domain vertical integration is most often considered and implemented as an approach to teaching and learning in general practice [14, 21], medical school curriculums [22, 23], and postgraduate training [24]. In medical education, the term can refer to integrating basic and clinical sciences with respect to learning outcomes [14], integrating graduate, postgraduate and continuing professional development resources and infrastructure with respect to delivery [21], or teachers addressing the needs of learners at different stages [21, 25].

Outlining a framework for vertical integration in general practice education and training, is defined by Thomson [26] as the *'coordinated, purposeful, planned system of linkages and actives in the delivery of education and training throughout the continuum of the learner's stages of medical education.'* [21]. The 2003 General Practice education and training report defines vertical integration as: "The coordinated, purposeful, planned system of linkages (level of students as well as assignments) and activities in the delivery of education and training throughout the continuum of the learner's stages of education." [27]. Dick [14] developed a conceptual model, known as VITAL (Vertical Integration in Teaching and Learning), based on educational theory about vertical integration. The VITAL model represents a possible implementation strategy for the GPET national integration framework [14]. There are several contexts for which vertical integration has been defined; however, there is minimal published literature directly addressing vertical integration of data visualization courses.

2   Related Work

2.1   Deep Learning and Education

The deep learning approach has at its core a focus on problem-solving [28]. Deep approaches to learning were first identified by Marton and Säljö [29, 30] in a series of studies that examined the way students tackled reading tasks. These studies identified students who used deep-level processing aimed to grasp the underlying meaning of the text [28]. Marshall [31] conducted a year-long study of 13 students who were doing a first-year engineering foundations course in the United Kingdom. Marshall's work identified a 'procedural deep approach' to student learning. The 'procedural deep approach' is characterized by the extent to which students showed evidence of seeking out relationships – with parts of the task and the whole, or with other related knowledge [28, p. 609]. This approach is similar to the problem-solving approach taken by students in the data visualization major when solving data visualization challenges.

Deep learning is associated with curiosity, personal interest, lack of external pressure—so called internal motivation [23]. Prerequisites for deep learning include conditions that simulate the student's own interest and removal of factors leading to external motivation, such as insecurity, fear and anxiety [23]. For this work we adopt the definition of deep learning provided by Warburton [10]: "Deep learning is a key strategy by which students extract meaning and understanding from course materials and experiences, it is associated with the use of analytic skills, cross-referencing, imaginative reconstruction and independent thinking." Warburton [10] present several factors thought to influence deep learning that include learning environment, course content, individual factors, and motivation of the student to understand (engagement with the topic) [10, Figure 1, p. 46]. Many of these factors are key components of the current data visualization curriculum. For example, the CGT 270 class learning environment introduces data visualization from a *hypothesis driven* perspective with datasets that are provided and predetermined research questions and from a *data driven* (exploratory) perspective where students gain experience letting the data drive the process. Visualization concepts are presented in a variety of ways to facilitate broad interests from students. Students are encouraged to reflect on prior knowledge and personal experiences for problem-solving assignments. Marton and Saljo [32] reports deep learning is internally motivated and is associated with an intention to understand rather than to simply pass an assessment task. It is dependent on a student's level of engagement with the topic [33]. Course related data visualization challenges closely relate to social issues with local impact providing students with a different lens through which to see where they can make a contribution, giving more meaning to their efforts beyond the classroom.

Pask and Scott [34] provided evidence for different styles of deep learning. They distinguished between a holistic (global) style that attempts to create a picture of the whole task (comprehension learning) and a serialist (step-by-step) style that pays more attention to details and processes (operation learning) [10]. Our work facilitates a combination of the holistic (comprehension) and serialist (operation) teaching and learning styles.

3   Vertical Integration Within the Data Visualization Major

3.1   Undergraduate Data Visualization Courses

CGT 270 Introduction to Data Visualization is the gateway course to the undergraduate major in data visualization at Purdue University's main campus. The course meets twice a week for a 50-minute lecture followed by a 50-minute lab. The three credit hour course is designed for students with little or no background in data visualization. It provides an introductory examination of data visualization through lecture, readings and hands-on experience with current visualization tools. Students learn the fundamentals of the visualization process for information and examine detail visualizations workflows. After taking the course students have both the theoretical foundation and practical skills needed to create insightful visualizations for a wide range of data types. This class is open to students in their second year or higher in the data visualization major.

CGT 470 Data Visualization Studio is a three credit hour course that teaches visualization design and development of interactive data visualization systems to communicate and analyze complicated datasets. Students learn interaction and visual design principles, draw from human perception and cognition theories, and focus on hands-on practice of developing interactive data visualization systems that enable users to see, understand, and analyze complex data and relations. Upon completing the course, students demonstrate the ability to apply design principles learned in class and use proper technologies to create a comprehensive interactive visualization system for data analysis. This class is open to junior and senior level data visualization majors.

3.2   Indy Big Data Visualization Conference and Challenge

The annual Indy Big Data Visualization Challenge serves as a mechanism for vertical integration of the two classes (CGT 270 and CGT 470) in the major. Data is provided by the sponsors of the challenge and made available two weeks before the submission deadline. Traditionally visualization challenges have a social theme with a local impact. For example, in 2017 participants were asked to track Indiana's highest area of opioid abuse and identify up to 10 contributing factors to the abuse using data sets provided by the conference.

In 2018 the data contained information about employment patterns and higher education activities in Indiana. The challenge was to answer questions about how the higher education sector responds to changes in the demand for skills in the economy. Potential questions could include (from the Indy Big Data Visualization Conference website (https://2018.indybigdata.com/visualization-challenge/#challenge-statement): What trends do you find in talent and workforce alignment? Did you find any barriers to employment or education in areas of misalignment? What ideas do you have to better identify and improve the alignment of Indiana's talent pipeline with the present and future needs of employers in the state? For the last two years, the Indy Big Data Visualization conference has coincided with the CGT 270 fall semester course schedule.

4   Approach

Participation in the Indy Big Data Visualization competition is optional. A student's decision to participate (or not) in the competition does not impact the student's grade in the course; however, the class is required to complete the visualization challenge as a course assignment. The competition timeline is short, intense, and described below.

Week 1–2. Introduction to data visualization in CGT270: 7-stage visualization process examined and explored. Students in CGT 270 complete individual visualization challenges in preparation for the class group visualization challenge; students are made aware of the Indy Big Data Visualization Challenge's web site for more details about the challenge.

Week 3–4. Students in CGT 270 and CGT 470 interested in completing volunteer to join the competition team. Datasets made available by the conference on the Indiana Data Hub. Competition team members organize and brainstorm ideas for the challenge. The team agrees on a challenge topic/theme. Tasks to be performed, based on individual skills and interests, are determined and agreed upon.

Week 5–6. Team registration deadline. Team continues to work on the visualization challenge, meeting and connecting regularly. Team presents to a panel of judges at the Indy Big Data Conference.

5 Results

The 2018 team consisted of five undergraduates. Four students (75%) were from the CGT 270 class and one student (25%) from the advanced class, CGT 470. The team was made up of students in their fourth (33%) and third (66.7%) academic year in the data visualization major. After the competing in the visualization challenge members of the team were asked to complete a feedback survey on the vertical integration experience. The survey consisted of 31 questions. Completion of the survey was optional and anonymous. Completion of the survey (or not) had no impact on students' course grade in CGT 270 or CGT 470. Three of the five team members (60%) completed the survey and provided feedback. A summary of survey responses is provided.

Respondents were asked to indicate how many data visualization courses they had taken, including any classes enrolled in at the time. There was an even split: 33.3% indicated having taken only one class, 33.3% indicated having taken two classes and 33.3% indicated having taken three data visualization courses. All team members had either taken CGT 270 in a previous semester or were enrolled in CGT 270 at the time of the competition. One student reported having completed an intermediate data visualization course (CGT 370) and having some work experience. All respondents (100%) indicated they felt the CGT 270 class prepared them for the competition. All respondents (100%) mentioned learning Tableau as a visualization tool in CGT 270 was beneficial for the class and for the competition as part of the vertical integration.

Respondents were asked to indicate statements that most accurately reflect their opinions using a four-point Likert scale of "strongly disagree," "disagree," "agree" and "strongly agree." Respondents (66.7%) strongly agreed with the statement, "My participation in the Indy Big Data Visualization challenge increased my interest in the subject of data visualization"; 33.3% agreed. Respondents (66.7%) strongly agreed with the statement, "My participation in the Indy Big Data Visualization Challenge showed me how useful knowledge of data visualization as a process can be"; 33.3% agreed.

Respondents were asked to rate the level of experience they feel is needed to be successful in the Indy Big Data Visualization Challenge. Respondents (33.3%) indicated, "The challenge required slightly more experience than I have;" 66.7% indicated, "The challenge required much more experience than I have." The team placed 5th in the presentation to judges and did not advance to the next round of presenting during the main conference.

Using a four-point Likert scale of "very likely," "somewhat likely," "somewhat unlikely," and "very unlikely," 33% of respondents indicated they are somewhat likely and 66.7% indicated they are very likely to recommend participating in a similar type of experience with students from CGT 270 and CGT 470 to a friend or other students.

Respondents were asked to rate the overall Indy Big Data Visualization Challenge Experience (Competition) using a four-point Likert scale with the following options: poor, fair, good, or excellent. Respondents (33.3%) rated the Indy Big Data Challenge as fair; 66.7% rated the conference as excellent.

6 Discussion and Conclusions

Vertical integration takes a lot of time and effort to plan and organize [23]. Limitations of this first attempt at vertical integration include: (1) dealing with variability in prior learning experiences of students [14], and (2) small team size. The team consisted mostly of students new to data visualization; only one student from the advanced class participated. Given only two weeks to produce a viable solution, the team would have benefited from more team members at the advanced level. Having more members on the team, with more data visualization experience would have made the short challenge window more manageable for the team. The advantages of the vertical integration through the Indy Big Data Visualization Challenge include: near pear mentoring of junior students by advanced students, the identification of areas in the approach to improve, increase in student's confidence in applying skills and techniques learned in class out of class and the real-world experience of working within the conference guidelines. Faculty and students agree, the vertical integration and competition was a good experience for data visualization majors. For future implementations, faculty will encourage more participation from upper level students enrolled in 300 and 400 level data visualization courses to facilitate more near peer mentoring with a wide range of skillsets on the team.

References

1. Byrd, V.L., McGraw, T., Chen, Y., Connolly, P.: Curriculum development for visualization capacity building. In: Proceeding of the ASEE Engineering Design Graphics Division, 71st Mid Year Conference, pp. 45–49, 16–18 October 2016
2. Byrd, V.L.: Introducing data visualization: a hands-on approach for undergraduates. Paper accepted to be presented at 2018 Association for the Advancement of Computing in Education, E-Learn Conference, Las Vegas, Nevada, 15–18 October 2018
3. Byrd, V.: Parallels between engineering graphics and data visualization: a first step toward visualization capacity building in engineering graphics design. In: ASEE EDGD 72nd Midyear Conference, 3–8 January 2018
4. Johnson, A.: Teaching data visualization in evl's cyber-commons classroom. In: Pedagogy Data Visualization, IEEE VIS Workshop (2016)
5. Beyer, J., Strobelt, H., Oppermann, M., Deslauriers, L., Pfister, H.: Teaching visualization for large and diverse classes on campus and online. In: Pedagogy Data Visualization. IEEE (2016)
6. Domik, G.: A data visualization course at the university of paderborn. In: Pedagogy Data Visualization, IEEE VIS Workshop (2016)
7. Zoss, A.: Challenges and solutions for short-form data visualization instruction. In: Pedagogy Data Visualization, IEEE VIS Workshop (2016)
8. Hearst, M.A.: Active learning assignments for student acquisition of design principles. In: Pedagogy Data Visualization, IEEE VIS Workshop, October 2016
9. Craft, B., Emerson, R.M., Scott, T.J.: Using pedagogic design patterns for teaching and learning information visualization. In: Pedagogy Data Visualization, IEEE VIS Workshop (2016)

10. Warburton, K.: Deep learning and education for sustainability. Int. J. Sustain. High. Educ. **4**(1), 44–56 (2003)
11. Mckenna, S., Mazur, D., Agutter, J., Meyer, M.: Design activity framework for visualization design. IEEE Trans. Vis. Comput. Graph. **20**(12), 2191–2200 (2014)
12. Information Visualization Wiki. https://infovis-wiki.net/wiki/Visualization_Pipeline. Accessed 26 Jan 2019
13. Fry, B.: Visualizing Data (Safari Books Online). O'Reilly Media, Sebastopol (2008)
14. Dick, M., King, D., Mitchell, G., Kelly, G., Buckley, J., Garside, S.: Vertical integration in teaching and learning (VITAL): an approach to medical education in general practice. Med. J. Australia **187**(2), 133–135 (2007)
15. Wang, Y., Faath, A., Goerne, T., Anderl, R.: Development of a toolbox for engineering in project teams for Industrie 4.0. In: Proceedings of the International MultiConference of Engineers and Computer Scientists, vol. 2 (2018)
16. Machta, R., Maurer, K., Jones, D., Furukawa, M., Rich, E.: A systematic review of vertical integration and quality of care, efficiency, and patient-centered outcomes. Health Care Manage. Rev. **44**(2), 159–173 (2018)
17. Rehber, E.: Vertical Integration In Agriculture And Contract Farming. IDEAS Working Paper Series from RePEc, IDEAS Working Paper Series from RePEc 1998 (1998)
18. Yoo, C.: Vertical integration and media regulation in the new economy. Yale J. Regul. **19**(1), 171–300 (2002)
19. Theuvsen, L.: Vertical integration in the European package tour business. Ann. Tourism Res. **31**(2), 475–478 (2004)
20. Buehler, S., Schmutzler, A.: Intimidating competitors—Endogenous vertical integration and downstream investment in successive oligopoly. Int. J. Ind. Organ. **26**(1), 247–265 (2008)
21. O'Regan, A., et al.: Towards vertical integration in general practice education: literature review and discussion paper. Ir. J. Med. Sci. **182**(3), 319–324 (2013)
22. Vidic, B., Weitlauf, H.: Horizontal and vertical integration of academic disciplines in the medical school curriculum. Clin. Anat. **15**(3), 233–235 (2002)
23. Dahle, L., Brynhildsen, J., Fallsberg, M., Rundquist, I., Hammar, M.: Pros and cons of vertical integration between clinical medicine and basic science within a problem-based undergraduate medical curriculum: examples and experiences from Linköping, Sweden. Med. Teach. **24**(3), 280–285 (2002)
24. Wijnen-Meijer, M., Ten Cate, O., Van Der Schaaf, M., Borleffs, J.: Vertical integration in medical school: effect on the transition to postgraduate training. Med. Educ. **44**(3), 272–279 (2010)
25. Kennedy, E.: Beyond vertical integration–community based medical education. Aust. Fam. Physician **35**(11), 901–903 (2006)
26. Thomson, J.: A framework for vertical integration in general practice education and training. General Practice Education and Training Ltd., Canberra (2003)
27. General Practitioners Education and Training: A Framework for Vertical Integration in GP Education and Training. General Practice Education and Training Ltd., Canberra (2003)
28. Case, J., Marshall, D.: Between deep and surface: procedural approaches to learning in engineering education contexts. Stud. High. Educ. **29**(5), 605–615 (2004)
29. Marton, F., Säljö, R.: On qualitative differences in learning: I—outcome and process. Br. J. Educ. Psychol. **46**(1), 4–11 (1976)
30. Marton, F., Säaljö, R.: On qualitative differences in learning—II outcome as a function of the learner's conception of the task. Br. J. Educ. Psychol. **46**(2), 115–127 (1976)
31. Marton, F., Säljö, R.: Approaches to learning. In: Marton, F., Hounsell, D.J., Entwistle, N. J. (eds.) The experience of learning, 2nd edn. Scottish Academic Press, Edinburgh (1997)

32. Marshall, D.: The Relationship between Learning Conceptions, Approaches to Learning, and Learning Outcomes in Foundation Year Engineering Students (1995)
33. Ramsden, P.: The context of learning in academic departments. Experience Learn. **2**, 198–216 (1997)
34. Pask, G., Scott, B.: Learning strategies and individual competence. Int. J. Man-Mach. Stud. **4** (3), 217–253 (1972)

Language Learning in a Cognitive and Immersive Environment Using Contextualized Panoramic Imagery

Samuel Chabot[1,2]([✉]), Jaimie Drozdal[1,2], Yalun Zhou[1,2], Hui Su[1,2], and Jonas Braasch[1,2]

[1] Rensselaer Polytechnic Institute, Troy, NY, USA
{chabos2,drozdj3,zhouy12,braasj}@rpi.edu
[2] IBM T.J. Watson Research Center, Yorktown Heights, NY, USA
huisuibmres@us.ibm.com
https://cisl.rpi.edu

Abstract. Immersive technologies augmented with AI for foreign language learning are currently uncommon. The Rensselaer Mandarin Project is a cognitive and immersive classroom that facilitates cultural and foreign language learning beyond a traditional classroom setting. Students perform tasks through intelligent interactions including authentic dialogues with multiple AI agents and multimodal gestures. Street View technology has the potential to further enhance foreign language learning and cultural knowledge acquisition in the Mandarin Project. Real-world panoramic scenes immerse learners in new locations and can provide richer context for more meaningful language learning. Students embark on "field trips" with cultural, historical, and lingual relevance at human-scale. Multiple learning opportunities and interactions are constructed for the various types of scenes students visit: vocabulary games, relevant AI agent dialogues, and informational lessons on cultural elements. The Mandarin Project will be assessed during a six-week classroom experience in the summer of 2019.

Keywords: Immersive learning · Virtual environment · Chinese as a foreign language · Multimodal interaction

1 Introduction

The Rensselaer Mandarin Project[1] is at the forefront of advanced research in cognitive and immersive classrooms for language learning. The AI-equipped immersive room, also referred to as the Cognitive and Immersive Room (CIR), currently allows learners of Chinese as a foreign language to experience a virtual trip to China through explorations and interactions in a virtual Chinese restaurant, Chinese street market, and Chinese garden. These explorations are facilitated

---

[1] https://apnews.com/3babfede5f6e4190ba5cebaa4eaebc81.

C. Stephanidis (Ed.): HCII 2019, CCIS 1034, pp. 202–209, 2019.
https://doi.org/10.1007/978-3-030-23525-3_26

by unique dialogues with various AI agents and include multimodal interactions such as scene navigation, scavenger hunts, and tai chi practice [2]. The Mandarin Project focuses on task-based language learning and supports the eight pedagogical requirements laid forth by Willis [19].

The ways in which the Mandarin Project currently supports these requirements are described in detail in [9]. It should be noted that the Mandarin Project is a supplemental tool and is designed for students who have learned the vocabulary and sentence structures required to complete these tasks through their classroom instruction.

1.1 Street View Inspiration

Google Maps with Street View provides 360° street-level imagery of global locations [17]. The inspiration to include Google Street View images into the Mandarin Project alongside the virtual world content came from a project for rapidly displaying real-world locations at human-scale in the CIR. The application of this technology in the language and cultural acquisition realm quickly became apparent. Using Street View panoramic images provides efficient production of content that is highly immersive and realistic.

1.2 Summer 2019 Course

In the summer of 2019, the Mandarin Project will be incorporated into a six-week summer course at Rensselaer Polytechnic Institute. *AI-Assisted Immersive Chinese* includes in-class instruction with a professor and lab hours in the CIR with two complementary experiences that make up the Mandarin Project. In addition to three existing virtual world scenes [2], the summer course includes a virtual university campus and immersive static, panoramic scenes displayed using Google Street View imagery. Students travel across China via these scenes, from major cities to ancient water towns.

The goals of *AI-Assisted Immersive Chinese* are to **immerse** students in real-life locations and scenarios that allow them to **explore** and that **expose** them to authentic speaking situations and linguistic and cultural norms across China. Students **connect** with each other and **compare** the cultural and linguistic differences between their own daily life and that of others living in China, as well as the cultural variety across places and generations.

2 Literature Review

2.1 Immersive Language Learning

Virtual immersive learning is recognized by many experts in the community and the applications to language learning are constantly explored. Interactive simulations and games are associated with superior cognitive outcomes in comparison to respective traditional teaching methods [13]. To achieve immersion, an educator can use multimedia (e.g. videos) or AR/VR applications. Taguchi, Li and Tang [18] had success in creating a scenario-based interactive environment to teach formulaic expressions by presenting videos and having students enter answers to questions about the videos. Canto and Ondaraa [5], Guzel and Aydin [10], and Yamazaki found significant effects of Internet-based 3D worlds on language performance. More literature on immersive environments for educational purposes can be found in [3,7,13].

2.2 Google Street View for Learning

Currently there are only a handful of tools that utilize Google Street View technology for learning and even fewer for foreign language learning. Google has its own tool, Google Expedition[2], that allows educators to tag points of interest in Street View images with descriptions and narratives. In addition to this tool, Google developed Google Cardboard[3], a VR headset that enables a virtual reality experience for students via Google Expedition [6].

Blue Mars Lite is an integration of Google Street View and Bar Mars a virtual world with 3D avatars. Ya-Chun Shih explored the use of this environment for language and cultural learning through a qualitative case study and found that it improved student attitudes but lacked the versatility needed to support language learners [16]. Shih similarly explored the integration of Street View images into the virtual world of VEC3D for facilitating the acquisition of English as a foreign language [17]. Learners navigate the virtual environment to accomplish two goal-based scenarios by controlling their animated avatars and collaborating with others through text and/or voice chat. The students and teacher found the system to be beneficial for language learning.

3 Enabling Street View

3.1 The CIR

Most VR-related initiatives now focus on personal devices, such as head-mounted displays, which remove an individual from his or her environment. Our system takes a different approach to empower group activities. The Cognitive and Immersive Room (CIR) features a nearly 360° circular panoramic screen measuring 3.8 m tall and 12 m in diameter. A single PC utilizes a specialized warping software to blend five projectors into a seamless desktop. The screen is of a microperforated PVC material for acoustic transparency. This allows a spatial audio system (currently eight loudspeakers, expandable up to a 512-channel wave field synthesis array) to be located behind the screen. The CIR is spatially aware of its users through a network of Kinect sensors and Point-To-Zoom cameras. Gesture controls, such as pointing and selecting (shown in Fig. 1), are enabled via software utilizing the data of these sensors [8]. Users may speak to the system

[2] https://edu.google.com/products/vr-ar/expeditions/.
[3] https://vr.google.com/cardboard/.

using a series of microphones. Natural Language Processing (NLP) performed by the IBM Watson Assistant service[4] discerns an appropriate action or response based on the interpreted intent of the user.

Fig. 1. Left: student approaching police officer for dialogue interaction, right: student using gesture to engage cultural information (Street View imagery: Google ©2019)

3.2   Developing Street View Content for the Mandarin Project

Content development for the summer course expands on our research into the linguistic and cultural knowledge necessary when one travels abroad to China, and the two experiences of the summer course are developed in parallel. In collaboration with the professor who will teach the summer course, we consult Chinese textbooks, online resources, and various books on Chinese culture and travel. Survival phrases and dialogues essential to study abroad programs, such as greetings, asking for help, exchanging currency, taking a taxi, etc. are the language elements of focus. We explore cultural elements in two parallel ways: by location and by theme. We start with important cities and towns in China that the professor requests: *Beijing, Shanghai, Suzhou, Yiwu, Wuzhen, Guangzhou, Lizhou.* We simultaneously search for content relating to the following themes: *hobbies, western culture, seasons, festivals, holidays, shopping, commerce, historical sights, arts, transportation, food, gardens, and temples.* This research provides the content to be supported by Street View imagery. To search for Street View content we explore various locations on Google Maps[5] and also developed a tool of our own using the Maps API to quickly search and explore panoramic images on the immersive screen in the CIR. For each high-quality panoramic image we asses its pedagogical value with respect to its linguistic and cultural elements. This content is chosen and developed in combination with the various technologies of the room for three specific types of interactions for students: vocabulary practice, dialogues with AI agents, and cultural presentations.

---

[4] https://www.ibm.com/cloud/watson-assistant/.
[5] https://www.google.com/maps.

3.3 Scene Navigation

Students carry out larger quests comprised of individual scenes, which are linked using navigable waypoints. For example, students navigate multiple locations along a popular pedestrian street in Shanghai to emerge at the Bund along the Huangpu River with views of the skyline. Along the way, students are presented with the three interactions, described in Sects. 3.4, 3.5 and 3.6. Student progress (dialogues performed, vocabulary words practiced, etc.) is logged and made available to both student and professor. Navigation between and interaction within the scenes occur through multiple modalities. The gesture and tracking systems in the CIR enable students to select interactive objects and waypoints by pointing an open hand at them and closing it into a fist. The system is also aware of students' spatial positions, and approaching the screen automatically activates content at that location [15]. Along with gestures, students can issue verbal commands such as "take me there" to transition between scenes. Audio feedback is spatialized for the multichannel array to provide directional cues for focusing attention to a particular location [12]. Cultural immersion is further enhanced using in-situ audio recordings of China. Scene navigation and the tools that enable it support "learner-regulated thoughts and actions for developing specific skills and general proficiency" that are necessary when learning a culture and language [14].

3.4 Cultural Elements

A powerful advantage of panoramic Street View imagery is the vast amount of real-world cultural content that can be found within images. Entire lessons can be constructed using direct examples of topics and concepts studied in a classroom setting. Students may learn about the martial art of tai chi in the classroom, practice it in the virtual Chinese garden, and visit scenes with practicing groups in public gardens and parks in the CIR (see Fig. 1). Many of these cultural elements are explicitly identified to the students through interactive tags. Opening these presents a concise explanation and its cultural significance. Additionally, students may want to know more about untagged elements in the scene, prompting spontaneous asides from the professor.

3.5 Vocabulary Practice

Each interactive scene offers the opportunity to practice vocabulary associated with objects found within it. The vocabulary are manually embedded in on-screen tags near the target objects, and selecting one opens a practice panel. This panel is populated with four vocabulary words, one of which is the target object and the other three are randomly chosen from the course vocabulary bank. This creates a multiple-choice minigame experience. After a student makes a choice via the gesture or voice controls, the correct answer is revealed and the minigame continues using images chosen at random from our database. The Watson Assistant Visual Recognition service[6] classifies the images based on the

---
[6] https://www.ibm.com/watson/services/visual-recognition/.

vocabulary bank and provides the next correct answer to the minigame. For each correct answer a student earns a reward in the form of virtual RMB that is added to his or her in-game wallet.

3.6 Dialogue Practice

When traveling in a foreign place it is imperative to know survival phrases. These are everyday and emergency words or phrases needed for navigating life such as "Where is the bathroom?", "I don't understand.", and "Help, I am lost.". Persons and objects within the scene provide context for practicing these phrases. Using the Watson Assistant Natural Language Processing service, we construct short and natural dialogues and use relevant people and objects in the scene to embody them. For example, a police officer in the scene, shown in Fig. 1, may prompt a student with "Can I help you?" to which a student may reply with what they are looking for. In a 2018 user study with the Mandarin Project, 15 students interacted with the AI waiter in the virtual Chinese restaurant. On the post-study survey one student stated "I loved the fact that it was a place to experience real life interaction while being able to make mistakes".

3.7 Integration

The Mandarin Project utilizes Google Street View panorama differently than existing methods for the following reasons: Our system is enabled in the CIR, a state of the art 360° panoramic display that stands 14 feet tall and provides human-scale immersion. This large scale environment does not require students to wear headsets to be immersed in a scene, and therefore, allows them to physically traverse the space and collaborate on tasks. The CIR enables multimodal interactions, a new paradigm in immersive language learning environments. Students use dialogues and gestures to communicate with the system and can approach an object or person in the scene to interact with it. Interactions are student-led as students can select which content to engage with and can independently explore and navigate scenes. This enhances student ownership of the learning. Language is practiced through multiple choice mini-games and interactive dialogues with AI agents embodied by people and objects in the Street View imagery. Our system includes gamification elements not seen in other tools utilizing Street View, such as earning virtual currency for completing interactions.

3.8 Challenges

While the tremendous amount of available Street View images provides a plethora of scenes to choose from, the process of sifting through to find the most appropriate and relevant can be tedious and time-consuming. While popular locations are inundated with choices, imagery at lesser known sites may be scarce or nonexistent. Additionally, restrictions on Google in China limit the company from collecting imagery as it does in other countries. Therefore, much of the content is user-submitted and not vetted for quality before posting.

4   Future Directions

The current system allows for single or compound words in vocabulary practice. We plan an update to include grammatical structures and phrases. Similar to [18], the incorrect answers can be specifically generated to help pinpoint what types of errors students are making.

Another step in the continuing development of the Street View tool is creating a user-friendly interface for those with no computer science expertise (i.e. teachers and students) to create and add content. Google provides two web-based tools for creating storytelling content: Tour Builder[7] for Google Earth and Tour Creator[8] for Google Expeditions. However, our system is designed for in-depth content and interactions that these tools do not support.

4.1   User Study

The effects of immersive Street View panoramic imagery on foreign language learning require further research [17]. Throughout the six-week summer course we will be running a user study to assess student progress and satisfaction with the different tools. We will use performance-based standards to assess the learning outcomes following the guidelines of the American Council on the Teaching of Foreign Languages (ACTFL) outlined in the World-Readiness Standards for Learning Languages [4].

5   Conclusion

In 1976, Hall [11] developed the iceberg analogy of culture. Just as only 10% of an iceberg is visible above water, only 10% of a group's cultural characteristics are obvious or explicit (e.g. food, clothing). The remaining 90% is hidden and includes beliefs, values, and attitudes [1,14]. Hall proposes that the only way to see below the surface is to actively participate in the culture. Applying Google Street View images in the cognitive and immersive classroom allows students to do so. In the Mandarin Project, students are able to experience cultural norms, acquire vocabulary knowledge, and practice common tasks across a number of themes, thereby beginning to uncover the hidden 90% of the "cultural iceberg".

Acknowledgments. This research is supported by the Cognitive and Immersive Systems Laboratory (CISL), a collaboration between Rensselaer Polytechnic Institute and IBM Research through IBM's AI Horizon Network. The authors would like to express gratitude to all of the researchers contributing to the Mandarin Project.

---

[7] https://tourbuilder.withgoogle.com/.
[8] https://vr.google.com/tourcreator/.

References

1. The iceberg model, localization and cultural context, August 2018. https://unitedlanguagegroup.com/blog/iceberg-model-localization-cultural-context/
2. Allen, D., Divekar, R.R., Drozdal, J., Balagyozyan, L.: The Rensselaer Mandarin Project - A cognitive and immersive language learning environment (2019)
3. Blyth, C.: Immersive technologies and language learning. Foreign Lang. Ann. **51**(1), 225–232 (2018)
4. Board, N.S.C.: World-readiness standards for learning languages (2015)
5. Canto, S., Ondarra, K.J.: Language learning effects through the integration of synchronous online communication: the case of video communication and second life. Lang. Learn. High. Educ. **7**(1), 21–53 (2017)
6. Clark, H., Duckworth, S., Heil, J., Hotler, D., Piercy, D., Thumann, L.: The Google Cardboard Book: Explore, Engage, and Educate with Virtual Reality. EdTech Team, Irvine (2017)
7. Divekar, R.R., et al.: Interaction challenges in AI equipped environments built to teach foreign languages through dialogue and task-completion. In: Proceedings of the 2018 on Designing Interactive Systems Conference 2018, pp. 597–609. ACM (2018)
8. Divekar, R.R., et al.: CIRA: an architecture for building configurable immersive smart-rooms. In: Arai, K., Kapoor, S., Bhatia, R. (eds.) IntelliSys 2018. AISC, vol. 869, pp. 76–95. Springer, Cham (2019). https://doi.org/10.1007/978-3-030-01057-7_7
9. Divekar, R.R., Zhou, Y., Allen, D., Drozdal, J., Su, H.: Building human-scale intelligent immersive spaces for foreign language learning. iLRN 2018 Montana, p. 94 (2018)
10. Güzel, S., Aydin, S.: The effect of second life on speaking achievement. Online Submission **6**(4), 236–245 (2016)
11. Hall, E.T.: Beyond Culture. Dobleday & Company, New York (1976)
12. Lee, W.: Using Auditory Cues to Perceptually Extract Visual Data in Collaborative, Immersive Big-Data Display Systems (2017)
13. Lin, T.J., Lan, Y.J.: Language learning in virtual reality environments: past, present, and future. J. Educ. Tech. Soc. **18**(4), 486–497 (2015)
14. Oxford, R.L., Gkonou, C.: Interwoven: culture, language, and learning strategies. Stud. Second Lang. Learn. Teach. **8**(2), 403–426 (2018)
15. Sharma, G., Braasch, J., Radke, R.: Interactions in a human-scale immersive environment: the craive-lab. In: Cross-Surface 2016, in Conjunction with the ACM International Conference on Interactive Surfaces and Spaces (2017)
16. Shih, Y.C.: A virtual walk through london: culture learning through a cultural immersion experience. Comput. Assist. Lang. Learn. **28**(5), 407–428 (2015)
17. Shih, Y.C.: Contextualizing language learning with street view panoramas. In: Integrating Multi-User Virtual Environments in Modern Classrooms, pp. 74–91. IGI Global (2018)
18. Taguchi, N., Li, Q., Tang, X.: Learning chinese formulaic expressions in a scenario-based interactive environment. Foreign Lang. Ann. **50**(4), 641–660 (2017)
19. Willis, J.: A Framework for Task-Based Learning. Pearson PTR, Harlow (1996)

Perception Differences Between Students and Teachers of Undergraduate Industrial Design Core Courses

Wenzhi Chen[(✉)] [iD]

Chang Gung University, Taoyuan 33302, Taiwan, R.O.C.
wenzhi@mail.cgu.edu.tw

Abstract. The perception of education will influence the learning and teaching process and achievement. The purpose of this study is to explore the perceptions of the undergraduate industrial design core courses. First, 32 students and 9 instructors were interviewed to collect the qualitative data for formulating the framework. The framework consisted of seven scales, including Image, Motivation, Objectives, Activities, Resources, Evaluation, and Future Development. Then, the questionnaire was designed according to the framework. There were 406 students and 24 instructors participating in the survey. The Results demonstrated that students' perceptions are similar to instructors. The major difference is the degree of perception. The main differences of the perceptions are on the learning process/method and career development.

Keywords: Design education · Core course · Learning perception ·
Teaching perception

1 Introduction

The perception of education will influence the learning and teaching process and achievement [1]. The students and teachers are the stakeholders in a learning system. They have their own perceptions of learning and teaching. Congruent perceptions contribute to better teaching-learning processes and help students achieve the best learning outcomes [1].

The design is one of the important capabilities of enterprise transformation from Original Equipment Manufacturer (OEM) to Original Design Manufacturer (ODM)/ Original Brand Manufacture (OBM) and success. It is important to educate the excellent designer for the industry. The core courses are the most important in industrial design education. Students integrate and practice the knowledge and skills learned from surrounding courses [2]. The main pedagogy of the industrial design core course is the studio. Interaction and communication are the main activities involving learning to design.

In the actual teaching experience, it is found that the learning/teaching process and outcome affect by students and instructors' different feelings and perceptions of the curriculum and design learning projects.

© Springer Nature Switzerland AG 2019
C. Stephanidis (Ed.): HCII 2019, CCIS 1034, pp. 210–216, 2019.
https://doi.org/10.1007/978-3-030-23525-3_27

The purpose of this study is to investigate the perceptions of students and instructors of the undergraduate industrial design core courses and to explore the relationship and influences between them.

2 Literature Review

Learning is a complex process of skill and knowledge development. The outcome of learning cannot be only presented by exam score, but by other indicators including student interest in the subject, their critical thinking skills, interpersonal outcomes, and other broad course outcomes [3, 4].

The perception of learning as something not just represented by the outcome will also affect the learning process. Könings and Seidel [1] illustrated that students and instructors have their own perceptions of education. A positive perception can lead to a better learning and teaching process and achievement. Velada and Caetano [5] also found that occupational satisfaction and affective and utility reactions are associated with the perception of learning and the perceived training transfer. Further, the results also reveal that the perception of learning fully mediates the relationship between occupational satisfaction and perceived training transfer, which partially mediates the relationship between affective reactions, utility reactions, and perceived training transfer. Marzano [6] point out that positive attitudes and perceptions are important factors for learning.

The perceptions of education include different scales. Könings, Seidel [1] used the Inventory of Perceived Study Environment Extended (IPSEE) to collect the perception data, which includes 8 scales: (1) Fascinating contents: the learning contents are interesting, challenging, and personally relevant for students. (2) Productive learning: indicates little emphasis on the sole reproduction of learning contents. (3) Integration: concerns integration of new knowledge with prior knowledge, different knowledge domains, and knowledge and skills. (4) Student autonomy: measures attention paid to students' self-steering concerning the content of learning, the way of learning, and time planning. (5) Interaction: incorporates collaboration with peers and interaction with the teacher. (6) Differentiation: inquires about opportunities for students to choose and tackle different tasks, solve problems in different ways, and use different learning materials. (7) Clarity of goals: includes items about the clarity of instructional goals and task demands. (8) Personalization: measures the distance between teachers and students, and the availability of support from teachers. Kennedy [7] also developed an inventory scale that includes: (1) Supervising teacher support; (2) Administrative support; (3) Fellow teacher support; (4) Student teacher involvement; (5) Clarity; (6) Autonomy; (7) Task orientation; (8) Work pressure.

3 Method

A two-phase study was designed to explore the perceptions of the undergraduate industrial design core course. First, the interview was conducted to collect qualitative data. Then, the questionnaire was designed according to the results of the interview and related references. The quantitative data was collected through a survey with a designed questionnaire to verify the results of the interview.

3.1 Interview

The interview was conducted to explore and formulate the framework of the perception of the undergraduate industrial design core course. The focus group interview of students and the individual interview of instructors was conducted to collect the data. There were 32 undergraduate industrial students and 9 instructors who participated in the interview. Of the 32 students, 6 were in first year, 8 were in second year, 7 were in third year, and 11 were in fourth year. 14 were male and 18 were female. There was 1 professor, 3 associate professors, and 5 assistant professors.

Each interview took about one hour, the content was recorded and analyzed using the qualitative data analysis and research software ATLAS.ti. Finally, a framework of the perception of undergraduate industrial design core courses was formulated.

3.2 Questionnaire Survey

A questionnaire survey was developed to collect data to understand the perceptions of students and instructors. A survey was conducted to collect quantitative data with a questionnaire designed according to the results of the interview and related references. All the answers were on the 5 levels Likert scales, with 1 representing "Strongly disagree", and 5 representing "Strongly agree".

There were 406 undergraduate industrial students from public universities, private universities, public universities of science and technology, and private universities of science and technology that participated in the survey. There were 158 (38.9%) male and 248 (61.1%) female students. There were 24 instructors participating in the survey, including lecturers (16.7%), assistant professors (58.3%), associate professors (16.7%), and professors (8.3%). Their teaching experience was from 2–26 years (average = 13.7, SD = 7.4).

All the data was entered into a Microsoft Excel datasheet, and then sorted and checked. Finally, the data was analyzed using IBM SPSS Statistics software with factor analysis and correlation analysis.

4   Results

4.1 The Results of Interview

The content of the interview was coded with a ground theory approach. The 1.306 codes were then produced and categorized. Finally, the framework of the perception of undergraduate industrial design core courses was formulated consisting of seven scales, including *Image*, *Motivation*, *Objectives*, *Activities*, *Resources*, *Evaluation*, and *Future Development*. The framework and the items were presented in Fig. 1.

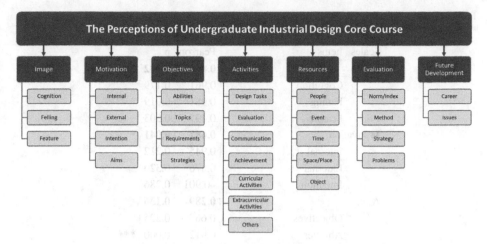

Fig. 1. The framework of perception of undergraduate industrial design core course.

The main findings of the interview include:

- *Image*: The images of core courses are different between students and instructors. The images of students are related to their learning experiences, but instructors' images are related to their teaching experiences. They have the same image with the problem solving on design.
- *Motivation*: The main motivation of student learning is interesting and necessary for their future career. For instructors, their main motivation is their ideal.
- *Objectives*: The main objective of students' learning is to focus on learning design skills. But instructors think students should learn more professional abilities, including skills, knowledge, and design thinking.
- *Activities*: Both students and instructors regard "learning by doing" as the best way for learning design.
- *Resources*: Students and instructors think the working space and classmates are important. Students care more about money.
- *Evaluation*: The criteria and the standard are important. But students more care about their design can be recognized.
- *Future Development*: Students care about their career, but instructors care about the trends of the design industry.

4.2   The Results of Questionnaire Survey

The perceptions of undergraduate industrial design core courses were collected through a questionnaire survey.

Table 1 presents the results of the correlation analysis of perceptions between students and instructors. They were significant moderately correlated in total. All the scales have significant correlation, except the *Aims* scale. They are highly correlated with *Activities*, *Image*, *Evaluation*, and *Future Development*.

Table 1. The correlation analysis of perceptions between students and instructors. (* p < 0.05, ** p < 0.01, *** p < 0.001)

Scales	Items	Pearson	p	
Image		**0.803**	**0.002**	**
	Cognition	0.961	0.179	
	Felling	0.981	0.019	*
	Feature	0.497	0.503	
Motivation		**0.687**	**0.041**	*
	Internal	0.945	0.212	
	External	0.876	0.320	
	Intention	−0.901	0.286	
Aims		**0.289**	**0.136**	
	Objectives	0.660	0.225	
	Abilities	0.912	0.000	***
	Topics	0.991	0.084	
	Requirements	0.113	0.887	
	Strategies	0.936	0.064	
Activities		**0.833**	**0.000**	***
	Design tasks	0.808	0.052	
	Evaluation	–	–	
	Communication	0.098	0.938	
	Achievement	1.000	0.000	***
	Curricular activities	0.959	0.041	*
	Extracurricular activities	0.986	0.106	
Resources		**0.597**	**0.005**	**
	People	0.735	0.038	*
	Event	0.966	0.166	
	Time	−1.000	0.000	***
	Space/place	0.987	0.104	
	Object	−0.078	0.922	
Evaluation		**0.734**	**0.000**	***
	Norm/index	0.538	0.213	
	Method	0.835	0.371	
	Strategy	0.938	0.226	
	Problems	0.349	0.396	
Future development		**0.712**	**0.047**	*
	Career	0.891	0.042	*
	Issues	0.571	0.613	
Total		**0.585**	**0.000**	***

The results demonstrated that students' perceptions are similar to their instructors according to the results of a descriptive statistic. There are still a little different from instructors' perceptions of some scales and items. The majority of differences are not different perceptions, but rather, different degrees.

Some students' scores were significantly higher than instructors. These items demonstrated that students have more ideals about design impact and value. They think design can change the world. They pay more attention to their own design abilities and design achievements, and hope that they will be recognized through these performances. In addition, students also pay more attention to their own design style and worry that the skills and knowledge learned in the school cannot meet the needs of the industry in the future.

The instructors' perceptions demonstrate that they think the core courses are most important for learning design. It can increase the abilities of students for their career development. They also think the learning process and design process are important.

The main differences between students and instructors are the learning process, methods, and career development. The instructors believe that students should follow the rules and requirements they proposed in the learning/teaching process. But, students hope they can control their design directions and style by themselves. The instructors also hope students can do design related jobs when they graduate. But, students do not agree.

5 Concluding Remarks

This study used a mixed approach with the qualitative interview and quantitative survey to explore the perceptions of students and instructors on undergraduate industrial design core courses.

The results have shown that students' perceptions are similar to instructors. But there are some differences on the degree. The perceptions of education will affect the learning and teaching process and outcomes. It needs to be verified through inferences with the perception differences.

User experience is important in contemporary design. For the education system, it is helpful to have a better experience in the learning/teaching process and performances. If the students and teachers' experiences and perceptions can be understood and apply to improving communication and interaction quality.

The results of this study can deepen the understanding of industrial design education and provide a reference for student and teachers' teaching. The results also can be referenced for further study.

Acknowledgments. This research was funded by the Ministry of Science and Technology of Taiwan under grant numbers MOST 104-2410-H-182-018 and MOST 105-2410-H-182-011. Thanks are extended to all participants and research assistants for their contributions to these projects.

References

1. Könings, K.D., et al.: Differences between students' and teachers' perceptions of education: profiles to describe congruence and friction. Instr. Sci. **42**(1), 11–30 (2014)
2. Demirbas, O.O., Demirkan, H.: Learning styles of design students and the relationship of academic performance and gender in design education. Learn. Instr. **17**(3), 345–359 (2007)

3. Centra, J.A., Gaubatz, N.B.: Student perceptions of learning and instructional effectiveness in college courses. Educational Testing Service (2005)
4. Koon, J., Murray, H.G.: Using multiple outcomes to validate student ratings of overall teacher effectiveness. J. High. Educ. **66**, 61–81 (1995)
5. Velada, R., Caetano, A.: Training transfer: the mediating role of perception of learning. J. Eur. Ind. Training **31**(4), 283–296 (2007)
6. Marzano, R.J.: A Different Kind of Classroom: Teaching With Dimensions of Learning. ASCD (1992)
7. Kennedy, J.: A study of learning environment in the extended practicum of a pre-service teacher education course at a Catholic university [electronic resource]. In: Research Services. Australian Catholic University (2006)

Towards an Augmented Reality-Based Mobile Math Learning Game System

Lin Deng[1]([✉]), Jing Tian[2], Christopher Cornwell[2], Victoria Phillips[2], Long Chen[1], and Amro Alsuwaida[1]

[1] Department of Computer and Information Sciences, Towson University, Towson, MD, USA
{ldeng,lchen13,aalsuw2}@towson.edu
[2] Department of Mathematics, Towson University, Towson, MD, USA
{jtian,ccornwell,vphillips}@towson.edu

Abstract. Learning math is critical in every student's life. Even though math educators designed many teaching and learning approaches, students' low passing rates indicate that they have not found an effective methodology for studying math. In this paper, we propose an interdisciplinary approach to help students learn mathematics during and after classes, practice mathematics exercises, and increase the readiness for taking the exams in mathematics. Specifically, we design an Augmented Reality (AR) and mobile game-based mathematical learning approach for students to improve learning outcomes. Through the game, students gain the interest in the concepts of math and, at the same time, they have ongoing practice on the concepts and have gained the experience of solving math problems. The portability characteristic of the mobile game enables students to learn whenever and wherever they would like. The entertainment characteristic of the mobile game boosts and maintains students' interest in learning and practicing mathematics. The integration of text, graphics, video, and audio into a student's real-time environment by AR provides a rich enhancement comparing to the traditional learning and teaching approaches. Blended with our educational gamification techniques and pedagogical methodologies, our game will increase student motivation towards preparing for math exams by being highly engaging, and students will enjoy the game to help prepare for exams. We will collect experimental results and students' feedback from our experimental study and conduct quantitative and qualitative analysis and report our findings. Eventually, this research will be a valuable avenue for mathematics teachers, students, and parents.

Keywords: Augmented Reality · Math education · Gamification

1 Introduction

From elementary school to college, people learn different levels and subjects of mathematics, and use mathematics in every aspect of their life and career.

© Springer Nature Switzerland AG 2019
C. Stephanidis (Ed.): HCII 2019, CCIS 1034, pp. 217–225, 2019.
https://doi.org/10.1007/978-3-030-23525-3_28

However, many students are not good at mathematics. Statistical data show that, in 2017, in a county of USA only a third of students passed a national math exam [2]. There are many reasons a student fails the exam, such as insufficient practice, boring lectures and in-class activities, inappropriate learning pace, etc.

As a research group consisting of mathematics scientists, computer scientists, and educational scientists, we propose an inter-disciplinary approach to help learn the concepts in mathematics during and after classes, practice mathematics exercises, and increase the readiness for taking the exams in mathematics. Specifically, we design an Augmented Reality and mobile game-based mathematical learning approach for students to improve learning outcomes. Through the game, students gain interest in the concepts of math and, at the same time, they have ongoing practice on the concepts and have gained the experience on solving math problems. The portability characteristic of the mobile game enables students to learn whenever and wherever they would like. The entertainment characteristic of the mobile game boosts and maintains students' interest in learning and practicing mathematics. The integration of text, graphics, video, and audio into a student's real-time environment by Augmented Reality provides a rich enhancement compared to the traditional learning and teaching approaches.

This paper introduces our motivation, design principles, main features and architectures of the game, and also describes the experiment we use for evaluating the game. The contributions of our study can be summarized as follows: (1) Our proposed game employs an emerging technology, Augmented Reality, to provide an enhanced level of gaming and studying experience; (2) Our mobile game gives students a new way of learning math and practicing exam questions; (3) Our mobile game initiates a new learning approach by incorporating customized learning pace, remote learning progress management, and parental control.

The rest of this paper is organized as follows: Sect. 2 goes through the background of the research; Sect. 3 describes the system design; Sect. 4 introduces the experimental study. Section 5 gives an overview of related work, and Sect. 6 includes conclusion and suggestion on future work.

2   Background

Gamification [6] is a methodology that applies game elements, such as competing, rewarding, and entertaining, to non-game environment or circumstances, to provide a much more pleasant experience, to motivate and engage people's interest, and to generate more effective outcomes. It has been found to be very helpful in educational application [11].

AR is an emerging technology that provides rich enhanced information in the form of text, graphics, audio, and video integrated into the real-world environment. With the rapid development of mobile computing power and image processing algorithms, AR is no longer a very expensive technology that requires advanced equipment to facilitate. A camera and screen of a smartphone are already enough to enable us to virtually step into an "augmented" new world.

3 System Design

This section introduces our design ideas regarding the functionality of the AR-based educational game, and provides an overview of the system architecture.

3.1 Functionality of the AR-based Educational Game

This section introduces the motivation, design and main features of the game.

AR Integration: As an emerging technology, AR has started to be employed by IT practitioners in many fields. Many games also start to leverage AR to increase entertainment and provide players with an enhanced level of gaming experience. One of the major features of our game is to incorporate AR, to give students a new type of learning experience. Specifically, our game leverages the AR Foundation package [1] in Unity [3], one of the most popular 3D game design platform. Aided by AR and location sensors in mobile devices, our game enables students to play and practice math questions at home, interact with their virtual pets and collectibles within the environment of their own home settings. Figure 1 shows an example screenshot of our game. The game can render virtual pets in students' physical environment. Our motivation of having AR embedded into the game is that we would like to encourage students to practice math questions at home, to give students more opportunities to expose the world of math, to boost their interest in playing and learning, and to ultimately increase their math skills.

Fig. 1. An example AR screenshot of our game

Timing: It is acknowledged that most math exams require students to finish a number of questions within a fixed time limit. During our class visits to a local middle school, we also observed that math teachers specifically designed their class activities to enable students to practice math questions in a given time limit, with the goal of increasing students' speed of solving and answering questions. With the similar motivation as teachers' in-class activities, we introduce timers to every scenario when students answer questions in our game, so that the game can indirectly help students practice their math skills and get students prepared for math exams.

Self-Paced Learning: Educators should accommodate students' diverse background and provide personalized learning and study experience. According to this principle, in this game, we design this self-paced learning feature that provides students a customized learning experience. For example, if a student finds that it is so easy to answer the questions, he/she may be bored and may not like to play the game anymore. To prevent this from happening, the game can automatically adjust the difficult levels of questions sent to the student's device, so the student can get challenged by harder questions and learn more knowledge. Teachers can customize the learning pace for every student based on students' progress. Also, the game AI can customize questions based on an individual student's frequent mistakes to let the student have more practice on the type of questions he/she is weak on.

Rewards and Incentives: Like playing regular games, rewards and incentives play a significant role in increasing the entertainment of games, recognizing users' achievement in games, and boosting users' interest. In our game, for example, students solve the most questions can receive in-game rewards from teachers, such as special badges, or out-game incentives, such as homework extra credits. Collectibles, such as tools, question hints, virtual foods and drinks, can help students answer questions, raise their in-game pets, and reward their study progress.

3.2 System Architecture

Figure 2 illustrates the general architecture of our proposed system. Our system includes four major interfaces for different types of users:

Student interface is the primary app installed on mobile devices that are used by students. It is also the medium that leverages AR technology to provide students with the innovative learning and gaming experience. Students play the AR game by practicing and solving math problems. The *central database* records every student's progress and performance, such as the number of correctly answered questions, the number of questions answered every day, the average speed of answering questions, etc.

Teacher's terminal is the interface provided to teachers to monitor students' progress, manage the database of practice questions, receive/send system-wide or personalized notifications, etc.

Knowledge experts is a special portal that enables math education experts to design and load new practice questions for students.

Parental control is the interface for students' parents to provide the necessary supervision to their children. For example, parents can set a time limit for the maximum hours that students can play the game every day, so that students do not get addicted to playing.

In addition to these four front-end interfaces, our proposed system includes the following major back-end modules:

Notification module is used to broadcast system-wide and personalized notifications, to students and teachers. For example, if a teacher uploads a new set of practice questions, he/she can initiate a system-wide notification to all the students. If a teacher finds a student has never practiced any questions for a while, she/he can notify the student regarding his/her progress.

Collectible management module and *Reward management module* provide the features of managing rewards and incentives. As described in the previous section, rewards and incentives are indispensable for a game to maintain students' interest, and they are one of the major advantages of our game compared to traditional learning approaches, because we can keep students playing and practicing as often as they can, wherever and whenever they like to.

Learning pace management module lets teachers manage students' different learning progress. This module provides self-paced learning features described in the previous section.

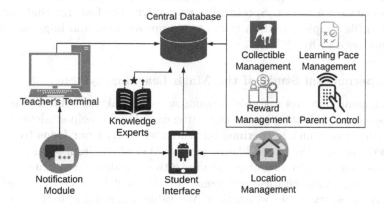

Fig. 2. System architecture

4   Evaluation and Experimental Study

Collaborating with local middle schools in USA, we design an experimental study to comprehensively evaluate the mobile game proposed in this paper and obtain important data for our future research. The students in the school need to take the PARCC assessments, in which math is an important part. The PARCC assessments were instituted in the state of Maryland in 2015. The PARCC assessments in math test a wide range of skills beyond problem-solving, including reading comprehension and analysis. According to 2017 PARCC results, less than half of students in grades 3–8 passed the English and math portions of the exam [2]. Underlying these results are genuine challenges that students and teachers face in their preparation for such a test, in and out of the classroom. This also highlights the urgency to implement a new mathematical learning approach, targeted at minimizing these new challenges.

4.1 Evaluation for the Game Development

For most software systems, obtaining users' feedback, observing how the systems are used, evaluating the functionality, usability, and performance are essential. Thus, in this research, we design an evaluation specifically to study how our users, i.e., students and teachers, use our game.

For the development of our game, we use the Agile software development process [5]. We organize each feature as a user story, and list acceptance tests of the user story. We bring the prototype to a small set of users and observe how they use the features. After that, we conduct a 30 min user interview, in which, 20 min are used for closed interview with prepared questions, and 10 min are used for open discussion, focusing on documenting and recording users' feedback, preference, and requirements. We conduct qualitative analysis based on the information we collect. Specifically, we analyze the features that our users like and dislike, implementation that needs improvement, and bugs and quality issues that need to fix.

4.2 Experimental Study of the Math Learning System

After our game becomes a stable version, we would like to conduct an experimental study to evaluate whether our game can actually help students improve their math. In our initial experimental study, we restrict our focus to the middle school students. We would like to recruit 20 students from local schools, by distributing the introduction of our study to these students. Students are free to participate our study and use our game. The consent from every participant's parents is necessary in our evaluation. We value maintaining participants' privacy as our highest priority task, so that we ask all of our team members to go through necessary training courses regarding behavior and human subjects experiments. All the data we collect are anonymized by a third party from the schools of participants. Every step of our experimental study is approved and monitored by the IRB from our university and local county public school board.

Among all the math subjects, Algebra is the most difficult for the middle school students because it involves a lot abstract concepts. In the middle school, students need to learn the fundamentals of algebra including variables, functions, quadratic equations, logarithms, etc. Therefore, as a first stage of a long-time project, our initial experimental study starts with middle school algebra as the subject. We will go onsite to the school and collect necessary experimental data, such as whether students are using our program, how long and how often they use it, what grades they receive from exams, what feedback they on the game, etc. Based on the experimental data we collect, we will further conduct quantitative and qualitative analysis, such as statistical analysis using appropriate statistical methods.

5 Related Work

Researchers have shown significant interest in investigating using computer games as a complement for standard teaching and learning approaches for many years. The research conducted by Kebritchi et al. [12] finds that educational mathematics computer games had a significant positive effect on students' mathematics achievement. In their study of 193 high school students and 10 teachers, students who played the games scored significantly higher on the district-wide math benchmark exam than students who did not play the games. Similarly, the research of Boyce et al. [4] finds that middle and high school students who played their computer game showed statistically significant learning improvement. The game they developed was able to increase student motivation and achieve higher learning gains in as little as 90 min. The latest empirical study involving 153 students, conducted by McLaren et al. [14], showed that a mathematics educational computer game can⁶ provide superior learning opportunities, be more engaging, and lead to significantly better gain scores in solving decimal problems.

The portability and convenience of mobile devices are expected to initiate a new trend of educational games. The paper of Diah et al. [7] discussed the development of an early prototype of an educational math mobile game. The paper of Ebner [8] introduced math mobile games they developed, and described their technical and pedagogical strategy. However, very few empirical studies are conducted based on mobile educational games, especially math games. Also, AR technology has been reported to be very effective in helping the understanding and improving the learning of different subjects for students, such as chemistry [13], physics [9], and physical education [10]. However, there are not many AR-based educational mobile games that can help students learn mathematics, practice mathematics problems, and prepare for standardized mathematical exams. There are also not many comprehensive applications provided to teachers to monitor students' learning, reviewing, and practicing progress. These are the aims of this project.

6 Conclusion and Future Work

Learning math is critical in every student's life. Even though educators designed many different teaching and learning approaches, students' low passing rate indicates that they have not found an effective methodology for studying math. There are many math games on the market. However, very few of them are designed for the comprehensive practice of the subject of math. Meanwhile, very few of them are based on mobile platforms. None of them incorporate AR, the emerging technology. None of them provide teachers a convenient approach to monitor students' learning and practicing progress and enable students to learn based on their own pace.

As an inter-disciplinary research team, in this paper, we propose an AR-based mobile math learning game, to help students learn math and practice math exams. We design a controlled experimental study to evaluate our approach. Our game will increase student motivation towards preparing for math exams by being highly engaging, and students will enjoy the game to help prepare for exams. This platform will also increase students' practice of skills needed to be successful on the math exams because it is not the traditional drill style practice. It will encourage mathematical independence and bridge the gap between in-school and at-home exam preparation. We hope that this AR-based mobile learning game will not only increase student performance on mathematics exams, but also increase student confidence in the area of mathematics as a whole.

The research into an AR-based mobile math learning game has just started. There are still avenues for future research, evaluation, and improvement. This research will prove to be a valuable avenue for mathematics teachers, students, and parents. We will collect experimental results and students' feedback from our experimental study. We will conduct quantitative and qualitative analysis and report our findings. We will also further improve the functionality of the game based on the data we obtained.

Acknowledgments. This research project is supported by School of Emerging Technology (SET) at Towson University via the Faculty Seed Research Funding.

References

1. About AR Foundation—Package Manager UI website. https://docs.unity3d.com/Packages/com.unity.xr.arfoundation@1.0/manual/index.html
2. Less than half of Maryland students pass English, math assessments - Baltimore Sun. http://www.baltimoresun.com/news/maryland/education/bs-md-parcc-scores-20170821-story.html
3. Unity. https://unity.com/
4. Boyce, A., Campbell, A., Pickford, S., Culler, D., Barnes, T.: Experimental evaluation of beadloom game: how adding game elements to an educational tool improves motivation and learning. In: Innovation and Technology in Computer Science Education (ITiCSE) Conference, pp. 243–247 (2011)
5. Collier, K.: Agile Analytics: A Value-Driven Approach to Business Intelligence and Data Warehousing. Addison-Wesley, Upper Saddle River (2012)
6. Deterding, S., Dixon, D., Khaled, R., Nacke, L.: From game design elements to gamefulness. In: Proceedings of the 15th International Academic MindTrek Conference on Envisioning Future Media Environments - MindTrek 2011, p. 9. ACM Press, New York (2011), http://dl.acm.org/citation.cfm?doid=2181037.2181040
7. Diah, N.M., Ehsan, K.M., Ismail, M.: Discover mathematics on mobile devices using gaming approach. Procedia - Soc. Behav. Sci. **8**, 670–677 (2010). https://www.sciencedirect.com/science/article/pii/S1877042810021981
8. Ebner, M.: Mobile applications for math education - how should they be done? In: Crompton, H., Traxler, J. (Eds.) Mobile Learning and Mathematics. Foundations, Design, and Case Studies, pp. 20–32 (2015)
9. Gu, J., Li, N., Duh, H.B.L.: A remote mobile collaborative AR system for learning in physics. In: 2011 IEEE Virtual Reality Conference, pp. 257–258. IEEE, March 2011. http://ieeexplore.ieee.org/document/5759496/
10. Hsiao, K.F.: Using augmented reality for students health - case of combining educational learning with standard fitness. Multimedia Tools Appl. **64**(2), 407–421 (2013). https://doi.org/10.1007/s11042-011-0985-9
11. Kapp, K.M.: The gamification of learning and instruction: game-based methods and strategies for training and education. Pfeiffer & Company (2012)
12. Kebritchi, M., Hirumi, A., Bai, H.: The effects of modern mathematics computer games on mathematics achievement and class motivation. Comput. Educ. **55**(2), 427–443 (2010)

13. Maier, P., Klinker, G., Tönnis, M.: Augmented Reality for teaching spatial relations. Conf. Int. J. Arts Sci. (Toronto), 1–8 (2009). http://wwwnavab.in.tum.de/pub/maierp2009ijas/maierp2009ijas.pdf
14. McLaren, B.M., Adams, D.M., Mayer, R.E., Forlizzi, J.: A Computer-based game that promotes mathematics learning more than a conventional approach. Int. J. Game-Based Learn. **7**(1), 36–56 (2017). http://services.igi-global.com/resolvedoi/resolve.aspx?doi=10.4018/IJGBL.2017010103

Human Computer Interaction in Education

Alexiei Dingli[✉] and Lara Caruana Montaldo

University of Malta, Msida MSD 2080, Malta
alexiei.dingli@um.edu.mt

Abstract. The Artificial Intelligence Assisted Learning application has been created to help Mathematics students at primary school level and assist their teachers. The application generates classwork and homework worksheets based on each student's ability level, corrects the worksheet, and gives immediate feedback to both the student and teacher. A crucial Human Computer Interaction concept implemented in the AIAL system is usability since the target audience is primary students and teachers who may have a basic proficiency in IT skills. Through the use of clearly partitioned sections, for classwork, homework, results and trophies, and intuitive controls, the application is easy to use and has a very low learning curve. Gamification and reinforcement elements were included in this application to further increase student engagement and enjoyment levels. The AIAL application can also be used for continuous assessment purposes. In the testing phase, it was noted that students enjoyed using the app.

Keywords: Artificial Intelligence (AI) · Human Computer Interaction (HCI) · Artificial Intelligence Assisted Learning (AIAL)

1 Introduction

Human Computer Interaction (HCI) can be defined as "a sociotechnological discipline whose goal is to bring the power of computers and communications systems to people in ways and forms that are both accessible and useful in our working, learning, communicating, and recreational lives" (Wtec.org 2018). The Artificial Intelligence Assisted Learning (AIAL) application has been created to help Mathematics students and assist teachers in primary schools. HCI ideas have been implemented in the AIAL app in order to make the app more accessible and helpful to users.

2 Usability of the AIAL Application

2.1 App Partitioning

An important HCI concept which was implemented in the AIAL system is usability and ease of use. This is an essential feature since this app is designed for primary school students and their teachers, who may have only a basic proficiency level of IT. One way in which usability was implemented is through clearly differentiated parts of the application.

© Springer Nature Switzerland AG 2019
C. Stephanidis (Ed.): HCII 2019, CCIS 1034, pp. 226–229, 2019.
https://doi.org/10.1007/978-3-030-23525-3_29

In the application there are different sections for classwork, homework, results and trophies. Therefore the user can easily navigate through the application. This is an essential feature to ensure that no unnecessary time is spent searching for the worksheet given by the teacher and the student only spends time working on the material of the given worksheet.

It is for this reason that the sections for classwork, homework, the student's user profile that contains trophies and work due have been programmed in a way to ensure that the student can easily find the work or information he/she is looking for.

The 'work due' section is composed of worksheets, mainly for homework purposes. These worksheets are found in separate sections, sorted by date, to help the child remember and keep up to date with the work that is due for that particular Mathematics topic.

In addition, the structured application aims to provide this app with a low learning curve for both teachers and students to be able to independently access all the features being offered in the app and master using it in a relatively short time.

2.2   User Controls

A user friendly interface for both students and teachers has been implemented in the Artificial Intelligence Assisted Learning (AIAL) application. By implementing intuitive and easy to learn controls to use the app, the app will assist learning in classrooms. Rather than using a mouse and a keyboard, the students just interact directly with the tablet through tap and/or drag motions for the numbers, operators or words. The student can also write/draw using either their finger or a stylus in the workings section as if it was rough paper. Similarly, when the teacher inputs a topic and sample question into the AIAL system, they use a drag and drop block style, similar to a visual programming language. The AIAL system then understands the input given and generates personalized classwork and homework depending on the level of the student that is recorded in the student's user profile. Every time a student completes work (classwork, homework or tests), the AIAL system updates the student's profile on the app. The student profiles of all the students in the class can be accessed by the teacher in order to provide the teacher with ready-made analytics and also indicate to the teacher which questions have been misunderstood and which students are struggling with a particular topic.

3   Human Learning

Another area which has been studied as part of HCI research is human learning and understanding. From previous literature it was learnt that continuous assessment is a better tool to aid student learning in comparison to final exams (Rezaei 2015; Kornell 2009). Moreover, when students have fun during the lesson, they are more concentrated and learn more.

3.1   Student Enjoyability Levels

During the testing phase of the AIAL application, it was evident that most students enjoyed using the app as they were very immersed in the content and were competing to see who could obtain the highest score by answering most questions correctly in the worksheet. Moreover, it was also noted that students were very eager to show the teachers the trophies they had unlocked. These trophies reflect the work completed and the student's performance in this aforementioned task.

In the AIAL system, the use of continuous assessment occurs through the use of periodic tests which are generated by the system. Moreover, the interactive application will enable students to remain interested in the classwork/homework they are performing and reduce boredom, which in turn promotes learning (Holmes 2015) This AIAL app can be used periodically as an additional tool in classrooms to provide an engaging and stimulating classwork activity in conjunction with other pen and pencil exercise worksheets given out by the teacher.

3.2   Gamification and Engagement

The use of a timer was also employed to increase the gamification in the app. This timer adapts according to the user level and the time increases and decreases accordingly. The time increases gradually if the system realizes that the user is running out of time as the answer box is repeatedly left empty when the timer reaches 0. On the other hand, if the student is never running out of time (timer does not reach 0) and answers a high proportion of the questions correctly, the time given to the student to answer the question will be decreased, thereby making the task more challenging to complete. A minimum and maximum time limit is set to ensure that the time is not decreased to such a low value that the student is unable to answer the question in time while also keeping the timer as a competition/game feature to ensure that the student is being challenged when answering the question and to ensure they do not get distracted and forget to answer the question. Students also have the option of switching off the timer should they require more time to answer the questions (than the maximum time) or do not like working under pressure/timed.

The colours used in the AIAL app were also specifically chosen to increase student engagement and personalize the app to each user. The screen flashes red when the time is running out to inform the user and remind them about the timer. Moreover, in the working section the user can change the colour of the pen. This allows the student to work out the problem in their preferred colour. The working space allows the students to work out the questions 'by hand' and not mentally. In this way, the student is able to solve the problem using any method that they have previously learnt.

3.3   Reinforcement

A further important aspect in student learning, especially in primary students, is that of reinforcement. Positive reinforcement is given to the students when they achieve a pre-set goal set by the teacher. An example of a goal is completing all the homework given in the week. If the student reaches this goal, a trophy will be given to the student which he/she will be able to view on their personal user profile. Viewing the trophies and seeing an ever-increasing number on their profile could act as an incentive and increase motivation in the students. This also helps students to respect deadlines without adding extra pressure. On the other hand, the AIAL system also provides constructive feedback to the student. This occurs immediately after the students complete a classwork/homework worksheet. The AIAL system corrects the personalized worksheet and shows the students which problems are correct and also which problems were wrongly answered. The student may then opt to either rework the worksheet or else view the answers with the solutions to the problems they got incorrect. This allows the students to recognize their mistakes and allows them to focus on understanding the process behind the solutions to the problems they answered incorrectly.

The application also involves two-way communication between the AIAL system and the student by acting as a tutor if the student encounters any difficulties. The system can offer assistance by showing other similar or related problems to the student, depending on where in the problem the student has misunderstood or is struggling with the problem. This can be done by the system analyzing the student's partial answer/s to try to get an understanding on what the student has already understood and where he/she actually needs help.

4 Conclusions

In conclusion, various Human Computer Interface techniques were used throughout the development of the Artificial Intelligence Assisted Learning (AIAL) app to ensure that the user was kept as a top priority throughout.

A user friendly interface for both students and teachers was implemented in the AIAL application. By implementing intuitive and easy to learn controls to use the app, the app has a low learning curve and students are able to focus all their attention on working out the material of the given worksheet rather than on navigating the application. The HCI concept of human learning and understanding is also prevalent in the AIAL application through the gamification, reinforcement and other engagement techniques used. A few examples of these techniques are the trophies, timer and colours. These aspects are thought to contribute to the student enjoyability and increase focus on the worksheet questions given.

References

Wtec.org: Chap 1: Human-Computer Interaction (2018). http://www.wtec.org/loyola/hci/c1_s1. htm. Accessed 30 Sept 2018

Rezaei, A.R.: Frequent collaborative quiz taking and conceptual learning. Act. Learn. High Educ. 16(3), 187–196 (2015)

Kornell, N.: Optimising learning using flashcards: spacing is more effective than cramming. Appl. Cogn. Psychol.: Off. J. Soc. Appl. Res. Mem. Cogn. 23(9), 1297–1317 (2009)

Holmes, N.: Student perceptions of their learning and engagement in response to the use of a continuous e-assessment in an undergraduate module. Assess. Eval. High. Educ. 40(1), 1–14 (2015)

Human Factors in New Personal Learning Ecosystems: Challenges, Ethical Issues, and Opportunities

Helene Fournier[1]([⊠]), Heather Molyneaux[2], and Rita Kop[3]

[1] National Research Council Canada, Moncton, New-Brunswick, Canada
helene.fournier@nrc-cnrc.gc.ca
[2] National Research Council Canada, Fredericton, New-Brunswick, Canada
heather.molyneaux@nrc-cnrc.gc.ca
[3] Yorkville University, Fredericton, New-Brunswick, Canada
rkop@yorkvilleu.ca

Abstract. This paper highlights over a decade of research on emerging technologies and learning innovation by the National Research Council, starting in 2008 with Personal Learning Environments (PLEs), connectivist-type MOOCs (cMOOCs) and more recently, new learning ecosystems. Late breaking research on human factors involved in critical learning on an open network will highlight participants' experiences in a recent cMOOC on distributed learning technologies - E-Learning 3.0. Human factors research is essential in identifying the types of support structures needed to create a place or community where people feel comfortable, trusted, and valued, as part of critical learning on an open network. Gaps and limitations in current research and development efforts in the area of new learning ecosystems are addressed as well as future areas of research worth exploring.

Keywords: Personal Learning Environments · PLEs · cMOOCs · Connectivism · Learning ecosystems · Human factors

1 Introduction

The National Research Council has been conducting research on emerging technologies and learning innovation since 2008, starting with Personal Learning Environments (PLEs), connectivist-type MOOCs (cMOOCs) and more recently, new learning ecosystems. A decade of research has identified important gaps, especially around the types of support mechanisms required by learners to be successful in these new open and accessible learning environments.

New learning technologies are emerging outside formal education, and academics and technologists are experimenting with these in formal and informal settings. Personal Learning Environments (PLEs) are part of the new learning ecosystem landscape, offering a wide range of open and accessible learning opportunities to learners across the world. A PLE is define as a single user's e-learning system that allows collaboration with other users and teachers who use other PLEs and/or Virtual Learning Environments and contain 'productivity' applications that facilitate the owner's learning

C. Stephanidis (Ed.): HCII 2019, CCIS 1034, pp. 230–238, 2019.
https://doi.org/10.1007/978-3-030-23525-3_30

activities, and are generally under the user's control as to use and personalisation [1]. PLEs are usually conceived of as open systems that are concerned with the coordination of connections made by the learner across a wide range of open systems [2]. MOOCs are included in PLE design efforts: as a massive multi-user environments, with open and distributed content that encourages cooperative learning, fully online delivery, and the packaging of these as an online course [3]. Novel technologies have prompted a new era of information abundance, far beyond the era of information scarcity and inaccessibility [4].

Tenets of emergent theories of knowledge and learning, such as connectivism, argue that online social networks can help interpret and validate information [5–7]. They promote a learning organization whereby there is not a body of knowledge to be transferred from educator to learner, and where learning does not take place in a single environment. Rather, it is distributed across the Web and people's engagement with it constitutes learning [7]. cMOOCs are 'based on a philosophy of connectivism and networking' [8] and 'are defined by a participative pedagogical model'[6].

Key principles of learning in networks [9, 10] are: distributed platforms, autonomy, diversity, openness, and connectivity. Downes and Siemens (conveners of the first cMOOC in 2008, CCK08) have described four key MOOC activities as: aggregation (filtering, selecting, and gathering personally meaningful information); remixing (interpreting the aggregated information and bringing to it personal perspectives and insights); repurposing (refashioning the information to suit personal purposes); and feeding forward (sharing the newly fashioned information with and learning from other participants) [11].

It is now possible for self-directed learners to participate informally in learning events on open online networks, such as in Massive Open Online Courses. In order to develop empowering learning environments that foster active learning, designers and developers of such environments first need to understand the factors that influence people's attitudes, intentions and behaviours. They must also understand the prerequisites for people to thrive in such environments in order to create favourable components and conditions, to encourage agency and autonomy to participate wholeheartedly.

2 Background

2.1 Human Factors in Self-directed Learning

Recognizing the challenges posed by innovations in Web-based learning, learning technologists have started developing structures to support autonomous learners in the negotiation of this new and ever-changing learning landscape. The creation of a place where people feel comfortable, trusted, and valued is the crux to engaging learners in an online environment [11]. The task would be to move towards a space that aggregates content and imagine it as a community, a place where dialogue happens, where people feel comfortable, and interactions and content can be accessed and engaged with easily: a place where the personal meets the social with the specific purpose of the development of ideas and of learning. In a learning environment characterized by change, the tools and application recommended to learners and the connections to others and resources are vitally important to create meaningful learning experiences. The flow of learning in a learning environment that supports learner self-direction on online networks, as is the case in cMOOCs, has been visualized in Fig. 1 [12].

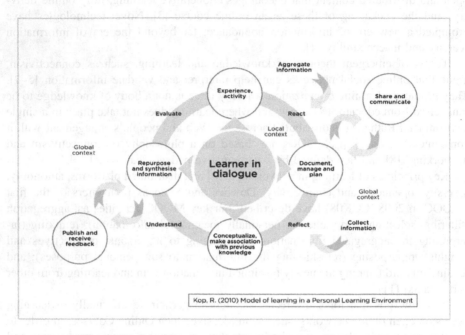

Fig. 1. Model of learning in a Personal Learning Environment

2.2   Disruptive Pedagogy

Connectivist MOOCs have been described as being pedagogically disruptive [13] and this can have a significant impact on participant learning experiences and their sense of personal identity. Connectivism is based on the idea that knowledge is essentially the set of connections in a network, and that learning therefore is the process of creating and shaping those networks. E-Learning 3.0—a cMOOC on the topic of 'Distributed Learning Technology' was offered from October 18 to December 17 2018. The course lasted nine weeks and each week covered a different topic, as follows: Data, Cloud, Graph, Identify, Resources, Community, Experience and Agency, as illustrated in Fig. 2.

Features of the course included: synchronous and asynchronous videos, course events and feeds. The gRSShopper application [14] and the Daily newsletter derived from it, facilitated resource aggregation and information dissemination relevant to the MOOC. gRSShopper has been a central tool across several MOOCs, helping learners to map the terrain of the conversation without telling them where to go specifically. Aggregation of independent points of view is one of the key mechanisms to cultivating

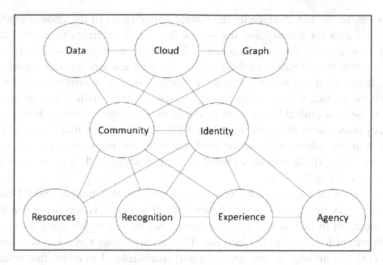

Fig. 2. E-Learning 3.0 topics

and harnessing the wisdom of the crowd. As part of a pedagogically disruptive learning experience, the course instructor expressed the following:

> *"You might be thinking: this course looks too difficult, too technical, or too high level. This will be true for everyone, even me. But the course is structured so you can focus on what's interesting and accessible for you, and you can ignore the rest."*[15].

Table 1 describes components of the course, including the course philosophy, technology, media and education.

Table 1. Components of the course.

Philosophy	What are the underlying concepts, systems and ethics?
Technology	What applications and systems will address this topic?
Media	What do we create and how do we communicate?
Education	What are the processes of learning, inference and discovery?

2.3   New Ethics and Privacy Issues in Networked Environments

Increasingly, information about individual learners and their online behaviors are now made available and harvested from their participation in MOOCs, which makes it possible to do these types of analyses. However, researchers need to carefully consider the ethical implications related to how personal learning data is collected, analyzed, and reported. The complexity of researching networked learning has been highlighted along challenges of human agency and the multitude of issues involved, such as the dynamics of the network, power-relations on the network, and the amount of content generated [16]. It might also mean that qualitative analysis in addition to quantitative analyses are necessary to obtain meaningful answers to research questions. Effective analysis would require a multi-method approach and would need to address new ethics and privacy issues.

Every researcher has to consider the ethical implications of the chosen methods of obtaining the data for a study and the use made of it. Sometimes obtaining data is a matter of accessing statistics or documents. When human subjects are involved in the research, careful consideration of the level of informed consent by participants is also required. It has been argued that gaining informed consent is problematic if it is not clear what the participant is consenting to and where "participation begins and ends" [17, p. 53]. Several ethical issues were raised in the literature, of which misuse of data and privacy issues were the most important. Researchers caution that data could pose a threat to subjects when misused, or used for different purposes than what it was supplied for [18, 19]. Researchers should at least anonymize data in order to respect privacy issues [18–20].

It has also been suggested by network researchers that people should have the choice to opt in or opt out of the use of their data. If someone is not aware that the data is being collected or how it will be used, he/she has no real opportunity to consent or withhold consent for its collection and use. This invisible data gathering is common on the Web [18] and highlights new decisions and issues related to ethics that researchers will have to address. Ultimately, researchers have a responsibility to carefully consider the context of their research, and also the process that takes place between observing, collecting and analyzing "Big Data"; data that is left by traces of activities that might not at all be related to the visible participation of learners [20].

3 Research Methodology

A survey was conducted in the context of the E-Learning 3.0 course in order to collect feedback from participants on their experiences within the MOOC, their background as well as information about their participation in the course, including their preferred modes of interacting within the MOOC, learning activities they participated in, as well as privacy and trust concerns. Links to the survey were sent to the email addresses of those who signed up for the course newsletter. The course instructor also mentioned the survey in two of the course videos as well as in a tweet.

General statistics were also collected through the gRSShopper aggregator as follows: newsletter subscriptions (177), harvested feeds (15), with the number of unique visitors to the E-Learning 3.0 course website reaching 3000. A total of 39 participants completed the survey, which contained demographic questions as well as questions related to general interest in the course, privacy and trust and preferred modes of interaction. The results of the survey are presented in the next section.

4 Survey Findings

4.1 Demographics

The majority of participants in the survey were well educated (76% master's or professional degree; 16% doctorates) and from an older demographic (65% were 55+). A majority of participants were male (65%), had a high degree of IT proficiency

(68% professional), with significant experience in online learning (58% with 11+ years involvement in online learning). Participants also had a high level of experience in MOOCs, with 95% reporting previous involvement in MOOCs.

4.2 Privacy and Trust

Even though all participants had concerns over privacy online in general, most (66%) survey respondents did not read the privacy policy for the MOOC. Some report not seeing it (the link is listed on the course outline) while most noted that they didn't have time or they trusted the course creator and didn't see the need to read the policy.

This could be connected with the idea of the creation of a community—in fact, one of the weekly topics (of 9 in total), was that of community, and 22/39 participants identified community as a topic of interest. The term community also came up in quite a few of the text responses where participants were asked to share their thoughts and experiences on the MOOC. "It's good to 'see' old familiar faces again, and be able to interact with them (people I connected with in some way in CCK11 and other cMOOCs of the era") (R20). The facilitator of the MOOC is indeed a part of the MOOC community and a friendly face, which created trust between him and the MOOC participants. When a connectivist course is working well, one can see a cycle of content and creativity that begins to feed on itself with people in the course reading, collecting, creating, and sharing. One of the survey questions asked participants to identify their preferred modes of interacting within the MOOC. Details regarding participants' preferred modes of interaction are presented in the next section.

4.3 Preferred Modes of Interacting Within the MOOC

Most of the participants responded that they read the daily newsletter and watched the videos on a regular basis. There was also moderate participation reported in the social media aspects of the MOOC. Blogging attracted the least amount of participation, with 39% of survey respondents reporting never blogging. (see Fig. 3).

Still, blogging was one of the most popular modes of interaction, with many participants choosing to read blog posts by their peers. Blogging and social means of interaction were mentioned with greater frequency by participants as their preferred mode of interaction. The importance of synchronous and asynchronous means of interacting were highlighted in the text responses of the survey. As one participant pointed out:

> *"I'm a free range learner and like to take my own route through a course, often checking out related resources and ideas along the way. But I do appreciate the sense of a shared experience that synchronous components of a course creates [...] it's the surprising, sometimes disconcerting and shocking discoveries in a rich, deep, multilayered, unplanned environment that makes the experience memorable and, perhaps transformational." (R24).*

Others pointed out the utility of accessing resources after the fact, stating preference for "Twitter and blog to blog because of the asynchronicity aspect. I love "the daily" because if I didn't get an email with the resource I'd most likely put the "course" even further back on the backburner." (R20). "Asynchronously, because the time zone of

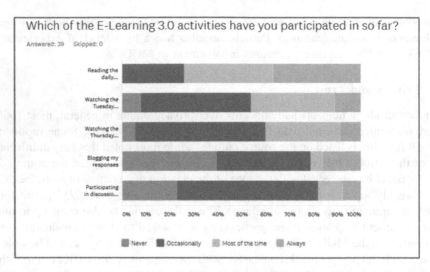

Fig. 3. Preferred mode of interaction in the E-Learning 3.0 MOOC

live events takes place in the middle of my night. I very much appreciate learning about the gRSShopper software and seeing how the course is mounted and use the concepts, if not the software itself, in my own course". (R39).

And others pointed out their appreciation for including multiple means of interaction, noting that "There isn't 'one' [preferred mode] they contribute in unique ways to the whole experience." (R1).

When asked to share their thoughts and experiences on the MOOC the terms community, open and interaction were frequently mentioned (see Fig. 3). Certainly the users written responses to the preferred modes of interaction speak to this theme of openness and interaction within a community. When asked to share their thoughts and experiences on the MOOC the terms community open and interaction frequently mentioned. Many thanked the MOOC producer for the opportunity for gathering the community and the facilitation of their interactions. Several participants called for more interaction, especially during the live sessions, and perhaps some webinars where the MOOC participants could have the opportunity to interact with each other synchronously to complement the asynchronous interactions. One common issue mentioned was that of time constraints, with several participants indicating intent to follow up on course material after the official end of the course.

"I wish I could have contributed more and engaged with others more. But, for me, these courses never really end. It's a bit like knowing that you can drop into your favourite bar or cafe anytime and know that you will find good people and good conversations there. No one expects you to turn up every day or at pre-determined times. And it's OK if you're away for a while. You'll just have more news to share on your next visit. A MOOC isn't like listening to a finished symphony, it's more like warming up in the pit with everyone else. It's improvised jazz." (R24)

5   Conclusions and Discussion

Working across distributed platforms allows learners considerable autonomy, but also requires the associated technical, navigation, and critical thinking skills. For new-comers to MOOCs, the experience may be difficult and disorienting. Fostering and encouraging learner autonomy is an essential part of the learning process and design but the constraints on autonomy must be recognized as part of the human factors involved in critical learning on an open network. The type of support structures needed to create a place or community where people feel comfortable, trusted, and valued, and can access and interact with resources and each other remains fertile ground for research in human factors in computer systems. The notion of what it means to learn in a new learning ecosystem continues to expand, with opportunities for individuals to manage their own learning, improve on their competencies, add a new skill set for career advancement or pursue learning for personal enjoyment.

Current research and development efforts in new personal learning ecosystems include powerful data-driven visualizations aimed at providing valuable and mean-ingful feedback to learners based on trace data of their learning activities, machine-learning techniques to personalize the learning, learning analytics, recommender sys-tems, big data and educational data mining applications, as well as the provision of safeguards for data protection and privacy in a complex networked environment. Specifically, research in the area of AI and data-based learning systems such as rec-ommender systems will help learners filter information and online social interactions, but the challenge also lies in the human factors that make people want to participate in a course and learn.

With the advent of social media and opportunities to connect people on a massive scale, we have now entered a new era of communication and trust. Learners, partici-pants, and consumers of technologies should be encouraged to make informed deci-sions about what they share, who they share with, and what might be the potential risks and benefits in contributing and participating. Transparency as well as sound data privacy, security, and trust practices by those producing new technologies and learning environments are now a priority.

Acknowledgement. We would like to acknowledge Stephen Downes, E-Learning 3.0 course facilitator. His philosophy on open and accessible learning has made this research possible and has contributed to over a decade of research and development on Personal Learning Environ-ments and MOOCs in particular.

References

1. Van Harmelen, M.: Personal learning environments (2006). https://pdfs.semanticscholar.org/3a80/0f41a3431cd05b37e882c34dc434aa27bbf3.pdf
2. Wilson, S.: Architecture of virtual spaces & the future of VLEs (2005). https://www.slideserve.com/Sophia/architecture-of-virtual-spaces-the-future-of-vles
3. Downes, S.: Design elements in a personal learning environment. Half an hour blog (2015). https://halfanhour.blogspot.com/2015/03/design-elements-in-personal-learning.html

4. Weller, M.A.: Pedagogy of abundance. Span. J. Pedagogy **249**, 223–236 (2011)
5. Downes, S.: What connectivism is [Web log post] (2007). http://halfanhour.blogspot.ca/2007/02/what-connectivism-is.htm
6. Siemens, G.: What is the theory that underpins our moocs? (2012). http://www.elearnspace.org/blog/2012/06/03/what-is-the-theory-that-underpins-our-moocs/
7. Bell, F.: Connectivism: its place in theory-informed research and innovation in technology-enabled learning. Int. Rev. Res. Open Distance Learn. **12**(3), 98–118 (2011). http://www.irrodl.org/index.php/irrodl/article/view/902/1664
8. Daniel, J.: Making sense of MOOCs: musings in a maze of myth, paradox and possibility. J. Interact. Media Educ. **2012**(3), (2012). https://jime.open.ac.uk/articles/10.5334/2012-18/
9. Downes, S.: Connectivism dynamics in communities. https://halfanhour.blogspot.com/2009/02/connectivist-dynamics-in-communities.html
10. Downes, S.: The MOOC of one (2014). https://www.slideshare.net/Downes/2014-03-10-valencia
11. Kop, R., Carroll, F.: Cloud computing and creativity: Learning on a massive open online course. EURODL, 1–11 (2011). http://www.eurodl.org/?p=special&sp=articles&article=457
12. Kop, R.: The design and development of a personal learning environment: researching the learning experience. In: Proceedings of the European Distance and E-learning Network Annual Conference 2010, 9–12 June, Valencia, Spain (2010). https://nrc-publications.canada.ca/eng/view/accepted/?id=0728bc9b-1907-49c1-90bd-0f7ea87a0cad
13. Mackness, J., Waite, M., Roberts, G., Lovegrove, E.: Learning in small, task-oriented, connectivist MOOC: pedagogical issues and implications for higher education. Int. Rev. Res. Open Distrib. Learn. **14**(4) (2013). http://www.irrodl.org/index.php/irrodl/article/view/1548/2687
14. Downes, S.: About gRSShopper (2018). https://grsshopper.downes.ca/about.htm
15. Downes, S.: Approaching E-Learning 3.0 (2018). https://halfanhour.blogspot.com/2018/09/approaching-e-learning-30.html
16. De Laat, M.: Networked learning. Doctoral thesis (2006). https://eprints.soton.ac.uk/20358/1/Maarten_De_Laat_Networked_Learning_2006.pdf
17. Miller, T., Bell, L.: Consenting to what? Issues of access, gate-keeping and 'informed' consent. In: Mauthner, M., Birch, M., Jessop, J., Miller, T. (eds.) Ethics in Qualitative Research, pp. 53–69. Seven Oakes, London and Sage Publications, New Delhi (2002)
18. Van Wel, L., Royakkers, L.: Ethical issues in web data mining. Ethics Inf. Technol. **6**, 129–140 (2004)
19. Boyd, D., Crawford, K.: Critical questions for Big Data. Inf. Commun. Soc. **15**(5), 662–679 (2012)
20. Prinsloo, P., Slade, S.: Ethics and Learning Analytics: Charting the (Un)Charted, Handbook of Learning Analytics, 1st edn., Chapter 4, pp. 49–57 (2017)

A Supporting System for Teaching Assistant to Control Assistant Behavior by Adjusting Instruction Time

Ryuichiro Imamura, Yuuki Yokoyama, and Hironori Egi(✉)

The University of Electro-Communications,
1-5-1 Chofugaoka, Chofu, Tokyo 182-8585, Japan
i1510027@edu.cc.uec.ac.jp, hiro.egi@uec.ac.jp

Abstract. In this study, we propose a Teaching Assistant (TA) support system to assist the TA in instructing students more effectively. The TA is expected to support students properly without decreasing the learning impact of the students. Hints for exercises should not be given excessively to let the students work by themselves. The proposed system controls the TA's behavior by preventing the TA from overrunning the instruction time. To measure the instruction time, the position data of the TA in the classroom is used. The system detects the beginning of a TA instruction based on the still position in a fixed period. When the instruction time overruns a specific time, the system notifies the TA by sending a signal to vibrate the mobile device worn by the TA. The TA is assumed to conclude the instruction and leave from the student when the mobile device vibrates. We introduced the experiment in the classes of basic programming course. From the results of the experiment, the notification affected the TA adequately and the instruction was concluded as anticipated.

Keywords: Teaching Assistant · Programming course · Assistance dilemma · Mobile device · Behavior analysis

1 Introduction

Many students in abasic programming course are beginners at writing code. Levels of understanding about programming vary among students. To tackle this situation, a Teaching Assistant (TA) is introduced to support the students who need help working the exercises in the course. The TA often gives hints based on requests from the students. However, the students are expected to acquire the ability to solve various problems by writing code, not just the knowledge learned in the course [1]. If the TA supports the students excessively, the students might not be able to acquire this ability. Therefore, the TA is expected to support students properly not to decrease the learning impact on the students. This dilemma is called the assistance dilemma [2].

In this study, we propose a system to support the TA in instructing more effectively. The system aims to prevent overruns of the TA's instruction time. It is intended to divide a long instruction time into separate segments. The students are led to ask the TA for further assistance only after they have attempted to solve the problems by

© Springer Nature Switzerland AG 2019
C. Stephanidis (Ed.): HCII 2019, CCIS 1034, pp. 239–246, 2019.
https://doi.org/10.1007/978-3-030-23525-3_31

themselves. Another merit of introducing the system is the TA can instruct a greater number of students in each class. The purpose of the system is to correct the bias of learning opportunities that the students obtain from the TA.

2 Related Works

A TA should support students working exercises in a course actively, not excessively. The assistance dilemma's effect has been studied. Miwaet al. reported on the tradeoff between problem-solving and learning goals [3]. The hypothesis is a high level of support improves problem-solving performance but reduces the learning effect that the learner obtains through a task. To test this hypothesis, they conducted two types of experiments. Both experiments set the level of support that subjects received in the learning experiment, and tests were imposed during and after learning. The relationship between test score and level of support was examined. Consequently, subjects who learned with a high level of support got a higher score on the test given during learning than subjects who learned with a low level of support. However, on the test given after learning, the result of the grade for the two subjects group was reversed. These results indicate that high-level support improves problem-solving but does not lead to effective learning. This research also suggests that no or a very low level of support does not lead to effective learning. In the first experiment, the test scores of subjects who learned without support were lower than those of subjects learned with support.

From the results of the research, it is necessary for the TA to support the students enough when working exercises; however, when excessive support is given, the leaning impact on students is decreased.

3 Proposed Method

The proposed method in this research is to manage the TA's instruction time for each student. If the instruction time exceeds a certain time, the TA is notified to conclude the instruction. The goals of this study are equalization of learning opportunities that students can be given by the TA and splitting instruction time during a lecture. The equalization of the learning opportunities is intended to maximize the chance for the students to be instructed individually by the TA. The TA is encouraged to give brief advice and to walk around the classroom so that other students can ask questions of the TA. Splitting the instruction time is intended to divide a single long instruction session to several short segments. It is intended to prevent the TA from teaching too much within one instruction instance. Students can use this between-segment time to consider the problem and make step-by-step progress within the shortened instruction time.

4 TA Support System

Figure 1 shows the outline of the proposed system. When the TA stops near a student, the system detects the student and starts to measure the instruction time. The device issues a notification if the instruction time exceeds the specified time. The TA is assumed to conclude the instruction and to show the plan for how to proceed with the exercises. If the TA finds it better to continue to instruct the student, the TA is not restricted to concluding the instruction.

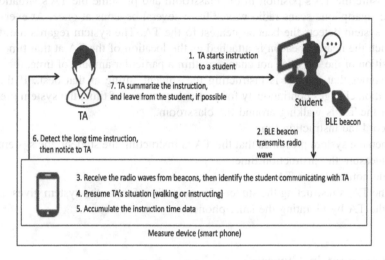

Fig. 1. Outline of the proposed system

4.1   Measurement of the TA's Position in the Classroom

To make it possible to use the system in ordinary classrooms, the system is implemented only with devices that are portable and easily equipped. To detect the students instructed by the TA, the position data of the TA, measured by Bluetooth low energy (BLE), is introduced. FCS1301 by Focus Systems is used as a BLE beacon for this measurement [4]. BLE beacons are attached to every seat in a classroom. The TA brings a smartphone to measure the BLE signals. During a lecture, the TA brings a textbook and a notepad so that devices of the system do not hinder the TA instructing with gestures. Figure 2 shows a TA assisted by the system. By carrying smartphones attached to the waist and the arm, the TA can use his hands freely and work without disturbing the devices. To measure the radio wave from the BLE beacons, the Beacon Scanner measurement application by Nicolas Bridoux is used [5]. This application can send JavaScript Object Notation data of the measured beacons to a server at every scan.

Fig. 2. Devices worn by TA

4.2   Presuming the TA's Instruction Time

The following steps are required for the system to presume the TA's instruction time.

(1) Measure the TA's position in the classroom and presume the TA's situation.
     The smartphone scans radio waves from several beacons at once. At every scan, the system detects the beacon nearest to the TA. The system regards the desk to which the nearest beacon is attached as the location of the TA at that time. If the position of the TA does not change within a particular amount of time, the system presumes that the TA is instructing the student sitting at that desk. If the TA's position changes continuously for particular amount of time, the system presumes that the TA is walking around the classroom.
(2) Record the instruction time
     When the system presumes that the TA is instructing the student, the system starts to measure the instruction time.
(3) Issue notices to the TA
     If the TA is instructing the student for more than 5 min, the system gives a notice to the TA by vibrating the smartphone.

5   Experiment in Classes

We introduced the system to classes of a basic programming course offered ata science and technology university. Table 1 shows the overview of the course.

Table 1. Overview of the course

Course title	Basic programing exercises for undergraduate students
Programming language	Ruby and C
Number of students	About 70
Number of teachers	1 or 2
Number of TAs	2
Number of lectures	15 lectures in 5 months
Length and frequency of classes	90 min, once a week

We conducted an experiment in six classes for the last 5 weeks of the course. The system was used in three classes (the experiment group), and the system was not introduced in the other three classes(the control group). At the first 3 weeks, the system was not used ineither group. Forthe last 2 weeks, the system was used in only the experiment group. Video was recorded in every classto observe the TA's response to students. Throughout the experiment, three types of the results are analyzed. The first result is the accuracy of presuming the TA's situation. The second result is whether the TA's behavior of instruction has changed before and after introducing the system. The third result comes from an interview with the TA about the system.

6 Result and Discussion

6.1 Accuracy of Presuming the TA's Situation

The system presumes the TA's situation at every scanning BLE beacon; therefore, we analyzed how many scans presumed the TA's situation accurately in each lecture. The correct situation for the TA is derived from observation recorded on video. As a result, the average accuracy over all lectures in presuming the TA's situation was 67.2%. The accuracy varied among TAs, from 50% to more than 70%. We considered this to be caused by the TAs' posture while the TA was instructing a student. We found it difficult to presume whether the TA was instructing the student based on the data of single scan. Therefore, the system presumes the TA's situation based on data from recent several scans. The operator monitors the instruction time and manually stops the system if it sends wrong notifications. Because of the limitation of the accuracy of presuming the TA's situation, some instructions exceeding the specified time are not detected. Still, there was at least once notification for every TA in the experiment group.

6.2 Change of the TA's Behavior Before and After Introducing the System

Because of a lack of collected data and variations in the working styles of the TAs, we analyzed two classes each for the experiment group and the control group. To investigate how the system affected the TA's behavior, we calculated every TA's average instruction time per student. We named this time the single instruction time. Figure 3 shows the distribution of every TA's single instruction time before and after the system was introduced.

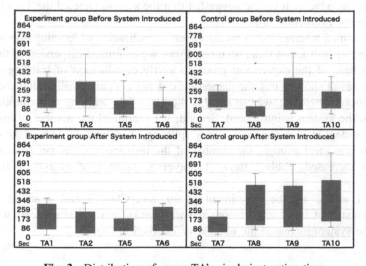

Fig. 3. Distribution of every TA's single instruction time

The two upper graphs show the single instruction time in both groups before the system was introduced. The lower two graphs show the single instruction time in both groups after the system was introduced in the experiment group. These graphs show that there is no remarkable difference between before and after the system was introduced in the experiment group. However, the single instruction time of the control group became longer in the last 2 weeks when the system was introduced in the experiment group. This is caused by the increase in difficulty in the progress of the lectures.

Then, we compared the overall average single instruction time of all TAs between the experiment group and the control group. Figure 4 shows the average single instruction time of both groups before and after the system was introduced.

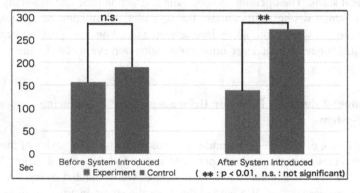

Fig. 4. Average single instruction time of the experiment group and the control group

We verified whether there was a significant difference between the two groups. From the result of Mann-Whitney U test, a significant difference was seen only after the system was introduced. It can be suggested that the system affected the TA's behavior to decrease the instruction time.

We examined whether the expected effects, equalization of learning opportunities, and splitting of instruction time, occurred. First, we examined dispersion of the single instruction time of the experiment group to verify equalization of learning opportunities. The result showed that the dispersion did not become smaller after the system was introduced. Therefore, we can say that the bias of the learning opportunities exists even when the system is introduced. Second, we examined the number of instruction times per student in each lecture to verify splitting of instruction time. If the effect of the system was great enough, the number of the instruction times per student would have been increased. Table 2 shows the average number of instruction times per student.

Class 1 and 2 are the experiment group, and Class 3 and 4 are the control group. Comparing Class 1 and 2 before and after the system was introduced, we cannot say that the system increased the number of instruction times.

Table 2. Average number of instruction times per student

Lecture	Class 1	Class 2	Class 3	Class 4
11	1.27	1.30	1.25	1.59
12	1.00	1.42	1.33	1.21
13	1.50	1.30	1.33	1.42
14	1.29	1.12	1.17	1.29
15	1.36	1.40	1.20	1.23
Average before the system was introduced	1.26	1.34	1.30	1.41
Average after the system was introduced	1.33	1.26	1.19	1.26

To increase the number of instruction times, we need to improve the system to encourage students to more actively ask questions of the TA. Additionally, it is necessary to motivate the TA to instruct the students who had already been instructed.

6.3 Analysis of the Interview

We found that some TAs might feel hurried by carrying notification-activated mobile devices, even when the system did not give a notification. We need to conduct an experiment to examine the effectiveness of the system excluding this psychological impact.

We asked the TAs whether notification after 5 min of instruction was appropriate. Some TAs answered that the duration was suitable as a default setting because the notification tended to occur when an instruction was almost finished. However, most TAs answered that when instructing students who did not understand the lecture well, the current setting to notify after 5 min is not appropriate. The setting time of the notification should be dynamic and should depend on the characteristics of the students and the lectures.

The TAs reported that carrying the devices did not hinder their tasks in classrooms. It can be suggested that it is possible to introduce the system in various types of lectures.

Finally, some TAs found the possibility of using the system in another way. In this study the system notices when the instruction time exceeds the specified time. However, some TAs said that they expected the system to notify them at regular intervals. In such cases, the TAs can know the passage of instruction time and might be able to control the instruction time by themselves.

7 Future Work

The accuracy of presuming the TA's situations needs to be improved. To solve this problem, we will consider combining the proposed notification system with other sensors, such as gyroscopes. After that, we will introduce this system in a long experimentto evaluate how this system will affect TA behavior. Adding some features can also be considered. It is also necessary to decide on the time to notify depending on the characteristics of the students and the lectures. Another experiment would be related to the use of this system as a regular notification timer.

8 Conclusions

In this study, we proposed a system to support the TA in instructing more effectively. The system presumes the TA's situation, depending on whether the TA is walking or instructing a student, and measures the instruction time. If the instruction time exceeds the specific time, the system notifies the TA. Using the system, we aimed to equalize the learning opportunities that students can be given by TAs and split the instruction time during a lecture into segments. To presume the TA's situation, BLE beacons were used. We found it difficult to presume the TA's situation using only the position data of the TA measured by BLE. Further investigation is required for the system to notify the TA at an appropriate time. The instruction time was shortened with the proposed system so that the TA's behavior would be affected positively. To increase the number of instruction times, we need to improve the system to encourage students to more actively ask questions of the TA. Additionally, it is necessary to motivate the TA to instruct the students who have already been instructed.

Acknowledgements. This work has been partly supported by the Grants-in-Aid for Scientific Research (No. 18K18657) by MEXT (Ministry of Education, Culture, Sports, Science and Technology) in Japan.

References

1. Okamoto, M., et al.: Computer programming course materials for self-learning novices. In: Herrington, J., Montgomerie, C. (eds.) Proceedings of ED-MEDIA 2010–World Conference on Educational Multimedia, Hypermedia & Telecommunications, pp. 2855–2861. Association for the Advancement of Computing in Education (AACE), Toronto (2010)
2. Kenneth, R.K., Vincent, A.: Exploring the assistance dilemma in experiments with cognitive tutors. Educ. Psychol. Rev. **19**(3), 239–264 (2007)
3. Kazuhisa, M., Hltoshi, T., Ryuichi, N.: Tradeoff between problem-solving and learning goals: two experiments for demonstrating assistance dilemma. In: Proceedings of the Annual Meeting of the Cognitive Science Society, vol. 34, no. 34 (2012)
4. Focus Systems FCS1301. https://www.fcs-mimamori.com/english.php. Accessed 21 Feb 2019
5. Nicolas Bridoux, Beacon Scanner. https://play.google.com/store/apps/details?id=com.bridou_n.beaconscanner&hl=ja. Accessed 21 Feb 2019

A Gamified Mobile-Based Virtual Reality Laboratory for Physics Education: Results of a Mixed Approach

Diego Iquira[✉], Briseida Sotelo, and Olha Sharhorodska

Department of Systems Engineering, Universidad Nacional de San Agustin de Arequipa, Santa Catalina 117, Arequipa, Peru
{diquira,mgbsotelo,osharhorodska}@unsa.edu.pe

Abstract. Virtual reality has an important role in learning physics since it provides students a virtual environment that simulates real-world situations. Virtual laboratories are a new alternative for teaching, as they provide safe environments where the student can repeat a practice without risk of damaging the equipment. Gamification allows motivating students through the application of game-design elements. The objective of this paper was to perform a mixed evaluation of the influence of immersive virtual reality and gamification on the learning of physics in a mobile learning environment. The proposed application is a low-cost alternative for both schools and universities that do not have the infrastructure to create a physics laboratory and a tool for distance learning in physics. 86 students of university education were tested and we analyzed the information generated by the students.

Keywords: Virtual reality · Education · Physics · Virtual laboratory · Mobile · Gamification

1 Introduction

In recent years VR technology has become more accessible [1] with the creation of commercial products such as the Google Cardboard that offers virtual reality experiences at an accessible price [2], which has allowed its application in different areas.

One of these areas is education, in which VR is used through learning situations, that allows large groups of students interact with each other in three-dimensional environments [3].

Among the advantages of using VR in the classroom is to represent complex data and concepts in a simple way, also VR generates learning motivation because students can interact with different objects [4].

In education, gamification has been used to motivate students to learn, where the goal is to increase the fun, participation, and motivation of the students [5].

© Springer Nature Switzerland AG 2019
C. Stephanidis (Ed.): HCII 2019, CCIS 1034, pp. 247–254, 2019.
https://doi.org/10.1007/978-3-030-23525-3_32

2   Proposed Application

The proposed virtual laboratory consists of a set of activities which are divided into theoretical and practical activities.

The theoretical activities are all the activities in which the student is asked questions related to the theoretical classes, 3 different activities have been established which are: multiple questions, true and false and connect concepts;

On the other hand, practical activities consist of exercises located in immersive virtual environments, 2 different practical activities have been established which are: solving an exercise: where, based on a set of data, the student must find the correct answer and free experimentation where the student is in a simulated environment where he can change the data and obtain different results.

The users chosen to use the virtual laboratory are students from the National University of San Agustin (UNSA) in the city of Arequipa, who have courses related to physics.

For the use of the virtual laboratory we have selected a set of gamification techniques which are: Narrative, Domain Opportunities, Player Control, Feedback, Progression by levels, Challenges, Music.

3   Implementation of Proposed Application

For the development of the virtual laboratory, we have used the Extreme Programming methodology and the development environment chosen is Unity3d.

The mobile devices selected to perform the tests requires a gyroscope and an accelerometer, additionally, we connected wireless controls to perform the interactions on the virtual scenario.

The components of the application are: A menu system, a level system, a save system, a VR navigation system, a music system and an activity control system.

The menu system contains the main interface that is used in the virtual laboratory, we used a minimalist design, where icons representing the different tasks are shown and are easy to identify by the students as viewed in the Fig. 1.

Additionally, a descriptive text indicating the task to be performed is shown as shown in the Fig. 1, we choose to make an intuitive design that allows the student to make full use of the application without the need to read manuals or ask for help.

This application saves the information generated by the student, process this information in the virtual environment and show it through the VR lenses allowing the student to select the objects through a reticle, which indicates what objects can be selected and shown a text message that describes the objects as shown in the Fig. 2.

Arrows are used to guide the student, as they indicate the position of a certain object when it is out of the student's vision, for example, a square icon replaces the arrow icon when the object is out of view the student as observed in the Fig. 2.

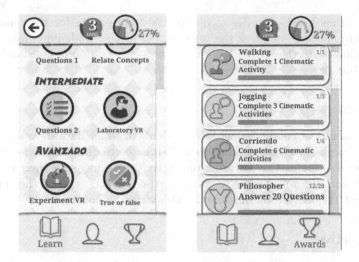

Fig. 1. Left side Icons of the activities available in the virtual laboratory, right part name and description of the activity to be carried out (Source: Own Elaboration)

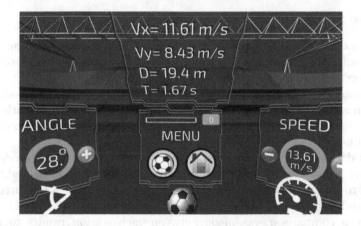

Fig. 2. Elements of navigation in the virtual environment (Source: Own Elaboration)

4   Methodology

4.1   Types of Research

Mixed research was conducted with two approaches qualitative and quantitative:

- On the qualitative side we surveyed the students after using the virtual laboratory, the questions focused on measuring the usability of the virtual laboratory.

– On the other hand, in order to obtain the information for the quantitative approach, the system saves the information of the students regarding their interactions with the virtual laboratory; this information is saved online from the mobile device.

4.2 Sample

The experiment was conducted with 86 students of which 32 were women and 54 were men. Six sessions lasting from 10 to 15 min were conducted, where the first test session was focused on carrying out activities to measure their theoretical knowledge and the following 5 sessions focused on the use of the immersive environment to measure the usability of the virtual laboratory.

4.3 Objective

The objective of the case study was to determine if students can easily use a virtual laboratory and if the students improve their answers after several sessions.

4.4 Case Study

In order to carry out this case study, students were presented with an activity, which in order to be completed, a series of exercises must be completed, based on the exercises solved, the student's attitude will be evaluated.

Six sessions were held with the students, in the first session the students had to solve an activity to measure their theoretical knowledge of kinematics, in the remaining sessions the students had to use the virtual laboratory to carry out the experiments.

It was decided to carry out several sessions to measure if the students had learned how to use the virtual laboratory, in each session we measured the time they took to complete each experiment, the objects observed in the virtual environment and the answers, both correct and incorrect.

Finally a comparison was made between each session results to measure whether the student has reduced the time necessary to complete the exercise, if the number of correct answers has increased and the number of incorrect answers has decreased.

A framework for evaluating the educational effectiveness of VR experiences was used as a basis to determine how to process the information generated by the students, of which four categories have been selected, which are [6]:

– Technician: Time to learn an interface, understanding of instructions, physical and emotional comfort
– Orientation: Time to feel comfortable in the virtual environment
– Pedagogical: Knowledge of the concepts that are being taught.

4.5   Usability VR Applications

To evaluate Usability, 12 measurement categories are being used, which are [7]:

- Level of realism in the virtual environment.
- Level of realism when performing tasks.
- Freedom of movement in the virtual environment.
- Response time on the screen.
- Realism in the physics of educational software.
- Level of perception of the virtual environment.
- Level of navigation and orientation.
- Ease of entry and exit in the virtual environment.
- Comprehensive menu.
- Easy use of educational software.
- Organized and understandable tasks.
- Feeling of being present in the virtual world.

5   Results

5.1   Case Study

At the technical level, based on the time taken to carry out the activities and objects viewed to complete each exercise of the virtual reality activities, it was determined in Fig. 3 that there is a reduction of 60% of the time and a reduction of 30%, of the number of objects viewed in the first exercise compared to the

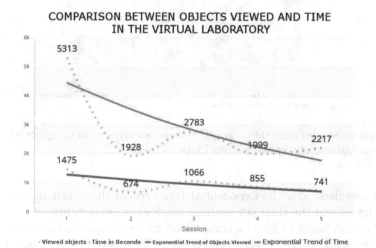

Fig. 3. Comparison between the time to complete an exercise and the objects viewed to complete an exercise in the virtual laboratory (Source: Own Elaboration)

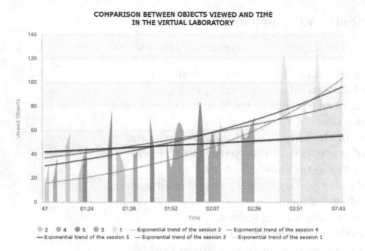

Fig. 4. Comparison between the objects viewed to complete an exercise and the time to complete an exercise in the virtual laboratory between the exercises (Source: Own Elaboration)

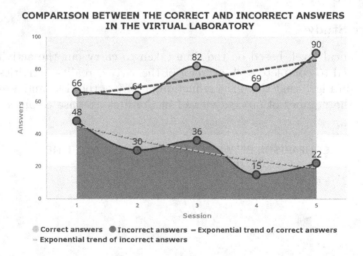

Fig. 5. Comparison between the correct and incorrect answers to complete an exercise in the virtual laboratory (Source: Own Elaboration)

following exercises; also the exponential trend shows that both the number of objects viewed and the time per exercise reach an average value.

On the other hand in Fig. 4 a comparison was made on the time to complete an activity based on the objects viewed where they were grouped based on the exercise, and a big difference is noted in the first exercise and the following ones changing a maximum time of 7 min and 43 s to one of 2 min and 36 s per exercise.

Based on the comparisons made, we have concluded that there has been an understanding of the students regarding the activities they carried out.

At the orientation level, we compared the number of objects viewed to complete the exercises, in Fig. 3 we determined a 60% reduction in time and a 30% reduction in the number of objects viewed in the first exercise compared to the other exercises.

Finally, at the pedagogical level, the correct and incorrect answers were compared based on the exercises as shown in Fig. 5, where an increase in the correct responses of 14% and a reduction of 50% of the incorrect answers was observed.

5.2 Usability VR Applications

Finally, the students were presented with a questionnaire of 12 questions about usability in VR applications where 19% of responses were completely in favor, 43% of responses in favor, 29% of neutral responses, 9% of Disagreeable answers as viewed in Fig. 6,

Usability in the virtual laboratory

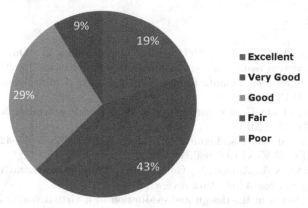

Fig. 6. Average of the results of the evaluation of usability VR applications (Source: Own Elaboration)

6 Conclusions and Future Work

6.1 Conclusions

The conclusions that have been reached after having completed the experiments proposed in this paper are:

- After analyzing the information obtained by the surveys it was observed that there is a 72% of responses in favor of the usability of the virtual laboratory that we have developed, for this reason the virtual laboratory is easy to use, but it would be necessary to perform more tests in order to improve usability.

- There has been a reduction of 60% and 30% of the time and number of objects viewed respectively per sessions, we notice that students after several sessions already knew the virtual laboratory and needed a smaller amount of time to perform the experiment and they already knew which objects to interact with in order to perform the experiment.
- Finally we have analyzed that the students presented a reduction of incorrect answers per session, where the incorrect answers were reduced by 50% and the correct answers increased by 14%, therefore the students have taken interest in solving the experiments correctly and have not lost their motivation in multiple sessions.
- With all the results obtained we can determine that students can easily use a virtual laboratory of physics to perform experiments, but a virtual laboratory does not replace the teacher but is a complement to the educational process.

Acknowledgments. The present investigation is part of the project "Implementación de un Laboratorio virtual inmersivo de Astronomía usando Técnicas de Gamification dirigido a Alumnos de Secundaria" BA-0026-2017-UNSA, thanks to the financing granted by the Universidad Nacional de San Agustin de Arequipa.

References

1. Callaghan, M., Eguíluz, A.G., McLaughlin, G., McShane, N.: Opportunities and challenges in virtual reality for remote and virtual laboratories. In: 2015 12th International Conference on Remote Engineering and Virtual Instrumentation (REV), pp. 235–237. IEEE (2015)
2. MacIsaac, D., et al.: Google cardboard: a virtual reality headset for $10? Phys. Teacher **53**(2), 125 (2015)
3. Helsel, S.: Virtual reality and education. Educ. Technol. **32**(5), 38–42 (1992)
4. VRS: Virtual reality - virtual reality (2017)
5. Azmi, S., Iahad, N.A., Ahmad, N.: Gamification in online collaborative learning for programming courses: a literature review (2006)
6. Roussos, M.: Issues in the design and evaluation of a virtual reality learning environment. Master's thesis, University of Illinois at Chicago, Chicago (1997)
7. Sutcliffe, A., Gault, B.: Heuristic evaluation of virtual reality applications. Interact. Comput. **16**(4), 831–849 (2004)

Providing Recursive Functions to the Tangible Programming Environment for Smartphones

Yasushi Kambayashi[1]([✉]), Katsuki Tsukada[1],
and Munehiro Takimoto[2]

[1] Department of Computer and Information Engineering,
Nippon Institute of Technology, 4-1 Gakuendai, Miyashiro, Minamisaitama,
Saitama 345-8501, Japan
yasushi@nit.ac.jp, cll55320@cstu.nit.ac.jp
[2] Department of Information Sciences, Tokyo University of Science,
2641 Yamazaki, Noda, Chiba, Japan
mune@is.noda.tus.ac.jp

Abstract. This paper reports an implementation of functions including recursive functions in a tangible programming environment. In the previous paper, we proposed a tangible programming environment which the users use on a smartphone. Our goal was to provide those who possess only a smartphone programming environment so that they can start learning programming without any preparations. It is well known that visual programming languages are suitable for young programmers. The most famous one is Scratch. When programming, users manipulate visual joining blocks that represent syntax elements. Today, almost everybody has a smartphone and it has significant computing power. On the other hand, what hinders users from widely using it in programming is its small screen. It is not suitable for fine operations because of the poor operability, which causes frequent recognition errors. Therefore we proposed a tangible programming environment where the user can program not in a screen but on a table by using physical cards. Scratch 2.0 and 3.0 provide recursive functions. Therefore we have expanded our previous implementation to provide functions including recursive functions. As the other syntax card, the user can define a function as a series of "function" card and "argument" cards, and can store entire function definition in one QR code. After creating the function QR code, the user can print that card and use it as a part of his or her program. Thus, the user of our programming environment can construct any program as the current Scratch user can without using personal computers.

Keywords: Tangible programming · Visual programming · Smartphone · Recursive function

1 Introduction

Recently, the programming is getting popular and integrated into the grade school's curriculum. The programming is said to be effective to cultivate the thought process that is so called "logical thinking." Ministry of Education, Culture, Sports, Science, and

© Springer Nature Switzerland AG 2019
C. Stephanidis (Ed.): HCII 2019, CCIS 1034, pp. 255–260, 2019.
https://doi.org/10.1007/978-3-030-23525-3_33

Technology has decided to make the programming education in the elementary schoolas a part of compulsory curriculum starting 2020 [1]. We can expect the programming is a common practice for everyone.

We proposed a tangible programming environment which the user uses on a smartphone [2]. Our goal was to provide those who possess only a smartphone programming environment so that they can start learning programming without any preparations. It is well known that visual programming languages are suitable for young programmers. The most famous one is Scratch that Mitchel Resnick et al. developed [3]. The user manipulates visual joining blocks that represent syntax elements to construct programs. Visualization requires certain region, i.e. large screen. This may be a restriction for providing programming experience for those who do not have personal computers. Today, almost everybody has a smartphone and it has significant computing power. On the other hand, what hinders users from widely using it in programming is its small screen. It is not suitable for fine operations because of the poor operability, which causes frequent recognition errors.

In order to mitigate this problem, we have implemented a tangible programming environment where the user can program not in a screen but on a table by using physical cards. Each card used in the environment represents a certain command of an abstract imperative programming language. The user places cards on a table by hand and combined them to create programs. Each card has a QR code, which the user makes his or her smartphone read. After reading all the codes, the user makes them execute on the smartphone and validates the results on the tiny screen. In addition, the user can draw arbitrary animation characters on a paper, which they input as a photo into their smartphones and use it in their programs just as the Scratch user can manipulate characters called sprits. Thus, the user of our programming environment can construct any program as the Scratch user can program without using personal computers.

On the other hand, our programming system had failed to provide any means for structural decomposition; the system did not have a method to define function, procedure or objects. Scratch 2.0 and 3.0 provide recursive functions. Therefore, in this paper, we expand our previous implementation to provide functions including recursive functions. As the other syntax card, the user can define a function as a series of "function" card and "argument" cards, and can store entire function definition as one QR code. After creating the function QR code, the user can print the code and make a card and then use it as a part of his or her program.

2 Programming Environment

The user of this application program can learn programming while producing programs such that they can construct them in Scratch. The user can use up to three arbitrary images in the programs by taking their photos into their smartphones. When the user starts the application, first, the user is asked to take drawings called sprites as shown Fig. 1. A sprite must be identified by the identification marker.

Fig. 1. The identification marker and a marked sprite

A program is constructed by combining command blocks that instruct a sprite how to move. A command block has a label that shows what the command block represents, and a QR code that represents a command for the corresponding sprite. Figure 2 shows a part of a program that uses five command blocks and how they are read though the camera on the smartphone. A command block consists of three items, namely ID, the explanation, and the command. ID is a six digit integer that is used for identifying each blockto avoid reading the same command block more than once. The explanation is a short description showing what the block does. When the user read a command block by the smartphone, the explanation appears on the screen so that the user can confirm its read. The command is the instruction given to the sprite. This is corresponding to one statement of an ordinary procedural programming language. The commands are stored in an array in the system, and picked one by one during the execution.

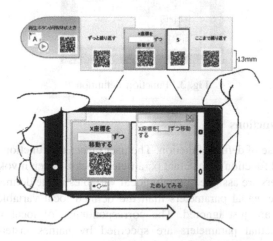

Fig. 2. Command blocks and how they are read

There are eleven kinds of command blocks the programming environment provides; they are start blocks, instruction blocks, numeral blocks, variable blocks, wait/terminate blocks, repetition blocks, conditional branch blocks, cloning blocks, and newly added function definition blocks, function invocation blocks and recursion blocks. The syntax and the semantics of our visual programming language is described in [1].

3   Functions

In the same manner as building a program, we can construct a functions by combing command blocks that instruct a sprite how to move. The created function is represented as a QR code, and the user can invoke the QR coded function in an arbitrary place in a program.

3.1   Creating Functions

A function definition is just like a complete program except it does not have the start block that specifies the sprite the program is applied. Figure 3 shows the definition of a function. After reading the command blocks that construct the function, the user push the "creating QR code" button to create and store the function in the smartphone. In our programming environment, formal parameters are defined as variables without values, and treated as local variables in the execution time.

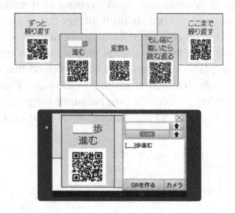

Fig. 3.   Function definition

3.2   Invoking Functions

Figure 4 shows a use of defined function. The user places the function invocation block to call the specified function with actual parameter blocks. When invoking the function, the actual parameters are assigned into the local variables in the defined function. If the user specifies more actual parameters than the defined local variables, the excessive actual parameters are just ignored. The correspondence of local variables (formal parameters) and actual parameters are specified by names instead of the order. Therefore the user can specify certain local variables and make some variables are left unspecified. Figure 4 shows a program that moves a sprite forward units indicated by the value of A, and reverses the movement at the edge of the screen. In the figure, the variable A is assigned value fifteen. The left green block indicates function invocation and the right green block indicates the end of actual parameters (and the end of the function invocation).

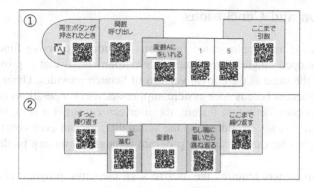

Fig. 4. Use of a function

3.3 Recursive Functions

In order to create a recursion, the user use the recursion block. The recursion block is only used in the function definition, and the invocation is performed as a normal non-recursive function. Figure 5 show the recursive function that compute the factorial of a given integer.

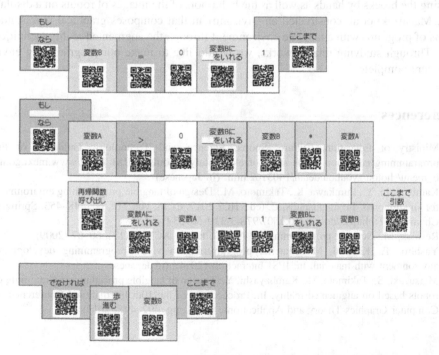

Fig. 5. A recursive function that compute the factorial of N

4 Discussion and Conclusions

We have proposed and implemented functions including recursive functions in our previously developed tangible programming environment so that it provides enough features almost the same as the current version of Scratch provides. Using QR codes is the key of our success because our system suppresses users' operations on the screen. By using the function definition feature, the user can construct a large scale program through function abstract. In addition to the scalability, we can even construct function library so that the user can construct a program through combining predefined library functions.

The previous system required the user to scan the entire program at once [2]. By compressing a subprogram into a QR code, the user can not only take advantages of library functions but also can add new program constructs into our programming environment. The user, however, have to print the QR code that represent the defined function to integrate it in a program. If we integrate user-defined functions into the programming environment, we can enhance the usability of the system. This can be one of the future directions.

There are a few tangible programming environment inspired by Scratch. Yashiro et al. extended the instruction blocks of the Scratch to physical blocks, designing a tangible interface where users can program the behaviors of physical robots by composing the blocks by hands as well as the behaviors of the images of robots on a display [4]. Matsuzaki et al. constructed an environment that composes graphical representations of programs with a tangible environment through the augmented reality technique [5]. Through studying related works, we would like to make our programming environment complete.

References

1. Ministry of Education, Culture, Sports, Science, and Technology: Guideline of the programming education in the stage of elementary schools (2018). http://www.mext.go.jp/b_menu/shotou/zyouhou/detail/1403162.htm. (in Japanese)
2. Kambayashi, Y., Furukawa, K., Takimoto, M.: Design of tangible programming environment for smartphones. In: Stephanidis, C. (ed.) HCI 2017. CCIS, vol. 714, pp. 448–453. Springer, Cham (2017). https://doi.org/10.1007/978-3-319-58753-0_64
3. Resnick, M.: Scratch: programming for All. Commun. ACM 52(11), 60–67 (2009)
4. Yashiro, T., Kazushi, M.: Material programming: a visual programming development environment with material. In: IPSJ Interaction (2014). (in Japanese)
5. Matsuzaki, S., Takimoto, M., Kambayashi, Y.: Design of tangible procedural programming of robots based on augmented reality. In: Proceedings of the 10th International Conference on Computer Graphics Theory and Applications, vol. 1. pp. 492–497 (2015)

Visual Poetry: Nurturing Children's Creativity Through Appropriate Blank Spaces

Ying Tung Liu(✉)

Chang Gung University, Taoyuan, Taiwan
M0742003@cgu.edu.tw

Abstract. This design study focuses on the importance of primary school students' reading and visual association. According study of the readability of Chinese books, to help establish the background information of the primary school children reading comprehension. However, among the styles less discussed is children's poetry which is often used in primary school education to nurture children's creativity. Described by Lin Liang as "the art of plain language", the verse's legibility and readability are explained and underwritten by rhyming or easy to understand sentences. The poet often uses the technique of "constant meaning, not text", whilst deliberately fragmented text represents the poet's "blank" space. This blank, or imaginary space, is the part that the reader can infill. This process demonstrates the reader can read between the line. This pilot study through the children's poetry of Lin Liang, aims to present the pictures that children see, along with the appropriate blanks will become elements in illustration through looking at the picture to practice illustration communication and inspire young readers' poetic imagination.

Keywords: Children's poetry · Illustration communication · Visual poetry · Children's creativity · Association

1 Introduction

Children absorption through reading can facilitate knowledge accrual, help them get into the habit of reading and learned writing skill from primary school education. In addition, children's poetry which is often in primary school education to nurture children's creativity [1, 2].

By establishing the database, artificial intelligent (AI) imitates the human's brain to think humility and more abstract thinking. Human communication can read between the line through high socialization and knowledgeable, different from computer information such as exactly; but children might have less social experience or ability to understanding high abstract meaning, hence this study was expected children reaching closeness to abstract thinking and be able to describe the meaning with abstract illustration have (missing) words into images, which poet's "blank" space or imaginary space, is the part that reader can infill.

This research was a pilot study to investigate poetic communication through appropriate illustration can be described by children without databased through visual

C. Stephanidis (Ed.): HCII 2019, CCIS 1034, pp. 261–269, 2019.
https://doi.org/10.1007/978-3-030-23525-3_34

association. The rest of the paper discusses relevant background context, design concept and methodology, followed by the result from the experiment with five children aged 9 to 11 years old.

2 Background

As are following on grades, children in primary school increasing the use of academic language, and flexibility in abstract and figurative thinking [3]. In children education, children's poetry has been an important role between children and literature. At aged between 7–12 years old children were at the stage started to learn writing skill and nurturing association in the following years.

2.1 Visual Poetry

On the grounds that visual association contains information transmission, this allows children to imagine comprehension beyond content; therefore, this research will investigate on children's understanding of pictures, and the possibilities for practicing associations, beyond imagery.

The characteristics of poetry's language can be traced to artistic mood, feeling or status as represented by a combination of words. The poet often uses the technique of "constant meaning, not text", whilst deliberately fragmented text. In the study of the readability of Chinese books, to help establish the background information of the primary school children reading comprehension, common (reading) texts for children considers themes and ideas, language and literary features, words and sentence complexity.

2.2 Illustration Communication

Reading text and viewing illustrations is integrated with composing with writing sound, and images, that has the potential to be highly engaging and productive for students. [3]

From Arakelian to discussed the factors of format the picture book's style, who mentioned the relationship between the text and illustration. The drawings of each of books complement the text of each panel in one of three ways: They can provide an example by explaining or giving details for a general statement in the text. They can provide a setting which does not deal with any specific statement in the text, but establishes a general scene. Finally, they can provide an illustration reproducing some statement in the text [4].

In Fig. 1, Maurice Sendak often use the first way of text-illustration relationship, provides a lot of details in picture to supply the missing part in the text. In Fig. 2, Original book text: In the spring when birdies sing. Something suddenly went "zing!". The picture applies the second way of text-illustration relationship, provide a setting which does not deal with any specific statement in the text, but establishes a general scene.

Fig. 1. 《*Where The Wild Things Are*》 By Maurice Sendak

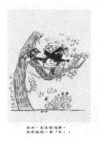

Fig. 2. 《Madeline and the Bad Hat》 By Ludwig Bemelmans

Fig. 3. 《Too *Noisy*》 By Wu Min Er

In Fig. 3, They applies the third way of text-illustration relationship: they can provide an illustration reproducing some statement in the text.

We knowing poem teaching strategy were applied in education in primary school, but poetic illustration are less discuss and following paper will discuss children explains poetic in children poetry.

3 Methodology

As we are still in the early phase of the project, in this study, we mainly focus on poetic communication through appropriate illustration. Color is not in the discussion, we will exclude the use of color in order to avoid having different interpretations. Following section, we will present the stories with pencil drawing, conducts storytelling and observation, and provide The little red riding hood as control group compare with other poetry, to discuss children's association strength difference.

3.1 Design Concept

To create illustrations, the content was based on the Lin-Lian's children poetry, the verse's legibility and readability is explained and underwritten by rhyming or easy to understand sentences. Through separate the verses, and followed the three types of text-illustration relationship, assemble pictures elements to make the sentences.

Fig. 4. The Little Red Riding Hood

The first story, The Little Red Riding Hood, we chooseCharles Perrault's vision: As she was going through the wood, she met with a wolf, who had a very great mind to eat her up. Children are familiar with the background of this story, in this image describes little red riding hood brought a basket on the way to grandma's house, met a big wolf in the forest. Children can imagine if she will get into trouble or not? There is provides an illustration reproducing some statement in the text.

《想家的獅子》

動物園是監牢，
一頭獅子住在裡面，
天天吼個不停。
好像在說：
放我回到森林吧！
我好想回家......

《Homesick Lion》
The zoo is a prison.
A lion lives in it,
roaring day after day.
It seems to said,
let me go back to the forest!
I really wanna go home…

Fig. 5. Homesick Lion

The image describes the lion is screaming, and the fence where it lives is restricted. There are trees and birds on its head, which represent the places where the lion wants to go back. This concept comes from sculpture, which connects the relationship between objects. In the view of the text-illustration relationship, is only for the content stated in the text.

《磨菇》
磨菇是
寂寞的小亭子。
只有雨天
青蛙才來躲雨。
晴天青蛙走了，
亭子裡冷冷清清。

《Mushroom》
Mushroom is a lonely pavilion.
Only on rainy days,
Frogs came out to take shelter.
On sunny days,
The sky clean, frogs leaving,
Pavilion was chilly and quietly

Fig. 6. Mushroom

The image was divided into two parts, the left show frogs taking shelter from the rain, and the right part shows the rain stopped that frog prepare to leave. This picture applies the first type of text-illustration relationship, that picture provides more details such as kinds of mushroom, and frogs emotional, these are not mentioned in verse. Moreover, the verse front part and back part have comparison feeling as lively and lonely.

《金魚》

我是一隻
表演的魚，
不能躺在缸底
沉睡。
二十四小時
跳著水上芭蕾，
沒有下班，
而且不能喊累。

《Goldfish》

I am a
performance fish,
Couldn't lie on the bottom
of the tank, falling asleep.
Twenty-four hours,
Water ballet dancing,
Cannot get off work,
and cannot complain.

Fig. 7. Goldfish

According to the first graph, the drawing provides an example by explaining or giving details for a general statement in the text. The image tells that the goldfish is a ballet dancer, couldn't get off work or complain. Use the clockwork on the back of the goldfish to express the feelings expressed in the text with the physical objects, the concept was personal point. Expect reader can understand the statement of the text through such details.

3.2   Experiment

Five Taiwanese primary school students (3 were females), age 9 to 11 years participated as subjects from one class (aged 8 to 12 years of eighteen children). Participants be arrangement the order as rising hands to participate. The experiment conducted in a room, which for writing skill and preceded was each participant can express their opinion verbally about illustrations with different stories. The experimental procedure is followed by: (1) researcher introduce to participants and decide the order of participants (2) all participants started looking at the picture (no poetry), viewed the first poetic illustration. (3) the participant was instructed to verbalize their feelings(opinions) one by one. (4) repeat steps (2) and (3) until the participant had viewed four illustrations.

All pictures provide same size 12 × 15 (cm), then projection in the room. All illustrations content are based on different children poetry by the same author, but one of them is based on classic fairy tale as a control group, in order to investigate the difference in the length of the child's statement.

Fig. 8. The participants describe story one by one.

4   Result

All users study were audio recorded, to be later analyzed by recorded keywords from children's looking at the picture. One of the participant couldn't describe more than one sentence to be excluded. This study classifies the participants mention in verbal content into 5 attributes: (1) Character (2) Character's emotion (3) Description event (4) Place (5) Association. By collating the result found, Homesick Lion and Mushroom extend more association statements. In addition, removing the color like reduce the cue, such as appearance of fogs, participants are classified into different characters (e.g. frogs, groundhog, smurf) for children, it can develop into any stories. Participants describe The little red riding hood, that her situation of meet the wolf, all participants are describe similar story, less association. The fourth picture Goldfish, the element set clockwork result positively. From recorded keywords, which show the participants can understand deliberate arranged objects, and through clockwork associate to goldfish turning never stop, repeat continually or controlled by someone.

5   Discussion

This paper to investigate whether the poetic communication through appropriate illustration can be recognized by children. According to the keywords recorded, Homesick Lion and Mushroom extend more association statements, that might be the character's emotion are not obvious directly, also without color, provide less emotional characteristic cue than other two pictures content more flexibility. Regarding the poetic illustration elements, Homesick Lion, trees and the bird on the lion's head, which concept refers to sculpture as meaning as every object connecting, but children are not this way to think significantly. Moreover, participants were according to objects relationship and around environment surmise characters emotion and rationalize the unreasonable elements in an illustration based on their own experience and interests.

While discuss background context, the three types of text-illustration relationship, provide way can transmit narrative to picture, that based on the human can read between the line. Another point worth to discussed was Goldfish, which including more abstract meaning in narrative. Therefore, we provide the explanation by our point that through clockwork present the 24-h can't rest. From participants positive result, the text-illustration relationship might be including one more way that: illustration can provide specific visual object convey abstract text. One of the limitations in this project is experiment set up, it's all participate in the same classroom at the same time, they have chance to affect each other. Illustration style was another point might produce bias, which although provide pictures as same way.

6 Conclusion

While our project is still in the early stage, we also conduct storytelling experiment, as a preliminary user study. As such provide set of poetic illustrations classify by children to be beneficial to the illustration communication and found children can create more story difference beyond the pictures. Although a lot of well-established research, however the mandarin is slightly different. In our further work, that doing more research considered how "blank" in poetry can inspire children's creativity.

Appendix

Table 1. Keywords recrode

Subject	Story and poetry			
	The little red riding hood	Homesick lion	The mushroom	Goldfish
Main character	S1: Little red riding hood and Big wolf S2: Little red riding hood and big wolf S3: Little red riding hood S4: None S5: The big wolf	S1: Lion S2: Lion S3: Lion S4: None S5: Lion	S1: Mushroom, leaves or smurf S2: Groundhog S3: None S4: Four frogs S5: four frogs	S1: Mermaid S2: Toy mermaid S3: Toy S4: Toy S5: Fish
Character's emotion	S1: Contemplate S2: Scared S3: None S4: Worried S5: Unhappy	S1: Happy or surprise S2: Surprise S3: Angry S4: Angry S5: Happy	S1: Want to eat the mushrooms S2: None S3: None S4: Distressed S5: Happy	S1: Helpless S2: Enjoy S3: Bored S4: Tired S5: Unhappy

(*continued*)

Table 1. (*continued*)

Subject	Story and poetry			
	The little red riding hood	Homesick lion	The mushroom	Goldfish
Place	S1: Forest S2: Jungle S3: House S4: None S5: Forest	S1: Cage S2: Zoo S3: House S4: None S5: House	S1: Damp corner S2: None S3: None S4: None S5: Besides the pond	S1: Toy shop S2: None S3: In a children's home S4: Someone's home S5: Toy shop
Description event	S1: The little red riding hood worried about big wolf will eat her S2: She doesn't know what the big wolf will do S3: Maybe big wolf like little red riding hood S4: She stare at the big wolf, that worried she will be attacked from behind S5: The big wolf looks unhappy, it might eat the little red riding hood	S1: The lion was happy or surprise, because its had lots of beautiful flowers on its head S2: Lion have trees and flowers growth on its head S3: Lion has zebra stripes. The bird licking its head, so its angry S4: The lion should be violent, but everyone like him causes a lot of cute flowers on his head. But, he hates someone love him S5: The Lion was happy because he found flowers growth on his head	S1: It might happen that they climb the mushroom to eat it, in a damp place on the corner S2: They want to get into soil so they dig with the shovel, that work hard for survive S3: They under the leaves to take shelter from rain, there was a coffee shop but they can't afford the money to pay entrance fee S4: One of these four frogs take a shovel to digging mushrooms, take it to eat, but the roots are too deep to dig up S5: Frogs dig mushroom beside the pond, and take a shovel since roots grow deep	S1: The character is a mermaid who is dancing ballet, and felt helpless since its has been controlled by a battery for toys S2: Its has happy mood for dancing ballet, but its broken result turning and turning to dizziness S3: This creature dancing ballet, who has a clockwork on the back. It has a dream but controlled by a bad guy forced it dancing never stop S4: It's a toy fish, which has fish head and human leg, and it's love dance but too tired to sleepily S5: The character is fish, dance in the toy shop

(*continued*)

Table 1. (*continued*)

Subject	Story and poetry			
	The little red riding hood	Homesick lion	The mushroom	Goldfish
Association	S1: None S2: The Little red riding hood S3: The Little red riding hood S4:None S5: Associated to little red riding hood hates the big wolf	S1: Butterflies and bees will come to collecting honey S2: Waiting for those flowers drop off, the lion will become normal S3: Associated to story lion ate people S4: None S5: The lion think will have more birds come to his head later	S1: I think the following little things may be was blue fairy S2: They're work hard to survive S3: Coffee shop below leaves S4: None S5: They dig up mushrooms and bringing back to share to their friends	S1: It's pitiful S2: None S3: None S4: Associated to broken toys in factory S5: It forced by owner to dancing

References

1. Tsai, C.H.: An Action Research on Process of Applying Association Strategies to the Fifth Grade Students' Collection Material toward Narrative Poem Writing (2018)
2. Wen, N.P.: Research of combination teaching to creative child poetry teaching with Mandarin teaching in the fifth grade of elementary school (2006)
3. Dalton, B.: Engaging children in close reading. Reading Teacher **66**(8), 642–649 (2013). International Reading Association 2013
4. Arakelian, P.G.: Text and illustration: a stylistic analysis of books by Sendak and Mayer. Children's Lit. Quart. **1**(3), 122–127 (1985)

Implementation of a Design Thinking Didactic Strategy Aimed at Challenges and Their Impact on the Development of Generic Competencies: Bootcamp #PascualChallenge

Carlos Ocampo-Quintero, Carlos Moreno-Paniagua,
Sara Ibarra-Vargas, Rocío Torres-Novoa, Nicolás Restrepo-Henao,
Francisco Gallego-Escobar, Juan Henao-Santa[(⊠)],
Luis Muñoz-Marín, and Saúl Emilio Rivero-Mejía

Pascual Bravo University Institution, Medellín, Colombia
{c.ocampoqu, c.moreno1975, s.ibarrava, rocio.torres,
nrestrepo, francisco.gallego, j.henaosa, luis.munoz,
saul.rivero}@pascualbravo.edu.co

Abstract. Competency-based training is a trend in the university context, as well as an effort to educate professionals capable of solving current and real world problems. Under this perspective, competencies are developed at the conceptual, attitudinal and procedural levels, interacting with environment socio-cultural factors. In this requirement the Institución Universitaria Pascual Bravo, based on experiences from other universities, worked on a learning strategy based on challenges through an event called Bootcamp #PascualChallenge, which allows students to discover and develop alternatives to improve specific situations in an interdisciplinary manner and thus train in generic skills. Likewise, in the event, a 3-day contest, Design Thinking elements were implemented to solve complex problems in a creative way, from systemic perspectives, in which a set of solar recharge systems for mobile devices were conceptually redesigned, these systems were in a critical functional and aesthetic state, due to the deterioration of their structures, technical faults and obsolescence. In this way, the Boot-camp #PascualChallenge event is proposed as a pedagogical alternative that enhances significant learning experiences in tune with the development of generic competencies, under a perspective of Challenge-Based Learning.

Keywords: Generic competencies · Challenge based learning ·
Design Thinking · Bootcamp

1 Introduction

In the university context, competency-based training has become a trend approach that seeks to educate professionals capable of solving the current and real world problems [1]. From this perspective, the student accounts for the development of competencies at the conceptual, attitudinal and procedural levels, interacting with the socio-cultural

C. Stephanidis (Ed.): HCII 2019, CCIS 1034, pp. 270–277, 2019.
https://doi.org/10.1007/978-3-030-23525-3_35

factors of the environment in which he or she develops as a professional [2]. At the Institución Universitaria Pascual Bravo (*IU Pascual Bravo*), the application of this competency-based training approach is part of the question: what should students learn in order to answer to the needs, interests, problems and solutions (NIPS) of Colombia's productive and social sectors? This is planned autonomously and contextually by the Institution, which results in a contextual know-how development. In this way, as shown in Fig. 1, IU Pascual Bravo plans competencies through elements of competency which are characterized by: (1) cognitive, procedural and attitudinal performance criteria; (2) contextual knowledge and comprehensions; (3) disciplinary or application context; and (4) evidence required for certification [3].

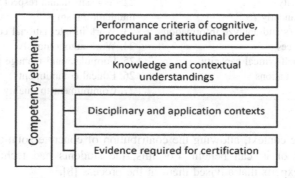

Fig. 1. Competency element characterization.

One of the most internationally recognized approaches to competency-based training is that presented by the Tuning Project [4], which began in the European Union with 135 universities from 27 countries and was replicated in other regions of Europe, Asia, Africa, Oceania, North America and Latin America. The Tuning Project opens a debate to exchange information that can generate improvement and collaboration between higher education institutions in different countries. This debate resulted in 27 generic competencies, shown in Table 1, defined for the field of education in Latin America [5].

From this standpoint, the IU Pascual Bravo has worked explicitly on the education of generic competencies through research projects with undergraduate students [6]. Furthermore, the Design Management programme of the IU Pascual Bravo, in dialogue with Professor Jan Erik Baars of Lucerne University of Applied Sciences and Arts (HSLU), among others, explored as a significant academic experience, the BootCamp model as an alternative to Challenges Based Learning -CBL-, which allows students to engage in the search for solutions to problems affecting local and global issues, including cooperative and interdisciplinary learning and developing different generic and specific competencies. It is common for the CBL to address a generic issue and pose one or more challenges related to the topic. In the case of Boot-Camp-PascualChallenge, it was enhanced with the Design Thinking Methodology [7], given that its structure promotes the development of innovation centered on people, creative work and teamwork through tools of empathy, ideation, prototype and pertinent details

Table 1. Generic competencies in Tuning Project.

1. Abstraction, analysis and synthesis	14. Creative ability
2. Apply the knowledge in practice	15. Identify, pose and solve problems
3. Organize and plan the time	16. Make decisions
4. Knowledge about the area of study and profession	17. Team work
5. Social responsibility and citizen commitment	18. Interpersonal skills
6. Oral and written communication	19. Motivate and drive towards common goals
7. Communication in a second language	20. Preservation of the environment
8. Use of information and communication technologies	21. Commitment to socio-cultural environment
9. Research capacity	22. Assessment and respect for diversity and multiculturalism
10. Update permanently	23. Work in international contexts
11. Search, process and analyze information from diverse sources	24. Work autonomously
12. Critical and self-critical capacity	25. Formulate and manage projects
13. Act in new situations	26. Ethical commitment
	27. Commitment to quality

for the academic context, allowing the contribution of concrete solutions from which society, or part of it, can benefit. For this, the students had technological tools, resources, and experts that advised them in the process [8].

One of the key objectives of education is to make it easier for students to think critically and creatively, although, it is usually believed that they are not prepared to solve disorderly and unstructured problems that do not have easy solutions in the real world, for this, in recent years, Design Thinking as a methodology has begun to be used strongly for problem solving, business modeling, strategic planning and development of ideas. Companies increasingly require the use of this concept, giving it the validity to be used in the student environment as a learning process and the acquisition of generic and specific competencies [9].

2 Methodology

Under the premise of the interdisciplinary exercise, 10 teams of students were formed to solve a challenge over three days of intensive work. Through this activity, teachers expected students to demonstrate the development of generic competencies and generic descriptors that are often not perceived in the execution of formal courses [10].

The first day of the Bootcamp began with the presentation of the participating students, the team of teachers accompanying the exercise and the working facilities for the event. The teams were formed in a pseudo-random way, using a proprietary software that assigned each student their work unit. The software ensured the conformation of the team with students of engineering and design programs, in order to guarantee interdisciplinary and active participation with technical knowledge of both fields of study. During the presentation of the challenge, the exercise was described, the work guide directed by elements of Design Thinking, the definition of deliverables for socialization and the evaluation rubric. Likewise, each team was given a box with the working materials: colored pencils, paper, adhesive tapes, glue, cardboard and electronic parts for the realization of a low fidelity functional prototype.

On day 2, the teams worked on their project, within the facilities of the Institution. The team of teachers organized an "operations center" with furniture for each team to plan, design and develop their proposal. During this time, teacher orientation sessions were reserved, through the assignment of appointments, in which specific concerns were solved in functional, aesthetic, quality and decision-making areas in the resolution of the problem posed. Likewise, the teachers accompanied the "operations center" to follow the progress of the projects, to promote the exchange of knowledge.

On day 3, its purpose was to carry out a pitch for the socialization and evaluation of the projects, with external juries, formed by 5 guest professionals from the energy, services and the cultural sector and the creative industry, with the purpose of feedback the experience to the students from their business realities and work projection. Each jury was given an evaluation rubric that it contained:

- **Project documentation:** Final report, workflow planning schedule, user and client characterization, summary of the creative and development process, list of technical and design requirements, approach to costs and value proposition.
- **Evidences of process:** Photographs showing the activities carried out, materials used and final product (prototype).
- **Model:** Functional projection in 1:10 scale, with description of the technical component and photomontage representation in context.
- **Order:** Folder with evidences and documentation suitably named to facilitate its identification.
- **Pitch:** A coherent and fluid oral presentation that allows to fully understand the proposal in 7 min.

For the pitch, each team prepared the design proposal in a 10 slides audiovisual presentation with the information regarding the formal, functional, interaction, construction and value proposal attributes, showing the scopes and results obtained, based on a systemic and strategic thinking of design and engineering.

Then, the jurors proceeded to discuss and analyze the factors of the rubric, verifying the information provided by the teams. Collective feedback was presented to the teams, emphasizing the positive contributions of immersion in terms of knowledge exchange, the capacity and commitment to teamwork, the forms of communication and justification of the project and the feasibility of continuing the proposals in the real context. At the end, the 3 winning groups were identified in a hierarchical order to grant public recognition and awards from the Institution and sponsors.

After the exercise, the students were asked to complete a perception survey regarding the achievement of the generic competencies identified in the Tuning project. Prior to the event, teachers were given a survey to identify generic competencies that the event could develop.

3   Results Analysis

All the information of the pedagogical strategy, images and experiences, were compiled in order to evaluate the different activities carried out, identify key points to implement continuous improvements in future academic events. In Fig. 2, a causal diagram is shown where it is observed that the development of generic competencies can be presented as a module based on the competency approach of the IU Pascual Bravo. It is observed that there is a gap between the expected level of generic competencies development and the existing one, the higher the expected level, the greater the gap. Equally, the higher the existing level, the smaller the gap. The larger the gap, the more there is a need to develop didactic strategies such as the Bootcamp #PascualChallenge event. At in the same way, the greater the number of strategies, the greater will be the development of existing generic competencies narrowing the gap. Thus, it is expected to identify the generic competencies that are developed with an CBL strategy.

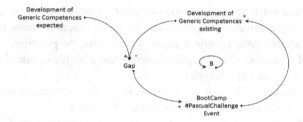

Fig. 2.   Causal diagram of development of generic competencies.

In order to verify the perception of the development of generic competencies during the execution of the event, a previous survey was conducted among teachers regarding generic competencies, rating from 1 to 5, the contribution of the event to each competency. Then, the students who participated in the event were also asked how much the event contributed to each of the generic competencies, rating them from 1 to 5 [11]. In both surveys, the results were counted and grouped to qualitatively assess, considering grades 1 and 2 as disagreement, 4 and 5 as agreement, and finally 3 as indecisive. In the analysis of the data, as shown in Table 2, there is a correlation of 0.74 between the student population and the teacher population, which indicates coincidence in the consensus of the generic competencies developed. Likewise, observing kurtosis and centrality data (mean, median, and mode), it is observed that in both populations there is a good coincidence in the responses. When calculating the coefficient of variation (standard-to-ground/average deviation), it was observed that it is very small, which strengthens this assessment.

In order to determine the generic competencies that were most developed in the event, those that reached more than 75% of coincidence in each population were identified, as shown in Table 3. From this result it can be deduced that, in short, there are 6 generic competencies developed in the Bootcamp event: creative capacity, teamwork capacity, research capacity, capacity to identify, pose and solve problems, capacity to make decisions and capacity to act in new situations.

Table 2. Statistical analysis of data from surveys on generic skills.

	Students	Teachers
Mean	63,9%	78,2%
Typical error	3,5%	4,5%
Median	65,2%	87,5%
Mode	60,9%	100,0%
Standard deviation	18,2%	23,2%
Coefficient of variation	28,5%	29,6%
Sample variance	0,03327248	0,05359687
kurtosis	1,56170875	1,93249324
Asymmetry coefficient	−1,2738391	−1,43084185
Rank	0,69565217	0,875
Minimum	0,17391304	0,125
Maximum	0,86956522	1
Sum	17,2608696	21,125
Account	27	27
Population correlation factor	0,74	

Table 3. Results of surveys on generic competencies.

Evaluated generic competencies		Students	Teachers
No	Description		
14	Creative capacity	**87,0%**	**100,0%**
17	Teamwork	**87,0%**	**87,5%**
4	Knowledge of the area of study and profession	**82,6%**	75,0%
9	Research capacity	**82,6%**	**87,5%**
2	Apply knowledge in practice	**78,3%**	75,0%
15	Identify, pose and solve problems	**78,3%**	**100,0%**
16	Make decisions	**78,3%**	**87,5%**
25	Formulate and manage projects	**78,3%**	**100,0%**

From these results, as shown in Table 4, a proposal for the event was structured as a module based on the competency-based training approach developed by IU Pascual Bravo. It was identified as an element of competency "to develop a technological challenge using elements of Design Thinking". The generic competencies agreed in the event were identified as performance criteria. Contextual knowledge and comprehensions were defined around the field of Design Thinking knowledge. The solar recharging systems for mobile devices of the IU Pascual Bravo was the scope of application on this occasion. Finally, the knowledge evidences that were identified are those that answer questions related to moments, tools and elements of Design Thinking, the performance evidences, direct or indirect observations related to the elements of Design Thinking; and, the behavioral evidences, the evaluation of the elements of Design Thinking and their evaluation before juries.

Table 4. Learning module of the BootCamp #PascualChallenge event

Competency Element: to develop a technological challenge using elements of Design Thinking	
Performance criteria	To develop, under a technological challenge: • Creative ability • The ability to work in teams • Research capacity • The ability to identify, raise and solve problems • The ability to make decisions • The ability to act in new situations
Wisdom/Knowledge/Contextual understandings	Design thinking: • User-centered design perspective • Moments of design thinking • Design thinking tools • Elements for the communication of the product and the project: – Plans, diagrams and sketches – Low-fidelity prototype model – Presentation type pitch – Brief – Evidence of the process
Disciplinary and application contexts	Solar systems for recharging mobile devices of the Institution
Evidences	• **Knowledge:** Respond to questions related to moments, tools and elements of Design Thinking • **Performance:** Direct or indirect observations related to the elements of Design Thinking • **Behavior/product:** Evaluation of the elements of Design Thinking and its evaluation in the face of juries

4 Conclusions and Recommendations

The Bootcamp #PascualChallenge event allows students to discover and develop alternatives to improve specific situations in an interdisciplinary manner and thus train in generic competencies. It is therefore an interesting pedagogical alternative to enhance meaningful learning experiences in tune with competency development, under an CBL perspective and, for the IU Pascual Bravo, it becomes an important competency-based learning strategy, which enables it to train professionals capable of solving current and real world problems. In addition, the importance of implementing Design Thinking elements to solve complex problems in a creative way from systemic perspectives was proved, which for the Institution also represents an opportunity to work in a joint and integrated manner, with different academic programs and with other universities in the local and global spectrum, so that design problems such as the one presented by solar recharge systems for mobile devices can be solved; all of which were in a critical functional and aesthetic state, due to the deterioration of their structures, technical failures and obsolescence.

All the information of the pedagogical strategy, images and experiences were gathered in order to evaluate the different activities carried out, identify critic points to implement continuous improvements in future academic events. Within the possibilities observed, it is expected to refine the learning module instrument for the event, incorporating more performance criteria, which will be visualized in the next Boot-Camp events. Likewise, a set of application ranges are identified, in which the linkage of sponsoring companies of the event is strengthened. Finally, it is important to incorporate more elements of Design Thinking, so that it integrates even more the interdisciplinary work in the development of competencies based curriculum of the IU Pascual Bravo.

References

1. Henri, M., Johnson, M.D., Nepal, B.: A review of competency-based learning: tools, assessments, and recommendations. J. Eng. Educ. **106**, 607–638 (2017). https://doi.org/10.1002/jee.20180
2. Irigoyen, J.J., Jiménez, M.Y., Acuña, K.F.: Competencias y educación superior. Rev. Mex. Invest. Educ. **16**, 243–266 (2011)
3. Gaviria, Y.: Guía de Apoyo: Planificando la Competencia y sus Elementos. Medellín, Colombia (2016)
4. Tuning Project: Tuning Educational Structures in Europe II. Bilbao, España (2006)
5. Beneitone, P., Esquetini, C., González, J., et al.: Reflexiones y Perspectivas de la Educación Superior en América Latina. Tuning Project, Bilbao (2007)
6. Lemmel-Vélez, K., Rivero-Mejía, E., Ocampo-Quintero, C.A.: Experiences of the SICAP Research Seeding in the Development of Soft Skills. Learn. Collab. Technol. Learn. Teach. LCT **10925**, 446–460 (2018). https://doi.org/10.1007/978-3-319-91152-6_34
7. Buchanan, R.: Wicked problems in design thinking. Des. Issues **8**, 5–21 (1992)
8. Fidalgo, Á., Sein-Echaluce, M., García, F.: Aprendizaje Basado en Retos en una asignatura académica universitaria. Rev. Iberoam Informática Educ. **25**, 1–8 (2017)
9. Castillo-Vergara, M., Alvarez-Marin, A., Cabana-Villca, R.: Design thinking: how to guide students and business entrepreneurs in the application. Ing. Ind. **35**, 301–311 (2014). https://doi.org/10.1016/j.destud.2013.03.001
10. Salazar, C.A.: Competencias transversales en los planes de estudio de las titulaciones de grado : los esfuerzos de Bolonia en calidad universitaria Efforts of Bologna in University Quality, pp. 61–72 (2012)
11. Nallaperumal, K., Krishnan, A.: Engineering Research Methodology A Computer Science and Engineering and Information and Communication Technologies Perspective. PHI Learn Priv Limited, New Delhi (2013). https://doi.org/10.1111/ibi.12062

Impact of Motivational Factors on the Learning Process in the Use of Learning Management Systems: An Empirical Study Based on Learners' Experiences

Melissa Rau[✉], Claudia Hösel, Christian Roschke,
Rico Thomanek, and Marc Ritter

University of Applied Sciences Mittweida, 09648 Mittweida, Germany
mrau2@hs-mittweida.de

Abstract. Learning management systems (LMS) are increasingly being used in the academic field as a supplement to face-to-face learning and are intended to effectively support knowledge transfer through individually integrable e-learning modules. In practice, however, it can be observed that LMS often does not live up to these expectations. Although the learning effectiveness of LMS is discussed in the literature, it is sometimes limited to the system level. Previous studies on the learning effectiveness of LMS have dealt in particular with the usability and adaptivity of the system. However, the one-sided focus on the system seems insufficient in the context of learning effectiveness, since motivational factors at the learner level are largely ignored. This study addresses the motivational factors in the use of LMS by students and uses a prototype to determine which e-learning modules have a positive effect on learning motivation. For this purpose, an e-learning prototype is developed on an LMS with various e-learning modules, and the extent to which the individual modules have an effect on learning motivation is investigated. The results of the study show that e-learning modules which demonstrate individual learning progress are suitable for promoting the learning motivation of students when using LMS.

Keywords: E-learning · Learning management system ·
Learning effectiveness · Motivation

1 Introduction

In the last ten years, the new information and communication technologies (ICT) have led to the increasing integration of e-learning into educational processes and the associated changes in the acquisition and transfer of knowledge [1]. E-learning, as a form of technology-mediated education, uses electronic tools and information technologies to provide learning content and enable learning

© Springer Nature Switzerland AG 2019
C. Stephanidis (Ed.): HCII 2019, CCIS 1034, pp. 278–283, 2019.
https://doi.org/10.1007/978-3-030-23525-3_36

experiences [2]. While traditional teaching and learning offers set spatial and temporal limits, e-learners can flexibly access learning content and learn at their own pace [3]. Various forms of e-learning can be classified in higher education. For example, a distinction is made between pure e-learning environments, Massive Open Online Course (MOOCs) or blended learning arrangements. The latter is used in academic education as a supplement to face-to-face courses and is intended to support knowledge transfer through individually integrable e-learning modules [4]. The implementation of blended learning courses is primarily carried out via Learning Management Systems (LMS). Conventional LMS offer a web-based interface to provide learning content, organise learning processes and enable communication between teachers and learners [5]. E-learning via LMS requires learners to have higher technical competences and a greater degree of self-discipline than with conventional teaching and learning arrangements [4].

Approaches to measuring the learning effectiveness of such e-learning offerings within an LMS usually address the technical level in particular. In this context, Sánchez and Duarte (2010) [6] investigate the influence of user-friendliness on the perceived benefit of the learner. Costa et al. (2012) investigate the functionalities of LMS and their application in the teaching and learning process [7]. More recent studies that deal with motivational factors, on the other hand, either focus on concrete e-learning activities or examine general motivational factors in learning. Yilmaz (2017) [8] examines the effects of e-learning readiness in the flipped classroom model, while Neagu (2016) [9] focuses on motivational factors in adult education, but without reference to e-learning.

The aim of this paper is to show how motivational factors within a learning management system can be used to increase motivation among learners. In this context, a prototype has been developed which will be used in conjunction with the classroom event "Fundamentals of 3D Modelling" and on the basis of which an evaluation can be carried out in cooperation with the learners by means of suitable surveys.

2   Methods

The motivational factors in the use of LMS are empirically investigated at the learner level on the basis of the developed e-learning prototype Fundamentals of 3D Modelling. For the development of the e-learning prototype, the technical infrastructure of the learning platform OPAL (Online Platform for Academic Teaching and Learning) [10] will be used. OPAL is a cross-university platform for e-learning, which is based on the open source LMS Online Learning And Training (OLAT) [11] and contains many elements typical for e-learning platforms - such as content management, discussion forums, wiki, and various self-test components.

The content concept of the prototype is based on the "Lernhaus" by Stoller-Schai (2017) [12] and includes the following four learning form levels:

- self-directed forms of learning methods: include asynchronous e-learning
- collaborative learning methods: include e-learning elements for collaborative knowledge development, e.g. Wiki
- social learning forms: include relationship-oriented e-learning
- testing learning forms: include test-based e-learning, e.g. e-tests, assessments

The e-learning prototype consists of modular, self-contained knowledge units that follow a uniform system. A progress indicator is implemented as an orienting element, which shows the students the individual processing status of the knowledge units at any time. Figure 1 shows the basic systematics of the individual knowledge units as well as the individual building blocks used for the implementation of the learning form levels mentioned above.

Fig. 1. Schematic representation of the learning methods and forms used in e-learning prototype

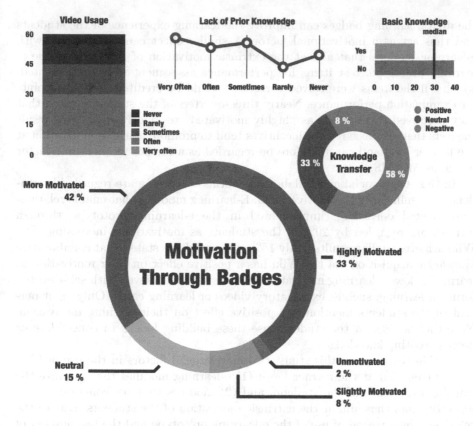

Fig. 2. Presentation of the results of the survey categories

The resulting prototype was offered for one semester to accompany the class-room event of the same name. At the end of the event, the prototype was evaluated by means of an online survey of 60 students with regard to the motivational properties of individual modules.

3 Results and Discussion

In an online survey, students were asked 20 questions about the complexes of "knowledge transfer", "prior knowledge", "basic knowledge", "video use", "badges" and "emotions". The aim was to assess the extent to which e-learning modules are used as motivational factors to promote motivation and how students perceive this. Figure 2 shows the results of the survey.

The results indicate that the motivation of students to learn when using LMS is increased, in particular, by means of verifying forms of learning such as open badges or test items. Over 78% of the students felt "highly motivated" to "motivated" to complete the subsequent knowledge unit when receiving a digital learning badge, so-called open badges. It can be assumed that the preservation of the digital learning badges can improve the learning experience of the students and thus act as a motivational factor. A similar effect can be observed with e-learning modules that aim at the extrinsic motivation of students. In the e-learning prototype, test items for performance assessment were implemented, which - if the items were solved correctly - could be credited as bonus points for examination performance. Nearly three-quarters of the students stated that they perceived this module as "highly motivated" to "motivated". This result suggests that extrinsic reward incentives tend to promote learning motivation at the learner level and can therefore be regarded as a further motivational factor in the use of LMS.

In this study, social and collaborative forms of learning are regarded by students as significantly less motivational. E-learning modules that enable relationship-oriented e-learning, implemented in the e-learning prototype through forums, are regarded by 20% of the students as motivational-increasing. The Wiki achieves similar results. Only 18% of the students stated that collaborative knowledge acquisition via the Wiki has a positive effect on their motivation to learn. The lowest learning motivation in this study is achieved with self-directed forms of learning, such as explanatory videos or learning cards. Only eight percent of the students mentioned a positive effect on their learning motivation. Nevertheless, 39% of the students use these building blocks to consolidate or deepen existing knowledge.

Within the scope of this study, two motivational factors in the use of LMS can be identified at the learner level: (1) e-learning modules that improve the learning experience of the students and (2) modules that set concrete reward incentives and thus aim at the extrinsic motivation of the students. Due to the relatively short period of use of the e-learning prototype and the low number of participants, these results cannot be regarded as representative. Rather, initial indications of motivational factors were identified, which are to be validated in further studies.

4   Conclusion

The aim of this study was to identify motivational factors in the use of LMS by students. For this purpose, an e-learning prototype was developed on an LMS with various e-learning modules and their effects on the learning motivation of the students evaluated on the basis of an online survey. Both e-learning modules that improve the learning experience of students and modules that set concrete reward incentives and thus promote the extrinsic motivation of learners were identified as motivational factors. These results are to be validated in further research. Furthermore, it should be investigated which e-learning modules can promote the intrinsic motivation of students. In addition, the e-learning prototype was designed according to the principle of "one size fits all". In future research, the prototype will be adapted to adaptive learning environments, and the motivational factors of individualized learning content will be investigated.

References

1. Felea, M., Albăstroiu, I., Vasiliu, C., Georgescu, B.: E-Learning in higher education: exploratory survey among Romanian students. In: The 14th International Scientific Conference eLearning and Software for Education, pp. 157–163, Bucharest (2018)
2. dong Kim, T., young Yang, M., Bae, J., Min, B., Lee, I., Kim, J.: Escape from infinite freedom: effects of constraining user freedom on the prevention of dropout in an online learning context. Comput. Hum. Behav. **66**, 217–231 (2017)
3. Mothukuri, U.K., et al.: Improvisation of learning experience using learning analytics in eLearning. In: Proceedings - 2017 5th National Conference on E-Learning and E-Learning Technologies, ELELTECH 2017 (2017)
4. Erpenbeck, J., Sauter, W., Sauter, S.: E-Learning und Blended Learning. Springer, Wiesbaden (2015). https://doi.org/10.1007/978-3-658-10175-6
5. Distefano, A., Rudestam, K., Silverman, R.: Encyclopedia of Distributed Learning. SAGE Publications Inc., Thousand Oaks (2004)
6. Sánchez, R.A., Hueros, A.D.: Motivational factors that influence the acceptance of moodle using TAM. Comput. Hum. Behav. **26**(6), 1632–1640 (2010)
7. Costa, C., Alvelos, H., Teixeira, L.: The use of moodle e-learning platform: a study in a Portuguese university. Procedia Technol. **5**, 334–343 (2012)
8. Yilmaz, R.: Exploring the role of e-learning readiness on student satisfaction and motivation in flipped classroom. Comput. Hum. Behav. **70**, 251–260 (2017)
9. Neagu, S.N.: A new vision of adult learning. Checklist - motivational factors involved in adult learning. eLearning Softw. Educ. **2**, 150–153 (2016)
10. OPAL. https://bildungsportal.sachsen.de/opal
11. OLAT. https://www.e-teaching.org/technik/produkte/olatsteckbrief
12. Stoller-Schai, D.: Lernhaus, Kompetenzenset und Learning Hub - Grundlagen für die Kompetenzentwicklung im Prozess der vernetzten Arbeit. In: Erpenbeck, J., Sauter, W. (eds.) Handbuch Kompetenzentwicklung im Netz. Bausteine einer neuen Lernwelt, pp. 449–472. Schäffer-Poeschel Verlag, Stuttgart (2017)

Development of Instructional Model App Design for User Experience

Sang-Duck Seo[(⊠)]

University of Nevada Las Vegas, Las Vegas, NV 89154, USA
sang-duck.seo@unlv.edu

Abstract. This study aims to develop an instructional model App design for effective user experience in self-learning acquisition of origami. In order to develop effective app design, this study conducted a pilot study to compare three formats of instructional models: printed, time-based video, and App instruction. To make the comparison, the study evaluated user tasks in three main areas: (1) time required to complete the given task, (2) number and kinds of errors, and (3) frequency of misunderstanding the instructional information. With an analysis of the result of the usability and exit interview, the findings suggest that users completed the task more effectively in the video and App instructions compared to the printed instruction. However, participants using the App instruction appeared more focused on the performance of each task and worked without interruption. According to both positive responses from the video and App instructions, this study proposes a conceptual framework for the new App design which provides an interactive user interface between static (graphic illustration) and kinetic (video simulation). The App also provides an effective learning acquisition through the online community where users can share their works and instruction model with other online users.

Keywords: Self-learning · Instructional model app · User experience · Visual literacy

1 Introduction

Self-learning, such as physical handcrafts, has further strengthened the concept of "do-it-yourself" through online domains. Mobile e-learning technologies and apps have introduced diverse contents and interactive user interface for effective learning acquisitions. In contrast to this popularity of self-learning in an informal manner through many online platforms such as video, audio and interactive apps, there are still printed materials available for learning resources. However, there is no clear evidence found yet to determine whether provided digital media would be more effective for learning and performing physical handcrafts through mobile communication. This study investigates the efficiency and effectiveness of self-directed learning with a pilot study for measuring comprehensive instructions, attaining the difficulty level and completing the task successfully. With the findings of comparisons between different instructional models, this study aims to propose an effective mobile application for self-learning of physical handcrafts.

© Springer Nature Switzerland AG 2019
C. Stephanidis (Ed.): HCII 2019, CCIS 1034, pp. 284–292, 2019.
https://doi.org/10.1007/978-3-030-23525-3_37

1.1 Self-Learning of Physical Handcrafts

Learning a craft in more traditional ways is known as repeated practice until learners have a fully-comprehensive technique, and bodily and embodied knowledge from a master craftsperson's feedbacks [1]. Self-learning, however, lacks interactive communication between learner's watching and doing, therefore, there is missing of the delivery method with subtly detailed-feedbacks for the value of learning outcomes [2]. Learners in typical self-learning need to engage with understanding both process and the performance in order to complete successful tasks with accuracy and retention. However, learning and improving skills tends to limit the learner's ability to solve problems in self-directed learning. Fully understanding a craft task, for instance, takes longer time in terms of the cognitive complexity transitioning from an abstract visual information toward accurate action [3]. Learners may also challenge perceiving characteristics of physical objects that are identified as a creative problem solving during their tasks [4]. Therefore, self-instructional model would be more effective by allowing learners to achieve the intended learning outcomes [5].

1.2 Visual Literacy in E-Learning

Visual literacy is defined as a reader's ability to understand visual language identifying five categories: (1) semiotics and film-video conventions, (2) signs, (3) symbols and icons, images and illustrations, (4) multi-images, and (5) graphic presentations [6]. Today's digital technology is effectively used as a viable learning tool in the delivery of online instruction and contents. With a variety of digital forms in e-learning, many online users have utilized digital medium as an effective learning resource. In this perspective, Aisami [5] raised significant questions for acquiring e-learning competencies and performance of achieving specific tasks; *"how people learn, what are the learning style, and how it is determined."* As computer-aided tutorials of craft has increased an accessible availability for users through online, visuals need to be considered as effective instructional models for both learners and teachers [7, 8, 9]. Especially, e-learning utilization through smartphone can improve learning practices and understanding contents more effectively with learning theories: Sensory stimulation through seeing, Cognitive learning in human memory, Humanism in learner-centered, and Information process for the capacity of short-term memory. [10]. Therefore, visual literacy in e-learning need to enhance effective and efficient level with interactive instructions where learners' perceptive and cognitive comprehension can differ from other instructional models.

2 Design Methods

The research method is comprised of two phases: (1) demonstrating measuring the effectiveness and efficiency of instructional models in visual handcraft activity and (2) developing a mobile application based on the findings of effectiveness from printed and video instructions. First, this study conducted a small group of a pilot study to compare the three instructional models (Table 1). The user testing provides participants to complete the origami "Crane" based on the given instructions. Each instructional model provides visual information formatted as different delivery methods. The printed instruction is designed by 24 steps with a single-color illustration (line and mass in gray color) and written text (pure black) [11]. The video instruction provides a live simulation of a demo for paper folding process without audio and text [12]. According to the measurement of learning effectiveness and efficiency in video instruction, participants were allowed to control a video interface and time speed of a total 6 min and 52 s for their preference. The App instruction is comprised of a total of 14 steps with graphic images illustrated with red and yellow arrows to indicate a folding and opening one to another side. The App provides a button for the control of each step [13]. A total of nine (9) participants were divided into three groups for each condition of taking a task. None of the participants had any experience learning origami. The research assessed user success, behaviors, and experiences in response to the different delivery methods. Data from the three groups was measured and evaluated based on: (1) time required to complete the task, (2) number and kinds of errors and (3) incidents of misunderstanding the instructional information. We also gathered user experience data from observation, exit surveys and interviews to compare the three learning models at the experiential level.

Table 1. Three instructional models for learning origami

Print	Video	App

3   Findings

The Average time required to complete the task was 14.9 min using the App Instruction, 10.8 min using the Video Instructions, and 26.7 min using the printed Instruction. The results are shown in Table 2. The time measurement shows that participants using the Video instructions completed the task more rapidly. Two participants gave up and did not complete the task, one in print, and one on the App. Both participants encountered difficulty on the same step which may show the difficulty of static media in visual instruction compared to motion media. (Table 3). Even though the instructions were comprised of multiple steps detailing the necessary folds, in different sides simultaneously, the video group followed the steps easily without audio instruction while users encountered difficulty in both the printed and the App instructions even though those instructions were supplemented with a detailed written description. Participants appeared more relaxed and showed a much higher level of confidence when being guided to the next step through the video instruction.

Table 2. Time completed (minute)

N	Print	Video	App
P1	24	9.22	11.42
P2	38.31 (give up)	9.13	18.33
P3	29.31	14.20	10.20 (give up)

Table 3. Complex instruction of visual literacy

Print	App	Video

In the exit interview participants were asked to rate the difficulty of the origami task. All participants in the Printed Instructions group rated learning origami "difficult" while the App and Video instructions were rated easy to neural by participants in those groups (Table 4). This result underpins that the Printed Instruction was not effective even though there are more information compared with the Video and App Instruction.

Table 4. Difficulty level of the learning origami

N	Print	Video	App
P1	Difficult	Easy to Neutral	Difficult
P2	Difficult	Neutral	Easy
P3	Difficult	Easy	Neural

Measurement: very easy, easy, neural, difficult, very difficult

A similar exit interview question asked participants to rate the difficulty of the instruction. The Participants who had the Printed instructions gave the instructional materials the lowest effectiveness ratings while both the Video and App groups were positive about their visual comprehension of the instructions (Table 5). All of the participants in the App and Printed instruction groups tended to interact first with the illustrations as their primary approach to the learning task. The Video instruction, however, provided only live simulations without audio or text. Therefore, the Video group did not demonstrate the same behavior. The tendency to look first at image supports the belief that learners primarily engage with graphic instruction and only engage the written instructions when they encounter difficulty at the visual comprehension level.

Table 5. Comprehension of visual instruction

N	Print	Video	App
P1	Neutral	Easy	Easy to Neutral
P2	Neutral	Easy	Neutral
P3	Difficult	Very Easy	Difficult

Measurement: very easy, easy, neural, difficult, very difficult

In further discussions with the participants, we found that the written material in the printed instructions was difficult to understand in terms of constructing a visual image of the necessary steps. Participants from the App instruction group said that the wording did not help them to follow the task instructions when they (the instructions) required multiple folding steps. Participants in the Video instruction group stated that time-based instruction was easy to follow without any text and/or audio resources. In response to our question about which step the participants found most challenging, a frequently mentioned issue has been difficulty understanding multiple steps represented by a single image, even when the image was accompanied by textual instructions (Table 6). Even though the printed instructions provided more visual elements with the instructions, and regardless of the detailed written instructions, participants were still confused.

Table 6. The most challenging step

Print	App

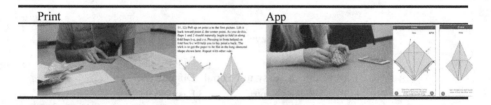

In their interviews, participants suggested improvements to the instructional model they had tested. The App instructions group suggested that the visual instructions should provide more accurate infographics, especially including clear definition of lines in the images and whether they (the lines) indicate a fold upward or downward. They also wanted more images detailing the steps. The Video instruction group had no suggestions for the improvement of the visuals, but one consideration with the video was speed control. The Printed instruction group recommended more images and more detailed steps. They also suggested that the line drawings should include folding methods again dealing with the proper direction of the fold, upward or downward.

4 A Proposed Development of Mobile App

In comparison of the three instructional models; printed, video and App instructions, this study found that the most effective visual instruction includes motion showing the folding of paper. The significant considerations based on the findings on users' experiences from the existing instruction models, this study proposed suggestions as follows: (1) Providing interactive user interface between static and kinetic instruction (Fig. 1), (2) designing enhanced informative structures in app design, and (3) sharing information between users through online community (Fig. 2).

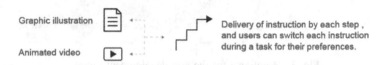

Fig. 1. Conceptual framework for tutorial delivery

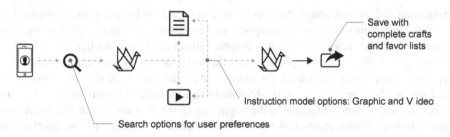

Fig. 2. Conceptual framework for the app development

4.1 Development for Wireframe

The prototype mock-up design was constructed by the learning process as how participants intended to interact with the given instruction model in the pilot study. Measured participants' performance and exit interview responses, usability test was re-evaluated with pros and cons between video and app instructions. With collected information and data from the pilot study, the wireframe work was effectively developed for enhancing an interactive delivery of instruction between graphic static information and kinetic video instruction without sound or additional written information (Fig. 3). Blue line indicates to transition of function, menu and page. The upper framework describes a delivery method of visual contents while the bottom framework illustrates user-centered design where each user can interact with personal preference options such as search engine, collection of tutorial examples, sharing the self-instruction with other online users.

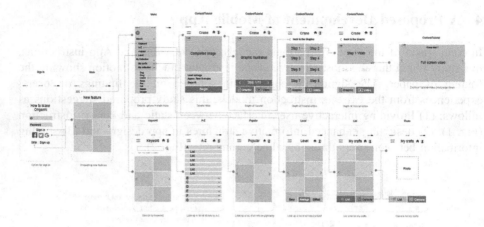

Fig. 3. Wireframe for the app development figure

4.2 User Interface and Design

Application design was under the significant consideration for the delivery method of the visual instruction for user's perception and cognition. A majority of existing App focused on static information with graphic illustration and written descriptions. According to both positive responses from the video and App instructions, this study proposes a conceptual framework for the new App design which provides interactive user interface between graphic static information and kinetic video instruction (Fig. 4). Users can choose their preference in the beginning of the instruction and the app allows them switch a different instruction mode between static and kinetic by the interface on the bottom of the screen (Fig. 5). Video instruction also provides a full screen mode where users are able to navigate and control each task step. This concept of the interactive menu and interface design will provide users effective self-control for

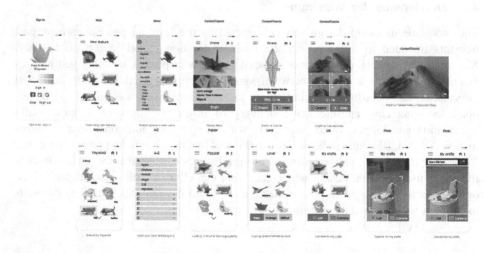

Fig. 4. A prototype design mock-up

Fig. 5. Interactive instruction mode options: left (Static graphic), middle (Kinetic video), and right (Full screen view of the video instructions)

retention, progression, and completion of self-learning instruction. The App also provides an effective learning acquisition through the online community where users can share their works and instruction model with other online users. The attached self-photo/video function allows users to create a video tutorial with completing tasks and upload it in "My Collection" which is automatically shared with other online users. This is a significant lacking in current App design, but it is highly recommended by participants in regards to their experience in the pilot study.

5 Conclusion and Discussion

This study investigated the learning effectiveness and efficiency of the three test models in the pilot study. Based on the result of the usability test, the study developed a new App design for user-friendly instructional delivery methods that allow users to control and manage their learning tasks and speed. Moreover, the conceptual framework developed for static and kinetic instruction mode options will provide a more effective and efficient experience for users for their own learning experience. A comprehensive review of how users respond to a new prototype App more effectively by a given task for self-learning has not yet been introduced. The proposed prototype mock-up will be examined through usability testing for future studies, and the results will be compared to current instructional models in the pilot study. If the results of the user experience are positive for effective self-learning acquisition, this app will be seen as effective for other instructional models such as a 'do-it-yourself (DIY)' projects with assembly processes.

References

1. Gamble, J.: Modelling the invisible: the pedagogy of craft apprenticeship. Stud. Continuing Educ. **23**(2), 185–200 (2001)
2. Torrey, C., Churchill, E.F., Mcdonald, D.W.: Learning how. In: Proceedings of the 27th International Conference on Human Factors in Computing Systems - CHI 2009 (2009)
3. Tenbrink, T., Taylor, H.A.: Conceptual transformation and cognitive processes in origami paper folding. J. Probl. Solving **8**, 1 (2015)
4. Anderson, J.R., Douglass, S., Qin, Y.: How should a theory of learning and cognition inform instruction? In: Experimental Cognitive Psychology and its Applications, pp. 47–58 (2005)

5. Aisami, R.S.: Learning styles and visual literacy for learning and performance. Procedia - Soc. Behav. Sci. **176**, 538–545 (2015)
6. Lohr, L.: Creating Graphics for Learning and Performance: Lessons in Visual Literacy. Merrill Prentice Hall, Columbus (2008)
7. Rosenberg, M.J.: E-learning: Strategies for Delivering Knowledge in the Digital Age. McGraw-Hill, New York (2001)
8. Aparicio, M., Bacao, F., Oliveira, T.: Grit in the path to e-learning success. Comput. Hum. Behav. **66**, 388–399 (2017)
9. Hubalovsky, S., Hubalovska, M., Musilek, M.: Assessment of the influence of adaptive e-learning on learning effectiveness of primary school pupils. Comput. Hum. Behav. **92**, 691–705 (2019)
10. Hashim, A.S., Ahmad, W.F.W., Rohiza, A.: A study of design principles and requirements for the m-learning application development. In: 2010 International Conference on User Science and Engineering (i-USEr) (2010)
11. Instructables: How to Make a Paper Crane. http://www.instructables.com/id/How-to-make-a-Paper-Crane-1/
12. Instructions, T.O.: Origami: Crane [tutorial]. https://www.youtube.com/watch?v=Ux1ECrNDZl4
13. Burlakov, S.: How to Make Origami. https://itunes.apple.com/us/app/how-to-make-origami/id472936700?mt=8&ign-mpt=uo=4

Interaction of Low Cost Mobile Virtual Reality Environments – Using Metaphor in an Astronomy Laboratory

Olha Sharhorodska and Diego Iquira[(✉)]

Department of Systems Engineering,
Universidad Nacional de San Agustin de Arequipa,
Santa Catalina 117, Arequipa, Peru
{osharhorodska,diquira}@unsa.edu.pe

Abstract. The virtual reality VR has become a tool to simulate events and situations that would be inaccessible for people such as travel in space and visit different planets, it is for this reason that the VR has become a new alternative for the teaching of courses such as astronomy. In this research a low cost VR environment has been created for the teaching of astronomy where metaphors are used to teach complex concepts, working with professors and experts in the area of virtual reality to create an intuitive environment for new users to VR technologies, tests were conducted with two educational institutions of 150 students where a comparison of four virtual reality environments was made.

Keywords: Astronomy · Virtual reality · Education · Mobile · Usability

1 Introduction

Virtual reality (VR) is a technology that allows users to interact and explore computer generated environments in real time [1], on education, VR technologies have been used to as complementary tools for teachers and students [2–7], this article present an immersive virtual environment for teaching astronomy, the platform for the application is android combined with Google Cardboard.

2 Astronomy Education VR Modules

An interactive interface has been developed which has three virtual modules, in each module different subjects are explained which are: the origin of the universe, solar system and a general view of the universe.

© Springer Nature Switzerland AG 2019
C. Stephanidis (Ed.): HCII 2019, CCIS 1034, pp. 293–300, 2019.
https://doi.org/10.1007/978-3-030-23525-3_38

2.1   Origin of the Universe

The module of the origin of the universe is the module that explains the origin of the universe through the theory of the big bang, divided into different scenarios but does not explain theories of higher education (quantum and relativity theories).

The module is divided into a series of scenarios, which are focused on describing the big bang process according to the curricula at the secondary level: At the beginning there is nothing, then the first particle appears that is smaller than an atom, in one bubble is stored the four forces of the universe (gravity, electromagnetism, internal nuclear force and external nuclear force), begin to separate forces, then separate forces, then the hydrogen and helium atoms appear, light begins to appear and finally a constellation appears.

The Fig. 1 shows the different scenarios of the module, in each scene an audio describes the different events that happen and you can see the animation of each process.

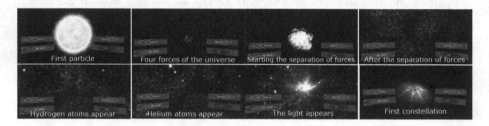

Fig. 1. This is a lot of figures that explains the different scenarios of the module origin of the universe (Source: Own Elaboration)

2.2   Solar System

In this module the different planets of the solar system are described, in this module you can perform the following actions: Approach the planets and the sun, visualize the order of the planets, visualize the translation of each planet and learn relevant information of each planet and from the sun.

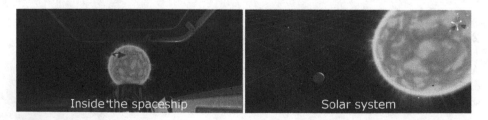

Fig. 2. The spaceship scenario and a view of the solar system (Source: Own Elaboration)

All the interactions of the module will be carried out within a ship in which the following movements can be made: Approaching the planets, traveling through the universe in a guided way, using controls to change scenes.

The Fig. 2 shows the solar system module where the interior of the ship is shown, and a general view of the solar system outside the ship.

2.3   General View of the Universe

This module focuses on showing relevant information about the different astral bodies of the universe such as: comets, asteroids, galaxies and satellites, in order to provide a general overview of the universe.

The visualization of a comet, asteroid and galaxy is done with the option of showing additional textual and auditory information, an approach to the objects can be made using the cameras, a label of the objects to which it is being observed is shown, the change of the scenes is done through the buttons of the ship simulating the displacement through black holes, all these actions are observed in the Fig. 3.

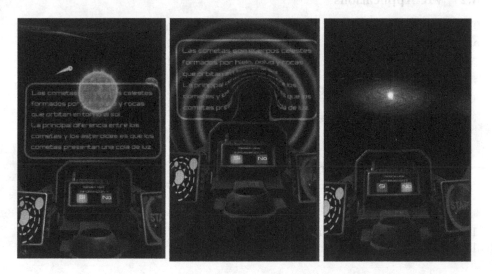

Fig. 3. View information of a comet and travel through a black hole to reach the Milky Way (Source: Own Elaboration)

3   Measurements and Usability Analysis

To evaluate the learning environment of astronomy, we have made measurements of two perspectives: Usability educational Applications and usability VR applications.

3.1 Educational Applications

For the evaluation of the system at the level of educational applications, 11 measurement categories are being used, which are [8]:

1. Immersion in the application.
2. Learning by realism.
3. Ease of interaction.
4. Educational utility.
5. Ease of use.
6. Presence.
7. Motivation in learning.
8. Intention to use.
9. Cognitive benefits.
10. Efficacy in learning.
11. Satisfaction.

3.2 VR Applications

The usability heuristics of virtual reality applications were measured, which are [9]:

1. Level of realism in the virtual environment.
2. Level of realism when performing tasks.
3. Freedom of movement.
4. Response time on the screen.
4. Realism in physics.
5. Level of perception.
6. Navigation level and orientation.
7. Ease of entry and exit.
8. Comprehensible menu.
9. Easy to use.
10. Organized and understandable tasks.
11. Feeling being present in the virtual world.

4 Results

4.1 Sample

The study case was conducted with 75 students of which 52 were men and 26 were women, from the city of Arequipa.

Three sessions lasting from 10 to 15 min were conducted, where the first session was focused on the origin of the universe, the second session on the solar system and the final session on a general view of the universe.

4.2   Results

For the analysis of results we opted for an analysis of the reliability of the instruments, we used the software package SPSS 23 for the analysis of the results, out of a total of 75 observations.

The reliability of the internal consistency of the items of the educational applications usability instrument was evaluated by calculating Cronbach's alpha. The reliability was considered acceptable with values that oscillate between 0.83 and 0.86 in the items (Table 1), additionally the total acceptable reliability of the instrument is 0.86 (Table 2).

Table 1. Item-total statistics on educational applications usability

Measurement items	Scale mean	Scale variance	Corrected item correlation	Cronbach's alpha
1	39,5897	35,564	,428	,860
2	39,4615	31,676	,584	,850
3	39,5897	32,985	,436	863
4	38,8462	32,923	,681	,844
5	39,0769	33,547	,540	,853
6	39,2821	32,682	,566	,851
7	38,9231	35,178	,429	,860
8	39,1282	33,325	,537	,853
9	39,1795	33,677	,611	,849
10	39,2051	31,957	,647	,845
11	39,2564	30,511	,728	,837

Table 2. Reliability statistics on educational applications usability

Cronbach's alpha	N of items
,863	11

The reliability of the internal consistency of the items of the educational applications usability instrument was evaluated by calculating Cronbach's alpha. The reliability was considered acceptable with values that oscillate between 0.83 and 0.86 in the items (Table 3), additionally the total acceptable reliability of the instrument is 0.86 (Table 4), with these results we have determined that both instruments are acceptable to evaluate the students.

Analyzing the results obtained from the students' tests we can see in the Table 5 that there is a great acceptance at the educational applications usability

Table 3. Item-total statistics on VR applications usability

Measurement items	Scale mean	Scale variance	Corrected item correlation	Cronbach's alpha
1	40,5641	43,779	,676	,840
2	40,8718	44,904	,537	,849
3	40,8718	42,536	,538	,850
4	40,4872	41,625	,638	,841
5	40,7949	42,852	,716	,837
6	40,4103	45,617	,496	,851
7	40,7949	41,957	,658	,840
8	40,5641	43,200	,676	,839
9	40,6154	45,717	,450	,854
10	40,1538	46,449	,342	,862
11	40,2821	49,260	,218	,866
12	40,4103	45,669	,514	,850

Table 4. Reliability statistics on VR applications usability

Cronbach's alpha	N of items
,860	12

Table 5. Educational applications usability evaluation results

Measurement items	Fair	Average	Good	Excellent	Total
1	0.07	0.20	0.52	0.21	1
2	0.05	0.36	0.50	0.09	1
3	0.09	0.32	0.47	0.12	1
4	0.08	0.29	0.48	0.15	1
5	0.05	0.37	0.46	0.12	1
6	0.02	0.33	0.50	0.15	1
7	0.15	0.16	0.51	0.18	1
8	0.10	0.26	0.49	0.15	1
9	0.05	0.24	0.48	0.23	1
10	0.04	0.27	0.40	0.29	1
11	0.08	0.23	0.48	0.21	1

evaluation, specifically in the categories immersion in the application and motivation in learning we found a greater number of Good responses, additionally in the categories efficacy in learning and cognitive Benefits obtained a greater number of Excellent answers.

Finally, we have considered the results obtained from the VR applications usability evaluation, where a greater number of positive responses have also been found on the Table 6. At a more detailed level, a greater number of Good responses have been obtained in the freedom of movement and level of perception categories, also in the easy to use and response time on the screen categories is where we found a mayor number of Excellent answers.

Table 6. VR applications usability evaluation results

Measurement items	Fair	Average	Good	Excellent	Total
1	0.06	0.41	0.42	0.11	1
2	0.15	0.31	0.45	0.09	1
3	0.09	0.36	0.50	0.05	1
4	0.11	0.19	0.38	0.32	1
5	0.15	0.27	0.41	0.17	1
6	0.12	0.23	0.50	0.15	1
7	0.16	0.28	0.43	0.13	1
8	0.11	0.34	0.39	0.16	1
9	0.06	0.33	0.38	0.23	1
10	0.02	0.25	0.38	0.35	1
11	0.09	0.22	0.48	0.21	1
12	0.14	0.18	0.49	0.19	1

5   Conclusions and Future Work

5.1   Conclusions

The conclusions we have reached after analyzing the results are the following:

- After analyzing the reliability of the internal consistency of the items of the educational and virtual reality applications usability we have determined that both instruments are acceptable to evaluate the students.
- The results obtained in the evaluation of usability of educational applications have shown that there is a higher percentage of positives responses in all the categories.
- Finally we also have analyzed the results of the evaluation of usability of virtual reality applications, which also show that there is a greater number of positive responses in all the categories.
- For this reason, analyzing all the results obtained, we can determine that the mobile-based astronomy education system allows students to use a virtual reality environment that is easy to use both at the educational and virtual reality application level, but we must take into consideration that this software does not replace teachers.

5.2   Future Work

As future work we propose adding new modules to the application, additional activities should be added to allow students to be evaluated within the application, more courses could be added which focus on science topics and finally a long term evaluation should be done to measure the students.

Acknowledgments. The present investigation is part of the project "Implementación de un Laboratorio virtual inmersivo de Astronomía usando Técnicas de Gamificacion dirigido a Alumnos de Secundaria" BA-0026-2017-UNSA, thanks to the financing granted by the Universidad Nacional de San Agustin de Arequipa.

References

1. Sherman, W.R., Craig, A.B.: Understanding Virtual Reality: Interface, Application, and Design. Elsevier, Amsterdam (2002)
2. Chakaveh, S., Zlender, U., Skaley, D., Fostiropoulos, K., Breitschwerdt, D.: Delta's virtual physics laboratory (case study): a comprehensive learning platform on physics astronomy. In: Proceedings of the Conference on Visualization 1999: Celebrating Ten Years, pp. 421–423. IEEE Computer Society Press (1999)
3. Martinazzo, A.A.G., Ficheman, I.K., Venancio, V., Corrêa, A.G.D., de Deus Lopes, R., Mantovani, M.S.M.: The mário schenberg spaceship: experiencing science in a collaborative learning VR environment. In: Ninth IEEE International Conference on Advanced Learning Technologies, ICALT 2009, pp. 626–628. IEEE (2009)
4. Roberts, D.J., Garcia, A.S., Dodiya, J., Wolff, R., Fairchild, A.J., Fernando, T.: Collaborative telepresence workspaces for space operation and science. In: 2015 IEEE Virtual Reality (VR), pp. 275–276. IEEE (2015)
5. Lintu, A., Magnor, M.: An augmented reality system for astronomical observations. In: Virtual Reality Conference, pp. 119–126. IEEE (2006)
6. Tan, S., Xu, C., Huo, J., Wang, X.: The remote education assistant system for the virtual physics experiment teaching system. In: 4th International Conference on Computer Science & Education, ICCSE 2009, pp. 1451–1454. IEEE (2009)
7. Wei, L., Huang, H.: Design and implementation of virtual simulation teaching system of solar system. In: 2018 International Symposium on Educational Technology (ISET), pp. 29–32. IEEE (2018)
8. Iquira Becerra, D.A.: Implementacion del laboratorio virtual inmersivo aplicado a la enseñanza de física usando fécnicas de gamification (2018)
9. Sutcliffe, A., Gault, B.: Heuristic evaluation of virtual reality applications. Interact. Comput. **16**(4), 831–849 (2004)

An Assistant Device for Piano Keyboard Self-learning

Adhemar Maria do Valle Filho[1]([⊠]) [iD], Claudia Regina Batista[1] [iD],
and Gabriel Vinicius Teixeira Kanczewski[2] [iD]

[1] Federal University of Santa Catarina, Florianópolis, Brazil
adhemar.valle@ufsc.br
[2] University of Valle do Itajaí, Itajaí, Brazil

Abstract. This is a multidisciplinary study involving the areas of computer engineering, electronics, musical education, playful learning and entertainment. This article shows the device design process for the assistant device for piano keyboard.

Keywords: Embedded systems · Music learning · Microcontrollers

1 Background

Playing piano keyboard is the dream of some people. A beginner music student needs to learn piano theory, reading the sheet music and practicing extensively to develop motor skills. Therefore, a beginner music student has a long way to go until the first satisfactory results. This long learning process can discourage the student who is eager to play their favorite songs.

Seeking to make a contribution in this area, a product (hardware & software) that uses programmable devices, sensors and actuators was developed to assist music students in keyboard self-learning. It must be coupled to the piano keyboard and through LED's in a box that lights up, the key to be played.

This is a multidisciplinary study involving the areas of computer engineering, electronics, musical education, playful learning and entertainment.

2 Methods

The device design process was performed in these four steps:

- Step 1: Analysis of similar systems.
- Step 2: Hardware design: Arduino control to MAX7921 (matrix 7 × 7).
- Step 3: Analysis of three possibilities: manual conversion of the music; development in C++ to read partitures in XML and serial tx to Arduino; sw integration with Synthesia, Hairless, LoopBe together with a computer.
- Step 4: Integration and final tests: it was chosen the third option and some tests of the integration is verified.

C. Stephanidis (Ed.): HCII 2019, CCIS 1034, pp. 301–305, 2019.
https://doi.org/10.1007/978-3-030-23525-3_39

In the first method, you picked up a song and manually converted it to a code indicating when a given LED should be lit and for how long the even if it was before going to the next led (Fig. 1). The downside of this method is that to manually convert all of the songs that were to be tested on the device, of the increase in conversion complexity as the music making it difficult.

```
acorde musica[] = {
    {{E},  500}, {{E},  500}, {{F},  500}, {{G},  500},
    {{G},  500}, {{F},  500}, {{E},  500}, {{D},  500},
    {{C},  500}, {{C},  500}, {{D},  500}, {{E},  500},
    {{E},  750}, {{D},  250}, {{D}, 1000},

    {{E},  500}, {{E},  500}, {{F},  500}, {{G},  500},
    {{G},  500}, {{F},  500}, {{E},  500}, {{D},  500},
    {{C},  500}, {{C},  500}, {{D},  500}, {{E},  500},
    {{D},  750}, {{C},  250}, {{C}, 1000}
};
```

Fig. 1. Music conversion – method 1

In the second method, it was developed a software using C++, to perform reading sheet music (Fig. 2) in XML and sending the song information in a serial way for the Arduino. This method worked with all sheet music tested. The problem encountered was that, how much bigger the sheet music was, the longer it would take the software to read the file and start transmitting the data to the Arduino.

Fig. 2. Sheet music – method 2

The third method used was Synthesia software (Fig. 3). In addition to Synthesia (free), two more softwares were used, one called Hairless (Fig. 4) also is free, so that MIDI information could be transferred to the Arduino by serial way. And the LoopBe1 software (Fig. 5) that is also free, used to transfer MIDI data between computer programs.

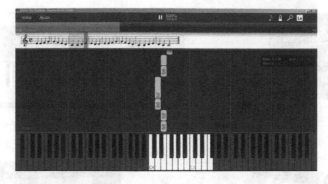

Fig. 3. Synthesia software

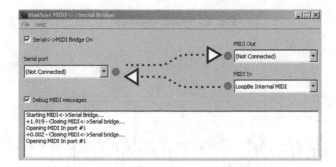

Fig. 4. Hairless

Fig. 5. LoopBe1

3 Development

The system overview can be seen in Fig. 6. The Arduino controls the MAX7921 circuit, which activates the LEDs to indicate the key that should be played. Each developed part will be shown in detail.

On the keyboard, above each key must have a led. When the led lights up the key must be touched. While it remains lit, the key must remain pressed. The row of LEDs was divided to form a matrix. This matrix was controlled by IC MAX7219. The IC has the ability to manage up to 8 × 8 matrices. For this work a 7 × 7 matrix was used. The connection sequence of the leds in groups of 7 is shown in Fig. 7 (Figs. 8 and 9).

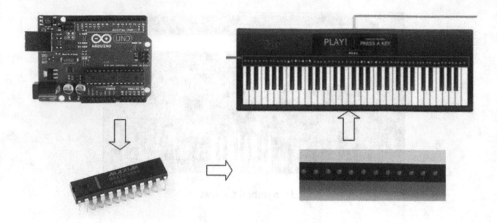

Fig. 6. System overview

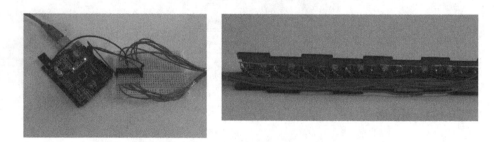

Fig. 7. Matrix circuit project

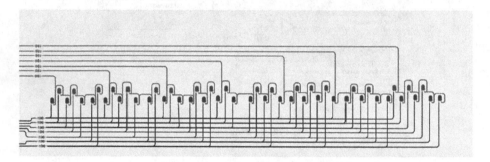

Fig. 8. Arduino + MAX7921 circuits + leds

Fig. 9. Prototype

4   Conclusion

After performing some tests with the three selected techniques, it can be observed that the third technique was the one that best satisfied the needs of the device. Since Synthesia software has countless free songs to use and had two trainee way, one that continues the music and the other where the music follows its normal rhythm. As a future work, the propose to develop a similar device, however fully developed with electronics, with active filters for each key, where the input would be a song and the circuit would try to identify the note and turn on the respective led.

References

1. Arduino: What is Arduino? (2017). http://www.arduino.cc. Accessed 24 Mar 2017
2. Wolf, W.: Computer as Components: Principles of Embedded Computing System Design, 3rd edn. Morgan Kaufmann Publishers, Burlington (2012)
3. Wiring: Wiring programming environment (2017). http://wiring.org.co/. Accessed 19 Mar 2017

"Do You Care Where I Come from?" Cultural Differences in the Computer Literacy Classroom

Simona Vasilache(✉)

Graduate School of Systems and Information Engineering,
University of Tsukuba, Tsukuba, Japan
simona@cs.tsukuba.ac.jp

Abstract. We live in a globalized world and multicultural environments are everywhere. Academic environments and classrooms are no different: students come from all over the world and participate in multicultural classes. The impact of cultural differences is receiving increased attention in many fields, including education. However, computer literacy classes are often excluded, with the so-called "computer language" considered universal, and not culturally dependent.

This work will focus on the cultural differences in the computer literacy class, on the perception of students with regard to these differences and on possible approaches by educators.

The results show that students are acutely aware of cultural differences in the classroom. Moreover, they believe that these differences are relevant when learning computer literacy, as much as they are in any other subject. The suggestions, comments, as well as the teacher's empirical observation reinforce the belief that, in an international environment, a culturally-adapted classroom style is needed in naturals science subjects, as much as in social science subjects.

Keywords: Computer literacy · International students ·
Multicultural environments

1 Introduction

Computer literacy has become an essential skill for the 21st century. As Jacob and Warschauer stated in 2018, "today's students will enter a workforce that is powerfully shaped by computing" [1]. Moreover, according to Hoar, "all undergraduate students, regardless of discipline, should be technologically literate" [2]. While there is no universally accepted definition of computer literacy, we can relate it to that of "literacy" and "computers". According to Poynton, the term "literacy" has changed within the past decades: in 1984, the Webster's New World Dictionary defined it as "the ability to read and write". In 2000, The American Heritage Dictionary of the English Language defined literacy as "The condition or quality of being knowledgeable in a particular subject or field" [3]. If we agree with the term "literacy" as reflecting familiarity with a given subject, we can consider computer literacy as the ability to interact with a computer.

More and more educational institutions are introducing computer literacy related courses, from an increasingly earlier age. In Japan, for instance, many higher education

© Springer Nature Switzerland AG 2019
C. Stephanidis (Ed.): HCII 2019, CCIS 1034, pp. 306–312, 2019.
https://doi.org/10.1007/978-3-030-23525-3_40

institutions include mandatory computer literacy classes. Wada and Takahashi have shown that there are "significant disparities in computer skills" with students entering universities in Japan [4]. Along with the increased number of international students, these disparities manifest on an even larger scale. The multicultural nature of education makes it essential that instructors "develop skills to deliver culturally sensitive and culturally adaptive instruction" [5]. Often the "computer language" is considered universal, and not culturally dependent. However, in computer literacy, just like in any other subject, the cultural differences must be taken into consideration. This work will highlight the students' perceptions on cultural differences in the computer literacy classroom, in the context of a multicultural classroom in an international program at a university in Japan.

2   Research Setting and Method

This work is based on data acquired during the past 4 years of teaching computer literacy courses at the University of Tsukuba in Japan. The course participants are students coming from more than 25 countries on 4 continents; they belong to a program aimed at international students, with the curriculum taught entirely in English. The students' age is generally between 18 and 35 years, although most of them are fresh high-school graduates. Three sets of data were used as follows. The first set of data is based on a questionnaire given to 42 student participants, enrolled in the mandatory course named "Information Literacy" in 2015. The course is made up of two parts: a lecture part (where students learn about computer hardware, the binary system, operating systems, security, the internet, intellectual property etc.) and a practice part (where the students use computers to edit documents, make presentations, create worksheets, send/receive emails using dedicated programs, create web pages, connect remotely to the university's servers etc.). The participants answered a questionnaire regarding their experience with teaching style, preferred class style and preferred evaluation methods. The same course taught in 2016 offered the second set of data, with 64 participants. At the end of the most recent computer literacy course, with 23 students enrolled in it during the 2018–2019 fall semester, the third set of participants answered a questionnaire regarding the following: advantages/disadvantages of an international classroom, opinions regarding differences in teaching style and learning depending on culture, whether cultural differences affect communication with peers/teachers or not, difficulties in class discussion and group work with other cultures, as well as general difficulties, comments and suggestions about computer literacy classes.

3   Results and Discussion

3.1   Class Style and Evaluation Method

The first set of answers was collected in 2015, at the end of an experimental class, in which the "flipped classroom" style was employed. The students were questioned with regard to their experience with various styles of teaching, as well as their preferred style of teaching. (Some of the results collected at the time appear in [10]. However, the mostly deal with the use of Learning Management Systems). The same questions were posed in 2018, in a similar setting. The students were asked whether they prefer the "classical" style (where the teacher lectures and the students simply listen), "flipped" style (where they study new concepts beforehand, then come to class, ask questions and discuss) or a combination of the two. Similarly, with regard to their experience, they were asked whether they are used to simply sit in class ("classical" style), whether they are rather used to studying at home first ("flipped") or whether they have "some" experience with studying first and then coming to class to clarify and discuss (equivalent to "combination"). The combined results for the two years are shown in Fig. 1.

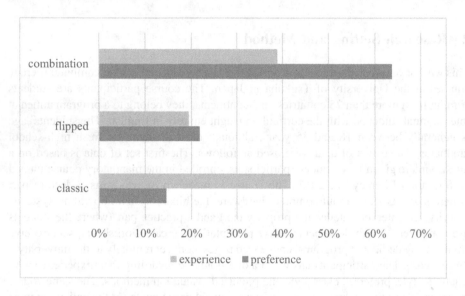

Fig. 1. Experienced vs. preferred style of teaching

We can observe that the majority of students preferred a combination of classical and flipped classroom style. When it comes to experience, about 40% or the participants have used the classical lecture style and a similar number have "some experience" with flipped classroom (thus considering a combination of the two styles as the commonly experienced class style). The comments received after the experimental class highlighted the fact that students enjoyed combining class styles, that they found the flipped classroom "refreshing" and "interesting". During the discussions with the class instructor after class, it became clear that the experience students have in learning environments is culturally-dependent. There are many related examples and studies in the education research. For instance, in [5], Parrish and VanBerschot proposed CDLF (Cultural Dimensions of Learning Framework) (based on the works in [6] and [7]). One of the cultural dimensions they consider is *equality and authority*. In societies with more authority, teachers are treated as unchallenged authorities and they are "solely responsible for what happens in instruction"; moreover, "the teacher is the primary communicator" [5]. On the other hand, in cultures with more equality, "students take responsibility for learning activities". The empirical observations of the class instructor confirmed these results. For instance, students coming from cultures considered as based on more authority are used to sitting in class, merely listening to the teacher lecturing, with almost no active participation/communication on their part.

When it comes to the preferred grading style, the results revealed that 53.3% prefer two tests (which was the current style adopted by the teacher at the time), 35.6% would like short, weekly tests, whereas only 4.4% prefer one final exam. At the same time, 6.7% suggested different methods, including a "take-home-exam" and two tests containing only "the important and useful information". Because the computer literacy course tries to cover many topics within a rather limited time frame, each topic is taught in concentrated form, with, from the point of view of the instructor, the most useful and significant parts included only. It is interesting to observe that the students were of the impression that some of the things they were being taught were not useful or important.

One more issue was analyzed with the students taking part in the 2016 course: their preference for the type of class materials. The majority of students, i.e. 60.3%, preferred a combination of printed and electronic materials. 22.2% preferred printed materials only, whereas 17.5% wished for electronic versions of class materials. Although no numerical data is available, based on the class instructor's observations, the demand for printed materials decreased exponentially within the past few years. In fact, the computer literacy classes offer the class materials using the institution's dedicated LMS, in electronic version only, and this is explained to (and immediately accepted by) the students during the very first class.

3.2 Cultural Differences in the Classroom

This section will highlight some of the cultural differences and their influence in the computer literacy classroom, using data from the third set of questionnaires, administered during the most recent computer literacy course, in winter 2018–2019.

The students were asked about the origin of their difficulties in working with colleagues from different cultures; they had to choose between differences in work style, personality or language skills. Furthermore, they were asked about the aspects which make class discussions difficult in multicultural class environments. The results are illustrated in Fig. 2.

We can observe that, in both cases, culturally-related aspects were not chosen as being the most relevant. In case of working with international colleagues, work style could be considered the most culturally-dependent aspect; however, it was chosen only by 22% of the participants. Personality was the most relevant for 65% of the participants, whereas language skills were considered by 13% of them. Similarly, cultural differences during class discussions were chosen only by 35% of the participants; self-confidence was considered the most relevant aspect, i.e. by 70% of participants, whereas language issues were chosen by 39% of the students.

Many researchers pointed out that communication faces challenges in multicultural environments. For instance, Xie et al. stated that "while globalization has resulted in shorter distances between individuals, cross-cultural problems arise in many aspects, especially communication conflicts caused by cultural diversity" [11]. The participants

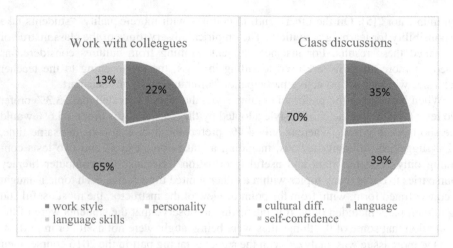

Fig. 2. Origin of difficulties in work with colleagues (left) and class discussions (right)

in the computer literacy course were also asked whether they feel that cultural differences affect communication with their colleagues, on one hand, and with their teachers, on the other hand. The possible answers were: "definitely yes", "yes, most of the time", "very little", "definitely not" and "I don't know". Figure 3 summarizes the results.

As can be observed from Fig. 3, "definitely yes" was chosen by 42% of the participants in the context of communication with their teachers, as opposed to only 17% when communicating with their peers. The cumulative responses of "definitely yes" and "yes, most of the time" is 63.4% in case of teachers and 56.5% in case of

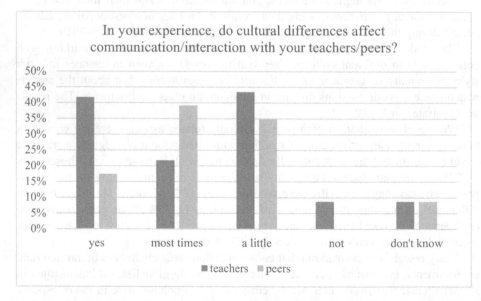

Fig. 3. Opinions regarding communication with peers/teachers in multicultural classrooms

peers. While these figures are not that different, the respective percentages of responses for "definitely yes" show that students feel strongly about communicating with their teachers in the context of multicultural education, to a larger extent than when communicating with their peers.

Last, but not least, the questionnaire aimed to highlight the students' general perspectives on learning computer literacy in a multicultural setting. Many researchers have pointed out that communication faces challenges in multicultural environments [8, 9]. When asked to compare computer literacy with other subjects, 65% stated that it is the same as studying any other subject, whereas 22% stated that it is easier than other subjects. No participants believed that computer literacy is more challenging than other subjects in a multicultural context (13% stated that they do not know). This finding underlines the importance of considering cultural aspects when studying computer literacy, just like when studying any other subject, and this is in line with research like that of Aronson and Laughter [12] or Civitillo et al. [13].

4 Conclusion

This work highlighted the perception of students with regard to cultural differences in international classrooms. The results show that students are undoubtedly aware of these differences and, furthermore, they believe that these differences are relevant when learning computer literacy, as much as they are when learning any other subject. The suggestions, comments, as well as the teacher's empirical observations reinforce the belief that, in an international environment, a culturally-adapted classroom style is needed when teaching computer literacy.

References

1. Jacob, S.R., Warschauer, M.: Computational thinking and literacy. J. Comput. Sci. Integr. 1 (1) (2018)
2. Hoar, R.: Generally educated in the 21st century: the importance of computer literacy in an undergraduate curriculum. In: Proceedings of the Western Canadian Conference on Computing Education, p. 6. ACM (2014)
3. Poynton, T.A.: Computer literacy across the lifespan: a review with implications for educators. Comput. Hum. Behav. 21(6), 861–872 (2005)
4. Wada, T., Takahashi, H.: Quantitative analysis of computer literacy class. In: INTED2012 Proceedings, pp. 5788–5793 (2012)
5. Parrish, P., Linder-VanBerschot, J.: Cultural dimensions of learning: addressing the challenges of multicultural instruction. Int. Rev. Res. Open Distrib. Learn. 11(2), 1–19 (2010)
6. Hofstede, G., Hofstede, G.J.: Cultures and Organizations: Software of the Mind, 2nd edn. McGraw-Hill, New York (2005)
7. Lewis, R.D.: When Cultures Collide: Leading Across Cultures, 3rd edn. Nicholas Brealey International, Boston (2006)
8. Alismail, H.A.: Multicultural education: teachers' perceptions and preparation. J. Educ. Pract. 7(11), 139–146 (2016)

312   S. Vasilache

9. Banks, J.A., Banks, C.A.M. (eds.): Multicultural Education: Issues and Perspectives. Wiley, Hoboken (2009)
10. Vasilache, S.: Student perspectives of computer literacy education in an international environment. Univ. J. Educ. Res. 4(6), 1426–1431 (2016)
11. Xie, A., Rau, P.L.P., Tseng, Y., Su, H., Zhao, C.: Cross-cultural influence on communication effectiveness and user interface design. Int. J. Intercult. Relat. 33(1), 11–20 (2009)
12. Aronson, B., Laughter, J.: The theory and practice of culturally relevant education: a synthesis of research across content areas. Rev. Educ. Res. 86, 237–276 (2016)
13. Civitillo, S., Juang, L.P., Badra, M., Schachner, M.K.: The interplay between culturally responsive teaching, cultural diversity beliefs, and self-reflection: a multiple case study. Teach. Teach. Educ. 77, 341–351 (2019)

How Parents Guide the Digital Media Usage of Kindergarten Children in Early Childhood

Franziska Zimmer[✉], Katrin Scheibe, and Maria Henkel

Department of Information Science,
Heinrich Heine University, Düsseldorf, Germany
{Franziska.Zimmer,Katrin.Scheibe,Maria.Henkel}@hhu.de

Abstract. In our modern society young children are getting in contact with digital media already in the early stages of childhood. Uncontrolled consumption of screen media and the media's content may have a variety of negative effects (e.g. social isolation) on the child's development. Parental mediation, the controlled, limited and supervised use of media plays an important role and may encourage positive effects of using media. The American Academy of Pediatrics (AAP) provided a list with some recommendations and tips about media and young children. Also, it is discussed that digital media literacy teaching should already start in Kindergarten. What are parents doing to mediate the media usage of their children? Are they setting limits? Do they act like a role model? And, what do parents think about digital media literacy instruction in Kindergarten? This study's researchers asked parents of 3 to 6-year-old Kindergarten children from Germany through a questionnaire as well as interviews about the mediation of their child's media contact. Likewise, parents were asked if digital media literacy should start in Kindergarten. A content analysis based on the tips from AAP was conducted as well. The results show that parents indeed try to limit the contact with media and are watching the usage. Kindergarten should be a tech-free zone according to nearly all parents.

Keywords: Parental mediation · Parents · Children · Kindergarten ·
Media usage · Digital media usage

1 Introduction

More and more young children are getting in touch with digital media devices earlier and earlier. They grow up in a digital environment with screen media since early childhood. According to Rideout [1], in 2011, 52% of households with under 8-year-old children have had access to mobile devices, this number increased to 75% by 2013. Also, the time spent by children aged under 8 years using and handling these devices rose from 5 min daily in 2011 to 15 min per day in 2013 and to 48 min daily in 2017 [2]. A variety of research projects report negative effects and developmental problems of children, like social isolation or anxieties, due to excessive and uncontrolled screen media usage [3, 4].

Apart from this, in all stages of childhood the content of the presented and used media plays an important role in the children's development as well [5, 6] There are not

© Springer Nature Switzerland AG 2019
C. Stephanidis (Ed.): HCII 2019, CCIS 1034, pp. 313–320, 2019.
https://doi.org/10.1007/978-3-030-23525-3_41

only bad effects, but also benefits of using new media, if usage and content of the media are controlled and chosen appropriately [7].

The regulation of the child's media usage, also known as 'parental mediation,' which is described by Warren [8] as "any strategy parents use to control, supervise or interpret media content for children," plays an important role for controlling children's media behavior, skills, and engagement. It is a relevant consistency to prevent negative effects and to manage the influence of the media on the child's development [9]. We can differentiate three types of parental mediation: instructive (also known as active or evaluative) mediation, restrictive mediation, and social co-viewing. Active mediation refers to communication about the media's content between parents and children. Restrictive mediation means to set rules, regulate the media usage and to set limits. Finally, social co-viewing describes the observation and viewing media together, but in contrast to active mediation without the active requirement to talk about the media's content [10, 11]. For children under five years, these three practices are all recommended by the child development research community [12]. The effects of parental mediation vary and are dependent on which type of mediation is exactly used by the parents [13]. There are also differences for the effects on early as well as later childhood years, which makes it necessary to study the younger group separately [14].

It was observed that children like to express themselves through media [15]. Even though there is some form of media implemented in Kindergarten, for example the children's cinema or gaming software for education, those should not be the only digital media that is used for digital media literacy. There already exist concepts to work playfully with pictures, audio, video, and even PCs [15]. Unfortunately, these impulses are seldom implemented by educators in Kindergarten. On one side, they do not feel equipped enough to teach the children digital media literacy, since training opportunities for educators are limited [16, 17]. Less than one-third of US pediatric residency programs teach about media exposure [18]. It was discovered that the way educators teach the children how to use media positively influences their willingness to learn how to interact with a medium, for example using a tablet to express their ideas through drawing and learning [19]. On the other hand, some educators claim that digital media education should be implemented by parents [20]. It is suggested that by the time children enter Kindergarten they should already have some media competency skills such as navigating computers and tablets, launching applications, and negotiating menus, since most of their classmates already have these skills [21]. But who do parents think is responsible for the digital media literacy instruction of their children?

The American Academy of Pediatrics [22] has listed health as well as safety tips for children handling and interacting with media. They recommend to limit the usage of digital media (restrictive mediation) and to promote off-screen playtime. Parents should cooperate with their child during screen media usage (active mediation and co-viewing); this will encourage social skills as well as their learning ability. Furthermore, it is necessary for parents to provide tech-free zones (restrictive mediation) and to act as role models, especially in relation to digital and screen media. Therefore, this study concentrates on what parents are adopting for their daily life in line with the mentioned recommendations. According to these key aspects the research questions of this study are as follows:

RQ1: Are parents limiting the media usage of their children, and if yes to what extent?

RQ2: How are parents acting as a role model for their children?

RQ3: Are parents always watching their child's media usage?

RQ4: Do parents see Kindergarten as a tech-free zone?

2 Methods

To answer the research questions, parents of children from Kindergarten filled out a questionnaire; additionally, some parents were interviewed. This study represents the parents' perspective and is only a small part of a much bigger and comprehensive study [23, 24]. 12 Kindergartens located in Düsseldorf, Germany agreed to perform the study with us in cooperation with their institution. The Kindergarten teachers were asked to select children of different social backgrounds and different ages to take part in the study. The selected families received detailed informational materials about the investigation as well as a consent form from us. The study was conducted from June 2015 to May 2016.

The questionnaire for the parents contained questions about their child's media behavior as well as about their own media behavior. First, demographic data about the children was asked about. Afterwards, the parents were asked to name the three most used media of their child, which were named in a pre-formulated list: TV, Smartphone, Phone, Tablet, Computer/Laptop, Audio, Magazines/Newspaper, Book/E-Books, Educational Toy, and Digital Camera. For the three most used media we asked the parents if they are setting limits for the usage of the media, and how long the children are using the media per day or week. Additionally, parents were able to state everything with comments. With the next question parents were also asked to name their three most used media and how long they are using them per day. Furthermore, the parents were asked if they are always present when their child is using digital media which could be rated from "agree" (1) to "not agree" (5) on a 5-point Likert scale. Next, they were asked if they have an internet child safety lock. Likewise, we wanted to know if parents think that digital media should be more present in Kindergarten and who is responsible for the media literacy instruction of children in Kindergarten as well. The questionnaire contains some more questions about the internet usage of the child, as well as about the usage of media for learning or entertainment purposes. Lastly, the parents were asked about demographic and personal data for both parents. Total 60 parents filled in surveys which were sent back to us for evaluation. Furthermore, personal interviews were conducted with 10 parents; each of the interviews took from 15 to 60 min in duration. The questionnaire served as a guideline, but the interviewer had the chance to ask additional as well as more precise questions and parents had the opportunity to explain everything in more detail.

The content analysis was implemented as follows. First, the interviews with the parents were transcribed by the researchers. Following this, a codebook was developed [25]. The code categories were deductively derived from the *Children and Media Tips from the American Academy of Pediatrics* [22]. Four code categories could be utilized based on the interviews. These were (1) "Set limits and encourage playtime" - do parents watch how long the children interact with the media and set limits? (2) "Be a good role model" - how often do parents use media and do the children notice it? (3) "Screen time shouldn't always be alone time" - are the children using media without the parents' guidance? (4) "Create tech-free zones" - do parents consider Kindergarten as a tech-free zone or should more media be implemented? If needed, the sorting of the sentences into the codes was discussed [26] and therefore an intercoder reliability of 100% could be reached.

3 Results

The results display how parents guide the children's digital media usage. The first research question concerns the limits parents set for their children and their media usage. The dissemination of the average hourly media usage per week of the children can be seen in Table 1. Furthermore, the table displays if the parents always accompany the child while using media. Most time is spent in front of the TV, making up 5.12 h per week, with one of the parents always being present. Even though the TV is used the most often, parents set rules for the watch time of their child.

Table 1. Children's average hourly use of media per week and parents' presence while the child is using media

Medium	N	Hours per week	N	Parents' attendance
TV	35	5.13	32	100%
Book/E-Book	36	4.88	31	9.68%
Audio	35	4.88	32	25%
Educational game	7	3.68	8	37.50%
Tablet	20	3.17	17	100%
Smartphone	8	1.75	7	100%

"No, she always asks me if she can watch something. But we have a rule that she can only watch one hour per day," as one mother states. "But this is really restricted, because I noticed, one episode and another one, another one, another one, another one, that quickly results in a snowball system that he quickly wants more", confirms another mother. Followed by this, books as well as audio, for example music or audio books are used 4.88 h per week. Here, most of the parents let the children use the media by themselves, only 9.68% of the parents are nearby when the child uses books, and 25% are present when kids listen to audiobooks or music. "One is not always nearby if he sits in his room and listens to an audiobook," as one father states. The medium that is used the least often is the smartphone with 1.75 h per week; here all parents attend their child. Overall, even if the parents are not nearby "subconsciously, I am always checking what the kids are hearing, what they are doing." Most parents (77.4%) do not utilize the opportunity of a child safety lock for their smartphone or tablet, only 20.8% make use of it. This rather small percentage can be explained with the parents always being present when their child uses a smartphone or tablet, making a child safety lock obsolete.

The second research question concerns the task of the parents regarding their media usage in their position as a role model. Table 2 displays the average number of hours they use a medium per week. The computer is used the most often, with 16.35 h. Since some parents use the PC for work at home the hourly use is comparatively high. But parents try to limit the use when the children are around: "I never work when the children are there. I only work when they are asleep." Even if the PC is used for games, parents want to shield their children, since "the games are not teddy bear stuff, I pay attention that he does not see any of it." One father also notes that "my son recognized that a computer is a complex medium and that I can do other things that he can't, which of course wakens a desire." Second and third are the smartphone (10.88 h) and the TV (10.52 h). Even the smartphone is used for work: "but for my work it sometimes happens that I get a call, even outside my office hours. Of course, he notices when I have to take a call." Furthermore, "if there is a message coming or something, the kids notice it. Then they say 'Mom, a text message is coming'." Non-digital media are used the least often, with books (5.25 h; N = 13) as well as magazines (4.33 h; N = 8) ranking second last and last, respectively (Table 2).

Table 2. Parent's average hourly media use per week.

Medium	N	Hours per week
Computer	34	16.35
Smartphone	34	10.88
TV	35	10.52
Tablet	14	8.14
Audio	12	7.44
Book/E-Book	13	5.25
Magazine/newspaper	8	4.33

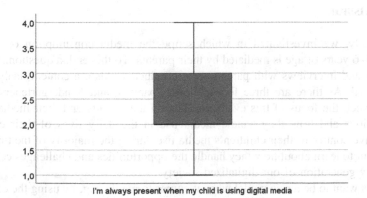

I'm always present when my child is using digital media

Fig. 1. Parents are present while the child is using digital media; "agree" (1) to "not agree" (5) (N = 59)

The third research question concerns the distribution of the parents' answers regarding their presence while the child is using digital media. The median is at 2 and the Interquartile Range (IQR) ranges from 2 to 3, which means that most parents want to be around their child while they interact with media. All parents are present while the child is using digital media. One of the parents states, "yes, I do not watch her all the time, but I am always in the same room." One mother puts emphasis on the fact that she is always with her child if electronic media is used. Exceptions are made if, for example, "it is a TV series I watched for the hundreds time or he watched for the hundreds time." On the other hand, the children are often not able to interact with the medium by themselves, for example, concerning smartphones or tablets. "This app that he is playing with my husband, he can't handle it from A to Z; he would not be able to progress in the game. One mini-game and he would need to quit."

The parents' opinion on whether Kindergartens should be a tech-free zone was also asked about (RQ 4), which was answered by 54 participants. 85.19% of them do not want digital media in Kindergarten. The biggest concern the parents have is the fear that the child may not have a "real childhood" if they were too engaged with media. Children are supposed to "play and sing," because "a Kindergarten is there so they can play [...], to have fun. The seriousness begins early enough". One parent addresses the question of how children learn: "they should make their experiences through touching, seeing, hearing, which can be done with physical things more easily than through computer games or apps". If the fun of children is concerned: "if they want entertainment, they can go outside to play, there they have toys, friends," as another parent states. 14.81% saw value in the approach of implementing more media in Kindergarten. "There are of course parents that do not own a PC, which can be seen as a minority, but considering which milieu the children are from [...], they could be in a disadvantage," "without any kind of media, the children will be left behind," as other parents affirm. One mother proclaims that by integrating media, no child needs to feel left out when it comes to, for example, popular movies: "if they watch, as a special occasion, a movie in the gym once a month, then all children will be integrated."

4 Discussion

In this study, we investigated in which scope the media consumption of children between 3–6 years of age is mediated by their parents. To this end, a questionnaire was developed and interviews with parents were conducted. Also, a content analysis was implemented. As there are three foci (children, parents, and Kindergarteners) in the whole project, the focus of this evaluation lies on the parents and their media habits, their opinions and how they handle media use in the daily lives of their children. Parents have control of their children's media use during the majority of the time, so it is important to learn about how they handle the opportunities and challenges connected with a new generation of our digitalized society.

Parents want to be a role model when it comes to media, e.g. by using the computer when the children are in Kindergarten or are asleep. Furthermore, parents make the effort to always be around their child if she or he is using media, especially digital media (e.g. smartphone, tablet, TV) or at least are aware of what the children are consuming while being in contact with those media. This way, they can shield their children from inappropriate content. But, a similarity in the media usage of parents and children cannot be observed. For example, parents prefer the computer and smartphone, while those media are seldom used by the child, if at all.

If parents want Kindergartens to be a tech-free zone, they are automatically responsible for the digital media literacy of their children. But comparing the results with other studies, children, e.g. in the U.S., are much more engaging with digital media a lot earlier. For example, according to a study in 2006, about 83% of children 6 years and younger use screen media (watching TV/DVDs, playing video games, using computers) for about 2 h each day [27]. Of course, too frequent media consumption is not a solution. Parents need to be aware about how to teach children. But, even many Kindergarteners do not feel equipped enough to teach children how to interact with media, how should the parents know how to do it reasonably? Therefore, a possible solution would be to implement special Kindergartens where children have a form of digital media literacy education alongside to more traditional Kindergartens.

Limitations of our research are that only a small sample of 10 interviews were conducted and could be evaluated. It represents only the opinion of a small number of parents which were very dedicated took part in the interviews. Parents have not been directly asked about active mediation (talking to the child while using the media) and only view of the interviewed ones talked about it. An interesting aspect to investigate in future research would be to conduct more detailed interviews about every type of parental mediation.

Acknowledgement. This study was initiated and led by Dr. Sonja Gust von Loh.

References

1. Rideout, V.: Zero to Eight: Children's Media Use in America 2013. Common Sense Media, San Francisco (2013)
2. Robb, M.: Kids' screen time shifts dramatically toward phones and tablets (2017). https://www.commonsensemedia.org/blog/kids-screen-time-shifts-dramatically-toward-phones-and-tablets
3. Pagani, L.S., Fitzpatrick, C., Barnett, T.A., Dubow, E.: Prospective associations between early childhood television exposure and academic, psychosocial, and physical well-being by middle childhood. Arch. Pediatr. Adolesc. Med. **164**(5), 425–431 (2010)
4. Certain, L.K., Kahn, R.S.: Prevalence, correlates, and trajectory of television viewing among infants and toddlers. Pediatrics **109**(4), 634–642 (2002)
5. Tomopoulos, S., Dreyer, B.P., Berkule, S., Fierman, A.H., Brockmeyer, C., Mendelsohn, A. L.: Infant media exposure and toddler development. Arch. Pediatr. Adolesc. Med. **164**(12), 1105–1111 (2010)
6. Linebarger, D.L., Walker, D.: Infants' and toddlers' television viewing and language outcomes. Am. Behav. Sci. **48**(5), 624–645 (2005)
7. Chassiakos, Y.L.R., Radesky, J., Christakis, D., Moreno, M.A., Cross, C.: Children and adolescents and digital media. Pediatrics **138**(5), 1–20 (2016)
8. Warren, R.: In words and deeds: parental involvement and mediation of children's television viewing. J. Fam. Commun. **1**, 211–231 (2001)

9. Vygotsky, L.S.: Thought and Language. MIT Press, Cambridge, MA (1986)
10. Valkenburg, P.M., Krcmar, M., Peeters, A.L., Marseille, N.M.: Developing a scale to assess three styles of television mediation: "instructive mediation", "restrictive mediation", and "social coviewing". J. Broadcast. Electron. Media **43**, 52–66 (1999)
11. Nathanson, A.I.: Identifying and explaining the relationship between parental mediation and children's aggression. Commun. Res. **26**, 124–143 (1999)
12. Warren, R.: Parental mediation of preschool children's television viewing. J. Broadcast. Electron. Media **47**(3), 394–417 (2003)
13. Ruh Linder, J., Werner, N.E.: Relationally aggressive media exposure and children's normative beliefs: does parental mediation matter? Fam. Relat. **61**(3), 488–500 (2012)
14. Duch, H., Fisher, E.M., Ensari, I., Harrington, A.: Screen time use in children under 3 years old: a systematic review of correlates. Int. J. Behav. Nutr. Phys. Act. **10**(102), 1–10 (2013)
15. Anfang, G., Demmler, K.: Medienarbeit im Kindergarten. Merz **50**(1), 47–52 (2006)
16. Plowman, L., Stephen, C.: Children, play, and computers in pre-school education. Br. J. Edu. Technol. **36**(2), 145–157 (2005)
17. Marci-Boehncke, G., Rath, M., Müller, A.: Medienkompetent zum Schulübergang: Erste Ergebnisse einer Forschungs - und Interventionsstudie zum Medienumgang in der Frühen Bildung. MedienPädagogik: Zeitschrift für Theorie und Praxis der Medienbildung **22**, 1–22 (2012)
18. Rich, M., Bar-on, M.: Child health in the information age: media education of pediatricians. Pediatrics **107**(1), 156–162 (2001)
19. Couse, L.J., Chen, D.W.: A tablet computer for young children? Exploring it's viability for early childhood education. J. Res. Technol. Educ. **43**(1), 75–98 (2010)
20. Six, U.: Förderung von Medienkompetenz im Kindergarten. In: Lauffer, J., Röllecke, R. (eds.) Kinder im Blick – Medienkompetenz statt Medienabstinenz: Dieter Baacke Handbuch, vol. 4, pp. 79–84 (2009)
21. Buckleitner, W.: What should a preschooler know about technology? Early Childhood Today (2013). https://www.scholastic.com/teachers/articles/teaching-content/what-should-preschooler-know-about-technology/
22. American Academy of Pediatrics: Children and media tips from the American academy of pediatrics (2018). https://www.aap.org/en-us/about-the-aap/aap-press-room/news-features-and-safety-tips/Pages/Children-and-Media-Tips.aspx
23. Gust von Loh, S., Henkel, M.: An app for measuring and promoting young children's media and information literacy. In: Proceedings of the 9th International Conference on Education and Information Systems, Technologies and Applications, EISTA 2015 (2015)
24. Henkel, M.: Exploring media and information literacy in early childhood with a digital app. In: Proceedings of the International Conference on Library and Information Science, LIS 2019, pp. 135–153. International Business Academics Consortium, Taipeh (2019)
25. Krippendorff, K.: Content Analysis: An Introduction to Its Methodology, 4th edn. Sage, Los Angeles (2018)
26. Mayring, P., Fenzl, T.: Qualitative inhaltsanalyse. In: Baur, N., Blasius, J. (eds.) Handbuch Methoden der empirischen Sozialforschung, pp. 633–648. Springer, Wiesbaden (2019). https://doi.org/10.1007/978-3-658-21308-4_42
27. Rideout, V., Hamel, E.: The media family: electronic media in the lives of infants, toddlers, preschoolers and their parents. Kaiser Family Foundation, Menlo Park, CA (2006)

HCI in Transport and Autonomous Driving

Plugin: A Crowdsourcing Mobile App for Easy Discovery of Public Charging Outlets

Salah Uddin Ahmed[1](✉), Fisnik Dalipi[1], and Mexhid Ferati[2]

[1] University of South-Eastern Norway, Hønefoss, Norway
{salah.ahmed,fisnik.dalipi}@usn.no
[2] Linnaeus University, Kalmar, Sweden
mexhid.ferati@lnu.se

Abstract. Nowadays, the growth of mobile apps is so fast and viral; they have the potential of transforming our everyday lives by creating huge opportunities to individuals and businesses. This translates into a growing demand for developing such apps, which need to be easy to learn and use. In this paper, we conduct an evaluation of an android mobile app, which we designed and developed to find and register power outlets in public spaces. Our evaluation of the prototype consisted of two stages. First, we provided the users with two tasks, with an additional option to indicate their perception of how easy it was to complete these tasks. Second, upon completing both tasks and offering their comments, participants were asked to take the SUS (System Usability Scores) questionnaire. The results of the evaluation indicate that the app usability and learnability is acceptable despite being a prototype. The findings and participants' comments give us a direction on how this app can be improved in the future.

Keywords: Usability analysis · Power outlets · Crowdsourcing · Mobile app · SUS evaluation

1 Introduction

Advances in mobile computing and technology have created immense opportunities for a wide range of useful applications to be developed and used. The usefulness and popularity of mobile devices, such as smartphones, tablets, and digital watches, is allowing users to perform various tasks in a mobile context. The pervasiveness of mobile devices in the modern society not only has transformed the way we communicate, but also has revolutionized the way we shop, do business or are entertained.

Several reasons have contributed to the prolific growth of the mobile devices and applications in recent times. First, they are meeting users' needs for mobility of computing and communication. Second, technological standards have matured sufficiently to provide mobile devices with high-speed wireless access to the Internet. Finally, users are now offered to customize their mobile platforms with apps that best serve their needs.

Our need of using internet and being connected with the world seamlessly anywhere and everywhere also demands that we can connect to power outlets everywhere we go; restaurants, cafes, train stations, airports, shopping malls, theatres, libraries. Power outlets in public spaces are often hidden, placed under a table or behind a sofa or another furniture, and often, there are no signs to tell about their location.

Inspired by the need of integrating the crowdsourcing technique to develop and populate mobile apps, in this paper, we are presenting the Plugin android mobile application, which we designed and developed to find and register power outlets in a public space. Using this app, users are able to find easily an outlet when needed or register a new outlet to make it available for future users. Our app, Plugin, adopts the crowdsourcing technique to let users populate and locate public electrical outlets that can be used to charge phones, tablets or laptops. Crowdsourcing approach is a technique of online activity participation where a group of individuals of varying knowledge, heterogeneity and number are voluntarily conducting any sort of task [1].

The described Plugin app has only been tested preliminarily, and the main objective of this paper is to conduct an interface evaluation analysis and find out whether the current app interface is satisfactory for the users.

The rest of the paper is structured as follows: in Sect. 2, we present the related work in this topic. Section 3 provides some descriptions of the interface design, whereas Sect. 4 presents the experimental setup. In Sect. 5, we present the findings and discussions. Lastly, Sect. 6 concludes this paper.

2 Related Work

Many mobile apps are utilizing GPS and other sensors to provide services of locating objects, businesses and people. For instance, Urbanspoon [2] is an app that helps people locate restaurants by user-selected criteria. Car Locator [3] app helps people locate their car in a parking lot and provide guidance to its location. Similarly, Best Parking [4] app, besides showing available parking spaces, also shows parking prices in order to help users find the cheapest available parking. The list of such apps is extensive. A common feature is that many of such apps rely on crowdsourcing techniques to populate their data.

A well-known app that utilizes crowdsourcing is Waze [5], where users can add information about speeding cameras, construction zones, and accident locations in roads. Furthermore, authors in [6] describe an app that uses users' input to populate ATMs and let users locate one in their city. Similarly, Merchant and Asch [7] report of an app that lets users populate and locate Automated External Defibrillators (AEDs), which are located in public places, such as airports, schools, shopping malls, etc.

Nevertheless, in the literature, the research addressing the benefits and needs of mobile apps for locating and registering power outlets is very scarce. To the best of our knowledge, there is no app developed yet in this direction. The only app that partially addresses this issue is FLIO app [8], which only merely mentions the power outlets in an airport in textual description. It has neither location-based services nor any options for users to add any power outlets. It is worth to note that we came across an unreleased android app named Outlet Finder [9], which is still in the process of development. Therefore, we cannot draw any further conclusion related to this app and compare it with Plugin.

On the other hand, the main advantage of Plugin is that it is not restricted to any location. Besides, it provides detailed description of the outlet found along with images for easy discovery by the user. In addition, the app provides a feature for commenting and voting for a particular outlet, through which users can contribute as well as rely on the trustworthiness of the location of the outlet. Sometimes, some outlets may become unavailable, broken, or removed due to physical changes of the space. Moreover, it has been also reported in newspapers [10, 11] that in several US airports pranksters placed fake power outlet stickers that caused frustration among the travelers. Our app with the possibility of negative voting can help in minimizing the frustration by providing users with accurate information of active power outlets.

3   User Interface Design and Interactions

The Plugin app has a very simple minimalistic user interface. The Home screen of the app opens Google Maps with the user's current position on it and showing the nearby power outlets.

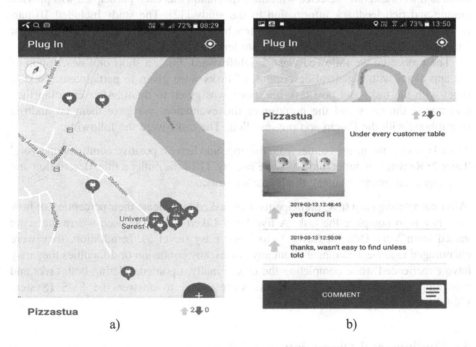

Fig. 1. Plugin user interface. (a) Marker selection, it shows brief information of a selected outlet in a place called Pizzastua. (b) Marker Information dialog, it shows outlet's details with image and comments.

The app has a GPS button on the top right corner that zooms in current user location. Outlets on the map are shown as small "outlet icons" which can be clicked to view more information about it (Fig. 1a). When clicked, it shows the name of the outlet and the user votes below the map. Users can move down to get a further detailed view of the outlet, such as, see the image of the outlet and all the previous users' registered comments (Fig. 1b). Users can add their comment and vote for that particular outlet.

If a user wants to register a new outlet on the app, this can be done by clicking on an action button on the bottom right corner of the home screen. When the action button is clicked, it opens the map in user's current location from where the user can zoom to fine tune the outlets location and put a marker on the map to register the new outlet. The user can provide a title, a description and an image while registering the outlet in the app.

4   Experimental Setup

The experiment was conducted with the participation of students and staff from University of South-Eastern Norway, campus Ringerike, which is a public university in Norway. For this research we used purposive homogeneous sampling method, where all participants were members belonging to one similar subgroup (academic institution), and were carefully selected with the expectation that each participant will provide unique and rich feedback information to the study [12]. The study included 10 participants, who were mostly students and teaching staff. Students varied from first year bachelor IT students to PhD Marketing students.

The procedure we followed was straightforward. First, a short oral description of the app along with a general description of tasks were given to participants. Next, a sheet with the tasks and post-task questions was given to them. After ensuring they understood the tasks and the purpose of the evaluation, we gave them an android smartphone with the Plugin app pre-installed. The tasks were the following:

Task 1: Locate the nearest outlet from the app, and leave a positive comment and vote!
Task 2: Register an outlet that you have nearby. Give the outlet a title, description and
provide an image by using the phone's camera.

After completing each task, participants were asked to indicate their perception of how easy it was to complete the task. A five level Likert scale was used where the score varied from Very Difficult (level 1) to Very Easy (level 5). In addition, they were encouraged to leave a comment about any issues, any confusion or difficulties they may have experienced while completing the task. Finally, upon completing both tasks and providing their comments, participants were asked to answer the SUS (System Usability Scores) questionnaire [13].

5   Findings and Discussion

The overall score for the evaluation of the app was 70. Despite this score being relatively low, it still indicates that the app usability and learnability is acceptable, according to [14]. Figure 2 shows SUS scores per participant, where a red line indicates the average score among all participants.

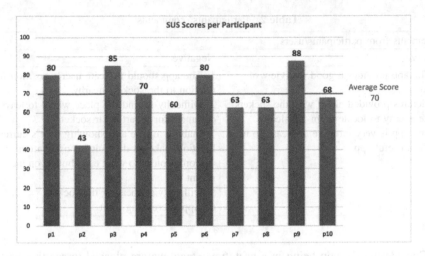

Fig. 2. System Usability Scores per participant

For each of the two tasks, participants were asked to score their difficulty while completing it. On average, task one and two scored 4 and 4.2, respectively, indicating that both tasks were easy to complete. Table 1 shows individual scores provided by each participant for each question, as well as the scores for the tasks. When comparing the SUS score with tasks scores, they seem to correlate well; participants with high SUS score also reported high scores on the easiness of performing the tasks.

Table 1. SUS scores for each participant and question along with the scores for the tasks

Participants	Questions										SUS score	Task 1	Task 2
	Q1	Q2	Q3	Q4	Q5	Q6	Q7	Q8	Q9	Q10			
P1	4	1	4	2	4	1	5	2	3	2	80	4	5
P2	3	2	2	4	3	3	2	4	2	2	43	2	4
P3	4	1	4	1	4	3	5	1	4	1	85	5	3
P4	4	3	4	3	4	1	4	1	3	3	70	5	5
P5	2	2	4	2	3	3	4	2	2	2	60	4	3
P6	2	1	5	1	5	3	5	2	4	2	80	4	4
P7	1	2	4	2	4	2	4	3	2	1	63	4	5
P8	4	3	3	2	3	2	4	3	3	2	63	4	4
P9	5	1	3	2	5	1	4	1	4	1	88	5	5
P10	3	1	4	3	1	2	5	3	1	2	68	3	4
Average											70	4	4,2

Upon finishing the tasks, participants were encouraged to provide their comments concerning their experience with the app. In Table 2 below, we provide positive and negative comments aggregately:

Table 2. Participants' comments

Comments from participants/users	
Positive	Negative
1. The app provides a good overview of sockets	1. The app should indicate user's position in relation to the sockets nearby
2. Pictures provided along with the sockets make it easy to locate them physically	2. Difficulty to find the place where to leave a comment for a particular socket
3. The app is very intuitive and easy to use	3. Inability of the app showing user's current location makes it difficult for orientation
4. Very useful app	4. Confusion as to what each button on the app meant
	5. Difficulty in locating the sockets
	6. App is crushing a lot

Considering the app being in a prototype stage, we are pleased to see that participants recognized the usefulness of the app. On the other hand, we also expected the negative comments, which provide us with guidance on how we could improve this app. For example, the negative comments 1 and 3 point to the drawbacks of our app while others (comments 2, 4, 5) point towards future work for improving usability. The comment that reports that the app was crashing a lot (comment 6) can be linked to a particular mobile phone, which was having low resources; as the app was running mostly without crashes on the other mobile phone. Apart from these, some participants also provided suggestions for further improvement of the app such as:

- Indicate user's position in relation to sockets nearby
- Provide a direction and guidance to locating the nearest or desired socket
- Implement a reward system to encourage users to register sockets
- Provide more detailed map (3D and birds eye view)

From our observation, we noticed that, many participants could not figure out the action button to add a power outlet. They were asking about it. Nevertheless, not many have mentioned this as an issue except one of the participants. Perhaps, it is only an issue when used for the first time.

6   Conclusion

In this paper, we reported the design and evaluation of the Plugin app. We briefly described app's main features that help users locate and register power outlets in public spaces. We also report an evaluation of the app we conducted with 10 participants. The main purpose of the evaluation was to measure app's usability, discover issues, and finding ways to improve it. The overall usability and learnability of the app was satisfactory despite the app being a prototype.

For future work, we have several points to improve the overall features of the app such as upvote or downvote others comments, ability to edit/delete a registered outlet via an admin panel. Participants' suggestions provided a good indication for future work direction. We also plan to make a heuristic evaluation of the app to complement the SUS evaluation and improve the usability of the app.

Acknowledgement. We would like to thank Alexander Gerrud, Torkel Velure, Agne Hesten and Ivarr Reyna who participated in the process of designing and developing the app.

References

1. Estellés-Arolas, E., González-Ladrón-de-Guevara, F.: Towards an integrated crowdsourcing definition. J. Inform. Sci. **38**(2), 189–200 (2012)
2. Urbanspoon: Google Play Store. https://play.google.com/store/apps/details?id=com. urbanspoon&hl=en. Accessed 12 Mar 2019
3. CarLocator: Google Play Store. https://play.google.com/store/apps/details?id=com. edwardkim.android.carlocatorfull. Accessed 12 Mar 2019
4. Best Parking. https://www.bestparking.com/. Accessed 12 Mar 2019
5. Waze. https://www.waze.com. Accessed 12 Mar 2019
6. Lončar, M., Aldan, J.A., Ivašić-Kos, M.: Mobile application for finding ATMs. In: 38th International Convention on Information and Communication Technology, Electronics and Microelectronics (MIPRO), pp. 1638–1642. IEEE (2015)
7. Merchant, R.M., Asch, D.A.: Can you find an automated external defibrillator if a life depends on it? Circ.: Cardiovasc. Qual. Outcomes **5**(2), 241–243 (2012)
8. FLIO app: Google Play Store. https://play.google.com/store/apps/details?id=com.getflio. flio&hl=en. Accessed 12 Mar 2019
9. Outlet Finder App: Google Play Store. https://play.google.com/store/apps/details?id=net. heinousgames.app.outletfinder&hl=en. Accessed 12 Mar 2019
10. https://www.nytimes.com/2015/05/07/business/the-power-grab-at-airports-has-a-new-headache.html . Accessed 12 Mar 2019
11. https://www.dailymail.co.uk/travel/travel_news/article-6043117/Travellers-fury-sparked-fake-power-outlet-STICKERS.html. Accessed 12 Mar 2019
12. Onwuegbuzie, A.J., Collins, K.M.: A typology of mixed methods sampling designs in social science research. Qual. Rep. **12**(2), 281–316 (2007)
13. Brooke, J.: SUS: a "quick and dirty" usability scale. In: Jordan, P.W., Thomas, B., Weerdmeester, B.A., McClelland, A.L. (eds.) Usability Evaluation in Industry. Taylor and Francis, London (1996)
14. Bangor, A., Kortum, P., Miller, J.: Determining what individual SUS scores mean: adding an adjective rating scale. J. Usabil. Stud. **4**(3), 114–123 (2009)

Smart Traffic Light Request Button – Improving Interaction and Accessibility for Pedestrians

David Barabas, Daniel Banzhaf[✉], Waldemar Titov,
and Thomas Schlegel

Institute of Ubiquitous Mobility Systems,
Karlsruhe University of Applied Sciences, Moltkestr. 30,
76131 Karlsruhe, Germany
iums@hs-karlsruhe.de, daniel.banzhaf93@gmail.com

Abstract. The aim of this paper is to test the suitability of a smart traffic light request button, equipped with a contactless pedestrian detection and a green time extension for certain target groups. Within a preliminary analysis the primary factors hygiene, usability and comfort are considered. Based on this groundwork, a concept of a smart traffic light request button is developed, which includes a pedestrian detection with ultrasonic technology and the extension of the green light time via radio frequency identification. Furthermore, the technical implementation is finally composed in a drafted prototype. With the help of a sample group an experimental evaluation of the prototype is carried out. The evaluation results show, that the smart traffic light request button is widely accepted, and a benefit is generated for pedestrians. In addition, the hypothesis, which is developed in the preliminary analysis and assumes the benefit of a smart traffic light button, is confirmed by this evaluation.

Keywords: Contactless pedestrian request button ·
Traffic light green time extension · RFID · Ultrasonic ·
Individualization in traffic management

1 Introduction

Pedestrians are often not given enough attention in the mass of road users. In order to reduce the daily-motorized city traffic, pedestrians should be more recognized as traffic participant. More and more affordable and new technologies ensure that outdated and established concepts should be reconsidered to examine their current state of the art. To improve interaction and accessibility of traffic light request buttons for pedestrians a preliminary analysis is carried out, evaluating possibilities in optimization of hygiene, signal cycle time as well as usability and comfort. Further development for pedestrian request buttons could lead to major improvements regarding the described aspects.

1.1 Hygiene

Pedestrians taking part in public life are sharing the mobility infrastructure with other pedestrians. This also includes buttons to request a safe signalized crossing.

C. Stephanidis (Ed.): HCII 2019, CCIS 1034, pp. 330–337, 2019.
https://doi.org/10.1007/978-3-030-23525-3_43

Conventional request buttons require a physical contact between human and device. Therefore, a pedestrian willing to request a safe crossing needs to physically contact the request button, usually mounted on the pole of the traffic light, which leads to an exposure of the potentially contaminated surface. According to Spörrle, bacteria can survive on these kinds of request buttons for several days leading to people avoiding contact with such devices [1].

1.2   Signal Cycle Time

Aiming to reduce the signal cycle time and in accordance with the German law [2], for the calculation of the green time provided to pedestrians, only half of the crosswalk length can be considered (Fig. 1). This means, that the signal light turns red before pedestrians have finished crossing the road (Fig. 2). Certainly, there is a safety time, which ensures that there are no conflicts between pedestrians and other road users. However, many people feel insecure to cross large crosswalks, especially people with slower walking speed might turn around to abort the crossing [3].

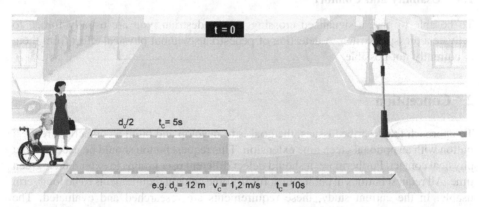

Fig. 1. The green time is calculated, considering only half of the street distance that pedestrians need to cross (Color figure online)

Legend: s_0 = distance, v_r = clearance speed, t_r = clearance time, t = time.

At signalized intersections with a high rate of crossing pedestrians with restricted mobility, a slower walking speed is assumed for the calculation of the green time [2]. For those cases in Germany, the slowest predetermined walking speed of the traffic system guideline (1 m/s) is assumed for the calculation of the green time. This leads to longer green times in general, even if there is no mobility-restricted pedestrian crossing the road. According to the traffic system guideline, the standard value for the walking speed of pedestrians is assumed 1.2 m/s, ranging from 1.0 m/s up to 1.5 m/s [2].

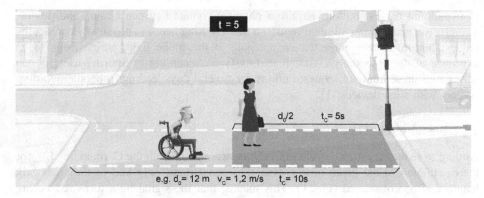

Fig. 2. If the walking speed of a pedestrian is too slowly they may still on the street and sometimes not even half way through when the traffic light turned already red. (Color figure online)

1.3 Usability and Comfort

To be able to pass a signalized crossing as a pedestrian, you are usually forced to activate a pressure switch. A detection of pedestrians without physical effort from them is currently not possible.

2 Conception

To approach the described issues, the goal is to develop and build a contactless request button with an optional green time extension. This request button should be used without physical contact. Furthermore, it should detect different user groups to extend their green time. All request buttons in public must fulfill some general requirements to be long term usable. In the current study, these requirements are researched and evaluated. The focuses of this study are functionality, reliability, usability and costs. Protection against vandalism and tech specific standardizations are not considered here [4, 5].

2.1 Contactless Detection

The detection of pedestrians at a crossing is realized with the help of an ultrasonic sensor by checking the distance of an object in front of the request interface. If the distance is shorter than a predefined value, the control module detects a request of a pedestrian.

2.2 Target Groups and Pedestrian Assignment

To implement an extension of the green time, first the qualified user groups were defined. Possible user groups that can benefit from the optional extension of the green time are pedestrians with restricted mobility, particularly those who are unable to reach a walking speed of one meter per second or faster. People with a walking disability or pensioners are mainly considered. Their walking speed often does not correspond to the speed used in the usual calculation of the green time [4]. To identify the qualified pedestrians, a concept of contactless identification is used. Therefore, RFID technology is chosen because of the compatibility with the student ID cards that are available during the study.

2.3 Prototype Case

In addition, to keep all the sensors in place and to create a usable interface, which can be visually connected to regular traffic light request systems for pedestrians, a case is drafted. During the evaluations of the prototype later in the study, the case is not only used to present a usable interface, but also the design of the case itself is evaluated. In the design of the case for the contactless request prototype the conventional design of already existing request devices are considered. Users should immediately recognize the purpose of the new device to ensure that the basic function of the pedestrian detection is understood. In addition to the similarity between conventional request buttons and the contactless request button, there must still be a recognizable difference to suggest the user that the operations of the two request buttons differ. This is achieved, on the one hand, by the fact that the prototype has no moving parts, which could imply a wrong operating method, such as a common pressure plate, and, on the other hand, by a smooth and simple design. There are no unusual design curves or edges that can be recognized as a push button. Furthermore, with pictograms it is attempted to convey the method of operation to the user in an uncomplicated way.

3 Implementation

To work cost-efficient for the implementation of the Prototype low-cost sensors are used to contactless detect human presence. A cost effective but reliable Arduino microcontroller operates as the Control Module to coordinate the used sensors. Furthermore, the case is drafted and printed using a 3D-printer.

3.1 Detection

The distance from the nearby pedestrian in front of the sensor is checked every 0.1 s and as soon as the distance falls below the defined limit of 13 cm, a request is detected. As visual feedback, a LED lights up. Tests during the study have shown that 13 cm is an appropriate value, which prevents passing pedestrians from triggering the request but still allows a detection of a requesting pedestrian well. For a final product, this distance must be checked even more accurately in a test environment.

3.2 Green Time Extension

To implement the described concept in Sect. 2.2, RFID-Cards with certain ID-numbers are used to match an ID-number stored in a database to identify the qualified pedestrian groups. Therefore, a RFID sensor reads out the ID-number of the chip built into a personal RFID-Card. Based on the voluntariness of the predefined pedestrian groups, the identification can be carried out with for example senior citizens cards, student ID cards or disabled ID cards. With bigger investments in RFID-Gates, an even more comfortable solution for the users could be created. The bigger the antenna, creating an electromagnetic field to power the RFID Chip, the bigger the detection range of the chip. You could be identified, without even pulling your ID card out of your pocket.

4   Experimental Evaluation

The evaluation was carried out as part of a laboratory test. For this purpose, a scenario has been developed in a controlled environment, with the aim to answer some predefined questions. The developed prototype is the basis of the evaluation. The contactless detection and the design of the case are supposed to be evaluated. Furthermore, the green time extension with the RFID chip is also a part of the evaluation.

4.1   Sample Group

As a sample group to be evaluated, the two greatest opposites in terms of technical affinity have been chosen representatively. One sample consisted of a group of five students who supposedly had a high affinity for technology and the second sample consisted of five people over the age of 60 years. The second sample was assumed to have less technology affinity. The aim was to test the prototype at the two social extremes.

4.2   Questions

The aim of the evaluation was to test the user's acceptance for a contactless push button with optional green time extension. For this, the following questions should be evaluated: Is the comprehensibility of the technical operation obvious? Is there a right to exist in the comparison to conventional request buttons? How user-friendly is the button and thus will the button be accepted? Moreover, are there any deficiencies in the technical design?

4.3   Study Design

The questionnaire can be divided into two parts. First, gender and age are asked to assign the participant to one of the two sample groups. It then indirectly queries its affinity with other contactless technologies and familiarity with request buttons.

The second part of the questionnaire attempts to answer the questions described in Sect. 4.1 by asking questions that relate directly to the request device and questions that contrast the prototype with conventional request devices.

4.4   Procedure

To produce the same conditions for each evaluation participant and to reduce external influences as far as possible, the oral communication between the participants and the evaluation manager is minimized. After the greeting, the participant is asked to a table with two sheets. One of these sheets outlines the following evaluation process and describes what a request button is to set all participants to a similar level of knowledge. In addition, the participant is instructed not to communicate with other people in the room if possible. This is to avoid, for example, unintentional assistance given or to manipulate the natural behaviour. On the other sheet, there are two tasks, which should be fulfilled one after the other. For this purpose, a scenario has been set up that stands for a real pedestrian crossing on a signalled intersection. The prototype button is attached to a pole; the pedestrian crossing is marked with Sticky tape on the bottom. A notebook at the end of the pedestrian crossing represents the signal for pedestrians (Fig. 3). In task one, the participants are asked to request green time with the help of the prototype request button and then cross the street. In task two, the participants are asked to request a green time extension, with the help of an RFID chip card. Based on these two tasks, the participants can familiarize themselves with the prototype to get an idea of the use of such a request button in the real world. After the participants have completed the tasks, they are brought back to the table to answer a questionnaire. After this has been completed, the evaluation is over. Depending on the participant, the duration of the evaluation runs between 7 and 15 min.

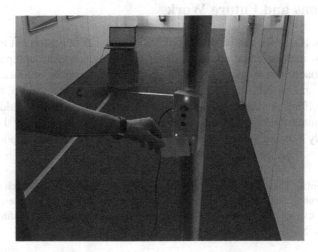

Fig. 3. The activation of the green time extension with a RFID card (Color figure online)

4.5   Results

The results show that it is widely accepted and has according to the participants the right to exist, especially in terms of the mentioned hygiene issues. Ten out of ten participants can imagine using the evaluated device in everyday life. Furthermore, the study participants stated the satisfying functionality and the simplicity in usage. Eight out of ten participants confirm that the usability with the tested device is instinctive. In terms of comprehension, two out of ten participants touched the device to be detected; thus, pedestrians preferring to touch the request device are satisfied as well since the detection still works fine. Among the advantages of the prototype over the conventional request buttons, higher comfort, better hygiene and the advantage of the green time extension have been mentioned.

5 Conclusion

Although ultrasound technology is not necessarily the most suitable technology when considering the requirements to be met, it has proven its worth in implementation due to its simple functionality and reliability. In design and technology, first steps have been taken in the direction of a fully developed contactless request button with optional green time extension. The results of the evaluation show that there is a need for such a product from the point of view of the participants, since it not only improves hygiene, but also reduces the physical effort compared to conventional request buttons. Furthermore, the optional green time extension and its advantages were well received by the participants. These advantages mentioned in the results were already hypothesized at the beginning of the work and could be confirmed within this work.

6 Limitations and Future Work

Looking ahead, this work can be used as a basis for further development approaches. It makes sense to include other non-considered technologies in the comparison to join with new approaches to this work. The results so far can also be optimized with other sensor models and raised to a more suitable everyday level. In addition, a larger-scale evaluation involving the target groups for the green time extension would be useful to be able to estimate the benefit. Within this work, the consideration of the implementation in already existing systems from a technical and data protection point of view is still pending.

Acknowledgments. This work was conducted within the scope of the research project "Real-labor GO Karlsruhe" and was funded by the German Ministry of Science, Research and Art, Baden-Württemberg as part of the science for sustainability initiative (Funding ID: MWK-0421.915-5(15)/HSKA).

References

1. Zeit.de Homepage. https://www.zeit.de/2014/30/fussgaengerampel-funktion. Accessed 12 June 2018
2. Forschungsgesellschaft für Straßen- und Verkehrswesen – FGSV: Beispielsammlung zu den Richtlinien für Lichtsignalanlagen (RiLSA), pp. 25–26, Köln (2010)

3. Alrutz, D.: Verbesserung der Bedingungen für Fußgänger an Lichtsignalanlagen. In: Bericht zum Forschungsprojekt FE 77.0493/2008, p. 9. Bundesanstalt für Straßenwesen, Bergisch Gladbach (2012)
4. VDE Homepage. https://www.vde-verlag.de/normen/0832014/din-en-50556-vde-0832-100-2011-09.html. Accessed 14 June 2018
5. Nullbarriere Homepage. https://nullbarriere.de/din32981-sig-nalgeber.html. Accessed 5 April 2018

Tinted Windows Usage in Vehicles: Introducing a Game that Evaluates It's Impact on Driver's Vision

Luiz C. Begosso[1,2](✉), Luiz R. Begosso[1], Cristiane Freitag[1],
and Gabriel B. Berto[1]

[1] Fundacao Educacional do Municipio de Assis – FEMA, Assis, SP, Brazil
begosso@gmail.com, begosso@femanet.com.br,
cristiane_freitag@hotmail.com,
gabriel.b.berto@hotmail.com
[2] Faculdade de Tecnologia de Assis – Fatec, Assis, SP, Brazil

Abstract. In this paper we present our experience with the development of a simulation software for evaluating the use of tinted windows on the vehicle windshield as well as their effects on drivers' vision. The motivation for the development of this study lies in the fact that simulation software can contribute to studies of human performance and its consequences in the area of vehicular technology. We present the specification of the application and the details of its implementation, as well as an analysis of the quantitative and qualitative results of the use of the simulation software.

Keywords: Tinted windows · Vehicular technology · Game

1 Introduction

Vehicle technology is intended to discuss concepts that enhance the driver's (or user's) performance and behavior, as well as understanding the differences and needs of specific user groups. In many countries, especially in tropical climates, it has been common for vehicle owners to opt for changing the transparency or color properties of the automobile's glass by applying a polycarbonate thermal film that aims to act as an ambient temperature controller. Also, several people believe that tinted windows give them some additional security and the fact of daring all the glasses of the vehicle can guarantee them some anonymity.

Automobiles play an important role in modern society, not only as a means of transportation, but also as a way to meet work needs and to master space and time through speed. In some cases, automobiles are considered as objects of flaunting and power and, in this sense, some studies emphasize that automobile arouses various emotional issues in people, such as the feeling of safety and security, comfort and style [1]. Other studies highlight the main advantages pointed out by the drivers for using tinted windows on the vehicle windshield, as described in [2]:

- Reduction of the incidence of sunlight and heat inside the car;
- Reduction of air conditioning usage and fuel consumption;

C. Stephanidis (Ed.): HCII 2019, CCIS 1034, pp. 338–343, 2019.
https://doi.org/10.1007/978-3-030-23525-3_44

– Improvement of passengers' privacy by providing a sense of security;
– Improvement of cars' aesthetics.

Several countries formalized the use of tinted windows on the vehicle windshield. In Brazil, the National Traffic Council (Contran) regulated this item through different norms and regulations [3]. Figure 1 illustrates the values regulated in Brazilian legislation.

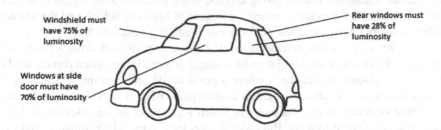

Fig. 1. Tinted windows values regulated in Brazilian legislation.

As highlighted by [2], the use of tinted windows on the vehicle windshield can decrease the driver's visibility at night and, consequently, endanger passengers, pedestrians and other vehicles.

In this work we will describe the specification and the details of implementation of a software that allows the simulation of the effects on drivers of various properties of transparency and color of tinted windows on the vehicle windshield. We will also present an analysis of the quantitative and qualitative results of the use of the simulation software. We believe that the use of a software simulating the effects of various properties of transparency tinted windows on vehicle windshield may contribute to the study of important consequences in the area of vehicular technology.

2 Background and Related Works

There are several arguments in the literature, which are favorable to the use of tinted windows in the daytime period, but at night the effects are not yet widely discussed. At this point, it is important to highlight that one of the goals of this work is to verify the behavior of drivers using tinted windows in the vehicles during the night. In cases where the car is driven by an elderly person, the use of such tinted windows may further aggravate the situation. The vision of the elderly driver may be compromised by age and the darkening of the windshield may further compromise the vision, increasing the risk of an accident.

An important study was conducted by [4] to verify how much the darkening of vehicle's windows impairs the younger and older drivers. The authors performed maneuver tests in two conditions (daytime and night time) and placed obstacles at different distances. They analyzed the speed, the distance and the time of maneuver of each driver. They found that both drivers are affected by the tinted windows, however the elderly drivers were the most impaired ones.

Another study conducted by [5] is in accordance with [4], and reports that the use of tinted windows in the vehicles can harm the elderly driver, since it takes more time to become familiar with the environment than a younger driver. In tests performed by the authors, the response time to an obstacle was greater for the elderly drivers, since they already have certain difficulties due to age and to the use of tinted windows under certain conditions, their performance tends to worsen with the use of tinted windows under certain conditions. For the young drivers, tinted windows have negative effects in extreme conditions, for example, when the degree of blackout is high and the ambient conditions are not adequate, their performance were also unsatisfactory.

According to the study conducted by [6], more experienced drivers have more perception of risk situations in relation to younger drivers. Experienced drivers tend to analyze the environment and check where a possible risk situation might occur, as the younger ones tend to analyze a situation as dangerous when it is evident or in the case of a certain situation change, for example when a person is on the sidewalk and may cross the street without looking. But older drivers look at the whole situation and may see risks where younger drivers do not or do not realize as a dangerous situation. For these authors the age of the driver does not interfere in the perception of dangerous. On the contrary, young drivers have advantages because they can analyze the situation as a whole and analyze certain situations that may be dangerous. The younger ones focus on situations where danger is imminent.

The study carried out by [7] concerns about the reduction of the perception of risk with the increase of the age of the elderly drivers, because with the age the problems of vision may increase and so it can reduce the perception of danger situations.

Another study conducted by [8] indicates that elderly drivers have the ability to perceive risk affected by age, when they are compared to younger drivers. Old drivers may lose their notion of risk or anticipates some maneuvers that can end up leading to an accident. An alternative in lowering this risk would be training elderly drivers to learn new skills and improve old ones.

In Brazil, there are no studies or statistics of accidents with regard to the use of tinted windows in vehicles, and also it is not known, if the use of tinted windows can significantly reduce the internal temperature of the vehicles.

Another point to be investigated is related to security, this is, if tinted windows would protect cars' passengers and if they would be less susceptible to the action of fringe.

In Brazil, the use of tinted windows is regulated by Contran, as illustrated on Fig. 1, and it must follow the following rules: on the windshield the light transmission should not be less than 75% and colored windscreens and other indispensable windows must have at least 70%. For areas that do not interfere with handling, transparency cannot be less than 28%. The name of the brand, manufacturer and degree of luminosity shall appear on the films and shall be visible on the outside of the glass.

However, in practice there is no effective supervision, the traffic agents do not have this device and usually in case of an inspection the agent verifies the information contained in the film, but without the device he has to use his own intuition if he is really inside the standard. If the vehicle has tinted windows out of the norm, the driver will suffer the penalties provided for in subsection XVI of art. 230 of the Brazilian Traffic Code, which consists of serious infraction, fine and vehicle retention for regularization.

3 Specification of the Software

The software we have developed is a simulation game, it simulates events that can occur when a driver is using his car, and that needs quick reflexes and enough visibility to avoid obstacles.

The mechanics of the game is described as follows: the driver must conduct the car in a route, and during that course several objects will appear before the car. The objective of the player is to click on the object before it hits the car, at the end of the route will appear the amount of objects hit by the car during the route. There are several objects in the game, and they have different behavior, some of them run towards the car, others are standing in the middle of the road. To increase the difficulty, there are 3 levels of tinted windows the driver can choose, from 70% visibility, 50% visibility and 30% visibility, it is also possible to choose the time of day, it can be day and night, Fig. 2 illustrates the simulator screen to choose film levels and the time of day.

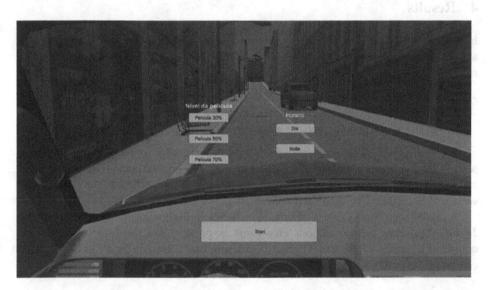

Fig. 2. Simulator screen used by player to choose tinted levels and the time of day

Our software is focused on simplicity. In the main menu the user can start the game, quit the application, or go to the options menu. In the options menu the user can change the resolution of the game and the graphic quality. During the game, the player can pause at any time and have the option to continue playing, go to the main menu or exit the software.

For the sound of the game we used audios available by Unity 3D. The sound used was the sound of the vehicle engine, to give a greater immersion to the player, and a sound effect whenever the player can hit the object before the collision. No music was used so as not to detract from the player's attention.

Figure 3 illustrates the features of our software.

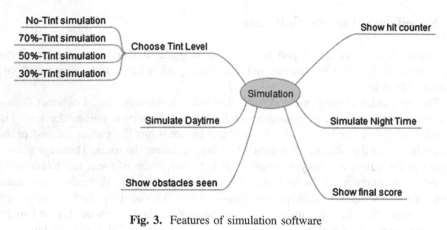

Fig. 3. Features of simulation software

4   Results

In order to verify the objectives defined in this work, we conducted an experiment with a convenience sample of 48 participants of both sexes. The population was divided as follows:

- Group 17_30: 20 people between 17 and 30 years old;
- Group 31_59: 10 people between 31 and 59 years old; and
- Group 60_+: 18 people aged 60 and over.

We performed 9 sessions with people of those groups playing the game, each session lasting 10 min, on different days and with the population mixed between sex and age. The game was set up to simulate the driving of the vehicle in the evening and with a 50% visibility in the tinted windshield.

It can be seen from Table 1 that the players belonging to Group 60_+ collided with 18 objects during the simulation. This value is greater than the sum of the objects collided by groups 17_30 and 31_59. Considering that these results are still initial, we can argue favorably to the works of [4, 5] who found answers similar to ours.

Table 1. Summarizes the results obtained after the nine game sessions:

User groups	Results
Group 17_30	5 objects
Group 31_59	6 objects
Group 60_+	18 objects

5   Conclusion

In this paper we present our experience with the development of a simulation software for evaluating the use of tinted windows on the vehicle windshield as well as their effects on drivers' vision. We present the specification of the application and the details of its implementation, as well as an analysis of the quantitative and qualitative results of the use of the simulation software.

Although the results of this study should not be considered as conclusive, as the sample used consists only of a few representatives of different age groups, it is imperative to discuss about blackening the vehicle windshields and the development of this simulator can contribute to studies of human performance and its consequences in the area of vehicular technology.

The purpose of this work was to consider the visual barriers imposed by the blackening of vehicle windshields. However, to verify the validity of the results obtained so far, further research must be carried out comparing samples of homogeneous sizes and applying new methodologies.

References

1. Machado, A.P.: A obsessão pelo automóvel. http://www.qualitapsi.com.br/wp-content/uploads/2014/avaliacao_textos/05-A-Obsessao-pelo-atuomovel-AdrianePicchettoMachado.pdf. Accessed 10 June 2015
2. Racv, Window tinting. http://www.racv.com.au/wps/wcm/connect/racv/internet/primary/my+car/car+safety/window+tinting/window+tinting. Accessed 27 July 2015
3. CONTRAN Homepage. http://www.ctbdigital.com.br/?p=Artigos&artigo=230. Accessed 20 Sept 2016
4. Sayer, J.R., Mefford, M.L., Blower, D.: The effects of rear-window transmittance and backup-lamp intensity on backing behavior. https://deepblue.lib.umich.edu/bitstream/handle/2027.42/49443/UMTRI-2001-6.pdf?sequence=1&isAllowed=y. Accessed 20 Dec 2018
5. Arbesman, M., Pellerito Jr., J.M.: Evidence – based perspective on the effect of automobile-related modifications on the driving ability, performance, and safety o folder adults. Am. J. Occup. Ther. **62**(2), 173–186 (2008)
6. Borowsky, A., Shinar, D., Gilad, T.O.: Age, skill, and hazard perception in driving. Accid. Anal. Prev. **42**(4), 1240–1249 (2010)
7. Horswill, M.S.: The hazard perception ability of older drivers. J. Gerontol. **63**(4), 212–218 (2008)
8. Horswill, M.S., Kemala, C.N., Scialfa, C., Pachana, N.A.: Improving older drivers' hazard perception ability. Psychol. Aging **25**(2), 464–469 (2010)

Using Simulation to Accelerate Development of User Interfaces for Autonomous Vehicles

Christopher R. Hudson$^{(\boxtimes)}$ (iD), Ryan Lucius, Robert Gray, Brandon Powell,
Matthew Doude, and Daniel W. Carruth (iD)

Mississippi State University, Starkville, MS 39759, USA
{chudson,bpowell,mdoude,dwc2}@cavs.msstate.edu,
{ral264,rg1071}@msstate.edu
http://www.cavs.msstate.edu/

Abstract. This paper outlines work being conducted at the Center for Advanced Vehicular Systems at Mississippi State University using simulated data to enable interface development for real world vehicles when hardware systems are not available. The ANVEL modeling and simulation tool was used to generate simulated video feeds. These videos feeds were provided to an information server, which was written to accept both simulated and real world camera data, and convert that data into an MJPEG over HTTP stream. An interface was written in Unity 2017 using simulated camera data received as an MJPEG from the information server. This user interface was then tested on a real world autonomous vehicle project, by passing camera data to the information server for conversion to a common vehicle interface format as the simulated camera data. This method allowed for the parallel development of user interface, without the need for physical hardware for testing, while maintaining real-time video capability.

Keywords: HCI · Autonomy · Simulation

1 Introduction

Autonomous vehicles present new user interface design challenges not present on traditional vehicles. An autonomous vehicle has several end users who need to understand and interact with different systems on a vehicle. A passenger requires a means to interact with the vehicle to provide goal locations. A researcher working on development of the system will need to visualize and understand the data provided to the system via on board sensors and how the system process that information. A mechanic working to resolve mechanical and electrical issues on the system will need to understand the complex layout of the autonomous vehicle, and which systems are reporting normal data. Autonomous vehicles are a

Supported by the Center for Advanced Vehicular Systems, Mississippi State University. NVIDIA hardware was provided through a partnership with NVIDIA Corporation.

C. Stephanidis (Ed.): HCII 2019, CCIS 1034, pp. 344–350, 2019.
https://doi.org/10.1007/978-3-030-23525-3_45

new technology still being developed. Many research teams operate with a limited number of vehicles shared among several teams working to meet deadlines. Given the need to make progress on various projects in parallel: design, development and deployment of user interfaces are often assigned lower priority for access to the physical hardware. Given these real-world problems, the implementation of these interfaces is often delayed due to the general need for increased access to the hardware. To address the issue of limited access to a shared platform, we propose using simulation to allow user interface designers to access the data they need to evaluate their designs. Many systems on an autonomous vehicle already rely on modeling and simulation of systems to facilitate faster development. Extending this simulation to enable the development and testing of user interfaces has significant benefits.

This paper outlines the use of the Autonomous Navigation Virtual Environment Laboratory (ANVEL), a real-time modeling and simulation tool for ground vehicle robotics, to accelerate the development of interface applications for an autonomous off-road vehicle project known as HALO at the Center for Advanced Vehicular Systems at Mississippi State University [2]. Using ANVEL, we can simulate numerous cameras, LIDAR, IMU, and GPS sensor data in real time. ANVEL provides APIs to access and pass real time data to external user interfaces and devices. To demonstrate this capability, we have implemented a Unity-based interface on an Android tablet. Simulated data is generated by ANVEL and provided to the information server in the same format as the real-world vehicle. The information server then processes and provides reduced vehicle data to the Android tablet for display. Because data coming from the simulator is processed and provided to the information server in the same format as data from the autonomous vehicle, we can directly transfer the interface from simulation to vehicle. This allows for a hardware in the loop capability. Because the tablet can leverage both real world and simulated data, designers are able to rapidly iterate on the interface using simulated data streams and test with vehicle hardware when it is available. By leveraging simulation techniques used by other development processes in autonomous vehicles, the quality of the interface can be improved while reducing development time and resource requirements.

2   Related Work

This systems mimics a hardware in the loop simulation. This method allows the interface device (Android Tablet) to use data generated in a simulation for development and testing, in replacement of data coming from physical cameras on the vehicle, since the vehicle is not available for the interface development team. Hardware in the loop simulation is a common method, used to provide unit testing for physical devices under specific circumstances [3]. It is known that hardware systems can often be unavailable due to time requirements for the development of different systems. Using model based system design helps developers of hardware systems implement different systems which can be tested in simulation at any level [5]. The notion of designing user interface for these same hardware systems can be included in this design paradigm. By allowing for the simulation of the hardware systems generating the data that needs to be visualized, model based system engineering can be applied to interface design.

3   Implementation

To enable simultaneous implementation of both user interface elements and physical systems without competing for resources, the HALO project vehicle was leveraged as a platform for this work. By leveraging a system that was undergoing powertrain electrification, the notion of working in parallel on a system that was unavailable for testing could be achieved. This section outlines the different platforms and tools leveraged, as well as the layout and function of the information processing server which provides data to the interface.

3.1   HALO Project

At the CAVS at MSU, the HALO project is converting a factory issued 2014 Subaru Forester into an all-electric vehicle. This electrification will result in the replacement of the powertrain for the vehicle. As a stock vehicle, the Subaru Forester has 24 city and 32 highway MPG with 250hp with a total weight of 3600lbs. After converting the vehicle to all-electric drive, the 90 kWh nickel-manganese-cobalt (NMC) lithium-ion battery pack gives it an estimated range of 240 miles, 536hp and a total weight of 5300lbs. Additionally during the process of reconfiguring the vehicle, 6 cameras were added to the vehicle. Two forward facing cameras (60° FOV), a left facing Camera (190° FOV), a right facing camera (190° FOV) and two rear-facing cameras (120° FOV). Additionally three LIDAR units were installed, two forward LIDAR on the bumper angled down towards the drive path of the vehicle and one LIDAR unit on top of the vehicle.

3.2   Nvidia Drive PX2

To enable the development of autonomous system behavior, as well as gain access to the LIDAR and cameras installed on the HALO vehicle, an Nvidia Drive PX2 was leveraged. The Nvidia Drive PX2 is a GPU/CPU supercomputer designed for autonomous vehicles [4]. In order to pass camera data from the Drive PX2 to the information server, Gstreamer and OpenCV software libraries were leveraged. Gstreamer was used to capture the image data from the camera devices. The raw image stream was then compressed and sent over UDP to the information server which received the compressed image data in OpenCV. The OpenCV image was made available as an MJPEG stream over HTTP. By leveraging a simple HTTP server, real time video could be accessed by multiple devices on the same network. This is outlined in Fig. 1.

3.3   ANVEL

The Autonomous Navigation Virtual Environment Laboratory (ANVEL) is a real-time physics based simulation environment, designed to model autonomous systems driving through various environments. ANVEL provides several simulated systems such as LIDAR, GPS, IMU as well as calculations of different forces acting on the simulated vehicle. In order to model the vehicle, ANVEL uses of definition files which describe each component of the simulated vehicle (battery, engine, wheels, mass, etc.). The ANVEL API was leveraged to extract the image data from the simulation environment. The data was received on the information server, and made available over HTTP as an MJPEG stream, in the same way the HALO car provided the video data. This is outlined in Fig. 1.

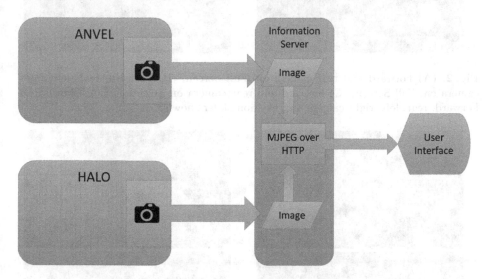

Fig. 1. The flow of video data from source to interface.

3.4   Unity

The user interface was designed using Unity 2017 [1]. Unity was chosen due to its ability to easily deploy to multiple devices such as Android, iOS, and Windows. Additionally, Unity provides scalability in user interfaces to account for a variety of display sizes so that the interface can be deployed on phones, tablets, laptops and desktop systems. This dynamic resolution management combined with ease of deployment made Unity 2017 ideal for implementing the user interface. No plugins were used in this implementation to ensure maximum capability with all systems during deployment.

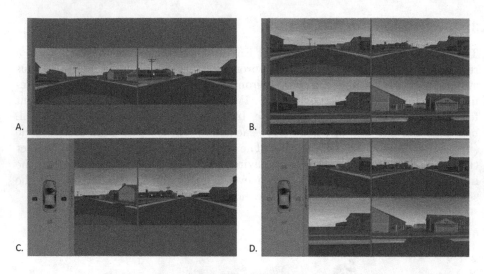

Fig. 2. (A) Forward and rear camera on, Full Screen, (B) Forward, rear, left, right camera on, Full Screen, (C) Forward and rear camera on, selection slider shown, (D) Forward, rear, left, right camera on, selection slider shown

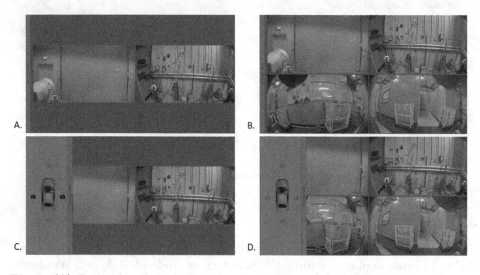

Fig. 3. (A) Forward and rear camera on, Full Screen, (B) Forward, rear, left, right camera on, Full Screen, (C) Forward and rear camera on, selection slider shown, (D) Forward, rear, left, right camera on, selection slider shown

4   Results

Video data was successfully integrated into the Unity interface and deployed to phone and tablet devices for monitoring vehicle feeds. The interface software was able to leverage both simulation and real-world data passed through a common information server and provided to the user interface through a common method. Example video feeds from ANVEL can be seen in the user interface in Fig. 2. By leveraging MJPEG over HTTP real time performance was achieved.

The capability of the user interface can be seen when connecting to the HALO vehicle. While the simple video monitoring user interface was designed using simulated video feed data, the format of the information was provided to the interface in the same way as real world data. This allowed for the interface to immediately work with the HALO vehicle when it was turned on, without the need for reconfiguration. The integration of video data can been seen in Fig. 3.

5   Discussion

Through the use of an information processing server, we have shown that data can be collected from both simulation and real world vehicle and forwarded in a common format to user interfaces. By leveraging simulation, we have shown that tasks such as integration of real-time video displays which rely heavily on the availability of physical hardware in order to test, can leverage simulation in order to speed up the implementation process of user interfaces. The user interface development team was able to develop and iterate on designs while the HALO vehicle was undergoing major system replacement and was unavailable for system testing.

6   Conclusions and Future Work

We have demonstrated use of simulation in order to mimic real world data, specifically leveraging real time video feeds, to design, develop and test user interfaces without the need for physical hardware. By enabling the user interface designer to use simulated data sources that match real-world data sources, work can be conducted in parallel which allows for a more rapid deployment of both physical system, and it's user interface, without having to resolve conflicts in system availability for development. In the future, we hope to expand this work to integrate additional systems present on both the physical and simulated vehicle. Additionally, we would like to explore using the same user interface for multiple vehicles without changing any internal implementation to the user interface, providing only changes to the information processing in the information server, which is vehicle dependent.

References

1. Unity Game Engine. http://www.unity3d.com
2. Autonomous Navigation Virtual Environment Laboratory (ANVEL). http://anvelsim.com/
3. Isermann, R., Schaffnit, J., Sinsel, S.: Hardware-in-the-loop simulation for the design and testing of engine-control systems 7(5), 643–653 (1999)

4. Nvidia Drive Px2. https://www.nvidia.com/en-us/self-driving-cars/drive-platform/
5. Rousseau, A., et al.: Electric drive vehicle development and evaluation using system simulation. IFAC Proc. **47**(3), 7886–7891 (2014)

Spaceship, Guardian, Coach: Drivers' Mental Models of Advanced Vehicle Technology

James Jenness[1]([envelope]), John Lenneman[2], Amy Benedick[1],
Richard Huey[1], Joshua Jaffe[1], Jeremiah Singer[1], and Sarah Yahoodik[3]

[1] Westat, Rockville, MD 20850, USA
JamesJenness@westat.com
[2] Toyota Collaborative Safety Research Center, Ann Arbor, MI 48105, USA
[3] Old Dominion University, Norfolk, VA 23529, USA

Abstract. Advanced driver assistance systems (ADAS), including automated driving features, can reduce the driver's workload by assuming control of driving subtasks such as steering (lane centering system), or maintaining speed and safe following distance (adaptive cruise control). Although these systems show promise for improving safety and efficiency, they also pose challenges regarding consumer understanding of their operation. Little is known about how new vehicle owners learn about the capabilities, limitations, and operational design domains for ADAS and how their personal understanding (mental model) influences their use of the systems and their driving behavior. This paper describes empirical work-in-progress aimed at delineating the dominant characteristics and changes over time in users' mental models of ADAS. We discuss results of the first phase of the research (user focus groups), along with the methods and preliminary findings for two additional phases of research. The second phase is a longitudinal study of 2018/2019 passenger vehicle owners (n = 41) who were interviewed nine times during their first six months of ownership. The third phase includes new Toyota owners (n = 12) who were video recorded while driving, and interviewed periodically. All interviews were audio recorded and analyzed to extract information about participants' understanding of the operation, capabilities, and limitations of ADAS. The objective of the analysis is to determine the characteristics of mental models that best describe differences observed between individuals. Two candidate characteristics are levels of complexity and anthropomorphism. User generated analogues such as "spaceship," or "elderly aunt" also show promise for distinguishing mental models.

Keywords: Drivers · Mental models · ADAS · Adaptive cruise control ·
Lane centering · Naturalistic · Consumer education · HMI · Automated driving

1 Introduction

Advanced driver assistance systems (ADAS), including automated driving features, show significant potential for improving safety and efficiency on our roadways [1]. However, new and changing ADAS technologies pose challenges to the formation and maintenance of mental models (i.e., understanding) of their operation [2]. The purpose of this project is to characterize users' mental models of ADAS technologies, including

© Springer Nature Switzerland AG 2019
C. Stephanidis (Ed.): HCII 2019, CCIS 1034, pp. 351–356, 2019.
https://doi.org/10.1007/978-3-030-23525-3_46

how they develop and evolve. This project will generate insights for improving system design and educating consumers. The three-phase research approach includes focus groups, a series of multiple interviews with vehicle owners, and data collection of actual driver experience under real-world driving conditions. Westat's IRB approved the protocols used in this project to ensure the welfare of human research participants.

2 Phase 1: Focus Groups

2.1 Approach

Phase 1 of this project consisted of three focus group sessions conducted to gain initial insights into variants of drivers' ADAS mental models and the mental model formation and evolution process. Researchers extracted information relevant to mental models from transcripts of the sessions. We focused on the language that drivers used to describe their ADAS and the experiences that influenced initial formation and subsequent changes to drivers' mental models of ADAS systems. Based on this qualitative analysis, we created a preliminary list of candidate dimensions or features of mental models that could serve as a basis for creating a taxonomy (i.e., a classification system) of mental models for ADAS technologies.

2.2 Methods

Prior to participating in a focus group, potential participants were screened for self-reported technology savviness. Based on their responses, they were assigned to high- (5 men, 5 women), low- (1 man, 6 women), or mixed high and low (4 men, 5 women) technology savviness focus groups. To be eligible, potential participants had to have purchased a new vehicle within the previous 12 months and the vehicle had to have at least two ADAS. There were no other restrictions about vehicle make or model.

The focus group moderator followed a script of topics and questions designed to extract information about each participant's understanding of their vehicle systems and underlying technology, their confidence in the systems, and system use patterns. Researchers made audio and video recordings of the sessions, and later transcribed the audio to capture the exact words that participants used when describing the ADAS on their vehicles.

Three researchers independently reviewed the session transcripts, noted sections that were relevant for understanding participants' mental models, and provided interpretations regarding the meaning of what the participants said. Then they met and discussed their interpretations to reach consensus on the meaning of participants' comments. Based on the notes from all three groups, the researchers each proposed candidate dimensions or characteristics of mental models for ADAS that could explain similarities and differences observed between participants' comments. Researchers reviewed and discussed the candidate dimensions and characteristics of mental models to reach agreement.

2.3   Results

Throughout the course of the focus groups, several participants described their vehicle and its ADAS using metaphors. Some examples are a teacher or coach, a robot, a computer, an elderly aunt, and a toolbox. In the qualitative analysis, researchers noted that such analogues seemed to be an efficient way for some participants to express their understanding of, and feelings about their ADAS.

Based on the analysis of the focus group transcripts, the strongest candidates for characteristics to include in a taxonomy of ADAS mental models are:

- Level of complexity: The level of detail in participants' descriptions of their vehicle's technologies varied substantially. Some participants went into extensive detail while trying to explain various system components and processes, while others simply described their system using the outcome. In other words, participants with a simple mental model tended to focus on what the system does, while participants with more complex mental models also tended to think about how the technology works.
- Level of holism: The perceived level of integration of ADAS technologies in the vehicle varied across the participant's descriptions. Some participants described the systems as a set of individual components with differing purposes and capabilities, while at the other extreme, other participants spoke about their vehicle as a single entity that performed actions to assist them and keep them safe.
- Level of anthropomorphism: The use of human characteristics by participants to describe their vehicles and ADAS technologies varied.

Researchers noted some additional candidate components of a mental model taxonomy that seemed to be associated with differences in system use. These were emotional connectedness and subjective evaluation of system performance. The emotional connectedness component captures emotions (positive or negative) associated with the participant's vehicle and ADAS technologies. Participants frequently used words like "love" or "annoyance" when discussing their vehicle's ADAS. The subjective evaluation components include constructs of perceived usefulness, trust, and system reliability. Participants often described their systems using one or more of these constructs. However, the focus group moderator did not pose follow-up questions that would have helped to distinguish between these constructs, and some participants used the terms interchangeably.

Finally, in addition to developing a preliminary set of characteristics to include in a taxonomy of ADAS mental models, researchers also identified sources of information that played a role in the development of participants' understanding of ADAS. From the discussions, it was clear that trial and error played a significant role in generating mental models of ADAS technologies. Several participants said they gained the most understanding through experimentation with the systems. Other participants indicated that their learning and understanding of ADAS was based on one or more memorable safety events. Some participants mentioned learning experiences at the automobile dealership where they purchased their vehicle as an important influence.

3 Phase 2: Longitudinal Interviews

3.1 Approach

Phase 2 is a longitudinal exploration of vehicle owners' perception of and experience with ADAS technologies over the first six months of vehicle ownership. It consists of a series of structured interviews conducted to gain a deeper understanding of mental model formation and evolution. The goal of phase 2 is to validate, refine, and augment the previously mentioned candidate characteristics for our mental models of ADAS taxonomy. We have nearly completed data collection for phase 2 and are currently reducing the extensive set of interview and questionnaire data.

3.2 Methods

Forty-one new vehicle owners enrolled in this study. To participate, participants must have purchased a new vehicle within the previous month that is equipped with at least two ADAS technologies. All participants completed an initial in-person intake interview aimed at gathering information about their initial level of understanding about the ADAS technologies in their car. Participants also filled out four scales (Hoyle Brief Sensation Seeking Scale, Driver Behavior Questionnaire, a technology acceptance questionnaire, and the Rotter Locus of Control) to gain insight into personality traits or other characteristics that may be associated with aspects of drivers' mental models [3–6].

Following an initial in-person interview, participants drove their vehicles as they normally would, and over the course of six months, and they participated in a series of seven structured phone interviews. In each of these interviews, a researcher gathered information about the participant's use and understanding of their ADAS to determine how their thoughts about ADAS may have evolved. In addition, the researcher asked questions regarding sources of information and new experiences that may have contributed any changes (or lack thereof) in the participant's understanding of ADAS. A final in-person interview was conducted six months after the initial interview to determine how the participant's mental model had changed, and the sources of information and experiences that influenced its evolution. During the final in-person interview, participants again completed the technology acceptance questionnaire so that researchers could assess whether changes in acceptance of the technologies had occurred during the six months of driving experience.

As part of the planned analysis, researchers will reduce data from the interviews and questionnaires to create a set of variables that includes specific information reported by the participants, such as changes in their system use, and summary variables that depend on researchers' interpretations, such as dominant emotions expressed toward ADAS (if any). Researchers will use both qualitative analyses and statistical techniques to explore associations between the variables and to determine which sets of variables best discriminate between participants who have clearly different understandings about ADAS. Such variables may be most useful for constructing a taxonomy of mental models.

4   Phase 3: Naturalistic Driving Evaluation

4.1   Approach

Phase 3 is a naturalistic driving study, conducted to refine and finalize the mental model taxonomy by assessing the specific impact that real-world driving events may have on ADAS mental model formation and evolution. For example, some participants may have mental models strongly influenced by events such as a near collision, while other participants may have misunderstandings about ADAS that are consistent with their real world experiences. Data collection for phase 3 is nearing completion.

4.2   Methods

Researchers recruited 12 owners of 2018 or 2019 Toyota Rav4, Corolla, Camry, or Highlander vehicles to participate in this study. Eight of the participants purchased their vehicle less than four weeks prior to enrolling in the study. They participated for 12 weeks. The remaining four participants had much more extensive experience with their vehicles (up to 18 months). They participated in the study for four weeks.

In each participant's vehicle, researchers installed a custom-built data acquisition system (DAS) that includes multiple accelerometers, and three cameras (capturing the road, the driver's face, and the instrument panel). The DAS also includes an audio capture device. By pressing a button on the device while driving, the participant could record 15-s verbal notes. Researchers received these notes on a daily basis via cellular phone connection to the DAS.

Participants were told to record notes about their experiences using the driver assist features of their vehicle. Specific written instructions also provided the following guidance for noteworthy events:

- "Something the vehicle did or did not do that surprised you."
- "Something you just discovered about the system."
- "Something that was especially helpful or annoying."
- "Something that happened that was safety related, perhaps another vehicle almost collided with you, or you almost drifted off the road, or you had any type of 'close call' or 'near miss'."

As in the phase 2 protocol, a researcher interviewed each participant in-person when he or she enrolled and exited the study, and intermittently (by phone) throughout the data collection period. The content of the interviews for phase 3 was similar to that in phase 2, but in phase 3 the researcher also asked the participant to discuss the circumstances of any new audio notes that they had recorded.

As part of the data analysis for phase 3, researchers will reduce data from the vehicle, including video data, for each noteworthy event reported by the participant. The DAS data will be examined to determine exactly how each participant was driving in terms of their speed, braking behavior, and where they were looking in the moments before they recorded their verbal note. These data, collected during drives, will be compared to reduced interview data from the same participants to assess whether specific driving experiences are associated with changes in participants' mental models.

5 Outlook

The combination of broad focus group discussions, targeted longitudinal interviews, and the naturalistic data collection procedure provide a strong basis for the creation of a taxonomy of ADAS technology mental models, and should provide additional insight into their formation and evolution. In turn, we expect that a data-driven taxonomy will serve as a useful tool when developing approaches designed to foster efficient and appropriate mental models of ADAS technology. These include, but are not limited to, consumer education approaches, training methods, and human-machine interface design strategies.

References

1. Kuehn, M., Hummel, T., Bende, J.: Benefit estimation of advanced driver assistance systems for cars derived from real-life accidents. In: Proceedings of the 21st International Technical Conference on the Enhanced Safety of Vehicles, Paper no. 09-0317. National Highway Traffic Safety Administration, Washington, DC (2009)
2. McDonald, A., McGehee, D., Chrysler, S., Askelson, N., Angell, L., Seppelt, B.: National survey identifying gaps in consumer knowledge of advanced vehicle safety systems. Transp. Res. Rec. J. Transp. Res. Board **2559**, 1–6 (2016)
3. Hoyle, R., Stephenson, M., Palmgreen, P., Lorch, E., Lewis, R., Donohew, L.: Reliability and validity of a brief measure of sensation seeking. Pers. Individ. Differ. **32**, 401–414 (2002)
4. Reason, J., Manstead, A., Stradling, S., Baxter, J., Campbell, K.: Errors and violations on the roads: a real distinction? Ergonomics **33**, 1315–1332 (1990)
5. Van der Laan, J., Heino, A., De Waard, D.: A simple procedure for the assessment of acceptance of advanced transport telematics. Transp. Res. Part C Emerg. Technol. **5**, 1–10 (1997)
6. Rotter, J.: Generalized expectancies for internal versus external control of reinforcement. Psychol. Monogr. **80**, 1–28 (1966)

Peripheral HUD Alerting and Driving Performance

Abram J. Knarr, Alexander Nguyen, and Thomas Z. Strybel[(⊠)]

California State University Long Beach, Long Beach, CA, USA
abeknarr@gmail.com, alexander.nguyen@gmail.com,
thomas.strybel@csulb.edu

Abstract. We examined driving performance using the Lane Change Test combined with a Peripheral Detection Task (PDT) that approximated stimuli crossing in front of the driver's vehicle, in order to measure performance on driving and critical event detection. For the PDT task, critical events were signaled by either a color cue, a flashing cue or combination color-flashing cue. These were compared to a no-cue condition. Driving performance and event detection were measured. All effects of the PDT on driving performance were nonsignificant. Color cues significantly reduced reaction time, but flashing cues increased reaction time. These results indicate that cues to events in the driver's periphery did not impair driving performance, at least for the simple driving task used here. Moreover, color cueing by itself was more effective than either flashing or color-flashing cues in detecting peripheral events.

Keywords: Driving · Peripheral event detection · Lane Change Test

1 Introduction

From 2014 to 2016, the number of people killed in motor vehicle collisions jumped from roughly 35,000 to over 40,000; in 2018, the number of traffic fatalities has remained at the 2016 level [1]. The increase in the death toll rate is somewhat surprising given the increased numbers of safety features found on new vehicles although these are available only in recent models. Even more surprising is the finding that, since 2010, cyclist fatalities increased by 25% and pedestrian deaths rose by 45% [2]. Possibly some of the increase in pedestrian deaths is due to increased emphasis on walking and biking in many cities. Nevertheless additional research and development is needed for improving the detectability of pedestrians, cyclists and other crossing traffic.

1.1 Heads up Displays

HUD technologies, due to their success in aviation, are being introduced in automobiles. It is important to examine how to design these displays so that information is displayed without interfering with information in the driver's environment. Therefore, most investigations of driving performance with HUDs have focused on whether the projected image impairs driving performance. For example, Watanabe et al. [3] examined the effect of HUD on driving. Participants viewed a video of driving and

C. Stephanidis (Ed.): HCII 2019, CCIS 1034, pp. 357–360, 2019.
https://doi.org/10.1007/978-3-030-23525-3_47

were instructed to report when certain events (road signs, turn signals, and passing cars) were detected. Participants also detected triangles at varying locations that were projected on the HUD. Results showed that responses to warning triangles increased with eccentricity; however, the HUD task did not significantly interfere with detection of road events. Liu [4] examined whether HUDs affected driving performance by manipulating whether drivers attended to the HUD or the outside environment. Lui showed that drivers attending to the HUD responded faster to road events under both low and high driving loads. Moreover, variability in speed was lower in the HUD condition.

In one of the few tests of HUDs for pedestrian detection, Kim et al. [5] compared pedestrian detection performance in which pedestrian crossings were signaled either with a traditional "BRAKE" symbol or a virtual "Shadow" display that notified drivers of the pedestrian's direction of travel. These were compared to pedestrian detection task with no cue. Both displays were shown to reduce braking reaction time and increase stopping distance. Therefore, HUD technologies may be useful tools in alerting drivers to objects in their periphery that are possible hazards.

The purpose of the present study was to examine the effects of visual warnings for obstacles that appeared in a driver's periphery and crossed into the driver's lane of traffic. We investigated whether the presence of a crossing alert affected driving performance, and three formats for signaling this event in a simulated HUD display. The Lane Change Task (LCT) and Peripheral Detection Task (PDT) were used [6].

2 Method

2.1 Participants

Twelve participants with at least 3 years driving experience were tested. All participants reported normal or corrected-to-normal vision and no color-vision deficits. Each participant completed two hours of testing and received a $20 gift card upon completion.

2.2 Apparatus and Materials

The LCT requires a participant to drive on an otherwise empty, three-lane road and change lanes in response to signs located on the shoulder of the road. The LCT was projected on a large screen, and participants completed the test using a Logitech gaming steering wheel. The LCT consists of 3-km straight-lane track and presents lane change signs roughly every 150 m, making a total of 18 lane changes per track. Performance on the LCT was assessed by the MDEV, the average deviation between the driver's path and a normative model. The PDT stimulus consisted of a sequence of four small white circles each 200 ms in duration, giving the appearance of an 800-ms moving stimulus. The initial circle appeared in the participant's peripheral view on the side of the road. The remaining circles appeared in sequence (ISI = 0 ms) and produced movement either toward or away from the center of the traffic lane. Participants responded to critical PDT events - movements toward the center lane, using a number pad located next to the steering wheel.

Four PDT conditions were tested based on whether critical events were cued, and the format of the cue, either color, flashing or color and flashing. For the color cue, the initial circle of the PDT event was yellow when movement was toward the center lane. For the flashing cue, the initial spot flashed when movement was toward the center lane. For the color-flashing cue, the initial spot appeared yellow and flashed for the critical event. For the flashing cue, the initial stimulus flashed twice. These cues were compared to a No-Cue Condition in which direction of movement was not cued.

2.3 Procedure

For each of the PDT cue conditions, three tracks each were run under low-workload or high-workload conditions in random order. For low workload, the PDT stimuli were presented between lane changes while the driver was lane keeping. For high workload, the PDT stimuli appeared while the driver was changing lanes. Within each track, nine PDT stimuli moved toward the center lane (critical events) and nine moved away from the road. Each participant was given time to practice the LCT prior to data collection. Baseline tracks with no PDT task, were run at the beginning and end of the cue conditions to determine the effect of the PDT on overall LCT performance. Driving performance was assessed with MDEV; performance on the PDT was assessed by reaction time and a non-parametric measure of sensitivity, A'.

3 Results

A one way repeated measures ANOVA was run to determine the effect of the conditions on driving performance (MDEV), with the factors baseline (no PDT), and the four cue conditions. The effect was nonsignificant (p = .582). A three-factor ANOVA was run on MDEV to determine the effects of cue conditions. Again, all main effects and interactions were nonsignificant (p's > .39).

PDT performance was measured by A', a non-parametric measure of sensitivity, and reaction time. A' determines a participant's sensitivity to signals in noise based on the number of hits and false alarms. A' ranges from 0.5, indicating no sensitivity to 1.0 indicating perfect sensitivity. Overall sensitivity on the PDT task was high, as the mean A' across conditions was .96. A three-factor repeated measures ANOVA with factors Color Cue (color vs. no color), Flash Cue (flash vs. no flash) and Workload (high vs. low) was run. Results indicated significant main effects of color, $F(1,11) = 7.390$, p = .020, $np^2 = .402$, and workload, $F(1,11) = 6.722$, p = .025, $np^2 = .379$. Sensitivity was higher for color cues, and for the high workload condition. The main effect of flash and all interactions were non-significant (p's > .289). For reaction time, main effects of Color $F(1,11) = 7.136$, p = .022, $np^2 = .393$, Flash, $F(1,11) = 46.546$, p < .001, $np^2 = .809$, and workload, $F(1,11) = 10.900$, p = .007, $np^2 = .498$ were obtained. Color cues (M = 642.3 ms, SEM = 24.3 ms) reduced reaction time compared to no-color cues (M = 665.8 ms, SEM = 20.8 ms). Surprisingly, reaction time to Flashing Cues (M = 708.0 ms SEM = 25.3 ms) was higher than for non-flashing cues (M = 600.0, SEM = 20.6 ms), and reaction time for the low workload condition

(M = 665.3 ms, SEM = 23.0 ms) was higher than for the high-workload condition (M = 642.7 ms, SEM = 21.9 ms). All interactions were non-significant (p's > .096).

4 Discussion

These results indicate that cues to events in the driver's periphery did not impair driving performance, at least for the simple driving task used here. For detection of critical events, color cues significantly reduced detection times, and color cues were more effective than either flashing or color-flashing cues. In fact, flashing cues disrupted detection somewhat as the mean reaction time was higher for flashing cues compared with non-flashing cues. This surprising result may have been the result of the brief presentation time of the PDT event. Given a total duration of 800 ms for the PDT event, the flashing stimulus appeared only for the first 200 ms, producing only 2 flashes. This brief flash event may have been insufficient to properly alert the driver.

Also somewhat surprising was the finding that detecting the peripheral stimulus was faster when the participant was engaged in making a lane change, yet performance on the lane change task was unaffected. It is possible that in the low workload condition the driver was anticipating the upcoming lane-change sign, which reduced sensitivity to peripheral events.

References

1. Shaper, D.: Even as cars get safer, traffic fatalities still high (2018). https://www.npr.org/
2. Short, F.: Why US cities are becoming more dangerous for cyclists and pedestrians. The Conversation, 20 February 2019
3. Watanabe, H., Yoo, H., Tsimhoni, O., Green, P.: The effect of HUD warning location on driver responses. In: Proceedings of the ITS World Congress on Intelligent Transport Systems, pp. 1–10 (1999)
4. Liu, Y.: Effects of using head-up display in automobile context on attention demand and driving performance. Displays 24, 157–165 (2003)
5. Kim, H., Anon, A.M., Misu, T., Li, N., Tawari, A., Fujimura, K.: In: Proceedings of the 21st International Conference on Intelligent User Interfaces, pp. 294–298. ACM, Sonoma (2016)
6. Mattes, S., Hallén, A.: Surrogate distraction measurement techniques: the lane change test. In: Regan, M.A., Lee, J.D., Young, K.L. (eds.) Driver Distraction: Theory, Effects, and Mitigation, pp. 107–121. Taylor & Francis Group, Boca Raton (2009)

ActoViz: A Human Behavior Simulator for the Evaluation of the Dwelling Performance of an Atypical Architectural Space

Yun Gil Lee[✉]

Hoseo University, 20, Hoseo-ro, 79beon-gil, Baebang-eup,
Asan-si, Chungcheongnam-do 31499, Korea
yglee@hoseo.edu

Abstract. The demand for atypical building shapes around the world is growing, and the use of tools, such as Rhino, for designing them is increasing in architectural design schools and firms. However, these design outcomes and processes often fail to recognize the requirements of convenience and safety for human behavior in a dwelling machine. In an architectural space, the users' behavior is one of the dominant factors that determine the value of a building. This is why we should not ignore the role of human behavior in the process of atypical building design. Most existing user-behavior simulation technology has been developed to evaluate a structure's emergency evacuation plans; there is no current technology to simulate the interaction of the built environment and its users based on the concept of "affordance," which refers to the properties of an object that show the possible actions users can take with it. The purpose of this study is to develop a technology that simulates human behavior to evaluate the residential performance of the design of an atypical architectural space. The proposed technology focuses on simulating the affordance of an atypical building during the design process. The results of this study are related to the intelligence of agents who respond to various types of spaces and situations, unlike the existing human behavior simulation technology that has been used for only a limited range of situations, such as escape simulations.

Keywords: Human factors · Human behavior · Atypical architectural design · Simulator · Evaluation

1 Introduction

The demand for atypical building shapes around the world is growing, and the use of tools, such as Rhino, for designing them is increasing in architectural design schools and firms. However, these design outcomes and processes often fail to meet the requirements of convenience and safety for human behavior in a dwelling machine. In an architectural space, the users' behavior is one of the dominant factors that determine the value of a building. This is why we should not ignore the role of human behavior in the process of atypical building design. Most existing user-behavior simulation technology has been developed to evaluate a structure's emergency evacuation plans; there is no current technology to simulate the interaction of the built environment and its

C. Stephanidis (Ed.): HCII 2019, CCIS 1034, pp. 361–365, 2019.
https://doi.org/10.1007/978-3-030-23525-3_48

users based on the concept of "affordance," which refers to the properties of an object that show the possible actions users can take with it.

The purpose of this study is to develop a technology that simulates human behavior to evaluate the residential performance of the design of an atypical architectural space. The proposed technology focuses on simulating the affordance of an atypical building during the design process. The results of this study are related to the intelligence of agents who respond to various types of spaces and situations, unlike the existing human behavior simulation technology that has been used for only a limited range of situations, such as escape simulations (Fig. 1).

Fig. 1. The design results of atypically shaped playgrounds using human-figured shapes [7].

2 Effectiveness of Human Behavioral Representation in the Atypical Architectural Design

In the previous study, we investigated the effectiveness of human behavioral representation in the atypical architectural design process. That focused on the relationship between a human behavior evaluation based on behavioral descriptions and creative problem finding. According to the results of the previous study, the human representations in the atypical architectural design process improved the designers' self-confidence in evaluating the usability and value of the design results. With human behavioral representation, designers can find more various functions of design results. As well, human behavioral representation had a positive effect on designers' reliability concerning the safety and comfort of the playground users. Taken together, the results showed that the representation of user behavior in atypical architectural design had an overall positive effect. In other words, human representation affects architects' problem finding and relevant design development not only in the field of conventional design but in atypical design as well [6, 7].

3 ActoViz: Human Behavior Simulator for Atypical Design Process

We are suggesting a tool with which designers can figure out the residential performance of a space in real time through the digital representation of the various behaviors of agents. The proposed system, called ActoViz, is intended for use in the design process for atypical architecture. It is an add-on module for Grasshopper, a tool that is frequently used for atypical building design throughout the world. ActoViz is a type of export system that can simulate human behaviors while taking into account design geometry. After the geometrical shapes of the structure have been designed using Rhino and Grasshopper, ActoViz can deploy non-player characters (NPCs) into the design alternatives. These NPCs play freely and behave in a variety of different ways in the simulation. The autonomous behavior of the NPCs is based on the intelligence of recognizing geometric affordance. Figure 2 illustrates the system structure of ActoViz.

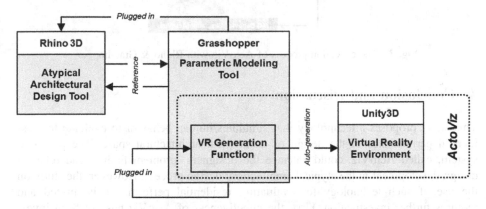

Fig. 2. The system structure of ActoViz

Figure 3 shows the process of executing ActoViz. When modeling of atypical architectural space and outer wall pattern modeling are done using the functions of Rhino and Grasshopper, the developed ActoViz module can be placed in Grasshopper and connected with existing algorithms to construct a simulation environment. When the simulation is executed on the ActoViz module, ActoViz delivers the modeled atypical space to Unity3D to generate the 3D virtual space in real time. Autonomous characters are deployed to the virtual space, and they behave freely on the atypical architectural surface. The behavioral representation of autonomous characters can influence the designers' decision-making process.

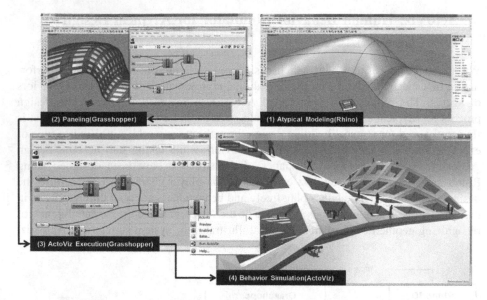

Fig. 3. The execution process of ActoViz with Rhino & Grasshopper

4   Conclusion and Discussion

This study proposes a technology that simulates human behavior to evaluate the residential performance of the design of an atypical architectural space. The proposed system, called ActoViz, could enhance the designers' problem finding and relevant design development in the atypical architectural design process. However, the study on the use of such technology for evaluating residential performance is limited and requires further investigation. First, the effectiveness of ActoViz has not been investigated. Second, the autonomous characters behaviors are quite limited and inadequate to the atypical shapes. Last we need to apply newer technologies to ActoViz for more proper behavior simulation like model predictive control.

Acknowledgment. This work was supported by the National Research Foundation of Korea (NRF) grant funded by the Korea government (MSIT) (NRF-2018R1A2B6005827).

References

1. Steinfeld, E., Kalay, Y.E.: The impact of computer-aided design on representation in architecture. In: Proceedings of ARCC Conference on Representation and Simulation in Architectural Research and Design (1990)
2. Lee, Y.G., Park, C.H., Lim, D.H.: A study on the development of the user behavior simulation technology using a perceived action possibilities. J. Korea Multimed. Soc. **17**(11), 1335–1344 (2014)

3. Dourish, P.: Where the footprints lead: tracking down other roles for social navigation. In: Munro, A.J., Höök, K., Benyon, D. (eds.) Social Navigation of Information Space. Computer Supported Cooperative Work, pp. 273–291. Springer, London (1999). https://doi.org/10.1007/978-1-4471-0837-5_2
4. Murase, H., Nayar, S.K.: Visual learning and recognition of 3-D objects from appearance. Int. J. Comput. Vision **14**(1), 5–24 (1995)
5. Norman, D.A.: Affordances, conventions, and design. Interactions **6**(3), 38–43 (1999)
6. Paletz, S.B.F., Peng, K.: Problem finding and contradiction: examining the relationship between Naïve dialectical thinking, ethnicity, and creativity. Creativity Res. J. **21**(2), 139–151 (2009)
7. Lee, Y.: A study on the effect of human factor for atypical design in the architectural design studio. In: Ahram, T., Karwowski, W., Taiar, R. (eds.) IHSED 2018. AISC, vol. 876, pp. 130–134. Springer, Cham (2019). https://doi.org/10.1007/978-3-030-02053-8_21

Analysis of Barriers and Incentives for the Introduction of Electric Vehicles in the Colombia Market

Estefanya Marin Tabares(✉), Carlos Andrés Rodríguez Toro(✉),
Sebastian Mazo García(✉), and Saúl Emilio Rivero-Mejía(✉)

Pascual Bravo University Institution, Medellín, Colombia
{e.marin407,c.rodriguez64,s.mazo5544,
saul.rivero}@pascualbravo.edu.co

Abstract. The entry of Colombia into the OECD, the acceptance of the Paris Agreement and the adoption of the Sustainable Development, is an evidence of the commitment of the country with the sustainability. A feature of sustainable cities is that through their public policy mitigation of greenhouse gases is guaranteed, which implies that their inhabitants use public transport in a greater proportion. To address the issue of pollution in the world, the introduction of electric vehicles has been stimulated.

Taking into account the upper lines, this project identifies some barriers and incentives for the introduction of electric vehicles in Colombia, in aspects of regulatory, economic, technological and perception by potential buyers of automobiles. The following strategy was carried out: a state of the art review was carried out to identify experiences of other countries in terms of market incentives for electric vehicles and related services. Subsequently, interviews were conducted with potential buyers of vehicles directly in some dealerships in the city of Medellin, with the purpose to know their perceptions regarding the performance, incentives and technological, economic or cultural barriers of electric vehicles in Colombia and the city. Finally, a mechanical engineer was interviewed, to determine the advantages and disadvantages of reconversion of a conventional vehicle to electric, in aspects such as performance, support costs and maintenance. Perception barriers were found among potential buyers of vehicles, in aspects with the technological infrastructure of the city and also for high prices compared to other countries in the region.

Keywords: Electric vehicles · Incentives · Sustainable mobility

1 Introduction

The entry of Colombia into the OECD, the acceptance of the Paris Agreement and the adoption of the Sustainable Development, is an evidence of the commitment of the country with the sustainability [1]. In that way, a sustainable city should be develop in four dimensions. One of them refers to the need to promote transport and sustainable urban mobility. Similarly, another feature of sustainable cities is that through their public policy mitigation of greenhouse gases is guaranteed, which implies that their

C. Stephanidis (Ed.): HCII 2019, CCIS 1034, pp. 366–372, 2019.
https://doi.org/10.1007/978-3-030-23525-3_49

inhabitants use public transport in a greater proportion [2]. While encouraging the use of mass public transport improves mobility, the problem of environmental pollution is not solved. To address the issue of pollution in the world, the introduction of electric vehicles has been stimulated.

In order to sell and buy electric vehicles, it is necessary to adopt tax incentives for supply and demand. Tax incentives are mechanisms of fiscal policy used by most countries to promote a specific industrial sector through exemptions or tax exemption [3]. On the other hand, non-tax incentives do not include tax exemption, but flexibility in the application of rules and regulations [4]. Tax incentives are instruments that affect the estimates of costs and benefits of initiatives open to economic agents [5]. Economic instruments modify prices, it is a matter of common sense; an economic instrument is basically responsible for rewarding good behavior and punishing bad behavior [6]. In addition to tax incentives, in the case of sustaining a vehicle, an adequate technological infrastructure is also needed, which is linked to the related services of buying and selling the vehicle.

Taking into account the upper lines, this project identifies some barriers and incentives for the introduction of electric vehicles in Colombia, in aspects of regulatory, economic, technological and perception by potential buyers of automobiles.

2 Methodology

In this project an exploratory type research was carried out, given that to date the market of electric vehicles in Colombia is still incipient and also in the laws and regulatory issues there are still legal gaps to be addressed by the national government and technical aspects to regulate. As a special case for the study, the city of Medellín was taken into account. On the other hand, the study focused only on the market of light electric vehicles without counting motorcycles and bicycles.

The following strategy was carried out: Firstly, a state of the art review was carried out to identify experiences of other countries in terms of market incentives for electric vehicles and related services. Subsequently, interviews were conducted with potential buyers of vehicles directly in some dealerships in the city of Medellin, with the purpose of their perceptions regarding the performance, incentives and technological, economic or cultural barriers of electric vehicles in Colombia and the city. Finally, a mechanical engineer expert in reconversion of conventional vehicles to electric vehicles was interviewed, to determine the advantages and disadvantages of reconversion of a conventional vehicle to electric, in aspects such as performance, support costs and maintenance of the vehicle.

3 Results

Until the beginning of 2019, reviewing the market data of electric vehicles in Colombia, it is appreciated that the introduction of this new technology to the market has been slow, given that the proposal of Law 230 of 2016 of incentives has not been approved by the Congress of Colombia and that also the incentives have been focused only towards the buyers leaving aside the related services.

3.1 Electric Cars Market in Colombia

According to the Association of Sustainable Mobility (Andemos), the most sold conventional cars brands in Colombia during the year 2018 were in their order: Chevrolet (49,916 units); Renault (49,741), Nissan (23,190), Mazda (21,520) and Kia (21,013). For the particular case of electric vehicles, 932 electric and hybrid cars were sold, where the BMW brand is consolidated as the brand with the highest number of cars sold with a total of 285 units, followed by Renault that sold 220 and Kia with 183 vehicles. with these characteristics [7].

On the other hand, Table 1 shows the prices and technical characteristics of some of the electric vehicles offered in the Colombian market.

Table 1. Brands and technical characteristics of the most sold cars in the Colombian market.

Brand	Power (HP)	Autonomy (km)	Time of charge (hour)	Price of sale (USD)
BMW i3	170	250	4,5	53,400
BYD e5	121	300	6	32,383
BYD e6	121	400	8	48,575
Hyundai Ioniq	118	250	4	29,469
Kia Soul EV	110	250	5	41,775
Mitsubishi i-Miev	67	160	8	29,113
Nissan Leaf	109	175	6,5	35,622
Renault Kangoo Z.E	60	170	6,5	27,523
Renault Twizy	17	80	3,5	12,950
Renault Zoe	92	300	6,5	32,380

Source: Own elaboration based on information observed on the website www.carroya.com in October 2018

According to Table 1, it is observed that except for the Renault Twizy, the price of the cheapest vehicle is over 84 million pesos, aspect that evidently has limited the increase in the sales of these vehicles. On the other hand, the cost of importing a hybrid vehicle (fuel and electric motor) is three times higher than that of a conventional car, while hybrid plug-in electric technology (electric motor and fuel, plus batteries) is four times higher and the value of a pure electric vehicle can be up to five times higher than that of a traditional one [8].

3.2 Incentives in the Electric Vehicle Market in Some Countries in Latin America and the World

The main policy incentives to captivate customers of electric vehicles (EV) are three: direct subsidies, tax incentives and savings in fuel costs. Tax incentives are used to reduce taxes when buying an EV. The saving of energy costs encourages users of electric vehicles to drive their car, which reduces the cost of charging energy [9].

Table 2 shows the tax structure for the vehicle market both with internal combustion engine (ICEV) and electric vehicles (EV) in some Latin American countries.

Table 2. Tax structure for electric vehicles in six Latin American countries

Tax	Argentina		Brasil		Chile		Colombia		México		Perú	
	ICEV	EV	ICEV	EV	ICEV	EV	ICEV	EV	ICEV	EV	ICEV	EV
Tax on the amount	0.5%	35.5%	0%	35%	6%	6%	35%	35%	0%	0%	9%	9%
Value added	41%	41%	43%	43%	19%	19%	16%	16%	16%	16%	17%	17%
Other	8.5%	58.5%	11.6%	11.6%	0%	0%	8%	0%	4%	0%	37%	37%
Total (sum)	50%	135%	54.6%	89.6%	25%	25%	59%	51%	20%	16%	63%	63%

Table 2 shows that the country with the highest taxes for the purchase of an electric vehicle is Argentina. Colombia, within the group of these six countries, has intermediate taxes.

Table 3 compares the final price of a BMW brand electric vehicle of reference i3, powered by a 94 Ah electric battery, which allows a range of approximately 200 km.

Table 3. Final price of a BMW i3 vehicle

Country	Price in american dollars (USD)
Argentina	43,900
Brasil	51,987
Chile	56,985
México	46,635
Perú	43,889
Colombia	53,400

3.3 Results of the Perception Survey of Vehicle Buyers in the City of Medellín

During the month of February of 109 a survey was carried out with 74 potential buyers of vehicles in the city of Medellín, which were in some dealerships selling vehicles in the city. The purpose of the survey was to know their perceptions regarding the performance, incentives and technological, economic or cultural barriers of electric vehicles in Colombia and the city. The survey consisted of 7 questions and was designed according to the Likert scale with 5 alternatives. The following results are obtained.

First question: Would you be willing to buy a hybrid or electric vehicle?
78.4% of the respondents (participants) answered that they strongly agreed (MD) or agreed (DA) to buy an electric vehicle, 17.6% said they were undecided, while 4.1% said they disagreed (ED) or strongly disagree (MED) in buying an electric or hybrid vehicle.

Second question: Do you consider that the increase in the value of gasoline will encourage the purchase of electric vehicles?
64.9% of the people surveyed responded strongly (MD) or agreed (DA) with the increase in gasoline as an incentive for the purchase of an electric vehicle, 18.9% said they were undecided in front of that measure, while 16.2% of respondents said they disagreed (ED) or strongly disagreed (MED).

Third question: When buying a vehicle, would you be willing to pay more money for an electric vehicle knowing that these are more environmentally friendly compared to a conventional vehicle comparatively speaking?
68.9% of respondents answered that they strongly agreed (MD) or agreed (DA) to pay more money to buy a hybrid or elective vehicle, 13.5% said they were undecided and 17.6% He said he disagreed (ED) or strongly disagreed (MED) against paying more money for the purchase of an electric vehicle.

Fourth question: Do you think that the biggest inconvenience that an electric vehicle has in the autonomy or battery life?
67.6% of the people surveyed responded strongly (MD) or agreed (DA) that the biggest drawback of an electric vehicle is the autonomy and battery life, while 18.9% expressed undecided and 13.5% answered that they disagreed (ED) or strongly disagreed (MED) against this inconvenience.

Fifth question: Do you consider that the country's current infrastructure and government initiatives are enough to encourage the purchase of electric vehicles?
27.0% of respondents said they strongly agree (MD) or agreed (DA) that the country's infrastructure and government initiatives are enough to encourage the purchase of electric vehicles, while 16.2% He was undecided and the remaining 56.8% responded to disagree or strongly disagree with the question.

Sixth question: Do you think that for the purchase of hybrid or electric cars the state should grant some type of incentive?
86.5% of the respondents answered that they strongly agree (MD) or agreed (DA) that the government grants some type of incentive for the purchase of these vehicles, while 8.1% were undecided and the 5.4% responded to disagree (ED) or strongly disagree (MED).

Seventh question: Do you think that electric vehicles have a lower mechanical performance compared to conventional vehicles?
40.5% of the people surveyed responded strongly (MD) or agreed (DA) that electric vehicles have a mechanical performance lower than a conventional vehicle. Conversely, 20.3% were undecided and 39.2% said they disagreed (ED) or strongly disagreed (MED).

4 Discussion and Conclusions

In Colombia, 932 electric and hybrid cars were sold last year, a figure that is very small compared to the total sales of the sector that exceeded 256,000 units. It shows significant growth compared to the figure for 2017, when only 196 units were sold. In the case of the city of Medellín, there are about 350 electric cars registered, and 19 loading points are installed throughout the city. On the other hand, despite the interest of potential buyers in acquiring an electric vehicle, the sales of this type of car compared with the sales of a conventional vehicle are still very low, which indicates that there are indeed barriers that must be overcome as is the need to have tax and non-tax incentives and, as far as possible, differentiated so that owners of vehicles with more than 10 years of age can acquire a new electric or hybrid vehicle. Similarly, the expert engineer expressed that it is necessary that the state should grant tax incentives and not tributary so that more and more people buy electric vehicles. In addition, he disagreed that an incentive for the sale of electric vehicles is to increase the price of gasoline.

According to the statements made by the people surveyed, although they agreed or agreed to pay more money for an electric car, the price remains a difficult obstacle to avoid. The price of an electric vehicle with similar conditions to a conventional vehicle costs up to 3 times more. On the other hand, the expert engineer expressed his agreement that transforming a conventional vehicle into an electric vehicle is cheaper than buying a new electric vehicle. Perhaps one of the disadvantages of an electric vehicle versus a conventional vehicle is its autonomy. Virtually the electric vehicle for the city of Medellin should be used at the urban level, since the nearest city that is Manizales is located more than 200 km away. It also happens with the battery charging time, since the minimum time required by the vehicles that are distributed in the Colombian market need at least 3.5 h.

On the other hand, it is evident that the technological infrastructure of the city of Medellin and the country related to charging stations is concentrated in some neighborhoods or shopping centers, that is, there are many sectors of the city of Medellín that lack technological infrastructure for future or potential buyers of electric vehicles. The expert engineer said he agreed that the country's technological infrastructure is insufficient for the entry of more electric vehicles. Perhaps one of the great advantages of the electric vehicle is the saving in energy costs, since charging the electric vehicle can be up to 75% cheaper than load a traditional vehicle. For example, a petrol vehicle for one person requires approximately US $ 32 per week, while an electric vehicle with similar characteristics only requires approximately US $ 9 for similar journeys. On the other hand, the expert engineer said that the maintenance tasks of an electric vehicle are cheaper than the maintenance of a conventional vehicle.

Likewise, it appreciates that potential buyers believe that the mechanical performance of an electric vehicle is inferior to that of a conventional vehicle with similar characteristics. The city of Medellín is built in a mountainous area and therefore for a vehicle user to move quietly needs a vehicle with a good torque. On the other hand, contrary to what was said by the people surveyed, the engineer disagreed with the fact that an electric vehicle presents a lower performance compared to a conventional vehicle. He also said the engineer agreed that the electric vehicles sold in the Colombian market are in line with the topography of the country. Also, there is a barrier in the country, the limited supply of related services for electric vehicles, such as the existence of specialized workshops with skilled labor to perform maintenance tasks in these vehicles. Also, from the normative point of view has not yet been updated in terms of tests and tests which are those of strict compliance for electric vehicles. Likewise, the sale of spare parts is still limited given the limited supply of suppliers of parts and supplies. On the other hand, the expert engineer said he agreed that a current barrier in the market is the shortage of skilled workers to perform maintenance tasks in electric cars.

References

1. Chavarro, D., Vélez, I., Tovar, G., et al.: Los Objetivos de Desarrollo Sostenible en Colombia y el aporte de la ciencia, la tecnología y la innovación. Colciencias. Subdirección Gen Diseño políticas 1, 1–30 (2017). https://doi.org/10.13140/RG.2.2.31118.87368
2. Findeter: ¿ Qué es una Ciudad Sostenible? (2016). https://www.findeter.gov.co/publicaciones/300613/_que_es_una_ciudad_sostenible/. Accessed 5 Mar 2019
3. Artana, D., Templado, I.: La eficacia de los incentivos fiscales, El caso de las zonas francas de exportación de Costa Rica, p. 107. El Salvador y República Dominicana, Banco Interam Desarro (2015)
4. Gómez-Gélvez, J., Mojica, C., Kaul, V., Isla, L.: La Incorporacion De Los Vehiculos Electricos En America Latina, p. 48 (2016)
5. CEPAL: Guía metodológica: Instrumentos económicos para la gestión ambiental, p. 73 (2015)
6. Silva, M., Correa, F.: Los instrumentos económicos como incentivos a la internalización de costos ambientales en empresas floricultoras. Pensam y gestión, p. 29 (2010)
7. Andemos: Cifras y Estadísticas (2018). https://www.andemos.org/. Accessed 10 Oct 2018
8. Revista Semana: Subió la venta de vehículos eléctricos e híbridos en Colombia durante 2018 (2018). https://sostenibilidad.semana.com/negocios-verdes/articulo/subio-la-venta-de-vehic-ulos-electricos-e-hibridos-en-colombia-durante-2018/42618. Accessed 17 Feb 2019
9. Longo, M., Zaninelli, D., Viola, F., Romano, P., Miceli, R.: How is the spread of the electric vehicles? (2015). https://ieeexplore.ieee.org/document/7325137. Accessed 15 Mar 2019

Towards Flexible Ridesharing Experiences: Human-Centered Design of Segmented Shared Spaces

Aaron Ong[1], Joaquin Troncoso[1(✉)], Arnold Yeung[1], Euiyoung Kim[1,2], and Alice M. Agogino[1]

[1] Berkeley Research for Autonomous Vehicles Opportunities (BRAVO), University of California, Berkeley 94720, USA
Joaquintroncoso@berkeley.edu
[2] Industrial Design Engineering, Delft University of Technology, 89807 Delft, The Netherlands

Abstract. The increasing usage of ride-sharing and autonomous vehicles has presented a need for personalized mobility experiences. This research defines these needs through an investigation from passengers who have used or will use these services. User-behaviors and user pain-points were categorized through in-depth interviews and observations. The most pressing categories were defined to be safety, privacy, and comfort. The variety of responses and user pain points defined a need for a flexible solution that employ a safe, private, and comfortable experience during a shared ride. We present a human-centered design solution that segments the shared space and provides a sense of security through personal physical space, privacy through asymmetrical viewing of neighboring passengers, and comfort through increasing the field of view of the passenger.

Keywords: User behavior · Ride-sharing · Privacy · Semi-autonomous

1 Introduction

Overcrowded cities and unpreventable traffic are the results of (1) considerable demographic growth of the last few decades [1] and (2) an increasing number of registered vehicles on the road [2]. People in the US spend on average 200 h per year commuting [2] and 6.9 billion driver hours are wasted due to traffic. According to Texas A&M Transportation Institute (TTI) and Irinx, inc., this issue yields in a total cost of $160 billion from time lost and fuel consumption implied [3]. Avoiding wasted time on unnecessary activities is a main public concern and there is a great opportunity to try and improve this problem.

The development of autonomous vehicle (AV) technology had opened new possibilities for future mobility solutions. It had created new ways of solving

---

A. Ong, J. Troncoso, A. Yeung—Contributed equally.

C. Stephanidis (Ed.): HCII 2019, CCIS 1034, pp. 373–380, 2019.
https://doi.org/10.1007/978-3-030-23525-3_50

the increasing traffic issue and the existing commuting inefficiency [4]. Current automotive companies, ride-sharing companies, and academia are spending a considerable amount of time and resources in developing research and market testing on AV's role to address ground transportation challenges. However, AV's are facing many challenges regarding safety, reliability, and technological unemployment; the transition to this technology will need to consider many different aspects to achieve a high market penetration.

During the last five years, the ride-sharing industry has increased its market participation in transportation exponentially [5] and has revolutionized urban mobility and helped address the increasing problems in congestion and commuting time [4]. This trend is projected to continue, especially with advances in AV leading to an expected switch from car ownership to ride-sharing services [6]. As the autonomous vehicle and ride-sharing platform converge within the next decade, with the growth of Waymo and Uber's Advanced Technologies Group (ATG), the ride-sharing passenger dynamics and experience within the vehicle become an increasing concern. For example, simple passenger matching is an exponentially difficult problem to tackle [7], which is dependent on not only matching route compatibility, but also personal features such as gender, social status, and social interaction types.

Current methods already satisfy the most important features that end-users seek: getting from point A to B. Hence, why high occupancy public transportation is still in business. Consumers do not mind standing in a sea of other commuters, as long as the bus/subway/train brings them to their destination. Additionally, micromobility has dented short-range transportation solutions, and their growth has overshadowed even Uber and Lyft's rapid growth back when they were still starting [8]. Moreover, there is still a preference for using personal vehicles because also mobilize their personal items and require the comfort/accessibility of storage. Despite these alternatives, there is a gap in the market for flexible-customize and premium services.

The scope of this project is to address problems and user's needs under a scenario where the vast majority of the people will commute through autonomous ride-sharing vehicles, using Human Centered Design (HCD). By aiming to satisfy ride-sharing users, whose needs are currently not being completely met, the focus is on generating an easily implementable solution, with a target timeline of 5–10 years. By possibly working with ride-hailing organizations in the future, such as Uber/Lyft, who are providing real-time solutions to address current needs in mobility [9], we hope our approach will actively contribute on the future mobility problem.

2   Methods and Approach

To explore new opportunities for the future of autonomous-rideshare vehicles, a human-centered design approach was utilized. Human-centered design is a creative approach to problem solving where a product is designed through strong empathy with the end user [10]. With the increasing usage of new vehicle types, autonomous vehicles, new users, and ride-share users, a human-centered app-roach will be utilized to find new opportunities to address newly discovered user needs.

2.1   In-Depth Interviews

In-depth user interviews were first conducted to understand what were the main pain points of users while riding a vehicle and their perceptions on ride-share and autonomous vehicle technologies. Twenty interviews were conducted, inter-acting with users from different backgrounds and diverse commuting preferences to identify the main mobility problems that each of them had experienced. The interview protocol was based on 19 questions within six different categories: Pre-survey (4), Background (5), Ride-share (3), Sensing (1), Autonomous Vehicles (3) and Conclusion (3). The outcomes of the interviews were classified by identi-fying core user's needs through quotes. Each of the quotes represented a specific user need and was then clustered into labeled groups, allowing for analysis of each interpretation collectively. They were assigned to seven categories: Safety, Privacy, Entertainment, Comfort, Convenience, Hygiene and User's Control.

Quotes and user's needs corresponding to these classes were grouped and analyzed through 2×2 matrix analysis. The main objective of this technique was to identify gaps in a two-dimensional graph which labels all users interviewed under specific criteria.

The first analysis compared people's willingness to talk in a ride and their preference between using a personal vehicle and having shared rides. The main conclusions were: (1) people that are more likely to prefer a quiet ride prefer using a personal vehicle rather than a ride-sharing service, (2) people that mainly use ride-sharing services for commuting tend to be more talkative. Therefore, considering that an increase in ride-sharing commuting is expected with the development of AVs [6], there is a gap that current ride-sharing services are not addressing; giving more quiet people more privacy in their ride while pooling with another passenger. This is one of the main opportunities obtained from the insights of this research and was considered in the development of the proposed final solution.

The second 2×2 matrix analysis constructed compared user's trust in AV technology with the amount of time they spend weekly inside of a car for com-muting. The analysis found that people that spend more time inside of a car tend to be more confident about AVs. One possible explanation may be that people who stay longer on the road experience more pain points related to their commuting experience. Taking this into account, the solution will try to fit the needs of short distance commuters with different demographics and help improve their perception of autonomous vehicle safety.

The final analysis was conducted to understand what passengers of different ages would like to do while commuting in an AV. It was found that people older than 25 years old preferred to rest while commuting, while those below 25 preferred to engage in other activities. Thus, the possible solution will need to give the users the flexibility to decide between a quiet and restful ride or a social experience with people looking for the same commuting experience.

2.2   Concept Generation

User interviews and previous research with academic and industry experts provided the foundation for our concept generation activities. These experts covered the fields of mechanical and product design, interaction design, and user experience (UX) design.

With the main user needs and current gaps in ride-sharing solutions identified, 72 concepts were developed and then clustered and filtered based on feasibility, ease of implementation, and ability to address the core user needs. The final three concepts obtained were the following:

1. Customized Vehicles: The idea of this concept was to create a flexible mobility service according to user's preferences. By delivering a vehicle with a different configuration representing a particular concept, users would be able to enjoy a variety of commuting experiences according to their mood and preference. Possible configurations designed were the coffee shop vehicle, social bar vehicle, hotel room vehicle, and office vehicle.
2. Segmented Space-Based Ride-Share Solution: This provides both a private and personal space through segmented spaces. Passengers who want to spend their commuting experience are matched with people who requested the same; this solution aims to solve the unsatisfied need of quiet users for ride-sharing services. This solution also provides a modular option, allowing the passenger to interact with other riders who also requested a social experience. Through the construction of automatic configurable partitions, the same physical car will allow different types of people to experience a vehicle that is adjusted to their preferences.
3. Personal/Ride-share Automatic Configuration: A completely automated vehicle that will allow passengers to perform several activities while having a ride. The main idea is to enable people with the ability to configure their vehicle at will (collapsible tables, rotating chairs, personalized entertainment systems) and then return to the default mode when the vehicle is parked.

Our expert feedback provided valuable insights in our concept selection process. Even though changing the expectation of regular rides was considered a valuable and innovative option, the variable expectation vehicle solution was discounted because of its difficulty to implement into the current automobile industry. For the personal/ride-share automatic configuration solution, industry experts warned us that this idea would be challenging as the targeted user base was too broad for a feasible solution. The solution was trying to tackle multiple problems at the same time and may result in a solution that is undesirable to any one user-base. The partition-based ride-share solution was recommended by the experts for further development. It was interpreted as a practical and short-term implementable solution that could be useful in the near future of ride-sharing services.

2.3   User Testing

To understand the strengths and flaws of the proposed concept, different user tests were generated using multiple Minimum Viable Products (MVP). The objective of this method was to replicate on a real-scale the concept through a low fidelity prototype. With the creation of the MVP, fast product testing was possible, helping to better understand users reactions and pain points. Through user testing, the configuration of the prototype was iterated several times according to the users' feedback, recommendations, and concerns, collected through interacting with a diverse group of users. The final product obtained in this process is the resulting version of the iterated prototypes.

The first round of user test was utilized to determine the reactions of users when they were on-board a partitioned vehicle, as shown in Fig. 1a. The goal of the test was to determine whether the partition helped improve the privacy, comfort, and safety of the user. The user test consisted of ten participants, all of whom experienced the partitioned vehicle on a fifteen-twenty minute ride to their destination within a five mile radius from their pick up point. Initial perceptions from the users were collected right after the ride was completed along with an in-depth survey.

3   Results

From the surveys, the partition was rated at an average of 3.7/5 for comfort, 4.2/5 for privacy, and 3.1/5 for safety. From the user feedback, some key insights on the design included:

- Positive
  - Quiet environment to get work done
  - Personal space without being disturbed by others
  - Prevents awkward situations where the user does not want to talk to others sharing the ride
- Negative
  - Safety concerns, due to not being able to see the driver or situate oneself on the road
  - Feeling of awkwardness caused by not knowing whether there is someone sitting next to you
  - Lack of windows created a claustrophobic feeling

The feedback received proved that the initial goals of creating a quiet and personal environment for the user during a commute was achieved. However, other negative features of the design were also discovered. To address the negative features of the design, a second round of user testing was conducted.

A/B testing was utilized to determine whether having a user looking at a screen that projects the front view of the vehicle is able to help improve the claustrophobic feeling and safety concerns addressed in the previous user test. The experiment was set by conducting five user tests on each of the two setups.

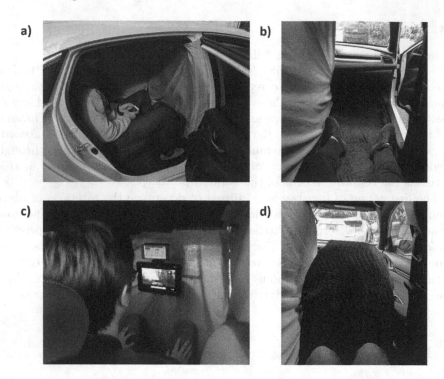

Fig. 1. Iterations and four different setups for experiential prototyping from the generated concepts. (a) Demonstrates a completely enclosed private space with partitions. (b) Demonstrates a premium user seating configuration with removed front seat and open leg room, more than doubling the physical space for the user. (c) Configuration A demonstrates an enclosed space but provides the user with real-time information and tracking of the vehicle and surroundings. (d) Configuration B demonstrates open field of view for live vehicle and surrounding status but physical space was restricted to the default size.

The first setup, Configuration A (Fig. 1c), consisted of a partitioned space on a vehicle with monitor displays that show the frontal view from the vehicle along with the route information provided through Google Maps. The second setup, Configuration B (Fig. 1d), consisted of a partitioned space with a partial view of the front windshield.

Comparing the results from the two tests, it was found that Configuration A created a better feeling of privacy compared to Configuration B. Configuration A was rated at 4.2/5 for privacy while configuration B was rated at 3.6/5. Configuration B, however, was rated higher on comfort. Configuration B was rated at 3.8/5 for comfort, while configuration A was rated at 3.6/5. Analysis of the recorded videos of the user test and the comments addressed by the users showed that although Configuration A helped situated the users with the outside environment, the screen increased their sense of motion sickness. Furthermore, the location of the screen caused the user to constantly stare at the screen over the course of the ride.

Through the feedback from the A/B test, it was determined that the screen-based perception mechanism was not sufficient at addressing the claustrophobic feelings and safety concerns originally expressed by the users. The final solution, therefore, will utilize a different mechanism to allow the users to have a wider view of the outside environment.

Another feature that was tested was the prime seating arrangement (Fig. 1b). This was to see if users were willing to pay extra for the extended space and legroom. Five users were tested on short fifteen to twenty minute rides and their initial thoughts and ride experience were recorded through video capture and surveys.

Analysis of the user feedback found that four out of five users enjoyed the extra legroom and were willing to pay more for the extra legroom, especially on a long ride. One female passenger, however, felt that the extra legroom could not be effectively utilized by her. Although this looks like a promising solution, more testing will be required before implementation into the final solution.

4   Conclusion

The increasing trends in shared spaces has presented a need for safety, privacy, and comfort. After performing 20 in-depth interviews, the need was defined and categorized. Following, a thorough list of concepts was generated, clustered, and finally, a solution was selected after considering research and industry expert feedback. We implemented this solution to user tests with an MVP to obtain feedback directly from end-users. After multiple iterations of the design solution, we consolidated the feedback from the initial user interviews, experts, and user testing to propose a solution that addresses the three main concerns: safety, privacy, and comfort.

5   Future Work

From the feedback gathered, we have synthesized the final solution (Fig. 2), which will be an automatically-deployable partitioning that governs the field of view for all passengers to enhance comfort and safety, as well as provide a physical separation to increase privacy.

The separations are designed as pillars with a diamond cross section, which will be actuated to collapse (Fig. 2). A scaled vehicle prototype is in progress, which will demonstrate this.

TOP VIEW OF VEHICLE SEATING ARRANGEMENT

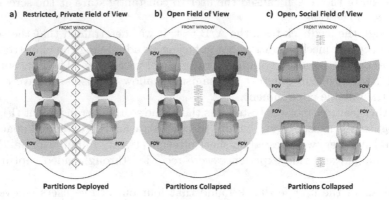

Fig. 2. Field of view (FOV) configurations for partitioned and social arrangements. (a) Demonstrates deployed partitions, restricting the FOV of adjacent passengers. (b) Partitions are collapsed but seats configuration discourages social interaction. (c) Collapsed partitions and reconfigured seats for socialization.

References

1. World Bank: Population, total. https://data.worldbank.org/indicator/sp.pop.totl. Accessed 06 Jan 2019
2. U.S. Department of Transportation: Bureau of Transportation Statistics National: Transportation statistics. https://www.rita.dot.gov/bts/sites/rita.dot.gov.bts/files/publications/nationaltransportationstatistics/index.html. Accessed 12 Nov 2018
3. Schrank, D., Eisele, B., Lomax, T., Bak, J.: 2015 urban mobility scorecard (2015)
4. Ingraham, C.: The American commute is worse today than it's ever been, February 2017
5. Wagner, P., Richter, F.: Infographic: ride-hailing apps surpass regular taxis in NYC, April 2018
6. Hampshire, R., Simek, C., Fabusuyi, T., Di, X., Chen, X.: Measuring the impact of an unanticipated disruption of Uber/Lyft in Austin, TX (2017)
7. Ghoseiri, K.: Dynamic rideshare optimized matching problem. Ph.D. thesis (2012)
8. Dediu, H.: Micromobility summit 2018/09/05, Copenhagen. http://www.asymco.com/2018/08/02/micromobility-summit-2018-september-5-copenhagen/. Accessed 16 Jan 2019
9. Gargiulo, E., Giannantonio, R., Guercio, E., Borean, C., Zenezini, G.: Dynamic ride sharing service: are users ready to adopt it? Procedia Manuf. **3**, 777–784 (2015)
10. Human centered design 101 - a course by IDEO & Acumen, 02 November 2018. https://www.plusacumen.org/courses/introduction-human-centered-design. Accessed Feb 2019

Design Development of the Support Tool to Prevent Secondary Accidents on Highway

Keitaro Sato[1(✉)] and Wonseok Yang[2]

[1] Shibaura Institute of Technology, Graduate School of Engineering
and Science, 3-7-5, Toyosu, Koto-ku, Tokyo, Japan
md18041@shibaura-it.ac.jp
[2] Shibaura Institute of Technology, Engineering and Design,
3-9-14, Shibaura, Minato-ku, Tokyo, Japan
yang@shibaura-it.ac.jp

Abstract. In Japan, when an accident occurs on a highway, the driver is required to move the vehicle 50 m behind the stopped vehicle and put a warning triangle and a warning flare. However, about 4,700 secondary accidents by following vehicles have occurred annually. In order to clarify the problem of the evacuation procedure, we conducted experiments to measure the working time of the process evacuating outside of the stopped vehicle. The recorded average time was 88.5 s, and only 40% of subjects completed all the steps. After the experiment, in the interview the majority opinion was that "It is difficult to grasp the accurate position of 50 m behind the stopped vehicle". From examining the findings, this is one of the causes of the secondary accident. Therefore we conducted the other experiment to measure the error between the point expected to walk 50 m and the actual distance. Less than 30% of the subjects could walk within 3 m of the error. From examining the experiments, the drivers who do not know the evacuation procedure and have no experience using the warning triangle and the warning flare need support to accomplish the evacuation procedure in a short time without mistakes. Therefore we designed the smartphone application that is able to support the evacuation procedure. The drivers can use it from just after they get out of the accident vehicle and inform the following vehicle of the existence of the stopping vehicle, to their safety is secured.

Keywords: Secondary accidents on highway · Evacuation procedure · Smartphone application

1 Introduction

In Japan, the rate of traffic fatalities has tended to increase in recent years the proportion of traffic fatalities among people over the age of 65 remains at a high level, and the traffic accident situation remains severe [1]. A brief comparison of the conditions of traffic accidents on ordinary roads and expressways for a period of 10 years up to 2015, shows that the reduction in death and injury during accidents on expressways is low and that driving on expressways might be highly risky. The percentage of fatal accidents during each weather is also high—with the highest percentage of 11.1% in foggy weather and the lowest rate of 1.75% in clear weather [2]. As the speed of vehicles on

© Springer Nature Switzerland AG 2019
C. Stephanidis (Ed.): HCII 2019, CCIS 1034, pp. 381–388, 2019.
https://doi.org/10.1007/978-3-030-23525-3_51

expressways is higher than on ordinary roads, there is a risk that the damage from an accident would be serious.

There is also the problem of secondary accidents wherein a moving vehicle collides with a halted vehicle and its driver. There are about 4,700 accidents a year if such secondary accidents are also considered. Among these accidents, 46.5% of the total accidents in 2014 were considered to be secondary accidents, and these are fatal in nature because of the high risk involved in a human-to-vehicle collision [3]. For example, a driver who got off the car and evacuated to the road shoulder was hit by a moving car, which was turned in the direction of the road shoulder to avoid a collision [4], and there was an accident in which the driver who was making an emergency call from within the stopped vehicle was hit by a subsequent truck and died [5]. The causes of the accident are the victim's over-reliance on the fact that the moving car would notice the stopped vehicle and the moving car's preconception of "no pedestrians at high speed" [5].

To prevent such accidents, in Japan, the driver who has made a stop on the expressway is obligated by law to notify the other moving vehicles of the halted state of the vehicle by installing a stopped car display device and flame tube 50 m behind the stopped car. However, the current situation is such that even evacuation procedures cause secondary accidents.

Some prior research includes verification of the scenarios related to the occurrence of the accident and safety measures employed by the Tokyo Metropolitan Expressway [6], current and future safety technology in automobiles [7], and possibility and issues of disaster prevention applications for software disaster prevention [8]. However, no research has been focused on the reduction of secondary accidents on freeways.

2   Background Research

In the event of an accident, because the driver might not be in the best logical state of mind and hence fail to take appropriate safety actions on time, there is a high risk of death or injury caused in a collision with a moving vehicle. Therefore, in this research, we have proposed a support method to prevent the secondary accident by safely performing the evacuation measures at the time of the accident. We first studied the issues with the current evacuation procedures and then developed a support methodology to aid evacuation procedure in case of an accident. In addition, drivers who are unaware of the evacuation procedure and have no experience using stop indicator devices and burners for the evacuation procedure will be able to do so in a short time without failure.

3   Experiment to Identify Issues with the Current Evacuation Procedure

3.1   Outline of the Experiment

We confirmed the procedure of the recommended action in case of a breakdown or an accident on the expressway and evacuated the car after stopping [9]. We photographed and reproduced the various points of action after the breakdown or accident. Then, we observed and interviewed the participants of the experiment and identified the underlying issues.

3.2 Details of the Experiment

【Experimental period】 September 22, 2017–September 29, 2017
【Participants of experiment】   14 men and women in their 20 s
【Experimental procedure】

1. A flame tube was placed in the front passenger seat and the stop display device in the trunk.
2. A burner and emergency stop were installed 50 m behind the car.
3. Evacuation to a point 10 m in the rear on the left side of the car to ensure safety.

【Experimental conditions】

- The conditions of vehicle was reproduced in the chairs.
- The subject imagined the situation wherein the car stopped because of an accident or breakdown.
- We marked the points of 50 m and 10 m behind the car.
- We explained to the subject how to use the flame tube and the stop indicator before the experiment.

3.3 Experimental Results and Discussion

Installation of a Smoke Tube and Stop Indicator
The instructions were to install the burner first at a point 50 m behind the car and then install a stop indicator. The correct method was to place the smoke tube on the ground [10]; eight out of the 14 subjects were able to do so. The incorrect methods used by subjects included putting up a smoke tube and returning without holding it (Fig. 1).

Fig. 1. Incorrect installation of the flame tube

Fig. 2. Incorrect installation of stop indicator

Because the stop indicator has a reflector on only one side, it is necessary to turn the reflector side in the direction from which the moving vehicle approaches [11]. 9 out of the 14 subjects were able to do so successfully. Incorrect usages included cases in which the reflector was put in such a way that it was invisible to the approaching vehicles or it was not erected perpendicular to the main body (Fig. 2).

Duration of Experiment and Evacuation Procedure

The average time recorded for the entire procedure was 88.5 s and about 40% of the subjects, that is, six people performed the entire procedure correctly. However, during the evacuation procedure, there is the possibility that a secondary accident occurs because of an inadequate display of the presence of a halted car in surroundings and the incorrect use of tools for own safety; therefore, it is necessary to address these issues.

3.4 Participants' Opinion and Discussion After the Experiment

When the subjects were interviewed after the experiment, the following comments were obtained. None of the subjects had any prior experience with using the stop indicator and the light bulb. One of the subjects did not know the location of the box of the stop indicator, whereas another one did not know how to assemble the stop indicator and had to read the instructions at the back of the box many times. In this experiment, we made a mark at 50 m behind the vehicle, but the subjects were worried that they might not be able to identify the position in an actual scenario.

4 Experiment to Confirm the Accuracy of the Sense of Distance

4.1 Outline of the Experiment

In a real-life accident scenario, there is no mark at 50 m as we had explicitly provided in the previous experiment. There was the possibility that a secondary accident could occur because the distance between the installation place of the emergency stop device and flame tube and the stopped car was unknown. Therefore, we conducted an experiment to measure the error between the actual distance of 50 m and the point people predict to be 50 m.

4.2 Details of the Experiment

〖Experimental period〗 November 17, 2017–November 24, 2017
〖Participants of experiment〗 28 men and women in their 20 s (14 people divided into 2 groups)
〖Experimental method〗 The experiment was conducted as follows.

  Group 1: Participants were made to move to a point they thought was 50 m under normal conditions
  Group 2: Participants were made to assume that the car was moving on the road and it had to stop due to an accident or a breakdown, and then they had to move to a point they thought was 50 m.

4.3 Results of the Experiment and Discussion

Group 1: Experiment Results
Three of the subjects in Group 1 moved to a position that was within 3 m of the actual position of 50 m and hence were within an error margin of 3 m. There were six people with an error margin of more than 10 m, and three people moved to a distance of more than 60 m. Moving the extra distance should be avoided as it increases the risk of being hit by a car. The average time recorded was 64 s.

Group 2: Experiment Results
Four of the subjects in Group 2 moved within an error margin of 3 m and three moved to a distance over 50 m. The average time recorded was 34 s, 30 s less than Group 1.

Consideration
It is difficult to accurately guess a distance of 50 m without the 50 m mark that we had provided. Further, it appears that looking back and forth to confirm the position of a distance of 50 m takes time. This raises the risk of being hit while looking back by an incoming vehicle on expressways with a lot of traffic. In a real-time scenario of an accident, it is required to evacuate quickly in a calm state to ensure safety. Therefore, I think that the actions of looking back as done in this experiment and moving to a longer distance than necessary have a high probability of causing a secondary accident.

5 Suggestion of Support Method to Prevent the Secondary Accident

From the experimental results in Sects. 3 and 4, we were able to recognize the issues with the recommended evacuation procedure. Hence we proposed to provide additional support to the recommended evacuation procedure by using a Smartphone on the driver's side to offer suggestions for each step of the procedure, thereby preventing the secondary accidents.

5.1 Design Requirements from Experiments and Surveys

Prompt Not to Stay in the Car After an Accident or a Breakdown
There is a risk of being hit by a following vehicle if one stays in the car at the time of an accident or a breakdown; therefore, we propose a functionality that prompts the driver to evacuate quickly after confirming the safety of the surroundings.

Support for Safe Travel on the Road
We need a functionality that checks whether the car is running properly and issues instructions to move safely on the road.

Support and Guide of the Evacuation Site
We need a functionality that can indicate a distance of 50 m from the car, which is a standard distance for installing a stop indicator and flame tube, and a distance of 40 m from the installation, which is the standard evacuation place for ensuring safety.

Installation Method of Flame Tube and Stop Indicator
We need a functionality that provides detailed instructions about installing the flame tube and the stop indicator to those who have never used them before.

5.2 Final Proposal

How to Launch the Application
We intend to use the Bluetooth functionality of the Smartphone, the car navigation system, and the shock detection function of the car navigation system. When the car navigation system detects an impact due to an accident, a notification is sent to the Smartphone through the Bluetooth connection and the application is activated (Fig. 3).

Fig. 3. Launch of application by detection of impact

Measurement of Moving Distance
This functionality can be used when walking and moving outside the guardrail before installing the flame tube and stop indicator, and it reduces the time lost in measuring the distance manually, thereby notifying the moving vehicles about the halted vehicle (Fig. 4).

Fig. 4. Measurement of moving distance

Installation Method of Stop Indicator
We discussed the method to install the stop indicator in four steps in Sect. 3 so that few people would become familiar with this. I think that the pictorial illustrations of the steps make it easier for use by people who have no prior experience with the installation. We designed the pictorial illustrations because there were people who did not fit the joint part of the reflective well (Fig. 5).

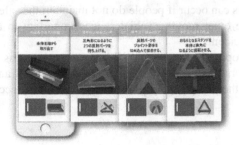

Fig. 5. Installation method of stop indicator

How to Install the Flame Tube
The installation method of the flame tube is divided into three steps and is explained in Sect. 3 so that few people could install it correctly in the experiments conducted. We think that the pictorial illustration of the situation after activating the flame tube makes it easier to install even for people with no prior experience (Fig. 6).

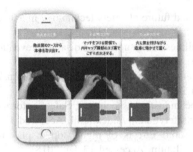

Fig. 6. How to install the flame tube

6 Conclusion

In this study, we initially confirmed the issues with the recommended evacuation procedure and then aimed to support the evacuation procedure in the event of a secondary accident on an expressway. The survey confirmed the evacuation procedures that are currently recommended during secondary accidents and the current status of products used in the event of an accident. The root cause analyzed was that people were unaware of the recommended evacuation procedure or could not perform the procedure accurately. Hence, we conducted various experiments through which we identified the issues with the recommended evacuation procedure and confirmed the difficulty of accurately estimating a distance of 50 m.

The experimental results concluded that approximately 40% of people could not install the safety equipment properly and that people also had difficulties in approximating the correct distance of 50 m to set up the safety equipment. Because it is assumed that accidents can occur if people do not maintain the safe evacuation distance of 50 m to notify the other moving vehicles, it is important to address this issue to prevent secondary accidents.

Hence we have proposed an application that creates awareness about the evacuation procedures and supports the necessary actions, in the event of an accident or failure, using a Smartphone, thereby possibly preventing a secondary accident.

References

1. The Metropolitan Police Department Transportation Bureau. The occurrence situation of traffic accident during 2014
2. Traffic Accident General Center: Traffic statistics 2015 version
3. Government Public Relations Online: Three points of safe driving on expressways. https://www.govonline.go.jp/useful/article/201307/5.html. Accessed 10 Jan 2018
4. The Asahi Shimbun, 22 November 2016
5. The Nihon Keizai Shimbun, 02 April 2013
6. Kurita, H., Kamijo, S., Tanaka, A., Goto, H.: Verifying the accident occurrence situation and safety target effect on the Tokyo Metropolitan Expressway. Civil Engineering Planning Lectures (2004)
7. Miraiki, M.: The present and future of safety technology in automobiles. DENSO Technical Review, vol. 12 (2007)
8. Masahiro, A.: The possibilities and issues of the disaster prevention app for software disaster prevention. Yokosuka 11, vol. 2 no. 2, pp. 145–155 (2017)
9. Japan Automobile Federation: Any questions about cars. http://qa.jaf.or.jp/drive/highway/07.htm. Accessed 13 Jan 2018
10. Japan Safety Flame Tube Industry Association: Safety information on the proper use of flame burner. http://www.safetyflare.jp/index.html. Accessed 13 Jan 2018
11. Japan Automobile Federation: Effects of night stop display board. http://www.jaf.or.jp/ecosafety/usertest/sign/detail;.htm. Accessed 13 Jan 2018

Projection Mapping for Implementing Immersive User Scenarios in Autonomous Driving: Insights from Expert Interviews

Jae Marie Tabuada[1], Tiffany Liaw[1], Kevin Pham[1], Jaewoo Chung[2],
Euiyoung Kim[1,3(✉)], and Alice M. Agogino[1]

[1] University of California, Berkeley, CA 94720, USA
euiyoungkim@berkeley.edu
[2] HP Inc., Palo Alto, CA 94304, USA
[3] Delft University of Technology, Delft 89807, The Netherlands

Abstract. We propose the use of projection mapping as a prototyping tool to create an experimentation environment to design, evaluate, and control immersion experience in future autonomous vehicles. As the first step, we conducted expert interviews with professionals in the automotive industry to understand the general implications of prototyping tools in future mobility solution development and their usefulness in concept test settings. The interview results reveal that projection mapping is one popular prototyping method for automotive professionals to demonstrate immersive future user scenarios. The paper includes additional insights from the interviews and current work-in-progress.

Keywords: Expert interview · Immersive user scenario ·
Autonomous vehicle · Sensor integration ·
Flexible experimentation environment

1 Introduction

The automotive industry is looking towards autonomous vehicles as the next platform for innovation. Without the need for a driver, autonomous vehicles provide an opportunity for new experiences based around the concept of mobility. In order for autonomous vehicle companies to dissuade an influx of tech companies into their market, autonomous car experiences should not rely on tablet or screens and should enhance the experience of travel. Automotive companies are proposing the use of projection mapping for displaying visual effects and driver assistance [1, 2] and HCI (Human Computer Interactions) researchers have been using projection mapping as a rapid prototyping technique [3]. In the field of autonomous vehicle research, an auditory based system of keeping user's aware of on-road events in autonomous vehicles was explored. This system lacked in the sense that the user's comfort, familiarity levels, or situational awareness with the vehicle did not change [4]. Research from the MIT AgeLab suggests that adults between the ages of 25 to 34 are more likely to be comfortable with full autonomous driving. It is also seen that older generations are less likely to be comfortable with relinquishing full driver control. It is suggested that the gradual adoption of assistive technologies would be beneficial to the acceptance of full autonomous driving [5]. Future mobility experiences should be explored beyond the themes of comfort, safety, or notifications by creating new meanings. For instance, a research team at the University of California, Berkeley has investigated in developing a new concept: a car seat with a haptic array on an armrest that produce different patterns of motion to make passengers feel as if they are at sea [6]. This exploration of novel experiences in the autonomous vehicle space allows for the forging of future implementations of technology in the user's experience.

In order to create a platform for exploring said novel experiences in autonomous vehicles, we propose an exploration into the immersion provided by multiple sensors during a daily commute and an exploration of the following overarching question: *Does projection mapping portray a compelling immersive environment for subjects to accurately visualize mobility concepts?* As the first step, we conducted 5 expert interviews with current employees in the automotive industry to understand general implication of prototyping tools in future mobility solution development and their usefulness in user test settings. The results of the expert interviews are included. We end our paper by showing a work-in-progress experimental setting that will be used to explore the effect of immersion on the user's trust with the autonomous vehicles as part of future research.

2 Methods and Analysis

2.1 Preliminary Research

We hosted a demo day at the Richmond Field Station, the location of our experimental location, and several experts from the automotive industry were invited to attend. Preliminary feedback on the concept of projection mapping and connected sensors in future mobility solutions was collected. Some expressed a concern with the safety of such technologies which lead us to pursue the sub question of how the feeling of safety, more specifically *trust*, can be addressed inside autonomous vehicles. We also presented a lower fidelity version of our experiment environment at the 3rd International Symposium for Academic Makerspace (ISAM) at Stanford [7]. Our testing scenario consisted of individual sensors being compared to a holistic sensory experience and our feedback suggests that users prefer the combination of visual and audio sensors. It was also suggested to incorporate a reclining option to the chair and combine it with ceiling projections; The test results are integrated in developing questionnaires for the expert interviews (Sect. 2.2) and current work (Sect. 4).

2.2 Expert Interviews

To obtain insight into industry methods, expert interviews were conducted with 5 individuals with positions in the mobility industry. The current use of projection mapping and techniques for building future mobility scenarios in autonomous vehicles were topics of interest. Expert interview participants were selected and recruited with a key criterion that they had multiple years of experience in the automotive industry or experience in future mobility innovation projects. Participants were recruited through emails sent throughout personal networks. Participant experiences ranged from concept car development to full projection mapping inside of a concept car, to human-centered design ambassador in their organization and Human-Machine Interaction prototyping. The participants' work experience ranged from 2 years to 17 years, and current job responsibilities ranged from User Experience Designer to Product Design Engineer to Prototyper. We conducted semi-structured interview procedure by ask the following primary questions:

(a) What kinds of mobility solutions (e.g., futuristic mobility solutions, interior, exterior, security, etc.) does his/her company deal with?
(b) What prototyping or mock-up tools (e.g., visual, haptic, auditory, etc.) does your company employ? What do you use them for?
(c) What do you know about projection mapping?

In addition, we also asked them questions regarding individual cybersecurity perceptions with respect to the risks around the data collection through the sensors inside of the vehicles. The thematic analysis [8] was used to uncover common themes in the interview transcripts. In this research, we aim to carry out emerging trends in implication of prototyping tools in future mobility concept development and how useful they are in the setting of concept tests.

3 Results

The audio data collected from each expert interview were transcribed in 110 code lines and independently reviewed by three coders. The results of review uncovered four themes that were compared to examine emerging trends. In this section, we report the common themes mapped with our primary research questions provided in the interview scripts.

Areas of Future Mobility Solution Design
The areas of future mobility concept development embrace a wide range of spectrum from commercial vehicles to concept cars. Front-end prototyping development platforms are used to facilitate not only the development of the entire concept vehicle development, but also the visual/sensorial representation of the partial user experience inside/outside of the vehicle environment. One participant addresses that their company does business in a full product line of commercial products. The new concepts are conceived in the innovation center they are involved in and the proved concepts are transferred to the company headquarters. Another participant mentions their company deals with not only automotive vehicles, but also micro-mobility services such as e-bikes and an eco-system development around sustainable mobility solution. The organization they are involved in particularly addresses they employ human-centered design in the process of creating better features for customers across all areas of future mobility exploration phases.

Main Purpose of Prototyping Tools
Prototyping tools mentioned by the experts tended to vary based on the team they were involved with. Those in UI/UX working with software-driven prototyping tools focused on idea generation or feasibility, while those working in hardware design tended to heavily use 3D printing or CAD software to rapidly build physical prototypes. Their choice of methodology or tools for prototyping mainly relied on the effectiveness to rapidly develop the prototype as fast as they can to go through many iterations. One mentioned, while describing tools for visual prototyping, the use of integrating projectors to visualize whether or not an immersive environment would improve the user experience. Several experts mentioned the term, 'immersive experience', as a main purpose of the prototyping tool development to demonstrate futuristic concept of user experience.

Effectiveness of Projection Mapping
We asked the professionals about their knowledge of projection mapping and how effective this method is in demonstrating concepts and user testing. They all knew and have seen projection mapping used as a prototyping or showcase tool, while two have used projection mapping currently or previously, before professionally, in their prototyping process. Projection mapping appears to mainly be used to provide an immersive visual environment for the target groups in order to create a realistic scene of vehicle content and road context, whether for the purpose of showcasing a new concept car or even conducting a performance test. One of the participants mentioned about using projection mapping for immersion effectiveness:

> *We don't want that [HMI/UI experiences] to be tested in a vacuum where you're sitting in someone's office pushing buttons on a screen. So, we project certain things like basically the road or the drive. – Participant 2*

These experts mentioned that projection mapping UX tools are used to identify user experiences to begin with. It was noticed that the projection mapping was useful as they are generally easy for users to navigate the interaction flow through the display. Projection mapping was good enough to show animation and wireframes, hence it is powerful software tool to illustrate future user scenario with a low-cost investment.

Risk Around Data Collection Under Immersive Mobility Environment
Several participants address possible concerns in passenger's privacy risk and safety issues when the autonomous driving arrives in the market. One participant mentioned that during user testing their company have previously collected personal passenger data on fingerprints, eye movements, facial recognition, heart rate and foot tremors. All participants mentioned how the movement towards autonomous vehicles in the automotive industry creates more risks in the automotive space (such as cybersecurity or vehicle hacking with increasing amount of software). The automotive industry struggles or does not focus on these issues since autonomous vehicle technologies are not fully developed. Therefore, there is difficulty in effectively implementing safeguards against these problems that are not currently present. One of the participants addresses:

> *While our company does work with cybersecurity and understands the importance of it, it is hard to integrate data protection and privacy at this moment without running fully autonomous vehicles and test it out. – Participant 3*

Hence, to reflect the emerging concern in users; privacy and safety issues while sitting in the inside of vehicles, we will continue examine potential risks around the data collection through the sensors inside of the vehicles.

4   Current Work

In tandem with the expert interviews, we propose the use of projection mapping as a prototyping tool to create an experimentation environment to design, evaluate, and control immersion experience in future autonomous vehicles. We currently explore the following sub questions to examine the implementation of immersive in car user scenarios in future autonomous driving using projection mapping:

(a)   What are the consequences of sensorial inputs (e.g. *visual with projection mapping, sound, and tactile*) within an environment and impact on user's immersion?
(b)   What's the line between a compelling immersive environment and an autonomous vehicle environment that users can trust?

4.1   Creation of the Experimental Environment

Airstream Projection Surface and Projection Mapping. A mock wall was designed to cover distracting features of our experimentation environment and provide an even projection surface; The wall was manufactured using panels of laser cut cardboard overlaid with projector screen material. With the Madmapper projection mapping software [9], we plan to manipulate each video to adapt on the projection surface, as well as edit the video for any additional visual effects required to accurately portray the scenario to the users.

Fig. 1. The projection surface

Area of Projection. The projection surface will be separated into three sections to correspond with the driver's point of view. These sections will be labeled as seen in Fig. 2. Projection locations of the chosen scenario and of the street view will vary as described in Table 1. Trial 1 and 2 will address the overarching question of whether or not the user feels immersed inside of our experimentation environment.

Audio and Haptic Sensors. Binaural audio speakers and speakers will be integrated into the headrest and base of the chair to create the audio sensors. The haptic sensors

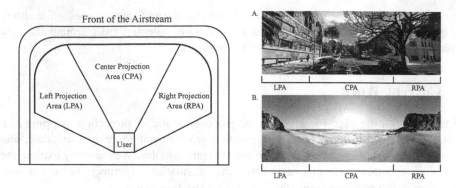

Fig. 2. Projection surface layout (Left) Scenario layouts A. Street view scenario [10] B. Beach scenario [11] (Right)

Table 1. Projection layout for experimental trials

Trail	LPA	CPA	RPA
1-No Immersion	Street	Street	Street
2-Full Immersion	Beach	Beach	Beach
3-Semi Immersed	Street	Beach	Street
4-Reverse Semi Immersed	Beach	Street	Beach

consist of a massage chair attachment and the bass boosted on the base speaker to create vibrations in the chair. The full immersion trial of all screens showing the same scenario will be used for visuals. Observations of user reactions and analysis of user interviews while varying the use of binaural audio, haptics, and projections will be used to determine is a paired experience is impactful on immersion. Trials will be conducted as seen in Table 2.

Table 2. Sensor testing trials

Trail	Audio	Haptic	Visual
1	×		×
2		×	×
3	×	×	×

4.2 Data Collection Methods

An initial survey will be conducted to determine the user's initial opinion on autonomous vehicles and immersive mobility environment. Then, video recording method (e.g., GoPro camera) will be used to capture the behavior during the user test. After the user test, we will record the audio of our expert and general user interviews to get their feedback on the overall satisfaction and reflections on their feelings of immersion, feeling of trust with an autonomous car, and overall experience.

5 Conclusion

This paper aims to shed light on the emergence of projection mapping as a prototyping tool to create an immersive experimentation environment for the exploration of opportunities in future autonomous vehicles. As an initial step, we conducted expert interviews with professionals in the automotive industry to apprehend the general usage of prototyping tools in future mobility concept exploration and testing. The expert interviews reveal that automotive companies have been using a variety of prototyping tools to demonstrate futuristic products, user interactions, user experience concepts, and concept testing. The projection mapping was one of the most popular methods among many in creating an immersive experience of unveiled concepts with a low-cost investment. We also found it notable to mention that there is a risk around implementing immersive user scenarios. Integration of connected prototyping tools and advanced sensors inside of future vehicles would result in collection of more personal data from users. Lastly, the current works-in-progress experimental environment setting is detailed as current research areas we focus on.

Acknowledgement. We would like to thank the Berkeley Research for Autonomous Vehicle Opportunities BRAVO team members and mentors for their continued constructive feedback and support with us.

References

1. Beaudouin-Lafon, M., Mackay, W.: Prototyping tools and techniques. In: Human Computer Interaction-Development Process, pp. 122–142 (2003)
2. Raij, A., Pollefeys, M.: Auto-calibration of multi-projector display walls. In: Proceedings of the 17th International Conference on Pattern Recognition, ICPR 2004, vol. 1, pp. 14–17 (2004)
3. Raskar, R., et al.: Multi-projector displays using camera-based registration. In: Proceedings of the conference on Visualization 1999: Celebrating Ten Years, pp. 161–168. IEEE Computer Society Press (1999)
4. Gang, N., Sibi, S., Michon, R., Mok, B., Chafe, C., Ju, W.: Don't be alarmed: sonifying autonomous vehicle perception to increase situation awareness. In: Proceedings of the 10th International Conference on Automotive User Interfaces and Interactive Vehicular Applications, pp. 237–246. ACM, September 2018
5. Abraham, H.: Autonomous vehicles, trust, and driving alternatives: a survey of consumer preferences, pp. 1–16. Massachusetts Institute of Technology AgeLab, Cambridge (2016)
6. Cantu, S., Kanagaraj, S., Marecal, E.: Human-centered Design – Renault: Creation of a Multi-Sensory Experience for Autonomous Vehicle Users. Master's Thesis, University of California at Berkeley, May 2018
7. Cholsaipan P., et al.: Reimagining onboard experiences for autonomous vehicle in academic makerspaces. In: the 3rd International Symposium for Academic Makerspace (ISAM), Stanford University (2018)

J. M. Tabuada et al.

8. Braun, V., Clarke, V.: Using thematic analysis in psychology. Qual. Res. Psychol. **3**(2), 77–101 (2006)
9. MadMapper Software website. https://madmapper.com. Accessed 29 Mar 2019
10. Google earth V 9.2.73.2. 2598 Hearst Ave Berkeley, CA. 37.87°N 122.27°W. http://www.earth.google.com. Accessed 9 Dec 2018
11. Erickson, G.M.: NWicon. http://www.nwicon.com/point-dume-beach-ii-360.htm. Accessed 9 Dec 2018

Effects of Time Headway and Velocity on Drivers' Trust in the HMI of ACC System – a Simulator-Based Study

Jianmin Wang[1], Wenjuan Wang[1], Xiaomeng Li[2], and Fang You[1(✉)]

[1] Car Interaction Design Lab, College of Arts and Media,
Tongji University, Shanghai, China
{wangjianmin,1731723,youfang}@tongji.edu.cn
[2] Centre for Accident Research and Road Safety-Queensland (CARRS-Q),
Institute of Health and Biomedical Innovation (IHBI), Queensland University
of Technology (QUT), Kelvin Grove, Brisbane 4059, Australia
xiaomeng.li@qut.edu.au

Abstract. Adaptive Cruise Control (ACC) system has been gradually accepted and popularized in the market. Rational trust level in the system Human Machine Interface(HMI) facilitates the drivers to use ACC in a safe and appropriate manner. In this paper, we tested participants' trust in the HMI of ACC system in cut-in conditions in a simulator, and aimed to investigate factors affecting the trust level. 24 participants joined in the simulator experiment in which the videos recorded in real-world driving were played as scenarios. Experimental results show that both driving velocity and time headway (THW) between vehicles affect the trust of ACC system HMI significantly. Drivers' trust level increases with the increase of THW at certain velocity condition, and drivers' trust level also increases with the increase of velocity at certain THW condition. Future research will focus on the HMI design of ACC with multiple modality of information output and validate the results in a varied driving environment.

Keywords: Human Machine Interface (HMI) · Trust · Driving simulator · ACC · Cut-in conditions

1 Introduction

In order to enhance driving comfort and improve safety, much effort has been engaged in the development of advanced driver-assistant systems (ADAS), such as ACC which is one of the most popular ADAS in recent decades. As a semi-automatic system, ACC requires drivers to collaborate with vehicles. The confidence of the human driver on ACC plays a vital role in the process of cooperation [1]. William Payre et al. found that the efficiency of an automated system often depended on the operators' level of trust in that system [2]. Lee and Moray also found that trust between humans and machines had influences on operators' control strategies [3]. Moreover, Lee et al. proposed that when a system was used excessively beyond its capabilities (overtrust), it led to misuse; however, when automation was not used when it would actually work and provide

© Springer Nature Switzerland AG 2019
C. Stephanidis (Ed.): HCII 2019, CCIS 1034, pp. 397–403, 2019.
https://doi.org/10.1007/978-3-030-23525-3_53

positive effects (distrust), it led to disuse [4]. Therefore, the appropriate use of ACC largely depends on drivers' trust.

As a crucial part of ACC system, the ergonomic design of HMI is a complex, interdisciplinary challenge. Besides the technical aspects, the challenge also lies in the need to choose interaction patterns that fit the mental model of the user [5]. Trust has been regarded as one of the leading HMI issues [6]. Designing an HMI that encourages appropriate trust is essential for the safe use of the semi-automatic system [7].

The real-world HMI test usually consumes a lot of resources. Most importantly, it could expose the participants into unpredictable risky situations. One promising approach for this concern is to provide users a relatively realistic driving environment with driving simulators. It is suggested that the more immersive driving environment facilitates the drivers to perceive themselves as more present in the (simulated) situation [5]. Thus in this study, we used the videos recorded from a real world driving as the driving scenario in the driving simulator.

2 Research Question

In this paper, an experimental study is presented to evaluate the drivers' trust in the ACC system HMI in the different cut-in conditions using a driving simulator. The study aims to investigate the factors that affect the driver's trust level, based on which, suggestions are proposed for the improvement of HMI design of ACC.

3 Method

3.1 Participants

In total, 24 participants (12 male, 12 female) took part in the study. The participants aged from 21 to 30 years, with a mean age of 24 years (SD = 2.11). They all have a valid driving license and know about how the ACC works basically as well as how to use an ACC.

3.2 Experimental Design

The cut-in event is a typical scenario of ACC [8, 9] and it's fairly common in day-to-day driving. Previous research has summarized the statistical characteristics of THW (distance/velocity) in various cut-in situations [10], and it was found that the influence of THW on subjective driver states in ACC is significant [11]. In addition to the THW, velocity is another important parameter in driving. Therefore, the real-world driving in the study was designed considering two independent variables, THW and velocity. 6 video scenarios were extracted from the real-world driving that met the condition requirement of simulator test. The specific parameters of test conditions are shown in Table 1.

Table 1. Specific parameters of six conditions.

	Velocity (km/h)	THW (s)
1	60	1.2
2	60	0.7
3	50	1.2
4	50	0.7
5	30	1.2
6	30	0.7

In the simulator test, a within-subjects experiment design method was adopted. The Latin square experiment design method was used to eliminate the influence of learning effect and experiment order effect [12]. All the participants were divided into six groups, with four in each group. The experiment test sequence of each group was different, and each group conducted six conditions in accordance with the designated order. The ACC function was turned on in all conditions, with the side vehicle cutting in from the left side at a same speed as the subject vehicle.

3.3 Experimental Procedure

The real-world driving was carried out in a professional automobile (Volvo S90). The videos of driver's front view (see Fig. 1) and corresponding dashboard (see Fig. 2) was recording in the real-world driving under various cut-in conditions.

Fig. 1. The video of driver's front view   **Fig. 2.** The corresponding dashboard video

Before the laboratory test, the participants were asked to read the ACC manual to further familiarize themselves with its operation and function. They were introduced of the interface elements (see Fig. 3) and interaction logic of ACC system HMI in Volvo in detail. They were also told that ACC function would work normally in all scenarios. They were required to make a comprehensive driving judgment according to the environment and HMI display. When the participants were familiar with the ACC operation and HMI information, they were arranged to take a practice drive of the simulator for 2–3 min.

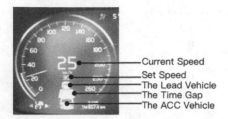

Fig. 3. Interface elements of ACC   **Fig. 4.** Testing scene

During the simulator driving, the front view videos and dashboard videos of different conditions were played in the driving simulator to provide the participants a sense of driving immersion as much as possible (see Fig. 4). If the participants believed that the scenario was risky, they could press on the foot brake pedal or turn the steering wheel to terminate the ACC automated driving. The whole driving process was videotaped to record the drivers' behavior.

At the end of each test driving, trustworthiness of HMI about ACC was measured by twelve questions with a 5-point Likert-type scales (1 = totally disagree, 5 = totally agree). This 12-item questionnaire was adapted from previous studies [13–15] and supplemented with new items. Scale's example items included "I can assume that this HMI will display the correct information" and "I don't care about the display of the dashboard", etc. Answers to these questions were averaged to form a reliable measure of trustworthiness. Responses were coded such that higher scores indicate more trustworthiness. After all the tests were completed, a simple interview was conducted with the participants about their driving experience. Example questions in the interview included" Did you notice the change of HMI when the side vehicle cut in?" and "Was the ACC system HMI helpful when you were driving?".

4   Result

According to the videos recorded during the experiment, all participants took over control of the vehicle by pressing the brake pedal while no one turned the steering wheel. The statistical result of drivers' braking behavior was shown in Fig. 5. As the THW decreased, the proportion of drivers that pressed the brake pedal to take over increased, indicating an increase of distrust on the ACC. Besides, the proportion of brake generally increased with the decrease of the velocity under both THW conditions. Since the lower velocity corresponds to a shorter distance between vehicles at certain THW condition, the decrease of trust level along with decrease of velocity implies that drivers might be more sensitive to the distance between vehicles instead of speed when they make a take-over decision.

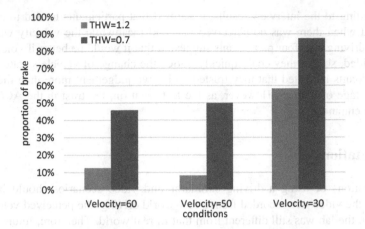

Fig. 5. Proportion of people who press the brake in different conditions

The trust scores of HMI was compared under different conditions. Figure 6 showed that regardless of velocity, the trust score when THW was 1.2 s was generally higher than that when THW was 0.7 s. This suggested again that drivers tended to be more confident of the HMI at large THW condition. For the same THW condition, the change of trust score did not follow a consistent pattern with the change of driving velocity.

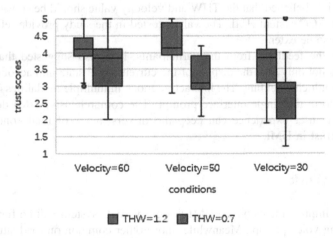

Fig. 6. Boxplot of trust scores

To identify the impact of THW and velocity on driver's confidence in the HMI, a repeated two-way ANOVA ($\alpha = 0.05$) was conducted and the results show that both THW (F $(2,138) = 3.06$, $p < 0.05$) and velocity (F $(1,138) = 3.91$, $p < 0.05$) had significant impact on the trust score while the interaction effect was not significant (F $(2,138) = 3.06$, $p > 0.05$).

According to the interview results, it seemed that participants tended to check the dashboard when there was no perceived risk and meanwhile the velocity was stable. After the driving test, four participants suggested that it would be better if voice prompt was provided, so that they could quickly notice the change of vehicle's state. Most of the participants indicated that they trusted their own judgement more than the HMI at the early stage of the test. However, as the test went on, the trust in the ACC system HMI was enhanced.

5 Limitations

The limitations of using a driving simulator and video scenarios should be noted. Although the video was recorded from a real-world driving, the perceived velocity and distance in the lab was still different from that in real world. Therefore, future research on field is necessary to generalize the findings of this study. Besides, the study only involved cut-in situation as the test scenario, which also composes a limitation to form a comprehensive evaluation of the HMI.

6 Conclusion and Discussion

In this study, we present an approach of using the driving simulator to test the level of trust in ACC system HMI in cut-in conditions. Results show that both velocity and THW have significant influence on the driver's HMI trust level. Based on the experimental data, it is believed that the THW and velocity value should be considered when designing the ACC system HMI. The values tested in the study provide references for the design to some extent.

Based on the feedback from the participants, it is also suggested that the HMI design should not only take the display of the current ACC state into account, but also consider the multichannel hint. The interactive mode in multiple modalities (e.g. audio) might outperform the single interface prompt. The comprehensive HMI design combined with the user experience can keep the drivers aware of road conditions and improve the trust in HMI.

7 Future Work

In the future, improvements on the HMI design of ACC system will be further tested, such as adding voice prompt. Meanwhile, more other common on-road situations, for example, car-following, will be involved in the test so that drivers generate an overall comprehension of the HMI performance.

Acknowledgments. This work was supported by the National Key Research and Development Program of China (#2018YFB1004903), the Fundamental Research Funds for the Central Universities (#22120180075) and National Science Foundation of China for Young Scholars (#71804126).

References

1. Beggiato, M., Pereira, M., Petzoldt, T., Krems, J.: Learning and development of trust, acceptance and mental model of ACC. A longitudinal on-road study. Transp. Res. Part F Psychol. Behav **35**, 75–84 (2015)
2. Payre, W., Cestac, J., Delhomme, P.: Fully automated driving: impact of trust and practice on manual control recovery. Hum. Factors J. Hum. Factors Ergon. Soc. **58**(2), 229–241 (2016)
3. Lee, J., Moray, N.: Trust, control strategies and allocation of function in human-machine systems. Ergonomics **35**(10), 1243–1270 (1992)
4. Lee, J.D., See, K.A.: Trust in automation: designing for appropriate reliance. Hum. Factors J. Hum. Factors Ergon. Soc. **46**(10), 50–80 (2004)
5. Meixner, G., Müller, C. (eds.): Automotive User Interfaces. HIS. Springer, Cham (2017). https://doi.org/10.1007/978-3-319-49448-7
6. Ekman, F., Johansson, M., Sochor, J.: Creating appropriate trust in automated vehicle systems: a framework for HMI design. IEEE Trans. Hum.-Mach. Syst. **48**(1), 95–101 (2018)
7. Carsten, O., Martens, M.H.: How can humans understand their automated cars? HMI principles, problems and solutions. Cogn. Technol. Work **21**(1), 3–20 (2018)
8. Gu, R., Zhu, X.: Summarization of typical scenarios of adaptive cruise control based on natural drive condition. In: Proceedings of the 11th International Forum of Automotive Traffic Safety, Chongqing, China, pp. 387–393 (2014)
9. Feng, Z., Ma, X., Xia, L., Zhu, X., Ma, Z.: Analysis of driver initial brake time under risk cut-in scenarios. In: The 14th International Forum of Automotive Traffic Safety, Changsha, China, pp. 113–122 (2018)
10. Siebert, F.W., Oehl, M., et al.: The influence of time headway on subjective driver states in adaptive cruise control. Transp. Res. Part F Traffic Psychol. Behav. **25**(Part A), 65–73 (2014)
11. Xiuyan, G.: Experimental Psychology. 1st edn. People's Education Press, China (2004).
12. Jian, J.-Y., Bisantz, A.M., Drury, C.G.: Foundations for an empirically determined scale of trust in automated systems. Int. J. Cogn. Ergon. **4**(1), 53–71 (2000)
13. Lyons, J.B., Stokes, C.K., et al.: Trustworthiness and IT suspicion: an evaluation of the nomological network. Hum. Factors J. Hum. Factors Ergon. Soc. **53**(3), 219–229 (2011)
14. Verberne, F.M.F., Ham, J., et al.: Trust in smart systems: sharing driving goals and giving information to increase trustworthiness and acceptability of smart systems in cars. Hum. Factors **54**(5), 799–810 (2012)
15. Forster, Y., Naujoks, F., Neukum, A.: Increasing anthropomorphism and trust in automated driving functions by adding speech output. In: 2017 IEEE Intelligent Vehicles Symposium (IV). IEEE, Los Angeled (2017)

Design Exploration for Driver in Traffic Conflicts Between Car and Motorcycle

Jianmin Wang[1(✉)], Zejia Cai[1], Preben Hansen[2], and Zhenghe Lin[1]

[1] Tongji University, Shanghai 201804, China
wangjianmin@tongji.edu.cn
[2] Stockholm University, Kista, 164 55 Stockholm, Sweden

Abstract. In our work, we focused on the traffic conflict between car and motorcycle, which is common in China. In our design requirement process, we presented two traffic conflict situations and analyzed their key factors. Initial positioning and trajectory of encountered motorcycles were found to be the most important but difficult point in car driver's awareness. Therefore, we propose two different prototypes of a LED visualization components for the car driver. This include changing color schemes and alteration of the amount of light in lamps. The goal was to design support to help the driver to detect motorcycles in the two corresponding traffic situations. The results show that changes in the amount of light in the lamps was performing better. In addition, a large set of qualitative feedback was collected and analyzed in the experiment.

Keywords: Car-motorcycle conflicts · LED visualization · Ambient light · HMI

1 Introduction

The extensive use of motorcycles in developing countries has brought both convenience as well as hazards to people. As a means of transportation, motorcycles are very popular in mainland China, for its agility in busy traffic and ease when parking even in narrow streets [1]. According to a Field Operation Test of Cars [2], carried out in Shanghai City, China, from July, 2014 to December, 2015, hazards involving electric motorcycles made up 16.67% of all kinds of hazard event, making it the third highest, just after the rear-end hazards and cut-in hazards. Furthermore, lots of disorderly conducts of motorcycles were identified, such as running the red light, fast lane-changes without using steering lights, reserve driving and so on. This dangerous driving behavior, involving also other road users such as car drivers. The light weight and small volume give a motorcycle both flexibility and mobility, but also poor stability, which easily lead to traffic conflicts and accidents with other vehicles [3]. Wang et al. [4] found, when analyzing the characteristics of traffic accidents involving motorcycles in China, that motorcycle accidents mainly involved in forward collision and flank collision are most common. Before designing, we made an exploration in requirement, to learn about the characteristics of traffic conflict between car and motorcycles. The following specific characteristics was considered important: The left-turn accidents between motorcycle and car was rank highest among motorcycle accidents. The reason for this problem is within the context of

© Springer Nature Switzerland AG 2019
C. Stephanidis (Ed.): HCII 2019, CCIS 1034, pp. 404–411, 2019.
https://doi.org/10.1007/978-3-030-23525-3_54

the road intersection conflict with vehicles going straight forward. Secondly, overtaking of the motorcycle is another problematic hazardous situation. Thirdly, the technology for vehicle-vehicle communication is developing rapidly, which can help driver to make a judgement in advance by data transmission and analysis [5]. However, at present, the communication between car-motorcycles received much less attention.

Based on the above reviews on mechanical capacities, the main characteristics of accidents between car and motorcycles in urban traffic flows was found, including suddenness of motorcycle's appearance and complexity of road condition. They may increase the difficulty in car driver's situation awareness and reaction.

To summarize, car driver's detecting motorcycle in traffic conflict between car and motorcycle in urban city situations is an important issue that deserves more attention. Our focus was to establish requirements for the design of driver's Human-Machine Interaction (HMI) through developing situations between car and motorcycle. The aim of this HMI design is to improve the condition for the detection of the surrounding motorcycles and decrease the rate of traffic conflicts and accidents.

2 Method and Study Set-up

Shalev-Shwartz et al. [6]. proposed a formal model that covers all the important elements of an autonomous vehicle: sense, plan and act to get the minimal requirements that every autonomous vehicle must satisfy and also how they can verify the requirements. Following their method in our situations between motorcycles and cars, relative position, trajectory and difficulty in detection were taken into consideration.

In our study, we use three different classifications of traffic situation between cars and motorcycles. All have their own different characteristics. In situation 1, motorcycle and car appears in the same lane and both drives in the same direction. The nature of this kind of situation is that the car shares the same lane with the motorcycle, so they have the conflict of right-of-way in a very limited space. In this situation the difficulty of car driver's detection is based on the uncertainty of the motorcycle's appearance. Due to the small volume and strong mobility, motorcycle can appear at any side of the car with unpredictability. Therefore, the requirement of the car driver is more about the direction of the motorcycle approaching at the side. Situation 2 illustrates the oncoming motorcycle. The nature of the conflict is their travelling direction, bringing the conflicts of right-of-way. In this situation, car driver will notice the motorcycle through the windshield more easily, because the motorcycle comes in front of the car's way. In summary, the uncertainty lies in the trajectory of the oncoming motorcycle. In Situation 3, car and motorcycle travel on different lanes, but the motorcycle meets the car from a vertical direction. Obviously, compared with the straight way, this situation is more frequent in junctions. The car driver can't expect the initial position or the travelling trajectory of the motorcycle, therefore, the difficulty in the car driver's situation awareness is much higher than situation 1 and 2 To summarize, there are great uncertainty, suddenness and complexity in the traffic conflicts between cars and motorcycles as shown in situation 1–3 in Table 1 below. From the classification, the encountered motorcycle's initial position and travelling trajectory were identified as the most difficult points in car driver's detection. This is the focus of our study.

Table 1. Three kinds of situations

Situation 1	Situation 2	Situation 3
Car and motorcycle are in the same lane and direction.	Car meets the oncoming motorcycle	Car meets the motorcycle traveling from a vertical direction

To verify the classification of our scenarios and to learn more about their perspectives on situations involving car and motor cycle encounters, we interviewed 12 experienced drivers in Chinese Mainland. The average driving experience was 4.1 years.10 interviewees expressed their caution about the motorcycles. Others suggested that there should be special treatments for motorcyclists, while the car drivers should take on more responsibilities than they are doing at the present.

When making a turn at the crossroad, 7 interviewees regarded that encounter as the most hazardous scenario, since it involves a high level of uncertainty. In this process, more concern would be attached to the encountered motorcycles, including motorcycle's position, speed, and direction and so on. One interviewee said that, at the crossroad, when a motorcycle appears in front of the driver's car, the driver would reduce the speed until the motorcycle bear off. On the other side, if the motorcycle was positioned in the rear, the driver would keep the speed as usual completing the turning.

Based on the scenario classification and the interviews, we will focus on the scenario when the car driver is about to make a right-turn at the crossing, and at the same time when the motorcycle appears in front of, or at the rear of the car, in which attention is focused on the motorcycle's position.

Through the interview, we learnt about the differences between the situations that motorcycle appears in front of the car and the situation when the car appear at the rear. When an approaching motorcycle appears in front of the driver's car, 11 interviewees said they observed the target directly through the windshield and then adjusted the distance and speed to the situation. However, 5 of them said the a more sudden appearance of the motorcycle often caused a disturbing situation. As for motorcycles approaching in the rear, 8 interviewees express concern. Car drivers usually detect the target through the rearview mirrors. However, they found it hard to recognize them because of their small size. When they finally were aware of an approaching motorcycle, there was limited time to make a reaction or decision. Accidents occurred for two of the subject in the similar car situation. It was considered that more workload was taken up when motorcycle approached in the rear than in the front, since they had to look around. 4 interviewees mentioned Blind Spot Detection(BSD), which use sensors or image recognition to detect targets in the rear blind spot area. The detection area of BSD covers 30–50 m behind the car and 3–3.5 m on both sides [7]. When a motorcycle is detected, the lamps installed on rearview mirrors (left and right sides) will light up. The detection area usually covered is the rear blind spot area. The interviewee thought well of its acuity but still felt uneasy. They needed to turn their head sideway especially when a warning signal was on the right side (Chinese cars are all left-hand-drive vehicles).

3 Design and Solution

To enhance car driver's possibilities to detect potential traffic conflicts between cars and motorcycles and create a better user experience, a Human-Machine interface was designed with the LED lamp.

The LED lamps were installed on the front windshield, which is one of the most fixed areas in a car. As described above, in the traffic conflict between cars and motorcycles, some of the important elements are (a) the direction of initial position and (b) trajectory of the encountered motorcycle. Accordingly, lamp bands are grouped into four sections (group 1–4) and placed on the left and right border of the front windshield to indicate the direction of the encountered motorcycles. BSD only indicates right and left approaches. In our study, right and left, front and rear were all taken into consideration to make a comprehensive trial.

Through the above analysis of situations, considering the driver's horizon and head movement, the detection area in traffic conflicts between car and motorcycle can be divided into the four sections corresponding to Group 1, 2, 3 and 4 (see Fig. 1): front-left, front-right, left rear and right rear. Different parts of the windshield are corresponding to different position of the encountered motorcycles. For example, when motorcycle is approaching a car from the left rear, the lamps in Group 3 will be triggered and turn on. The interaction is dynamic, when the position of encountered motorcycle changes, the position of lightened lamp will also change.

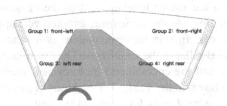

Fig. 1. Layout of the interface on windshield

The interaction of lamp is an important issue and two kinds of display were set: (a) as the emergency degree is getting higher, the color of light get darker (Display 1), and (b) which includes more light in a pyramidical shape (Display 2). The emergency degree is defined in terms of the distance between the driver's car and motorcycles. When the distance is shorter, the emergency degree is higher. In Display 1, when encountered motorcycles entered the detection area of the ego car, one light would be on. While distance between car and motorcycle is shrinking, there is a progressive increase in amount of lamps that are lit up. There is a maximum of five lamps. In Display 2, the amount of lamps are fixed, and the important interface feature is the color of lamp. When the encountered motorcycle entered the detection area, the lamp will turn on and go yellow. As the motorcycle approaches, the color of lamp will turn darker, for example orange. When the emergency degree reaches the top, the light will turn red (Table 2).

Table 2. Two kinds of displays

Trigger Condition: Distance between ego car and motorcycle	Display 1	Display 2
50m	●	●
40m	●	●●
30m	●	●●●
20m	●	●●●●
10m	●	●●●●●

4 Implementation and Test

The prototype is implemented and displayed in driving simulator, which was developed with Unity 2018 and Logitech's Driving force racing wheel. There are two reasons why we used the simulator and software rather than hardware and filed test with real car. Using simulator can guarantee the both the subjects and property security. Furthermore, when connecting the serial port of Arduino and Unity, using LED lamp band as the interface, there were too large delays between the trigger and the reaction, which brought great uncertainty in interaction process. As described earlier, we will focus on the scenarios involving a car driver turning right at the crossroads, and motorcycle approached it at the same time. At the same time, a motorcycle appears in front of or at the rear of the driver's car. In our implementation, two kinds of prototypes were displayed on A pillar and B pillar in the simulators. They were triggered by the distance between the driver's car and the encountered motorcycles. Their conditions and corresponding interfaces is shown in the Table 3. Two kinds of prototypes by two kinds of scenarios, therefore there were 4 tests for every participant.

To minimize the effect of sequence, we used Latin square design in the arrangement of participant's test. A Latin square design is the arrangement of t treatments, each one repeated t times, in such a way that each treatment appears exactly one time in each row and each column in the design [10].

Every participant's sequence was shown in the Table 3 and the numbers correspond to the different situations: Situation 1 (front & colors) corresponds to a scenario when the driver's car encounter an oncoming motorcycle and the HMI provide guidance with changes in colors. Situation 2 (rear & colors) involves a situation when the motorcycle approaches a car and the guidance is based on lamps with changing colors. The difference between Situation 2 and Situation 3 (rear & amount) is in the way the guidance is done. In Situation 3, the lamps changes regarding the amount of light. In Situation 4 (front & amount), involving oncoming motorcycles, the lamps changed in amount of light as in Situation 3.

Table 3. Participant's sequence with Latin square design

Participants	Sequence of situation
A	1,2,4,3
B	2,3,1,4
C	3,4,2,1
D	4,1,3,2

Before the experiment, every participant was offered time to practice and acclimatize themselves to the simulator, including handled feelings, test environment, different meanings behind every sequence. When the experiment began, we told them how the lamp in cars would change in advance, but we did not tell them in what direction the approaching motorcycle would appear.

We used two methods in our experiment. Eye tracker Tobii Pro Glasses 2 was used to collect data from participants, such as eye fixations. After experiment, we interviewed the participants. The data and feedback would be used for the assessment of prototypes.

5   Result and Discussion

12 subject participated in our experiment, using Latin square design. After the experiment, we analyzed the data from both the eye tracking and interviews.

In order to learn about what role of the interface played in car drivers' detection, we made a count about how car drivers recognized the encountered motorcycles. We identified two patterns. The first pattern was based on their eyes directly and the other way was through the help of the lamp (Table 4). The figure showed that the lamps played a more important role when the motorcycle approached the driver's car from the rear, especially with the lamps that changed the amount of light. However, in the oncoming motorcycle situation, the car drivers were apt to observe the approaching motorcycle with their eyes. No statistical significant difference between the two prototypes were detected in the scenario where the motorcycles appeared in the rear, although the result may be seen as indicative. However, in the interview, 11 participants considered that the lamp in Display 1 was much more eye-catching, due to the changes in color.

Table 4. The way how participant detect the motorcycle and frequency

Situation	Participant who detect motorcycle by lamps	Participant who detect motorcycle directly
1 (front & colors)	3	9
2 (rear & colors)	10	1
3 (rear & amount)	12	0
4 (front & amount)	3	9

In the experiment, one of the participants (#2) was involved in a car accident in the simulator. The motorcycle approached at the left rear and the lamp got dark to provide warning signal. This situation ended in a collision, and the driver's car knocked into the motorcycle in the front right. In the interview, the participant pointed to that he/she was not aware of the lamp at all. This reasons for this accident could be: (a) the changing color of the lamp may not have been eye-catching enough; or (b) the participant was not familiar enough with the simulator.

The eye tracker also showed the gaze movement patterns, which showed how the driver interacted with the lamps on A pillar and B pillar. When the participants recognized that the lamp turned on, they observed the road condition on corresponding side. This behavior was especially clear when the motorcycle appeared in the rear. Participants was apt to observe the road condition in the rearview mirror. At the same time, the road condition in the front would be paid attention to, so the gaze movement would become a triangle in this situation as shown in Fig. 2. Seven participants showed this pattern of behavior within the experiment. When they found the lamp turning on, they would glance the rearview mirror on the same side, and then looked back to the road condition in front of the ego car through the windshield. The lamp's role in situations when motorcycles appeared in front of the driver's car was much smaller. Even when participants detected targets through the lamp, they said they just took a brief glance, then focused on the target itself.

Fig. 2. Habit formed in the use of lamps demonstrated by eye-tracker

Based on the results, we may elaborate the following. The lamps on pillar A and B can play a more important role in detection of approaching motorcycles and in turn lowering the driver's uncertainty in that traffic situation. However, most participants preferred using the lamps that changed the amount of light, rather than color, since the lamp with increasing/decreasing amount of light was more eye-catching according to the interviews. When an approaching motorcycle comes in from the rear, the lamps play a more important role in detecting hazards. When lamps are turn on in order to act as warning signals in front, they may cause distraction to the car drivers.

We collected lots of feedback about the prototypes. Most participant did not think it was necessary to show guidance when there was an oncoming motorcycle, since they could detect it directly by eye-sight. As for motorcycles in the rear, it is necessary to provide guidance as early as possible. One participant suggested that the light triggering distance alerts, could be made through personalized settings. As regards to the mode of interaction, most participants thought the lamp was better than steering wheel vibration or voice alerts, because the vibration will make them nervous easily and voice alerts will take up more time to make a reaction.

One limitation of our study is that there is rather vital differences between an experiment set-up like ours and a real-life test scene with actual road condition. A next step, could be to try our prototypes in cars in a more controlled field experiments.

References

1. Cheng, A.S., Ng, T.C.: Development of a Chinese motorcycle rider driving violation questionnaire. Accid. Anal. Prev. **42**(4), 1250–1256 (2010)
2. Ma, X., Zhu, X., Ma, Z.: An analysis on traffic classification and violation behavior of intersections with the approach of open field test. In: Proceeding of the 14th International Forum of Automative Traffic Safety, p. 14 (2017)
3. Yong, L.: Analysis on traffic safety of motorcycle in China. J. Guizhou Univ. Technol. (Social Science Edition) **05**, 126–130 (2007)
4. Wang, H., Riguang, N., Xichan, Z.: An analysis on characteristics of motorcycle accidents. Automot. Eng. **11**, 1009–1012 (2008)
5. Dey, K.C., et al.: Vehicle-to-vehicle (V2 V) and vehicle-to-infrastructure (V2I) communication in a heterogeneous wireless network – Performance evaluation. Transp. Res. Part C Emerg. Technol. **68**, 168–184 (2016)
6. Shalev-Shwartz, S., Shammah, S., Shashua, A.: On a formal model of safe and scalable self-driving cars. arXiv preprint arXiv:1708.06374 (2017)
7. Liu, G., Zhou, M., Wang, L., Wang, H., Guo, X.: A blind spot detection and warning system based on millimeter wave radar for driver assistance. Optik Int. J. Light Electron Opt. **135**, 353–365 (2017)
8. Dodge, Y.: Latin Square Designs. The Concise Encyclopedia of Statistics, p. 297. Springer, New York (2008). https://doi.org/10.1007/978-0-387-32833-1

The Research on Basic Visual Design of Head-Up Display of Automobile Based on Driving Cognition

Fang You, Jinghui Zhang$^{(\boxtimes)}$, Jianmin Wang, Mengting Fu,
and Zhenghe Lin

Car Interaction Design Lab, College of Arts and Media, Tongji University,
Shanghai, China
{youfang, 1733470, wangjianmin}@tongji.edu.cn

Abstract. As a new type of vehicle vision interactive device, head up display (HUD) has a good assistant effect on alleviating the visual distraction and action distraction caused by reading vehicle information. At present, the automobile equipped with HUD mainly concentrates on a small number of high-end brands, and the promotion of HUD is in the initial stage. Most of the HUD visual interface designs do not take account the specific needs of the driver in specific scenarios, so drivers need more cognitive resources and workload to read information from these HUD, which easily causes distraction. According to this background of the industry, and based on the size of the important design elements on HUD, this paper carries out the design research of HUD visual interactive interface with the driver workload as the core.

Firstly, the author of this paper investigated the HUD in China auto market in 2018, and organize the information architecture, information layout and main design elements. Then, the ISO standard illumination was simulated in the room, and different sizes of design elements were placed on the optical machine, 36 participants were tested for reaction time (RT) and workload.

This experiment takes weather and age as independent variables and reaction time (RT) as dependent variables, and combines with the evaluation of the workload of the subjects, the results of the test are analyzed. This experiment puts forward a basic research method for new vehicle equipment from the perspective of visual design and cognitive workload, which is of great significance in this experiment.

Keywords: Head-up display · Visual design elements · Response time · Workload

1 Introduction

In the process of human-vehicle-environment interaction, the driver obtains a certain amount of on-board information through the visual interaction interface in the vehicle, which is the cognitive process of the driver, and it is the basis of all driving behavior and driver performance [1]. The driver observes the change of the interface visually, and determines the type and meaning of the information by thinking channel. After

C. Stephanidis (Ed.): HCII 2019, CCIS 1034, pp. 412–420, 2019.
https://doi.org/10.1007/978-3-030-23525-3_55

that, the driver will make decisions and perform corresponding interactions for the content of the information. Finally, the interaction will get feedback in the vehicle interaction system. Throughout the process, the driver will inevitably need to shift the sight of driving and think about it [2]. If the visual interface is not designed properly, the driver will need to spend more cognitive resources to identify the information. In the process of identification and thinking, the driver's line of sight and attention are not placed on the main driving tasks, it is easy to cause driving distraction behavior that affects safety [3]. Wickens describes cognitive behavior from the perspective of resource capacity. He believes that the occupants have a group of cognitive resources with similar nature, limited function and certain capacity. When task difficulty increases or resource competition among multiple tasks leads to resource shortage, system performance will decline [4].

Psychological workload is a multi-dimensional concept, which is used to describe people's psychological pressure or information processing ability at work. It involves many factors, such as work requirements, time pressure, task difficulty, operator's ability, effort and so on [5]. Under the background of the rapid development of automation, the relationship between people and the system has changed greatly. At present, the main methods of measuring mental workload are subjective evaluation scale, performance measurement and physiological measurement [6].

It is reasonable to measure mental workload with subjective evaluation scale, because it is a psychological structure itself. In the study of HART and Staveland, they described the TLX mental workload measurement method, which had been proved by experiences at that time, probably the closest approach to the essence of mental workload mining, and could provide the most common, effective and sensitive indicators. At the same time, they also noticed that subjective methods are also subject to operator bias and preconceived notions, and that the results of subjective evaluation are based on the operator's memory or abstraction from experience. Although there are many subjective factors for uncertainty in using the subjective rating scale method, the results of the evaluation using TLX are relatively stable after years of experimental measurement and verification [7].

The NASA Task Load Index (NASA-TLX) provides a multi-dimensional scoring process that derives the overall score based on six psychological workload factors: mental load, physical burden, time stress, task performance, effort, and frustration. The TLX consists of two measurement evaluation processes: weight and rating [7]. This experiment also used the NASA TLX multi-dimensional rating scale for workload testing of different sizes.

The appearance of the head-up display plays in mitigating the distracting behavior caused by the in-vehicle information reading process. HUD can reduce the frequency and duration of the driver's eyes-off-the-road by projecting the required information in front of the driver. This enables the driver to steer easily and to respond quickly to information provided by the road conditions and communication systems. According to the statistics, HUD can reduce vehicle collisions by 25% [8]. It is of great significance to study the visual interaction interface of HUD on the basis of driving cognition and human-computer interaction. With the popularization and promotion of HUD, it is very important to explore and establish a set of effective HUD visual interaction principles and norms. The research content of this paper will provide certain reference value for this exploration process.

This paper investigates and sorts out the information architecture and information layout of existing automotive HUDs, then extracts the main design elements. According to the illumination standard provided by ISO 15008, the light conditions of daytime direct light (45000 lx) were simulated, and the optical calibration was performed by the brightness meter. The experiment were carried out in the daytime and snowy scenarios, the three main design elements of text, numbers and icons were tested for different sizes of recognition responses. Besides, the participants were asked to evaluate the workload in six dimensions. The integrated subjective and objective test parameters provided a theoretical basis for the HUD interface design.

2   Method

2.1   Experimental Environment

In this experiment, HUD optical machine is used to put the test content on. The communication interface of optical machine is connected with a tablet computer. A tester is responsible for controlling the tablet computer. ISO 15008 proposed that the test of vehicle visual display needs to simulate night (maximum illumination is less than 10 lx), evening light (about 250 lx), daytime direct light (about 45000 lx) [9]. The purpose of the experiment is to test the minimum size and comfort domain size range that the user thinks can be accepted in the HUD visual design, and provide a theoretical basis for the HUD interface design. Therefore, this experiment selects the daytime direct sunlight with the smallest contrast between the simulated environment and the optical machine. Light was tested and optically calibrated using a luminance meter. In terms of weather, due to the greater reflection of the road surface during snowy days, the effect on the image of the light machine is more obvious. Therefore, this experiment selects two weather conditions, sunny and snowy, and explores whether the weather affects the identification of the subject. The experiment used a projector to project a picture containing weather and road conditions in front of the driving field of view, statically simulating environmental conditions (Figs. 1 and 2).

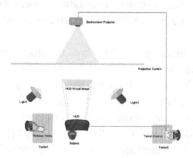

Fig. 1. Test environment.

Fig. 2. Test site.

2.2 Subjects

36 participants aged between 21 to 46 years old participated in the experiment (mean age = 32.8, SD = 6.8 years). All subjects had at least one year of driving experience, non-color blindness. Their visual acuity (including corrected visual acuity) is 4.8 or above, all of whom have a certain understanding of HUD before the experiment. But 36 subjects did not drive a car with Windshield-HUD.

2.3 Test Contents and Test Steps

The size range is larger than the size of the text, numbers, and icons obtained by the market survey, that is, the text and number values are 24px, 30px, 36px, 48px, and the icon size values are 50 * 24px, 50 * 40px, 68 * 70px, and 71 * 88px. Moreover, in order to avoid the learning effect, the text, numbers and icons in the sunny and snowy scenes are different. At the same time, all elements are displayed in white.

After the participant enters the test area, the tester will ask the participant to read the informed consent form, fill in the basic information, and perform the vision test. Next, the tester will let the tester read a test documentation including test purpose, test content and test task. In this experiment, the experiment was carried out according to the test sequence of the sunny day scenario after the sunny day scenario, and the three types of elements were divided into three groups according to small, medium, large and super large groups. The experiments were carried out in the order of Latin squares (Fig. 3).

Fig. 3. Test contents.

The test used the Unity to create a display program that was confirmed by the tester before the experiment. Then, when the subject pressed the right button of the keyboard, the task started. After two seconds of black screen, the HUD presented the test content.

When the subjects recognize the contents of number, text or icon, press the space key, and then dictate what they see, after which the tester's tablet computer interface will show the reaction time of the subjects. Then, after the testers record the time, they inform the subjects that they can start the next experiment of identify reaction time. After the test of each group of three elements is completed, the participants are asked to fill in the NASA-TLX questionnaire to score the Workload value under this size group.

3   Results

3.1   The Influence of Weather Conditions on RT

By calculating the average recognition reaction time of each element in the sunny and snowy scenarios, the data of 36 people showed that only the text, number and icon in the small size group had 85.80%, 88.57% and 91.43% completeness in the sunny scenario, and only the text, number and icon in the small size group had 97.14%, 91.41% and 68.57% completeness in the snowy scenario respectively, and the other size groups can be fully recognized.

As shown in Fig. 4, the change of the overall recognition response time in sunny and snowy scenarios conforms to the general cognitive law, and the response time of icons is generally higher than that of words and figures. The average response time of icons with small size is close to 2 s, this indicates that the cognitive resources occupied by the small icon are high and should not be used in the design. It can be observed that in sunny and snowy scenarios, the number of medium is generally higher than that of small in response, which may be related to the shape of the number itself.

In the small text test, the average RT of snow day is 0.4 s higher than that of sunny day, while in the other sizes, the average value of sunny day is more time-consuming than that of snowy day. In the RT test of number, the overall response time in sunny days is slightly larger than that in snowy days. For icons, due to the influence of graphical complexity, 71 * 88px size icons have a certain degree of increase in response time.

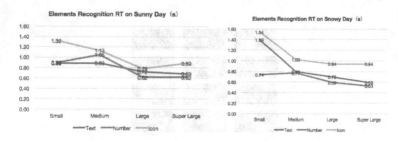

Fig. 4. Elements recognition RT on sunny day and snowy day.

Through one-way ANOVA analysis, when the independent variable is weather, the experiment finds that the weather has no significant effect on the identification RT of different elements with different sizes under daytime direct light (Table 1).

Table 1. One-way ANOVA analysis of weather conditions

Size	Text	Number	Icon
Small	0.15	0.20	0.44
Medium	0.41	0.42	0.62
Large	0.78	0.53	0.29
Super large	0.21	0.08	0.76

3.2 The Influence of Age on RT

Thirty-six subjects were tested in this experiment. Among them, 16 were 21–30 years old and 20 were 31–46 years old. From Fig. 5, it can be seen that the average identification RT of different sizes of texts, numbers and icons in sunny day shows that the 31–36 age group is higher than the 21–30 age group in all sizes, indicating that the 21–30 age group's cognitive ability is better than the 31–46 age group in all sizes.

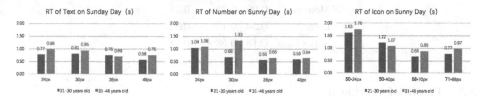

Fig. 5. Elements recognition RT on sunny day of 2 age groups.

However, it can be obtained by one-way ANOVA analysis that in the case of sunny day, the effects of different age groups on different size identification RT are not significant (Table 2).

Table 2. One-way ANOVA analysis of age groups on sunny day.

Size	Text	Number	Icon
Small	0.37	0.40	0.22
Medium	0.99	0.35	0.76
Large	0.54	0.13	0.32
Super large	0.18	0.68	0.48

In the snowy day scenario, experiments with different contents but the same size were carried out. As shown in Fig. 6, the average recognition RT of different sizes of texts, numbers and icons showed that the 31–46 age group was lower than the 21–30 age group in all sizes, while the smallest size of words, numbers and icons was just the opposite. It is indicated that for the smallest size elements, the identification of the 31–46 age group is more difficult than the 21–30 age group, but the difference between the two groups is small, and the group with the older age is more recognized. Similarly, the effect of different age groups on the identification response was not significant under the snowy day conditions by one-way ANOVA test (Table 3).

Fig. 6. Elements recognition RT on snowy day of 2 age groups.

Table 3. One-way ANOVA analysis of age groups on snowy day.

Size	Text	Number	Icon
Small	0.37	0.40	0.22
Medium	0.99	0.35	0.76
Large	0.54	0.13	0.32
Super large	0.18	0.68	0.48

3.3   Trends of Workload

According to the selection of the scores and the selection of the weights, the average value of workload under each size is calculated. It can be seen that the workload value gradually decreases as the size becomes larger. In the snowy day, the change from small to medium size is large, which indicates that in the size range of this experiment, the fastest driving force for workload reduction is the range from small size to medium size, but for daytime sunny scenario, the range is from medium to large. In both weather conditions, the difference between large and super large Workload value is not significant (Fig. 7).

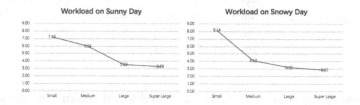

Fig. 7. Workload trend of each size groups.

4   Discussion

Considering the dimension design of elements on HUD display terminals from the perspective of RT and workload, we can find that it is difficult to define the minimum range among the four levels selected from the market survey results, which may be related to the indoor simulation static experiment rather than the dynamic test of actual driving scenarios. As for the comfort range of size, it is suggested that in HUD interface design, the text size should be between 36–48px and the digital size should be between 36–48px. Due to the influence of semantics, the icon size should not be less than 68 * 70px. At the same time, for the icon with warning meaning, designers should make more thoughtful considerations on size, color, layout and dynamic effects.

By observing the influence of weather conditions on the size identification, it is found that the influence of the weather is not significant; by observing the influence of the two age groups on the size identification, it is found that for the small size, the age group has a higher recognition response to the size. For the smallest size, the RT of older group is generally slower than the younger group. At other sizes, the difference between the different age groups was not obvious.

In addition, because this experiment is carried out under a standard illumination condition and the brightness of the optical machine itself is restricted, the experimental results have certain limitations, but this experiment proposes a basic research method from the perspective of visual design and workload for the new in-vehicle equipment, which is a great significance of this experiment.

5   Future Work

Along with the rapid development of intelligent networked vehicles, new in-vehicle terminals and human-computer interaction interfaces have emerged. The car has become a personal space for information acquisition, transmission, communication and entertainment, which will make the car human-computer interaction show a high degree of complexity, but also bring a lot of user experience problems. For the interface design of the new vehicle terminal, there are still many research points, such as layout, color, dynamic effects and multi-channel design. The results of this experiment can be used as a reference for research in subsequent directions. Moreover, for this experiment, in the future work, more in-depth comparison can be made for different standard lighting conditions, and the problem can be further studied in detail from the direction of optics and ergonomics.

Acknowledgments. This work was supported by the National Key Research and Development Program of China (#2018YFB1004903), the Fundamental Research Funds for the Central Universities (#22120180075) and National Science Foundation of China for Young Scholars (#71804126). We would like to thank Dr. Zhejun Liu and Yunshui Jin for support and feedback.

References

1. Schmidt, R.: Unitended acceleration: human performance considerations. In: Peacock, B., Karwowski, W. (eds.) Proceedings of Automotive Ergonomics, Taylor and Francis, London, pp. 633–662 (1993)
2. Bergasa, L.M., Nuevo, J., Sotelo, M.Á., et al.: Visual monitoring of driver inattention. In: Computational Intelligence in Automotive Applications (2008)
3. Alm, H., Nilsson, L.: The effects of a mobile telephone task on driver behaviour in a car following situation. Accid. Anal. Prev. 27(5), 707–715 (1995)
4. Parasuraman, R., Sheridan, T.B., Wickens, C.D.: Situation awareness, mental workload, and trust in automation: viable, empirically supported cognitive engineering constructs. J. Cogn. Eng. Decis. Making 2(2), 140–160 (2008)
5. Recarte, M.A., Nunes, L.M.: Mental workload while driving: effects on visual search, discrimination, and decision making. J. Exp. Psychol. Appl. 9(2), 119 (2003)
6. Wickens, C.D.: Multiple resources and performance prediction. Theor. Issues Ergon. Sci. 3(2), 159–177 (2002)
7. Hart, S.G.: Nasa-task load index (NASA-TLX); 20 years later. Proc. Hum. Factors Ergon. Soc. Ann. Meet. 50(4661), 904–908 (2006)
8. Hibberd, D.L., Jamson, S.L., Carsten, O.M.J.: Managing in-vehicle distractions: evidence from the psychological refractory period paradigm. In: International Conference on Automotive User Interfaces & Interactive Vehicular Applications (2010)
9. ISO 15008: 2003: Road vehicles – Ergonomic aspects of transport information and control systems – Specifications and compliance procedures for in-vehicle visual presentation (2003)

A Survey on the Intention to Use a Fully-Automated Vehicle

Liang Zhang[1,2(✉)], Jingyu Zhang[1,2], Li Lin[1,2], Han Qiao[1,2], and Xiangying Zou[1,2]

[1] Key Laboratory of Behavioral Science, Institute of Psychology, Chinese Academy of Sciences, Beijing, China
[2] University of Chinese Academy of Sciences, Beijing, China
zhangl@psych.ac.cn

Abstract. Automated vehicles, with the rapid development in recent years, are closer to becoming a reality. The fully-automated bus is going to be open to the public in China this year. Thus, it is indispensable to know the public attitudes to automated vehicles. This study surveyed 725 participants on their intended use of full-automated vehicles. Particularly, nearly 200 of them had a similar experience as passengers of the fully-automated vehicles. Overall, results revealed that participants were "somewhat agree" to take an automated vehicle (mean score = 5, rang 1–7, 7 represents extremely agree). In general, 6.62% of the participants were moderately or extremely willing to use an automated vehicle (score 6–7), and 25.52% of the participants were somewhat willing to use an automated vehicle (score 5–6). 30.21% of the participants were unwilling to use automated vehicles (score < 4). Moreover, the participants with similar experience, were more willing to use an automated vehicle than those without experience. These results show that, in general, the Chinese people hold an inclusive and acceptable attitude towards fully-automated vehicles. Enhancing the understanding of automated vehicles, such as take a test ride, will help to further promote the intention to use the automated vehicles.

Keywords: Automated vehicle · Behavior intention · Experience

1 Introduction

Automated vehicles are regarded as safer than traditional vehicles for its potential to reduce severe crashes resulting from human errors. With the increasing development in recent years, they are going to be put into use in recent years. In China, the fully-automated bus is going to be open to the public this year. Full driving automation is ranked as the highest level of automation (Level 5) according to the SAE International Standard J3016 [1]. This level of automation requires no human attention, which means the human driver is completely eliminated.

In China, it is a critical and urgent for the government to know the public attitudes toward fully-automated vehicles since they are going to be deployed soon. The public intention to use a fully-automated vehicle has significant implications for the successful implementation of the technology. Recent studies have examined drivers' intended use

© Springer Nature Switzerland AG 2019
C. Stephanidis (Ed.): HCII 2019, CCIS 1034, pp. 421–426, 2019.
https://doi.org/10.1007/978-3-030-23525-3_56

of automated vehicles [2, 3] and passengers' perception of automated vehicles [4]. Given that those studies mostly focused on conditional automation, and the surveys were completed in western countries, an investigation into the attitude towards fully-automated vehicles is needed in the Chinese background.

To date, most online surveys have mainly investigated the intention to use automated vehicles as either drivers or passengers [5–7]. However, few studies have looked into the difference between the two perspectives. Besides, there are other perspectives that should also be taken seriously. For example, pedestrians' intention has been overlooked. Therefore, the current study aimed to extendedly examine the behavior intention to use an automated vehicle, including the purchase intention, the self-usage intention both as driver and passenger, the intention to take significant others to ride, and the intention as pedestrians.

Previous studies have suggested that age and gender might be factors that influence the perception and intended use of automated vehicles [3, 4, 8]. For example, a large-scale survey across the US, the UK, and Australia found that older participants and females were more unlikely to ride in an automated vehicle [4]. However, there can be other factors, apart from demographic variations, that influence the intention to use automated vehicles. We assumed that the experience with automated driving helps enhance the confidence in the safety of automated vehicles.

The aim of the current study was to investigate the behavior intention towards the use of automated vehicles in an extended scope, based on the Chinese population. We hypothesized that the intention of purchase, self-usage as drivers and passengers, significant-others-usage, and pedestrian would be different. In addition, we also hypothesized that similar experience with automated vehicles would enhance the intention of use.

2 Method

2.1 Participants

A total of 779 participants answered the paper-based or online questionnaires. The paper-based questionnaires were collected from local vehicle inspection sites in Beijing and on-the-job postgraduate classes in Shenzhen. The online questionnaires were collected through a social media platform (WeChat). For the online questionnaires, the rejection criterion was as follows: (1) the answer time was less than 500 s; (2) the error rate of the check questions was over 75%; (3) from the same IP address. Finally, 725 valid questionnaires remained for analysis. Among the 725 respondents, 373 were from Beijing and 352 were from other cities in China. The number of participants with similar experience was 175 (23.9%). The average age of participants was 30 ± 14, ranging from 18 to 60. The average driving year was 4.65 ± 5.73, ranging from 0 to 32 years. The number of male participants was 360 (50.3%).

2.2 Measures

Demographic Variables. The demographic variables composed of age, gender, education, marital status, number of children, annual income, driver license, driving years.

Behavior Intention. The behavior intention was measured with 17 items. The behavior intention was measured from five perspectives, including purchase, driver, passenger, significant-others-usage, and pedestrians. The purchase perspective composed of 3 items, such as, "If automated vehicles were available for a reasonable price, I will buy one" (Cronbach's alpha = .807). The perspective of drivers composed of 3 items, such as, "I'm willing to drive an automated vehicle on the road" (Cronbach's alpha = .899). The perspective of passengers composed of 4 items, such as, "I'd like to ride an automated vehicle as a passenger" (Cronbach's alpha = .865). The perspective of significant-others-usage composed of 3 items, such as, "I will consider taking my child/children to ride an automate vehicle" (Cronbach's alpha = .957). The perspective of pedestrians composed of 4 items, such as, "I'm willing to walk on a road with automated vehicles" (Cronbach's alpha = .938).

3 Results

3.1 Behavior Intention of the Whole Sample

General Behavior Intention. The general behavior intention to use automated vehicles was collapsed across all the items. The average score was 4.48 ± 1.00. The distribution of general behavior intention was shown in Table 1. 6.62% of the participants were moderately or extremely willing to use an automated vehicle (score 6–7), and 25.52% of the participants were somewhat willing to use an automated vehicle (score 5–6). Only 30.21% of the participants were unwilling to use automated vehicles (score < 4).

Behavior Intention in Specific Perspective

Intention of Purchase. The average score of intention to purchase an automated vehicle was 4.10 ± 0.72. The proportion of "moderately or extremely agree" (score 6–7) was 0.97%, and that of "somewhat agree" (score 5–6) was 13.93%. And 31.59% of the participants were unwilling to purchase automated vehicles (score < 4).

Intention of as Driver. The average score of intention to drive an automated vehicle was 5.23 ± 1.15. The proportion of "moderately or extremely agree" (score 6–7) was 37.38%, and that of "somewhat agree" (score 5–6) was 29.52%. Only 10.07% of the participants were unwilling to drive automated vehicles (score < 4).

Intention of Passenger. The average score of intention to ride an automated vehicle as passengers was 4.86 ± 1.17. The proportion of "moderately or extremely agree" (score 6–7) was 20.03%, and that of "somewhat agree" (score 5–6) was 27.86%. Only 17.52% of the participants were unwilling to ride automated vehicles (score < 4).

Intention of Significant-Others-Usage. The average score of intention to consider taking significant others to ride an automated vehicle was 3.85 ± 1.56. The proportion of "moderately or extremely agree" (score 6–7) was 14.90%, and that of "somewhat agree" (score 5–6) was 15.59%. And 43.59% of the participants were unwilling to ride automated vehicles (score < 4).

Intention of Pedestrian. The average score of intention to walk on a road with automated vehicles was 4.29 ± 1.40. The proportion of "moderately or extremely agree" (score 6–7) was 15.86%, and that of "somewhat agree" (score 5–6) was 20.41%. And 45.24% of the participants were unwilling to ride automated vehicles (score < 4).

Comparison of Different Behavior Intention. The average score and distribution of each specific behavior intention were shown in Table 1.

Repeated-measures of ANOVA was conducted for the average score of different behavior intention. The result revealed a significant effect of different behavior intention, $F(4, 2896) = 340.488$, $p < 0.001$, $\eta^2 = 0.320$. Post hoc analysis showed that all specific behavior intention was significant with each other, $ps < 0.001$. The rank of intention was as follows: driver > passenger > significant-others-usage > pedestrian > purchase.

Table 1. The descriptive statistics of behavior intention.

	Mean (SD)	Extremely agree	Somewhat agree	Neutral	Don't agree
General intention	4.48 (1.00)	6.62%	25.52%	37.66%	30.21%
Intention of purchase	4.10 (0.72)	0.97%	13.93%	53.52%	31.59%
Intention of driver	5.23 (1.15)	37.38%	29.52%	23.03%	10.07%
Intention of passenger	4.86 (1.17)	23.03%	27.86%	31.59%	17.52%
Intention of significant-others-usage	3.85 (1.56)	14.90%	15.59%	25.93%	43.59%
Intention of pedestrian	4.29 (1.40)	15.86%	20.41%	18.48%	45.24%

3.2   Comparison Between Samples with and Without Experience

General Behavior Intention. Among the whole sample, 186 respondents had experienced automated vehicles, and 535 didn't, with 4 missing data. The independent t-test showed that the respondents with the similar experience (4.86 ± 0.96) were more willing than those without similar experience (4.35 ± 0.98) to accept automated vehicles, $t(719) = 6.136$, $p < 0.001$.

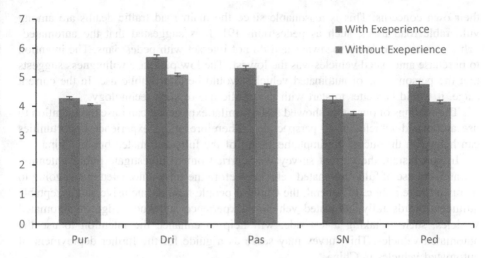

Fig. 1. Comparison of behavior intention between two samples. Pur: Intention of purchase. Dri: Intention of drivers. Pas: Intention of passengers. SN: Intention of significant-others-usage. Ped: Intention of pedestrians.

Behavior Intention in Specific Perspective. For every specific perspective, we also conducted an independent t-test to compare the two samples (see Fig. 1). The results showed that the behavior intention was significantly higher in the sample with experience, in all specific perspectives, $ps < 0.001$.

4 Discussion

The present study examined the behavior intention to use automated vehicles in five specific perspectives and the role of experience. We found that, in general, 6.62% of the participants were moderately or extremely willing to use an automated vehicle (score 6–7), and 25.52% of the participants were somewhat willing to use an automated vehicle (score 5–6). And 30.21% of the participants were unwilling to use automated vehicles (score < 4). In addition, our results showed that participants' intention was different from one perspective to another, as the intention to be a driver of automated vehicles was the top one. Moreover, our survey also suggested that participants with similar experience were more intended to use automated vehicles in all perspectives.

Our results showed that the intention to use automated vehicles as drivers was the highest among all perspectives. One possible explanation is that drivers are mostly benefited from the automated vehicles for they can reduce the manual effort. Following that, the intention to ride automated vehicles as passengers ranked the second place. Interestingly, when it comes to significant others, the intention dropped compared to self-usage. This difference may suggest that the public still hold concerns on the safety of automated vehicles when their children or parents are taken into consideration. The proportion of unwillingness was highest for pedestrians, indicating that although the drivers might not worry about the safety of automated vehicles, the pedestrians have their own concerns. This is reasonable since the main road traffic deaths are among vulnerable road users, such as pedestrians [9]. It is suggested that the automated-vehicles run on enclosed roadways and do not interact with pedestrians. The intention to purchase automated vehicles was the lowest. The low purchase willingness suggests that the personal use of automated vehicles would be after public use. In the current stage, it would be better to start with the public use of such technology.

The findings of our study showed that a similar experience can raise the intention to use automated-vehicles in all perspectives. Therefore, more experience opportunities can help with the successful implementation of the fully-automated bus in China.

In conclusion, the current survey was carried out to investigate public intention towards the use of fully-automated vehicles, before the fully-automated bus is going to be open to the public. In general, the Chinese people hold an inclusive and acceptable attitude towards fully-automated vehicles. Experience and knowledge of automated vehicles, such as taking a test ride, will help to enhance the intention to use the automated vehicles. This survey may serve as a guide for the further deployment of automated vehicles in China.

References

1. SAE International. SAE J3016: Taxonomy and Definitions for Terms Related to Driving Automation Systems for On-Road Motor Vehicles (2018)
2. Buckley, L., Kaye, S.-A., Pradhan, A.K.: Psychosocial factors associated with intended use of automated vehicles: a simulated driving study. Accid. Anal. Prev. **115**, 202–208 (2018)
3. Hulse, L.M., Xie, H., Galea, E.R.: Perceptions of autonomous vehicles: relationships with road users, risk, gender and age. Saf. Sci. **102**, 1–13 (2018)
4. Schoettle, B., Sivak, M.: A Survey of Public Opinion About Autonomous and Self-Driving Vehicles in the US, the UK, and Australia. University of Michigan Transportation Research Institute, Ann Arbor, MI (2014)
5. Bansal, P., Kockelman, K.M., Singh, A.: Assessing public opinions of and interest in new vehicle technologies: an Austin perspective. Transp. Res. C: Emerg. Technol. **67**, 1–14 (2016)
6. Kyriakidis, M., Happee, R., de Winter, J.C.F.: Public opinion on automated driving: results of an international questionnaire among 5000 respondents. Transp. Res. Part F: Traffic Psychol. Behav. **32**, 127–140 (2015)
7. London: YouGov. https://yougov.co.uk/topics/lifestyle/articles-reports/2016/08/26/majority-public-would-be-scared-take-ride-driverle. Accessed 15 Mar 2019
8. Rahman, M., Lesch, M.F., Horrey, W.J., Strawderman, L.: Assessing the utility of TAM, TPB, and UTAUT for advanced driver assistance systems. Accid. Anal. Prev. **108**, 361–373 (2017)
9. WHO Road Traffic Injuries. https://www.who.int/en/news-room/fact-sheets/detail/road-traffic-injuries. Accessed 20 Mar 2019

HCI for Health and Well-Being

Comparison of Gaze Patterns While Diagnosing Infant Epilepsies

Hirotaka Aoki[1(✉)], Satoshi Suzuki[2], and Makiko Aoki[2]

[1] Tokyo Institute of Technology, 2-12-1 Oh-okayama Meguro-ku,
Tokyo 152-8552, Japan
aoki.h.ad@m.titech.ac.jp
[2] Kanagawa Institute of Technology, 1030 Shimo-ogino,
Atsugi-shi, Kanagawa 243-0292, Japan

Abstract. To identify differentiator of infant epilepsies diagnosis skills, eye movement data were recorded from nineteen nurses and nine nursing school students during performing clinical reasoning processes for the diagnosis. Nineteen nurses includes one expert having rich experiences in caring for infants with severe physical and intellectual disabilities, nine specialists having relatively long experience as nurses in pediatrics/obstetrics as well as research/teaching experiences in pediatrics/obstetrics department in university, and nine intermediate nurses having relatively short experiences in pediatrics/obstetrics department in hospital. Nine nursing students are in 2nd/3rd-year at a nursing school. In the experiment, twenty video movies showing an infant were exposed. Each infant in the videos showed some epilepsies-like symptoms. Each participant was asked to make his/her diagnosis whether each of infants' body motions may be serious or not. An expert and specialists showed different visual perception patterns compared with other participants. They paid more attention to a face of an infant, which is directly connected with a major root cause of the severe epilepsies (i.e., a malfunction of neurotransmitter function in brain), but less attention to physical symptoms such as unintentional motion in hands/foot. Based on the results, possible interpretations regarding characteristics of diagnosis strategies of expert, specialist, intermediate nurses and nursing school students are given.

Keywords: Visual perception patterns · West syndrome · Clinical reasoning processes

1 Introduction

1.1 Epilepsies-Like Symptoms and West Syndrome

Epilepsy is defined as a disorder of the brain characterized by an enduring predisposition to generate epileptic seizures, and by the neurobiologic, cognitive, psychological, and social consequences of this condition [1]. There are many types of epilepsies including West syndrome, Lennox-Gestaut syndrome, Rolandic epilepsy and so forth. In this paper, West syndrome is focused as an example of serious epilepsies.

© Springer Nature Switzerland AG 2019
C. Stephanidis (Ed.): HCII 2019, CCIS 1034, pp. 429–433, 2019.
https://doi.org/10.1007/978-3-030-23525-3_57

West syndrome is characterized as a severe epilepsy syndrome. This occurs in between 3–7 months old [2]. It is conjectured that the cause of the syndrome is a malfunction of neurotransmitter function in brain. As symptoms of the syndrome, brief but not so frequent attacks are observed. In typical cases, sudden flexions occur in a tonic style of the body, arms and legs, periodically. The typical symptoms of the West syndrome, such as brief attacks found in arms, are very similar with those of unproblematic primitive reflexes (e.g., Moro reflex). Caused by the similarity, it is quite challenging for doctors/nurses to accurately detect potential infant patients having severe disease (e.g., West syndrome).

1.2 Objective

One of the most critical clinical processes in infant epilepsies diagnosis is to detect abnormal symptoms by careful observations of infants showing epilepsies-like body motions. This process can be characterized as a mixture of intuitive and analytical processes. In some cases, the former process (i.e., intuitive process) seems to be a key factor to make better clinical decisions. Considering the background, the objective of the present study is to identify differentiator of infant epilepsies diagnosis skills by analyzing eye movement data obtained in experiments.

2 Experiment

2.1 Participant

Nineteen nurses specializing in maternal/child nursing and nine students at a nursing school participated in our experiment. The nineteen nurses were divided into three groups of expert (1), specialist (9) and intermediate (9). An expert was a university researcher working in a department of nursing. She had more than 20-year experience in a hospital, and had more than 11-year experience in a special hospital for infants with severe physical and intellectual disabilities. Nine specialists had relatively long experience (more than 10 years) as nurses in pediatrics/obstetrics department in hospitals. They were also working as university researchers in nursing departments at several universities. Nine intermediate nurses are now working in obstetrics department in hospitals. Their years of experiences ranged from 5–10. Additionally, nine nursing students majoring in nursing science at an identical nursing school (2nd or 3rd year) participated in our experiment. In total, the participants consisted of the following four groups: Expert, Specialist, Intermediate and Student.

2.2 Stimuli

Twenty of 30-s video movies each of which showed an infant were exposed. Each of infants in the videos showed some body motions similar to typical epilepsies-like symptoms, but not all of them were caused by severe health problems. The severe cases in the movies are those of the West syndrome.

2.3 Apparatus

Eye movement recording was conducted with either Tobii X3-120 eye tracker (Tobii Technology) or TalkEye III (Takei Scientific Instruments).

2.4 Procedure

On arrival, a participant was given a detailed explanation about the task to make his/her diagnosis decisions whether each of infants' body motions were relating to some serious cause or not. Then he/she was escorted to the display with eye tracking system. After calibration procedure, each one of twenty video movies were started to play. The participants eye movement were recorded during playing the twenty movies.

3 Result

3.1 Data Processing

According to Blascheck's eye movement data taxonomy [3], there exists one category called "dwell" in eye movement visualization techniques. The dwell is referred to as a condition where a specific area of interest (AOI), which is determined by considering semantic information involved in visual stimuli, is continuously looked at. In other word, a dwell is successive fixations if the fixations are within a specific AOI. The reason why the dwell was adopted in our data analysis is caused by the fact that we used two different types of eye tracking system. To elicit gaze patterns from raw eye movement data, we first determined AOIs in movies. As for infant body, we classified it into the following seven AOIs: Head, eye, mouth, upper arm, forearm, trunk and leg. Then we counted the number of dwells for each AOI and measured their duration.

Based on the durations of dwell for each AOI, gaze patterns were analyzed in terms both of holistic attention allocations and attention allocations just after epilepsies-like symptoms (i.e., motions in some places in infant body that may be unintentional/problematic ones.) In order to analyze holistic attention allocations, cumulative durations of dwell for each AOI were obtained for each participant. As for attention allocations just after epilepsies-like symptoms, this was analyzed by focusing on data around occurrence of the symptoms.

Table 1 summarizes the rate of duration for each AOI (holistic and after symptoms) for each participant group. The durations were calculated by summing up all durations for each AOI in each group. As for the data in after symptoms condition, we calculated the rates by using eye movement data for 3 s just after some symptom was observed.

3.2 Holistic Attention Allocation

By comparing the rates of duration of dwell for each AOI among four groups, we can find clear tendency along with expertise level. We think that the expertise level in infant epilepsies diagnosis is sophisticated in the following order: Student, intermediate, specialist and expert. It is conspicuous that more attention is paid to eyes by well-skilled nurses (i.e., Expert and specialist nurses). Expert and specialist nurses seemed to recognize that areas near eye (eye, head and mouth) are key areas since most of their attention was paid to very specific areas. The intermediate nurses seemed very close to the well-skilled nurses. As for nursing school students, however, they seemed to pay attention more widely. We can interpret that well-skilled nurses tended to pay their attention to eyes, while others tended to pay their attention to whole part of infant body.

3.3 Attention Allocations After Epilepsies-like Symptoms

As for the tendency in attention allocations after epilepsies-like symptoms, no clear difference was found from holistic attention allocations. Even though some problematic body symptoms occurred, the participants' attention allocation strategy seemed not to be influenced.

Table 1. Rate of duration of dwell for each AOI

AOIs	Expert		Specialist		Intermediate		Student	
	Holistic	After symptoms	Holistic	After symptoms	Holistic	After symptoms	Holistic	After symptoms
Head	16.5%	14.4%	2.9%	4.0%	5.3%	8.6%	14.8%	17.1%
Eye	66.5%	71.9%	64.6%	63.2%	60.3%	59.1%	44.7%	42.4%
Mouth	2.9%	3.7%	16.5%	19.0%	12.0%	16.6%	10.9%	10.6%
Upper arm	1.0%	0.6%	1.9%	1.5%	1.9%	2.2%	3.3%	3.7%
Forearm	2.6%	2.6%	1.6%	3.0%	2.4%	3.2%	6.1%	6.3%
Trunk	2.3%	6.4%	2.3%	2.3%	2.4%	1.8%	3.9%	1.9%
Leg	7.8%	0.5%	9.4%	7.0%	11.9%	3.5%	9.5%	8.2%
Others	0.4%	0.0%	0.8%	0.0%	3.9%	5.1%	6.9%	9.8%

4 Discussion

Considering the background/experience of expert and specialist nurses, we can expect that they have rich knowledge about the West syndrome and its phenomenology. The West syndrome's major root cause is a malfunction of neurotransmitter function in brain. This root cause is directly connected with not only unintentional motion in hands or foot, but also some unnatural eye movements. In primitive reflexes like Moro reflex, for example, unnatural eye movement is not observed in general. From our data, we can interpret that the well-skilled nurses paid more attention to face of an infant, which is directly connected with a root cause of the West syndrome (i.e., some malfunction of neurotransmitter function in brain), but less attention to physical symptoms such as unintentional motion in hands/foot. As a monitoring strategy, they may try not to miss critical sign of brain-related symptom during diagnosing infant epilepsies by keeping their gazes to eyes of the infant at any moment. As for nursing school students, they learnt basics of West syndrome in lectures. Their gaze pattern showing widely allocated attention tendency may reflect that they adopted an analytical process during diagnosing where each part of infant body was scanned.

There is clear convergence between the tendency found in our data analysis and previous visual expertise research in medical domain. As a grand tendency, it is said that expert tends to fixated to task-related key areas (such as areas directly connected with abnormality in mammograms tasks) more compared to novices [e.g., 4] Our result showing that the well-skilled nurses paid much of their attention to eyes and tried to keep it seems to coincides with the previous eye movement data-based expertise research in medicine.

5 Conclusion

This paper analyzed eye movement data during diagnosing infant epilepsies-like symptoms obtained from four different level of skill groups. We examined the tendency in both of holistic attention allocation and that just after epilepsies-like symptoms. By comparing the tendency among four nurses groups, we could identify well-skilled nurses' clear characteristics of the attention allocation processes. The well-skilled nurses tried to keep giving their attention to eyes of infant, meaning that they may recognize that the eyes were critical area since they are directly relating to the root cause of the West syndrome.

As a follow-up study, we are now conducting a research where medical doctors' eye movement data are recorded during performing the identical tasks. In the data analysis, the individual differences in gaze patterns will be examined by considering their expertise levels/clinical experiences. We also plan to discuss convergence between the tendency found in nurses and doctors.

Acknowledgement. This research was partly supported by Grant-in-Aid for Scientific Research (C), No. 18K04599, the Japan Society for the Promotion of Science. We also acknowledge our participants in the experiment, Hiroyuki Nishimagi and Shunta Seki for their great assistance for this research.

References

1. Fisher, R.S., et al.: ILAE official report: a practical clinical definition of epilepsy. Epilepsia 55(4), 475–482 (2014)
2. Dulac, O.: What is West syndrome? Brain Developement 23(7), 447–452 (2001)
3. Blascheck, T., Kurzhals, K., Raschke, M., Burch, M., Weiskopf, D., Ertl, T.: Visualization of eye tracking data: a taxonomy and survey. Comput. Graph. Forum 36(8), 260–284 (2017)
4. Reingold, E.M., Sheridan, H.: Eye movements and visual expertise in chess and medicine. In: Liversedge, S.P., Gilchrist, I.D., Everling, S. (eds.) Oxford Handbook on Eye Movements, pp. 528–550. Oxford University Press, Oxford (2011)

Technology-Enhanced Training System for Reducing Separation Anxiety in Dogs

Carlos Arce-Lopera[✉], Javier Diaz-Cely, Paula García, and María Morales

Engineering Faculty, Universidad Icesi, Calle 18 No. 122-135, Cali 760031, Colombia
{caarce, jgdiaz}@icesi.edu.co

Abstract. Separation anxiety in dogs is a common condition that is manifested by destructive behavior when dogs are left alone. The most successful treatment for canine separation-related problems requires dog's behavior modification via a time consuming training. Moreover, this type of training needs a high commitment from the dog's owner. Here, a canine wearable interface connected to a mobile application was designed to monitor and guide a training program aiming at behavior modification in dogs. The objective was to design a system that enhances user engagement while monitoring dog's biometrical signals. Preliminary testing of the system revealed significant behavior changes. Significant decrease in dog's overall destructive behavior was recorded. Specifically, when using the technology-enhanced vest, dogs were quieter and reduced their anxious movements. These preliminary results support the idea that technology-enhanced training is a feasible alternative to motivate and guide owners to implement separation training with their dogs.

Keywords: Wearable · Separation anxiety · Dog training

1 Introduction

Dogs are highly social animals capable of forming social attachments to members of their own or other species [1]. However, the ease to form social attachments also make them prone to disruptive behavior when separated. Indeed, separation anxiety in dogs is a common condition and is manifested by dogs adopting destructive behavior when left alone, like barking, chewing or eliminating in the house [2]. One of the most successful treatment for canine separation-related problems is behavior modification. Particularly, systematic desensitization combined with counter-conditioning has proven to be a successful solution that does not involve expensive medication [3]. However, to implement such a strategy the owner requires a strong commitment. Here, a technology-enhanced training system that guided owners through the behavior modification process was developed. The objective was to design a system that improves user engagement and uses biometric feedback from the dog.

© Springer Nature Switzerland AG 2019
C. Stephanidis (Ed.): HCII 2019, CCIS 1034, pp. 434–439, 2019.
https://doi.org/10.1007/978-3-030-23525-3_58

2   Methods

The system is divided in two main components: a wearable vest and a mobile application. The vest communicates with the mobile application via Bluetooth and the Internet. The mobile application monitored the process of the behavior training for the dog and guided the owner through the different exercises in the separation anxiety training routine.

2.1   Wearable Design

The wearable vest (see Fig. 1) included an inclinometer, four vibro-tactile actuators, a Bluetooth module, a power module and an e-textile microcontroller (LilyPad Arduino). All electronic components were sewed using conductive thread. The vest was designed for dog's comfort using soft but durable breathable materials. The upper part of the vest used an anti-fluid type of cloth to prevent water to access the electronic components. Moreover, to enable testing of different breeds of dog, the vest used a one size fits all design using adjustable Velcro strap and buckles for improved fit.

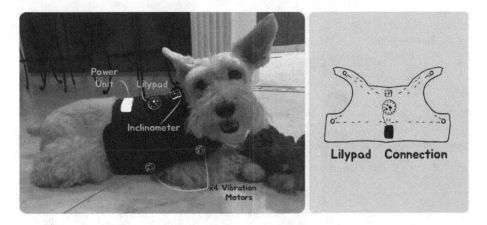

Fig. 1. A schematic view of the wearable system.

The inclinometer values were used by the system to predict the dog's behavior using their movement. The inclinometer was positioned at the back of the dog's neck and transmitted data via Bluetooth to the stand alone application connected to the internet (see Fig. 2B). The inclinometer monitored three dimensional accelerations, three dimensional angular velocities and three dimensional angles of the module. To calibrate the system and to build the behavior predictive model for each dog, a calibration period was performed. In this calibration phase, the user had to label the behavior of the dog using the mobile application. After the calibration period, a behavior prediction model for each dog that participated was developed using machine learning techniques and the data outputs of the inclinometer.

The four vibro-tactile actuators serve as stimuli to be used as counterconditioning when the system classified the dog's behavior as anxious. The system was design such that the vibro-tactile stimuli was interpreted by the dogs as a positive stimulus similar to a petting session with the owner. This association between the vest tactile stimuli as a positive interaction must be trained to the dog. The mobile application has a calibration module designed for ensuring that this association was met.

2.2   Mobile Application Design

On the other hand, the mobile application was designed to guide the use of the system allowing the owner to personalize and record dog's training process. The vest communication is via Bluetooth to a local host computer. The computer uses a cloud-based database service to record each event. The mobile application was connected to the cloud-based database via the Internet (see Fig. 2B). Moreover, the mobile application was designed to contain three modules and allowed training control and fostered motivation for continued monitoring of the training (see Fig. 2A).

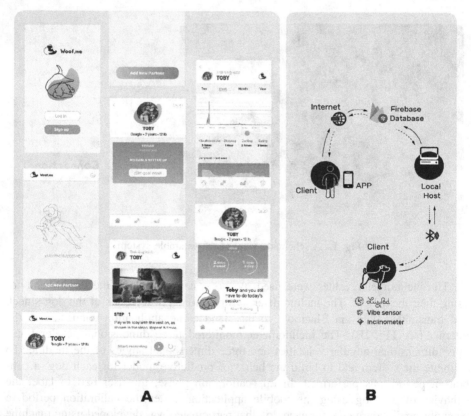

A   **B**

Fig. 2. Mobile application design. The left side 2A shows a mockup version of the main features of the mobile application. The right side 2B shows the communication schematic of the system.

The first module of the mobile application allowed the personalization of the training. In this module, all information about the training configuration were set allowing dog and owner characterization based on time scheduling and goal expectations in time. Moreover, the module provided guiding through the necessary calibration of the vest's actuators and sensor based on the particular dog's behavior. The calibration routine was set as a list of activities needed to be performed by the owner and dog to characterize the particular biometrics of the dog.

The second module was the training breakout and activity guide tailored to the specific dog. The designed training session take into account the information recorded in the calibration phase. Furthermore, each training session had a video explanation of the routine. When the owner was ready to begin, the mobile application guided the interaction with the dog and monitored the dog's biometrics. In the latter phases of the training, the behavior predictive model activated automatically the actuators depending on the state of the dog.

Finally, the third module was a report visualization module, targeting at showing the history of the training to evaluate performance and to boost motivation.

2.3 Experimental Design

The system's modules were tested using five dogs. Three of the dogs were Beagles, one was a Pug and the other was a Schnauzer (see Fig. 3). All dog owners were informed about the purpose of the study and consented voluntarily to participate.

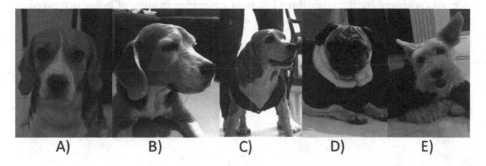

A)   B)   C)   D)   E)

Fig. 3. Subjects of the study.

First, a video recording of all dogs when they were left alone was taken to analyze the particular anxious behavior of the dogs in a separation condition. After the video was taken, each owner had to fill a questionnaire when watching and rating the video. The owner had to fill the perceived behavior modification of their dogs using a 5-step Likert scale. The questionnaire asked to describe the behavior in four main categories: perceived anxious vocalizations, perceived physical distress, perceived destructive behavior and perceived aggressiveness towards people.

Perceived anxious vocalizations referred to the amount of barking, howling, crying and growling made by the dogs while alone, as perceived by their owners. Perceived physical distress referred to the physical uneasiness displayed by the dog's anxious motion and other body language, like having their ears back or their tail tucked between the legs. Perceived destructive behavior was the amount of perceived damage the dog inflicted when left alone, for example, when dogs scratched walls or bit objects and furniture. Finally, the perceived aggressiveness towards people referred to the perception of hostile behavior when strange people approached them.

After the characterization of the severity of the separation anxiety problem, the owners were instructed to familiarize the dog with the vest. Then, they had to calibrate both the sensor and the actuators. The mobile application suggested different activities to be able to perform this calibration as fast as possible. After the calibration was completed, the training could start. The owners were instructed to put the vest on the dog and leave. Video was recorded while the dog was alone wearing the vest. Using the same questionnaire and new video, owners were asked to describe the dog's behavior. Moreover, movement of the dogs was analyzed to determine the differences between vest and no vest conditions.

3   Results

Preliminary testing of the system revealed significant behavior changes in the dogs. Particularly, a statistically significant decrease ($t(5) = 2.8$; $p < 0,05$) in their overall destructive behavior was recorded (see Fig. 4). Indeed, dogs without the vest were significantly perceived as more destructive ($m = 3.5$; $SD = 2.3$) than when they had the system on ($m = 1.6$; $SD = 1.0$). On the other hand, no statistically significant difference was achieved for the other three behavior categories in spite of being perceived as being on average lower for the condition when dogs wore the system.

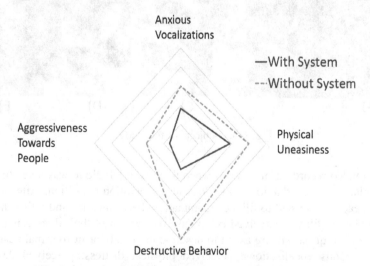

Fig. 4. Results of the perceived behavior modification for the dogs.

Using the video recordings, analysis of the dog's movement revealed that the dogs reduced their anxious movements when wearing the vest. Figure 5 shows the overview of the location of the dog Fig. 3C as a two dimensional heat map for both conditions: wearing the vest (see Fig. 5B) and without the vest (see Fig. 5A). This example showed that the system prevented dogs to wander in the enclosed space when left alone. This pattern was consistent for all dogs.

A)   B)

Fig. 5. Heat map of the movement of dog Fig. 3C. The left image 5A shows the movement of the dog when left alone in the balcony without wearing the system. The right image 5B shows the movement when the dog is wearing the technology-enhanced vest.

In-depth interviews with dog's owners revealed that the vest was comfortable for their dogs and did not restrict their movement. Also, the owners perceived decrease in all negative behaviors related with separation anxiety. However, full continued training sessions with the dogs remain to be performed to assess the real impact of the system on dog's behavior. Also, the mobile application needs to evaluate the user engagement as the application design emphasized ways so the owner had a high motivation and persisted with the training. Finally, the vest needs to incorporate an efficient energy control and management to be able to record dog's behavior for long-lasting training sessions.

4 Conclusion

These preliminary results support the idea that technology-enhanced training is a feasible alternative to motivate and guide owners to implement separation training with their dogs. Further research is needed to implement the training in different days and test for long term effects.

References

1. McCrave, E.A.: Diagnostic criteria for separation anxiety in the dog. Vet. Clin. North Am. Small Anim. Pract. **21**, 247–255 (1991)
2. Borchelt, P.L., Voith, V.L.: Diagnosis and treatment of separation-related behavior problems in dogs. Vet. Clin. North Am. Small Anim. Pract. **12**, 625–635 (1982)
3. Sargisson, R.J.: Canine separation anxiety: strategies for treatment and management. Vet. Med. Res. Rep. **5**, 143–151 (2014)

Persuasive Design Strategy of Health Education in Interaction Design for the Elderly Adults

Yongyan Guo[1,2], Wei Ding[1,2(✉)], and Yongjing Guo[1,2]

[1] School of Art Design and Media, East China University of Science and Technology, Shanghai, China
g_gale@163.com, dw.6789@163.com, 57619873@qq.com
[2] Satellite TV Channel of Jiangsu Broadcasting Corporation, Nanjing, China

Abstract. There are three points in the current situation and problems of health education for urban elderly in China. First, the health education service for the elderly adults is simple and with low technology. Second, the service object is narrow to the sick people. Third, because of the decline of the information contact ability, the elderly adults have some difficulties in learning health education information. To use persuasive strategies to improve the educational effect with the help of the new technology is a good choice for them. Therefore, this paper focuses on using the Persuasive Strategy Design(PSD) to promote elderly adults participation in health education.

Research methods: The Likert five scale was used to investigate the seniors' perception experience evaluation on the questionnaire of interactively persuasive strategies. The evaluation data was analyzed by Spass 20. The most important strategic factors were extracted by the factor analysis for the elderly adults to accept health education easily. Then these strategies were explained to help design a health education prototype to meet needs of the elderly adults.

Keywords: Aging · Health education · Persuasive strategy · Interaction design

1 Introduction

1.1 Problems of Aging Population Development and Health Education

With the acceleration of population aging, the issue of health care is attracting more and more attention in China. By the end of 2010, China's population over the age of 60 has reached 178 million, accounting for 13.26% of the total population. In 2008, the results of the national health service survey showed that by the end of June 2012, the number of people aged 65 and above was 97 million 122 thousand, and half of them had been suffering from a variety of chronic diseases. If the corresponding health education and health management is 5-10 years ahead of schedule, the incidence of the elder adults will be reduced, which will reduce social medical insurance by a large proportion.

Health education is an important part of the health management system for the elderly. The aim is to make elder adults get necessary health knowledge that are

© Springer Nature Switzerland AG 2019
C. Stephanidis (Ed.): HCII 2019, CCIS 1034, pp. 440–445, 2019.
https://doi.org/10.1007/978-3-030-23525-3_59

beneficial to physical and mental health through various organized activities, to prevent and reduce the occurrence of senile diseases, enhance physical and mental health and prolong life [1, 2].

1.2 Persuasive Technology

The persuasion theory was first put forward by Fogg [3], an experimental psychologist at Stanford University. Persuasive technology was defined as an interactive computing system to form, change or enhance people's attitudes and behaviors. This theory is built on the basis of psychology and behavior research, and has been valued gradually along with the development of information technology.

Persuasive design (PSD) is a new field of research. System Process Model (Oinas-Kukkonen and Harjumaa) [4] is a model of persuasive design for information system based on previous research. This model is composed of three different parts:

(1) understand the key factors behind the persuasive system; (2) analyze the persuasion background; (3) choose and design the system strategy. It gives seven assumptions behind the persuasion system, and proposes a framework model for improving the persuasive effect of the system, which is mostly used in the design of the information architecture of the interaction system.

1.3 The Practical Significance of Persuasive Theory in Health Education

The theory of persuasion is the basis for the development of information technology [5, 6]. The research content is how to make it easier for the elderly to accept the information of health education in a non coercive way through persuasive design [7].

In 2013, *Suggestions on Promoting the Development of Health Service Industry* was proposed to promote the development of the medical information industry, make full use of the existing information and network facilities, and realize the sharing of medical security, medical services, health education and other information as soon as possible [8].

In conclusion, it is important to improve the health education level of the elderly by persuasive technologies. The study of the persuasive design theory and the persuasive design methodology established in the health field will contribute to the innovation of the intelligent service and the health education, and make a positive contribution to the "healthy aging" goal of the aging society in China.

2 Factor Analysis Method

The factor analysis method is a statistical analysis method, which is based on the dependence of the research variables, and some complex variables is summed up into a few comprehensive factors. The four basic steps in the factor analysis are as follows: (1) To confirm the original variables to be analyzed is suitable for factor analysis. (2) To structure factor variables. (3) Rotation matrix is used to make factor variables more interpretable. (4) The name and interpretation of factors are done.

3 Factor Analysis of Persuasion Design Strategy

3.1 Questionnaire Design

The health questionnaire is designed according to three steps: first is to compare the existing persuasion design models according to the literature retrieval at home and abroad. The second is to design the questionnaire according to the special needs of the persuasive design model (Oinas-Kukkonen and Harjumaa) and the health education interactive system. The third is to modify the factors in the questionnaire according to expert consultation and small-scale user research.

The subjects of this study were people over 50 years old. The subjects were asked to evaluate the persuasive strategy of health education in the questionnaire. The scores are set by the Likert five scale, of which 1 represents very disapproved, 5 represents very agreeing, and 3 represents indifferent. Finally, 300 questionnaires were issued online and offline, and 287 were recovered, with a recovery rate of 95.7%.

3.2 Questionnaire Analysis

The factor exploration method is used to analyze the data with SPSS software as follows (Table 1):

Table 1. KMO and Bartlett's Test

Kaiser-Meyer-Olkin Measure of Sampling Adequacy		.923
Bartlett's Test of Sphericity	Approx. Chi-Square	10453.578
	df	595
	Sig.	.000

Factor analysis requires strong correlation between original variables. In KMO (Kaiser-Meyer-Olkin) test, if KMO value is closer to 1, it is more suitable for factor analysis. In this case KMO > 0.8 which is considered very suitable for factor analysis. The significance coefficient of Bartlett's sphericity test is 0, which is less than 0.01. It means that this study reaches a remarkable level (Table 2).

Table 2. Total variance explained

Component	Initial eigenvalues			Extraction sums of squared loadings			Rotation sums of squared loadings		
	Total	% of variance	Cumulative %	Total	% of variance	Cumulative %	Total	% of variance	Cumulative %
1	20.074	57.355	57.355	20.074	57.355	57.355	5.389	15.397	15.397
2	1.465	4.187	61.542	1.465	4.187	61.542	5.311	15.175	30.572
3	1.184	3.384	64.925	1.184	3.384	64.925	5.219	14.911	45.483
4	1.175	3.358	68.283	1.175	3.358	68.283	4.647	13.278	58.762
5	1.006	2.876	71.158	1.006	2.876	71.158	4.339	12.397	71.158

According to the factor analysis, 5 main factors are extracted, and characteristic root values are more than 1, accounting for 71.158% of the total variance, which can explain most of the differences of variables. These 5 factors are the main factors that constitute the 35 project variables of the original questionnaire. This extraction effect can also be seen from the scree plot. It is appropriate that 5 factors were extracted before the sharp turning of the curve.

In order to clearly explain the meaning of the main factor, the factor matrix is used to carry out variance maxima orthogonal rotation to get a project with high load on every main factor. The contents of each item and the value of the load are as follows (Table 3):

Table 3. Rotation matrix

Factor1		Factor2		Factor3		Factor4		Factor5	
Variable	Load value	Variable	Load value	Variable	Load value	Variable	Load value	Variable	Load value
E33	.676	E20	.736	E1	.676	E28	.780	E25	.759
E34	.672	E2	.632	E35	.624	E26	.666	E29	.631
E10	.616	E23	.632	E19	.609	E7	.658	E30	.592
E12	.609	E11	.591	E21	.590	E6	.621	E17	.583
E8	.580	E4	.561	E5	.568	E16	.590	E15	.508
E14	.549	E31	.551	E3	.522	E27	.515		
E22	.543								
E18	.519								

3.3   Factor Analysis

The five categories of factors that have the greatest contribution to the results of the analysis are named as follows: F1 "Factor of value-added service", F2 "Factor of system trust support", F3 "Factor of major task support", F4 "Factor of Game strategy" and F5 "Factor of incentive mechanism". These five factors account for 71.158% of the total contribution. Designing and improving these five factors will greatly enhance the perceived satisfaction of elderly users to the health education system. Factor interpretation is as the Table 4 below.

Table 4. Factor Interpretation

Factor	Subitem	Content
F1 Value-added service	E33	Buying medicine service
	E34	Interpretation of medical information
	E10	Feedback of graphic information
	E12	Medical help
	E8	Emotional supervision
	E14	remind
	E22	Clear guidance
	E18	Interface professionalism
F2 System Trust Support	E20	Interface for the elderly
	E2	Simulation process

(continued)

Table 4. (*continued*)

Factor	Subitem	Content
	E23	Authoritative
	E11	Historical information record
	E4	Health monitoring
	E31	First aid measures
F3 Major Task Support	E1	Reduce the amount of information
	E35	Imitation and guidance
	E19	Privacy protection
	E21	Convenience and reliability
	E5	Diet information
	E3	Individualization
F4 Game strategy (E16, Exchange of Accumulated points)	E28	Cooperative question and answer
	E26	Competitive learning
	E7	Sleep supervision
	E6	Sports supervision
	E16	Exchange of accumulation point
	E27	Game learning
F5 incentive mechanism	E25	Making friends
	E29	Social incentive
	E30	Interest
	E17	Medal incentive
	E15	Ranking incentive

4   Conclusions

Through literature review, the persuasive theory is introduced. The study was conducted in the way of interviews and small seminars. At the same time, persuasion strategies were analyzed by the methods of online and offline questionnaires, and five major factors of health education for the elderly were found by factor analysis. Finally, based on the above research results, the interactive prototype of health education APP for elder adults is designed to explore the health education mode which is more in line with the Chinese elderly needs and Chinese culture.

Acknowledgements. This study is supported by the Youth Fund for Humanities and Social Sciences Research of the Ministry of Education, No. 17YJCZH055. This paper is supported by the Shanghai Open Fund for Class IV Top Disciplines of Design in 2018, No. DA18304. This study is supported by key curriculum projects in Shanghai, No. YZ0126121.

References

1. Han, H.: The effect of prevention and treatment of chronic diseases in the health education and management in the community. Chin. Med. Sci. **14**, 99–101, 144 (2017)
2. Ning, X., Aiping, Z.: Evaluation of effect of health education on hypertension patients. J. Clin. Nurs. **1**, 27–30 (2011)
3. Fogg, B.J.: Creating persuasive technologies: an eight-step design process. In: Proceedings of the 4th International Conference on Persuasive Technology (Persuasive 09), Claremont, CA, pp. 1–6 (2009)
4. Oinas-Kukkonen, H., et al.: Persuasive 2008. LNCS, vol. 5033, pp. 164–176. Springer, Heidelberg (2008). https://doi.org/10.1007/978-3-540-68504-3
5. Yusoff, M.F., Zulkifli, A.N., Mohamed, N.F.F.: The model of persuasive Hajj learning environment. Jurnal Teknologi (Sci. Eng.) **77**(5), 141–147 (2015)
6. Tørning, K.: A Review of Four Persuasive Design Models (2013). https://doi.org/10.4018/ijcssa.2013070103
7. Jiancaro, T., Jamieson, G.A., Mihailidis, A.: Twenty years of cognitive work analysis in health care: a scoping review. J. Cogn. Eng. Decis. Making **8**(1), 3–22 (2013). https://doi.org/10.1177/1555343413488391
8. Ye Jilin, W., Ailian, W.D.: New requirements for health education of the chronic disease under the background of the aging. Chin. Contemp. Med. **28**, 166–168 (2014)

Commercial Activity Trackers Overestimate Step Count: Implications for Ambulatory Activity Monitoring

Albert Hernandez, Toyin Ajisafe[⊠], Byung Cheol Lee, and Junfei Xie

Texas A&M University – Corpus Christi, Corpus Christi, TX, USA
toyin.ajisafe@tamucc.edu

Abstract. Guidelines for Physical Activity (PA) include a minimum of 150 min of moderate PA each week for adults, and at least 60 daily minutes of moderate-to-vigorous PA for youth aged 6–17 years. The burden to monitor self-compliance lies on the individual and involves tracking content, intensity, and temporal breakdown of daily activities while delineating these as light-, moderate-, or vigorous-intensity. Presenting PA recommendations as steps per day makes them more accessible. Inaccurate step counts can mislead individuals looking to meet recommendations using a step count paradigm. This research evaluated the degree to which wrist and hip worn activity trackers misattribute steps to non-ambulatory activities and overestimate total step count. An adult male (age: 41 years; height: 1.7 m; mass: 74 kg) wore a Fitbit Versa and Apple Watch on his wrist and a Withings Go and an Apple iPhone 7-deployed Pedometer++ application on his lateral hip. The participant walked and ran for a total of 84 and 100 steps, respectively, and performed 20 vertical jumps, 20 bilateral hops, 20 squats, and 20 sit-to-stand tasks. The mean step count and percent error between observed step count and total step count output from each device were calculated. Fitbit Versa, Apple Watch, Pedometer++, and Withings Go overestimated total step count by 110%, 126%, 48%, 97%, respectively. It was concluded that both low- and high-end commercial activity trackers attribute steps to non-ambulatory activities and consequently overestimate step count. This can mislead individuals who rely on these activity trackers to monitor their step count. Therefore, there is need for algorithms with improved activity recognition.

Keywords: Commercial activity trackers · Step count · Wrist worn sensors · Physical activity recommendations · Non-ambulatory activities

1 Introduction

Recurrent physical activity (PA) is critical to controlling or preventing excessive body weight and decreasing the risk of adverse metabolic outcomes, including many types of cancer [1, 2]. Physical Activity Guidelines for Americans recommends a minimum of 150 weekly minutes of moderate PA for adults, and at least 60 daily minutes of moderate-to-vigorous PA for children and adolescents aged 6–17 years [2]. Although

C. Stephanidis (Ed.): HCII 2019, CCIS 1034, pp. 446–451, 2019.
https://doi.org/10.1007/978-3-030-23525-3_60

the requisite PA level to maintain a healthy weight or decrease excess body weight would expectedly vary between individuals, it is commonly thought that for many, greater than 150 weekly minutes of moderate-intensity PA is necessary to maintain their current weight [2, 3]. PA tends to prevent weight gain when done at moderate- or vigorous-intensity and is aerobic in nature [2]. Monitoring self-compliance necessitates that an individual tracks the content, intensity, and temporal breakdown of their daily activities and delineate them as light-, moderate-, or vigorous-intensity PA. There has been a strong interest among researchers to present PA recommendations as number of steps accumulated over the course of different temporal scales, in order to make them more accessible and tractable to the lay public.

De Craemer et al. [3] found varying step count equivalents depending on the regression cut-point used; therefore, they proposed a daily step count of 11,500 to approximate 180 min of PA activity in preschoolers. Conversely, Gabel, et al. [4] proposed that 6000 steps approximate 180 min of daily PA. Guidelines for American children 3–5 years old have since been updated from 180 daily minutes to being physically active throughout the day [2]. Tudor-Locke, et al. [5] concluded that walking at an average cadence of 100 steps per minute correspond to moderate-intensity among young adult males and females. Silva, et al. [6] suggested 12,000 daily steps as the optimal count for children and adolescents for meeting PA recommendations. Fitbit encourages a goal of 250 steps every hour to break up sedentary behavior and engender healthy benefits.

Biomechanically, a step is the interval between initial contact on one foot and initial contact on the contralateral foot along the plane of progression [7, 8]. While lateral hip wear is considered optimal for tracking PA, it likely constitutes a new habit and may require reeducation for many users. Hip-worn accelerometers do not detect activities like cycling [9, 10]. Wrist watches are widely used accessories. Wrist-worn activity trackers (equipped with time display) seamlessly fit into everyday sartorial habits, thereby precluding the need for user re-education. This may explain the ubiquity of wrist-worn commercial activity trackers. Although pedometers and accelerometers have demonstrated convergent and criterion validity (i.e., for step count) during running and walking [11, 12], the extent to which wrist- and hip-worn accelerometers may misattribute steps to non-ambulatory activities and consequently overestimate step count is not lucid.

The purpose of this research was to evaluate the degree to which both wrist worn and hip worn activity trackers misattribute steps to non-ambulatory activities and misestimate overall step count.

2 Experiment

2.1 Protocol

An adult male (age: 41 years; height: 1.7 m; mass: 74 kg) wore a Fitbit Versa (Fitbit, San Francisco, CA) and Apple Watch (Apple Inc., Cupertino, CA) on his right and left wrists, respectively. The participant also secured a Withings Go tracker (Nokia, Espoo, Finland) and an Apple iPhone 7-deployed Pedometer++ application (Cross Forward Consulting LLC) to his lateral hip using an attached clip and an elastic waist band, respectively. The participant walked and ran for a total of 84 and 100 steps, respectively, on a non-motorized single belt CURVE treadmill (WOODWAY, Waukesha, WI). The participant then performed 20 vertical jumps, 20 bilateral hops (at their preferred frequency), 20 squats and 20 sit-to-stand tasks. A sit-to-stand task was delineated as rising from a seated position in a chair (i.e., with hips and knees at approximately 90° flexion) to a fully upright standing position (i.e., with the hips and knees at approximately 180° extension), and lowering back down to a seated position. The participant performed three separate trials of each task. The frequency of each task criterion, e.g., number of steps and jumps, was counted by a direct observer. Texas A&M University – Corpus Christi Institutional Review Board approved this study.

2.2 Data Analysis

The number of steps on the respective device application dashboards were recorded before and after each task. The difference between the initial and final step count was the step attributed to the task by the device. The mean and standard deviation (SD) of the step count were calculated across three repeated trials for each device. Corresponding coefficients of variation (i.e., quotient of SD and mean expressed as a percentage) were also calculated. The percent error between directly observed step count and overall step count output from each device was calculated.

3 Results and Discussion

The current work explored the degree to which commercial activity trackers increment step count during non-ambulatory activities. Fitbit Versa, Apple Watch, Pedometer++, and Withings Go had errors of 4%, 1%, 0.4%, and 1% (Fig. 1a), respectively, for running; the respective errors for walking were 11%, 8%, 5%, and 2% (Fig. 1b). The increased errors for walking are consistent with previous findings of decreased pedometer accuracy at slower ambulatory speeds [11]. Each device (even when worn on the hip) incorrectly attributed steps to non-ambulatory tasks (Figs. 1c–f) and consequently overestimated overall step count by considerable margins (Table 1). This work has several limitations, including the absence of hypothesis testing owing to the sample size. The research needs to be furthered with additional participants and more non-ambulatory tasks, including hand clapping.

(a)

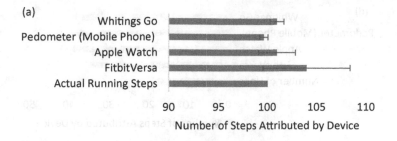

(b)

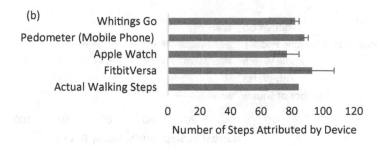

(c)

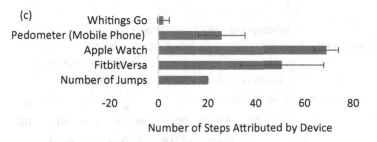

Fig. 1. Steps attributed (by devices) to (a) running, (b) walking, (c) vertical jumping, (d) hopping, (e) squatting, and (f) sit-to-standing

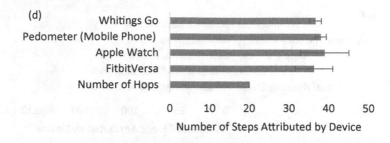

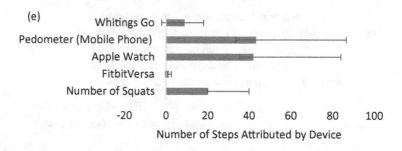

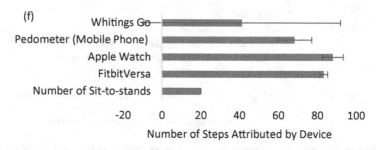

Fig. 2. Steps attributed (by devices) to (a) running, (b) walking, (c) vertical jumping, (d) hopping, (e) squatting, and (f) sit-to-standing

Table 1. Overall step count error by device

Device	Total step count attributed	Actual/Observed step count	Percent error
Fitbit versa	387	184	110%
Apple watch	415	184	126%
Withings go	272	184	48%
Pedometer++	363	184	97%

4   Conclusion

It was concluded that both low- and high-end commercial activity trackers attribute steps to non-ambulatory activities and consequently overestimate step count. This can mislead lay individuals who rely on achieving their PA goals by monitoring their step count. There is a need for algorithms with improved activity recognition, especially while leveraging the popularity of wrist worn sensors.

References

1. Lauby-Secretan, B., et al.: Body fatness and cancer-viewpoint of the IARC working group. N. Engl. J. Med. **375**, 794–798 (2016)
2. Physical Activity Guidelines for Americans, 2nd edn. U.S. Department of Health and Human Services (2018)
3. De Craemer, M., De Decker, E., De Bourdeaudhuij, I., Verloigne, M., Manios, Y., Cardon, G.: The translation of preschoolers' physical activity guidelines into a daily step count target. J. Sports Sci. **33**, 1051–1057 (2015)
4. Gabel, L., et al.: Step count targets corresponding to new physical activity guidelines for the early years. Med. Sci. Sports Exerc. **45**, 314–318 (2013)
5. Tudor-Locke, C., Sisson, S.B., Collova, T., Lee, S.M., Swan, P.D.: Pedometer-determined step count guidelines for classifying walking intensity in a young ostensibly healthy population. Can. J. Appl. Physiol. **30**, 666–676 (2005)
6. Silva, M.P., Fontana, F.E., Callahan, E., Mazzardo, O., De Campos, W.: Step-count guidelines for children and adolescents: a systematic review. J. Phys. Act. Health **12**, 1184–1191 (2015)
7. Whittle, M., Richards, J., Levine, D.: Whittle's Gait Analysis. Churchill Livingstone, London (2012)
8. Winter, D.A.: Biomechanics and Motor Control of Human Movement, 4th edn. Wiley, Hoboken (2009)
9. Bassett Jr., D.R., Ainsworth, B.E., Swartz, A.M., Strath, S.J., O'Brien, W.L., King, G.A.: Validity of four motion sensors in measuring moderate intensity physical activity. Med. Sci. Sports Exerc. **32**, S471–S480 (2000)
10. Hendelman, D., Miller, K., Baggett, C., Debold, E., Freedson, P.: Validity of accelerometry for the assessment of moderate intensity physical activity in the field. Med. Sci. Sports Exerc. **32**, S442–S449 (2000)
11. Tudor-Locke, C., Williams, J.E., Reis, J.P., Pluto, D.: Utility of pedometers for assessing physical activity: convergent validity. Sports Med. **32**, 795–808 (2002)
12. Godfrey, A., Del Din, S., Barry, G., Mathers, J.C., Rochester, L.: Instrumenting gait with an accelerometer: a system and algorithm examination. Med. Eng. Phys. **37**, 400–407 (2015)

iGlow: Visualizing a Person's Energy Level Through Hand Motion

Triet Minh Huynh, Bhagyalakshmi Muthucumar,
and Dvijesh Shastri[(✉)]

Department of Computer Science and Engineering Technology,
University of Houston-Downtown, Houston, TX, USA
{huynht32,muthucumarb1}@gator.uhd.edu,
shastrid@uhd.edu

Abstract. This research proposes a novel approach of providing fitness feed-back in wearable devices. Current fitness wearables on the market primarily provide statistical feedback in the forms of graphical representations of the collected data such as activity tread lines, activity rings, activity bars, etc. We propose a wearable wristband with a built-in LED whose light intensity is altered according to the users' physical activity – higher the activity level brighter the LED light. More specifically, we have designed and developed an Arduino-based prototype device that collects accelerometer data from hand motion, and then maps the hand motion data into light intensity. Such a device can have numerous applications in health and fitness as well as for entertainment purpose, as the device can emit light accordingly to hand motion, which gives users visual feedback/cues on their energy exertion.

Keywords: Fitness wearables · Physical activity · Accelerometer

1 Introduction

Recently, there has been a surge in demand for "smart" devices such as Apple Watch, Samsung Watch, or Fitbit due to their ability to provide fitness feedback which acts as a reward to help motivate users to stay on the fitness track. The feedback is typically in the forms of graphical representation (e.g., activity tread lines, activity ring, activity bar graphs) of the physical activity data such as number of steps or calories burned. Through this research, we propose a different fitness feedback approach. We introduce a wearable wristband that maps physical activity data to light intensity of a built-in LED on the surface of the wristband. Depending on the brightness of the LED, the users will be aware of how vigorous they are performing a particular physical activity, so that they can strive to adjust their effort accordingly. This visual form of feedback is both more straightforward and convenient compared to the statistical feedback. The proposed device can use not only for fitness activities but also for entertainment purpose such as a dance party.

Our research was inspired from a case study that was conducted to see how nightclubs of the future might be impacted by the collaboration of creative industries [1]. This case study was conducted over a period of two days by the Dutch National

© Springer Nature Switzerland AG 2019
C. Stephanidis (Ed.): HCII 2019, CCIS 1034, pp. 452–456, 2019.
https://doi.org/10.1007/978-3-030-23525-3_61

Research Institute for Mathematics and Computer Science (Centrum Wiskunde & Informatica or CWI). The objective was to see how a nightclub experience can be curated and enhanced with technologies by appealing to all five senses of the participants.

For this study, a fashion label expert was hired to design custom food menus, sound, lighting and scents. The researchers' goal was to analyze the impact of the surrounding environment on the participants of the dance event. To do this, CWI designed wristbands using Raspberry Pi that were fitted with Bluetooth transmitters and have the participants wear these wristbands. A venue was rented out for a period of two days which was fitted with dozens of Bluetooth sensors in the walls. The point of this was to have the data of the wearer to be transmitted to the base stations which then be transmitted to a control center [2]. There was a total of 900 guests who were invited to the event, so the traffic of data was extremely high. The dataset consisted of temperature and accelerometer readings, and depending on the readings, the researchers could customize the environment of a specific room by changing the lightning and sound. After that, the researchers observed to see how the participants responded to the interference being made to the environment, which would indicate the effect of using technology for enhancing environment to create desired response.

Our device is geared toward reflecting individual's energy exertion more than a group setting. We have designed and developed a wristband using Arduino board, an accelerometer and a LED. The aim of this research is to develop a wearable device providing visual cues to motivate and influence people in terms of fitness and entertainment.

2 Methodology

The research is broken down into 5 major phases as shown in Fig. 1.

2.1 Data Collection

Our initial hardware consideration for this project was Arduino board to quickly develop a usable prototype as a proof of concept. Arduino provides built-in libraries for a variety of tasks which make the process of data extraction easier [3].

We built a simple circuit consisting of the Arduino Nano board, the Adafruit LIS3DH triple-axis accelerometer, HC-05 Bluetooth module, and a LED. The circuit measures acceleration of the user's hand on three axes using the LIS3DH accelerometer, and the data can then be sent serially to a computer using the HC-05 Bluetooth module. Like any other wearable, it is a miniature embedded computing system [4].

The accelerometer generates two sets of signals. One set is consisted of three positional vectors – one vector per axis – which represent hand position in the 3D space. The other set is consisted of three acceleration vectors – one vector per axis – which represent hand acceleration in the 3D space. In this design, we mainly focused on the acceleration vectors. Data is collected at 10 Hz frequency.

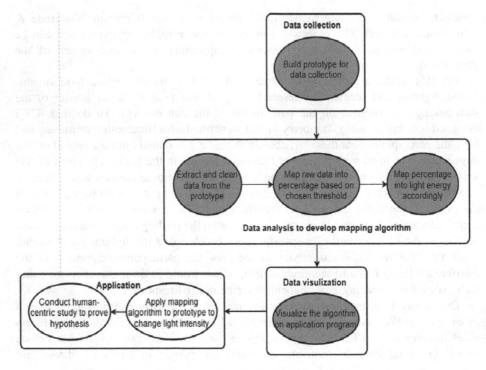

Fig. 1. Project pipeline (finished phases are colored)

2.2   Data Analysis

Once the data is collected, the next step is to analyze the data and come up with an algorithm to map the acceleration data collected to light intensity. The digital LED installed on the circuit takes values in the range from 0 to 255. Therefore, the algorithm must map the accelerations in all three axes to a single light intensity in that range such that it would provide smooth transition of light intensity while the circuit moves around in space. The algorithm we have come up with achieves this mapping in three steps: (1) normalize the raw data, (2) map the normalized data to light intensity, and (3) update the light intensity.

Normalize the Raw Data

The raw data normalization requires the information of the maximum and minimum values of the acceleration on all three axes. The minimum value represents no activity and maximum value represents highest possible acceleration of the human hand. Through lab trials, we found average values of no activity of our device are 0.0925, 0.5638, and 9.4508 m/s^2 for x, y, z axes respectively, and average values of highest acceleration are $\pm$ 40.0 m/s^2 for x, y, z axes respectively. The normalized values at any given time $t(x, y, z)$ is calculated using the following formula:

$$Normalized\ Data(x,y,z)_t = \frac{\left|Raw\ Acceleration(x,y,z)_t - No\ Acceleration(x,y,z)\right|}{\left|Highest\ Acceleration(x,y,z) - No\ Acceleration(x,y,z)\right|}$$

$$(1)$$

The normalized values are in the range of 0 to 1 where 0 represents no activity and 1 represents maximum activity at a given time (t).

Mapping Normalized Data to Light Intensity

Normalized data at a given time (t), is a vector of three values (x, y, z). We average these values and generate a single value which represents energy of the hand motion at time, t. Finally, the hand motion energy is mapped to light intensity by multiplying the average value to 255 as shown in the following equation.

$$Light\ Intensity_t = \frac{Normalized\ Data(x,y,z)_t}{3} \times 255 \qquad (2)$$

Update Light Intensity

This step of the algorithm helps with the smooth transition of light intensity level in real-time. This is to prevent the LED from changing light intensity too abruptly. We implement a signal processing technique called "sliding window" to help accomplish the above goal. A three-second window, which is consisted of 30 samples (3 s × 10 samples per second) is maintained and updated continuously. This strategy can be thought of as a queue with FIFO operation. Once new data sample is collected and mapped to light unit, it will be added into the end of the queue, and the first entry in the queue will be discarded. Average intensity of the sliding window is used to set the intensity level of the LED.

3 Results

To study the feasibility of the algorithm we developed a Win-Form application that processes the row data and visualizes the activity level. Figure 2 shows outputs of the application in which the number represents an LED intensity value and the color simulate LED intensity. The application simulate LED brightness by changing the opacity level of the red-colored square.

Fig. 2. LED simulation tool. The number in each visualization shows light intensity. The color in each visualization simulate LED. (Color figure online)

4 Conclusion

This research introduces the concept of providing fitness feedback by altering light intensity of a wearable device. This approach complements the current approach of graphical representations of fitness activities that the most fitness wearables use. Furthermore, the concept can be used to apply toward entertainment activities such as dancing in nightclubs. We believe that the visual form of fitness feedback may have impact beyond the individual level. A case in point is a group exercise or a dance party in which individuals' energy level can be visualized through the proposed device, and noticed by others, which in turn motivate them to be engaged in the fitness or dancing activity. When everyone in the group exercise or dance with full energy, a beautiful mosaic of lights can generate positive energy in the room.

5 Future Work

Our next task is to develop a full-scale product such that it would capture and process data in real-time on the Arduino board itself, without needing to communicate with the computer. Next, we will have to miniaturize the device to fit it on the wrist. Finally, we will design a human-centric experiment incorporating the use of our device to explore the impact it can have on the users.

References

1. Cabrero, S., Jansen, J., Röggla, T., Guerra-Gomez, J.A., Shamma, D.A., Cesar, P.: CWI-ADE2016 dataset: sensing nightclubs through 40 million BLE packets. In: Proceedings of the 8th ACM on Multimedia Systems Conference (MMSys 2017), pp. 181–186. ACM, New York (2017). https://doi.org/10.1145/3083187.3083213
2. Barros, S., Jansen, J., Cesar, P., Röggla, T., Shamma, D.A. Designing the club of the future with data: a case study on collaboration of creative industries. In: Extended Abstracts of the 2018 CHI Conference on Human Factors in Computing Systems (CHI EA 2018), Paper CS06, 9 p. ACM, New York (2018). https://doi.org/10.1145/3170427.3174358
3. Badamasi, Y.A.: The working principle of an Arduino. In: 2014 11th International Conference on Electronics, Computer and Computation (ICECCO), Abuja, pp. 1–4 (2014). https://doi.org/10.1109/ICECCO.2014.6997578
4. Williamson, J., et al.: Data sensing and analysis: challenges for wearables. In: The 20th Asia and South Pacific Design Automation Conference, Chiba, pp. 136–141 (2015). https://doi.org/10.1109/ASPDAC.2015.7058994

Systematic Review of Mobile Phone Apps Currently Available to Norwegian Users to Support Diabetes Self-management

Julia Jacoby[✉]

Oslo Metropolitan University, 0167 Oslo, Norway
julia.jacoby@oslomet.no

Abstract. Diabetes is a chronic illness that affects millions of people world-wide. Patients who find it difficult to adhere to its complex treatment regimen face severe health implications. For example, many patients find it challenging to meet diabetes self-management demands such as frequent blood sugar checks, regular insulin and/or medication use, and consistent dietary and exercise regimens. Studies have shown that mobile health (mHealth) solutions and mobile applications (apps) offer unique opportunities for meeting these challenges and achieving better treatment adherence. With increasing mobile phone adoption, many commercial diabetes self-management apps have become available. Such fast-paced developments make it difficult for patients and healthcare providers to stay current. This systematic review of diabetes apps available to Norwegian users aims to give an overview of the apps on the market. By comparing and reviewing results across various themes, this study identifies important ones for successful diabetes self-management. This will enable identifying other areas that should be considered in the design and development of diabetes self-management apps.

Keywords: mHealth · Mobile apps · Diabetes · Self-management · Systematic review · Design

1 Introduction

Today, around 415 million people suffer from diabetes worldwide [1]. According to the World Health Organization, the management of this disease and its ensuing complications remains a global health emergency that currently accounts for 12% of healthcare expenditures [2].

Diabetes, in addition to its various physical impacts, also often leads to deteriorated quality of life and increased rates of depression and anxiety among patients [3, 4]. Mobile health (mHealth) studies found that the use of mobile phone applications (apps) for diabetes self-management has a positive impact on individuals [5]. However, these studies note various positive and negative impacts, indicating that such apps may be a convenient and viable support system for many but not all diabetes patients depending on their preferences, health literacy, economy, etc. [6–9]. This study sheds light and begins to build an understanding of diabetes apps and their implications for users, with a special focus on apps that are currently available for Norwegian patients. The findings

© Springer Nature Switzerland AG 2019
C. Stephanidis (Ed.): HCII 2019, CCIS 1034, pp. 457–466, 2019.
https://doi.org/10.1007/978-3-030-23525-3_62

are relevant for identifying areas for further consideration in the use of mobile apps that are designed and developed for diabetes self-management.

1.1 Overview of Current Apps

Compared to early mobile phones, today's mobile phones and tablet PCs offer a considerably wider range of functionalities. Apps are increasingly used in managing various tasks in daily life. Currently, just under two million apps are available in the Apple App Store (operating system: iOS, developer: Apple) and more than 2.1 Million apps, in the Google Play Store (operating system: Android, developer: Google) [10].

As such, the app market is immense and constantly growing. In the Norwegian context, this is an important development because its large geographic area relative to its small population often implies long travel times for diabetes patients to speak directly to a healthcare provider. The implementation of apps as a means to communicate and self-manage illness in daily life is therefore particularly interesting in this context. Accordingly, the Norwegian Ministry for Healthcare has established a Directorate for e-Health to actively implement strategies and policies and to manage the integration of mHealth into the Norwegian Healthcare System [11].

The number of health-related apps available in Norway increased by 57% in 2016 to 259,000 apps [12]. This growth reflects a global trend, and it is particularly interesting in the context that the saturation of mobile phone usage among the Norwegian population is estimated to be 88% [13]. Here, the digitalization of the healthcare sector with digital patient files and other measures has to a large extent become a part of daily life for patients with chronic illnesses. It is important to note that according to a 2016 report by the National Center for e-Health Research (Nasjonalt Senter for E-Helseforskning), diabetes is one of the fastest developing sectors among health apps in Norway [14].

Among the categories of medicine, health, and fitness, thousands of apps, including those that target diabetes nutrition and dietary behavior for diabetes patients, are available. These apps can deliver healthcare anywhere by overcoming geographical and organizational barriers as well as time constraints [15, 16]. As noted earlier, some parts of Norway are sparsely populated and therefore travel times to healthcare providers can be high. Therefore, apps for diagnosis, self-management, mitigation, treatment, or prevention of diseases such as diabetes [17] can be particularly valuable in the Norwegian geographic context. Apps can provide diabetes patients with greater autonomy, with the possibility to self-manage and track their illness progression on a daily life basis in real time. Diabetes self-management includes monitoring of glucose levels, lifestyle modifications, medication management, prevention of complications, and psychosocial care [18]. Self-management of a chronic illness such as diabetes often contributes to minimizing risks and complications associated with its chronic nature.

2 Method

2.1 Information Sources and Search

A systematic review of mobile phone apps in English and Norwegian in the two mobile app stores—Google Play (Android) and App Store (iOS)—was conducted from November to December 2018.

A search was conducted among apps within comparative categories, and their specifications were identified according to the Preferred Reporting Items for Systematic reviews and Meta-Analyses (PRISMA) (Table 2) [19, 20]. A list of relevant search terms was assembled in English and Norwegian and entered into the search engines of these two app stores. The search strategy consisted of the terms "diabetes," "diabetes mellitus," "diabetes mellitus type 1," "diabetes type 1," "diabetes mellitus type 2," "diabetes type 2," "diabetic ketoacidosis," "blood sugar," "blood glucose," "diabetes manager," "diabetes management," "diabetes diary," and "diabetes tracker" (Table 1). The specific search strategy for each app store can be provided by the author upon request. Subsequently, an app review based on the information given in the Google Play Store, Apple App Store, and the apps themselves was conducted. The review of available mobile apps for diabetes self-management is based on criteria for promoting diabetes self-management as defined by Goyal and Cafazzo (monitoring blood glucose level and medication, nutrition, physical exercise, and body weight) [6].

Table 1. Search terms applied in the Apple App Store and the Google Play Store

Search terms in English	Search terms in Norwegian
diabetes	diabetes
diabetes mellitus	diabetes mellitus
diabetes mellitus type 1	diabetes mellitus type 1
diabetes type 1	diabetes type 1
diabetes type 2	diabetes type 2
diabetes mellitus type 2	diabetes mellitus type 2
diabetic ketoacidosis	diabetic ketoacidosis
blood sugar	blod sukker
blood glucose	blod glukose
diabetes manager	diabetes assistent
diabetes management	diabetes rådgiver
diabetes diary	diabetes dagbok
diabetes journal	diabetes journal
diabetes tracker	diabetes sporing

2.2 Eligibility Criteria

To be eligible, an app has to be available in one of three Scandinavian languages (Norwegian, Swedish, or Danish) to be useful to local Norwegian users. This criterion was relaxed in that an app could also be available only in English if it fits all criteria

Table 2. PRISMA flowchart

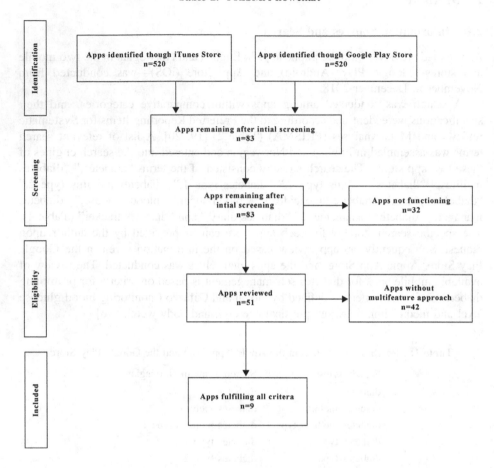

described as the basis for successful diabetes self-management according to Goyal and Cafazzo. Through their research, they have defined the following criteria: monitoring blood glucose level and medication, nutrition, physical exercise, and body weight [6]. These five aspects had to be present in the app for it to be considered eligible. Additionally, the app has to specifically address diabetes self-management, although whether it targeted Type 1 or Type 2 diabetes could be unspecified. Lastly, the app had to appear among the first 20 rankings for one of the search terms to be considered viable according to the two app stores' search algorithms.

2.3   App Selection

After the search according to the abovementioned search terms, the first 20 apps in the ranking were reviewed according to the eligibility criteria. Apps had to match the inclusion and exclusion criteria set a priori. Only the first 20 apps were considered owing to the algorithms used by the two app stores for ranking various apps. Duplicates were removed and the remaining apps were screened according to the following criteria: title, introduction text, user reviews, and language availability. The remaining eligible apps were downloaded and reviewed more thoroughly based on the criteria set by Goyal and Cafazzo [6]. The levels of inclusion of features based on the selection criteria in the selected mobile apps can vary. The results were discussed with two other design researchers. In some cases, app developers were contacted to clarify the design and to determine whether the app was developed according to a specific theory and if so, which one. In cases of a nonresponse, one reminder was sent.

3   Results

3.1   Functions of Apps

During the study, 520 apps were initially found in the two app stores (Google Play and Apple App Store), of which every hit was reviewed in terms of its relevance and explicit link to diabetes mellitus. This pre-screening process was important owing to the large number of misleading descriptions of apps that were caused by the low admission requirements for new apps entering these app stores.

From this initially large number, 83 were identified as likely to be matching the criteria in the initial screening. These apps were then tested and evaluated. Of these, 32 did not meet even minimal requirements or did not work properly. While a wide range of mobile applications is available for diabetes self-management, ranging from fitness apps, carbohydrate counters, glucose trackers, to diabetes meal-planners, few combined a number of these features. This multifeature approach is, according to Goyal and Cafazzo, a key element for the promotion of diabetes self-management. The current results show that only nine out of 51 reviewed mobile apps were versatile and useful enough for successful diabetes self-management based on the selection criteria.

4   Discussion

4.1   Principal Findings

App Audience. In this review, one outcome was the realization that diabetes patients are the primary users/customers for the apps available today. In fact, 96% of apps were targeted at individuals with diabetes. Physicians or health professionals were the targeted users of a smaller proportion of apps.

Language. Many apps were available in multiple languages; however, few were in a Scandinavian language (Norwegian, Danish, or Swedish), leading to the small number of apps reviewed. Further, even though many apps offered Norwegian as a language setting, some seemed to be translated by a translation algorithm. This occasionally led to misleading translations that could be detrimental in a healthcare context. Additionally, the availability of Norwegian as a language did not necessarily make the app user-friendly in the Norwegian cultural context. This is because user reviews often noted an inherent lack of local products to be found among the food databases. This was often related to comments on poor usability of an app by Norwegian users. It also points to the fact that simply providing linguistic readability is not enough; users also require cultural readability to consider the app useful. If this is not possible, as was often the case for Norwegian users, in a small country and subsequent market, the possibility of easily adding to or building a database of local food is considered helpful.

Usability. An important consideration of mobile applications is the ease with which the user and the product interact. Usability, according to Nielsen [21], involves comprehensibility, image and text presentation, understandability, and intuitiveness among other features to determine how easily users can interact with apps.

Among diabetes apps, most appear to be comprehensible. However, many did not have good fault tolerance, which refers to the ability of the app to respond well to unexpected hardware or software failures. Another technical detail was that only a small number of apps were constantly updated and that the user reviews were rather old. This could imply that the app has fallen out of favor or that the developers have lost interest in the app after a few years.

Accessibility features (i.e., screen reader, large type, color contrast) were available in many apps, with 41% of Android apps offering a large font (versus 0% of iOS apps). Paid apps tended to have more usability strategies for patients with low health literacy, such as, plain language, clearly labeled links, and organization features. Here, it is also interesting to note that "design," "usability," and "easy to use" were frequently mentioned in the user ratings and seemed directly correlated to users' positive ratings and satisfaction with the app. This is something that will be examined closer in the field-work following this review.

Integration with other mobile applications (e.g., email, calendar, maps) was available in 44% of apps. Interestingly, the number of functions available that also correlated with positive usability according to the app reviews were functions related to self-monitoring and visual presentation of data patterns, such as graphs of glucose ratings over time and being able to export and share these with others.

Overall, apps appear to be primarily available in English, with limited available user rating data. At a broader level, paid apps do not seem to offer major advantages over free apps other than some improved features for those with low health literacy. Finally, user ratings and number of downloads do not appear to be reliable indicators of app quality.

Security. Given the large amount of physiologic data available in apps with monitoring features, data security is an issue to be considered. In the age of private data becoming a commodity traded by large companies, protection of privacy and health data has become a growing concern. This is true especially because commercial app developers often adhere to different ethical standards than healthcare providers. This inherently raises concerns, especially considering that only one of the 9 apps reviewed indicated HIPAA (U.S. Department of Health and Human Services regulations protecting the privacy and security of certain health information) [22] compliance. Most apps did have long privacy and terms of use contracts that the user has to agree to if he/she wishes to use the app. As tracking and communicating physiological data becomes increasingly prevalent and providers become accustomed to using apps to monitor such data with their patients, having security measures will likely become an important app feature.

4.2   Limitations of the Review

This review has the following limitations. A systematic search was performed by applying rigorous methods; however, the lack of transparency on the side of the apps stores in how their algorithms affect ranking and possible language biases within the search terms does not allow for a fully transparent process. Additionally, according to Martínez-Pérez et al., owing to the dramatic rate of app development, the number of available commercial apps is a moving target [23]. In particular, when considering the rate of updates and redesigns, apps often change their user interaction or visual layout quite significantly from one update to the next to stay up to date with current trends. Further, this review did not assess the quality of use of the apps found during the study as this was beyond the current scope.

4.3   Implications of Using Mobile Apps for Diabetes Self-management

Considering the great need for diabetes patients to manage and adapt to their illness in daily life, the wide range of diabetes apps available to them can be considered positive. The wide variety of apps available on the market likely allows patients to find a fitting solution for their individual needs. However, the ever-growing number of apps available can also be overwhelming for both healthcare staff and patients who are searching for reliable and well-designed apps to support them in their diabetes management efforts. Therefore, a better understanding of the usefulness and quality of apps available on the market is necessary. To achieve some kind of clarity or to establish a framework within which to operate, it is necessary to further rigorously study the development and impact of apps on diabetes self-management.

Currently, user ratings seem to be the most feasible way for patients (and possibly developers) to evaluate app options and quality. Nonetheless, many apps found in this review lack user-ratings or might be outdated. Among apps with recent user ratings, the information they contain is very varied in the actual feedback they provide. Additionally, the lack of transparency in how app stores provide user ratings raises concerns about biases arising from the algorithms employed by the various App Stores. In the Apple App Store, for example, a minimum of reviews are required before an average review rating is produced [24]. Further, the search functions in app stores tend to be cumbersome for users to navigate, with limited possibilities for advanced searching and filtering. Independent reviews and ratings exist in the form of blogs, magazines, and websites. However, diabetes and other medical apps are in a unique position in that higher risks might be involved in the use of low-quality apps as they might provide misleading information or suggestions.

This review also highlights the fact that few apps base their design and development on validated behavioral theories, such as for example the Theory of Planned Behavior. Apps also lack variety in the theories that are implemented. Primarily, the apps reviewed in this article seemed to base their approach on tracking health variables such as blood glucose levels, carbohydrate intake, and physical activity. mHealth research suggests that self-tracking and monitoring of blood glucose levels are particularly critical components of successful diabetes management [25]. More frequent monitoring, especially with the provision of feedback on the monitored data, is a key factor in health behavior change interventions according to Miltenberger [26]. However, outside of this approach to behavior change, few evidence-based tools or theories seem to have been employed in commercial apps for diabetes self-management. It seems that apps that are developed based on specific behavior change theories for diabetes management are primarily research probes rather than commercially available apps. Though these apps often clearly communicate their goals and intentions, they often only exist for the duration of the study because the researchers simply lack the funding, capacity, and, potentially, interest to further develop and support the app after the study is completed. The implementation of behavior change theories in addition to patient-centered motivational strategies in the design and development of an app seems to hold promise. The outcome of integrating features such as goal setting and problem-solving of barriers could be positive for use. In addition, individualized features such as local eating habits, personalized feedback, and tailored reminder features would likely improve user engagement and adherence.

4.4   Conclusion

This article is part of doctoral research that explores the role design can play in the daily experience of diabetes as a chronic illness. As such, it represents a preliminary study to act as groundwork for fieldwork illuminating how diabetes patients interact with, experience, and use diabetes apps. By using this study as a guideline, a new app will be developed to test the findings. However, the study results can also be used as a basis to provide app developers or designers with recommendations on what to consider when creating or re-designing a commercial app for successful diabetes self-management. There is a need for mobile apps for diabetes self-management with more specific features to increase the number of long-term users and thus influence better diabetes self-management. It might even prompt interest in attempting to integrate a larger variety of behavioral theories, learning theories and/or motivational theories among others, into new commercial app developments. This could act as a novel approach in a market with tough competition. Alternatively, it might prompt developers and designers to consider a partnership with researchers. This could also be of interest to researchers, as it would allow them to build apps that increase in lifespan and integrate multiple perspectives into the development rather than a pure research outcome focus.

Further, this study can provide other researchers interested in this field with a dataset to build upon to potentially act as a local case study. As such, it can be used by others who would want to understand app development over time. In this regard, it can provide a snapshot of a very specific point in time, or it can act as a local case that can be compared to other countries to understand what apps are available in their local language and how they receive reviews in a local cultural context.

References

1. Guariguata, L., Whiting, D.R., Hambleton, I., Beagley, J., Linnenkamp, U., Shaw, J.E.: Global estimates of diabetes prevalence for 2013 and projections for 2035. Diabetes Res. Clin. Pract. **103**(2), 137–149 (2014)
2. da Rocha, F.J., et al.: IDF diabetes atlas estimates of 2014 global health expenditures on diabetes. Diabetes Res. Clin. Pract. **117**, 48–54 (2016)
3. Schram, M.T., Baan, C.A., Pouwer, F.: Depression and quality of life in patients with diabetes: a systematic review from the European depression in diabetes (EDID) research consortium. Curr. Diabetes Rev. **5**(2), 112–119 (2009)
4. Lin, E.H., et al.: Depression and advanced complications of diabetes: a prospective cohort study. Diabetes Care **33**(2), 264–269 (2010)
5. Whitehead, L., Seaton, P.: The effectiveness of self-management mobile phone and tablet apps in long-term condition management: a systematic review. J. Med. Internet Res. **18**(5), e97 (2016)
6. Goyal, S., Cafazzo, J.A.: Mobile phone health apps for diabetes management: current evidence and future developments. QJM **106**(12), 1067–1069 (2013)
7. Hood, M., Wilson, R., Corsica, J., Bradley, L., Chirinos, D., Vivo, A.: What do we know about mobile applications for diabetes self-management? a review of reviews. J. Behav. Med. **39**(6), 981–994 (2016)
8. Caburnay, C.A., et al.: Evaluating diabetes mobile applications for health literate designs and functionality. Prev. Chronic Dis. **12**, E61 (2015)
9. Klonoff, D.C., Kerr, D.: Digital diabetes communication: there's an app for that. J. Diabetes Sci. Technol. **10**(5), 1003–1005 (2016)
10. Statista, App stores: Number of apps in leading app stores (2018). https://www.statista.com/statistics/276623/number-of-apps-available-in-leading-app-stores. Accessed 29 Jan 2019
11. Directorate for e-Health. https://ehelse.no/english. Accessed 20 Mar 2019
12. Research 2 Guidance, mHealth App Developer Economics (2016). http://research2guidance.com/product/mhealth-app-developer-economics-2016. Accessed 26 Oct 2016
13. Malmlund, J., Behnk, F., Moen, H., Suortti, J.P.: More than just a phone-A study on Nordic mobile consumer behaviour. Deloitte Global Mobile Consumer Survey: The Nordic Cut. p. 6 (2017)
14. Saadatfard, O., Årsand, E.: "m-health for diabetes management," Fact Sheet No. 9/2016 (2016)
15. Akter, S., Ray, P.: MHealth - an ultimate platform to serve the unserved. Yearb. Med. Inform. **19**(1), 94–100 (2010). https://doi.org/10.1055/s-0038-1638697
16. Thakkar, J., et al.: Mobile telephone text messaging for medication adherence in chronic disease. JAMA Intern. Med. **176**(3), 340 (2016). https://doi.org/10.1001/jamainternmed.2015.7667
17. Silva, B.M., Rodrigues, J.J., Díez, I.D., López-Coronado, M., Saleem, K.: Mobile-health: a review of current state in 2015. J. Biomed. Inform. **56**, 265–272 (2015)
18. US Department of Health and Human Services. http://www.hrsa.aquilientprojects.com/healthit/mhealth.html. Accessed 17 Oct 2018
19. Moher, D., et al.: Preferred reporting items for systematic review and meta-analysis protocols (PRISMA-P) 2015 statement. Syst. Rev. **4**, 1 (2015)
20. Shamseer, L., et al.: Preferred reporting items for systematic review and meta-analysis protocols (PRISMA-P) 2015: elaboration and explanation. BMJ **349**, g7647 (2015)
21. Nielsen Norman Group. https://www.nngroup.com/articles/usability-101-introduction-to-usability. Accessed 23 Mar 2019

22. Department of Human Health and Human Services. https://www.hhs.gov/hipaa/for-professionals/security/laws-regulations/index.html. Accessed 23 Mar 2019
23. Martinez-Perez, B., la de Torre-Díez, I., Lopez-Coronado, M.: Mobile health applications for the most prevalent conditions by the world health organization: review and analysis. J. Med. Internet Res. **15**(6), e120 (2013)
24. Apple Developer. https://developer.apple.com/app-store/review/guidelines. Accessed 20 Mar 2019
25. Knapp, S., Manroa, P., Doshi, K.: Self-monitoring of blood glucose: advice for providers and patients. Clevel. Clin. J. Med. **83**, 355–360 (2016)
26. Miltenberger, R.G.: Behavior Modification: Principles and Procedures, 6th edn. Cengage Learning, Boston (2015)

Design Mobile App Notification to Reduce Student Stress

Ann Junker[✉]

DePaul University, Chicago, IL 60604, USA
ann.junker@gmail.com

Abstract. College is the first time many students spend extended time away from their parents' homes and take on new responsibilities of independence. Encountering different lifestyles and values, they begin to define their adulthood. Newfound freedom increases stress they have not learned to cope with. This paper discusses recognizing stress, learning coping skills, and social sharing toward designing a personalized mobile application used to monitor students' stress and help them set goals. The application uses a reward system to reduce stress levels and facilitate a healthier lifestyle.

Keywords: Student stress · Stress reduction · Health and wellness · Signs of stress · Stress recognition · Coping mechanisms · Skill building · Social sharing · Behavioral change · Gamification · Mobile application notifications

1 Introduction

College students encounter new situations they may not know how or be mature enough to handle, elevating their stress levels. Students report academics, finances, time management, and socialization as top stressors. School/life balance is challenging to manage and affects academic performance. Students feel cannot achieve desired grades because of these new responsibilities [9]. The Healthy Minds Study 2016–2017 Data Report found students reported stress impaired academics between one and six days over a four-week period [3].

1.1 Signs of Stress and Seeking Help

Many college counselors report that the majority of students are not aware that habit changes are signs of stress. These habits, like changes in sleep routine or appetite, social withdrawal, smoking, or excess alcohol or drug use, can become unhealthy coping mechanisms. Students may also experience difficulty concentrating; feel overwhelmed, depressed, or anxious; and experience stomach issues, headaches, or skin reactions when stressed. Such changes in habits can have unintended consequences, like health or academic issues, engaging in violent acts, or encounters with police [9].

The Healthy Minds Study 2016–2017 Data Report found 24% of students sought out mental health counseling during that academic year. Reported reasons for students not seeking help were lack of time, money, relevant services, or appointment times, or

© Springer Nature Switzerland AG 2019
C. Stephanidis (Ed.): HCII 2019, CCIS 1034, pp. 467–475, 2019.
https://doi.org/10.1007/978-3-030-23525-3_63

students wanting to deal with their issues on their own [3]. Students who want to appear "grown up" may feel embarrassed about seeking out help, delay seeking out help, or prefer researching options on their own before talking with others about their issues. Due to underfunding of in-person clinics, campus counseling services have implemented online services and found that such services were accessed earlier than in-person counseling and met self-efficacious needs [9].

1.2 Behavioral Change and Gamification

People perceive stressful situations differently; one feels very stressed while another is less stressed. Perceived stress is dependent on one's ability to cope. Those with high perceived stress are more likely to rely on unhealthy coping mechanisms. Goal-setting and monitoring reminds us to take care of ourselves with healthy habits, like exercising, healthy eating, sleeping well, participating in hobbies, socializing, and meditating. Time management skills, like activity prioritizing, help us focus our time on personal goals and create a balanced schedule. Recounting past successes with affirmations helps us focus on positive experiences. Friends and family may be supportive but may lack the knowledge to effectively help students experiencing stress. Conversely, support networks are experienced and trained to help people with specific stress related issues. These networks provide a sense of belonging, create accountability, and encourage us to continue with our goals [9, 11].

Behavioral change theories encourage us to pursue our path toward a healthier life. These theories share similar steps, like learning the effects of unhealthy coping mechanisms, learning to recognize one's unhealthy habits, believing one can overcome barriers, creating desire for positive change, learning healthy coping mechanisms, and building mastery of healthier habits [4, 12, 14]. The goal of behavioral change is to replace unhealthy habits with healthy ones—in other words, to build new skills. New skills are not easy to learn, use, or remember, so we often rely on old habits in stressful situations. Gamification shares elements of behavioral change theories, such as gaining self-purpose through personalized achievable goals designed to reinforce desired changes. Gamification monitors and notifies us about progress, creates accountability, encourages us to improve our skills, and sets up rewards when reaching milestones. "Successful games all have something in common: the intrinsic joy of skill-building. It feels good to engage our brains to improve our skills and make progress along a path toward mastery [10]." Games are about "character transformation"—or behavioral change.

Learning new skills can be tedious and complicated. Healthcare professionals have found game-like therapy is engaging, beneficial, and encourages longer-lasting change. Studies involving children with asthma and diabetes found children's confidence in managing and reducing symptoms of their disease improved when such skills were learned though a game [1]. Studies examining Consumer Health Informatics applications related to weight loss, exercise, alcohol intake, and mental health found that personalization was key to encouraging behavior change [6].

2 Student Stress Surveys

I conducted two surveys to gather more information about stress levels, coping mechanisms, and goal setting. Both surveys were conducted online using Google Forms.

The first survey focused on academic stress, coping, and perceived stress levels (see Table 1). Eight out of nine participants were female, and one was male. The age range was from 18–47. Participants were in Bachelor's, Master's, and Doctor of Nursing Practice programs in the United States. Using the Perceived Stress Scale (PSS) seven of nine participants scored moderate stress with a range of 19–24, two scored high stress with scores of 24 and 27, and no one scored average or low-stress levels.

Table 1. Academic stress, coping, and perceived stress levels survey highlights.

Top stressors	Academics, finances, work/school/life, followed by time management and healthy eating
Effect of stress on life	Fatigue, feeling overwhelmed, time-management issues, poor life balance, unhealthy dietary choices, and lack of motivation
Campus services	Four of nine were aware of campus counseling services; none used them. Lack of time and knowing where to go were common barriers. One preferred to use other resources
Finding help	Friends, family, search mobile apps, and search online
Activities to relax	Exercise, social, sleep, hobbies, baking, crafts, read, TV, music, eating well, and meditate
Stress reduction activities for application design (participants were given list of options to choose from)	Learn new skills was the top choice, followed by track activities, set goals, help recognize stress, track mood, relaxation, and scheduling help. Sharing, music, and meditate had one vote each. No one choose health professional services or learn about stress in general

The second survey focused on stress recognition, symptoms, and setting/achieving goals (see Table 2). Seven of nine participants were female, and two were male. The age range was from 18–47. Participants were in Bachelor's, Master's, and Doctor of Nursing Practice programs in the United States.

Table 2. Stress recognition, symptoms, and setting/achieving goals survey highlights.

Activities that caused stress	School work, work, finances, and school group activities
Activities to reduced stress	Sleep, friends/family, hobbies, read, relaxing music, exercise, plan better, create to-do lists, deep breath, and vacation
Physical symptoms of stress	Breath incorrectly, exhaustion, frequent illness, headaches, dizziness, inability to fall/stay asleep, high blood pressure, inability to focus, irritability, and picking nails
Goals and action plans	Six of nine used goals and action plans to feel less stress
Types of goals	Bike, weight loss, career-related learning, read more, schedule assignments, set reminders, and place less emphasis on work
Barriers to achieving goals	Difficulty achieving goals when busy, not motivated when tired or stressed, and experiencing distractions
Sharing goals and progress	More likely to share positive progress with friends and family, not likely to share with social media or health care professionals
Reasons for sharing	"Appropriate with people I trust," "I didn't think of sharing," "I feel like no one would care," and "I'm a bit of a private person."
Encouragement to achieve goals	"Knowing the end goal," "deadlines," "the effects after—feeling less stressed," "family," and "inner need for accomplishment."
Stress reduction activities for application design (participants were given list of options to choose from)	Activity tracking/goal setting were top responses, followed by mood tracking, help recognizing when stressed, learning new habits, relaxation, and scheduling help. Connecting with mental health professionals and learning about stress received one response each. Connecting with others received no responses
Wearables to detect stress	Five of nine tried wearables, one mentioned the notifications helped them recognize stress
Wearable information to track progress and goal achievement	Encouraging visuals, update/track goals reminder, track self-care stress levels, monitor heart rate and blood pressure, ask what you did to take time for yourself, and sense nail-biting to alert one of the behavior

3 Smartphone Design Ideas for Behavioral Change

Mary Czerwinski points out "the hardest human/computer interaction is the intervention itself. You have to design an intervention that is not annoying, is not patronizing, and is actually sticky [7]." Smartphones are ideal to track goal progress because they encourage self-efficaciousness, are often on hand, and contain much of our personal information [13]. Connected to smartphones, biometric wearable devices create "body awareness" where we learn over time how to recognize symptoms of stress and adjust our behavior on our own [8].

Personalized notifications and activities appropriate to the user's context encourage behavior change. Such notifications can be of two types: user-initiated or just-in-time (JIT). The user-initiated type allows users to proactively set up notifications and to record completed activities when the user choses. JIT notifications, used with a biometric wearable device, reactively and automatically notify users when certain conditions are detected. JITs help users recognize stress symptoms and guide users through a stress-reducing activity in the moment [2, 5].

4 Digital Wireframe User Testing

4.1 Method and Participants

Two sets of mid-fidelity wireframes were created to test if users felt the notifications were easy to follow, engaging, and included activities appropriate to the user's context. Wireframe set one was a user-initiated task to notify the user to bike at a time the user pre-scheduled. In the user's context, the activity of this notification type can be more time consuming and physically activity. Wireframe set two was a JIT task to alert the user to meditate when stress was detected. In the user's context, the activity of this notification type can be done quickly and in almost any environment without additional equipment. Both notification type gave options for other types of activities.

For the wireframe user tests, participants were required to be university students who used a smartphone. There were one male and five female participants with an age range of 21–30.

Fifteen-minute remote unmoderated tests were set up, conducted, and video-recorded with UserTesting.com. Participants used their personal computers to access the wireframes to log stress levels and activity completion. Participants were not asked to perform the stress reduction activity. I reviewed, transcribed, and coded the videos. Allowing users to focus on tasks, the wireframes were pre-set with activity preferences and pre-logged data. Participants completed both tasks in the same order with user-initiated tested first and JIT tested second.

4.2 Evaluation Measures

I used an observation log to capture notes for time on task, completion rates, navigation, and think-aloud feedback. Successful completion criteria included number of mistakes made (see Table 3) and whether participants reached the last step of the task.

The user-initiated task involved completing the activity and socially sharing their progress. The JIT task involved completing the activity and viewing the progress screen. Post-task and test questionnaires gathered qualitative data on the users' satisfaction and attitudes.

Table 3. Success rate determined by number of mistakes.

Rate	Completion measure
Success	Participants completed task without mistake and filled in all the content
Partial success	Participants were able to complete the task but made mistakes < 2
Failure	Participants could not complete the tasks or made mistakes > 2

4.3 Results

Time on Task and Task Success. User-initiated notification averaged 1.28 min with times ranging from 1.10 to 1.50 min. JIT notification averaged 1.12 min with times ranging from 0.40 to 1.50 min. Table 4 outlines task success.

Table 4. Task success

Success rate	User-initiated	JIT
Success	4 users	6 users
Partial success	1	0
Failure	1	0

Ease of Use and Satisfaction for User-Initiated Notification. For ease of use, five of six participants gave a rating of 5 and one gave a rating of 4 (using the Likert Scale where 1 is very difficult and 5 is very easy). Participants liked the layout, task flow, and content, but disliked the bland wireframe visuals and would have preferred the app did more tracking instead of requiring self-reporting.

In feeling engaged in monitoring progress, two of six participants gave a rating of 5, one gave a rating of 4, one gave a rating of 3, and two did not provide a rating (using the Likert Scale where 1 is not satisfied and 5 is very satisfied). Participant 3 mentioned, "It's like a journal for me to keep track of how healthy I've been. Especially in moments where I feel as though I'm not doing anything, there's evidence right here to show that I'm actually trying to be active." P5 said, "They remind you that you have this many points [...which] helps encourage you to continue on."

Ease of Use and Satisfaction for JIT Notification. For ease of use, four of six participants gave a rating of 5, one a rating of 4, and one did not provide a rating (using the Likert Scale where 1 is very difficult and 5 is very easy). P3 said, "There are questions that you can answer, but you have the option of skipping them. So, the process is even quicker." P2 added, "I liked how it gave me clear and concise options to choose from." Participants mentioned they liked the layout, task flow, content, and tracking charts; they would have preferred more encouraging wording and visual design, friendlier ratings, and more personalization options to add their own activities.

In feeling engaged in monitoring progress, one of six participants gave a rating of 5, two a rating of 4, one a rating of 3, and two did not provide a rating (using the Likert Scale where 1 is not satisfied and 5 is very satisfied). P3 suggested including features like logging and tracking emotions for later reflection. P5 liked having activities to pick from because "I was worried that it would just have meditation."

Post-test Questions. Feedback regarding the usefulness of monitoring stress with different notifications included: "Yes, every kind of stress level for me personally has been treated differently" and "Knowing what triggers and discerning different stress levels would be very useful in helping me reduce stress." Responses regarding whether smartphone reminders to do an activity helped in reaching a goal included: "Works best for people like me who need guidance"; "Small nudges are very impactful and useful"; and "If it was something other than exercising, like learning a new language or hobby, then yes." Responses to preferred activities for each notification type included: "Task 1: I do not think there is a restriction to the types of activities. Task 2: I definitely think it depends on what you are doing [...] if you are taking a test or something that involves restrictions, then you couldn't strike a yoga pose or go for a walk." Responses to if and how participants recently shared progress with friends included: "I did it in person. People responded very positively and were incredibly encouraging"; and "I don't go out of my way to share progress or post things on social media."

5   Findings and Future Design Ideas

5.1   Tracking Automation

Automation to reduce self-reporting was appreciated by participants. P3 said they would prefer the app to do more tracking for them so they didn't need to self-report. P4 said, "I don't know, maybe I'm just dumb and want everything to be handed to me."

5.2   Visual Design and Wording/Messaging

Participants believed visual design and gentle wording encouraged them toward goal success and should be further researched. P1 mentioned, "More graphics would give much more satisfaction to seeing your goals and your progress." P1 also said it would "really help people like me—having a whole bunch of words thrown at you can be kind of stressful and having the graphics really does help make navigating the app all that much easier." P3 said, "It'd be nice if [...] I was greeted with words of affirmation."

5.3   Content and Activities

Future designs should clarify content and add reflection notes and personalized activities. P2 mentioned wanting milestone rewards on the progress page. P1 mentioned, "It would be good to maybe see it broken down a little bit more in terms of points on [...] a daily basis." P3 said in-app activity guidance was helpful "since if you're in a moment where you can't really focus on anything because your mind is going like a thousand miles per hour, you just need simple directions." P3 wanted a place to log their feelings to reflect on later.

5.4 Social Sharing

Participants were reluctant to share progress on social media, saying it felt "spammy and annoying," or did not want to share their "vulnerabilities." These attitudes run counter to current research discussed in the introduction. My second survey showed participants were more willing to share slightly positive progress with family and friends. This suggests research can be done solely on how comfortable users feel about social sharing and what types of progress they share.

5.5 Notifications Control

Future designs should consider allowing users to silence notifications at inappropriate times. One idea is to connect the user's calendar to the stress application. P1 said it would be useful "if there's a way to turn them off during certain hours, just so it wouldn't distract me if I was in school." P3 agreed, saying it would be awkward to have their smartphone notify them at any time when they might not be alone.

6 Limitations and Discussion

I researched many resources to learn about stress, coping mechanisms, behavioral change, gamification, and tracking activities and stress, though the design was limited to two notification user flows. Another limitation was the low number of participants used for surveys and wireframe testing. The design suggests a wearable device to detect stress levels, and the lack of such a device for real-life stress detection was a limitation.

While this study focused on student stress, many ideas can be carried over to other life stages. Even if we learn to cope with stress successfully, we can still fall into unhealthy habits and find we need new ways to cope. Learning new skills can be difficult and time-consuming. Having students learn these skills early in life can help them build stress-reduction skills and become able to recognize and successfully manage stress later in life. Creating an application addressing these issues can improve behavioral change success rates and encourage people to continue pursuing a healthier lifestyle.

References

1. Bandura, A.: Health promotion by social cognitive means. J. Health Educ. Behav. **31**(2), 143–164 (2004)
2. Czerwinski, M., Gilad-Bachrach, R.: Designing interventions for health and wellbeing (2016)
3. Eisenberg, D., Ketchen Lipson, S.: The healthy mind study 2016–2017. Study (2017)

4. Fishbein, M., Yzer, M.: Using theory to design effective health behavior interventions. J. Commun. Theory **13**(2), 164–183 (2003)
5. Gilad-Bachrach, R., Czerwinski, M., Iqbal, S., Mark, G.: Challenges for designing notifications for affective computing systems. Microsoft research (2016)
6. Gibbons, M.C., et al.: Consumer health informatics: results of a systematic evidence review and evidence-based recommendations. J. Transl. Behav. Med. **1**(1), 72–82 (2011)
7. Hewer, M.: Powering Products with Psychological Science. Observer. Association for Psychological Science, April 2014
8. Höök, K., Ståhl, A., Jonsson, M., Mercurio, J., Karlsson, A., Johnson, E.: Somaesthetic design. J. Interact. **22**(4), 26–33 (2015)
9. Kadison, R., DiGeronimo, T.: College of the Overwhelmed. Jossey-Bass, New Jersey (2005)
10. Kim, A., Kim, S.: Game Thinking: Innovate Smarter & Drive Deep Engagement with Design Techniques from Hit Games, 2nd edn. gamethinking.io, Burlingame (2004)
11. Monat, A. (ed.): Stress and Coping: An Anthology, 2nd edn. Columbia University Press, New York (1985)
12. Montano, D., Kasprzyk, D.: Theory of reasoned action, theory of planned behavior, and the integrated behavioral model. J. Health Behav. Health Educ. Theory Res. Pract. **4**, 95–124 (1985)
13. Morris, M.: Motivating change with mobile: seven guidelines. J. Interact. **12**(3), 26–31 (2012)
14. Wendel, S.: Designing for Behavior Change: Applying Psychology and Behavioral Economics. O'Reilly Media, Sebastopol (2013)

Human-Food Interaction Framework: Understanding Student-Athletes' Extreme Food Needs

Sohyeong Kim[✉], Da Hyang Summer Jung, Anand Upender,
Sahej Claire, Ion Esfandiari, and Eesha Choudhari

Center for Design Research, Mechanical Engineering, Stanford University,
Stanford, CA, USA
{sohkim, summerjung, anandx, saclaire, ionesfan,
eeshac}@stanford.edu

Abstract. The food and kitchen technology industry is quickly growing and changing as user lifestyle preferences shift. This shift is arguably occurring most rapidly in Silicon Valley. There has been tremendous growth in every aspect of the food process, from food delivery services to cooking robots and automation to the ingredients themselves. However, are such food and kitchen technologies addressing the future needs of users? To understand the future needs of Silicon Valley users, we decided to look at extreme users: student athletes. By interviewing six athletes at Stanford University with extreme food needs, we gained insights on the broader future of food. To analyze the needs, we developed a preliminary Human-Food Interaction (HFI) Framework, which allowed us to understand the overall user journey and the specific user needs in each step of this journey (ex. delivery, storage). After analyzing needs, we categorized Silicon Valley food tech services into the different steps in HFI framework. As a result, we found that there is a significant gap between extreme user needs, which are indicative of future needs, and the services currently available in the market.

Keywords: Human-food interaction · Extreme user · Stanford athlete

1 Background

Innovation in food technology is happening rapidly in Silicon Valley. Large companies are starting to recognize the value of the fast-growing food tech industry and are increasingly getting involved in this market by forming a corporate venture arm (such as Tyson and Kellogg), acquiring other innovative food-related companies (such as Nestle), or developing their own innovation teams (such as Google) [1]. Another huge signal of the rising food tech space is that even traditional tech-oriented venture capital firms are now tapping into the food market. In 2018, venture-capital firms invested in food and grocery delivery services more than triple the amount they invested in 2017 [2].

A myriad of food tech startups are automating the culinary food space, and food product innovations are attacking all areas of the food pyramid [3]. Food substitutes, healthy artisanal products, and an increase in food products catered to the lactose intolerance, gluten-free, vegetarian, and other alternative diet markets are contributing to this increase.

As researchers of Stanford University, which is located at the heart of Silicon Valley, we became curious whether the food tech services and products described above were addressing the future needs of the market. Our problem statement is as follows: are food and kitchen tech addressing future needs? If they are not, where are the gaps and opportunities?

2 Methodology and Framework

In order to understand the future needs of Silicon Valley users, we adopted von Hippel's extreme user research methodology, which is also widely used in Design Thinking methodology. Von Hippel asserts how looking at users with extreme users can help designers develop unprecedented high-technology products [4]. Extreme users' needs are amplified and their work-arounds are often more notable. This helps designers pull out meaningful needs that may not emerge when engaging with people in the middle of the "bell curve". Still, the needs that are uncovered through extreme users are often also needs of a wider population or indicative of future needs. When selecting the group of extreme users, we were inspired by Olympians, who have to follow strict diets and always be conscious of what they eat. Former studies have shown that food can directly affect athletes' performance [5].

We interviewed four Stanford athletes and one Olympian to gain an understanding of how food fit into their lifestyles. The interviews were conducted on Stanford campus over the course of two months. After interviewing the athletes, we interviewed over ten industry experts and food startup founders in Silicon Valley to gain an understanding of food tech trends and the startup ecosystem. We mapped all of the qualitative data we obtained from these interviews onto a framework we developed that outlines the food process from the consumer perspective (Fig. 1).

Fig. 1. Human-food interaction framework

The Human-Food Interaction framework starts with a user learning about his or her food ingredients. The user then purchases the ingredients in various platforms, such as a farmer's market. Next, the ingredients are delivered to the user's house by the user or a third party. Once the ingredients are delivered, the user stores them in different storage areas or appliances depending on their preservative capabilities. When the user decides to eat, the user turns the ingredients into a ready-to-eat dish by first ideating and then cooking. Lastly, the user consumes the food and disposes of the food waste from the meal. HFI framework allowed us to analyze the user needs in a more systematic way and parse down the problem space.

3   Preliminary Findings

3.1   User Persona

Based on athlete interviews, we created a user persona of our extreme users. Named Julia, our user persona embodies the lifestyle of the student athletes.

Julia is a sophomore in Stanford women's rowing team. She is always busy with her coursework and training, but she manages them by staying extremely disciplined. Her social life, such as going to frat parties on weekends, is often compromised. Nonetheless, she does not care too much because she has her team and coach who will always support her. Because she does not have time to cook nor knows how to cook, she eats at dining halls and snacks often. Although cooking is not her expertise, she cares deeply about what she puts in her mouth. She perceives her body as a system which she has to optimize by inputting optimal fuel, which is food. When eating food, she cares more about its nutrition and functionality than its flavor. Therefore, she refuses to eat highly processed food or eat it in a small amount if necessary. To make sure that she is optimizing her food consumption, she logs what she eats every day.

3.2   Interview Result

The main finding is that although the needs of athletes differ based on sport, the common ultimate goal is to optimize nutrition for performance through streamlined food process. Athletes view food similar to how they view their workouts and aim to efficiently optimize their portfolio of nutrients for performance of the human system, with no regard to the social or enjoyment aspects of food. The common trends among the athletes that we observed and the athlete's specific food needs in each step of HFI framework can be summarized as below (Table 1).

3.3   Need Mapping

After summarizing the user needs, we listed out a number of Silicon Valley-based food tech services and products, based on which step of HFI framework they were focusing on. When we compared currently available food technologies and our extreme user's needs, there were specific gaps in the step-specific needs in storage. Regarding storage, the users wanted to customize and personalize the size and temperature of the storage compartments, but such a service could not be found. Overall, there was only a dearth of services that tackled storage problems (Table 2).

Table 1. Stanford athletes' food needs

Process	Common trends	Needs
Ingredients	Wants to understand what is in the food Fresh, nutritious ingredients	Access fresh, nutritious food Understand food information
Shopping	Price matters Infrequent shopping Buy things that last long	Minimize time spent shopping for new ingredients Save money
Delivery	Minimize transportation Carry snacks	Eat frequently Transport fresh food Minimize transportation
Storage	Food has to stay fresh Store has to be user friendly Flexibility in temperature and size is desired Want a storage that is shared but does not feel like it is shared	Customize and personalize size, temp compartments, etc. Preserve fresh foods
Cooking	Having control over food choices Assembly (ex. sandwich) over cooking Lack of interest and time	Make healthy choices Choose what to assemble Minimize time and resources Maximize nutrition
Eating	Snacking Meal Supplement Convenience Logging Part of training (to optimize performance) Feels like a chore	Keep track of food Customize nutrition Optimize their nutrition to perform best

3.4   Lack of Interconnectivity

Interestingly, there were several steps in this framework that were desired to be connected for the user, but this connection did not exist. The connections were not apparent in the needs addressed by tech products because most of these solutions focused on only a single step of the process. There was a significant lack of services that enhance the connectivity between storage and the steps around it, such as delivery or cooking. For example, there was a need for bridging the gap between delivery and storage processes to essentially create a customized grocery store at home. This could also be in the form of on-demand ingredients in order to minimize storage (e.g. Amazon Dash for ingredients) (Fig. 2).

Table 2. Food tech startups/services and the needs that they address

Process	Startups and services	Needs addressed
Ingredients	Impossible Foods, New Wave Food, Tiny Farms, Sugarlogix, Clara Food, Food Composition Scanner, Soylent	Eat delicious food that's good for the people and the planet Ensure transparency Eat safely Eat fast and efficient
Shopping	AmazonGo, VR/AR (smart label), Block chain	Shop fast and convenient without waiting Ensure 24 h availability Save time and money
Delivery	Instacart, UberEats, Blue Apron, Drones, Autonomous Cars, Starship	Deliver faster with better selection and service Deliver fresh food for less food waste Be fast, smart, safe, and cost-efficient
Storage	Smart Fridges	Manage food to avoid food waste
Cooking	**Ideation** Chef Watson, AI rec engines, Yummly, Iniit, Pic2Recipe **Cooking** Blue Apron, Meal Kits, Food 3D printer, Robots (Zume, Moley, Momentum, Flippy), Nima, Nomiku **Eating** Miraculin, NuTekSalt, Eating w/VR, Soylent	Provide customized recipes based on ingredients Track and control cooking processes Cook faster and easier Know your body type and compatibility
Waste	Smart Fridge, Biodegradable utensils, Treasure 8, Automated Inventory, Smart Packaging	Keep food fresh and notify the expiration date Upcycle food waste

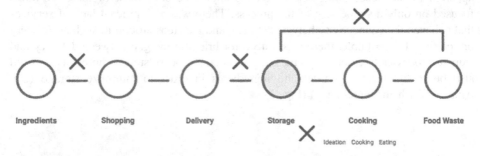

Fig. 2. Lack of interconnectivity around storage ("X" indicates a gap between two steps)

4 Conclusion and Limitations

In this study, we found that most food tech companies are not designing for the interconnected future user needs, resulting in an ecosystem of independent solutions to a codependent problem. To design for the future, the food technology industry needs to develop a concept based on the whole food process, not based on a single product, in order to address customized needs and lifestyles of users.

To focus on extreme users, the user studies in this research were conducted with exclusively Stanford athletes. For future research, it would be valuable to conduct user studies with a diverse range of extreme users, for example, children, people with disabilities, people with no refrigerator, etc. in order to compare and contrast how they use their kitchen and interact with food.

Expanding the research, both the user studies and industry/trend analyses, to less innovative contexts would be interesting, since our research was highly limited to the Silicon Valley context. It would also be valuable to gather and analyze quantitative data on usage of kitchen products, well-being indices, neuro/physical performance analyses, etc. to supplement the qualitative findings from the user studies. It would be useful to take these findings and research their managerial product implications based on the gaps and opportunities found and suggest new products and features.

References

1. Park, S.Y., Kim, S., Leifer, L.: "Human chef" to "computer chef": culinary interactions framework for understanding HCI in the food industry. In: Kurosu, M. (ed.) HCI 2017. LNCS, vol. 10271, pp. 214–233. Springer, Cham (2017). https://doi.org/10.1007/978-3-319-58071-5_17
2. Wall Street Journal. https://www.wsj.com/articles/tyson-launches-venture-capital-fund-1480939204. Accessed 28 Mar 2019
3. Wall Street Journal. https://www.wsj.com/articles/investors-are-craving-food-delivery-companies-1540375578. Accessed 28 Mar 2019
4. Von Hippel, E.: Democratizing innovation: the evolving phenomenon of user innovation. J. für Betriebswirtschaft **55**, 63–78 (2005)
5. Filaire, E., et al.: Food restriction, performance, psychological state and lipid values in judo athletes. Int. J. Sports Med. **22**, 454–459 (2016)

Computer Vision-Based System to Detect Effects of Aromatherapy During High School Classes via Analysis of Movement Kinematics

Ksenia Kolykhalova[1], David O'Sullivan[2(✉)], Stefano Piana[1], Hyungsook Kim[3], Yonghyun Park[3], and Antonio Camurri[1]

[1] Casa-Paganini - InfoMus, DIBRIS, University of Genova, Genova, Italy
[2] Division of Sport Science, Pusan National University, Busan, Republic of Korea
davidosullivan@pusan.ac.kr
[3] Department of Art Technology, Inha University, Incheon, Republic of Korea

Abstract. We present non-intrusive visual observation and estimation of movement parameters using RGB data for detecting the effect of olfactory stimulation (essential oils) on movement patterns of high school students during the lessons. In particular, we examine the effect of exposure to aromatherapy has on students' movement kinetics of upper-body: velocity, acceleration, jerk and energy. The Lavender essential oil was used because of antiseptic, antimicrobial, anti-inflammatory and calming properties that may be used for treating anxiety, insomnia and depression [8,11,12]. Two classes were studied, as control and experimental group during two days with week of pause in between. First group had both days without aromatherapy, instead the second - two settings without and with aromatherapy for separate days. For post processing of the recorded data we use OpenPose [7] for estimation of position of joints, Matlab for processing positional data and tracking of the subjects, EyesWeb XMI for the extraction of movement features at a small time scale. Data showed significant differences in velocity, acceleration and jerk for left shoulder and elbow joints of experimental group in comparison between aroma and no aroma settings with Mann-Whitney U test at $p < .05$. In conclusion, this is an ongoing study shows the possibility of using movement qualities, such as kinematic movement features, extracted ecologically using non-invasive equipment, as a method to measure change of movement behavior, in the cases when no other type of data capture is possible. Future studies will involve further experiments and wider collection of movement features with higher level notations as fluidity, smoothness, rigidity of the movements.

Keywords: Pose estimation · Skeleton tracking · Movement kinematics

This work was supported by Global Research Network program through the Ministry of Education of the Republic of Korea and the National Research Foundation of Korea [NRF-2016S1A2A2912583].

C. Stephanidis (Ed.): HCII 2019, CCIS 1034, pp. 482–487, 2019.
https://doi.org/10.1007/978-3-030-23525-3_65

1 Introduction

Korea is known for its high-stress professional and educational environments, in which it is customary to work or study long hours into the night. Adolescents and the elderly, widely considered vulnerable groups in society, are the most at risk for depression, anxiety, and suicidal intentions [9,10]. An increasing number of children and adolescents have been reporting psychosomatic symptoms (e.g., pain, fatigue and tension) in response to perceived stress [5]. Detecting stress in real life with an unobtrusive methods is a challenging task. The objective of this study is to find method for stress detection that can accurately and unobtrusively detect psychological stress in real life via movement analysis. The study is conducted in the framework of Project "Effect of olfactory stimulation on extending concentration behavior patterns in high school students". We are applying computer vision techniques for data processing and analysis of movement kinematics to detect the effect of aromatherapy on movement behaviour of high school students during the lesson. As a result, this study explores the possibility of using movement qualities, extracted ecologically using non-invasive equipment (only RGB cameras), as a method to measure change of movement behaviour due to aromatherapy.

2 Related Work

In the last few years, researchers have proposed various systems that use physiological signals to automatically detect stress as well as other human emotional states [13]. Treatment of stress-related disorders can benefit from automated estimation of human movements [1]. Numerous systems have attempted emotion recognition using cardiovascular activities (e.g., Electrocardiography and Blood Volume Pulse detection sensors), electromyography signals, and skin conductance, presented in a summary [6]. Furthermore, devices like mobile phones have begun featuring sensors (accelerometer, GPS and microphones etc.). In studies from Muaremi et al. [2] and Moturu et al. [3] heart rate variability data and iphone data was used to detect low, moderate and high stress conditions and investigate the connection between sleep and mood.

The high school classroom settings of Korea does not give a high flexibility for use of on-body sensor technology, despite the interesting results of recent studies. The non-intrusive methods are assumed harmless and can be incorporated in any scenario. The use of camera can be done to capture the image of the person and then processing on it, as optical flow to robustly track a person's movements [4]. In this study the experimental settings are based on non-intrusive data collection through HD video camera.

3 Experimental Setup

3.1 Participants, Testing Procedure and Equipment

Two high school class of 26 and 27 students participated in experimental recordings, during an the usual lessons. All of the students volunteered and agreed to be further analyzed in the framework of the study with the consent of the parents, however only data of 8 subjects who were sitting in the front tables are selected for further investigation. Due to quality of the video 7–9 subjects out of 26 could be tracked with good confidence. The example of recording frame is presented on Fig. 1(a). The settings of the experimental recordings were held ecologically, as a usual high school class.

Fig. 1. (a) Example frame of recorded video data. (b) Locations of 7 upper-body joints

The subjects were studied at two separate settings: one day without aromatherapy, and one with lavender aromatherapy. The Lavender essential oil was used because of antiseptic, antimicrobial, anti-inflammatory and calming properties that may be used for treating anxiety, insomnia and depression [8]. Two classes were studied, as control and experimental group during two days with week of pause in between in two different conditions: (i) without and (ii) with exposure to lavender oil (necklace with essential oil). Both classes were recorded with four high definition cameras installed in four different sides of the classroom, adequately covering the required space. Videos were recorded at full-HD (1920×1080) resolution and 100 frames per second.

4   Computational Details

4.1   Data Processing

In order to reduce the size of initial data and increase the processing speed the recordings were segmented into smaller 5–10 min parts, excluding the frames where teacher walk around the class, obscure the camera view or the irrelevant to the lesson parts of the recordings.

In order to acquire the whole posture data as a time-series, we used Convolutional Pose Machines (CPM) developed by The Carnegie Mellon University

(CMU) [7] for pose estimation. CMP is a novel technique, that consists of a deep neural network for estimating articulated poses [7]. We extracted the position of 7 joints per frame, that were the most visible in the recordings. The following upper-body joints are considered: right and left wrist, right and left elbow, right and left shoulder, C7 the point on the spine in the middle between two shoulders, see Fig. 1(b).

CMP allowed us to recognize skeletons of multiple subjects, using a RGB video camera. We considered that OpenPose a convenient tool that available open source for extracting accurate posture data.

4.2   Tracking and Matching of Subjects

The data output available from OpenPose is JSON files for each frame of the recording separately, that consist of people pose data saved by custom JSON writer. Each JSON file has a people array of objects, where each object has: an array containing the body part locations and detection confidence formatted asx and y coordinated and c - confidence. As notation, JavaScript Object Notation or JSON is an open-standard file format that uses human-readable text to transmit data objects consisting of attribute-value pairs and array data types (or any other serializable value). In order to work with JSON files and extract the meaningful data, we developed software modules separately in MATLAB, in order to solve the following tasks:

- Restructure the data from JSON format to a matrix of values.
- Rewrite the data of each frame from separate JSON file into one matrix.
- Eliminate the information of pose data that correspond to the people that we don't need for analysis.

We have set the lower and upper threshold for positional data in order to filter out the unnecessary information. We performed tracking and matching of subjects based on the minimum Euclidean distance of the body centroid, taking into account the assumption that people are siting and do not move from their places. In this step, we computed and filtered the positional data of the X, Y coordinated of 7 joints named previously, for each participant separately. The extracted skeletal data, then is used for calculation of meaningful movement related to kinematics: acceleration, velocity, energy and jerkiness.

4.3   Movement Features Extraction

Considering the limitations of the movements that can be executed during the school, we focused our analysis on upper-body movements. We extracted low-level motion features at a small time scale (i.e., observable frame-by-frame), such as velocity, acceleration and kinetic energy and jerkiness. We perform the movement feature extraction using EyesWeb XMI[1]. EyesWeb XMI was used to read

---

[1] (http://www.infomus.org/eyesweb_eng.php) is a development software, that supports multimodal analysis and processing of non-verbal expressive gestures.

positional data, generate bi-dimensional points (x,y) for each joint and for the calculation of kinematic values and features. EyesWeb XMI blocks developed specifically to carry on these operations. They can accept a coordinate as input and can calculate a single quantity that can be chosen among speed, acceleration, jerk and curvature. Each of the calculated quantity can be calculated as tangential (i.e., magnitude of the velocity) or as its components (i.e., components of velocity for x,y coordinate). The blocks are configurable using the following set of parameters:

- Input Mode: the blocks can accept two different types of input, the first type is a single coordinate of a point, the second one is a temporal sequence of coordinates stored in a multi-channel time-series, the type of input can be chosen using this parameter.
- Output Dim: used to choose the dimensionality of the desired output that can be tangential (mono-dimensional) or components (multidimensional)
- Output Feature: is the desired output quantity, the user can choose among velocity, acceleration, jerk and curvature
- Filter Order: is the order of the Savitzky-Golay filter used in the block, the higher is the order the more smoothing is applied to the computed values.

5 Results

We examined if the differences can be noticed for each of the joint of the body separately for the factor of Aromatherapy - No Aromatherapy respectively for velocity, energy, acceleration and jerkiness. The Mann-Witney U test was chosen due to possibility of an unbalanced dataset. Data showed significant differences for left shoulder and elbow joints of experimental group in comparison between aromatherapy and no aromatherapy settings with Mann-Whitney U test with a significance level of $p < .05$ in velocity ($p = .026$, $p = .037$), acceleration ($p = .018$, $p = .037$) and jerk ($p = .020$, $p = .036$) respectively.

6 Discussions and Conclusion

In conclusion, this is an ongoing study shows the possibility of using movement qualities, such as kinematic movement features, extracted ecologically using non-invasive equipment, as a method to measure change of movement behavior, in the cases when no other type of data capture is possible. The study showed the difficulties of applying this technology in a real classroom situation as there were several complications in using uncontrolled data settings, which resulted in a large amounts of discarded data and long processing time. However, the method and techniques used are very well suitable for data collected in non-invasive way. Future studies will involve further experiments and wider collection of movement features with higher level notations as fluidity, smoothness, rigidity of the movements.

References

1. Rani, P., Liu, C., Sarkar, N., Vanman, E.: An empirical study of machine learning techniques for affect recognition in human-robot interaction. Pattern Anal. Appl. **9**, 58–69 (2006)
2. Muaremi, A., Arnrich, B., Tröster, G.: Towards measuring stress with smartphones and wearable devices during workday and sleep. BioNanoScience **3**(2), 172–183 (2013)
3. Moturu, S.T., Khayal, I., Aharony, N., Pan, W., Pentland, A.S.: Sleep, mood and sociability in a healthy population. In: Conference Proceedings: Annual International Conference of the IEEE Engineering in Medicine and Biology Society, vol. 2011, pp. 5267–5670 (2011)
4. Smith, P., Shah, M., Lobo, N.: Monitoring head/eye motion for driver alertness with one camera. In: Proceedings of the 15th International Conference on Pattern Recognition (ICPR 2000), vol. 4, pp. 636–642 (2000)
5. Hjern, A., Alfven, G., Östberg, V.: School stressors, psychological complaints and psychosomatic pain. Acta Paediatr. **97**, 112–117 (2008)
6. Ćosić, K., Popović, S., Kukolja, D., Horvat, M., Dropuljić, B.: Physiology-driven adaptive virtual reality stimulation for prevention and treatment of stress related disorders. Cyberpsychol. Behav. Soc. Netw. **13**, 73–78 (2010)
7. Wei, S., Ramakrishna, V., Kanade, T., Sheikh, Y.: Convolutional pose machines. In: IEEE Conference on Computer Vision and Pattern Recognition, pp. 4724–4732 (2006)
8. Cavanagh, H.M., Wilkinson, J.M.: Biological activities of lavender essential oil. Phytother. Res. **16**, 301–308 (2002)
9. Kim, H., Song, Y.J., Yi, J.J., Chung, W.J., Nam, C.M.: Changes in mortality after the recent economic crisis in South Korea. Ann. Epidemiol. **14**, 442–446 (2004)
10. Lee, M.: Korean adolescents' "examination hell" and their use of free time. New Dir. Child Adolesc. Dev. **99**, 9–22 (2003)
11. Bartram, T.: Encyclopaedia of Herbal Medicines. Grace publishers, Dorset (1995)
12. PDQ Integrative, Alternative, and Complementary Therapies Editorial Board, 20 September 2018. https://www.cancer.gov/about-cancer/treatment/cam/patient/cam-topics-pdq
13. Lefter, I., Burghouts, G.J., Rothkrantz, L.J.: An audio-visual dataset of human-human interactions in stressful situations. J. Multimodal User Interfaces **8**(1), 29–41 (2014)

Semantic Analysis of Online Dentist Review: Toward Assessing Safety and Quality of Dental Care

Ye Lin[1], Simon Hong[1], and Chen Liang[2,3]($\boxtimes$) iD

[1] Western University of Health Sciences, Pomona, CA 91766, USA
{ye.lin,skhong}@westernu.edu
[2] Louisiana Tech University, Ruston, LA 71272, USA
cliang@latech.edu
[3] University of South Carolina, Columbia, SC 29208, USA

Abstract. Safety and quality measurement of dental care is important but shows a lack of standardized measure concept set. In recent years, patient review websites (PRW) emerged as a widely used platform for health consumers, including dental patients. The massive patient online reviews (POR) are a rich data source that captures various aspects of safety and quality of dental care, such as patient experience, cost, clinical efficiency, outcomes, etc. However, PORs consist of both structured data (e.g., ratings) and unstructured data (e.g., comments in free text). The processing of textual data is costly for traditional qualitative methods. This study aims to jointly leverage automated text processing and expert evaluation to extract safety and quality related semantic information from dental PORs. As an exploratory study, we sampled dental PORs of Los Angeles, California from RateMDs. Using the National Quality Measures Clearinghouse (NQMC) domain framework as a reference, we identified salient topics relating to clinical quality measures (e.g., patient experience), healthcare delivery measures (e.g., cost, management), etc. We also identified topics relevant to safety and quality but were not covered by any domains of NQMC, suggesting a possible gap of concepts. Finally, our study demonstrated great potential of adopting informatics, specifically, social media computing in POR study of dental care.

Keywords: Quality of health care · Social media · Dental care

1 Introduction

In the United States, 88% of adults gained health-related information from the Internet [1]. In the past two decades, the proliferation of web-based doctor review carries growing influence in patients' medical decision making, reflected in the increased number of patient review websites (PRW) and a high percent (59%) of patients who reported high importance of PRW when choosing a doctor [2–4]. The massive patient online reviews (POR) also provide a unique angle to the safety and quality of health care.

© Springer Nature Switzerland AG 2019
C. Stephanidis (Ed.): HCII 2019, CCIS 1034, pp. 488–494, 2019.
https://doi.org/10.1007/978-3-030-23525-3_66

Nevertheless, POR studies for oral health care is sparse as compared to general health care services. In the most recent systematic review of POR studies [4], there is only one study from Germany that focused on PORs of dentists [5]. Other than the lack of POR studies in dentistry, in fact, the safety and quality measures have been elusive generally in oral health care as suggested by the Institute of Medicine [6, 7]. In addition to the two official web-based sources of quality measure including dentistry (i.e., Hospital Compare and Dialysis Facility Compare), commercial PRWs are an important source of data about oral health care.

An important reason for the limited POR studies in oral health care is the challenge of harnessing and analyzing POR data from the Internet. PORs typically consist of both ratings on the Likert scale and comments in the free text. Arguably, textual data are time-consuming for traditional qualitative analysis while technically challenging for automated processing as they contain terminologies, ambiguous semantic information, expressions of informal language, etc. As for textual data from social media, tailored analytics is often needed to explore social networking and cognitive-behavioral features. Thus far, there is no specialized text mining method for extracting safety and quality-related information from the textual data of dental PORs.

Leveraging social media computing and text mining, the present study aims to explore safety and quality-related semantic information from PORs of dentists with the goal of understanding in patients' perspective the most salient problems and concerns during dental care experience. We extracted PORs of dentists from RateMDs, a popular PRW in the US. We incorporated customized natural language processing (NLP) techniques and manual evaluation to extract safety and quality-relevant semantic information from PORs.

2   Methods

2.1   Data

Ratings and reviews were collected from RateMDs (http://ratemds.com). RateMDs is a web-based platform for PORs in the US. The website accepts (1) an overall rating (1–5 stars) of the healthcare providers, (2) ratings (1–5 stars) on four dimensions, respectively, including staff, punctuality, helpfulness, and knowledge, and (3) comments in free text. Note that both (1) and (2) are structured data whereas (3) is unstructured. RateMDs also allows users to specify categories and specialties of healthcare, locations (city, state), gender, whether verified doctors, and whether accepting new patients during the search of healthcare providers.

We collected data for all of the dentists in the city of Los Angeles, California, that was documented on RateMDs, resulting in a total of 1669 providers. These web-based data were collected through in-house developed Python codes primarily building on *boilerpipe 3* package. There were 221 of the providers who received at least one review. Therefore, data for these 221 providers were used for analysis. Data collection was completed in February 2019.

2.2   Analysis

We firstly summarized the basic facts about ratings. Ratings were also used jointly in the semantic analysis of the comments. To facilitate the analysis of comments, we employed the probabilistic topic model based on latent Dirichlet allocation (LDA) algorithm [8]. The model was built on the input of free-text comments to automatically summarize a number of topics that the comments carry. Since this is an unsupervised approach, very limited hand processing was required, which largely reduced the processing time. To explore how topics that are associated with five different ratings vary, we developed five topic models using comments distinguished by associated overall ratings.

To ensure the validity of topic models, we finetuned the models by experimenting with different numbers of topics as the model parameter. The best parameter was identified when there was a maximized coherence value [9]. Therefore, it was expected to result in one best-performed model for every overall rating.

We employed *Genism* package along with a number of supportive text processing packages in Python for the text analysis and model development as described above. We followed the standard text processes including free text cleaning, tokenization, stop words removing, and lemmatization with the aim of preparing the data ready for topic modeling.

Next to the model development is the human evaluation of safety and quality related topics. We hand selected relevant topics for group discussion and qualitative analysis. The National Quality Measures Clearinghouse (NQMC) domain framework was used as a reference for the identification of relevant topics [10].

3   Results

3.1   Descriptive Analyses

Of the 221 providers who have at least one review, we identified 139 (62.9%) providers of 5-star, 25 (11.3%) providers of 4-star, 27 (12.2%) providers of 3-star, 18 (8.1%) providers of 2-star, and 12 (5.4%) providers of 1-star. These providers received as many as 74 reviews or as less as one review.

3.2   Semantic Analyses

Topic Models. We developed 5 topic models for comments associated with 1–5 star of overall ratings. In each model, we tested different numbers of topics as the model parameter ranging from 2 to 100 with a stepping of 2. Figure 1 shows the experimental results. For models for 1-star, 2-star, and 4-star comments, the coherence scores converged, indicating the existence of the most meaningful model identified by an explicit number of topics. Therefore, we selected the number of topics to be 10 for the 1-star model (coherence score = 0.67), 14 for the 2-star model (coherence score = 0.83), and 18 for the 4-star model (coherence score = 0.47) for the human evaluation. For models for 3-star and 5-star, the coherence scores did not converge, indicating that the semantics are too sparse to be summarized into salient topics. Considering a relatively high coherence score with a smaller number of topics, we selected the number of topics to be 8 for the 3-star model (coherence score = 0.46) and 42 for the 5-star model (coherence score = 0.44) for the human evaluation. The resulted models outputted a set of topics represented by 10 representative words. See Table 1.

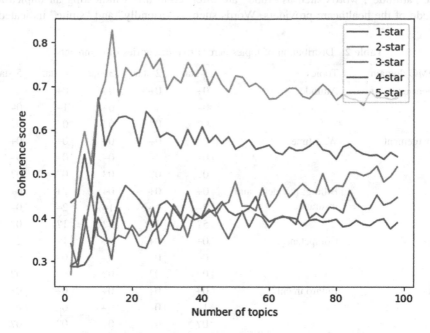

Fig. 1. Coherence scores affected by the number of topics.

Human Evaluation. After reviewing the topics, we identified topics that are relevant to the safety and quality of dental care. During this process, we used thesauruses from the NQMC domain framework as the reference of inclusion criteria for identification of safety and quality relevant topics. Table 2 shows the occurrences of topics across different NQMC domains.

Table 1. Selected topics with surrounding words.

Models	Surrounding words of a topic
1-star	"know" + "go" + "dentistry" + "dentist" + "horrible" + "experience" + "really" + "expensive" + "painful" + "receive"
2-star	"son" + "appointment" + "treat" + "rude" + "attitude" + "sign" + "knapp" + "strap" + "nasty" + "do"
3-star	"helpful" + "whitening" + "convince" + "stuff" + "expensive" + "unneeded" + "stand" + "disappoint" + "pressure" + "usually"
4-star	"painless" + "skilful" + "appointment" + "cosmetic" + "worth" + "recomend" + "julie" + "extra" + "sameni" + "hard"
5-star	"nice" + "office" + "organize" + "experience" + "several" + "staff" + "go" + "casellini" + "helpful" + "friendly"

A meaningful topic is typically represented by a couple of representative words. For example, the topic "billing/payment/insurance" is surrounded by words such as "insurance", "insurer", "charge", "bill", "billing", "pay", "payment", "cost", and "claim". There were also words co-occurred with the words above indicating a satisfaction or dissatisfaction to the billing, payment, and insurance issues. Words such as "expensive", "unneeded", "horrible", "disappointed", and "lie" indicated dissatisfaction. Words such as "awesome", "great", "amazing" were associated with satisfaction. With regard to the topic "attitude", words such as "rude" are often cooccurred indicating an unpleasant attitude of the healthcare providers. Words such as "friendly" and "smile" indicated a

Table 2. Distribution of topics across five categories of comments.

NQMC domains	Topics	1-star	2-star	3-star	4-star	5-star
Patient experience	Attitude	0+	0+	0+	0+	5+
		0–	4–	0–	1–	0–
		0?	0?	0?	0?	0?
Management	Wait time	0+	0+	0+	0+	0+
		0–	2–	0–	0–	0–
		0?	0?	0?	0?	0?
Cost	Billing, payment, and insurance	0+	0+	0+	2+	0+
		2–	1–	1–	2–	0–
		5?	2?	3?	1?	0?
NA	Competency	0+	0+	0+	1+	2+
		0–	0–	0–	0–	0–
		0?	0?	0?	0?	0?
NA	Environment	0+	0+	0+	0+	0+
		1–	0–	0–	0–	0–
		0?	0?	0?	0?	0?
NA	Recommendation	0+	0+	0+	4+	2+
Total relevant topics		8	9	4	11	9

Note: + indicates positive sentiment; – indicates negative sentiment; ? indicates unknown sentiment.

pleasant attitude.

We also found relevant topics that were not captured by any thesauruses from the NQMC domains (see Table 2). The topic "competency" was identified as relevant to describe the appropriateness and professionalism of using clinical skills. Although somewhat subjective, especially for patients who typically have limited medical knowledge, this topic is believed to be associated with the clinical quality measure as defined in the NQMC domain framework. The words "knowledgeable" and "skillful" were representative words surrounding this topic. We also found the topic that was possibly associated with the environmental aspect of the healthcare providers. Owing to the small sample size, we only found one such a topic with a negative sentiment, "nasty", from 1-star comments. In addition, the topic "recommendation" was identified from only 4-star and 5-star comments indicating whether patients were willing to recommend the healthcare providers.

4 Discussion

The present study is to the best of our knowledge the first pilot study that focuses on textual data analysis of PORs for dental care. Our findings have confirmed that data from PRWs are important to the measure of health care safety and quality, specifically, including oral health care. Although the health consumers' opinion and experience can be highly personalized and even subjective, we believe the PORs are an important data source for identifying indicators of oral health safety and quality. In this effort, a comprehensive research agenda is highly demanded to understand (1) the behavioral aspects of dental health consumers in the interaction between consumers, PRWs, and real-world providers, (2) effective and efficient social media computing methods tailored for dental care related data, (3) the role and usage of knowledge extracted from PORs with the scope of improving safety and quality measures and oral health care.

From the patients' perspective, the quality of dental care shares both common and unique aspects as compared to general health care. For example, patients of dental care providers also concerned about doctors' competency and patient experience in general. But dental patients weight heavy on providers' attitude and cost of care. Patients who rated 1-star for dental care providers mostly commented on the cost related problems whereas had very limited comments on procedures, outcomes, and patient experience.

Safety and quality measure for oral health care has been fell behind. Our findings suggested the significance of leveraging data from PRWs to improve the quality measure of oral health care. More importantly, our findings suggested a possible gap between traditional quality measure and data available on PRWs. For example, we found missing perspectives in the NQMC domain framework when it was used as a reference for identifying safety and quality relevant topics.

Although this work is a pilot study, we summarized the limitations and corresponding future directions as follows. First, our findings are based on a small sample of data from a single location (i.e., urban) and a single PRW (i.e., RateMDs). The small sample size may have affected the performance of topic modeling. Single location and single site study also limit the generalizability. The next step is to expand the data analysis on multiple data sources. Second, the granularity of data analysis could be improved. We will include tailored NLP procedures in the future studies. Third, the POR studies with the scope of assessing health care safety and quality are critiqued about providing less-objective data. It is also a limitation to the present study. Cross-evaluation is required to demonstrate the robustness of the findings.

References

1. Kadry, B., Chu, L.F., Kadry, B., Gammas, D., Macario, A.: Analysis of 4999 online physician ratings indicates that most patients give physicians a favorable rating. J. Med. Internet Res. **13**, e95 (2011)
2. Lagu, T., Hannon, N.S., Rothberg, M.B., Lindenauer, P.K.: Patients' evaluations of health care providers in the era of social networking: an analysis of physician-rating websites. J. Gen. Intern. Med. **25**, 942–946 (2010)

3. Hanauer, D.A., Zheng, K., Singer, D.C., Gebremariam, A., Davis, M.M.: Public awareness, perception, and use of online physician rating sites. JAMA **311**, 734–735 (2014)
4. Hong, Y.A., Liang, C., Radcliff, T., Wigfall, L., Street, R.: What do patients say about physicians and hospitals online? A systematic review of studies on patient online reviews. J. Med. Internet Res. 21, e12521 (2019)
5. Emmert, M., Halling, F., Meier, F.: Evaluations of dentists on a German physician rating Website: an analysis of the ratings. J. Med. Internet Res. **17**, e15 (2015)
6. Services: Improving access to oral health care for vulnerable and underserved populations. National Academies Press (2012)
7. Institute of Medicine of the National Academies Committee on an Oral Health Initiative: Advancing oral health in America. National Academies Press, Washington, DC (2011)
8. Blei, D.M., Ng, A.Y., Jordan, M.I.: Latent Dirichlet allocation. J. Mach. Learn. Res. **3**, 993–1022 (2003)
9. Newman, D., Lau, J.H., Grieser, K., Baldwin, T.: Automatic evaluation of topic coherence. In: Human Language Technologies: The 2010 Annual Conference of the North American Chapter of the Association for Computational Linguistics, pp. 100–108 (2010)
10. Agency for Healthcare Research and Quality: NQMC Measure Domain Framework. https://www.ahrq.gov/gam/summaries/domain-framework/index.html

Toward an Integrated Situational Awareness Measuring Function for Electronic Health Records

Vida Pashaei[✉] and David C. Gross

Department of Systems and Industrial Engineering, The University of Arizona,
Tucson, AZ, USA
vidapashaei1993@email.arizona.edu

Abstract. Although Situational Awareness (SA) has been an active area of research for decades, the integration of SA system frameworks specifically within the healthcare industry is a fairly new topic of interest. Recent, rapid advances in technology, especially in the field of biomedical informatics, have introduced many SA challenges; proven links between SA and patient safety warrants further studies as to identify and address the issues associated with these newly available tools. Electronic Health Records (EHRs) are one of the most adopted tools in the U.S. healthcare system that perform various functions, capturing many kinds of medical data. One subset of patients that makes use of EHRs are insomnia patients. Insomnia is the most common sleep disorder among the general population; approximately 10% to 15% of adults in America suffer from chronic insomnia [1]. Although many researchers have tackled issues associated with EHRs including the information chaos that negatively impacts SA, none of them have measured or analyzed actual SA Measures of Effectiveness (MOEs). Developing SA MOEs for impact of EHRs on SA effectiveness for the clinician decision-making process may yield improved quality of treatment for insomnia patients.

Keywords: Situational Awareness · SA · Electronic Health Records · EHR · Insomnia · Situational Awareness Global Assessment Technique · SAGAT · Virtual Reality · VR · Human-Computer Interaction · User interface

1 Introduction

1.1 Insomnia

Insomnia is defined as the subjective perception of the struggle to initiate and maintain a high-quality sleep on a nightly basis, which can lead to cognitive impairments [2]. Moreover, insomnia is categorized into two major sub-categories: chronic insomnia and transient insomnia, the root causes of which are very different [3].

Treatments for insomnia can come in the forms of pharmacologic and non-pharmacologic interventions. As most insomnia drugs reportedly cause many severe side effects, psychiatrists must exercise caution when seeking the most suitable drug specific to each patient [4].

© Springer Nature Switzerland AG 2019
C. Stephanidis (Ed.): HCII 2019, CCIS 1034, pp. 495–499, 2019.
https://doi.org/10.1007/978-3-030-23525-3_67

Epidemiologic studies support gender-based differences in sleep disorders [2–6]. However, these differences are prone to be overlooked by the physicians; the practitioners might not be situationally aware of the information even though it is readily available.

1.2 Situational Awareness

Perhaps the most adopted SA reference is Endsley's body of work. According to her, SA goes beyond information processing as it also counts for projection of the information to the future. Additionally, Endsley provides a framework of SA consisting of three levels, which was adopted in many domains including healthcare:

1. Perceiving important data in the environment,
2. Understanding the meaning of data and turning it into information, and
3. Projecting information to the near future [7].

As the quality improvement methodology Define, Measure, Analyze, Improve, and Control (DMAIC) suggests, the path to improvement involves measuring well-defined factors; therefore, having an integrated SA measuring function within EHRs may result in higher levels of SA for Physicians.

1.3 Electronic Health Records

Electronic Health Records (EHRs) are widely adopted in the U.S. healthcare system capturing health-related data; data that is included in EHRs can be either structured or non-structured. The information contained in EHRs may also support decision-making processes.

EHRs can be developed by commercial or non-commercial vendors. The Primary purposes of EHRs include setting objectives and planning patient care, documenting the delivery of care and evaluating the outcomes of care [8].

Some of the EHR functions are Physician Order Entries, messaging, patient summary, warnings for a drug on drug interactions, etc. [9].

One of the many challenges associated with EHRs is that the vast amount of available data in EHRs begs the need for improved search methods and creative visualizations to present the data at the time that is needed. There are also many other issues involved with EHRs including but not limited to, privacy concerns, data safety and security issues, system glitches, so on so forth.

Many studies have discussed the capabilities of EHRs for improving SA in the health care domain. For example, Lurio discusses how EHR alert systems can boost public health SA of clinicians [10]. However, most studies of this type do not actually measure SA to support their claims.

2 Literature Review

SA can be measured either directly or indirectly; one of the most common measures of SA is Endsley's Situational Awareness Global Assessment Technique (SAGAT), which requires freezing the process at random times and having queries completed by the operator [11, 12].

However, in most healthcare settings that cannot be the case, simply because freezing the process cannot be done. For example, resuscitation processes should not be stopped. That is when indirect measures (simulation-based measures) are used.

The nature of healthcare system is different from other complex environments, in that this system is directly affecting individuals' lives; therefore, not only SA measuring techniques should be different than those that are proposed for other dynamic environments, but also SA framework could be subject to changes.

For instance, to incorporate SA within the healthcare system, researchers proposed a fourth level to this model; "Resolution"; that is, choosing the best available solution based on the first three stages of SA and translating to patient care [13].

Moreover, a seven-level SA framework has been proposed for resuscitation teams that includes allocating resources, planning, avoiding fixation errors, calling for help when needed, prioritizing attention, re-assessing patient, and shared mental model [14].

The process of treating insomnia, however, can be stopped; therefore, direct measures of SA; such as SAGAT are applicable to this situation.

Virtual Reality (VR) is proven to be effective in enhancing SA scores through training by providing advanced user interfaces, which facilitates Human-Computer Interaction. A handful of Virtual Learning Environments (VLE); such as WebOnCOLL and Active World (AW) have been developed for the purpose of training clinicians over the past decade, neither of which have been utilized to measure SA within EHRs [15].

Consider Telehealth Outreach for Unified Community Health (TOUCH), a virtual environment for training medical students that enables real-time communication [16]. However, this VLE had many disadvantages including involving no eye-tracking capabilities in the system, which made it impossible to figure out what the remote users were looking at.

Simulation-Based Training (SBT) is a widely adopted technique in various areas of healthcare; on the contrary, automizing measuring process is fairly new for researchers [17]. Furthermore, Wald explains how complex user interfaces in EHRs adversely affect SA of the physician, which warrants the need for more optimal functions that are built-in to EHRs [18].

3 Methodology

The University of Arizona's Architecture-Driven Systems Laboratory (ADSL) developed the Systems Architecture Synthesis and Analysis Framework (SASAF), whose main objective is to find the optimal set of domain-specialized hardware, software, procedures, and policies for systems architectures using interoperable infrastructure shown in Fig. 1. SASAF tools allow for the creation of knowledge-based environments through ontology editing.

Fig. 1. ADSL SASAF operator hardware station

An ontological approach is proposed to be utilized based on the guidelines provided by the National Institutes of Health (NIH) for the evaluation and management of chronic insomnia. A SASAF ontology can link many insomnia clinical practice procedures developed by NIH to EHR data, thereby aiding practicing clinicians. The process of developing an SA measurement from the SASAF ontology can be built upon SAGAT.

For the purpose of this paper the optimal solution included the VR coding software Unity.

4 Results and Discussion

A prototype of the proposed integrated SA measurement function for EHRs extends the pre-existing ADSL Integrated Sensor Viewer, which has been successfully applied in other domains such as Space Situational Awareness. This prototype shall leverage the ADSL's Virtual Reality (VR) capabilities, including the rendering engine Unity. The prototype shall be capable of processing EHR data for insomnia patients, comparing them to NIH guidelines, generating SAGAT queries for physicians, and measuring SA scores from these queries. Finally, measuring SA regularly influences SA scores positively, which is the objective of this study.

5 Conclusion

The ADSL's Development Processes include future activities to be completed incrementally, including implementing the prototype, designing experiments with the actual integrated function for EHRs, and advancing the function for other healthcare purposes. All in all, this study shall develop an extendable SA measurement function for EHRs that can directly measure the SA of psychiatrists treating insomnia patients, allowing for unprecedented treatment through data immersion.

Future studies shall concentrate on integrating eye-tracking facilities to EHRs; that is the eye-tracker will capture at what part of the screen the doctor was looking, at any given time. In other words, better potential measures of SA could be proposed when using new technologies.

References

1. Roth, T.: New developments for treating sleep disorders. J. Clin. Psychiatry **62**, 3–4 (2001)
2. Hale, L., et al.: Does mental health history explain gender disparities in insomnia symptoms among young adults? Sleep Med. **10**(10), 1118–1123 (2009)
3. Shaib, F., Attarian, H.: Sex and gender differences in sleep disorders: an overview. In: Principles of Gender-Specific Medicine, 3rd edn., pp. 585–601. Elsevier (2017)
4. Soares, C.N.: Insomnia in women: an overlooked epidemic? Arch. Womens Ment. Health **8**(4), 205–213 (2005)
5. Pandi-Perumal, S.R.: Sleep and its disorders in women. Synopsis of Sleep Medicine, vol. 1. Apple Academic Press (2016)
6. Pusalavidyasagar, S., Abbasi, A., Cervenka, T., Irfan, M.: Sleep in women across the stages of life. Clin. Pulm. Med. **25**(3), 89–99 (2018)
7. Endsley, M.R.: Measurement of situation awareness in dynamic systems. Hum. Factors J. Hum. Factors Ergon. Soc. **37**(1), 65–84 (1995)
8. Häyrinen, K., Saranto, K., Nykänen, P.: Definition, structure, content, use and impacts of electronic health records: a review of the research literature. Int. J. Med. Inform. **77**(5), 291–304 (2008)
9. Hsiao, C.-J., Hing, E., Ashman, J.: Trends in electronic health record system use among office-based physicians, United States, 2007–2012. US Department of Health and Human Services, Centers for Disease Control and … (2014)
10. Lurio, J., et al.: Using electronic health record alerts to provide public health situational awareness to clinicians. J. Am. Med. Inform. Assoc. **17**(2), 217–219 (2010)
11. Endsley, M.R.: Direct measurement of situation awareness: Validity and use of SAGAT. In: Situational Awareness. pp. 129–156. Routledge (2017)
12. Endsley, M.R.: Situation awareness global assessment technique (SAGAT). In: Proceedings of the IEEE 1988 National Aerospace and Electronics Conference, NAECON 1988, pp. 789–795 (1988)
13. McGuinness, B., Foy, L.: A subjective measure of SA: the Crew Awareness Rating Scale (CARS). In: Proceedings of the First Human Performance, Situation Awareness, and Automation Conference, Savannah, Georgia, vol. 16 (2000)
14. O'Neill, T.A., White, J., Delaloye, N., Gilfoyle, E.: A taxonomy and rating system to measure situation awareness in resuscitation teams. PLoS ONE **13**(5), e0196825 (2018)
15. Rajaei, H., Aldhalaan, A.: Advances in virtual learning environments and classrooms. In: Proceedings of the 14th Communications and Networking Symposium, pp. 133–142 (2011)
16. Caudell, T.P., et al.: Virtual patient simulator for distributed collaborative medical education. Anat. Rec. B New Anat. **270**(1), 23–29 (2003). An Official Publication of the American Association of Anatomists
17. Lloyd, M., Watmough, S., Bennett, N.: Simulation-based training: applications in clinical pharmacy. Clin. Pharmacist **10**(9), 3–10 (2018)
18. Wald, E.R., Windell, D.: Dynamically optimizing user interfaces, February 2018

Development of Usability Guidelines for Mobile Health Applications

Bidisha Roy$^{(\boxtimes)}$, Mark Call, and Natalie Abts

MedStar National Center for Human Factors in Healthcare,
Washington, DC 20008, USA
bidisha.roy@medstar.net

Abstract. The healthcare space continues to embrace the convenience of mobile health applications, yet these app are not regulated nor standardized results in suboptimal results and potential patient harm. Xcertia aims to address this need by bringing together subject matter experts, stakeholders, academics, developers, and students to develop guidelines to steer mobile health app development. These team members were divided into five key workgroups: Privacy, Security, Content, Operability, and Usability. The current paper focuses on the Usability group and its process and development of its ten guidelines. Leveraging the unique strengths of academics and industry subject matter experts, the group researched, identified, and grouped key usability components into basic usability guidelines, each including its own set of detailed performance requirements. Employing an iterative process, the workgroup rigorously reviewed these requirements to capture only those that are vital to app efficiency and effectiveness. These ten guidelines cater to a wide audience with varying knowledge of usability and human factor principles and address the topics of visual design, readability and understandability, navigation, feedback, notifications, help resources and troubleshooting, historical data, accessibility, and app evaluation. The guidelines aim to guide mHealth stakeholders in developing safe and intuitive apps while also catering to target users within specific use environments.

Keywords: mHealth · Usability · Mobile health applications · Healthcare

1 Introduction

Current industry standards for development and evaluation of new medical products are largely focused on FDA-regulated products. However, mobile health (mHealth) applications have rapidly gained traction in health management and care, creating a need for stricter guidelines mHealth apps that may or may not be considered medical devices. Though some informal guidelines have been publicly available, the medical industry has lacked a reliable, standardized reference to address the specific design, development, and testing needs of mHealth apps. To address this need, Xcertia—an mHealth app collaborative founded by the American Medical Association (AMA), American Heart Association (AHA), DHX Group, and Healthcare Information and Management Systems Society (HIMSS)—released on Feb. 13, 2019 its initial draft of a

© Springer Nature Switzerland AG 2019
C. Stephanidis (Ed.): HCII 2019, CCIS 1034, pp. 500–506, 2019.
https://doi.org/10.1007/978-3-030-23525-3_68

new set of guidelines promoting more thoughtful development of mobile health applications (mHealth apps) [1]. These guidelines cover five key topic areas critical to app development: Privacy, Security, Content, Operability, and Usability. Because the authors of this poster belong to the Usability faction of the collaboration, this poster describes the content and development of the Usability Guidelines [2].

Notably, the creation of these guidelines was driven by the intent for application to a diverse array of mHealth apps. The Xcertia Guidelines apply to any app operating in the healthcare realm, from guided home-use data tracking and clinical decision support apps to apps that serve as medical information repositories and databases. Consequently, the guidelines cover apps used by a wide range of clinical and lay (i.e., patient) users for varied use cases across a range of use environments. The Xcertia Guidelines strive to achieve several goals across both the mHealth and overarching healthcare industries. Because the guidelines are a consolidated set of industry standards, it is expected that app developers will utilize them as a resource to improve products and decrease time to market. The guidelines also aim to reduce the burden on healthcare systems pursuing procurement of clinically-based apps: if healthcare systems can confirm that an app of interest meets the Xcertia Guideline's performance requirements, they can be confident they are implementing effective, well-designed apps into their care environments. Consumers, whether clinician or patient, can also be confident of the apps' ease of use, content accuracy, and confidentiality protection capability.

In addition to the overarching goals for the Xcertia Guidelines, the Usability Guidelines specifically aim to fulfill two primary purposes. Firstly, they aim to assess how a mobile health app is designed to be safe and easy to use by incorporating five key quality components of usability: learnability, efficiency, memorability, prevention of errors, and user satisfaction. Secondly, they strive to optimize apps for use by the specified users within the specified use environments.

2   Methods

Xcertia consolidated five working groups of industry experts across a variety of disciplines to develop the guidelines for each topic area. Workgroup members included academics, app developers, subject matter experts in the section topics, healthcare providers, and other industry stakeholders. The Usability Guidelines were informed by the following sources: industry experience and expertise, primary empirical research in mHealth and human-computer interaction, usability heuristics, and examination of secondary usability literature and user experience standards. After each group generated a subset of overarching individual guidelines for each of the five sections, members further elaborated on each guideline by providing a series of performance requirements. For example, the Operability group generated a "Connectivity" guideline composed of four individual performance requirements.

Over the course of seven months, members utilized an iterative development process to build upon existing guidelines drafts and generate new content. After individually generating and editing content on a collaborative document, all members participated in biweekly remote meetings to discuss and review generated content and determine progress targets for the next meeting. This iterative process fostered consistent critical review of the proposed guidelines as team members reflected on the relevance and robustness of research supporting draft content. In February of 2019, all five sections were combined, reviewed, and prepared for publication.

The Usability group identified high-level topics primarily by leveraging both insights from subject matter experts and recent research identified by graduate students. Graduate students performed a thorough review of the usability and human factors literature pertaining to mobile applications and presented their findings to the group. Both subject matter experts and graduate students collaboratively organized content, allowing the high-level categories (guidelines) to evolve organically. For example, "alerts, alarms, and notifications" was once considered part of the App Feedback guideline but was later separated into its own guideline after the group generated a high number of relevant performance requirements dedicated to the subject. Following categorization, key findings were consolidated into a document as guidelines, which were then reviewed multiple times to identify coherence to baseline standards, such as a consistent "voice" and use of accessible language to reach a broad audience (i.e., understandable to those without technical or design backgrounds).

3   Results

3.1   Introduction to Results

The Xcertia Guidelines contain five sections (Privacy, Security, Content, Operability, and Usability), each of which includes a subset of individual guidelines that is further broken down into a series of performance requirements. While each guideline provides an overarching theme or principle for consideration, the performance requirements provide detailed, prescriptive instructions directed at readers who are designing, developing, or evaluating mHealth apps. Key topics from each guideline section are summarized below, with an emphasis on the Usability Guidelines. Overall, the Usability Guidelines outline how to design for safety and ease-of-use by optimizing learnability, efficiency, memorability, error prevention, and user satisfaction, covering such topics as alerts/notifications, navigation, troubleshooting, user disabilities, evaluation techniques, and more.

3.2   Usability Guidelines

The Usability Guidelines emphasize the importance of designing for an app's specified target users and use environments to promote efficient and accurate operation resulting in safe, satisfying user experiences. Each high-level Usability Guideline is presented and defined in Table 1.

The first guideline, Visual Design, lists 10 performance requirements to help developers, designers, and managers follow usability standards that promote content legibility and clarity to support user engagement and minimize distractions. Some of the requirements address topics of formatting, layout, and adaptability. Selected examples of Visual Design performance requirements are highlighted below:

Table 1. Usability guidelines

Guideline	Definition
U1 Visual Design	Apps should follow standards of visual design that promote legibility, clarity of content, and user engagement without introducing unnecessary distraction. Apps that leverage user expectations in their design strategy shorten the learning curve and decrease user frustration
U2 Readability	Text used within the app must be readable, understandable, and adjustable to accommodate ease of operation for a variety of devices, users and use environments. Text size adjustments should not alter the screen layout in a manner that could confuse users or prohibit ease of use
U3 App Navigation	Users should be able to navigate quickly and easily between screens to complete tasks. Navigation should feel natural and familiar, and should not dominate the interface or draw focus away from content
U4 Onboarding	Apps should facilitate an intuitive process for launching, registering, entering personal information (if applicable), and preparing for first-time use. As the users' first introduction to the app, a simple and intuitive onboarding process is critical in instilling user confidence that the app will provide a satisfying overall user experience
U5 App Feedback	Apps should provide sufficient feedback to inform the user of the results of their actions and promote understanding of what is going on in the system. Feedback includes app reactions to user input, including providing messages to the user. Efficient and informative feedback ensures that users will be able to understand and perceive app actions without frustration. Guidelines associated with feedback related to notifications, alarms, and alerts can be found within Guideline U6
U6 Notifications, Alerts and Alarms	Notifications (general reminders or updates to the user), alerts (non-urgent indicators intended to capture user attention), and alarms (urgent indicators that may be safety-critical) must consider both safety and usability to inform users when attention is required
U7 Help Resources and Troubleshooting	Apps must incorporate help and troubleshooting features to guide the user when needed. Unavailable or unclear help features may lead to user confusion, frustration, and ultimately app abandonment
U8 Historical Data	Apps used to gather data should store historical data in a manner that is easy for users to access and understand
U9 Accessibility	Apps should be designed and built to accommodate a wide variety of users, including those with disabilities such as perceptual impairment (visual or auditory), cognitive impairment and learning disabilities, and motor impairment. Designs that are made to be adaptable will facilitate ease of use for all users, not just those with disabilities. Additionally, app design should aim to accommodate use with common assistive technologies (e.g., screen readers)

(continued)

Table 1. (*continued*)

Guideline	Definition
U10 Ongoing App Evaluation	Throughout the entire development lifecycle, apps should undergo robust, iterative evaluations that follow a user-centered design process. Understanding the user perspective and evaluating technology to test assumptions is critical in developing safe and usable products, and apps that do not meet user expectations or are cumbersome to use are unlikely to be adopted. Apps requiring review by the Food and Drug Administration (FDA) should undergo testing evaluation that follows the FDA's guidelines for applying human factors and usability engineering to medical device design

- U1.06 Important elements critical to app functionality and content understandability should be positioned above the scroll line to minimize the opportunity for missed information. Users should be able to clearly identify when screens extend beyond the scroll line.
- U1.09 When possible, reduce the probability of data entry error by providing users with selectable options rather than requiring text entry.

The second guideline, Readability, contains 6 performance requirements which provide clarity on such topics as default font size, text hierarchies, content clarity, and comprehension level.

Guideline U3, App Navigation, includes 5 requirements to address ease of use so that navigating an app feels natural and intuitive. This guideline outlines methods for users to navigate within an app, such as menus, swiping, and reversible actions. Selected examples of App Navigation performance requirements are highlighted below.

- U3.01 Users should be able to easily identify where they are in the app and how to navigate to different destinations. The navigational path should be logical, predictable, and easy to follow. For screens that users may need to access in succession, providing shortcuts may improve ease of navigation.
- U3.03 App design should facilitate reversible actions by allowing the user to navigate back to previous pages.
- U3.05 The app's main menu should be easily locatable and identifiable. Standard app design conventions would likely lead most users look for a menu on the top, left-hand side of the screen. A collapsed menu is often associated with the three-bar "hamburger" icon that frequent app users are expected to be familiar with.

The Onboarding guideline aims to create a natural method of registering and preparing users using an app for the first time. Onboarding performance requirements discuss the importance of clear launch screens, bypassing introductory information and steps, and tutorials within its six requirements.

Guideline U5, App Feedback, is a vital piece of user app interaction as it assists the user in understanding both the results of their actions and how the system is responding. This guideline contains 6 performance requirements that call out important feedback characteristics, app transparency, and error messages.

The importance of the Notifications, Alerts & Alarms guideline lies in its safety implications for users. Performance requirements address topics such as sensory output to elicit users' attention, cancelling alarms, and accessing alarms at a later time.

Guideline U7, Help Resources and Troubleshooting, addresses users' ability to access helpful documentation and address potential app issues, which is vital to user-app interaction. Performance requirements discuss walkthroughs and easy access to help features, as well as appropriate use of text and images to convey helpful content.

Historical Data is an important component that is often excluded in apps. This guideline encourages easily accessibility and understandability of historical information. This can be accomplished by adhering to the data manipulation, presentations, and storage capacity-related performance requirements.

Guideline U9, Accessibility, provides basic requirements an app must meet to support efficient use by physically- or cognitively-impaired users. This guideline contains 6 performance requirements addressing such topics as flexibility in various input modalities, content adaptability, and the need to retain functionality and ease of use.

Lastly, On-Going App Evaluation, guideline U10, emphasizes the importance of continuous app evaluations to foster continuous app efficiency to an ever-changing user population. Its 7 performance requirements discuss the need for targeting and researching user populations, the various methods and process of user testing, and the importance of testing in a realistic environment. This guideline stresses the importance of usability evaluations in developing safe applications.

3.3   Other Guidelines

Privacy

The Privacy Guidelines cover protection of user information, including protected health information. Key themes in this section include disclosing data collection and use, access to collected data, and obtaining user permission before data sharing. Compliance with important laws and regulations, including the Health Insurance Portability and Accountability Act (HIPAA), the Children's Online Privacy Protection Act (COPPA), and the European Union General Data Protection Regulation (GDPR), is also discussed. This topic is likely relevant in addressing concerns of patient users, who may be reluctant to utilize an app that stores and transmits personal health data.

Security

The Security section focuses on protecting apps from threats and ensuring data remains uncompromised. Security is critical for mHealth apps used in the clinical space, which may store data for many patients. These guidelines highlight a robust risk evaluation process and various threat identification methods, including scanning and encryption. HIPAA compliance is again discussed here, as well response to and recovery from data breach incidents.

Content

Ensuring that information is current and accurate is particularly important for mHealth apps, those providing clinical decision support, such as suggested medical treatments or interventions. The Content Guidelines emphasize transparency regarding information sources, including providing access to data for evidence-based claims, and advertised content. Additionally, medical information presented in an app must be up-to-date. If new data suggests that best practices be updated, any outdated content that could be medically dangerous should be removed.

Operability

Operability discusses correct app function through the install, load, and use processes. This differs from the Usability section in that the content focuses on inclusion of specific functionality rather than responses to user inputs. For example, the topic of onboarding is covered in both the Usability and Operability Guidelines, but the discussion in the Operability section focuses more on technical requirements and correct app behavior. Operability also covers information transparency (e.g., change history and medical device status), as well as connectivity (e.g., specific performance requirements for apps connecting to or serving as electronic health records (EHRs)).

4   Discussion

4.1   A Subsection Sample

The Xcertia Guidelines fill an important industry gap by consolidating information from a variety of sources to provide a reliable, standardized reference for addressing the specific design, development, and evaluation needs of mHealth apps. By utilizing a set of guidelines that can be applied to both regulated and non-regulated products, mHealth stakeholders can benefit from standardized processes that result in improved design and better user experience.

All working groups faced various challenges throughout the development of the guidelines. The Usability group's primary challenges included prioritizing topics for inclusion, determining an appropriate level of detail while also striving for a universally-applicable set of guidelines, translating for various audiences (e.g., design, development, human factors, psychology), and defining and maintaining voice and language use consistent with the greater Xcertia effort.

The Xcertia Guidelines are available for a public comment period through May 15, 2019 at https://www.xcertia.org/the-guidelines/. Comments will be utilized to generate updates that will be implemented in the final version.

References

1. The Guidelines – Xcertia. https://xcertia.org/the-guidelines/. Accessed 09 Mar 2019
2. App Usability Guidelines & Survey. https://xcertia.org/app-usability-survey/. Accessed 09 Mar 2019

Socialization of Veterans Using Virtual Reality

Joan Marie Savage[✉] and Lucas Stephane[✉]

Department of Computer Engineering and Sciences,
Florida Institute of Technology, Melbourne, FL 32901, USA
joanmariesavage@gmail.com, lstephane@fit.edu

Abstract. Real cognitive power comes from using external aids that enhance our cognitive activities; however, without such assistance, our memories, thoughts and reasonings are all constrained (Ware 2008). Exposure to trauma can cause damage to the area of the brain noted for value-based decision-making and can lead to a greater risk of mental health problems. However, evidence suggests that social support may provide a protective barrier on brain structure. A major factor in high suicide rate among military veterans is due to untreated mental illness. Unfortunately, there is a gap of service for veterans released from active duty and who are waiting to be treated by VA Medical Centers. Recently, there have been several press releases concerning the increase of suicide among veterans, and the inability of the VA to serve veterans in a timely manner. Numerous laws, blue ribbon commissions, Inspector General (IG) reports, Government Accountability reports, and hearings in both the Senate and House of Representatives Veterans' Affairs Committees are examining ways to fix this inefficiency (Heller et al. 2014; Ducharme 2018). The main objective of this research is to describe how players experience healthy socialization within virtual reality social environments using virtual ethnography and phenomenology. This exploration of healthy socialization using the emerging virtual reality social platforms may enable both positive socialization and positive emotional states (Stephane 2007 and Savage 2014) for both the short-term gap of service, and the long-term building of resilience.

Keywords: Military veterans · Socialization · Virtual reality · Resilience · Trauma · Suicide · Mental health · Post-traumatic stress disorder

1 Introduction

1.1 Gap of Service

Suicide is 10th leading cause of death in the United States, and worldwide suicide is high in countries like Lithuania, South Korea, and Japan (World Population Review 2019). The United States contains service gaps in that suicide prevention needs both reactive and proactive care (Aguirre et al. 2013); however, the focus is generally on reactive care in that a person would notify authorities only after someone threatens or attempts suicide. There are nearly 22 million veterans living in the United States, but only 5.9 million actually use VA health care services; therefore, 16 million veterans are not receiving health care benefits from the VA (Bagalman 2014). Many may depend on charity and local and state resources.

© Springer Nature Switzerland AG 2019
C. Stephanidis (Ed.): HCII 2019, CCIS 1034, pp. 507–513, 2019.
https://doi.org/10.1007/978-3-030-23525-3_69

Several press releases have been issued over the last few years making military veteran suicide prevention and intervention top priority of the Department of Veteran Affairs (VA) (Shinseki 2012; VA 2018a, b). The most recent press release at the time of this research was January 2019 from Robert Wilkie, the Secretary of Veterans Affairs, stating that veteran mental health is the top clinical priority of the VA (Wilkie 2019). However, very little is mentioned concerning a proactive treatment for sustainable mental health for veterans. Secretary Robert Wilkie explained that the critical time for high-risk veterans happens during the 12-month period following their discharge from the military. The release discusses accountability and transparency of the VA as an approach to treating the problem - providing very little explanation of what is being done to actually support veterans during this critical 12-month period.

Early interventions like developing necessary socialization skills and maintaining healthy relationships are lacking, causing a gap in service in the care of those struggling with suicide ideation stateside and globally. Both proactive and reactive responses are vital components in creating early intervention methods through socialization and both can be developed by advancements in technology (Aguirre et al. 2013). Socializing with these advancements include virtual reality social environments (VRSE); for example, AltspaceVR.

AltspaceVR is a social platform in virtual reality that assists people from over 150 countries to socialize in the most natural way possible. The main objective of this research is to describe how Players experience healthy socialization within VRSE and two of the research goals: (1) help provide veterans with healthy socialization experiences, and (2) help build resilience in Players while they are waiting to be seen by a health care professional.

2   Design Thinking

The iterative and incremental design thinking (DT) approach (Meinel and Leifer 2011) is employed for identifying and mapping appropriate human-centered design methods for each stage, i.e. problem statement(s), need-finding, ideation, prototyping and evaluation. In particular, in the evaluation stage, objective phenomenology and virtual ethnography (Creswell 2018; Boellstroff 2012, 2015) are investigated in terms of best fit for eliciting and understanding each player's unique perspective and unique experience related to expected positive socialization in social VR platforms such as AltspaceVR.

Previous research focused on online social environments (e.g. Second Life) which showed that players enjoyed creating things in VR, but most of them used the online environment primarily for socializing (Brahnam 2014).

Furthermore, social support seems to have a protective effect on Orbitofrontal (OFG) volume in the brain for veterans exposed to trauma. Traumatic experiences are associated with reduced OFG volume; this region of the brain plays a role in object identification, learning of stimulus-reward associations and value-based decision-making. Reduced OFG volume may affect the ability to recognize the implications of stimuli; like rewarding stimuli (Aupperle, Connolly et al. 2013) in social interactions. Recognizing positive and negative stimuli from another person is important for developing and maintaining healthy relationships.

3 Methods

This article is based on my current PhD research.

The problem statement and need-finding DT stages are based upon previous research and personal experiences, and the related methods are literature reviews and observations.

During the DT ideation stage, the main methods employed were brainstorming sessions and design rationale for identifying the best VR structure to enable studying the experiences of healthy socialization. Initially the research focused on thoughtful facial expressions (Savage 2014) and the real-time animation of virtual avatars. Facial expressions play a powerful role in social interactions from birth to adulthood (Université de Genève 2017), however, after several iterations over the course of 2-years, it was decided to shift toward VR social environments that enabled observation of players and elicited larger scale multi-player socialization.

The DT prototyping stage was aligned with the ideation stage for assessing the usefulness and feasibility of a VR environment within the scope of the current research. Over the course of 2-years, 3D software enabled the animation in real-time of an avatar's face based on the player's facial expressions. Different software and hardware were identified and compared, and a first successful prototype was implemented using Brekel Kinect Pro Face. However, the overall configuration, even though ready for experiments, was found quite complex, constraining, and expensive from a sustainability perspective, i.e. if deployed at a large scale, every player would need to be provided with a Microsoft Kinect and a VR-ready computer, and players would need to constrain their movements within the field of view of the Kinect sensor. Furthermore, the real-time integration of the facial expression capture and animation with various existing games was also found to be complex and not sustainable (e.g. upgrades over time). Therefore, the recent social VR environments were finally selected as the preferred design for the current research. As mentioned above, the main research focus shifted from facial expressions to social interactions in the ideation stage, and the prototyping shifted from hard-coding to customizing activity spaces in these social VR environments and utilizing all the advanced features offered by such environments, both technical (i.e. multi-player, multiple VR headset support, cross-platform support - Windows, Mac, mobile devices) and social (i.e. subscription rules and 24/7 moderation).

By consequent, for the DT evaluation stage, using the virtual space AltspaceVR, I began attending events over an 8-month period starting in March 2018 in an effort to establish prior ethnography. Events within Altspace are ongoing sessions/events dealing with different forms of socialization while offering a myriad of activities. For example, one event is called "Mental Wellness: Real-Life Superheroes," where players learn practical applications concerning mental wellness; another example is an event called "VR Church," where Players explore spirituality and meditation. As my virtual relationships developed, I began to host my own events, and as a result the initial methodology shifted from ethnography to phenomenology, for studying emergent phenomena.

Participant population currently consists of four virtual reality players called a "transient" sample. It is recommended for phenomenology methodology to have 3–25 players or until saturation is reached on the chosen phenomenon (Creswell 2013 and Ary et al. 2010). Sample demographics include United States and United Kingdom. Limitations include (1) age: 18-years and older, and (2) English speaking. Recruitment strategies emerged during development and hosting of events, and while participating in other events and activities for the purposes of recruitment, observation, and interviewing of players relating to healthy socialization within virtual reality.

Data collection consists of interviews and observations where a player signs a consent form agreeing to be observed and interviewed. After 8-months of player observation, an interview was set up with each of the chosen players in the transient sample. The University Institutional Review Board reviewed and approved the study in January 2019. Interviews were conducted in February 2019 and lasted roughly 30–45 min. They were completed by calling the player using the Discord voice and text chat application for gamers, and the interviews were recorded using OBS Studio.

3.1   Trustworthiness

Credibility (Creswell 2013) was addressed using different techniques such as prolonged engagement in the field (currently a total of 1-year from March 2018 – March 2019), member-checking, and triangulation of methods and data sources; both ethnographic methodology and phenomenology were used, and both observation of players in their natural virtual environment and interviewing players for confluence of evidence (2013).

Player interviews were coded using inter-rater and intra-rater (code-recode) validation to help confirm reliability. I started with the first interview from Player 1 and coded a page with higher level emergent themes. Some of these themes were: Safety, Silliness, Engaging, Privacy, Comfortability, and Real-World Likeness. After two weeks, I returned to the same section of the interview and recoded it again. I chose the same or similar codes. For example, 'Engaging' was the initial code used during the first time through, while 'Interesting' was used during the recode. After my second time through, I utilized inter-rater agreement and sent the interview and coded themes to another researcher who confirmed and agreed with my decisions. Additional considerations for dealing with trustworthiness will be addressed as this research is conducted and completed.

4   Results

Data reduction has been conducted throughout the process for observations of players in their natural virtual environment and during each interview. Data analysis is still in its early stages but there are already some very interesting findings. For example, preliminary research has already suggested that socializing in VR while discussing mental wellness has been extremely beneficial to real-world applications, and socializing through entertainment has impact in Real-World Likeness. Player 4 even stated that he/she finally felt the courage to seek counseling for extreme social anxiety.

Player 1 (P1) recently went through a major surgery and had been homebound for several weeks. For P1 the friendships that he/she developed within VR were similar to Real-World Likeness.

P1: "The more you're there and interact with the same people, you kind of bond with them a little bit and your comfort level is much better, you know, and that's how it works in the real world too".

5 Discussion and Recommendations

Qualitative research allows studying emergent properties. One of these emergent properties is what I have termed *'Transient'* sample unique to VR users. In this sample, each player is considered from both the virtual reality and the real reality standpoint; in terms of their chosen avatar (and name) representative of their unique character within VR, and in terms of the actual human in real reality. The transient sample represents:

(1) Randomness of and among the players within these virtual environments; they cross time zones, cultural, religious, and moral zones;
(2) Accessible within reason; they must also be receptive to the researcher's questions in and out of VR;
(3) Typical; (versus representative) differing in players already using VR verses willing-to-use VR technology (this is also a usability issue);
(4) Indiscriminate and genial (hospitable) for at-the-moment participation in both virtual and real world;
(5) Present and Settled (PAS): sticking around instead of event hopping. When asked a set of questions, some participants would just "pop-out" of the event and/or exit the game. There are three aspects to PAS - first, they do not wish their actual world identities to be compromised; second, they are having technical issues causing misunderstanding or making it difficult to connect and respond; third, they do not like the event (regardless of the researcher) and are unwilling to stay further;
(6) Constancy (or loyalty) to a particular environment (AltspaceVR), spaces (events or areas of interest), or avatars (other players). A player's fidelity to their chosen event, game, environment, etc. can be fiercely loyal or intensely duplicitous.

A research study was conducted on veterans (Savage 2015) using a video game called Suicide Intervention-Prevention Mini-Game (SIP-M). This video game was designed to teach players about mental wellness while distracting them through interactive entertainment (running around in third-person searching a warehouse for clues), and through gaming challenges (time constraints and time warnings). By distracting players with these gaming features, players would be inadvertently educated on suicide intervention-prevention. The results were that eventually all Users showed improvement in learning about suicide intervention-prevention or scored exactly the same. However, only one User scored worse during the initial attempt to play because they were unaccustomed to playing video games. When the User immediately played the game a second time, the User showed substantial improvement in learning the facts about suicide-intervention prevention.

512   J. M. Savage and L. Stephane

This study is important because information can be lost when there are technology malfunctions and misunderstandings concerning how to use or how to engage in a virtual reality environment. This is another reason why players in virtual reality are such a unique sample and interesting sample. One player could be using a Smartphone to attend events, another might use a PC, or they may be using one of several types of VR headsets on the market.

5.1   Future Direction

A poll was conducted by The Washington Post and Kaiser Family Foundation (2015) among a random national sample of 819 Iraq and Afghanistan war veterans. This poll revealed that 55% of those surveyed felt disconnected from civilian life and two-thirds missed the community of other solders. The poll showed that 51% personally knew a service member who had attempted or who had actually committed suicide. Finally, 51% believed the military nor the government are doing enough to help veterans transition.

My research efforts toward providing healthy ways of socializing through social VR environments and entertainment are supported at this stage by positive observations in the social VR platforms as well as positive feedback from players. Therefore, it is expected that continuing to create adapted activity spaces in these VR platforms as well as providing insights and guidance for meaningful socialization will contribute to a better veteran transition.

References

After the Wars - Post-Kaiser survey of Afghanistan and Iraq war veterans: The Washington Post, 20 October 2015. https://www.washingtonpost.com/page/2010-2019/WashingtonPost/2014/03/30/National-Politics/Polling/release_305.xml

Aguirre, R., McCoy, M., Roan, M.: Development guidelines from a study of suicide prevention mobile applications (apps). J. Technol. Hum. Serv. **31**, 269–293 (2013). https://doi.org/10.1080/15228835.2013.814750. Copyright © Taylor & Francis Group, LLC. ISSN 1522-8835 print/1522-8991

Ary, D., Jacobs, L.C., Sorensen, C.: Introduction to research in education, 8th edn. Wadsworth Cengage Learning, Belmont (2010)

Aupperle, R., Connolly, C., Stillman, A., May, A., Paulus, M.: Deployment and post-deployment experiences in OEF/OIF veterans: relationship to gray matter volume. PLoS One **8**(9), e75880 (2013). https://doi.org/10.1371/journal.pone.0075880

Bagalman, E.: The number of veterans that use VA health care services: a fact sheet. Analyst in Health Policy. Congressional Research Service (7-5700) (2014). http://fas.org/sgp/crs/misc/R43579.pdf

Boellstroff, T., et al.: Ethnography and Virtual Worlds: A Handbook of Method. Princeton University Press, Princeton (2012)

Boellstroff, T.: Coming of Age in Second Life: An Anthropologist Explores the Virtually Human. Princeton University Press, Princeton (2015)

Brahnam, S.: HCI prototyping and modeling of future psychotherapy technologies in second life. In: Kurosu, M. (ed.) HCI 2014. LNCS, vol. 8510, pp. 273–284. Springer, Cham (2014). https://doi.org/10.1007/978-3-319-07233-3_26

Creswell, J.W.: Qualitative Inquiry and Research Design: Choosing Among Five Approaches, 3rd edn. SAGE Publications, Los Angeles (2013)

Creswell, J.W., Poth, C.N.: Qualitative Inquiry and Research Design, 4th edn. Sage, Thousand Oaks (2018)

Ducharme, J.: The VA didn't spend millions of dollars meant for veterans suicide prevention, report finds. TIME, December 2018. http://time.com/5483823/veterans-affairs-suicide-preven-tion/?fbclid=IwAR3dMGYgvmXI8b7kWNjquc_udvzhchQBvobcYs2ZJVqKo4BdkQXtRVzjF48

Heller, D., Moran, J., Vitter, D., Casey, J.R., Heinrich, M., Tester, J.: (2014). http://www.casey.senate.gov/download/va-backlog-march-2014-report

Meinel, C., Leifer, L.: Design thinking research. In: Plattner, H., Meinel, C., Leifer, L. (eds.) Design Thinking: Understand, Improve, Apply, pp. 1–11. Springer, Heidelberg (2011). https://doi.org/10.1007/978-3-642-21643-5_1

Savage, J.: A Veteran's Guide to Civilian Living. CreateSpace, Scotts Valley (2014). ISBN/EAN13 1502753685/9781502753687

Savage, J.M.: Usability assessment of a suicide intervention-prevention mini-game. In: Stephanidis, C. (ed.) HCI 2015. CCIS, vol. 529, pp. 703–708. Springer, Cham (2015). https://doi.org/10.1007/978-3-319-21383-5_119

Shinseki, E.: President Obama signs executive order to improve access to mental health services for veterans, service members, and military families [News Release], 31 August 2012

Stephane, L.: Cognitive and emotional human models within a multi-agent framework. In: Harris, D. (ed.) EPCE 2007. LNCS (LNAI), vol. 4562, pp. 609–618. Springer, Heidelberg (2007). https://doi.org/10.1007/978-3-540-73331-7_67

Université de Genève: Do blind people express their emotions in the same way as people who can see? ScienceDaily, 4 July 2017. www.sciencedaily.com/releases/2017/07/170704093813.htm. Accessed 17 June 2018

VA: Veterans Benefits Administration Reports (2018a). https://www.benefits.va.gov/reports/detailed_claims_data.asp

VA: Veterans Benefits Administration Reports: Claims Backlog (2018b). https://www.benefits.va.gov/reports/mmwr_va_claims_backlog.asp

Ware, C.: Visual Thinking: For Design. Morgan Kaufmann, Amsterdam (2008)

Wilkie, R.: The VA is making real progress on suicide prevention for veterans [News Release], 14 January 2019

World Population Review. http://worldpopulationreview.com/countries/suicide-rate-by-country/. Accessed 25 Mar 2019

Wellbeing Technology: Beyond Chatbots

Eliseo Sciarretta[✉] and Lia Alimenti

Link Campus University, Via del Casale di S. Pio V, 44, 00165 Rome, Italy
{e.sciarretta,l.alimenti}@unilink.it

Abstract. Digitalization has revolutionized almost every sector of our life, including both the private and the professional one, just as the relationship between man and machine/computer is radically changing our lives.

Among many sectors, the authors have chosen to explore how digitalization and new technologies are mutating the healthcare, focusing in particular on the exploitation of chatbots and on the forms of interactions with them.

Human computer interfaces are becoming more important in a world whose complexity is increased by technology and in which certain groups of people risk being excluded. Fragile categories, health support services, are common keywords because one of the most important games is played on them and on the concept of social innovation through technology.

In this context, social differences can be smoothed out, but can also be magnified. In sectors like education or healthcare, such a level of inequality could be reached, that there could be A-class citizens, who would have access to technological prostheses, thus increasing their capacities in some way, and B-class citizens who would be excluded.

The authors start giving an overview of the main technologic innovations in the field of healthcare and explaining how they can magnify the risk of exclusion. Then the focus is shifted first on the interaction between people and chatbots used for generic purposes, and then on the central theme of health-bots. Finally, in the conclusions, the authors give a reading about the main interaction forms that can help people using these systems.

Keywords: Chatbot · Healthbot · Virtual assistant · AI · Machine learning · Human computer interaction · User experience

1 Introduction: Innovation and Inclusion in Healthcare

Interface, commonly intended as the space where interaction between people and machines occurs, becomes more and more important in today's world. Technology makes the complexity of systems increase and some groups of people risk being excluded. Among all the various kinds of end users, the elderly are those most likely to remain excluded from this process, but since they're growing in number and spending power, they are also potential recipients of projects and solutions.

Designing interfaces that can ease the interaction and reduce complexity is therefore critical. Above all in the healthcare sector, where senior citizens are the main target.

C. Stephanidis (Ed.): HCII 2019, CCIS 1034, pp. 514–519, 2019.
https://doi.org/10.1007/978-3-030-23525-3_70

In recent years, the medical sector has undergone a transformation driven by new technologies and innovation: telemedicine, wearable devices, health apps, drones, but also virtual assistants, big data, artificial intelligence, augmented reality and virtual reality have all become familiar terms not only to experts, but also to patients and their families.

These innovations have proven they can improve the quality of care and life of patients, while reducing healthcare costs. And they can allow people overcome physical barriers, provided they're designed properly.

2 The Centrality of the Interaction: The Case of Chatbots

In recent times, great attention has been placed on the design of conversational interfaces, through the use of chatbots, the technological tools that "pretend" to be human in order to help people in a variety of tasks. Almost seventy years have passed since "The Imitation Game", Turing's test [1], in which people had to guess if they were engaging in a conversation with a machine or with a human.

Interest in this topic today is higher than ever, probably because the latest technological advances make it harder to distinguish between an Artificial Intelligence (A. I.) and an actual human, almost to the impossibility.

The term chatbot refers to any software application that engages in a dialog with a human using natural language, as stated by Dale [2]. In other words, a chatbot is an A.I. based program that simulates an interactive human conversation by using pre-configured keywords and sentences, either via written text or speech. Nowadays chatbots are widely spread and used: from simple bots that follow question-and-answer patterns to more complex bots that make use of Artificial Intelligence and are able to learn. On the market and in the main app stores it's easy to find commercial bots, customer service bots, content-based bots, but also service-based bots, like, for instance, the ones which function as a night companion for those who suffer from insomnia [3].

In a world where people are accustomed to real-time 24/7 feedback, chatbots represent the best way for administrations and companies to connect to their users/clients. As a matter of fact, by 2020, 80% of companies are expected to employ a chatbot.

For this reason, one of the most important design goals is to make interaction with chatbots [4] enjoyable and to avoid possible frustrations, by trying to predict the reactions of the user and to respond to them in an appropriate way. In addition to the most common problems of understanding, an interesting aspect emerged from several studies [5] is that people tend to place themselves in a dominant position compared to a chatbot and often "test" it, by provoking it, aware that the one they are talking to isn't a person. This often ends up in vulgar sentences or more or less explicitly sexual approaches to female chatbots.

A chatbot designed to respond promptly and ironically can establish an empathetic relationship with the user, gaining respect and credibility [6]. People tend to anthropomorphize the world around them and if they face a well-defined chatbot they tend to establish a more positive and empathic relationship.

A further development of chatbot based interaction is for the bot to understand the emotions of its interlocutors through sentiment analysis and the use of emojis, gifs and other communication artifacts in conversations to make them more engaging.

The decisive threshold for making chatbots credible thus becomes the ability to create an empathic link with the user through a solid personality. For this reason, new professions need to be considered as employed in the design of a chatbot, such as conversational designers, A.I. interaction designers, character designers or even poets, television writers or dramatists as in the case of Microsoft Cortana [7].

A chatbot based service represents an essential resource today, and having one that can surprise us with his personality and be friendly is the new frontier for designers of conversational interfaces.

2.1 Chatbots in Healthcare: Healthbots

Chatbots are currently employed in a variety of sectors, such as insurance, banking services, retail. More recently, they have been applied to the evolving sector of healthcare.

Although this kind of bots, promptly renamed as "healthbots", are still experimental and in the first stages of evolution, they are already used today to reserve a service or to make an appointment with the doctor based on the severity of the symptoms, to monitor a patient's health status by sending notifications to the nurse or to the doctor, in case of abnormal parameters, or they are used as home helpers.

The ever-evolving digitalization of the medical sector is already showing enormous potential: apps, all-day health monitoring, personalized health systems, artificial intelligence and healthbots guarantee better results at lower costs.

Besides, the technology also aims at reaching full social inclusion in the health sector. Lower access costs to these devices means more access to a better care for more people, in the (maybe utopian) hope of a world where everyone, anywhere and at any time, can get the highest quality of care.

For example, it is common practice to seek medical solutions on Google [8, 9], but one can easily get lost in a maze of pages with solutions that are often inadequate and irrelevant, and that can cause a unjustified state of anxiety for the most disparate symptoms. An appropriately programmed healthbot could solve this problem.

Uses and implementations of healthbots, as mentioned, are still being tested, but there are already relevant examples, some of which are listed below:

- Sensely [10], a machine learning based virtual nurse;
- AiCure [11], which is able to analyze received images and to understand whether the patient is following the prescribed indications or not;
- Babylon Health [12], which uses artificial intelligence to identify the different pathologies and suggests the most suitable therapy;
- Woebot [13], a psychological help service to support people avoiding negative thinking.

Italian company MSD Health [14] has developed a healthbot to improve the quality of life of people suffering from Alzheimer's disease, which can respond to patients' questions, reminding them drug therapies, memorizing names and contacts of family members and eventually helping them to find their way back home.

Today, healthbots have the capacity to provide an answer to simple health related questions, but, in the future, they are expected to become more precise by integrating the data provided by wearable sensors, smart watches and digital medical records, in order to provide more accurate information on everyone's health status, while preserving, at the same time, personal data security.

Among the possible uses and benefits, healthbots could ease the interaction with several databases, thus providing precise information about a pathology or about the therapy that a specific patient is following.

In case of a common illness, such as a cold or flu, the healthbot is able to advise the patient which drug to take, to give explanations on how to take it and any interactions with other pharmacological compounds taken at the same time. In the event that the bot does not know how to respond to a certain problem, it can send a message to the doctor to inform him of any critical issues.

In general, the integration of healthbots can be advantageous, especially in responding quickly to simple but frequently asked questions, but, in the not-too-distant future, they could be used in different ways:

- To hand out information about diseases and related therapies to follow (the healthbot would provide precise information, both to the doctor, about the therapy to be prescribed, and to the patient, about the treatment to follow);
- To improve adherence to therapy, which is often changed autonomously by chronic patients (the healthbot would be able to "educate" the patient by providing information and by reminding how and when to take a certain medication).

3   Conclusions: How Can Interaction Be Optimized?

In this paper, the authors stated that among the different innovations affecting the healthcare sector, a prominent role can be assigned to the so called healthbots, which can be helpful in solving some problems related to the provision of trusted information, such as fake news.

Still, this particular application of chatbots is just one of the possible ways to interact with a machine: starting with the classic keyboard and mouse or touchscreen, the range goes all the way to more human-friendly ways, that are able to engage different senses and channels such as speech, vision, gestures and touch. This is happening also in the healthcare field, for example through the use of NAO (Aldebaran Robotics, 2006), the famous small robot, 60 cm high, capable of interacting with humans, thanks to specially designed software [15].

There are different interfaces for this type of interaction but there isn't an optimal way with defined characteristics; quite the opposite, each situation has its corresponding specific characteristics and its different strategies of interaction.

Choosing the interface to be used for a robotic system is a complex operation that deserves a careful evaluation of various factors, such as the users, the place and the time of communication, the level of interaction and the degree of reliability.

In any case, speech seems to be the most promising mode of interaction in most interactions.

This type of interaction is applied in the healthcare sector to provide support, especially to children, in the therapy. Overseas, Robot Therapy [16] is already a widespread alternative in some hospitals of excellence, in specialized centers of therapy and even in the homes of individual users.

Like the new trend of chatbots, even the interaction with a humanoid robot is becoming more and more natural, through the anticipation of user reactions, which makes the process less frustrating. This is made possible by the customization of the programming software that can be modified when needed.

This is just one example of how technology (robotics in this specific case) and the desire to develop technologically advanced solutions can encourage innovation and improve society.

The adoption of healthbots may be profitable and bring benefits to the society only if they are properly designed and programmed. The examples mentioned in the discussion show a strong interest in the use of chatbots in the healthcare, but for them to be fully effective, the design process needs to consider the interaction between people and healthbots, in order to find the "sweet spot" and the most suitable interface.

For years, user experience designers have struggled to find the perfect visual interface, but the use of natural language through a conversational interface could make these efforts almost useless, at least in this area, with a transition from the design of visual layout and interaction mechanisms to the design of conversation.

Research in this field is still in its early stages, and the authors intend to further explore the topic in future works.

References

1. Turing, A.M.: Computing machinery and intelligence. Mind **59**(236), 433–460 (1950)
2. Dale, R.: The return of the chatbots. Nat. Lang. Eng. **22**(5), 811–817 (2016). Industry Watch
3. InsomnoBot Homepage. http://insomnobot3000.com/. Accessed 18 Feb 2019
4. De Angeli, A.J., Graham, I., Coventry, L.: The unfriendly user: exploring social reactions to Chatterbots. In: Han, S.K., Youn, G. (eds.) Affective Human Factors Design. Asean Academic Press, London (2001)
5. Dibitonto, M., Leszczynska, K., Tazzi, F., Medaglia, C.M.: Chatbot in a campus environment: design of LiSA, a virtual assistant to help students in their university life. In: Kurosu, M. (ed.) HCI 2018. LNCS, vol. 10903, pp. 103–116. Springer, Cham (2018). https://doi.org/10.1007/978-3-319-91250-9_9
6. Duijst, D.: Can we improve the user experience of chatbots with personalisation? (2017)
7. Microsoft Cortana Homepage. https://www.microsoft.com/it-it/windows/cortana. Accessed 18 Feb 2019
8. Ruberto, M.G.: La medicina ai tempi del web. Medico e paziente nell'e-Health. FrancoAngeli, Milano (2011)
9. D'Amo, G.: Alle mie pazienti il dottor google dice che… Una nuova base sicura, decentrata in psicoterapia 3.0. In: Psicobiettivo, pp. 145–170, March 2014. https://doi.org/10.3280/psob2014-003010
10. Sensely Homepage. http://www.sensely.com/. Accessed 20 Feb 2019
11. AiCure Homepage. https://aicure.com/. Accessed 20 Feb 2019
12. Babylon Homepage. https://www.babylonhealth.com/. Accessed 20 Feb 2019

13. Woebot Homepage. https://woebot.io/. Accessed 20 Feb 2019
14. MSD Homepage. https://www.msdsalute.it/. Accessed 18 Feb 2019
15. SoftBankRobotics Homepage. https://www.softbankrobotics.com/emea/en. Accessed 18 Feb 2019
16. Robins, B., Dautenhahn, K., Boekhorst, R.T., et al.: Robotic assistants in therapy and education of children with autism: can a small humanoid robot help encourage social interaction skills? Univ. Access Inf. Soc. **4**, 105 (2005). https://doi.org/10.1007/s10209-005-0116-3

Measurement of Tech Anxiety in Older and Younger Adults

Kelly S. Steelman[✉] and Kay L. Tislar

Michigan Technological University, Houghton, MI 49931, USA
{steelman,cltislar}@mtu.edu

Abstract. Tech anxiety is an established barrier to technology adoption, and recent work suggests it may also impair the development of higher-order digital competencies. Researching this issue requires a reliable measure of tech anxiety. The widely-used Computer Anxiety Rating Scale was developed more than 30 years ago, but computer devices and use have changed dramatically during that time. We developed and tested a new Tech Anxiety Rating Scale (TARS) encompassing a range of modern devices, tasks, and scenarios. One hundred eight older adults and 150 college students completed the TARS and six other surveys related to computer use, anxiety, self-efficacy, proficiency, and attitudes. We present an exploratory factor analysis of the TARS for the combined datasets and separately for the older and younger adults. Overall, the EFA revealed common underlying factors for older and younger adults, suggesting that the TARS is appropriate for use with both populations.

Keywords: Older adults · Senior citizens · Aging · Tech anxiety · Computer anxiety

1 Introduction

Computer anxiety is an established barrier to using or purchasing computers [14–16] and is associated with poor task performance [8] and difficulty learning computer skills [7,13]. Understanding the relationship between computer anxiety and these factors requires a validated scale of computer anxiety. The most commonly used scale, the Computer Anxiety Rating Scale (CARS [8]), was developed more than 30 years ago when personal desktop computers were becoming popular at school, work, and home. The CARS contains a range of statements focusing on a person's worried thoughts (e.g., It scares me to think that I could cause the computer to destroy a large amount of information by hitting the wrong key), self-confidence (e.g., I am confident that I can learn computer skills), attitudes (e.g., You have to be a genius to understand all the special keys contained on most computers), and performance (e.g., I have difficulty in understanding the technical aspects of computers). Since its original development, the nature of computers and computer use has changed dramatically. Although some researchers [3] have modified the scale to eliminate obsolete

© Springer Nature Switzerland AG 2019
C. Stephanidis (Ed.): HCII 2019, CCIS 1034, pp. 520–527, 2019.
https://doi.org/10.1007/978-3-030-23525-3_71

questions (e.g., I am sure that with time and practice I will be as comfortable working with computers as I am in working with a typewriter) or to slightly modify the terminology (e.g., change *computer terminals* to *computer*), the CARS has not had a major update to reflect the broad range of modern computing devices, tasks, and concepts (e.g., smartphones, online shopping, and Wi-Fi). Finally, as noted earlier, CARS includes statements pertaining to self-efficacy and performance. Many researchers, however, are interested in understanding the relationship between computer anxiety and these factors. The inclusion of statements related to self-efficacy and performance, therefore, may result in an inaccurate assessment of the relationship between these constructs.

We developed the Tech Anxiety Rating Scale (TARS) to address these issues. We use the term *tech* to be more inclusive of the range of modern computing devices. Scale instructions specify that respondents consider the use of desktop computers, laptop computers, tablets, and/or smartphones when rating each statement. Second, we focused each question on worry and negative self-talk, two aspects of the cognitive component of anxiety [2,9], and avoided statements that might be more related to self-efficacy or the behavioral outcomes of anxiety. Finally, we included statements that targeted modern anxiety-provoking issues like viruses and malware, privacy and security, and frequent software updates [13]. The 26-statement scale is included in Table 1.

In the current study, we administered TARS to both older adults and college students and conducted an exploratory factor analysis to reduce the set of statements, identify underlying factors, and determine whether the factors were consistent for both groups. Notably, past research on computer anxiety has focused primarily on these two populations. It is plausible that older and younger adults may differ not only in their tech anxiety levels, but also in the types of activities or scenarios that may provoke anxiety in the first place. Both older and younger adults are likely to have a range of proficiency levels with computer technology, but they are also likely to have had different types of experiences with technology simply by virtue of differences in their interests, use characteristics, and the age at which they first started using technology. To be useful, therefore, TARS must be validated with both older and younger adults to ensure its items are relevant to a wide range of users and that the scale scores allow for meaningful comparisons between the two groups.

2 Methods

2.1 Participants

One hundred eight older adults ($M_{age} = 66.81$, $SD_{age} = 7.72$; 72 women) and 150 Michigan Tech college students ($M_{age} = 19.41$, $SD_{age} = 1.27$; 46 women) participated in the study. Older adults were recruited through a combination of digital (email, listservs, Facebook) and non-digital (flyers and table tents posted at the public library, grocery stores, coffee shops, etc.) advertisements and snowball sampling [6]. Recruitment materials specified that we were seeking participants age 55 and older who were brand new to computers, mid-level users, or pros.

Older-adult participants received $20 upon completion of the study. Younger adults were recruited through the Michigan Tech undergraduate research pool which includes students from a range of majors. Participation was restricted to individuals ages 18–30. Younger-adult participants received course credit for participation.

2.2 Materials

Computer and Internet Use Questionnaire (CIUQ). The CIUQ collected basic demographic information, details about participants' history of ownership and use of computer technology (smartphones, tablets, laptops, and desktop computers), frequency and location of Internet use, and an inventory of common technology-based tasks.

Tech Anxiety Rating Scale (TARS). TARS included 26 questions that encompass a range of modern technology-based tasks, devices, and scenarios. Responses were provided on a five-point, Likert-like scale ranging from strongly disagree to strongly agree. Scores could range from 26–130, with high scores indicating higher levels of tech anxiety.

Computer Anxiety Rating Scale (CARS [8]**).** We used the 19-statement version of CARS, with questions edited as suggested by Cooper-Gaiter [3]. Responses were provided on a five-point, Likert-like scale, ranging from strongly disagree to strongly agree. Scores could range from 19 to 95, with higher scores indicating higher levels of computer anxiety.

Computer Self-Efficacy Scale (CSES [4]**).** The CSES included 28 statements about the user's confidence with computer-related tasks. CSES scores could range from 28 to 140, with higher values indicating a greater confidence in one's ability to use computers.

Generalized Anxiety Disorder-7 Assessment (GAD-7 [12]**).** The GAD-7 asks participants to rate how often they have been bothered by seven different issues on a four-point scale: not at all, several days, more than half the days, and nearly every day. GAD-7 scores could range from 0 to 21.

Computer Proficiency Questionnaire (CPQ [1]**).** The original CPQ includes 33 items rated on a five-point, Likert-like scale: never tried, not at all, not very easily, somewhat easily, very easily. Items are divided into six subscales. CPQ scores are calculated by summing the average of each subscale. We modified the CPQ to add a seventh subscale about security and updated the Internet and General Skills sections to include modern technologies and tasks (e.g., touchscreens, trackpads, connecting to Wi-Fi, saving to the cloud, using cloud-based software like Google Docs). Modified CPQ scores could range from 7 to 35, with higher scores indicating a higher level of proficiency on technology-based tasks.

Attitudes Toward the Internet Scale (ATIS [10]**).** ATIS includes 16 statements, each rated on a 7-point Likert-like scale. High scores indicate more positive attitudes toward the Internet.

2.3 Procedure

After participants signed an informed consent, surveys were administered in group settings to older-adult participants at several community locations (e.g., libraries and community centers) and to younger-adult participants in classrooms at Michigan Tech. All surveys were administered on paper. Participants completed the CIUQ first followed by the other six surveys, with the order determined by a Balanced Latin Square design.

3 Exploratory Factor Analysis

Exploratory factor analysis (EFA) of the 26-question TARS was conducted separately for the older and younger adults and for the combined datasets. Principal Axis Factoring was selected as the factor extraction method [5] with PROMAX rotation [11]. For all three analyses, Kaiser-Meyer-Olkin measures were greater than 0.878, indicating sufficient data for EFA; Bartlett's test of sphericity indicated a patterned relationship between items (all $ps < .001$). Variables were dropped if cross-loading of greater than 0.3 occurred on two or more factors, if the variable did not have a factor loading of at least 0.4, or if the communality of the variable was below 0.3. For each dataset, the number of factors was determined by the scree test.

Factors and loadings are presented in Table 2. For the combined dataset, variables loaded onto four factors, explaining 72.8% of the variance. Three of the factors were labeled as *safety and security* (10.3%), *consequences of actions* (6.9%), and *judgment from others* (6.2%). The factor that explained the largest portion of the variance (49.3%) included three statements about negative self-talk and four questions regarding managing new tasks.

EFA of the older adult dataset produced the same four factors, which accounted for a total of 75.5% of the variance. The first factor (56.7%) contained eight statements, distributed between *negative self-talk* and *managing new tasks*. Five of the statements overlapped with those from the EFA of the combined dataset. The *safety and security* factor (5.0%) and *judgment from others* factor (4.9%) included the same set of statements as in the combined analysis. The *consequence of actions* factor (8.9%) included one additional statement.

For the younger adult dataset, the variables loaded onto five factors, with 72.6% cumulative variance. Three of the factors were consistent with the previous two analyses: *consequences of taking action* (7.1%), *safety and security* (12.5%), and *judgment from others* (9.0%). In contrast to the other two analyses, *negative self-talk* (37.2%) and *managing new tasks* (6.8%) were split into separate factors. The *negative self-talk* factor, however, contained two statements that were more related to the consequences of worry (feeling overwhelmed; difficulty concentrating) than self-talk.

Table 1. Tech Anxiety Rating Scale: Indicate how often you worry about or tell yourself each of the following items when using a computer device (desktop computer, laptop computer, tablet computer, and/or smartphone). Please circle one number to respond to each statement: (1) never, (2) rarely, (3) sometimes, (4) often or (5) always.

No.	Question
1	I worry that something I do will break my device
2	I worry that bad things will happen if I press the wrong button or click the wrong thing
3	I worry that something I do will accidentally delete important information or files
4	I worry about what might happen after I press a button or click something
5	I worry about whether it is safe to connect to the Internet (Wi-Fi) in public places
6	I worry that other people will see information that I don't want them to see
7	I worry that people I don't know (hackers) will steal my information or identity
8	I worry that my device will get infected with a computer virus or malware
9	I worry that people will think I'm stupid if I ask for help
10	I worry that I will look silly or foolish
11	I worry that people will watch and judge me
12	I worry that I will forget how to do something that I've already learned how to do
13	I worry that I won't be able to figure something out on my own
14	I worry that I won't be able to use my programs (or apps) if a new version comes out
15	I worry if I have to do something new
16	I worry when a window or message appears (pops up) on my screen
17	I worry about what will happen if I choose to install or accept an update to my device, program, or app
18	I worry that I won't be able to find something that I've saved on my device
19	I worry that I won't be able to get back to where I started after I click a link or open a new page or program
20	My worries overwhelm me
21	My worries make it difficult to concentrate on my task
22	I tell myself that I am too old to do this
23	I tell myself I'm not good with computers
24	I tell myself that I will never figure out a new task
25	I tell myself that I need to do things more quickly
26	I rehearse the steps that I need to take in my head

Table 2. Factor loadings for EFAs conducted on the combined dataset and separately for the older and younger adult samples. Column 3 contains the statement numbers from Table 1.

Label	Factor	No.	Combined	Older	Younger
Negative self talk	1a	24	0.992	0.919	0.601
	1a	23	0.846	0.637	0.592
	1a	22	0.759		
	1a	25		0.684	
	1a	26		0.932	
	1a	21			0.974
	1a	20			0.714
Managing new tasks	1b	14	0.733	0.690	0.534
	1b	15	0.729	0.672	
	1b	19	0.620		0.732
	1b	13	0.495	0.604	
	1b	16		0.511	
	1b	18			0.791
Safety and security	2	7	1.079	0.999	0.995
	2	6	0.751	0.729	0.811
	2	5	0.658	0.699	0.633
	2	8	0.572	0.695	0.460
Consequences of actions	3	2	0.942	0.942	0.911
	3	1	0.749	0.565	0.730
	3	3	0.626	0.960	
	3	4	0.606	0.825	0.578
	3	18		0.598	
Judgment from others	4	10	0.892	0.934	0.886
	4	9	0.869	0.946	0.852
	4	11	0.708	0.569	0.824

4 Discussion

As shown in Table 3, both TARS and CARS scores were significantly negatively correlated with attitudes toward the Internet (ATIS), computer self-efficacy (CSES), and self ratings of proficiency (CPQ). These relationships held when calculated for all participants and separately for older and younger adults. TARS scores were significantly positively correlated with generalized anxiety scores. CARS, in contrast, was not correlated with GAD-7 scores for younger adults or when calculated across all participants. Overall, CARS scores were more strongly correlated with measures of self-efficacy, attitudes toward the Internet, and self-ratings of computer proficiency than were TARS scores. This finding is not surprising given that many of the CARS statements are related to these factors.

Scores on the TARS were calculated using the reduced set of 18 statements from the combined EFA. As illustrated in Fig. 1, older adults generally reported higher levels of tech anxiety and had a wider range of tech anxiety scores than the college students. TARS and CARS scores were significantly correlated across all participants ($r = .50$, $p < .001$) and when calculated separately for the older adults ($r = .42$, $p < .001$) and younger adults ($r = .50$, $p < .001$).

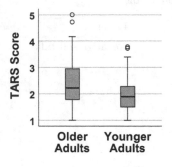

Fig. 1. Boxplots of TARS scores.

Table 3. Correlations between TARS and CARS and other measures. $**p < .01$ $*p < .05$

Scale	TARS			CARS		
	All	Older	Younger	All	Older	Younger
ATIS	−.34**	−.26**	−.25**	−.57**	−.60**	−.37**
GAD7	.17**	.34**	.35**	0.04	.23*	0.15
CSES	−.51**	−.39**	−.52**	−.76**	−.76**	−.73**
CPQ	−.37**	−.24*	−.38**	−.56**	−.58**	−.48**

5   Conclusion

In summary, the exploratory factor analyses revealed common underlying factors for both the older- and younger-adult samples and motivated the reduction of the TARS from 26 questions to 18. Follow-up analyses with the reduced scale indicate that the TARS is negatively correlated with measures of computer self-efficacy, attitudes toward the Internet, and self-ratings of computer proficiency.

Current work is focused on refining TARS based on the results of the current study. Specifically, we are adding questions related to negative self-talk and managing new tasks, the two categories of statements that loaded onto a single factor in the EFAs for the combined dataset and for the older adults, but into two separate factors for younger adults. The next step will be to administer the survey and to conduct a confirmatory factor analysis to validate the scale.

References

1. Boot, W., et al.: Computer proficiency questionnaire: assessing low and high computer proficient seniors. Gerontol. **55**(3), 404–411 (2015)
2. Borkovec, T., Inz, J.: The nature of worry in generalized anxiety disorder: a predominance of thought activity. Behav. Res. Ther. **28**(2), 153–158 (1990)
3. Cooper-Gaiter, E.: Computer anxiety and computer self-efficacy of older adults (unpublished doctoral dissertation) (2015)
4. Durndell, A., Haag, Z.: Computer self efficacy, computer anxiety, attitudes towards the internet and reported experience with the internet, by gender, in an east european sample. Comput. Hum. Behav. **18**(5), 521–535 (2002)
5. Fabrigar, L., Wegener, D., MacCallum, R., Strahan, E.: Evaluating the use of exploratory factor analysis in psychological research. Psychol. Methods **4**(3), 272–299 (1999)
6. Goodman, L.: Snowball sampling. Ann. Math. Stat. **32**(1), 148–170 (1961)
7. Harrington, K., McElroy, J., Morrow, P.: Computer anxiety and computer-based training: a laboratory experiment. Educ. Comput. Res. **6**(3), 343–358 (1990)
8. Heinssen, R., Glass, C., Knight, L.: Assessing computer anxiety: development and validation of the computer anxiety rating scale. Comput. Hum. Behav. **3**(1), 49–59 (1987)
9. Mathews, A.: Why worry? The cognitive function of anxiety. Behav. Res. Ther. **28**(6), 455–468 (1990)
10. Morse, B., Gullekson, N., Morse, S., Popovich, P.: The development of a general internet attitudes scale. Comput. Hum. Behav. **27**(1), 480–489 (2011)
11. Osborne, J., Costello, A.: Best practices in exploratory factor analysis. Pract. Assess. Res. Eval. **10**(7), 86–99 (2005)
12. Spitzer, R., Kroenke, K., Williams, J., et al.: A brief measure for assessing generalized anxiety disorder: the GAD-7. Arch. Intern. Med. **166**(10), 1092–1097 (2006)
13. Steelman, K.S., Tislar, K.L., Ureel, L.C., Wallace, C.: Eliciting best practices in digital literacy tutoring: a cognitive task analysis approach. In: Zhou, J., Salvendy, G. (eds.) ITAP 2017. LNCS, vol. 10297, pp. 447–460. Springer, Cham (2017). https://doi.org/10.1007/978-3-319-58530-7_34
14. Szaja, S., Charness, N., Hertzog, C., Nair, S., Rogers, W.: Factors predicting the use of technology: findings from the center for research and education on aging and technology enhancement (create). Psychol. Aging **21**(2), 333–352 (2006)
15. Torkzadeh, G., Angulo, I.: The concept and correlates of computer anxiety. Behav. Inform. Technol. **11**(2), 99–108 (2005)
16. Weil, M., Rosen, L.: The psychological impact of technology from a global perspective: a study of technological sophistication and technophobia in university students from twenty-three countries. Comput. Hum. Behav. **11**(1), 95–133 (2005)

A Novel Wearable Mobility Device Adapting to Posture of Wearer and Environments with Steps

Rintaro Takashima, Takashi Kuwahara$^{(\boxtimes)}$, and Masanobu Imahori$^{(\boxtimes)}$

Program in Empowerment Informatics, School of Integrative and Global Majors,
University of Tsukuba, Tsukuba, Japan
{takashima, kuwahara, imahori}@golem.iit.tsukuba.ac.jp

Abstract. Personal mobility devices that can extend mobility functions of healthy person have been developed. However, conventional personal mobility device has some aspects that restrict the mobility functions of person since these devices have no ability to go up and down steps and to use freely because of portability. Thus, we propose a novel concept of mobility device that has ability to wear and to take advantage of the walking functions of person. It seems that it is possible to extend the mobility functions even in environments with steps. In this paper, we propose and develop a novel wearable mobility device that can wear, and go up and down steps. Our wearable mobility device consists of seat, frame, in-wheel motors and casters. The seat which has two load-cells is used as an interface for connecting a wearer to our mobility device and controlling our mobility device. The frame has two free joints each leg. Thus, the frame can realize states of sitting and standing. We carried out experiments to confirm that a participant with our wearable mobility device has the ability to walk, go up and down steps, and run with in-wheel motors. As the results of experiments, our wearable mobility device has the abilities to walk, go up and down steps, and run with in-wheel motors. In conclusion, we developed a novel wearable mobility device and confirmed that our wearable mobility device has feasibility to extend mobility functions of healthy person by adapting to human posture and steps.

Keywords: Wearable device · Personal mobility device · Controlling interface

1 Introduction

Movement is an essential action in human society. Therefore, the quality of our lives can be improved by extending mobility function of healthy person. Above all, personal mobility, which is capable of moving indoors and outdoors while coexisting with pedestrians, is expected to be a next-generation transportation for achieving efficient movement of users, expanding the mobility function of individuals. For example, there are personal mobility devices used while sitting on a seat [1, 2]. However, conventional

© Springer Nature Switzerland AG 2019
C. Stephanidis (Ed.): HCII 2019, CCIS 1034, pp. 528–532, 2019.
https://doi.org/10.1007/978-3-030-23525-3_72

personal mobility has some aspects that restrict the mobility functions of person since these mobility don't have ability to go up and down stairs and to use freely because of portability.

Therefore, if it is an unprecedented new personal mobility device that enables movement beyond the step without getting off, it is considered that it is possible to extend the human movement function without obstructing the movement range. Thus, we propose a novel concept of mobility device that has ability to wear and to take advantage of the walking functions of person. It seems that it is possible to extend the mobility functions even in environments with steps.

In this paper, we propose and develop a novel wearable mobility device that can wear, and go up and down steps.

2 System Overview

We propose a novel personal mobility device which can wear and take advantage of the walking functions of person as shown in Fig. 1. Our wearable mobility device consists of seat, frame, in-wheel motors and casters. The seat which has two load-cells is used as an interface for connecting a wearer to our mobility device and controlling our mobility device. The frame is mainly made of CFRP and aluminum alloy, and has a shape along each leg. In addition, the frame has two free joints each leg. Thus, the frame can realize states of sitting and standing as shown in Fig. 2.

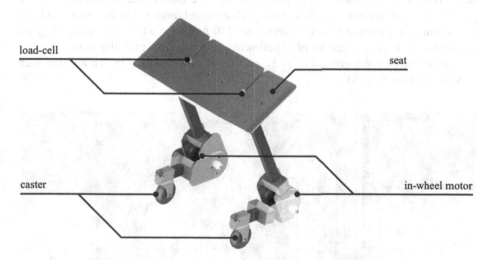

load-cell

seat

caster

in-wheel motor

Fig. 1. Overview of a developed wearable mobility device

Fig. 2. Standing and sitting state of a wearer with wearable mobility

3 Basic Experiment

We carried out three experiments to confirm that a participant with our wearable mobility device has the ability to walk, go up and down steps, and run with in-wheel motors. In basic experiments, we applied the wearable mobility to an able-bodied adult male (Weight: 60 kg, Height: 170 cm, Age: 24). We carried out experiments on flat ground when confirming to walk and run with in-wheel motors. On the other hand, we carried out an experiment at stairs which have 170 mm steps when confirming to go up and down steps. As the results of experiments, our wearable mobility device has the abilities to walk on flat ground (Fig. 3), go up and down steps (Fig. 4), and run with in-wheel motors (Fig. 5).

Fig. 3. A result of walking experiment

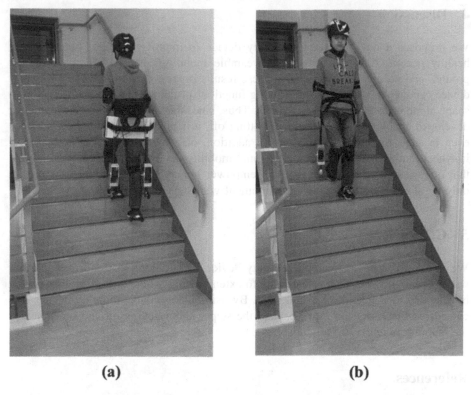

(a)   (b)

Fig. 4. A result of going up and down experiment. (a) is going up stairs. (b) is going down stairs.

Fig. 5. A result of running with in-wheel motors experiment.

4   Discussion

We proposed a novel wearable mobility device to improve mobility function of a healthy person. A user wearing our wearable mobility device could walk on flat ground, and go up and down stairs. These results suggest that our wearable mobility device can take advantage of the walking functions of human because the frame has a shape along each leg and has free joints. Thus, since the wearable mobility device we developed enable us to walk without getting off, it is possible to move beyond steps even in steps or stairs environment. In addition, our device enables us to run with in-wheel motors like conventional personal mobility devices. Therefore, it is thought that our wearable mobility device can empower human's mobility functions on not only the flat ground but also the environment with steps or stairs.

5   Conclusion

We developed a novel wearable mobility device. In addition, we confirmed that our wearable mobility device has feasibility to extend mobility functions of healthy person by adapting to human posture and steps. By using this wearable mobility device, it is considered that users can move beyond the step without getting off and be expanded the mobility function of individuals.

References

1. WHILL Inc. http://whill.us. Accessed 27 February 2019
2. Honda Global | UNI-CUB. https://global.honda/innovation/robotics/UNI-CUB.html. Accessed 27 February 2019

Interacting with Cultural Heritage

MRsive: An Augmented Reality Tool for Enhancing Wayfinding and Engagement with Art in Museums

Jad Al Rabbaa$^{(\boxtimes)}$, Alexis Morris, and Sowmya Somanath

OCAD University, Toronto, Canada
{jrabbaa,amorris,ssomanath}@faculty.ocadu.ca

Abstract. Most museums use printed methods to support indoor navigation and visitor engagement strategies. However, modern museum visitors' needs are not always met using static and conventional approaches, which are commonly employed in today's museums. This paper investigates how indoor wayfinding and visitor engagement in the museum might be improved through interactive augmented reality. We designed "MRsive", a handheld Augmented Reality (AR) tool using a user-centered design approach. The ultimate goal is twofold: the first is to simplify the required cognitive effort in navigating the museum space, and the second goal is to boost visitor engagement with museum artifacts through multisensory interaction. MRsive uses computer vision tools to read visual features in the space and achieve accurate indoor positioning of the directions and virtual cues anchored in the physical space. To evaluate our design, we followed a human-centered design approach. We conducted user testing at the Art Gallery of Ontario (AGO) followed by semi-structured interviews. The observations and answers of participants showed a considerable improvement in the speed, accuracy and ease-of-use when completing a wayfinding or engagement task. We hope our findings and discussion will contribute to the future development of this system and other AR tools that may improve wayfinding in complex indoor spaces and engagement with points of interest in other indoor environments.

Keywords: Wayfinding · Indoor navigation · Augmented Reality (AR) · Computer vision · Multisensory engagement · Museum environments

1 Introduction

First-time visitors commonly get lost in museums and experience spatial anxiety and challenges related to maintaining a strong understanding of many artifacts. This is often alleviated when having a guided tour that involves navigation to the artifact, multi-sensory engagement, and close observation of the art. However, in contrast to this, visitors generally rely on signs and printed maps. In the case of complex museums, this navigation would require considerable spatial reasoning and decision making, referred to as wayfinding. Allen [1] defines wayfinding as "purposeful movement to a specific destination that is distal and, thus, cannot be perceived directly by the traveler". According to the Society for Experiential Graphic Design (SEGD) wayfinding aids

© Springer Nature Switzerland AG 2019
C. Stephanidis (Ed.): HCII 2019, CCIS 1034, pp. 535–542, 2019.
https://doi.org/10.1007/978-3-030-23525-3_73

refer to the tools used to facilitate this decision-making such as maps, direction signs, and navigational assistants [2]. Using such wayfinding tools involves different cognitive processes [3] that normally add to the museum visitor's spatial anxiety. Reading maps, for example, requires mental rotation of 2D objects and identificationof symbols while matching the map to the environment [4]. This process gets more complicated in complex spaces and affects the speed and accuracy of navigation. Signage is another static wayfinding method that is time-consuming to interpret. It highly depends on the placement of signs, the clarity of text and design, and the level of complexity of pictograms [5]. Due to the digital advancement, mobile applications have started being introduced to the visitor experience in museums since 2009 [6] which offered new possibilities of communications between the museum and the visitor. Although the digital capacities of the mobile phone were leveraged toward wayfinding, indoor positioning of the user was the biggest limitation, as GPS signals are weak and inaccurate in enclosed places.

Further, the engagement with art in museums generally depends on simple written exhibition information which at times limit the visitor's understanding of the background or history behind each exhibit. Audio navigation guides provide more freedom to the visitor. They verbally describe the historical background of the arts of interest that are manually selected. However, they have an impact on the navigation process and risk being unsynchronized with the navigator's position and their line of sight. There has been a recent interest from museums to target Gen Y (1982–2002) known as the net generation [7], as Gen Y visitors prefer to interact with exhibits as opposed to being passive participants in the experience and expect instant gratification [8].

In our proposed approach, we unpack the benefits of augmented reality and its potential future development to provide both wayfinding and engagement in museum spaces. Through visual tracking, a dynamic indoor positioning is achievable as well as a digital and interactive engaging experience with the art. This approach attempts to further contribute toward addressing new visitors' needs and interests.

2 Related Work

Several indoor navigation systems using augmented reality have been proposed over the last few years. These systems utilize different indoor positioning techniques to localize and anchor content, which is divided into two approaches. The first approach is wireless connectivity using wireless technologies such as GSM, WLAN, Bluetooth, among others. INSAR [9], for example, uses the Wi-Fi fingerprinting technique and does not require an external server achieving a fast performance. However, the fluctuation in the positioning accuracy makes this technique unsuitable for a complex and precise augmented reality display. The second approach is visual tracking which can be marker based, markerless, or extensible tracking. Kim et al. [10] developed an AR application that relied on scanning markers at every decision point in the wayfinding (and navigation) process. While this achieved much more accurate results than wireless tracking, it is debatable if an experience that heavily relies on repetitively and manually scanning visual markers could provide a user-friendly navigation.

When it comes to encouraging visitor engagement, Various museums have recently incorporated AR features to interact with the art. For example, the Street Museum application in the Museum of London [11] allows visitors to overlay images from the museum's photography collections on present-day London street scenes. The Van Gogh Museum (Amsterdam, the Netherlands) uses AR to assist visitors to visualize x-rays, infrared and ultraviolet captures on top of original paintings [12]. The "ReBlink" at the AGO (Toronto, Canada) is another recent and good example of a successful AR application and exhibition. It allows visitors to view traditional paintings in a re-contextualized modern twist. While the ReBlink project succeeded in drawing a lot of attention to the museum by providing a modern look at the art [13], it was not aimed toward deepening the understanding of the original exhibits.

3 Designing *MRsive*

Tosolve the spatial anxiety and disconnection from the arts in a museum setting it is important to track the visitor's indoor position and orientation and detect the art they are looking at or interested in throughout their visit. Following a user-centered design approach, we propose MRsive, an AR solution that uses hand-held augmented reality, with computer vision tools for tracking and localization, as input to display virtual directions accurately anchored in the physical space to lead visitors to their destination. To bring exhibits to life and to enhance engagement, the system recognizes the artifact through visual detection of different feature points. The art is then activated by different multisensory interactions such as 3D virtual objects, animations, text, sound and vibrations to invite the visitors into a deeper engagement and understanding of the art.

3.1 System Overview

MRsive's system overview as shown in Fig. 1 is divided between input and output (horizontally) and between wayfinding and engagement (vertically). The prototype was developed using Unity 3D and exported to an iPhone, leveraging the camera positioning system, and the Placenote and Vuforia SDKs for localization and anchoring content during the wayfinding and engagement activities.

Wayfinding. Visual Simultaneous Localization And Mapping (vSLAM) [14] uses computer vision to triangulate and track thousands of points related to surface landmark features in the physical environment. This allows the system to provide an accurate pose estimation of the handheld device's viewpoint across a wide range of viewpoints in the scene. Similarly, the Placenote SDK uses the camera to collect different depths in the space through the detection of feature points. It generates a 3D point cloud and vertical and horizontal planes that are imported to Unity and used as a reference to the real world before accurately anchoring the directional cues in the 3D space as AR objects (see Fig. 2).

Engagement. To bring art to life, the Vuforia SDK uses the artwork as visual markers that trigger an AR multisensory interaction. Those exhibits are saved as image marker targets in Vuforia and are detectable by the system's camera. We used a painting called

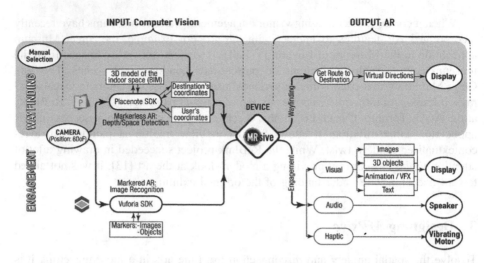

Fig. 1. MRsive's system architecture. (Left) Input architecture for wayfinding in grey, and engagement in white. (Right) AR outputs for wayfinding in grey and engagement in white.

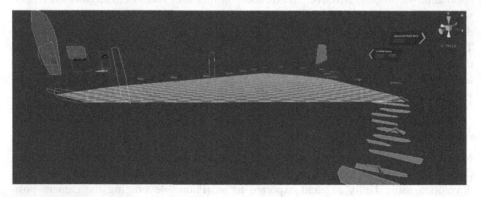

Fig. 2. 3D point cloud and planes representing the scan of the real world. (Obtained using the placenote SDK). Other AR objects are manually added to the model in unity.

"The Storm" as an example. When the painting is detected, MRsive triggers visual, auditory and haptic responses related to the artwork, toward a more engaging study of the exhibit.

3.2   User Experience

The visitors are provided with different navigation interfaces as shown in Fig. 3. First, the visitor chooses their point of interest on the map or from a list of destinations (Fig. 3(a)). Then, the camera opens and invites the user to scan the space around to identify the indoor localization (Fig. 3(b)). Behind the scenes, MRsive compares the different depths and feature points of the live view with the 3D model of the space already saved on the Placenote's database. The difference calculated between those two models enables the system to identify the coordinates and rotation of the visitor's device relative to the 3D space. Once MRsive finds the visitor's position, virtual and animated arrows appear on the ground level leading the user, turn by turn, to the location of the previously selected destination. To support a better understanding of the space, a dynamic track-up 2D map with a pin in the middle is shown on the corner of the display during this experience (Fig. 3(c)). Once arrived at the desired destination, the visitor is capable to augment the exhibits by scanning them. The scan of "The Storm" for example triggers the display of different virtual graphics such as 3D graphics, images and text that describe and complement the art (Fig. 3(d)). Moreover, a soundscape and a haptic response are triggered as well. The soundscape of wind, thunder, rain, and even the sound of the steps of a distant shepherd play in the background while the phone vibrates every time the sound of thunder plays.

(a)   (b)   (c)   (d)

Fig. 3. MRsive screenshots by order of user-flow: (a) Destination selection; (b) Scanning to localize the space; (c) AR wayfinding directions; (d) Interaction with 'The Storm'.

4 Evaluation

To test the usability of our system we conducted user testing with 12 participants that have never been to the AGO. The evaluation was divided between a wayfinding experiment and an engagement experiment and included observation of the participants' interaction with MRsive in the space followed by semi-structured interviews.

For the wayfinding experiment, participants were asked to locate and navigate to the same destination by first using any traditional, pre-existing wayfinding aids available at the AGO, and then using MRsive, to qualitatively compare the results. On average, it took participants 111 s less to complete the task when using MRsive; a significantly shorter duration. Participants were also asked to evaluate how intuitive they found both approaches by rating them on the Likert scale of 1 to 10, where 1 means not intuitive at all and 10 means extremely intuitive. Figure 4 shows the significant difference between the ratings and confirms the observations which noted frustration when using static approaches, which is contrasted against the confidence displayed when using our approach. Even though most participants complained from navigating the space while holding a phone, they were impressed with the easiness of the AR approach and commended the top view map at the corner of the screen as it followed their orientation and localization accurately during their navigation from origin to destination.

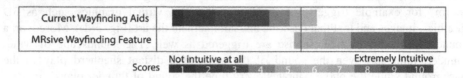

Fig. 4. Wayfinding scores in both approaches. MRsive's scores ranged between 5 and 9 while static wayfinding aids were rated between 1 and 6.

For the engagement experiment, participants were asked to interact with "The Storm" painting using our system after attempting to read the label next to it and engage with it. Through the think-aloud method, most participants expressed feelings of surprise and excitement when using MRsive, and they appeared totally focused and immersed in what they could see, hear and feel. Participants mentioned that the information gave the art more context. Three participants mentioned that the audio helped them notice the shepherd and sheep which were small details for them to notice. When compared to the traditional aids, the engagement with the painting through the multisensory interactions was, on average, four times longer than simply reading the label and looking at it with no aids. On the Likert scale of 1 to 10, Participants rated MRsive significantly higher than what they rated the static approach for engagement (see Fig. 5).

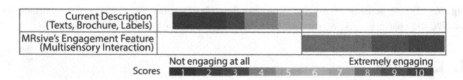

Fig. 5. Engagements scores of both approaches. MRsive's scores ranged between 8 and 10 while static engagement approaches were rated between 2 and 6.

5 Future Work

The findings of the conducted study indicated multiple opportunities for future improvements on two differentlevels, design and platform in use in MRsive:

Design Level. The image of AR virtual objects normally renders on top of the real world image in the camera view causing an incorrect depth occlusion, and a less immersive experience. In the future, we aim to introduce depth information to the AR scene for a more credible anchoring of virtual directions and stable navigation experience. Moreover, animating the system's interface and icons could be another addition that benefits the user experience and make the navigation of the system interface more intuitive.

Platform Level. Since most participants commented on the discomfort and disconnection caused by looking down to a screenwhile moving in the space, it is worth exploring a shift in platform. MRsive runs on a smartphone or a tablet and it is designed to be extended in the future so that the experience can be hosted on a head-mounted display (HMD). The current limitations of HMD-based AR technology, such as the low field of view, bulky form factor, and often tethered hardwarecontribute to the current difficulty to develop content for these platforms that can be applied readily in museum spaces [15]. However, in the future, we aim to explore a Do-It-Yourself (DIY) solution using mobile components, like an iPhone and a Google Cardboard with a cutout on the camera area to create a video see-through display (Fig. 6(b)). While it does not solve the limited field of view (FOV) challenge [16], the shift of the interface from the fingertips (Fig. 6(a)) to the face (Fig. 6(b) and (c)) allows a proper placement of graphical objects relative the user's line of sight (LOS) and offers hands free interactions with the system. Further investigations of the relationship between the placement of the display, type of user experience, and FOV would be very valuable to the research community and for preparing MRsive for the promising future of AR glasses (Fig. 6(c)) and their advancement currently lead by Microsoft HoloLens and Magic Leap.

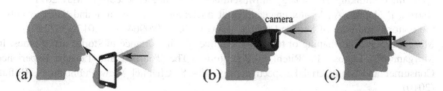

Fig. 6. DifferentAR displays: (a) Handheld device's display; (b) Video see-through display; (c) Optical see-through display (smart eyeglasses).

6 Conclusion

This work has presented the development and evaluation of MRsive, a novel mobile-based 3D augmented reality system that supports indoor wayfinding and engagement with art in museums; including the outcome of onsite user testing within the Art Gallery of Ontario (AGO) in Toronto, Canada, as a testbed. Results have shown that MRsive's approach to indoor localization of visitors, thanks to realtime vSLAM-based detection and tracking of feature points in the space facilitates indoor wayfinding and navigation. The displayed virtual wayfinding cues are accurately anchored in the physical space in the perspective view and the overall system framework proved to be intuitive; showing a significant improvement in wayfinding completion tasks, compared to traditional wayfinding aids. Moreover, MRsive's application of image recognition to turn exhibits into markers that trigger corresponding visual, auditory and haptic representation of the art for providing multisensory interaction proved to increase the engagement time with a selected museum testing artifact and showed a considerable potential in improving the understanding of this artwork. The latter hints toward future similar approaches to encourage general interest and deeper engagement withtoday's museum environments.

Acknowledgements. For their support of this research, we would like to thank the digital team and visitor research department at the Art Gallery of Ontario in Toronto.

References

1. Allen, G.L.: Spatial abilities, cognitive maps, and wayfinding: bases for individual differences in spatial cognition and behavior. In: Golledge, R.G. (ed.) Wayfinding Behavior: Cognitive Mapping and Other Spatial Processes, pp. 46–80 (1999)
2. SEGD: What is Wayfinding?. https://segd.org/what-wayfinding. Accessed 28 March 2019
3. Wiener, J.M., Büchner, S.J., Hölscher, C.: Towards a taxonomy of wayfinding tasks: a knowledge-based approach. Spat. Cogn. Comput. **9**, 152–165 (2009). https://doi.org/10. 1080/13875860902906496
4. Lobben, A.K.: Tasks, strategies, and cognitive processes associated with navigational map reading: a review perspective. Prof. Geogr. **56**(2), 270–281 (2004)
5. Passini, R.: Wayfinding in Architecture. Van Nostrand Reinhold, McGraw-Hill Book CO, New York, New York (1984)
6. Economou, M., Meintani, E.: Promising beginnings? Evaluating museum mobile phone apps. In: Rethinking Technology in Museums Conference Proceedings, May 2011
7. Barron, P., Leask, A.: Visitor engagement at museums : generation Y and 'lates' events at the national museum of Scotland (2017). doi.org/10.1080/09647775.2017.1367259
8. Moscardo, G.: The shaping of tourist experience: the importance of stories and themes. In: Morgan, M., Lugosi, P., Ritchie, J.R.B. (eds.) The Tourism and Leisure Experience: Consumer and Managerial Perspectives, pp. 43–58. Channel View Publications, Buffalo (2010)
9. Alnabhan, A., Tomaszewski, B.: INSAR : indoor navigation system using augmented reality. In: Proceedings of the Sixth ACM SIGSPATIAL International Workshop on Indoor Spatial Awareness - ISA 2014, pp. 36–43 (2014). https://doi.org/10.1145/2676528.2676535
10. Kim, M.J., Wang, X., Han, S., Wang, Y.: Implementing an augmented reality-enabled wayfinding system through studying user experience and requirements in complex environments (2015). https://doi.org/10.1186/s40327-015-0026-2
11. Zolfagharifard, E.: Streets of London now...and then (2014). http://www.dailymail.co.uk/ sciencetech/article-2567739/Streetmuseum-app-creates-hybrid-images-London.html. Accessed 28 March 2019
12. Van Eck, W., Kolstee, Y.: The augmented painting: playful interaction with multi-spectral images. In: 2012 IEEE ISMAR-AMH (2012)
13. Stephenson, B., Lorenzo, N., Manikoth, K., Yule, M., Chan, T.: A remedial and summative evaluation of the reblink installation at the art gallery of Ontario (2017)
14. Ventura, J., Arth, C., Reitmayr, G., Schmalstieg, D.: Global localization from monocular SLAM on a mobile phone. IEEE Trans. Vis. Comput. Graph. **20**(4), 531–539 (2014)
15. Billinghurst, M., Clark, A., Lee, G.: A survey of augmented reality navigation, **8**(2), 73–272 (2017). https://doi.org/10.1561/1100000049
16. Xiao, R., Benko, H.: Augmenting the field-of-view of head-mounted displays with sparse peripheral displays. In: CHI 2016, pp. 1221–1232 (2016)

The Interaction of the Public with the Show Museum: A Case Study About the Museum of Tomorrow

Cidomar Biancardi Filho[✉] and Priscila Arantes

Doctorate and Master's Degree Design Graduate Program,
Anhembi Morumbi University, São Paulo, SP 04705-000, Brazil
cidomar.bf@gmail.com, ppgdesign@anhembi.br

Abstract. This article discusses the interaction between the public and the Digital Museum, using as a case study the Museum of Tomorrow [Museu do Amanhã], in the city of Rio de Janeiro, Brazil. The study is based on the use of hashtag and its marking in social networks, making an analysis of the specific places, conceived in design, for the practice of selfies and later publication and marking. The study presents a typical relation of contemporary societies and their relationship with museum and technology, raising the possibility of construction and/or reconstruction of totally digital spaces earmarked for the exhibition of art and history.

Keywords: Digital museum · Show museum · Hashtag

1 Introduction

The discussion of the relationship between museum and technology is not recent. Nor is it recent the theoretical discussion that addresses art made and shown in alternative ways, such as digital installations. There are also new art concepts, increasingly linked to the relationship between aesthetic production and digital culture.

One of the discussions about art exhibited in previously unexpected spaces, such as refurbished factories, abandoned warehouses, among other spaces, is the article "The Cultural Logic of the Late Capitalist Museum", a text in which Krauss (1990) discusses - in a conversation with Tony Smith in 1990 - the art that begins to leave the frames and gain new ways of exhibiting themselves, of gaining life, in that period of still nascent minimalism.

Moreover, almost fifteen years later[1], Groys (2014) presents the idea of digital interaction between museum and spectator in the article "Self-Design and Public Space", in which he also presents the concept of "avatar", i.e. the character by which most of the contemporary digital citizens express themselves, who will also be the character through which they will make their exposure in social media.

---

[1] The text of Rosalind Krauss was originally published in September 1990, as read in the meeting of the International Association of Museums of Modern Art (CIMAM) in Los Angeles, and Groys text in 2014.

© Springer Nature Switzerland AG 2019
C. Stephanidis (Ed.): HCII 2019, CCIS 1034, pp. 543–548, 2019.
https://doi.org/10.1007/978-3-030-23525-3_74

In fact, the appearance of the avatar, described by Groys (2014), is the result of a series of social behaviors and living spaces, that will culminate with a way to act socially, in digital media, a striking feature of contemporary society.

Digital art, as already mentioned by Krauss (1990), will require adequate spaces for its exhibition. The collection, once physical and palpable, becomes ephemeral and produced and stored digitally.

This is where the definitely digital spaces, such as the Atelier des Lumières in Paris, emerge. First 100% digital museum in the French capital, it is dedicated to immersive exhibits: music and digital projections involve the viewer - who is free to make use of digital devices such as smart phones and tablets, for example - on a tour through the visual production of big names of world painting. The inaugural exhibition was dedicated to the work of Gustav Klimt, and now is showing the summary of Van Gogh's work.

In this same context there also appears the Museum of Tomorrow, in the city of Rio de Janeiro, Brazil. It is a building designed by the famous Spanish architect Santiago Calatrava, commissioned by the Roberto Marinho Foundation[2], to serve as a physical landmark for the transformation of the old port area of Rio de Janeiro, which is very degraded and forgotten. It is managed by the Municipal Secretariat of Culture of the city of Rio de Janeiro, and sponsored by global companies such as banks, oil companies and technology companies[3].

The Museum of Tomorrow was inaugurated on December 17, 2015, one year before the RIO/2016 Olympics. Several transformations took over the city, as happened with Barcelona on the eve of the 1992 Olympic Games. In Rio, the Museum of Tomorrow was undoubtedly one of the most important.

2 The Museum of Tomorrow

Dedicated to tomorrow, as its name implies, its conception and operation are geared to explorations and questions about the time of enormous changes in which we are inserted and which paths mankind will follow in the future.

The Museum's very electronic address provides a brief description of its activities: "… *a journey towards possible futures, from the great questions that Mankind has always asked. Where did we come from? Who are we? Where are we? Where are we going? How do we want to go? Guided by the ethical values of Sustainability and Coexistence, essential for our civilization, the Museum also seeks to promote innovation, disseminate the advances of science and publish the vital signs of the planet. A Museum to broaden our knowledge and transform our way of thinking and acting.*[4]

---

[2] The Roberto Marinho Foundation is a foundation linked to the largest network of telecommunications of Brazil, the Globo Group, owner of printed and digital newspapers, and also the television network with the largest audience in the country.

[3] The management of the Museum, since its construction, is classified as a public-private partnership, and their managers and sponsors can be found in the electronic address: https://museudoamanha.org.br/#. Accessed March 01, 2019.

[4] The full description is available at: https://museudoamanha.org.br/pt-br/sobre-o-museu.

For the development of activities related to the questioning of mankind, as well as for the proposed interaction, the Museum also presents a very peculiar needs program, evidenced also and mainly by its architecture project, basically composed by a mega-exhibition space of an interactive and digital character and a building whose main facade is one of the most photographed in recent times, as we will see next.

The building occupies an area of 15 thousand square meters, implanted at Mauá Pier, whose total area of the surroundings is 34.6 thousand square meters. "*The idea is that the building were as ethereal as possible, almost floating over the sea, like a boat, a bird or a plant*"[5], explains Calatrava, author of the architecture project, when he talks about the building.

The height of the two-story building does not exceed 18 m, in respect to the historic surroundings of the Port. The main exhibition space, upstairs, has almost 5,000 square meters and is 10-m high, overlooking the Guanabara Bay. The lower floor is occupied by more technical and administrative functions such as offices, educational support areas, research space, auditorium, a restaurant, archives, warehouses and docks. The main lobby and the Museum shop are also on the same floor.

The main exhibition, which occupies the whole large space of the upper deck, is called "A Course of Questions". Idealized by the doctor in cosmology Luiz Alberto Oliveira, it makes the user go through a structured narrative in five large areas, all of them interactive: Cosmos, Earth, Anthropocene, Tomorrow and Us. All 40 interactive experiences are available in Portuguese, English and Spanish.

3   The Interaction at the Show Museum

Based on the descriptions of the Museum of Tomorrow discussed above, it is now possible to present the study proposed here.

Having received more than 25,000 visitors in the first weekend of operation, and more than 3 million visitors since its opening, the Museum is clearly configured as a building of spectacular character, serving as a pole of attraction for people who do not always go in search of the digital and interactive experiences offered at their facilities.

Featherstone (1995) explains exactly this behavior in Consumer Culture and Postmodernism, when he describes the postmodern city and the cultural behavior of people in this city:

"... *The postmodern city, therefore, is much more aware of its own imagistic and cultural dimension: it is a center of cultural consumption as much as of general consumption, and this, as has already been emphasized, cannot be dissociated from cultural signs and imagery, so that urban life styles, daily life and leisure activities are influenced, to varying degrees, by post-modern simulational trends*".

FEATHERSTONE, Mike. 1995, p. 140

The study proposed here, based on the avatar of Groys (2014) and on the consumer society of Featherstone (1995), presents the survey of the use of the hashtag

---

[5] The above transcribed phrase, as well as other descriptions of Calatrava himself, can be read in full at the electronic address: https://museudoamanha.org.br/pt-br/content/arquitetura-de-santiago-calatrava.

corresponding to the Museum of Tomorrow; #museudoamanha on the Instagram social network, the main responsible for marking hashtags in all social networks available to the cyber user today.

Instagram began as an online social network in 2010, developed by two colleagues from Stanford University: Kevin Systrom (North American) and Mike Krieger (Brazilian). In two years it has reached over 100 million active users worldwide.

It revolutionized the way internet users share photo and also became one of the largest online paid advertising vehicles, a mode through which celebrities make a post using certain products and/or brands, making explicit reference to this. As a "digital influencer", he/she will propagate the use of the brand in question, as well as become directly or indirectly responsible for the choice at the purchase time. Through Instagram it is also possible to replicate the publication to other social networks, such as Facebook, Twitter, Tumblr and Flickr.

Going back to Groys (2014), social network users can be considered real avatars of the real people, and act as such, making direct reference to the places where they move around, as well as the digital brands they use to confirm presence in a certain place.

Here we have no relation to the brands mentioned in social networks, but rather the place marked, more specifically the Museum of Tomorrow.

Through a simple search, on Instagram itself, through the official hashtag of the Museum: #museudoamanha, we can see that it was quoted 252 thousand times until the date this article was written (February 2019). In a rather simple calculation, the Museum has roughly 1,160 days of existence, which leads us to understand that the hashtag #museudoamanha has been used on average 217 times a day since its inauguration.

As a comparison, the British Museum, for example, one of the most renowned museological institutions in the world, with more than 260 years of existence, registers only 460,000 #britishmuseum, in research in the same Instagram.

The Louvre Museum, in Paris, perhaps the most visited museum in the world, also presents only 370 thousand #louvremuseum in the same social network.

The ratio is absurd, comparing the three examples above.

While the first average is 217 times per day, the second is 0.00099 per day. The third average, considering the Louvre as a Museum starting in 1793, is 0.004 uses of the hashtag #louvremuseum per day.

In a second approach, comparing the use of the same #hashtags above, considering the existence and use of Instagram, we have:

- Museum of Tomorrow: 86.30 uses per day;
- British Museum: 157.53 uses per day;
- Louvre Museum: 126.71 uses per day.

However, it is important to note that the Museum of Tomorrow was inaugurated and opened to the public only five years after Instagram began to be used as a social network, a period in which both the British Museum and the Louvre Museum were already part of the imaginary for more than two centuries.

In addition to the use of hashtag #museudoamanha, the Museum building is deployed in a way to provide the user with a selfie with the entire building as background, proving that in addition to using the hashtag, the Museum is also one of the most used as a selfie point.

4 Conclusion and Possible Implications

With the information presented, it is possible to present some conclusions about the interaction of the Museum of Tomorrow and its user.

The first and most important is that buildings designed with the initial proposal of becoming spectacular, a pole of convergence of digital interaction and people, are undoubtedly better known and digitally coveted as places of "pilgrimage". This is what I call the Show Museum.

The second is that the Museum itself, as a digital institution, can and should take advantage of this interaction and promote physical and digital actions in the search for free digital marketing: the greater the number of markings for hashtags, the better known the building becomes, and more marketing actions are possible to accomplish. It is a more mature concept, yet still relevant, that can be clearly understood in depth in texts by Featherstone (1995) and Harvey (1989).

Last but not least, all Institutions can, in a digital world, take advantage of a collection that is in the cloud, in order to be able to reconstruct or even keep in the memory of a basically digital society, even though the "aura" (1955) of physical preciousness can never be replaced.

Recently, in the dawn of September 02 to 03, 2018, the National Museum, the oldest Scientific Institution of Brazil, suffered a fire of gigantic proportions and had almost 100% of its collection of more than 20 million items burned.

Since then, in a slow and gradual work, a group of researchers has been recovering part of the collection of the Museum through the mapping of publications in digital social networks, using #museunacional and its derivatives as an element of search and research.

Several sessions of nightly digital projection on the facades of the post-fire museum have taken place, showing the public who visits the museum, although burned, part of the lost collection and also part of the recovery work that is under way.

The Avatar Museum!

References

Benjamin, W.: A obra de arte na era de sua repordutibilidade técnica, 1st edn. L&PM, Porto Alegre (1955). https://doi.org/10.1096/fj.09-0701ufm
Featherstone, M.: Cultura de Consumo e Pós-Modernismo. Studio Nobel, São Paulo (1995)
Groys, B.: Self-design and public space. The Avery Review (2014). http://averyreview.com/issues/2/self-design-and-public-space
Harvey, D.: Condição Pós-Moderna, 11th edn. Blackwell, São Paulo (1989). https://doi.org/10.1017/cbo9781107415324.004. Loyola
Krauss, R.: The cultural logic of the late capitalist museum, vol. 54, p. 3, October 1990. https://doi.org/10.2307/778666

O que se sabe sobre o incêndio do Museu Nacional, no Rio. https://g1.globo.com/rj/rio-de-janeiro/noticia/2018/09/04/o-que-se-sabe-sobre-o-incendio-no-museu-nacional-no-rio.ghtml. Acessed 01 Mar 2019

The Museum of Tomorrow/Santiago Calatrava. https://www.archdaily.com/66019/the-museum-of-tomorrow-santiago-calatrava. Accessed 27 Feb 2019

Museu do Amanhã/Rio de Janeiro. https://calatrava.com/projects/museu-do-amanha-rio-de-janeiro.html. Accessed 27 Feb 2019

Sobre o Museu. https://museudoamanha.org.br/pt-br/sobre-o-museu, Accessed 28 Feb 2019

Quem somos. https://museudoamanha.org.br/pt-br/quem-somos. Accessed 28 Feb 2019

Um percurso de perguntas. https://museudoamanha.org.br/pt-br/exposicao-principal. Accessed 28 Feb 2019

Interactive Edutainment: A Technologically Enhanced Theme Park

Chryssi Birliraki[1(✉)], Nikos Stivaktakis[1], Antonis Chatziantoniou[1],
Vassiliki Neroutsou[1], Emmanouil Zidianakis[1], Ioanna Zidianaki[1],
Emmanouil Apostolakis[1], Emmanouil Stamatakis[1],
Michalis Roulios[1], Stavroula Ntoa[1], Michalis Sifakis[1], Maria Korozi[1],
Spiros Paparoulis[1], Thanasis Toutountzis[1], Nikolaos Patsiouras[1],
Antonis Dimopoulos[1], George Paparoulis[1], Nikolaos Partarakis[1],
George Margetis[1], and Constantine Stephanidis[1,2]

[1] Foundation for Research and Technology – Hellas (FORTH),
Institute of Computer Science, N. Plastira 100, Vassilika Vouton,
700 13 Heraklion, Crete, Greece
{birlirak,nstivaktak,hatjiant,vaner,zidian,izidian,
apostolak,stamatakis,roulios,stant,misi,korozi,
spirosp,atout,patsiouras,dimopoulos,groulis,partarak,
gmarget,cs}@ics.forth.gr
[2] Department of Computer Science, University of Crete, Heraklion, Greece

Abstract. Heraklion Christmas Castle is a joint effort between ICS-FORTH and the Municipality of Heraklion-Crete (Municipal Public Service Enterprise of Heraklion), trying to pioneer and be innovative in the presentation of Christmas customs and ideas by creating a festive neighborhood governed by interactive technology. The approach followed by this research work was to employ interactive systems to give a feeling of Christmas to children and adults through the combination of education and entertainment. This work presents the innovative systems designed and developed for the Christmas Castle to augment and enhance the festive spirit through multimodal interaction techniques, such as virtual environments, kinesthetic interaction, physical object identification and serious games. All the systems were designed and integrated within art artefacts (special constructions) that match the Christmas look-and-feel and provide a user-centric design.

Keywords: Interactive systems · Edutainment · Multimodal interaction ·
Information visualization · Kinesthetic interaction · Serious games ·
Public spaces · Public installations · Ambient Intelligence (AmI)

1 Introduction

The creation of systems that are innovative, interactive, playful, usable and fit the context of use is a challenging task especially when such systems are being deployed in public spaces, such as theme parks.

C. Stephanidis (Ed.): HCII 2019, CCIS 1034, pp. 549–559, 2019.
https://doi.org/10.1007/978-3-030-23525-3_75

Public spaces form an important part of our everyday life – they create a sense of belonging, provide a place where we can socialize, relax, and learn something new [5]. A public space is a social space that is generally open and accessible to people. We encounter public spaces everywhere we go: town centers, parks, and public streets are all common settings of our everyday life. Public spaces involve necessary, optional and social activities [11]. According to the authors, in contrast to the compulsory ones, optional activities are seriously related to the quality of the public spaces. Social activities that occur spontaneously as a direct consequence of people being in the same places are equally affected by the quality of the environment.

Public displays are for anyone to interact in a walk-up-and-use [14] manner. In public displays, a large proportion of users are passers-by and thus first-time users. Most of the research on public displays has been carried out by running installations in local communities, yet this research has only recently started.

Ambient Intelligence allows the user to interact with several means often simultaneously, such as speech, body movements, gestures, eye and head tracking or even with physical objects. Multimodal interaction is a part of everyday human discourse: we speak, move, gesture and shift our gaze in an effective flow of communication. Jaimes et al. [15] define a multimodal system as a system that "responds to inputs in more than one modality or communication channel, such as speech, gesture, writing and others".

"Play is a very serious matter….It is an expression of our creativity; and creativity is at the very root of our ability to learn, to cope, and to become whatever we may be" [6, 19]. Over the years, interactive games have evolved in a number of areas [13] in terms of both hardware and software. Such a change is based on users' diversity and on the fact that games are part of society and culture [23]. Especially for children [3, 10] it is easier to engage in activities when playing is their motivation [1, 2, 9].

The purpose of this work is to use different ways of interaction so as both children and adults may use applications that can educate them while playing. By providing a combination of image, sound and interaction, users can communicate Christmas customs, while at the same time get involved in the action of each system. The technologies used vary by application, so users learn to handle technological advances in many different ways, helping them in a later encounter with corresponding systems. Although this work presents the case study of interactive systems at Heraklion Christmas Castle, the logic behind is that the systems can be adapted to any context of use with small changes in the content and the visual composition that surrounds them.

2   Related Work

Human behavior and interaction, both among people and between a person and an interactive system, largely affect the way that users perceive and react to their surroundings. Human behavior can trigger engagement through the feeling of curiosity, the point being fully described as a 'honey-pot' effect [24]. The different phases of interaction between users and public installations range from the ambient and implicit to finally using them on an immediate and more personal manner [22]. Moreover, the setup of the public displays and the location's architecture strongly influence user interaction and social effects; as presented by Ten Koppel et al. [16], different display configurations can either promote or hinder interaction both with deployed systems and between users.

Moreover, playfulness constitutes another fundamental factor affecting the way people approach and interact with exhibits publicly accessible [2], fostering creativity, promoting social interaction and physical play. In the same context, edutainment [12] combines the domains of education with entertainment, thus presenting valuable input in a pleasant manner and allowing learning while enjoying interaction.

Interactive installations employ a diverse set of input methods which are often combined in order to provide the optimal user experience and further engage users, often being combined and providing multimodal interaction [4]. Gestural remote interaction constitutes a widespread approach for manipulating [7] public displays. In a similar manner, the entire body movement and posture can act as an input mechanism for deployed applications, providing less efficient but certainly more playful and enjoyable interaction between the end users and the system [8, 20, 21].

Finally, physical objects, often referred to as smart objects, are used as an interaction technique [18]. Tangible interaction has the advantage of the user using an everyday item which is enhanced by technological components (such as RFID cards, accelerometers, gyroscopes, distance sensors, etc.) and achieving more than initially expecting; as a result, users feel that the physical item or even themselves are empowered to perform actions otherwise impossible. An interesting example is presented by Marshall et al. [17], where authors use the concept of smart replicas in an effort to augment a museum and enhance the overall user experience of people's visit.

3 Heraklion Christmas Castle

In Heraklion Christmas Castle, four areas have been configured to host the interactive systems of the Institute of Computer Science of the Foundation for Research and Technology – Hellas (ICS-FORTH). These are: (a) the house of fairytales, (b) the house of the elves, (c) the house of surprises and (d) the sleigh with the reindeer. Each house is design-decorated to stimulate the Christmas spirit, but also to promote user participation, collaboration and fun. More specifically, the house of fairytales enhances user experience through kinesthetic interaction, immersion and playfulness. Users can become part of the system and interact with system's elements. The applications deployed in the elves' house combine education with fun. Through the use of the systems, users learn to operate with more ecological consciousness, but also educate themselves about geographical destinations around the world, enrich their knowledge about Christmas customs around the world and apply analytical thinking. The surprise house, on the other hand, is based on entertainment; through interactive games, which use controls found in everyday life, such as a steering wheel and a hand pump, the systems assist the development of skills like perception, speed and goalseeking. As far as the sleigh is concerned, the main goal for users is to familiarize themselves with the robotic technology through animatronics (servos, stepper motors, robotic equipment and electronics are integrated into the reindeer's body), but also to participate in a technological way in the experience of gift delivery, an established custom all over the world. All interactive systems developed are thoroughly described in the following sections.

3.1   The House of the Elves

Gift's Energy Efficiency. The main goal of this system is to develop ecological consciousness to users allowing them to contribute in the screening process of the gifts on their way to Santa Claus's bag. The system rates each gift with regard to its energy efficiency and allows users to interactively choose the more ecological material combination among several potential alternatives. In particular, users select one of the packaged gifts and place it in a suitable position on a belt. The belt is automatically activated as soon as a user has been tracked near it, and starts to move by promoting the present in a special area that hosts an "X-ray machine" (Fig. 1). As the gift reaches this area, virtual light beams scan the packaged gift and its interior are displayed on a digital screen. At the same time, aspects of gift's energy efficiency is revealed gradually via animations and related textual and imagery information. By studying the items displayed for each gift on the screen (Fig. 2), users are called upon to decide if it should be considered as ecological and make a selection using the appropriate buttons. When a gift is considered suitable for distribution, it is released and directed to the Santa Claus bag for delivery. If users feel that the gift's materials are not safe or friendly for the environment, they can change the construction materials' combination to be more environmentally friendly. If users' response is not correct then the system provides the appropriate feedback for users to review their choices. Upon choosing the correct combinations, the gift delivery progress is displayed on the digital screen. User interaction with the system is accomplished using physical controls (i.e., buttons).

Fig. 1. Construction design of the "Gift's energy efficiency" system

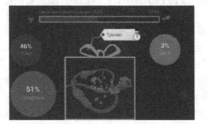

Fig. 2. System's game design

Global Gift Delivery. This system presents an interactive way of delivering Christmas gifts on the five continents. The information provided by the system helps to collect data from different sources and to broaden the analytical thinking of users as well as enrich their geographic knowledge.

In terms of the visual composition, specially shaped positions are created for the gifts that users can placeto see the letter accompanying each gift. A specially designed mechanism allows the wish to appear automatically on a digital display, when users place the gift in the specific position to be recognized. The wishes of each child are displayed on a digital screen, accompanied by all the necessary information the user needs (text, images) (Fig. 4) to recognize which continent each letter comes from.

A surface has the appropriate holders per continent for each gift. When users place the gift on the continent that they think the wish corresponds to, the system recognizes whether the answer is correct or incorrect (Fig. 3). Once the correct continent is selected, its border automatically turns green and a message on the screen informs the users that they have made the correct choice. In case of an error, an appropriate message appears on the screen to prompt users to refine their choice, while the wrongly selected continent blushes with special lighting. Then, users can choose the next gift and follow the same procedure to recognize the next wish. When the gifts have been distributed to all five continents, a light animation is activated throughout the map and a reward message appearson the screen. The goal of the system is to help users learn by playing. The system combines technologies for identifying physical objects on non-technological surfaces and for presenting augmented information to auxiliary projections.

Fig. 3. Construction design of the "Global Gift Delivery" system

Fig. 4. Game screen of the "Global Gift Delivery" system

The Basil Pie. The system consists of a custom wooden "new year cake" and allows visitors to randomly select any piece and see if it was the lucky one (the tradition is that one piece contains the lucky coin symbolizing health and good luck for the coming year). The system recognizes the location of the golden coin and a corresponding sound message is played when the matching piece is selected.

The system consists of wooden pieces of a "basil pie" decorated and placed on a platter. Users are able to choose their own piece in an attempt to try to find the hidden coin (Fig. 5). The system incorporates a special mechanical and electronic mechanism to randomly change the position of the coin each time a selection is being placed (Fig. 6).The system combines technologies for recognizing natural objects on non-technological surfaces.

Fig. 5. System setup and user interaction

Fig. 6. Construction in layers

3.2 The House of Surprises

Gift Collection Assistant. This system provides the ability to interact with physical objects in order for the players to use a virtual vehicle to collect gifts scattered around the environment and load them on Santa's sleigh.

In a virtual 3D environment, there is a snowy mountainous landscape full of Christmas gifts scattered on the snow (Fig. 8). The purpose of the system is for users to help Santa Claus place the gifts back to the sleigh in an interactive way. By using really augmented controls, such as a gear lever and a steering wheel (Fig. 7), players direct a special machine to collect as many gifts as possible at a predetermined time and put them on the sleigh for Santa to continue his journey.

The system allows interaction with actual augmented controls and enriches users' experience by displaying a 3D environment.

Fig. 7. Construction design of the "Gift Collection Assistant" system

Fig. 8. Real-time game view of the "Gift Collection Assistant" system

Santa Claus Brings the Gifts. The system is an interactive game in which users are called upon to help Santa Claus share the gifts to the children at a specific time by using natural controls.

A digital screen shows a virtual environment in which Santa's sleigh with the help of a balloon flies over the city (Fig. 10). Using pressure sensors (Fig. 9), users can start the game, direct the virtual balloon and take it to the chimneys of the houses to help Santa Claus drop the gifts. Users also try to avoid any obstacles that might show up during the flight. The virtual environment enriches users' engagement with the system via incorporating Christmas music and animated graphics. On the upper area of the screen, the remaining time and "lives" as well as the number of gifts delivered are being displayed. The system allows tangible interaction with physical objects via a sensor-equipped hand pump.

Fig. 9. Construction design of the "Santa Claus Brings the Gifts" system

Fig. 10. Game design of the "Santa Claus Brings the Gifts" system

3.3   The House of Fairytales

This system presents various interactive fairytales and through storytelling, animations and interactive gaming, each story comes alive and integrates users into the virtual environment, making them a part of each story's plot. The system allows players to participate in fairytales with natural kinesthetic ways of interaction, such as by freely moving in space to interact with on-screen elements.

The system presents interactive fairytales that are placed in a specially designed room consisting of three large projection surfaces that frame the users (in a cave-like format), giving the feeling that they are immersed into the story, as the virtual elements will surround them via wall projections. Through these views users are actively engaged in the story plot. A custom designed rotating mechanism allows triggering the start of the fairytale's narration. Sound effects, real-life narratives and animations motivate users to participate in the flow of the story through interactive games that have to be completed in order to continue with the story. Using special image and depth sensors, the hands and the entire body of users are recognized to act as a means of interaction with the game, without the need for a controller or other mechanical part. The software subtracts users' background and integrates users into the virtual environment of the story (Fig. 11), allowing multiple users to see live their image embedded in digital sceneries and interact with elements of the virtual environment.

3.4   The Neighborhood with the Lights

The system supports the remote control of smart lighting using arrays of LED lights and headlights. The aim is to highlight specially designed Christmas decorations that beautify the castle's walls. The software provides the ability to create and customize scenarios to control the state, intensity and color of each light unit. It also allows the scheduling of scenarios as well as the creation of specific photo rhythmic effects based on selected musical sounds. The system supports remote control of custom lighting in a continuous flow to reproduce lighting in figures (Fig. 13) that decorate the area outside the Christmas Kiosks. The figures are special constructions made of simple materials (such as metal, wood, Plexiglas). Inside the constructions, appropriate equipment is incorporated to support remote control of both the hue and light intensity of individual parts. The software provides scenario activation, which synchronizes the lights with selected musical sounds.

Fig. 11. Game design with user actively engaged

The system enriches the user experience by combining technology with art as well as with light and music (Fig. 12).

Fig. 12. Technology and art combination using lights

Fig. 13. Lighting in figures

3.5   Rudolph

At the entrance of the "Christmas Castle", visitors are welcomed by a novel system that combines a mechanical speaking doll with videos of flight over the city of Heraklion, the sleigh of Santa Claus with Rudolph the Red-Nosed Reindeer leading the pace (Fig. 15). Rudolph invites children to become Santa Claus' assistants and deliver presents to everyone in Heraklion, through a virtual interactive trip over the city center.

Users can get on the Santa's sleigh, start their trip to Heraklion city and share as many gifts as they can while seeing the city from above (Fig. 14). Interaction is done using joystick for navigation and a tablet for giving text input, as well as with a big screen where it shows video of the city that has been captured using a drone. In the end, users can send to their email their pictures, which have been taken by the traveling system using a camera.

Fig. 14. Users interacting on the sleigh   **Fig. 15.** Rudolph and the sleigh

4 Conclusion

This work has presented the technologically enhanced Heraklion Christmas Castle. In this context, eight interactive systems have been deployed which provide a more "innovative" view of Christmas. Through a combination of novel information visualizations and multimodal and playful interaction techniques the Christmas spirit is promoted. Users have the opportunity to live a unique experience in a theme park and use technology to discover their interests through different visualizations. Users' satisfaction and response justify that novel forms of interaction can enhance information provision capacity and increase their interest by providing more immersive and memorable experiences. As future work, an in-situ evaluation is necessary in terms of usability, interaction and user experience.

Acknowledgements. The installation at the Christmas Castle of the city of Heraklion was funded under a contract between FORTH and the Municipal Public Service Enterprise of Heraklion. The development of the interactive systems presented by this research work was supported by the FORTH-ICS internal RTD Programme 'Ambient Intelligence and Smart Environments'[1].

---

[1] FORTH-ICS AmIProgramme: http://ami.ics.forth.gr/.

References

1. Baranek, G.T., Barnett, C.R., Adams, E.M., Wolcott, N.A., Watson, L.R., Crais, E.R.: Object play in infants with autism: methodological issues in retrospective video analysis. Am. J. Occup. Ther. **59**(1), 20–30 (2005)
2. Bekker, T., Sturm, J., Eggen, B.: Designing playful interactions for social interaction and physical play. Pers. Ubiquit. Comput. **14**(5), 385–396 (2010)
3. Bratton, S.C., Ray, D., Rhine, T., Jones, L.: The efficacy of play therapy with children: a meta-analytic review of treatment out-comes. Prof. Psychol.: Res. Pract. **36**(4), 376 (2005)
4. Bressan, F., Vets, T., Leman, M.: A multimodal interactive installation for collaborative music making: from preservation to enhanced user design. In: Proceedings of the European Society for Cognitive Sciences of Music (ESCOM) Conference, pp. 23–26 (2017)
5. Carr, S., Stephen, C., Francis, M., Rivlin, L.G., Stone, A.M.: Public Space. Cambridge University Press, Cambridge (1992)
6. DeVary, S.: Educational gaming: interactive edutainment. Dist. Learn. **5**(3), 35 (2008)
7. Drossis, G., Grammenos, D., Birliraki, C., Stephanidis, C.: MAGIC: developing a multimedia gallery supporting mid-air gesture-based interaction and control. In: Stephanidis, C. (ed.) HCI 2013. CCIS, vol. 373, pp. 303–307. Springer, Heidelberg (2013). https://doi.org/10.1007/978-3-642-39473-7_61
8. Drossis, G., Ntelidakis, A., Grammenos, D., Zabulis, X., Stephanidis, C.: Immersing users in landscapes using large scale displays in public spaces. In: Streitz, N., Markopoulos, P. (eds.) DAPI 2015. LNCS, vol. 9189, pp. 152–162. Springer, Cham (2015). https://doi.org/10.1007/978-3-319-20804-6_14
9. Engelen, L., et al.: Increasing physical activity in young primary school children—it's child's play: a cluster randomised controlled trial. Prevent. Med. **56**(5), 319–325 (2013)
10. Fromme, J.: Computer games as a part of children's culture. Game Stud. **3**(1), 49–62 (2003)
11. Gehl, J.: Life Between Buildings: Using Public Space. Island Press, Washington (2011)
12. Grammenos, D., et al.: Design and development of four prototype interactive edutainment exhibits for museums. In: Stephanidis, C. (ed.) UAHCI 2011. LNCS, vol. 6767, pp. 173–182. Springer, Heidelberg (2011). https://doi.org/10.1007/978-3-642-21666-4_20
13. Haddon, L.: The development of interactive games. The media reader: continuity and transformation, pp. 305–327 (1999)
14. Izadi, S., Brignull, H., Rodden, T., Rogers, Y., Underwood, M.: Dynamo: a public interactive surface supporting the cooperative sharing and exchange of media. In: Proceedings of the 16th Annual ACM Symposium on User Interface Software and Technology, pp. 159–168. ACM, November 2003
15. Jaimes, A., Sebe, N.: Multimodal human–computer interaction: a survey. Comput. Vis. Image Underst. **108**(1–2), 116–134 (2007)
16. Ten Koppel, M., et al.: Chained displays: configurations of public displays can be used to influence actor-, audience-, and passer-by behavior. In: Proceedings of the SIGCHI Conference on Human Factors in Computing Systems. ACM (2012)
17. Marshall, M.T., Dulake, N., Ciolfi, L., Duranti, D., Kockelkorn, H., Petrelli, D.: Using tangible smart replicas as controls for an interactive museum exhibition. In: Proceedings of the TEI 2016: Tenth International Conference on Tangible, Embedded, and Embodied Interaction, pp. 159–167. ACM, February 2016
18. Price, S., Rogers, Y., Scaife, M., Stanton, D., Neale, H.: Us-ing 'tangibles' to promote novel forms of playful learning. Interact. Comput. **15**(2), 169–185 (2003)
19. Rogers, F., Sharapan, H.: How children use play. Educ. Dig. **59**(8), 13–16 (1994)

20. Salah, A.A., Schouten, B.A., Göbel, S., Arnrich, B.: Playful interactions and serious games. J. Ambient Intell. Smart Environ. **6**(3), 259–262 (2014)
21. Tieben, R., Sturm, J., Bekker, T., Schouten, B.: Playful persuasion: designing for ambient playful interactions in public spaces. J. Ambient Intell. Smart Environ. **6**(4), 341–357 (2014)
22. Vogel, D., Balakrishnan, R.: Interactive public ambient displays: transitioning from implicit to explicit, public to personal, interaction with multiple users. In: Proceedings of the 17th Annual ACM Symposium on User Interface Software and Technology. ACM (2004)
23. Wimmer, J.: Digital game culture(s) as prototype(s) of mediatization and commercialization of society: the world cyber games 2008 in cologne as an example. In: Fromme, J., Unger, A. (eds.) Computer Games and new Media Cultures, pp. 525–540. Springer, Dordrecht (2012). https://doi.org/10.1007/978-94-007-2777-9_33
24. Wouters, N., et al.: Uncovering the honeypot effect: how audiences engage with public interactive systems. In: Proceedings of the 2016 ACM Conference on Designing Interactive Systems, pp. 5–16. ACM, June 2016

Application Research on Human-Computer Interaction in Emotional Design of Science and Technology Exhibition Hall

Chen Chen[✉]

Industrial Design Department, School of Mechanical Science and Engineering,
Huazhong University of Science and Technology, Wuhan 430074, Hubei, China
M201870771@hust.edu.cn

Abstract. Rapid developments in Information Technology drastically changes many sectors including exhibition designing. The exhibition designing has evolved from the early exhibits, where the focus was on user's single-line interaction, to two-way interactive model which is more preferred and efficient. The physical environment layout was utilized to display the development of multi-dimensional virtual space, and the user is the sole controller of the display space. The exhibition space is not only a three-dimensional hall, but a multi-dimensional setting which can appeal to the user's sense of vision, smell and other perceptions. Such exhibitions can even create an experience of travelling through time and space. Based on the nature of public welfare science education institutions with educational exhibition as its main function, the science and technology exhibition hall mainly caters to the youth. Modern science and technology exhibition halls must utilize science and technology related to human-computer interaction and use its target audience's curiosity for new things to facilitate dissemination of scientific principles and technological achievements. This can be achieved through encouraging participation, creating experiences etc. through interactive exhibits and auxiliary displays means at the modern science and technology exhibition halls. This approach should be considered for its merits.

Keywords: Science and technology exhibition halls ·
Human-computer interaction technology · Adolescent

1 The Nature of Science and Technology Exhibition Halls and Service Population Survey

The Science and Technology Museum is an important window that reflects the image of a country's science, technology, culture and society, which main task is to popularize scientific knowledge, disseminate scientific ideas, advocate scientific spirit, publicize scientific and technological achievements and their role, cultivate public science and technology interest, meet public scientific and technological needs, and improve public scientific and technological literacy. As a platform for popularizing scientific and technological knowledge, disseminating scientific ideas and scientific methods, the Science and Technology Museum is an important position for the public,

C. Stephanidis (Ed.): HCII 2019, CCIS 1034, pp. 560–565, 2019.
https://doi.org/10.1007/978-3-030-23525-3_76

especially adolescents, to carry out regular and mass popular science education activities. Therefore, the design of the science and technology exhibition hall needs to meet the aesthetic needs of young people, enhance their own attractiveness, and pass knowledge to younger generations in a more interesting way.

2   Building Technology Hall of Emotional Experience

2.1   Designing Interesting Space Plots

Designing interesting spatial plots is one way approach to attract youngsters' attention. It refers to utilize a kind of display space with a series of specific theme props to create a story-like display atmosphere with affluent and vivid details and unexpected sequential changes, so that the display space shall be equipped with more vitality, which is based on the spatial experience of the recipient. "It is a spatial experience that transcends form, function, as well as form and function" [1].

The spatial plot comes from human perception. "In a broad sense, many perceptual activities are the arousal of memory" [2], and the emotional experience of reality. More often than not, the design of the spatial plot derives from the artistic expression of the plot of actual life, which is supposed to evoke fantasy and memory through the sensory activities of the recipient and through the role of space and time, establishing a connection with the plot of individual life. Actually, the artistic appeal of spatial plots often comes from specific material carriers in the spatial experience and the associated life plots in the process, as well as from the chain reaction of spatial experiences and the participation and interest of experiences. At the same time, the appeal of spatial plots also depends on a certain sequential change, because there is no necessary connection and correlation among plots, scenes, events, and props, and from the beginning of the scene, from the sense of sight, hearing, touch, smell to taste. Changes, climaxes, and endings are so diverse that layers of varying degrees are superimposed in the process of spatial experiences, which requires the orchestration of the sequence of scenes. Moreover, the information that the audience feels in the previous scene often affects the understanding of the information in the latter space scene. Therefore, the sequential programming is supposed to have the foreshadowing of changes in the beginning, and predicts the convergence of the latter scene, which forms a holistic feeling. This arrangement this arrangement has made the space got a focus, the primary and the secondary, changes, the rhythm as well as the appeal of the spatial plot.

2.2   Creation of an Attractive Space Scene

A scene generally refers to unit in space series, such as an exhibition hall in display space or shared area. Usually the scene is the place that contains the theme of the plot, the collision with visitors and is also the place where dialogue is the most active. Generally speaking, the scene mainly includes two attributes: one is the material environment in the scene; the other is the subject "person" in the place in which it contains the event and its implied meaning and the plot correlation between spatial elements.

As a scene, it is by no means a single isolated place in the exhibition space, involving the left and right, the upper and lower, the inner and the outer, and the spatial association between the human and the object. This association has created a sense of continuity in the space series, which seems that a movie has played a role in "contracting" and has brought anger to the exhibition space and strengthened the emotional experience of the recipient. Additionally, there are also internal relationship relationships among props, interfaces, forms, lights shadows, and textures, etc. This kind of association is not only a material function and visual connection, but also a plot association, implying a possibility between the transition in space and plots.

2.3   Utilizing the Appropriate Language Carrier and Coding

Fiction, drama, and films often describe stories and plots through words, languages, sounds, movements, etc., while emotional space is through material carriers such as form, structure, materials, colors, textures, paths, interfaces, function, and image. The narrative is the language of space, embodied in a non-verbal feature. To express the emotional design of space, we are supposed to first determine the concept of space, which is the soul of integrating spatial atmosphere. For example, the display of communication products with the concept of "communication". The second is the semantic system, which includes the semantics from two aspects of "signifier" and "referred": one refers to the material form, function, structure, and the activity event, etc; the second refers to the implicit subject and the symbolic meaning. Furthermore, syntactic and grammatical systems are needed, which is expressed as a kind of logic.

3   The Superiority of Human-Computer Interaction Technology in the Application of Emotional Technology Exhibition Hall

3.1   Haptic Application

Spatial page turning is also called interactive flip book, air flip book, virtual e-book, magic flip book, etc. It is a kind of visual effects of flipping books realized by infrared sensing technology and computer multimedia technology. Visitors rarely require standing in front of the booth and reach out to make the left and right swinging arms in the air. The computer will recognize the action of visitors and transmit the motion to the computer for processing. The application in the computer is based on the signals captured which drives the multimedia animation to perform the effect of flipping the book. This kind of virtual flip of books has a novel form and strong visual impacts, and quite a few exhibitions have its own figure. For example: the 60th anniversary of the founding of the individuals' Republic of China, the second National Geographic Surveying and Mapping Exhibition. Touch-based human-computer interaction is also available at the Canada Pavilion, the City Life Museum, and the Chongqing Pavilion at the Shanghai World Expo. Through LCD or PDP display, the resolution of virtual books gets to be greatly improved, and the sharpness and the color contrast are also able to be greatly improved, and the text, pictures and other materials will be highly restored. The color and gray scales are not worse than the printed ones, and can be embedded in animations and video as well as other materials.

3.2 Voice Control Application

The "power source" of the German Pavilion at the Shanghai World Expo is an innovative application of human-computer interaction technology in the design of display. The interactive metal ball weighing 1.3 tonnes with 400,000 LEDs (mainly used to display images) is placed in the 3-story hall at the end of the German Pavilion tour, as shown in Fig. 1. At the beginning of the interaction, the audience was divided into two batches and shouted following the instructions of the commentator. After hearing the shouts, one eye would flash first on the metal ball, automatically finding the direction in which the sound was loudest, which side shouted loudly, and the interactive ball would sway to that side more intensively. Through the loud screams of the public at the place, the metal ball gradually started to swing back and forth, rotating in a circular motion, and the color image of the spherical surface became more and more dense, and different scenes based various themes like "urban buildings" and "harmonious families" would be broadcast randomly. The human-computer interaction technology represented by the voice control has been also widely used in life, such as voice recognition technology, voice dialing and data entry services. People get to talk directly to machines, and their hands thus can be liberated. The "Power Source" metal ball of the German Pavilion at the Shanghai World Expo is unique in the world. The combination of human-computer interaction technology and modern display technology has enabled all the audience on the scene to participate in the interaction at the same time and to be cognizant of people are the source of power to create a "harmonious city."

Fig. 1. The metal ball hanging in the power source hall in German museum

3.3 Holographic Imaging Technology

In the course of the exhibition of the National Pavilion of the 2010 Shanghai World Expo, many viewers would stop in front of the "National Treasure" art - "The Riverside Scene at Qingming Festival". The interactive version of the "Qingming Shanghe Map" shocked all visitors, which was divided into two versions, day and night. There were 1,068 people, including 691 people during the day and 377 people at night, which were the prosperous scenes of Bianjing, the capital of the Northern Song Dynasty which was also the largest city in the world at that time. In order to enable people to see the many characters more clearly in the "Qingming Riverside Map" and appreciate the artistic conception, the Shanghai Science and the Technology Commission set up a "large-size screen human-computer interaction" project, which was developed by Crystal Stone Digital Technology. The "Qingming Shanghe Map" utilizing LED technology was like a movie screen, and the characters and scenery were vivid. By adopting computer technology to combine character dialogues, the Qingming Shanghe map had become an immersive human-computer interaction medium. Based on the ICE and Silverlight technologies of Microsoft Corporation, the original three-dimensional layout recovery algorithm and the virtual environment organization method were developed for the spatial modeling characteristics based on the scatter perspective of the Qingming Shanghe Map. Through the use of "horizontal block" and "vertical layering" data management strategies, the reasonable organization and seamless splicing of ultra-large data were realized, and the 5.1-channel stereo effect was used to make visitors fascinated by the prosperity of Bianliang, the capital of Northern Song Dynasty (Fig. 2).

Fig. 2. The virtual game in Shanghai Science and Technology Museum

4   Conclusion

The current era is featured with the "experience economy". The design of display space is not only the design of form and function, but also the sensory experience of the recipient who is full of interest and active participation. The spatial experience of force which is irreplaceable, pleasant and full of artistic infections is needed and a kind of necessities of the times. With the modern high-quality interactive technology, the emotional atmosphere of the space would be made stronger. The display of the science and technology carries the heavy responsibility of nurturing young generations, and transforms the science and technology exhibition hall from the past unchanging sense of science and technology into a richer emotional space, which is an inevitable trend of the development of the exhibition hall's designs. Interactive technology is the cornerstone of emotional space design, and emotional space display will also stimulate the interactive technology to advance.

References

1. Shaoming, L.: Architectural Experience – The Plot in Space. China Building Industry Press, p. 46 (2007)
2. (British) Brian Lawson: "Language of Space", translated by Yang Qingjuan. China Building Industry Press, Beijing, p. 47 (2003)
3. LUOJian-guo: Affect of Human Nature Evolvement on Machinery Development. In: Proceedings of 2010 Second Asia-Pacific Conference on Information Processing (2010)

Research on Design Process of Small Intangible Cultural Heritage Art Gallery Based on VRP-MUSEUM Technology—Taking the Art Gallery of Shanghai Style Lacquerware as an Example

Jingyi Ji, Janxin Cheng[✉], and Rongrong Fu

School of Art Design and Media,
East China of Science and Technology University, Shanghai 200030, China
chumoecho@qq.com

Abstract. This paper adopts the case analysis method and the field investigation method. By comparing the current situation of entity art gallery and virtual art gallery, VRP-MUSEUM technology is confirmed as the core technology of the design of intangible cultural heritage virtual art gallery. Then the design process of the virtual Art Gallery of Shanghai Style Lacquerware is developed by combining with 3D laser scanning technology, 3D modeling technology and other technologies to make the optimal final design plan. These methods contribute to develop a design process that is easy to use and can break the gap between visitors and intangible culture. The process aims to solve the problems existing in the existing art museum.

Keywords: Virtual art gallery · Intangible cultural heritage ·
VRP-MUSEUM technology · Design process

1 Introduction

As an important place for public art education, how art gallery display arts to the public becomes an important topic. The virtual art gallery means that the public can not only browse the virtual exhibits at home, but also realize the interactive experience with the virtual exhibits, thus stimulating their enthusiasm for online and offline browsing. This is also the fundamental purpose of countries to actively build virtual art galleries. However, it is worth noting that most of the domestic art galleries blindly follow the trend to build virtual art galleries, resulting in many virtual art galleries exist only in name. Many small art galleries have fallen into the embarrassing situation of poor performance and low network access due to backward management concepts, insufficient investment in software and hardware and lack of talents. This paper discusses the design process of the virtual art gallery on the above issues (Fig. 1).

© Springer Nature Switzerland AG 2019
C. Stephanidis (Ed.): HCII 2019, CCIS 1034, pp. 566–574, 2019.
https://doi.org/10.1007/978-3-030-23525-3_77

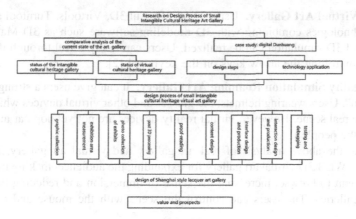

Fig. 1. Technology roadmap.

2 Research Review

2.1 Current Situation of Intangible Cultural Heritage Gallery

Current Situation of Real Intangible Cultural Heritage Gallery. The art gallery has entered a stage of rapid development in the context of the country's increasing emphasis on non-legacy protection and cultural undertakings.

However, there are still many problems in the development of China's non-legacy art galleries: (1) the display platform is limited. It cannot overcome the constraints of time and space, nor can it allow users to experience an all-round visit. (2) Form of presentation is too singular. (3) It usually has a planned and designed tour route that greatly weakens the subjective initiative of the viewers. (4) Its operating costs are high. Many private pavilions directly affect the scale and quality of them. (5) There are many problems about cultural relics in the real non-legacy art gallery.

However, compared with the traditional art gallery, the appearance of the non-legacy art gallery is closer to the people's life, but, virtual art gallery has changed the operation mode, and also created a good space for the inheritance and development.

Current Situation of Virtual Intangible Cultural Heritage Gallery. At present, virtual art galleries are mainly divided into four categories.

Website-Style Art Gallery. That is to say, the pictures, texts, video and audio and other materials are placed on the website for the users to browse. This method is simple to make, low in cost and fast in access, making it the first choice for online exhibitions. However, the user experience is poor [1].

Field Shooting Art Gallery. At present, there are many art galleries at home and abroad to carry out 360-degree panoramic shooting in the real art gallery. Then the photos are stitched together to form a spherical exhibition and published on the Internet that users can visit through the network. Generally, it has a good user experience [2].

WEB 3D Virtual Art Gallery. Using Unity3D, Cult3D, Virtools, Turntool and other similar technologies combining with 3D modeling software such as 3D Max, virtual roaming and 3D simulation can be realized. Users can freely travel through the virtual scene by controlling the arrow keys on the keyboard [2].

Virtual Reality Simulation Roaming Art Gallery. It can give users a strong sense of "immersion". Users wearing helmets, 3D glasses and other virtual devices which seems to be in the real scene. However, virtual reality devices are not yet popular and cannot satisfy all the people [3].

Combine the above analysis of real art gallery and virtual art gallery, I suggest building the WEB 3D virtual art gallery for expanding the audience, making more users are convenient to browse, increasing the sense of immersion and reducing the cost of small art galleries. The users can control the scene with the mouse and roam in it (Table 1).

Table 1. Real art gallery versus Virtual art gallery [4].

	Real art gallery	Virtual art gallery
Features	Display, educate, collect and research in a real way	Display, educate, collect and research in a digital way
Autonomy	Passive	Active
Convenience	Buy tickets at stores	Use the web
Interactivity	One-way interaction	Interaction, games, extended information, etc.
Control of environment	Uncontrollable or changeable	Window interaction
Display	Single and fixed	Varied
Presentation	Close quarters	All-around and digital
Expansion	Limited	Unlimited
Scale	Limited to buildings and access, hard to expand	Limited by network, server and hardware devices, but can be expanded and improved
Space	Limited by the distance between the viewer and the object	Can be reduced or enlarged, 360-degree view
Resource savings	High venue rental fees, exhibition fees, and long-distance exhibit transportation fees	Environmental protection, energy saving, low carbon

2.2   Case Study: Digital Dunhuang

Design Steps and Technical Application Overview. The "Digital Dunhuang" project will bring together a variety of data and literature data that have been acquired and form a digital library of grotto cultural relics combining diversification and intelligence [5]. The project consists of seven processes: image acquisition, scene measurement, pre-photography collection, post-image processing, proofreading and verification, VR production, and platform construction (Fig. 2).

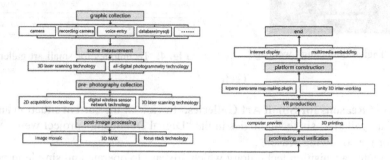

Fig. 2. Production process of "digital dunhuang" project.

Image acquisition technology is the use of digital cameras, digital video recorders, microphones and other tools for image, audio, video, text data collection. After data collection, the data is uploaded and stored through the mysql. The second step is scene scanning measurement. Firstly, using 3D laser scanning technology to quickly reconstruct the 3D model of the scene and various data such as lines, faces and bodies. Secondly, using the all-digital photogrammetry technology, the collected data is processed in the computer for numerical, graphic and image processing, so that the final product are in a digital form. Thereby, two-dimensional mural painting adopts 2D acquisition technology, which is combined with digital camera and tripod head. Three-dimensional sculpture uses the same 3D laser scanning technology for data acquisition. Fourth step, multiple cameras shoot at different angles of the same scene, then, correct, denoise, match and finally construct a high-quality, clear, smooth-edged, high-resolution image. The focus stack technology digitizes the murals, effectively solving the problem of the 3D surface. The three-dimensional sculpture building uses modeling technology to make the stereo effect realistic and optimize the design. After digitally integrating all the buildings and exhibits through post-processing, the model files are proofread and inspected by computer browsing, and 3DMAX files are used for 3D printing for more accurate inspection. The project uses a krpano panoramic map production plugin to make a panoramic roaming of 2Dl image. That is, all processed flat images are retrieved from the mysql database and imported into krpano to stitch the images. This allows to quickly generate a panoramic roaming project with basic functionality. The 3D building components of the project are interactively produced by Unity3D software, which facilitates network transmission. The final step is to insert all the data into the network platform through HTML, CSS, and JavaScript to form a virtual museum.

In view of the needs of building the WEB 3D virtual art gallery, the design process is relatively complete and suitable for small art galleries. But it needs to be adjusted according to the characteristics of the art gallery. Due to funding constraints, shortages of technology, and lack of staff, the technology used in the project is not fully applicable to small art galleries (Fig. 3).

Fig. 3. "Digital dunhuang" webpage

graphic acquisition technology	3D laser scanning technology
modeling technology (3D MAX)	2D acquisition technology
3D printing	web page production technology

Fig. 4. Techniques for small art galleries.

Tech-

niques and Reasons for Small Art Galleries. In view of the current situation analysis of small art galleries, six technologies in the "Digital Dunhuang" project were selected to use for the following reasons:

The graphic acquisition technology which are easy to operate and simple in process and can realize the collection and permanent preservation. 3D laser scanning technology can use of different types of venues. Besides, it is easy to process, analyze, output, and display. The 2D acquisition technology can also achieve image data collection and permanent preservation. 3DMAX modeling technology has an advantage in price. Its production process is simple. This technology can complete the real reproduction of 3D buildings and exhibits. 3D printing can achieve the inspection and proofreading of the model. The web design idea can embed all the data, images, audio, video, etc. into the network platform to form a virtual art gallery (Fig. 4).

The six technologies mentioned above are commonly used techniques, and their design time is short, easy to operate, low cost, and low hardware requirements are very suitable for the construction of small virtual art museums.

2.3   Key Technologies of the Small Virtual Art Gallery

Considering the database mysql and krpano panoramic map making plugin are more suitable for the construction of large virtual art galleries, the following two technologies are chosen instead to achieve the best results.

Python Crawler Technology. The database mysql is a relational database. Its management system is suitable for large websites with large databases, but there exist problems such as modular programming, low execution speed, low security and complicated operation. It is an recommendation that use Python crawler technology to write programs for forming a local database. It not only can obtain files in batches, but also easy to operate. Besides, it is suitable for websites with small data volume, which is convenient for later implantation into the network platform for retrieval.

VRP—MUSEUM. VRP—MUSEUM is a pavilion which suitable for all kinds of technology museums, experience centers, large-scale exhibitions. It is a three-dimensional interactive experience model that put exhibition halls, exhibits and temporary exhibits to the Internet for display, promotion and education [6]. VRP - MUSEUM can not only create krpano panoramic map making plugins in all-aspects, but also can integrate Unity3D interactive operation. It has the following advantages: Omnidirectional, three-dimensional and 360° browsing, strong sense of reality, automatic roaming and manual roaming switch freely, powerful interactive effects, easy to use and has a wide range of applications and the system requirements are low and the PC platform can operate.

In summary, the small virtual art gallery can use the 6 technologies in the "Digital Dunhuang" project and the VRP - MUSEUM virtual pavilion technology that replaces the Python crawler technology of the database mysql and replaces the krpano panoramic map production plugin.

3   Design Process of Small Intangible Cultural Heritage Virtual Art Gallery

3.1   Summary on Designing of Shanghai Style Lacquerware Art Gallery

According to the characteristics of different fields of the small art gallery and content frame design and interface design were added on the "Digital Dunhuang" project, so as

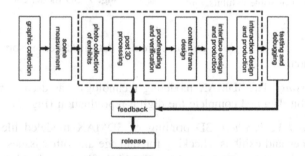

Fig. 5. Designing of Shanghai Style Lacquerware Art Gallery.

to better enhance the sense of immersion of the small virtual art gallery (Fig. 5).

Shanghai Lacquer Art Museum collect and inherit the lacquer ware is unique. It is the lacquer art museum with the largest number of lacquer wares, the most complete varieties and the most abundant collections in Shanghai. The following content will describe the combination between design process of the small non-legacy virtual art gallery and the Shanghai lacquer art gallery.

Data Collection

Graphic Collection. Use digital cameras, microphones, etc. and voice recorders to interview exhibitors and complete the collection of images, video, and text.

Scene Measurement Scan. The three-dimensional laser scanning technology is used to scan and measure the appearance of the Shanghai Lacquer Art Museum and its internal scenes. The 3D laser scanner is selected according to the structure of the venue.

Photo Collection of Exhibits. The Shanghai Lacquer Art Museum exhibits are divided into 2D and 3D. Most of the 2D exhibits are paintings and calligraphy, mainly using two-dimensional acquisition technology, namely tripod, tripod head, and digital camera. The 3D exhibits are mostly sculptures. The three-dimensional laser scanning technology is used to collect the three-dimensional data in order to restored into digital exhibits, and it is as same as the scene measurement.

After data collection, the program is written using Python crawlers technology to form a local database. Data retrieval and post production were achieved by storing the

Fig. 6. Collection of some exhibits.

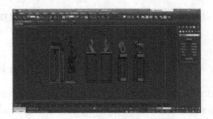

Fig. 7 3D model construction.

previous collected data in different sort (Fig. 6).

Venue Construction

Late 3D Processing. The 3DMAX modeling technology was used to reconstruct the venue and exhibit data and complete the digital reproduction (Fig. 7).

Proofreading and Verification. 3D printing of 3DMAX modeled files, comparison with actual scenes and exhibits, checking for damage and other issues.

After confirming the correctness, the 3DMAX file is embedded in the VRP-MUSEUM software to complete 3DMAX modeling, lighting, texture mapping, rendering, baking and exporting.

Virtual Build

Content Frame Design. Systematic content framework design for venues, exhibits, and graphic materials in VRP - MUSEUM. The first step is to determine the nature and content of the exhibition. According to the results of data collection, the exhibits in Shanghai Lacquer Art Museum can be divided into basic display and long-term display. The display content is divided into different eras and different types. The second step is to clarify the theme of the exhibition. Usually the theme is time, place, nature, purpose, etc. It should show ideological, scientific and artistic. The has set up four major museums in accordance with the four types of engraving, inlaying, screw-filling, and engraving. The third step is to classify the exhibits. The classification of exhibits is based on the types of the four special exhibition halls. The fourth step is to formulate the display structure. To determine the structure of the exhibits, refine the display of the main body and clearly show the logical relationship (Fig. 8).

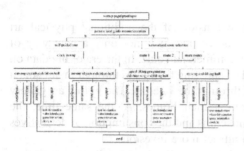

Fig. 8. Operation flow chart.   **Fig. 9** Virtual museum design.

Design and Product Interface in VRP - MUSEUM. According to the content of the art gallery, the design style conforms to the theme, which includes the overall picture style, start-up interface, browsing interface, tool buttons and so on. Shanghai Lacquer Art Museum is designed with a blend of design styles.

Interaction Design and Production. In the VRP - MUSEUM software, the venue, exhibits, and interfaces are organically combined to add interactive functions such as interactive games and multiplayers online communities. The main social functions are camera, compass, navigation map, hotspot trigger, data query, FLASH video picture call, voice introduction and so on (Fig. 9).

Test and Feedback. All data resource files are compressed and packaged into web-published WEB3D files. Then through HTML, JavaScript, CSS for web design, the virtual art gallery is embedded in the web page.

3.2   Features of Haipai Lacquerware Virtual Art Gallery

Through the construction of the virtual venue of Shanghai Lacquer Art Museum, we can compare the following characteristics: (1) Simulate the real object in a 1:1 way. The scenes created based on the real light and shadow environment are more immersive. (2) It is possible to observe exhibits at close range and at multiple angles, and to gather related information together and expand unlimited knowledge with limited space. Exhibits and props can be switched at will, fully exploring the functions of the exhibits, allowing users to better understand the exhibits. (3) Everyone can move, communicate and simulate the real pavilion environment in the same pavilion. The virtual pavilion can be used to further build a virtual community, so that create a virtual community full of knowledge and fun [4].

4 Prospect and Value

In summary, the virtual art gallery as an extension of the traditional physical art museum, in the future, its role positioning is diverse. It is not only a new way of cultural communication, but also has certain commercial value. In the era of big data on the Internet, people are more and more fond of showing their lives through major social platforms, and they will also live and learn through the Internet. The virtual art gallery can meet the needs of people without leaving their homes. At the same time, the development and application of virtual art museums and the consumption of derivatives not only attract more user groups, but also attract more investors.

The design process of the virtual art gallery can help the art gallery operators to establish a complete virtual art gallery system more quickly and efficiently, so as to obtain more channels of communication.

References

1. Liu, Q., Lei, S., Zhang, G., Huang, J., Zhang, X.: Digital protection and inheritance of Tujia instrumental music culture based on virtual museum. Journal of Hubei University for Nationalities (philosophy and social science edition) (2017)
2. Cai, Z.: Function analysis of digital music museum website at home and abroad. Music Communication (2015)
3. Zhu, X., Zhou, M., Geng, G.: Research on development mode of virtual museum. Comput. Appl. Soft. **2005**(06), 34–35 + 107
4. Baidu library. https://wenku.baidu.com/view/00f3510303d8ce2f0066237e.html. Accessed 25 June 2018
5. Digital Dunhuang. https://www.e-dunhuang.com/index.htm. Accessed 09 Dec 2018
6. Baidu encyclopedia. https://baike.baidu.com/item/VRP-MUSEUM虚拟展馆. Accessed 21 Nov 2018

Author Index

Printed in the United States
By Bookmasters

Printed in the United States
By Bookmasters